MOUNTAIN

DENNIS P. CHAPMAN

THE 10TH MOUNTAIN DIVISION

A History from World War II to 2005

SCHIFFER MILITARY
4880 Lower Valley Road   Atglen, PA 19310

This book is dedicated to the memory of Col. (Ret.) James E. Sikes Jr. and Spc. Scott P. Wiles, both of 2nd Battalion, 87th Infantry, 10th Mountain Division, Fort Drum, New York, and to the memory of the members of the 10th Division who succumbed to the great influenza pandemic at Camp Funston, Kansas, in 1918.

Designed by Justin Watkinson
Type set in Impact/Minion Pro/Univers LT Std

ISBN: 978-0-7643-6524-9
Printed in India

Published by Schiffer Publishing, Ltd.
4880 Lower Valley Road
Atglen, PA 19310
Phone: (610) 593-1777; Fax: (610) 593-2002
Email: Info@schifferbooks.com
Web: www.schifferbooks.com

For our complete selection of fine books on this and related subjects, please visit our website at www.schifferbooks.com. You may also write for a free catalog.

Schiffer Publishing's titles are available at special discounts for bulk purchases for sales promotions or premiums. Special editions, including personalized covers, corporate imprints, and excerpts, can be created in large quantities for special needs. For more information, contact the publisher.

We are always looking for people to write books on new and related subjects. If you have an idea for a book, please contact us at proposals@schifferbooks.com.

CONTENTS

I reported to the 10th Mountain Division's 2nd Battalion, 87th Infantry, at Fort Drum, New York, in early 1991, following my graduation from West Point and training at Fort Benning. A lot of water has gone under the bridge since then, but I have never forgotten my connection with the 10th Mountain and I still wear its emblem with pride, years after my retirement from the Army. Yet, perhaps surprisingly, other than a vague awareness of the division's service in Italy during the Second World War, my knowledge of the division's history was mostly limited to what I had experienced of it personally in Homestead, Florida, and in Somalia. I suspect that many 10th Mountain Division veterans have had the same experience. But as the following pages show, the history of the 10th Mountain Division is so much more than that. It is a story of physical endurance, American ingenuity, and extraordinary valor. It is a story that stretches across most of the Army's history during much of the twentieth century and all of the twenty-first century to date, from world war to the Cold War to the global war on terror. In writing this book I have sought to gather together the loose threads of the division's history and to weave them into an integrated narrative. My principal aim has been to broaden the perspective of all those associated with the division, past and present, so that both today's soldiers and the veterans of the past can see their own lived experiences with the 10th Mountain in a broader context—not merely as the isolated episodes of which they participated, but as parts of a much-larger adventure and a much-older tradition. In short, in writing this book, it is my hope to enable the mountain troopers of today to see themselves as part of a long, honorable and distinguished tradition stretching back more than a century.

I should also like to address certain aspects of this book that may raise some objections. One such is the inclusion in this work of the history of the US Army's 10th Division, formed during World War I, and of the 85th, 86th, and 87th Infantry Regiments, also formed during that conflict. Some may object that the Army has never treated these formations as part of the lineage of the successor entities by the same names formed during World War II and, in the case of the 10th Mountain Division and the 87th Infantry Regiment, that are still with us today. I made a conscious decision to part with the Army on this point and treat these formations as part of the overall 10th Mountain Division story for two reasons. The first is simply justice. While the war ended before those units made it to France, the men who served in them served nonetheless. This is especially poignant in the case of the 10th Division, formed under Maj. Gen. Leonard Wood at Camp Funston, Kansas. Many members of this division succumbed to the great influenza pandemic in 1918. While these men were spared the horrors of the trenches and died in the United States rather than abroad, they died nonetheless, died in the service of their country, and died in a strange place far from home. Their memory deserves to be honored, and I honor it by incorporating the history of the first 10th Division and the first 85th, 86th, and 87th Infantry Regiments into the history of the 10th Division that lives on today—the 10th Mountain Division. The second reason I include the original 10th Division in this account is that doing so provides a frame of reference through which the evolution of divisions as a permanent tactical echelon of command in the US Army can be told, thus more fully illustrating the evolutionary process that would eventually yield the modern 10th Mountain Division itself.

Another matter that should be addressed is my inclusion of two separate chapters on the history of the 87th Infantry Regiment apart from the 10th Mountain Division, these being the chapter on the invasion of Kiska in the Aleutians during World War II, and the chapter on the history of the 87th Infantry Regiment during the interregnum when the 10th Mountain Division was inactive after 1958. Again I have multiple reasons for doing so. First, the story of the 87th Infantry is integral to the history of the 10th Mountain Division in a way that even the history of the 85th and 86th Infantry Regiments is not. As discussed in chapter 2, the 87th Mountain Infantry Regiment was the first mountain infantry element formed in the US Army, along with the Mountain Training Center, and the first of the mountain infantry regiments recruited under the supervision of Minnie Dole; as such, it played a key role in developing the tactics, techniques, procedures, and equipment that would be used by the 10th Mountain Division and the other mountain infantry regiments once they were formed. The 87th Infantry also contributed subject matter experts to the Mountain Training Center who undoubtedly assisted with the formation of the 85th and 86th Mountain Infantry Regiments, and one battalion of the 87th Infantry trained alongside the 86th when the latter was formed; also, the 87th Infantry went through the famous D-series exercises with the rest of the 10th Mountain Division at Camp Hale upon return from the Kiska operation. In summary, the 87th Infantry Regiment is something akin to a patriarch of the 10th Mountain Division, providing, like Abraham did for the Israelites, the seed from which the 10th Mountain Division grew; as such, I tell the story of the 87th Infantry in full alongside that of the division itself. The second reason I address the history of the 87th Infantry Regiment separately is as a means of continuity, by which we can follow the development of the Army from 1958 to 1985, when the 10th Mountain Division was inactive and thus not contributing to that development, and as a bridge connecting the 10th Infantry Division of 1958 with the light infantry 10th Mountain Division of today.

I should also comment on some of the things omitted from this volume. While the 85th, 86th, and 87th Infantry Regiments are associated with the 10th Mountain Division's famous Italian Campaign during the Second World War, there have been many other units that have formed a part of the 10th Mountain Division, from the 90th Infantry Regiment, which briefly served with the division until displaced by the 87th Infantry returning from Kiska, to the many infantry battalions not affiliated with the 10th Mountain Division during World War II that have since served under its colors, to the many formations of other branches that have formed a part of the division. Each of these units deserves the same level of attention to their individual histories as has been given to that of three infantry regiments that served with the 10th Mountain Division in Italy. It is only the limitations of time and space that prevent me from giving them all the full attention they deserve here. Finally, some may note that my account of the 10th Mountain Division's participation in the Iraq and Afghanistan campaigns and other post-9/11 operations stops at 2005. As with the matters noted above, the limitations of time and space, aggravated by the barriers to research stemming from the COVID-19 pandemic in 2020, have made it necessary to limit the scope of my coverage of these campaigns here. As discussed further in the concluding chapter, a full accounting of the 10th Mountain Division's activities in the wake of the September 11, 2001, attacks will likely have to await a full accounting of the post-9/11 campaigns themselves.

A few acknowledgments are in order. First, I wish to thank my long-suffering wife for her patience throughout the months I spent working on this project. Second, I would like to thank Mr. Sepp Scanlin, director of the 10th Mountain Division Museum at Fort Drum, New York, for the access to the Annual Historical Summaries produced by the 10th Mountain Division since its reactivation in 1985. These are very valuable resources for anyone wanting to get a grasp of the division's very busy OPTEMPO over the past thirty-five years. I would also like to thank the staff at the US Army Heritage and Education Center at Carlisle Barracks, Pennsylvania, for their assistance in affording me access to what may be the only extant copy of the history of 5th Battalion, 87th Infantry, during its Panama service.

Last, I would like to acknowledge the many people, named and anonymous, whose work appears in the notes and bibliography throughout this work. The story of the 10th Mountain Division could not be told without the collective efforts of many ordinary people—staff officers and veterans, students at our many valuable military service schools, and, above all, the memoirists and amateur historians who lovingly recorded the histories of their units and their own experiences as an avocation rather than as a profession. It is thanks to the labor of all these ordinary people, much more than to the work of professional historians, journalists, and scholars, that the history of the 10th Mountain Division has been preserved for posterity.

First Creation: Leonard Wood and the Original 10th Division

According to the US Army Center for Military History, the 10th Mountain Division came to life on July 10, 1943, when the Headquarters, 10th Light Division, was constituted in the United States Army and activated at Camp Hale, Colorado, five days later.[1] But unknown to many, this was not the US Army's first infantry division designated as the "10th": on July 9, 1918—twenty-five years almost to the day before the 10th Light Division was organized—the War Department ordered organization of the first 10th Division.[2] Orphaned and rejected by the Army today,[3] the first 10th Division was organized at Camp Funston, Kansas, on August 10, 1918, and demobilized there less than six months later on February 13, 1919.[4] Only its Advance Detachment reached France, having departed Camp Funston on October 27, 1918.[5] It sailed from New York on November 2, 1918, arriving in France a week later on November 9; eight days earlier, the 210th Engineers and Trains departed Camp Funston for Camp Mills en route to France but never arrived—the Armistice was signed on November 11, two days after the 10th Division's Advance Detachment landed at Brest, and all overseas movement was suspended.[6]

The division as an echelon of command had not been a permanent feature in the US Army prior to the twentieth century. Following the Civil War, the Army was organized on the basis of geographical "departments," which could be further subdivided into districts.[7] "Recognizing the need for mobile commands larger than the regiment," the Army made plans to establish formal divisions and brigades in 1905 and attempted to implement the plan in 1910.[8] The Mexican Revolution of 1910 interrupted this effort, however, with a single "maneuver division"

being formed from Regular Army regiments instead, to be stationed at San Antonio, Texas, against any contingencies arising from Mexico's troubles; by August of that year this organization had disbanded.[9] This experience had confirmed the Army leadership in its belief in the need for divisions as a permanent echelon of command, as well as raising concerns that the Army needed to plan for future mobilization contingencies.[10] Under the auspices of Secretary of War Henry L. Stimson, the "Stimson Plan" was developed, under which the Army would be organized into four continental and two overseas geographic departments, three coast artillery departments, and a mobile army consisting of three infantry divisions and one cavalry division, two separate brigades in Hawaii, and twelve infantry divisions organized from the National Guard.[11] These "again proved to be largely paper units, though the 2nd Division was actually mobilized and concentrated once again in Texas due to troubles in Mexico."[12]* The National Defense Act of 1916 provided for organization of the Regular Army and National Guard into permanent divisions, and in May 1917 the War Department published new divisional tables of organization.[13] The Stimson Plan was modified in 1917, with the expansion of geographical departments to six and coast artillery districts to five, and the creation of the Panama Canal Department and the Panama Canal Coast Artillery District.[14]

The 10th Division had its genesis in America's entry into the First World War. Initially, Gen. Pershing had estimated that a field force of twenty divisions with associated supporting forces would be necessary to establish an independent American operational force in theater, and the War Department initially planned to deploy thirty

---

* For a contemporaneous account of National Guard service on the southern border during the Mexican Border War, as well as a discussion of some larger aspects of America's problem of military preparedness during that period, see Capt. Irving Goff McCann, *With the National Guard on the Border: Our National Military Problem*; for a broader overview of US Army operations on the US-Mexican border, see Matt M. Matthews, *The US Army on the Mexican Border: A Historical Perspective*.

divisions and supporting forces—a total of 1,372,000 men—by the end of 1918.[15] However, in light of a series of disastrous events,[16] including Russia's withdrawal from the war, thus freeing Germany to transfer forces from the former eastern front to the west for a renewed offensive, this request was ultimately increased to one hundred divisions.[17] In July 1918, President Wilson approved a ninety-eight-division force to be fielded by the end of 1919, with eighty divisions slated for deployment to France and eighteen to be kept in reserve in the United States; the secretary of war authorized the formation of twelve new divisions—the ninth through the twentieth—that month.[18]

The 10th Division was organized on August 10, 1918, at Camp Funston, Kansas, adjacent to Fort Riley, and was to consist of Regular Army and National Army elements.[19] The numerical designation of any given division represented neither the order in which it was created nor the order in which it deployed overseas (if it did). Rather, it indicates the original source of the division: Regular Army divisions were to be numbered 1–25, National Guard divisions were to be numbered 26 through 75, and National Army divisions—that is, units that were to be filled entirely with draftees—were to be numbered 75 and up. "The Regular Army divisions . . . were originally made up from Regular Army units plus voluntary enlistments and selective service men."[20] In practice, however, personnel from all sources were absorbed into units of all three categories.[21] The 10th Division's insignia consisted of a "Roman numeral X in gold in circle of same color, superimposed on a marine blue square,"[22] and it was organized with three brigades and supporting arms as follows: 19th Infantry Brigade, consisting of the 41st and 69th Infantry Regiment and the 29th Machinegun Battalion; 20th Infantry Brigade, consisting of the 20th and 70th Infantry Regiments and the 30th Machinegun Battalion; the 10th Field Artillery Brigade, consisting of the 28th and 29th Field Artillery Regiments and the 10th Trench Mortar Battery; the 28th Machinegun Battalion; the 210th Engineers; the 210th Field Signal Battalion; and division trains consisting of the 10th Train Headquarters and Military Police, the 10th Ammunition Train, the 10th Supply Train, the 210th Engineer Train, and the 10th Sanitary Train.[23]

Although the main body of the 10th Division never deployed overseas, service with the division would have been a lively time nonetheless. Camp Funston "was a huge, sprawling collection of unpainted, two-story, frame barracks which served as home for over 40,000 young trainees,"[24] and a veritable beehive of activity, as described by Old Army cavalryman Capt. W. F. Pride:

> The target range . . . was in constant use by troops from Funston, from morning till night. This was a modified range for trench firing, many of which were in use by the National Army. Funston was a huge armed camp, teeming with activity. Street cars ran every few minutes but . . . a seat on the cowcatcher was worth a dollar. Taxis were everywhere, charging whatever they thought the trade would stand, and with their cars never idle . . . Pawnee came to life again after over sixty years of lethargy, when the Cavalry Camp was established. Trains stopped there and it attained the dignity of a station. . . . Army City developed just outside the reservation boundary . . . being close to camp it got a great deal of soldier trade. It had paved streets, theatres, business houses and a city government . . . it was only very recently, 1925, that it finally went completely out of existence.[25]

Notwithstanding the ending of the war prior to its deployment, the 10th Division was nonetheless touched by history in at least two significant ways. The first was in the person of its commander, the single-minded and tenacious Maj. Gen. Leonard Wood.[26] Wood "was a polarizing figure. He was brash, aggressive, opportunistic, opinionated, and lacked patience with anyone who did not see things the way he did."[27] Although largely forgotten by the general public today except as the name of the sprawling active Army installation in central Missouri, Leonard Wood was one of the most prominent military figures of his day. He began his career in the Army in

1885 as a contract physician on the western frontier.[28] He was appointed to the Regular Army as a lieutenant and assistant surgeon in 1886,[29] just in time to be attached to Capt. H. W. Lawton's expedition against the Apaches to capture Geronimo.[30] When "persistent losses eventually left the infantry company in Lawton's command without any assigned officers[,] Wood volunteered and Lawton put him in charge of the company for the rest of the campaign."[31] Wood so distinguished himself in this capacity that he was awarded the Medal of Honor for his actions. The citation read that Wood

> voluntarily carried dispatches through a region infested with hostile Indians, making a journey of 70 miles in one night and walking 30 miles the next day. Also for several weeks, while in close pursuit of Geronimo's band and constantly expecting an encounter, commanded a detachment of Infantry, which was then without an officer, and to the command of which he was assigned upon his own request.[32]

During the Spanish-American War, Wood was instrumental in the formation of the First United States Volunteer Cavalry—the Rough Riders; having been appointed colonel of volunteers by the governor of Massachusetts, Wood served as the famous regiment's first commander, with Teddy Roosevelt as his deputy.[33] Wood later assumed command of the brigade of which the Rough Riders was a part (allowing Roosevelt to assume command of the regiment), and with that command, appointment as brigadier general of volunteers.[34] He was later appointed military governor of Santiago and then of Cuba.[35] When his commission in this rank was made permanent, he "jumped in regular rank from assistant surgeon to brigadier general"[36] over the heads of 509 other officers.[37] He went on to serve as a colonial administrator and military campaigner in the Philippines,[38] and ultimately as the "first effective Chief of Staff" of the Army.[39]

With such a stellar record, Wood might seem to have been a natural candidate for appointment as commander of the American Expeditionary Force (AEF) in France. But for all his brilliance and his truly remarkable accomplishments, Wood was a combative, confrontational, and arrogant officer who alienated many, often antagonizing even his supporters. "Shrewd, ruthless, and often insubordinate,"[40] some viewed him as "too politically powerful to be disciplined and not insubordinate enough to be court martialed."[41] As one commentator has written, "despite [his] sterling record, Wood's outspokenness on political matters, along with his close relationship with former President Roosevelt, led . . . [President] Wilson to distrust the general."[42] Put more bluntly, Wood's "open opposition to President Wilson" terminated his candidacy for the command.[43]

Instead, Wood was sent to Camp Funston, Kansas, where he took command of the 89th Division, which he prepared for deployment.[44] Though denied command of the AEF, Wood likely consoled himself with the prospect of leading the 89th Division to glory in France. It was not to be: when the 89th Division was alerted for deployment in May 1918, Wood was relieved of command.[45] He vigorously protested, securing meetings with the secretary of war, followed by a contentious meeting with President Wilson himself, but to no avail.[46] He had alienated the president and would remain in the United States. In Wilson's view, Wood was "an agitator, where he goes there is controversy and conflict. It is safer to have him here than on the war front."[47] Wood's poor relationship with Gen. Pershing had also contributed to this outcome: in the winter of 1917–1918, Pershing had recommended that seventeen senior officers be relieved of their commands and not sent to France—Wood among them.[48] Although Pershing cited Wood's health as the cause (he had suffered from a brain tumor for years),[49] in reality Pershing's long-standing "extreme animosity towards Leonard Wood"[50] was a major motivating factor. And Wood did not help himself by his behavior in Europe during an observation tour there in February 1918, where he "'launched into a freewheeling attack on Wilson and Pershing,' lamenting the poor preparation and leadership of the US Army, and criticizing the 'broomstick' training the soldiers were receiving at home,"[51] nearly scuttling Pershing's effort to keep the AEF together in its own sector on the front.[52]

So the 89th Division went to Europe without Wood, who stayed behind and saw to the training of the 10th Division. It does not appear, however, that the 89th Division itself shared their president's opinion on Gen. Wood, as an official history of the 89th recorded in 1919:

On June 1 [1918], General Wood was detailed elsewhere and Brigadier General Winn assigned to the command of the Division. The unexpected transfer of Gen. Wood on the very eve of the sailing of the Division which he had so carefully trained was keenly felt both by himself and by the officers and men from which he must separate. It was not possible to forget that the splendid esprit de corps and the high standard of military efficiency which had ever characterized the Division since its inception was primarily due to the wisdom, foresight, skill and character of General Wood. His division has never forgotten him.[53]

Wood was bitter at the slight of having his division sent to France without him, grumbling to a friend that "we are now developing another division, the troops to be taken over by someone else, without doubt; but nevertheless troops that I know will do their duty whether I am with them or not."[54] While disappointed, however, Wood does not appear to have felt himself demeaned at being asked to repeat his work of the 89th with 10th. On the contrary, he seems to have taken pride in the role, and to have demanded that the soldiers of the 10th take pride in themselves. "Look at your uniform as you look at your flag," he told them. "Remember it is just as deserving of respect as the robes of your clergy. It is the uniform in which many of you will make the supreme sacrifice. So keep it clean."[55] "We are trying to give you a discipline which is founded on respect for your officers and confidence in them," he wrote. "We do not want to give you the discipline of fear. We have the machinery to do it, but we never want to use that if we can help it, because it is not the right kind of discipline. That is the kind of discipline you are going to see fail when the break does come among the Germans."[56]

As to the enemy, "Do not believe that you have any special qualifications which will enable you to lick the Boche, the German, without special training," he wrote, "because that is not true. You have got to train just as you have for football or a game of baseball":[57]

You have got a hard job ahead of you. You are going into a war as severe, as remorseless and as cruel as men have ever known. It is almost a war without quarter. Now, we want as many of you to come back as possible, and the number that will come back will depend very largely upon whether or not you go over well trained. So go ahead with your training. You have got to learn all the tricks of a dirty enemy, a very brave enemy, but an enemy who is halting at nothing. . . . I am sorry to have to say this to you. We thought, in war, that we had reached an age where fair play would be the rule, but we have gone back to the early stages. It is simply a game of killing, nothing else, and the fellow who can stand the gaff the longest, who can smile last, is the man who is going to win.[58]

Training began in earnest soon after the division was formed; it reached an assigned strength of 22,300 officers and men by August 31 and would peak at an assigned strength of 24,829 by the end of November 1918, with most of the division coming from Illinois, Kansas, Missouri, Nebraska, and South Dakota.[59] As the war progressed, training improved; more equipment was available and units in training were not as harassed by levies of thousands of trained men, to be replaced by raw recruits; owing to these improvements, Gen. Wood was able to accomplish in three months with the 10th Division what it had taken him nine to accomplish with the 89th.[60] He was happy with the result:

The Division is made up of the same type of men as those who filled the ranks of the 89th . . . and a fine lot they are. We have had more in the way of training; we have had the same fine spirit of loyalty, and we had what we did not have before—freedom from changes in the personnel. . . . We received authority to organize the Division on August 10, 1918, and two weeks later, on August 24, we had a review of something over 23,000 men in line.[61]

Gen. Wood had to cope with one difficulty, at least, that would not trouble his successors in the 10th Mountain Division twenty-five years later: conscientious objection. "The conscientious objectors . . . proved an irritation out of proportion to their numbers."[62] They were also a source of yet more friction between Wood and the administration in Washington. While Selective Service rules allowed for exemption on the basis of conscience for objectors who were members of recognized religious groups in existence as of May 18, 1917,[63] War Department guidance extended the exemption even to those who objected not only on religious grounds, but on the basis of personal convictions unrelated to religion.[64] This Wood found obnoxious, since, in his view, it extended the shelter of conscientious objection to those whose objection to the war was not moral, but political—to men "who endeavored to convert their guards to communism, and posted at their quarters signs: 'Bolshevist Tent,' 'Lenin and Trotsky Tent,' or 'International Socialist Tent.'"[65] One Camp Funston military police officer likely spoke for Gen. Wood as well as himself when he observed that

through regulations coming down from the War Department . . . our hands were tied, and the worst of it was, the objectors knew just how closely our hands were bound . . . they flaunted their War Department protection in our faces and took great delight in doing so, knowing we could not expose the pacifist element of the War Department, as we were inferior officers to those protecting the obstructionists.[66]

The 10th Division's famous and colorful commander notwithstanding, its real brush with the great events of the time came from an altogether different, and tragic, quarter: the catastrophic Spanish flu pandemic of 1918. "Spanish" flu is a misnomer—the pandemic actually began in the United States, making one of its earliest appearances at Camp Funston. The first case was reported at Funston on March 4, 1918;[67] this soldier—Albert Gitchell—is often reported to have been "Patient Zero" in the pandemic, though this is disputed.[68] Camp Funston is widely believed to have been the epicenter of the first wave of the pandemic, though some scholars believe that it actually began 300 miles west at Haskell County, Kansas, and was brought to Camp Funston from there.[69] Wherever it began, it had a profound effect at Funston, where by March 29 over 1,100 men had been hospitalized with the infection.[70] This "first wave" occurred before the 10th Division was organized; however, the second, much-deadlier wave of the pandemic reached Camp Funston on September 16, 1918, just a few weeks after the 10th Division's organization the preceding month,[71] and spread "with appalling swiftness."[72] Even at the high of the first wave, deaths of soldiers in the United States from all causes never rose above about 0.25 per 1,000; during the second wave, however, deaths rocketed sixteenfold to nearly four per thousand.[73] This is *deaths*, not *infections*. Gen. Wood described the severity of the crisis at Camp Funston in a letter to the governor of Kansas, thus:

There are 1,440 minutes in a day. When I tell you there were 1,440 admissions in a day, or practically one a minute, you will realize the strain put upon our Nursing and Medical force. The Nurses and Medical Personnel did admirably. The influx of patients for two or three days was like the wounded coming back from the battlefront.[74]

Between September 16 and November 7, 1918, 16,983 Camp Funston soldiers were admitted for treatment, with the highest daily number of admissions occurring on September 30, at 785 admitted that day; 841 died of the disease during this "second wave."[75] While these figures do not differentiate by unit of assignment, it is absolutely clear that the pandemic reached into the ranks of the 10th Division. One 10th Division victim was Caleb Walton Hall, a private in the 28th Field Artillery Regiment, a Fairfax County, Virginia, native who succumbed to the pandemic at Camp Funston on September 29, 1918.[76]

The 10th Division never deployed to France. Overseas movement of personnel was suspended after the signing of the Armistice on November 11, 1918, and less than three weeks later, on November 29, 1918, the 20th Infantry Regiment was detached from the division, with units departing Camp Funston between December 12, 1918, and January 4, 1919; the 20th Infantry would be scattered to the four winds, with elements deployed to Camp Lloyd Wheaton, Rock Island, Denver, Nitro, Fort Brady, Fort Leavenworth, Fort Riley, and Fort Sheridan.[77] Demobilization of all elements of the division except the 20th Infantry and 41st Infantry was ordered on January 18, 1919; the 19th and 20th Infantry Brigade Headquarters and the 10th Field Artillery Headquarters were demobilized on February 13, 1919, and the 10th Division Headquarters itself was demobilized a few days later, on February 18, 1919.[78] The demobilization process was finally completed on March 31, 1919, when the 210th Engineer Trains disbanded.[79] The 19th and 20th Infantry Brigades were subsequently assigned to the Panama Canal Division, though with subordinate elements other than those assigned at Camp Funston,[80] until 1927.[81] Both were disbanded permanently in 1944.[82] Of the 19th Brigade's Camp Funston subordinate elements, the 41st Infantry Regiment saw active service in various designations and configurations during the Second World War;[83] the 69th Infantry was constituted in the Regular Army on October 1, 1933, as the 69th Infantry (Light Tanks), organized in approximately 1936 and disbanded on November 11, 1944.[84] Of the 20th Brigade's Camp Funston subordinate elements, the 20th Infantry Regiment, a Regular Army unit of long standing, went on to active service in the Second World War and Vietnam;[85] the 70th Infantry Regiment ceased to exist after being demobilized at Camp Funston.[86]

While the 19th and 20th Infantry Brigades (though not their subordinate units) formed the core of the Panama Division after the war,[87] the division itself was cast aside and is now considered as having no "current designation," on the grounds of having been "disbanded."[88] Perhaps the Army

did not view the 10th Division's brief tenure at Camp Funston as worthy of preserving in the history and lineage of the force, the unit having neither deployed nor carried out any operational tasks. If so, the Army does it a disservice. The 10th Division was commanded by one of the most noteworthy and successful American officers of the day, and its advanced party actually reached France during the course of hostilities. Thousands of soldiers reported for duty and trained with the division, and many, such as Pvt. Hall, died at Camp Funston, succumbing to the deadly Spanish flu or other causes while in the service of the United States with the 10th Division. The division was included in the general staff's 1921 historical summary of the US Army divisions activated during World War I, and a detailed summary of the division's history was included in the US Army's official order of battle for the First World War, originally printed in 1949 and reprinted in 1988.[89] What's more, the lineage and honors of at least three currently serving US Army battalions—5th Battalion, 20th Infantry; 1st Battalion, 41st Infantry; and 3rd Battalion, 41st Infantry—all reflect their assignment to the 10th Division during the First World War.[90] The 10th Division did not ignominiously lose its colors to the enemy like Rosemary Sutcliff's eponymous Ninth Legion;[91] on the contrary, the division and its soldiers rendered worthy service, and the loss of those who perished was no less grievous for their having died in Kansas rather than France. This Gen. Wood understood, as reflected in his message to them upon their discharge:

In the performance of military duty to one's Country in time of war, it is not for the citizen called to the Colors to select the kind of service to be done by him. One who has willingly and loyally responded to the call to arms and who has put his best efforts, mental and physical, into the training, and performed all military duties required of him to the best of his ability, standing ready always to make the supreme sacrifice of life itself, if need be, has done all that a good citizen and soldier could do to insure [sic] the successful prosecution of the war.[92]

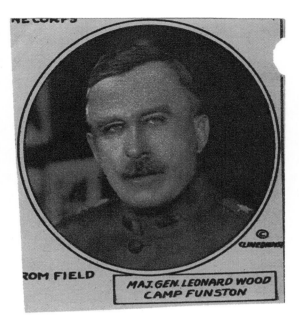

Shoulder sleeve insignia of the original 10th Division. *Author's collection*

Maj. Gen. Leonard Wood at Camp Funston, ca. 1918, as depicted in a 1918 *New York Times* pictorial. *Author's collection*

The long staircase leading to Leonard Wood's residence at Camp Funston. *Author's collection*

Another view of Maj. Gen. Wood's residence at Camp Funston. *Author's collection*

Drilling recruits at Camp Funston, during World War I. *Author's collection*

Unidentified Soldier of Company D,
70th Infantry Regiment, 10th Division,
World War I. *Author's collection*

Soldiers receiving instruction at Camp Funston during World War I. The caption reads "Reading the Camp Rules."
Author's collection

Tactical training at Camp Funston, World War I. The caption reads "Advancing by Squads." *Author's collection*

Enlisted collar insignia, Company E, 70th Infantry
Regiment, 10th Infantry Division, ca. 1918. *Author's
collection*

HEADQUARTERS TENTH DIVISION

February 20 1919.

From: The Commanding General.

To: *Mech Charles Miller Hdq Co 41st Inf*
Camp Funston Kan.

Subject: Discharge from service by reason of services being no
           longer required.

1. In the performance of military duty to one's Country in
time of war, it is not for the citizen called to the Colors to select the kind of service to be done by him.   One who has willingly
and loyally responded to the call to arms and who has put his best
efforts, mental and physical, into the training, and performed all
military duties required of him to the best of his ability, standing ready always to make the supreme sacrifice of life itself, if
need be, has done all that a good citizen and soldier could do to
insure the successful prosecution of the war.

2. Although I appreciate how keenly you feel the disappointment of your failure to secure duty overseas in the actual battle
area, I know you rejoice together with all Americans in the prospect
of a righteous and just peace imposed upon the enemy and the termination of the terrible conflict which has involved the whole civi-
lized World.   You have done your best.   You have cheerfully and
loyally discharged the clear duty of every citizen in time of war
and your work has been a part of the great National effort which has
aided in securing a victorious peace.

3. You are discharged from the Army because your services
are no longer required in the present emergency.   You will return
to your place in civil life all the better for the training you
have had, and I feel sure you will take with you a better and higher
appreciation of the obligations of citizenship, including the obli-
gation of every man to be trained, prepared and ready to render
service to the Nation in war as well as in peace.

LEONARD WOOD,
Major General, United States Army,
Commanding.

Discharge orders for a soldier of the 41st Infantry Regiment, 10th Division, Camp Funston, 1919. *Author's collection*

Headquarters

Sixty-Nineth Infantry

19th Brigade, 10th Division

Camp Funston, Kansas
January 11, 1919.

IN severing your connection from the service and from your Regiment, I desire as your Regimental Commander to assure you of my heartfelt wishes for your future success, and to express to you my appreciation of your qualities as a soldier and a man.

In the hard work of our intensive training, when we thought we would have our chance to go "over there," and through the days of our bitter disappointment when the Armistice was declared, your conduct and that of the men of the 69th Regiment was of the greatest pleasure and comfort to me.

No work has ever been too hard, no duty too difficult for you to perform, and now in going back to civil life you carry with you the proud knowledge that, although you did not go to France, you were ready and willing to go, and that you did your service for the Flag with equal patriotism here.

I hope to see you again and, believe me, I shall always be proud to meet a soldier who has served with me in the 69th Infantry.

I trust you will always keep this letter as a token of my friendship and esteem, and a remembrance of your service with this Regiment.

Colonel, 69th Infantry,
Commanding.

Discharge orders for a soldier of the 69th Infantry Regiment, 10th Division, Camp Funston, 1919. *Author's collection*

CHAPTER 2

Inception of the US Mountain Troops

Prior to the Second World War, the US Army had little in the way of specialized training or units with special capabilities. This is not to say that Americans were not aware of the specialized capabilities of other nations: for example, in 1935, the *Mid-Week Pictorial*, a tabloid weekly published by the New York Times Company, ran a one-page feature titled "Armies on Skiis," which included photographs of Austrian soldiers training on skis in Tyrol and Japanese troops conducting test maneuvers on skis preparatory to winter campaigning in Manchuria.[1] But given the small size of the Army and of its budgets during the interwar years, and, even more importantly, given the lack of clarity as to where or whether the United States might again fight, there was little incentive to invest limited resources in specialized training or in the development of specialized units.[2] By 1940, however, this attitude had begun to shift. One of the factors prompting that change was the fierce resistance mounted by tiny Finland against the invading forces of their gigantic neighbor, the Soviet Union.[3] The USSR invaded Finland on November 30, 1939,[4] following a period of negotiations beginning on October 12, in which the Finns refused to capitulate to a number of onerous Soviet demands upon their territory.[5,6] In these negotiations the Soviets had demanded adjustments in the USSR's favor to the Finnish-Soviet borders in the Karelian Isthmus and on the Rybachi Peninsula, they had demanded Soviet occupation of four Baltic islands belonging to Finland, and they demanded a lease of a naval base at Hangö and the right to station five thousand troops there.[7] Ultimately, the Finns offered to accept most of the Soviet demands but held firm against the leasing of Hangö; negotiations broke down on this point.[8] Because the Soviets considered this key to securing the northwestern approach to Leningrad, "the Soviet Union turned to a military solution."[9]

The Soviets committed approximately 500,000 troops to the attack on multiple axes, including thrusts in northern Finland, in the Lapland region in central Finland, and in the south on axes in eastern Karelia and the Karelian Isthmus.[10] This southern thrust was the Soviets' main effort, in which they launched the 350,000 soldiers of the Seventh Army Group against the Finns' Mannerheim Line, "a fortified zone of fire points, 'dragons teeth' tank traps, and trenches" across the Karelian Isthmus.[11] The Soviets largely relied on frontal assaults, while the Finns, a mainly infantry force principally composed of ten 15,000-man divisions, employed "*motti* tactics"[12]—fast-paced mobile warfare wherein small units of highly skilled ski troops would encircle and attack isolated enemy formations.[13] In these attacks,

battalions engaged in delaying actions aimed at bringing the enemy's forward group to a halt in every possible location. At the same time, where the terrain and conditions were favorable, the enemy column was broken up and isolated into small units. The breaking up of the column was done by strike forces that advanced from the cover of the flanking wilderness toward the road used by the enemy. Short distance slicing operations were performed by mobile ski units; ammunition, mines and explosives were either carried along or pulled in sleds.[14]

The Finns would also conduct blocking maneuvers, in which

blocking points on the road along which the enemy advanced were decided upon and marked on the map after careful planning and reconnaissance. Along the road, one or several small hills or outcroppings in the terrain, without any organized defense, were usually chosen as points to block the road. Another requirement was that if the enemy tried to move forward or retreat, the road could be easily cut and brought under fire. . . . The assault upon the point, which had been chosen for the roadblock, was done in the most surprising manner, taking the best possible advantage of the terrain and darkness.[15]

In a manner both echoing the recruiting of the Rough Riders in the Spanish-American War—those "rambunctious . . . cowboy volunteers"[16] that Congress had authorized to be formed into three regiments of cavalry, "to be composed exclusively of frontiersmen possessing qualifications as horsemen and marksmen"[17]—and foreshadowing the recruiting of the 10th Mountain Division a few years later, the Finns relied on a corps of tough outdoorsmen to provide them with operational mobility during these phase of their struggle: "Finnish farmers and lumberjacks were used to transportation with horses and sleighs in winter conditions. . . . In the pre-war winter maneuvers of the army, the methods of the farmers and the lumberjacks had been used. Sleighs, sleds and skis were chosen and developed in such a way that they could transport the heavy arms and equipment of the infantry in the roadless forests and across the frozen marshes"[18]—practice that would serve the Finns well in 1939 and 1940.

Contrary to the expectations of many of an easy Soviet victory, the Finns "surprised the world with the tenacity and effectiveness of their resistance," as their "ski troops, clothed in white to mask their moves disrupted Russian Supply columns and won victory after victory."[19,20] Their biggest victory was at Suomussalmi in east-central Finland, where Finnish forces destroyed one Soviet division and badly damaged another.[21] So effective was the Finnish resistance that "the Russo-Finnish campaign . . . seemed to destroy the belief that a new paragon of armed might had arisen in the East, and that the proletarian doctrine, grafted on the body of Russia, had given birth to a superlative new military organization, to a new skill in the art of war."[22] Although the Soviets under Marshal S. K. Timoshenko

ultimately "bludgeoned" the Finns into accepting a negotiated peace, it took nearly 1.2 million Soviet soldiers to subdue tiny Finland, and that at the cost of 68,000 killed and 130,000 wounded.[23] One scholar has succinctly summarized the outcome this way:

The Red Army achieved success in both campaigns against Finland through sound strategic planning, mass, and decisive tactical action to break through the Finnish defenses. However, Finland was able to systematically withdrawal to prepared secondary positions to prevent complete destruction of its army—the key Soviet operational objective.[24]

The Finnish success caught the attention of policymakers in the United States. Another campaign that piqued American interest in mountain and winter warfare was the Allied defeat in Norway,[25] where having landed troops in the vicinity of Narvik as early as April 15, 1940, they struggled "to take the town because of the difficulty of operating in deep snow over such broken country,"[26] thus "revealing the fact that the majority of the Allied ground units lacked adequate training and equipment for winter and mountain warfare. This fact strongly reduced their usefulness."[27] Other operations contributing to the interest in mountain and winter warfare were the success in the Balkans of German armored formations trained in mountain operations, and the failure of non-Alpini Italian troops in Albania.[28] Of the latter, the US military attaché in Italy observed that "the divisions were not organized, clothed, equipped, conditioned or trained for either winter or mountain fighting. The result was disaster."[29] He went on to conclude that

an army which may have to fight anywhere in the world must have an important part of its major units especially organized, trained and equipped for fighting in the mountains and in winter. The army and equipment must be on hand and the troops fully conditioned, for such units cannot be improvised hurriedly from line divisions.[30]

The Army took notice. On January 6, 1940, Assistant Secretary of War Louis Johnson made an inquiry to Army chief of staff George C. Marshall as to what thought the Army had given to the special requirements of matériel—supply, equipment, and logistics—that the Army would require to field an effective combat force "under conditions approximating those of the campaigns in Finland and Northern Russia."[31] Marshall replied that the Army had been studying this question with respect to the defense of Alaska, and that troops stationed in northern climates had been conducting winter training annually, pointing out as particularly successful the training at Fort Snelling, Minnesota, which had successfully incorporated skis.[32] Marshall further stated it as his "intention [to] continue, accelerating where practicable, tests of food, clothing, equipment and transportation in order to standardize for the purpose the types best suited to operations under severe winter conditions, [and that] the campaign in Finland is being studied and should be of considerable assistance."[33] Marshall added that "winter maneuvers, on a larger scale than yet attempted are desirable, but to date funds for this purpose have not been available."[34]

The Finnish resistance had not just caught the attention of military and government officials; it had also captured the public imagination.[*] As one scholar has noted, "Though Finland was previously little known to much of the world, throughout the winter of 1939–1940 readers around the globe anxiously followed stories of the heroic little nation battling alone in the cold north against the Soviet Union."[35] To the astonishment of Americans and the entire world, the Finnish army put up effective resistance. Finnish valor impressed Americans and elicited even more enthusiastic support as the David and Goliath struggle captured the national imagination.[36]

It caught the imagination of one American in particular—Charles Minot "Minnie" Dole. In February 1939, Dole and a few friends gathered for drinks at a local inn following a day's work supporting the activities of the annual skiing festival at Manchester, Vermont.[37] Years later, Dole would recall that

the conversation turned to the Russo-Finnish War, and inevitably—because we were skiers—we discussed the amazing job the Finns were doing on the Russians on the Karelian Isthmus. The isthmus was honeycombed with canals, marshes, and inlets which froze solid in winter. As marching columns of Russians advanced across the frozen wastes, they were met by fast-moving Finns on skis, who would attack from ambush . . . the number of separate attacks gave the Russians the impression that the Finnish army was double its size.[38]

Dole and his compatriots felt that the Finns were "a perfect example of men fighting under conditions and terrain with which they are familiar,"[**] and then reflected on the poor state of training of the US Army at the time: "If foreign troops should attack our northeast coast in winter, can you imagine our Army trying to slog through the sort of weather outside?" Dole asked, further observing that "they'd have a hard enough time getting up the roads, let along branching off into the woods."[39] That conversation was the genesis of a passionate quest by Dole and fellow skiing enthusiasts that would, eventually, lead to the formation of the 10th Mountain Division.

A "Connecticut insurance broker" and 1923 graduate of Yale University, Minnie Dole was an "avid skier" who learned to ski as a Boy Scout.[40,41]

---

[*] For a fictional account of the Russo-Finnish War, see Antti Touri, *The Winter War*, part of the Aspasia Classics in Finnish Literature series.

[**] These Finnish ski troops, together with the American ski troops for which they were, at least in part, the inspiration, would make a small, odd, but enduring appearance in American literature, In John Knowles's classic coming-of-age novel and perennial denizen of high school literature classes, *A Separate Peace*. In Knowles's novel, eastern prep school student Phineas compensates for his inability to join the war effort due to injury, by carrying on a running fantasy about the war not being real but, rather, being an elaborate hoax. Phineas continues his game when recruiters for the United States Ski troops make a presentation at his fictional school, objecting that the ski troopers in the film aren't Americans at all, but rather images of Finns about to attack Soviet troops. John Knowles, *A Separate Peace*, 109.

Two skiing accidents—one minor and one tragic—would shape his life: the first event occurred around New Year's Day 1936, when, on a skiing trip with a friend, Dole fell and broke an ankle. Help was difficult to find, and he ended up being taken down the mountain on a jury-rigged litter made of a tin sheet.[42] Two months later, Dole's friend Frank Edson was killed in an accident during a ski race.[43] These events inspired Dole to found the National Ski Patrol in 1938, and to serve as its director until 1950.[44]

The National Ski Patrol was formed as a "great co-operative movement organized by skiers," essentially a federation of "Registered Ski Patrols whose primary objective is to work towards greater safety and therefore greater enjoyment in the sport of skiing."[45] Among its stated goals was the development of skiing safety and first-aid education programs, establishing of new ski patrols and coordinating their operations, improving the efficiency the ski patrol system by bringing to bear the resources and experiences nationwide, management and improvement of ski slopes and trails, maintenance and improvement of first-aid resources in support of skiing, and other functions.[46]

As war clouds loomed in 1940, Dole turned his attention to the employment of skiing, and of the capabilities of the National Ski Patrol System, in the defense of remote mountainous parts of the United States and its possessions. In June 1940, he and colleague John Morgan traveled to Governor's Island, New York, to meet the II Corps Headquarters chief of staff, Gen. Irving I. Phillipson, and offer the services of the National Ski Patrol to the War Department.[47] Phillipson was well aware of the rigors of conducting training and operations in winter, having formerly commanded Pine Camp—the future Fort Drum and home of the modern 10th Mountain Division—in upstate New York—during wintertime.[48] Having experienced the truly harsh North Country climate with its brutal lake-effect snowstorms caused

by the camp's proximity to Lake Ontario,* Phillipson was supportive of Dole's proposal but felt that he would best prosper by taking the matter up directly with the authorities in Washington.[49] Dole and Morgan did so, setting off for Washington, DC, that very day, using a connection in the office of Senator Wadsworth to gain entrée to training expert Col. Charles Hubner of the general staff.[50] When Hubner was unreceptive, they wrote directly to President Roosevelt on July 18, 1940, telling the president[51]

of Finland's and Norway's heroic ski troops. [Dole's letter] offered the idea of American ski troops. It contended that only ski troops could defend the Aleutian Islands, Alaska, or the snowbound Rockies against invasion. In Europe, Norway was mountainous. So were the Balkans, and Italy with its Apennines and Dolomites and Brenner Pass.[52]

Suggesting that "it is more reasonable to make soldiers out of skiers than skiers out of soldiers," Dole proposed establishment of two training camps, one in the East and one in the Northwest, where two hundred men could be trained in winter warfare, then to be sent out as instructors to the rest of the Army.[53] Roosevelt referred the matter to the War Department and so notified Dole. Thus encouraged, Dole leveraged a Yale classmate's business connections to secure a meeting[54] with Special Assistant to the Secretary of War Arthur Palmer and, through him, other functionaries, and finally Gen. Marshall.[55] While many of the other officials Dole met reacted skeptically, Marshall showed interest.[56] Meeting in September 1940,[57] Dole, Morgan, and Marshall reviewed Dole's proposals; Marshall noted that he was "considering leaving several divisions in the north for winter training."[58] Dole responded with a pledge of full assistance from the National Ski Patrol System—on offer that Gen. Marshall

* The author experienced the ferocious winter climate of the upstate New York "North Country" directly when stationed at Fort Drum with the 10th Mountain Division in the early 1990s, when snow could accumulate fast enough to strand vehicles in a couple of hours and astounding quantities of snow might fall over the course of a day, due to lake-effect storms attributable to the proximity of nearby Lake Ontario. Wintertime post closures caused by snowfall occurred with regularity, and when the decision was made to close the installation, it was wise to head out for home immediately, since those sticking around a bit longer to finish up a few last details might find themselves struggling to make it home at all.

accepted.[59] Following this meeting, the War Department appointed two officers of the Army general staff to serve as liaisons between the NSPS and the Army, with whom Dole began the long and arduous process of developing suitable equipment for US Army soldiers engaged in winter operations.[60]

Following Dole and Morgan's meeting with Gen. Marshall, the National Ski Patrol received a small infusion of funds from the Army ($2,500),[61] and, in November 1940, Gen. Marshall formally requested the assistance of the National Ski Patrol System. In a letter dated November 9, 1940, Marshall asked "the personnel of the National Ski Patrol, acting as a volunteer civilian agency,"

> to become fully familiar with local terrain; to locate existing shelter and to experiment with the means of shelter, such as light tents, which may be found suitable for the sustained field operations of military ski patrol units; to perfect an organization prepared to furnish guides to the Army in event of training or actual operations in the local areas; and to cooperate with and extend into inaccessible areas the anti-aircraft and anti-parachute warning services.[62]

Eventually the NSPS received an annual stipend from the Army, initially $6,500, eventually rising to $25,000 per year.[63]

On December 5, 1940, Gen. Marshall, through the secretary of war, issued a directive to the 1st Division (Fort Devens, Massachusetts), 44th Division (Fort Dix, New Jersey), 5th Division (Fort Custer, Michigan), Division (Fort Leonard Wood, Missouri), and 3rd and 41st Divisions (Fort Lewis, Washington) that "the National Ski Association (Patrol System) would assist the Army in winter warfare training as well as experiment with light tents and other means of shelter, and would be prepared to furnish guides and cooperate in antiaircraft and anti-parachute warning service."[64] It further provided that these divisions were to establish ski patrols in their areas consisting of selected soldiers who would be taught to travel by ski and snowshoe, as well as camping and traveling in snow and mountain

terrain; each division was given $1,200 with which to purchase equipment.[65]

The 1st Division designated the 26th Infantry Regiment (minus one battalion) as its ski-training test unit; its training would be conducted at Plattsburg, New York. Additionally, groups of ten officers and one hundred enlisted soldiers traveled on a rotational basis to Lake Placid, where they received a week of "concentrated ski instruction from three-time US Olympic Team captain Rolfe Monsen. Ultimately nine rotations, totaling about a thousand men, received this training,[66] and "three officers and fifty-three men were formed into a ski patrol, which attained a high degree of skill."[67] The 26th Regiment completed its training on February 28, 1941. Summarizing what he had learned from the training, regimental commander Col. James T. Muir wrote that

> teaching troops to use snowshoes is simple. ... Any person who meets the Army physical requirements only needs a short course of instruction and then a short hardening or conditioning period to be able to maneuver proficiently on snow shoes. ... The problem of teaching troops to ski is comparatively simple. Young men of good physique, particularly those with well-coordinated sense of balance, can become expert on skis in a relatively short time. The major problems are those of supporting weapons, ammunition, evacuation, and supply.[68]

Col. Muir concluded with the observation that "ski training is an asset; like the Texan's six-shooter, you may not need it, but if you ever do, you will need it in a hurry, 'awful bad.'"[69]

The 3rd Division at Fort Lewis, Washington, established its ski patrol in December 1940 from a pool of "picked volunteers out of the 15th Infantry."[70] In 1948, the Army Ground Forces prepared its official history of the Mountain Warfare Training Center; that history described the 3rd Division's ski patrol as follows:

> Capt. Howard Crawford was administrative officer, and Capt. Paul B. Lafferty, former University of Oregon ski coach, was technical

adviser. Lt. Woodward acted as ski instructor. Eighteen men made up the unit which was quartered in a converted Park Service garage at Longmire on Mt. Rainier. . . . The first six weeks were spent in ski instruction on cross-country and stem turns. Route selection and camouflage discipline as well as trail discipline were stressed. Four overnight marches were made during this phase, starting with a two-day trip, and ending with a week's journey around the flanks of Mt. Rainier and across many of its glaciers.[71]

The 5th Division moved its training from Fort Custer, Michigan, to Camp McCoy, Wisconsin, to take advantage of better snow conditions there, and a Winter Warfare Training Board under Capt. Albert H. Jackman was established on December 8, 1940.[72] The Army Ground Forces history described the 5th Division's program as follows:

Patrol training was carried out by the 3d Battalion, 2d Infantry, consisting of about a thousand officers and men, using basic equipment. A ski patrol best detachment of about 5 officers and 250 enlisted men, using the best commercial equipment available, was set up. Two, later four, civilian instructors were hired. Training, mainly in cross-country work was carried on extensively all winter because of the flat nature of that immediate terrain. Intense cold prevailed. Lt. Col. Joseph L. Ready reported the following observations: It is comparatively simple to teach men the fundamentals of skiing on level ground, in soft deep snow. Personal hygiene instruction must be stressed to prevent frostbite of the hands, face, and feet. The technique of winter camping must be taught all men. All ski patrol members must be specifically trained.[73]

In the 6th Division, training was conducted separately by a number of detachments. I Company of the 1st Infantry Regiment trained on snow-shoeing and skiing at Fort Warren, Wyoming; at Fort Snelling, Minnesota, Company H, 3rd Infantry, conducted snowshoe training; while at Fort Warren a composite elements of the 20th

Infantry trained on skis and snowshoes.[74] The 6th Division also organized a twenty-two-man ski patrol, half officers and half enlisted men. This patrol received its first twenty hours of instruction from National Ski Association representative Alfred Lindley, and then another one hundred hours of instruction from a reserve officer on active duty, Lt. John Hay.[75] On the basis of their training, Maj. Gen. C. S. Ridley of the 6th Division recommended the following:

There was no need for changing the Tables of Organization. Specially trained patrols were required, to which the best qualified men should be detailed. One ski platoon for each battalion was suggested. A platoon of three squads of twelve men each should make up a ski patrol, one man in each squad to be armorer-artificer, carrying the spare parts and maintenance tools. All rifle companies in the Infantry should be ski-equipped. The weapons platoon should use snowshoes. Medical units should use both.[76]

Gen. Ridley further recommended "an instructors' school for officers and noncommissioned officers in winter warfare" and noted that the ski patrol had the same function as the cavalry patrol, and that troops expected to operate in winter environments "must be stationed at places known to be suitable for snowshoeing and skiing."[77]

On the West Coast, the 41st Division of Fort Lewis, Washington, began its ski patrol training on Mount Rainier in January 1940, being billeted at the Ashcroft Civilian Conservation Corps Camp near Rainier National Park.[78] Consisting of twenty-five men plus Lt. Phelps, its commander, the 41st Division patrol had little skiing experience, but its members "were distinguished for their athletic ability and general ruggedness."[79] Skiing instruction was carried out by a former Montana ski instructor, Sgt. Karl Hindermen, who focused on the fundamental skills necessary to carry out "the patrol's mission," which was to "cover great distances over snow safely with greatest possible speed, carrying their own food, supplies, and weapons, in an effort to determine the effectiveness of the training program."[80]

After completing its individual ski instruction, the 41st Division ski patrol carried out an aggressive program of long-distance patrolling. The first patrol consisted of a four-day crossing of the Olympic Mountains under the leadership of a former University of Washington ski-team captain, Lt. John B. Woodward; this patrol consisted of a 40-mile trek through woods, across rocky peaks, and over 12-foot snows—"the men and equipment stood up well."[81] The patrol then conducted a two-week movement "across the northern end of the Olympic Mountains, seldom travelled in winter."[82] Per the Army Ground Forces History:

After the first week the strain began to tell on both men and equipment; some boots and bindings fell apart, and some of the men developed blisters or became exhausted. Eight of the group were sent back, but the rest continued the trip for another week to a successful conclusion. On 20 April 1941, the 41st Division ski patrol was disbanded.[83]

The 44th Division established its ski-training unit from among personnel stationed at Fort Dix, New Jersey, in February 1941. Again, from the Army Ground Forces Mountain Training Center History:

In charge was Lt. Eric C. Wikner, formerly of Sweden, with considerable experience in cross-country skiing and winter camping. Pvt. Harold Sorensen, Olympic skier from Norway, who had been inducted into the Army a few days previously, was selected as coach for the patrol of twenty-three men. The area surrounding Old Forge, NY, was chosen as the training ground. For 3 1/2 weeks the men were given extensive training in military skiing and camping in extreme cold—sometimes as low as 20 degrees below zero. Detailed tests were conducted and reports written on various types of sleeping bags, clothing, skis, and general winter equipment. The men engaged in actual combat maneuvers during the last few days. As usual, the ski-vs-snowshoe argument was raised by the local inhabitants. Two test races were held between skiers

from the patrol and native snowshoers, the best in the Adirondack Mountains, including an Indian. Though the course had been laid out by the snowshoers themselves, with emphasis on uphill and deep woods terrain, each time the skiers won with ease, proving conclusively that skis are faster for general snow travel. For the most part, the members of the patrol had had previous skiing experience, but they could not in any sense of the word be termed expert military skiers. However, after nearly a month of concentrated instruction in the snow plow and the lifted stem Christiania, the 44th Division ski patrol was able to travel up to 25 miles a day with a 45-pound pack and be ready for combat on arrival— It had become a military ski patrol.[84]

The Army's experiment with ski troopers was noticed and reported on favorably in a write-up in *Life* magazine, featuring a photo of a US Army soldier engaged in ski training on the front cover, and a brief description, with illustrations, of **winter training on Mount Rainier.**[85] Notwithstanding its brevity and its tabloid format, the *Life* magazine piece correctly assessed the Army's objective in conducting such training, noting that the Army did not envision a vast force of skiers.[86] Given the breadth of the United States and its territories, and the diversity of the environments that those territories encompassed, as well as the uncertainty of where the Army might fight—not to mention the paucity of resources with which the US Army traditionally had to cope—specialization was a luxury that the Army felt it could ill afford. As the chief of staff of the Army noted in his biennial report in 1941:

The Army of the United States differs in one important characteristic from the armies of Europe. Ours must be an all-purpose Army as we are in an entirely different position from a European nation which knows its traditional or potential enemies and the terrain over which it will have to fight. We must be prepared to operate in the Arctic or the Tropics, in deserts or mountains, and the elements of our ground forces must be properly balanced to meet any contingencies. Our organization must be a balanced one with armored, air, and foot elements in proper proportion to provide maximum flexibility.[87]

The Army's objective, in this initial phase of winter training, was simply to identify the equipment and tactics best suited to defending Alaska or fighting in some other northern clime.[88] As Minnie Dole wrote,

At this time all thinking was on the defense of this country, strange as that may sound to readers now. But before we got into World War II, we were not the strongest military country in the world, only potentially so. It was to repel possible invasion of North America that United States mountain troops were first organized.[89]

The experiment was a success. "The purpose of the winter testing and training program in 1940–41 was not to build up a combat force of ski troops, but rather to lay a foundation for future winter training."[90] It did so. The winter training experiment produced a great deal of useful data pointing the way to the successful activation of mountain and winter units. While there were clearly obstacles to be overcome, the experiment established "that men with no previous skiing experience could be taught military skiing in two months well enough to become instructors themselves—provided they were picked for rugged health and athletic ability."[91] It also showed that mere facility with skiing was not enough: recreational skiing experience would not ensure success as a ski trooper—experience in winter camping was also a necessity if the skier was to be able to withstand the rigors of mountain and winter operations, and this would have to be taken into consideration as plans were laid to proceed with the activation of mountain and winter units.[92]

While the various divisions were carrying out their experiments in winter training, parallel work was ongoing on the critical matter of equipping units—on a permanent rather than an experimental

basis—for winter operations. This was not as simple a matter as going out onto the commercial market and purchasing equipment off the shelf. While there were more than two million skiers in the United States, the sporting-goods industry focused its efforts on supplying the needs of the large proportion of skiers who were hobbyists, who "knew only enough skiing to enable them to go out in the winter and slide down a packed slope for a few hours at a time," consequently producing equipment adapted for civilian rather than rigorous military use; furthermore, much of the suitable equipment that did exist was not made in the United States.[93] Nothing illustrates just how complex the issue of equipment was than the "battle of the bindings." This controversy began with a letter by Minnie Dole to the War Department vociferously protesting the use of toe-strap bindings by US Army ski troops, insisting instead on "diagonal down-pull bindings."[94] In 1940, the National Ski Association held its annual convention in Milwaukee, Wisconsin; Dole wrote to Gen. Marshall, asking that Col. Hubner and Col. Nelson Walker attend, which they did.[95] At this conference the National Ski Patrol System and the National Ski Association formed the National Volunteer Winter Defense Committee;[96] the matter of the proper equipping of ski troops was taken up at a meeting of that body, where "the battle of the bindings resumed," to the amusement of two Army lieutenant colonels who attended the conference, entertained by the fact that "even the skiing experts couldn't agree on the exact type of bindings."[97] The committee entrusted this vexing matter to a subordinate equipment committee chaired by Sierra Club member Bestor Robinson. Robinson and his committee took on the challenge of developing requirements for the myriad equipment items that ski troops would need, from items of clothing (parkas, pants, headgear, and mittens), to sleeping and shelter equipment (sleeping bags, mats, and tents), to equipment needed on the march, such as rucksacks, footwear, and the skis themselves.[98] The committee received advice from all corners of the globe, on matters ranging from sled dogs and motorized sleds to alpine climbing equipment.[99]

As a preliminary matter, the equipment committee conducted review of the foreign literature on winter tactics and equipment, which quickly revealed that developing doctrine for and equipping US ski troops would not be as simple as borrowing doctrine from nations with established winter and mountain troops: the US effort had in view the defense of Alaska, the northern plains, and the Rocky Mountains; American circumstances simply did not match those in these other lands.[100] As noted in the *History of the Mountain Training Center*,

It soon became apparent to the committee, however, that the American terrain presented unique problems that could not be solved by applying foreign techniques. In the matter of shelter, for example, the European technique depended largely upon the existence of near-by huts, barns, and farmhouses for overnight bivouac. These structures are common to much of the European and Scandinavian mountain terrain, but they are not found on the American continent, especially in Alaska. The Finns transported their equipment on horse drawn sleds, on which were carried heavy conical tents, housing as many as eighteen men, and kept warm by body heat alone. The Swiss even dug huge caves in their glaciers and cornices. No such procedures would work in the soft powdery snows and the roadless mountains of the Western Hemisphere. It must be remembered that at this time all thoughts were on defense against invasion—not invasion by us. It was to repel possible hostile attacks on North America itself that the United States Mountain Troops were first organized.[101]

Another concern was the lack of objective technical data on the specifications necessary for adequate winter equipment and the performance characteristics of the equipment that was available, a situation unacceptable to Robinson, who wanted equipment tested and scientific data collected.[102] Toward that end, the Army Medical Corps established a testing facility at Fort Knox, Kentucky, where test subjects lived for extended periods of time under artificially created arctic temperatures,

and doctors collected data on the results.[103] Probably the most progress was made, however, by the practical test conducted at Bestor Robinson's behest by the Sierra Club, which mounted a skiing expedition to test various articles of clothing and equipment;[104] one Capt. Lafferty of the 15th Infantry accompanied the expedition.[105] The "zero weather, blizzards, and gales met with by the group of twenty men" in the High Sierras "provided excellent conditions for testing the various items, and the results of these findings were incorporated into the Army recommendations sent to the Army during the summer."[106]

On April 2, 1941, the acting assistant G-3, Col. Harry Twaddle, sent a proposal to the Army chief of staff recommending allocation of $15,000,000 for the "immediate construction" of a high-altitude camp to facilitate training in mountain terrain, suggesting that it was "quite possible that part of our army will be called upon to fight in the mountains and we should not be totally unprepared as were the British in Norway."[107] That month, Colonels Walker and Hurdis and Forestry Service representative Bob Monohan were tasked to survey locations in the western United States capable of housing fifteen thousand men—a full division—for year-round mountain winter training.[108] Discussion about the proposal went on throughout the summer and was opposed on the theory that it ought to be feasible to develop competence in mountain warfare by training infantry units in mountain field camps located near their home stations.[109] Twaddle countered that

the training of units in mountain warfare by having such units move to suitable high mountain terrain and camp for short periods is a makeshift method and entirely inadequate. . . . Troops operating in mountains will normally encounter high altitudes, snow and low temperatures. They must be accustomed to life under such conditions. The camping problems alone are tremendous. Troops must actually live and train the year round under high altitude conditions if we are to obtain any worthwhile results. There is no case where realism in training is more appropriate. . . . Fort Lewis is about sixty miles from terrain which is barely satisfactory for this purpose. Camp Ord and San Luis Obispo are about one hundred miles from suitable terrain.[110]

Although debate continued, Twaddle's recommendation was tabled, at least temporarily, when on May 5, 1941, Gen. Marshall made the decision not to request funds for the construction of the high-terrain training camp. In part, the impetus for his decision had come from Lt. Gen. Lesley J. McNair, general headquarters chief of staff. McNair opposed proposals for the formation of a special mountain division unless and until the definite need for one arose; informing McNair's opposition was the fact that maneuvers in 1941 had convincingly shown—if it had ever been doubted—that the US Army was not ready for combat anywhere, much less in specialized mountain terrain. Also of concern were the competing demands for resources from advocates of other forms of specialization—aviation, armor, and mechanized forces—all of which conspired to render dedicated mountain forces "a luxury that could not be afforded unless there was a reasonable certainty that they would be required.[111] On receipt of this news, Minnie Dole objected, pointing out that America's northern border was snow covered at least four months of the year, that winter conditions had been a feature of the fighting in several countries during the ongoing war, that Germany could field fourteen mountain divisions, and that no one could predict where or when we might be called upon to fight.[112]

The door had not been completely closed on the prospect of dedicated mountain troops in the US Army, however. For while Gen. Marshall had opted not to request funding to construct the high-altitude training camp, his memorandum of May 5, 1941, *had* "ordered surveys to be made for a mountain division camp in the vicinity of West Yellowstone, Montana, and Pando, Colorado, so that full information would be ready if there was a further augmentation of the Army."[113] Marshall further supported establishment of a high-altitude training school to train select personnel and create the nucleus for a future mountain force if needed; for his part, Lt. Gen. McNair recommended the

creation of an infantry battalion and an artillery battalion capable of mountain operations.[114]

For all of Minnie Dole's advocacy, it appears that the true impetus for the creation of the school or test force suggested by Marshall and McNair came from the war in Europe. On August 5, 1941, Lt. Col. L. S. Gerow of the general staff noted in a memorandum that a decision on establishing such a test force had been postponed pending fiscal analysis. "He then went on," however,

to quote extracts from a recent report submitted by our military attaché to Italy, to the effect that the Italian army was defeated in the Balkan campaign by lack of well-equipped mountain troops. After the Greek counteroffensive had driven the Italians back across the mountains of Albania in the dead of winter, the Italian High Command could only throw piecemeal into the operations infantry divisions of the line as fast as they could be gotten to Albania. These divisions were not organized, clothed, equipped, conditioned, [or] trained for either winter or mountain fighting. The result was disaster. Twenty-five thousand were killed, ten thousand were frozen, large numbers made prisoners; loss in morale and prestige were irreparable . . . one of the important lessons learned from this was that an army which may have to fight anywhere in the world must have an important part of its major units especially organized, trained, and equipped for fighting in the mountains and in winter. . . . Such units cannot be improvised hurriedly from line divisions. They require long periods of hardening and experience, for which there is no substitute for time.[115]

Gerow then noted that "this was a powerful argument for specialized training, and he suggested that the plan for a test force in the mountains be again taken up with a view to reconsideration."[116] The German invasion of Russia also reinforced the need for units with specialized mountain and winter training. As early as mid-November 1941, the effect of Russia's winter climate was beginning to tell on the invaders, as they began to suffer from the lack of appropriate clothing and equipment in the harsh climate of the Soviet Union.[117]

Formation of the Mountain Training Center and the 87th Mountain Infantry Regiment

The War Department was reorganized in early March 1942; supervision of training activities was transferred from GHQ to the Army ground forces.[118] While the change in Army organization did not extinguish interest in winter and mountain training, resource and manpower limitations made the formation of any large-scale body of mountain troops infeasible. Instead, it was decided to continue work with a small-scale test force through 1942, and to defer activation of a division until early 1943.[119] Pando, Colorado, was selected as the sight of the Mountain Training Center, and contracts were signed for the construction of the future Camp Hale at a site 9,000 feet above sea level.[120] Pando was a tiny community located 6 miles from Leadville, Colorado, which had been hard hit by the Great Depression, which it endured by selling ice for refrigerator cars supporting California fruit growers.[121] Pando was deemed a good location for the Mountain Training Center because of its location in a long valley affording ample space for the construction of a camp, surrounded by 12,000-foot peaks as a training area for alpine training to come, and because it was accessible by both rail and a major highway.[122] Initially, however, mountain training would commence at Fort Lewis, Washington, where the 15th Infantry had already successfully conducted its ski patrol; so, on November 15, 1941, the 1st Battalion (Reinforced), 87th Mountain Infantry, was activated.[123] The following February the unit trucked to Mount Rainier, where they were billeted in two rented hotels leased until the following June, and where they would initially train.[124] Their temporary lodgings were

an ideal location because of the nearness to Ft. Lewis—62 miles over paved and ploughed highways. The buildings had a combined military capacity of about four hundred men—enough for almost three rifle companies. Rations were brought up daily

from Ft. Lewis by truck, and all meals were cooked by Army personnel in the capacious kitchens of the Lodge. But above all, this lodge was located right in the heart of the best snowfields of the State of Washington, and skiing started from the front door, or rather from the second-story windows, thanks to a 20-foot average snow depth.[125]

Like the 10th Mountain Division itself, the 87th Infantry Regiment had a predecessor of the same designation organized during the First World War. The original 87th was constituted on July 31, 1918; it was organized as a part of the 19th Division in September 1918, around a cadre of personnel drawn from the 14th Infantry Regiment,[126] with the bulk of other personnel being draftees.[127] The War Department ordered the formation of the 19th Division on July 31, 1918.[128] It was to be a Regular Division organized at Camp Dodge, Iowa;[129] the actual formation of the division began only in September 1918, after the 2nd and 14th Infantry Regiments were "concentrated" at Camp Dodge.[130*] Training began on a rolling basis as the division's subordinate units formed, and continued until January 1919.[131] The division was demobilized on January 29, 1919,[132] the 87th Regiment having demobilized two days earlier, on the twenty-seventh.[133] The new 87th was constituted on November 15, 1941, and activated at Fort Lewis, Washington,[134] under the command of Lt. Col. Onslow Rolfe, with an initial complement of twelve officers and one enlisted soldier, the latter having been "drafted to stoke the fires, [being] the only non-volunteer in the early days of the outfit."[135] Unknown to the new recruits that began trickling in to the unit at Fort Lewis, the 87th Infantry would go on to be the "first regiment to sail to both the Pacific and European Theaters,"[136] deploying first to the windswept wastes of Kiska in the Aleutian Islands in August 1943 as part of Amphibious Task Force 9,[137] and later deploying to Italy in 1945. But for now, the 87th Infantry was a "paper regiment,"[138] with the first recruits trickling in slowly. One of the first men recruited was Charlie McLane, former captain of the Dartmouth Ski Team. McLane had approached Dole and the NSPS about the mountain troops and was given authorization to proceed to Fort Lewis—he was the first to join the 87th, being told upon arrival, "Lad, you are the Mountain Infantry. You're a one-man regiment."[139] The 87th got off to a slow start. McLane's first night was "wretched":

His was an empty room in the barracks. Many empty cots made the room still emptier. . . . Each day this week brought new disappointments. A few dozen men who had never seen skis or snow arrived at Fort Lewis to make up the nucleus of the 87th.[140]

The absence of fellow skiers was not the only challenge facing the new mountain troopers in those early days, as McLane would later recall. "Those were the scary days when Fort Lewis was being evacuated," he wrote. "Troops scattered about in the hills to avoid a concentration. They knew there was possible trouble brewing in Japan, and that Japan had bombers and carriers that could reach us."[141]

The core of the regiment began to take shape. As John Jay* would later write in the *History of the Mountain Training Center*,

Because of the highly specialized nature of the training, it was essential that the proper personnel be picked to form cadres for the new outfit. With the exception of four Regular Army officers, all of whom had had experience in winter climates or with pack animals, the initial cadre was organized from a canvass of men from the 3rd Division, the California National Guard, the 41st Division, and from volunteers who had had previous skiing experience in Yosemite and similar ski areas along the West Coast. This group, commanded by

Lt. Col. Onslow S. Rolfe, himself a crack horseman, was soon augmented by a steady flow of volunteers and transfers from all parts of the country, but mainly from the New England area.[142]

By December 8, about seventy-five enlisted soldiers and officers had reported to the regiment from the 15th Cavalry, mostly being assigned to A Company but also establishing the skeleton of all the other companies in the regiment.[143] The Mountain Infantry was quite an adjustment for some of these "cavalrymen from New Mexico, artillerymen from California, [and] infantrymen from Washington":[144]

Particularly the cavalry demonstrated a violent animosity toward Mount Rainier. These men still loved the cavalry . . . The talk in the mess was horse talk until suddenly Capt. Lafferty appeared with a handful of men who had formed the 15th Ski Patrol the winter before. With these men came the first distinctive flavor of skiing, the splitkeins under the cots and the smell of burnished wax. The bragging and swaggering, too. Cautiously, the cavalry began to inquire about lifted stem Christianias.[145]

Upon the arrival of the 87th at Mount Rainier, training began in earnest. Again, as recounted in the *History of the Mountain Training Center*:

The best men in the outfit had previously been selected and interviewed to determine their fitness to teach military skiing, and a nucleus of about thirty men was designated as the instructional cadre. They came from all parts of the country—from Franconia and North Conway in the East; from

---

* Throughout much of the Army's history, the regiments of the Regular Army were often broken up and distributed at widely scattered posts rather than serving together as cohesive units at a single duty station.
** Jay was closely connected with the Mountain Training Center throughout its existence, initially serving as a meteorologist and photographer for the Mountain and Winter Warfare Board, joining the Mountain Warfare Center when it transferred to Camp Hale; he then served as S2 of the center and later as commander of the 10th Reconnaissance Troop. He would go on to have an interesting and distinguished career. A lineal descendant of John Jay, first chief justice of the United States Supreme Court, Jay would become a prolific producer of skiing films, stimulating the growth of skiing as a sport. See John C. Jay, *History of the Mountain Training Center*, i; Charles Minot Dole, *The National Ski Patrol System Manual*, 113; and Elaine Woo, "John Jay: Descendant of Chief Justice Pioneered Ski Films," *Los Angeles Times*, December 15, 2000.

Wisconsin in the Midwest; from Yosemite, Sun Valley, and Mt. Hood in West, to mention a few. Their techniques were as varied as their names, and a standard of military skiing had to be developed. A school for instructors was hastily organized by Capt. Lafferty, assisted by Peter Gabriel of Franconia and Arnold Fawcus of Yosemite, and a composite type of military skiing was established, [taking] cognizance . . . of the fact that most of the skiing was to be done with heavy packs, so that the graceful sweeping turns of civilian skiing were out. Emphasis was placed on safety and endurance rather than upon speed and daring.[146]

A rugged course of instruction ensued for the next week, six days a week in all weather, focusing exclusively on skiing, with all other training held in abeyance during this period.[147] Some soldiers were found simply unsuited to the task and were reassigned to other units elsewhere in the Army, but the vast majority succeeded.[148] At the end of the course they were put through a 2-mile "military ski qualification course" over various terrain; the soldiers were evaluated and awarded skill classifications on the basis of their performance.[149]

Training was conducted on a rotational basis, since initially Company D had been required to remain at Fort Lewis on guard duty; Companies A and B relieved Company D of this duty in mid-April. These two companies never performed that duty, however, the 87th having been relieved of guard duty upon their arrival back at Lewis; instead, they were able to commence a course of pack training. Company C had remained at Mount Rainier, training on snowshoes and unit-level training on skis. Company A relieved them at Rainier in early May, spending two weeks on the mountain conducting unit training while Company C returned to Fort Lewis. In the second half of May, Company A and Company B rotated, Company A returning to Lewis while Company B conducted unit training of their own. Company D—the heavy-weapons company—pursued a different course of instruction; this company focused more on snowshoe training,[150] since "ammunition packs and mortars weighing 70 and 80 pounds were dangerous loads for skiers, and could be carried more safely by the slower-moving but surer-footed snowshoers . . . tests found it imperative to back-pack the weapons and ammunition instead of hand-pulling on toboggans, which over variable terrain is a man-killing job."[151] The men acquitted themselves well in this training, as recognized by Rolfe in late April when he wrote to Maj. Gen. Mark Clark that

> I do not believe I have ever seen a better group of physically trained men in my life. For example, we just took a ski march with the battalion, seven miles with a thirty pound rucksack, from Paradise Lodge (5,500 foot elevation), to Sugarloaf (9,500 feet), then down the Paradise Glacier, and over Mazama Ridge to the lodge. This was done on the fifth day of a five-day test on K rations. Result: Every man completed the march and no accidents.[152]

Special arrangements had to be made for some aspects of the training. Instructions on rappeling and the use of pitons and ropes began on three 30-foot wooden climbing walls built at an old sand and gravel quarry near Fort Lewis stables, on the orders of one Capt. Woodward, an accomplished competitive skier from Washington.[153] Army engineers would later construct an artificial glacier at Camp Hale for instruction on ice training;[154*] as an interim expedient at Fort Lewis, a team traveled to Mount Rainier and made photographs and films of ice-climbing techniques for use as classroom training materials to familiarize soldiers back at Fort Lewis with ice climbing.[155]

Col. Rolfe would observe that "we have learned that you cannot take just any trained infantryman and make him a skier or mountaineer."[156] To address this, in the only arrangement of its kind at that time, the Army contracted with

---

* This effort would be not entirely successful, at first. When first constructed, the artificial glacier was built on a south-facing slope, which caused the ice to melt; it was later reconstructed on a north-facing slope, and training was able to proceed from March until mid-May 1942. Jay, *History of the Mountain Training Center*, 63–64.

the National Ski Patrol System to recruit skiers, "mountaineers, loggers, timber cruisers, prospectors, and rugged outdoor men"[157] for the 87th. Applicants would complete questionnaires, which the NSPS would evaluate; those approved by that body would be accepted into the mountain troops.[158] Eventually, the adjutant general of the Army directed that all men recruited by the NSPS would be routed directly to the Mountain Training Center at Camp Hale without further orders from the War Department.[159] The NSPS helped the Army assemble "a gathering of men with every conceivable background that was thought to be useful in forming [a mountain] division. There were skiers, snowshoers, Maine woodsmen, dogsled people, big-game hunters, [and] Norwegian farmers."[160] It was a "remarkable collection of people who were to have a truly distinctive stamp on the 10th Division."[161]

While the 87th conducted its initial training on the slopes of Mount Rainier, developments continued on other fronts. In late March 1942, word began to leak out about construction of a major training center at Pando, Colorado.[162] On April 20, 1942, this became official when the Army announced approval of the construction of a high-mountain training facility there—the future Camp Hale—to be ready for occupation the following November or December; a test force would occupy the site initially, to followed by activation there of a mountain division the following spring.[163] The camp was to be constructed in a valley near the Eagle River and would be subject to flooding—a problem cured by blasting fill material from the mountain.[164] The Mountain Training Center was initially activated at Camp Carson, Colorado, on September 3, 1942,[165] with Rolfe, now a full colonel, in command.[166] Augmented by a handpicked cadre of the best skiers in the 87th,[167] the Mountain Training Center moved to the newly completed Camp Hale—named for Spanish-American War veteran and Colorado native Irving G. Hale, who had participated in the founding of the Veterans of Foreign Wars[168]—on November 16.[169] Camp Hale was a difficult place to live and train—so much so that the soldiers assigned there promptly nicknamed it "Camp Hell."[170] Although imbued with an outward idyllic

charm by recent snowfall when the soldiers arrived to occupy the camp, the reality was quite different; first off, the snow covered a mass of debris and tools left strewn about by the Army Corps of Engineers workers who had constructed the camp, leading to punctured tires and disabled vehicles, as well as covering dirt roads that rapidly disintegrated into muck under the burden of vehicular traffic, leading to further stuck vehicles and blocked roads.[171] Virtually no amenities existed at first (a defect that would be cured later by further construction), and the housing for officers' wives was 70 miles away in Glenwood Springs.[172] A more serious and enduring problem was air pollution: because the camp was located in a natural depression shielded from the wind, smoke from the approximately five hundred coal-burning stoves in the camp, aggravated by soot from as many as a dozen trains supplying the camp daily, was not readily dissipated but rather hung in the air for extended periods, inflicting upon many soldiers the infamous "Pando hack."[173]

At the same time, the Mountain Winter Warfare Board was created within the 87th Infantry,[174] "to test and develop mountain and winter equipment [and] formulate, develop and recommend changes in mountain and winter warfare doctrine."[175] Headed by one Capt. Jackman, the board examined all aspects of winter and mountain warfare, from clothing, to tactics to equipment.[176] The board evaluated winter camouflage clothing for ski troopers and experimented with rations suitable for mountain operations, and it researched the winter warfare tactics of other nations such as Russia and Finland and tested out tactics on the slopes of Mount Rainier to figure out what would work; "the basic Field Manuals could be thrown away. All was different in the mountains."[177]

For all the progress made at Fort Lewis and on Mount Rainier, problems remained. One major handicap came in the form of land use regulations. Much of the 87th's training at Mount Rainier was conducted on federally owned land. Use of firearms was prohibited on Park Service land in the area; so seriously was this stricture taken that a waiver had to be obtained even to allow the soldiers to carry unloaded weapons during training. Even the firing of blank ammunition was prohibited for fear of disturbing the local wildlife. Because of these onerous restrictions, the 87th accomplished very little in the way of tactical training during their stay at Fort Lewis.[178]

Another burdensome distraction from the business of making mountain soldiers emanated from the Army itself. Stationed at Fort Lewis, the 87th fell under the command of the Fourth Army and the Western Defense Command. They not only failed to show much interest in the 87th's mission but actually actively interfered. West Coast blackouts disrupted Col. Rolfe's training program, and the threat of absorption into the Pacific coast defense forces loomed over the regiment like the Sword of Damocles.[179] Ultimately, the move to Camp Hale was motivated as much by the need to get the 87th out from under the officious meddling of the West Coast defense establishment as for other training reasons.[180]

Construction of Camp Hale had been challenging, due in part to problems with a labor force dissatisfied with the remote location and high altitude.[181] Life there continued to be challenging after the Mountain Training Center occupied it. Not only did the camp contain no extracurricular amenities,[182] but this was aggravated by the fact that the nearby town of Leadville was placed off-limits—to the detriment of morale[183]—despite the fact that the town had cracked down severely on prostitution and gambling in anticipation of Camp Hale's construction, even closing the "red-light district," which had existed as long as the town itself.[184] This restriction was finally lifted on February 24, 1943, and shortly thereafter the town held a "get acquainted" event attended by hundreds of soldiers.[185] Camp Hale held its first dance on March 12, 1943, and a USO opened shortly thereafter.[186]

As Camp Hale was under construction, the 87th Regiment itself was growing. The 2nd and 3rd Battalions were activated on June 1, 1942, and the decision was taken to expand the organization to a reinforced regiment of four thousand soldiers.[187] On November 18, 1942, 1st and 2nd Battalions entrained for movement to California, where they would conduct maneuvers with an element of the First Filipino Regiment[188] while 3rd Battalion

continued the process of formation at Camp Hale.[189] There they were to conduct an exercise at Camp Hunter Liggett, the objective of which was to "determine the proper training techniques and the most essential combat equipment, transport and organization necessary for elements of a standard division to operate under combat conditions in mountains, thick woods, heavy undergrowth and primitive roadnets"[190] and to prepare for the future amphibious attack to recapture Kiska.[191] The 87th "acquitted themselves very creditably indeed [during this exercise], impressing numerous high-ranking observers with their uniform ability, officer and men alike, to carry heavy packs and negotiate rugged terrain for days on end without a complaint."[192] The battalions had deployed with mules and built mule trails throughout the training area, maneuvering day and night over the course of a six-week exercise.[193]

Mountain and winter training took on a new level of sophistication after the establishment of the Mountain Training Center and the consolidation of the 87th at Camp Hale. Notwithstanding the critical recruiting work being done by the National Ski Patrol System, many personnel arriving at Camp Hale had no skiing experience; to correct this, Col. Rolfe directed a forty-day ski-training program.[194] Unfortunately, this program was not a success at first, since many of the officers involved refused to accept instruction from personnel junior in rank to them, interfering with the training or even boycotting it altogether.[195] Col. Rolfe remedied this problem in February 1943, appointing Lt. Paul Townsend as director of a new ski school, "with authority to enforce his orders"; Townsend assembled a staff of instructors and spent the winter teaching skiing and winter survival.[196] That summer, a mountaineering school was established, consisting of a week of rigorous classroom instruction followed by practical exercises on 100-foot cliffs near camp.[197] Among other initiatives, a detachment from the 87th was sent to Canada to assist in developing a motorized vehicle capable of operating in snow—a vehicle that would eventually become the M29 Weasel,[198] widely used by the mountain troops at Camp Hale and by others in other theaters; another detachment helped in the production of a Hollywood film about the 87th.[199] As described by one 87th infantry veteran, "Many new problems of winter-military training were presented by the extreme high altitude and weather";[200] training and testing were intensified:

> Over a hundred types of equipment and vehicles were tested. Units and detachments, to the size of battalions, bivouacked in the surrounding mountains at 12,000 feet, and ran problems and tests in the snow and extreme cold. Unusual schools were set up with experienced men in charge to teach— not only skiing, but snow-shoeing, snow-freighting, and trail breaking in toboggan. Dog teams were attached, and men were trained in their handling. Men were trained to build snow caves; taught to cook the mountain ration individually; trained in the prevention of avalanches; and instructed in rescue work. . . . Various manuals were written. A "manual of skis" for drilling and marching was developed.[201]

The influence of the Mountain Training Center and the 87th Infantry extended well beyond the boundaries of Camp Hale. Mountain Training Center personnel were dispatched to conduct training at Camp (now Fort) McCoy, Wisconsin;[202] Seneca Park, Virginia; the Porcupine Mountains, in northern Michigan; Lincoln, New Hampshire; and North Africa.[203] Particularly noteworthy was the training conducted in Virginia and West Virginia. An important impetus for this training was Operation Husky, the Allied plan for the invasion of Sicily, a rugged Mediterranean island of poor roads and mountainous terrain.[204] Training commenced in portions of the Jefferson and George Washington National Forests, where "heavy undergrowth, numerous large streams, limited observation and poor road net" would provide a reasonable facsimile of the terrain on Sicily.[205]

A detachment from the Mountain Training Center was initially dispatched to Virginia to assist the 36th and 45th Divisions in their preparations for the invasion of Sicily.[206] Two camps (North Camp and South Camp) were constructed for the training units, who would be instructed by a team from the Mountain Training Center.[207] According to the Army Ground Forces history on mountain and winter warfare training,

> A maneuver area was established at Buena Vista, Virginia with officers and enlisted men from the Mountain Training Center as instructors. Regimental combat teams of each of the divisions were given five days of preliminary exercises to accustom them to movement over rugged mountainous terrain, and they then participated in free, two-sided maneuvers under simulated combat conditions. While the majority of the troops were engaged in organizational training[,] selected individuals consisting of from five to ten men from each rifle company, one artillery liaison detail from each light artillery battalion[,] and five men from each regimental intelligence platoon were given technical rock climbing instruction.[208]

This training having been found valuable to the 35th and 45th Divisions during operations in Sicily, the decision was taken to continue it for other formations at Elkins, West Virginia. For nearly a year, combat elements of the 28th, 31st, 77th, 35th, and 95th Infantry Divisions conducted maneuver training in mountainous terrain before deploying to the theater of operations.[209] Select individuals from these units also received specialized instruction in technical rock climbing: "Roped climbing, belaying, rappelling, piton work, and even the difficult tension climbing were successfully taught in a series of two-week classes, culminating in an all-night 'assault' up a 300-foot cliff."[210] The training provided by the West Virginia branch of the Mountain Training Center (or, in its later configuration, the Mountain Training Group)[211] was to prove immensely valuable. As observed in the *History of the Mountain Training Center*,

> These four divisions [28th, 35th, 77th, and 95th], in addition to the 45th and one combat team of the 36th Division—which had been trained similarly a year previously—and the 2nd and 76th Divisions—

trained in over-snow movement in Wisconsin—all had opportunity to put to actual use in war the techniques learned from the Instructors of the Mountain Training Center. A study of the accomplish-ments of these divisions will prove the value of even a short period of mountain and winter warfare training for combat troops.[212]

Formation of 10th Light Division (Alpine)

The 86th Infantry Regiment was constituted on November 25, 1942;[213] on November 26, 1942—about ten days after the Mountain Training Center occupied Camp Hale—its 1st Battalion began organizing.[214] The regiment was formally activated in increments from December 12, 1942, through May 1, 1943.[215] Like the 87th before it, the 86th was recruited with the assistance of the National Ski Patrol System, which screened potential recruits for potential aptitude, as they had those of the 87th before it.[216] The 86th commenced its specialized training in mountain and winter warfare alongside the 3rd Battalion, 87th Infantry, while the remainder of the 87th participated in the Hunter Liggett exercise.

Although the Mountain Training Center was providing excellent instruction to infantry units, that training was narrow in scope. As the Army Ground Forces noted in one of its historical monographs, "The training given at the West Virginia Maneuver Area introduced standard units to some of the problems which they would encounter in combat in difficult terrain, but no attempt was made to transform these units into mountain troops or to fit them for operations at high altitudes."[217]

The problem of operations in the high mountains was not to be solved by the employment of standard units; rather, the conduct of combat operations in that environment was to be entrusted to a specialized formation. The 10th Light Division (Alpine) was activated for this purpose at Camp Hale on July 15, 1943, consisting of the 85th, 86th, and 90th Infantry Regiments along with organic artillery and other elements.[218] The 87th Mountain Infantry was not initially a part of the division structure, having decamped on June 11,

1943, to Fort Ord, California, for two weeks of amphibious training preparatory to the regiment's participation in the invasion of Kiska to reconquer that Alaskan island from the Japanese. The 87th would be redeployed to Camp Carson, Colorado, over the course of the months of November and December 1943, with the entire regiment back in Colorado by the first of January 1944, replacing the 90th Regiment in the 10th Mountain structure.[219] Those members of the 90th Regiment that had been recruited via the National Ski Patrol System stayed with the 10th Mountain Division, being cross-leveled out to other divisional units in exchange for other personnel not recruited by the NSPS.[220] The 87th Infantry returned in time to participate along with the 85th and 86th Regiments in the famous D-series exercises, a grueling six-week exercise in brutal winter conditions and rugged mountain terrain, before departing Camp Hale for Camp Swift, Texas, in December 1944 and thence Italy in 1945.[221]

The 85th Infantry was constituted on July 10, 1943,[222] activated on July 15, 1943,[223] and began organizing at Camp Hale on August 10, 1943, around a core of twenty officers and six hundred enlisted soldiers drawn from the 86th Infantry Regiment, a cadre drawn from the ranks of the 27th Infantry Division,[224] and fillers provided by Army Ground Forces.[225] The arrival of the 27th Division cadre from Hawaii—"the islands"[226]—provides an interesting illustration of the contrasting perspectives of the mountain infantry and other, "ordinary" infantry. One 85th Infantry veteran describes the meeting of these cadre from Hawaii and the enlisted soldiers at Camp Hale who had already received some mountain training:

> While we were still at Hale, they brought in this cadre from Hawaii, and they were going to teach us how to be soldiers. So we were all out walking through what to us was just foothills. And these guys from Hawaii, who had never been above forty-five feet, were suddenly at 9,000 feet, walking up and down what they called mountains.[227]

The 90th Regiment was reconstituted from its World War I predecessor on July 10, 1943, and activated five days later.[228] Like the 85th, the 90th was in large part built around personnel drawn from the 86th Infantry, along with cadre from II Armored Corps and Army Ground Forces fillers.[229]

All three regiments of the 10th Mountain Division had World War I antecedents. On July 11, 1917, the system of numbering infantry regiments that we know today came into being; under this system, the Regular Army was allocated regimental designations 1 through 100, while National Guard regiments were to be numbered 101 through 300 and National Army regiments were to begin at 301.[230] Among the Regular Army regiment allocation, 1 through 65 were raised as Regulars, 66 was skipped, and 67 through 90 were raised nominally as National Army formations, but with cadres from the previously formed Regular regiments.[231] The formation of the original 87th Infantry Regiment by this process has been described above. The earlier 85th and 86th Infantry Regiments were also formed in this fashion, organized as at Camp Travis, Texas, in September 1918, to be part of the 18th Division; neither ever deployed, being demobilized at Camp Travis on February 13, 1919.[232] The 85th Infantry Regiment—a part of the 35th Infantry Brigade— was built around a cadre drawn from the Regular Army 19th Infantry, while the cadre for the 86th came from the 35th Infantry Regiment; the 86th would form a part of the 36th Infantry Brigade.[233]* As with the 87th Infantry and the 10th Division itself, the World War I predecessors of the 85th and 86th Regiments were not recognized as part of the lineage of the newly formed regiments.[234] For reasons unknown, however, the 90th Infantry Regiment organized at Camp Hale is recognized as the descendant of its World War I predecessor organized at Camp Sevier, South Carolina, in August 1918 as a Regular Army regiment, assigned

to the 20th Division as part of the 40th Infantry Brigade, with regimental cadre drawn from the 50th Infantry Regiment.[235] The 90th demobilized on February 28, 1919, at Camp Dodge, Iowa,[236] without having deployed overseas. Ironically, distinctive insignia would ultimately be approved for all the infantry regiments associated with the 10th Mountain Division, *except* the 90th Regiment: the 85th Infantry's insignia was approved on August 21, 1951; the 86th Infantry's was approved on December 12, 1951; and the 87th Infantry's insignia was approved during the war on February 9, 1943.[237] The 90th Regiment remains without an approved distinctive insignia to this day.[238]

The Army began to take seriously the value of a division with mountain capability as early as the fall of 1942.[239] By early 1943, "the experience of the Mountain Training Center . . . [had] made it evident that it was possible for a tactical organization as large as a division to be organized and trained for mountain and winter warfare."[240] The 10th Light Division (Alpine) was activated on July 15, 1943, under Second Army and assigned to the XI Corps. In addition to the three infantry regiments, the division's complement of artillery consisted of the 604th, 605th, and 616th Field Artillery Battalions. The former two battalions had been activated previously and trained under the auspices of the Mountain Training Center. The third—the 616th—was a newly organized entity formed from personnel from the 604th and 605th, the Mountain Training Center, and 2nd Artillery Battalion. Other divisional units were formed from among the units and personnel of the Mountain Training Center, while the division's antiaircraft element—the 727th Antiaircraft Artillery Machine Gun Battalion—was sourced from outside the Mountain Training Center by the Antiaircraft Command.[241]

As organized, the 10th Light Division was intended to rely for transport primarily on pack animals, a fact that significantly marked the

---

* While there may be others, I am aware of only a single published reference, other than this work, that acknowledges the prior existence of the original 10th Division or of the original 85th, 86th, or 87th Regiments. *10th Infantry Division History*, published in 1957 to commemorate return of the division to Europe as part of Operation Gyroscope, provides a brief history of the 10th Mountain and of its three constituent infantry regiments. Describing recruits reporting to Fort Riley, Kansas (where the 10th Division was then stationed), it notes that "thirty-seven years before that cold 1955 night a similar group of men arrived at the same post to make up the Army's first 86th Regt. But World War I ended before they could be trained and the regiment was demobilized on February 13, 1919." See *10th Infantry Division*, *1957*, n.p.

division's early training efforts, as one 87th Infantry officer recalls:

> Can you imagine the task of learning and then teaching a regiment of new people how to take care of all those horses and mules? While some animals came from government remount stations, many were unbroken and untrained. Some of our personnel were old packers, and mule skinners etc. But it was largely a training job for all of us.[242]

Notwithstanding the emphasis on mules, the 226th Engineer Company was attached to ascertain whether it was feasible to construct roads and trails in mountain terrain to facilitate support of the division by motor transport.[243] To that end, the division's complement of pack animals was supplemented with a variety of light wheeled and tracked vehicles for experimental use, including the M28 and M29 cargo carriers,[244] known as the Weasel. The Weasel was a light, tracked vehicle designed by Studebaker in 1942 and 1943.[245] What would become the Weasel was conceived in preparation for Operation Plough, a proposed incursion into Norway to be conducted jointly by the United States and the British Commonwealth, wherein small teams of commandos would infiltrate Norway to attack hydroelectric facilities supplying Germany with power.[246] Operation Plough was the brainchild of Geoffrey Pyke.[247] Described as "one of the most original yet unrecognized figures of the twentieth century" and a "genius for coming up with radical ideas,"[248] Pyke was appointed by Lord Louis Mountbatten as director of programmes at UK Combined Operations Command. In a fifty-four-page proposal to Lord Mountbatten, Pyke argued that

> if there were to be landed by parachute, men with machines able to travel fast and far, not through, but ON the snow, over

and down the slopes of the Norwegian mountains, able to carry arms for attacking and explosives to destroy bridges, tunnels, railway tracks, hydroelectric stations, etc. etc., equipped to maintain themselves in any part of the country, however high and desolate, to launch frequent attacks on vital objects, simultaneously or in quick succession . . . the Germans would be compelled to put into Norway more men than they have there now.[249]

Pyke was a misanthropic, "belligerent" figure, and his "contempt for the military mind" created substantial friction between himself and the American and British military officers with whom he worked.[250] He was a brilliant figure nonetheless.* While his brainchild Operation Plough would be canceled due to "insurmountable logistical problems and insufficient aircraft,"[251] one of the fruits of his genius was the Weasel, which survived cancellation of its parent operation and went on to give good service on widely scattered battlefields.** As part of the US contribution to such a future operation in Norway, Gen. Marshall concluded that US industry could produce the light specialized vehicle to be an air-droppable vehicle transportable inside either an American glider or a British Lancaster bomber, envisioned to support the infiltrating commando teams.[252] Given 180 days to design a rugged, air-transportable vehicle that could easily traverse snow, Studebaker had a prototype ready in sixty days.[253] The 87th Infantry assisted in the development of this vehicle, participating in an expedition to Canada for that purpose. One veteran would recall, nearly forty years later, that

> good fortune became my lot when I became one of about seventy-five men to be sent to the Columbia Ice Fields, where a camp was being formed by the army to develop a snow vehicle called the Weasel to be used

---

* Pyke was also a tragic figure. He fell under suspicion of having been a Soviet agent during his work for Combined Operations, with "the case against him" being "detailed and substantial" (Henry Hemming, *The Ingenious Mr. Pyke*, 6). He committed suicide on February 21, 1948 (Hemming, *The Ingenious Mr. Pyke*, 3).
** Another fruit of the abortive Operation Plough was the creation of the joint US-Canadian First Special Service Force (FSSF), a commando brigade that would participate alongside the 87th Infantry in the recapture of Kiska from the Japanese in August 1943. See Kenneth Finlayson, "Operation Cottage: First Special Service Force, Kiska Campaign," *Veritas* 4, no. 2 (2008).

in snow country. We spent about two unbelievable months on the Saskatchewan Glacier working on this project. We were also trained in every phase of glacier mountaineering. When I look back on it now, it seems like a fairy tale.[254]

The Weasel first entered production as the M28, but, "aware of its shortcomings," Studebaker began working on a new version, which would become the M29, almost immediately after the M28 went into production.[255] The Weasel was a compact vehicle, measuring in at approximately 10 feet long; 5 feet, 5 inches wide; and just under 6 feet high in the M29 configuration (the M29C amphibious configuration was longer).[256] Weighing between 3,725 and 4,077 pounds empty (depending on configuration),[257] the Weasel exerted a ground pressure of 2.10 pounds per square inch when configured with 15-inch-wide tracks and 1.69 pounds per square inch in the 20-inch track configuration,[258] so that it "would float across snow," transporting troops and equipment at a top speed of 36 miles per hour.[259] An extremely versatile vehicle, the Weasel was deployed in a variety of configurations, including light cargo, signal line laying, and radio, ambulance, and command configurations, along with the M29C amphibious version equipped with stern rudders and watertight buoyancy cells.[260] It could travel over soft, powdered, or crusted-over snow,[261] or in marshland, and it could swim in deep water when suitably equipped.[262] Over 15,000 would be built by war's end.[263] The Weasel would be used extensively by 10th Mountain Division soldiers during training at Camp Hale,[264] and the Weasel would see service in Alaska, the Pacific, and Europe,[265] where, according to Pyke's biographer Henry Hemming, it would be "used to keep the Nijmegan bridgehead open and, when German forces flooded the Ardennes to halt the Allied advance, the first vehicles to get through the German lines were Weasels."[266] The Weasel continued in service after the war, including during mountain and winter warfare training by the 38th Regimental Combat Team at a reconstructed Camp Hale (the camp having been abandoned and its structures cannibalized

following the departure of the 10th Mountain Division, only to be rebuilt in 1947),[267] as shown in the photographs of the 38th Regimental Combat Team's commemorative annual for 1947–1948.[268] More dramatically, the Weasel would also be employed in Arctic and Antarctic expeditions in the years following the end of World War II.[269]

The division's mission was a continuation of the missions of the 87th Mountain Infantry and the Mountain Training Center before it, without whose groundbreaking efforts the division's mission would have been impossible. The 10th Light Division

was organized to test the organization and the equipment best suited to the employment of a division in high mountain warfare and was to be trained to attain ultimate combat efficiency high mountain warfare. It was designed to operate primarily in mountains and primitive terrain where road nets were poor or nonexistent and under adverse and extreme winter weather conditions.[270]

Appointed to command the newly formed 10th Light Division was Maj. Gen. Lloyd E. Jones, who previously had commanded a task force at the Aleutian island of Amchitka; the assistant division commander, Frank L. Culin Jr., also had Aleutians experience, having commanded the northern forces on Attu from early May 1943 until shortly before the 10th Light Division's activation.[271] Brig. Gen. David L. Ruffner was appointed commander of the division artillery; Ruffner was a particularly apt choice, being "a recognized authority on pack artillery," and having served as the commander of the Mountain Training Center artillery from that entity's activation until his appointment to the 10th Light Division's artillery.[272]

The 10th Light faced significant challenges in carrying out its early training mission. Manpower was one of them. The National Ski Patrol System had played a major role in manning the 87th Infantry and, later, the 86th. It continued to identify qualified recruits after the activation of the division, providing about 2,000 fillers. These NSPS-endorsed recruits reached the division through a number of routes: 770 reported directly to Camp Hale from reception centers; many others arrived at Camp Hale after having first completed basic training at infantry and artillery replacement centers, despite having been "earmarked" for service with the mountain troops; still others had already been assigned to units when they applied to the NSPS for service with the mountain troops.[273] Notwithstanding their indispensable efforts, however, the National Ski Patrol System simply could not supply all of the 10th Light Division's manpower needs, and personnel were soon brought in from other sources. In early August 1943, a reorganization of the 89th Division yielded thirty officers and 454 enlisted soldiers who were assigned to the 10th; the following October, the division received 1,333 soldiers from inactivated armored infantry regiments, and in early December a reorganization of tank destroyer battalions yielded another 409 fillers for the division; throughout, the NSPS's efforts continued.[274]

The necessity of incorporating fillers from outside the NSPS recruiting system had an effect on the quality of the recruits received into the division. According to the *History of the 10th Light Division (Alpine)*, "Most of the filler replacements were not volunteers for mountain troops. Many of them were from the south, unacquainted with snow and cold weather and with a lower educational and AGCT level than the original personnel." Although "the filler replacements from the armored infantry and tank destroyer units . . . proved to be satisfactory, . . . considerable training was necessary to bring them up to the standards of the remainder of the division."[275] Furthermore, previously learned lessons were again confirmed:

It was found that a soldier able to duty at a low altitude may find considerable difficulty doing duty in the mountains. To learn to live and fight in sub-zero and rarefied atmosphere was not an easy task. . . . From time to time lists of men not meeting the physical standards were submitted to higher headquarters for reassignment.[276]

By February 1, 1944, 982 men were assigned to other infantry divisions at lower altitudes by this process, and to the Special Troops headquarters of both 2nd and 3rd Armies.[277] Ironically, while the inability of some soldiers to meet the heightened requirements of the 10th Mountain Division led to some attrition, other losses were caused by the very exceptional quality of the mountain troops, as 10th Mountain soldiers volunteered for aviation-related training and airborne assignments. The extraordinary losses combined with the ordinary attribution experienced by all units to substantially delay the division's achieving its full complement of personnel, with the division not reaching full strength until March 22, 1944.[278] This personnel turnover, combined with the many "special 'details' going and coming constantly," had the effect of impeding "real comprehensive military training."[279]

Aggravating normal attrition for most infantry divisions was the War Department's practice of stripping personnel from those infantry divisions not yet alerted for deployment to provide combat replacements for deployed units—such stripping occurred "until the latest feasible date before . . . embarkation."[280] This process had begun by the end of July 1942, when the War Department ordered that "low-priority units in training" be levied for individual replacements when the flow of replacements from Recruit Training Centers ran short.[281] The process of levying stateside divisions for replacements was so severe that "in the last nine infantry divisions sent to the European Theater (those sent after October 1944) only a quarter of the enlisted men in the regiments has been in the regiments since the preceding January."[282]

Despite the severe need for infantry replacements in theater, the 10th Light Division was largely spared the requirement to provide large numbers of enlisted replacements for deployed units, save those made available as described above. Although the demand for replacements in theater was voracious—US-based divisions were levied for 92,000 enlisted replacements from April to September 1944, with every division programmed for deployment after September 1944 being aggressively stripped of personnel for replacements—the 10th Light was one of only two such divisions to avoid such cannibalization of its personnel (the other being the 14th Armored Division).[283] But this was decidedly not the situation in the case of officers—particularly among company-grade infantry officers—the officers who serve as platoon leaders and rifle company commanders.[284] Turnover among infantry officers was extremely high, since officers in units training in the United States were repeatedly ordered overseas as replacements. The scale of the challenge is illustrated by the comments of a regimental commander in the 65th Infantry Division on November 1, 1944:

> The turnover of commissioned personnel in this regiment since activation has been about 150 percent. The turnover has been heaviest among junior officers, principally among the lieutenants. Some companies have had as many as seven commanders and some platoons have had sixteen platoon leaders. Battalions have had as high as five commanders. The Regiment has had two commanding officers.[285]

The 10th Division bore its share of this burden, and "the losses of well qualified . . . line officers proved to be difficult for the division to overcome."[286] As stated in the *History of the 10th Light Division (Alpine)*,

> The division was called on to furnish numerous officer replacements to AGF [Army Ground Forces] replacement depots. Officer cadres for new field artillery battalions took many officers from the field artillery battalions. There was a constant shifting of infantry and field artillery officers in and out of command. The medical corps was hardest hit. From the date of activation until 1 May 1944 there had been at least two complete turnovers of medical officers. The medical battalions were forced to function with 1 or 2 medical officers in a company authorized 6. The infantry medical detachment operated with 2 medical officers in a detachment authorized 4.[287]

Training the 10th Light Division (Alpine)

Prior to the establishment of the 10th Light Division, the Mountain Warfare Training Center had carried out a an exercise in February 1943, in which a defensive position was to be established 13,500 feet above sea level at Homestake Peak, to be followed by various training maneuvers.[288] Bad weather hampered the exercise, including heavy snow and temperatures in the range of 25 degrees below zero; more importantly, the exercise revealed many deficiencies in the training on individual winter and mountain tasks, including proper use of equipment, overland movement capabilities, and basic survival skills such as preparing meals; nearly a third of the participants became casualties, including from frostbite.[289] Another serious problem, however, was exhaustion, including among the more experienced troops that had trained at Fort Lewis; this was in large part due to the carrying of excessive amounts of equipment, with members of the 87th Infantry carrying an average of 86 pounds—41 pounds more than the maximum specified in the applicable Army regulation for high-altitude training.[290] So serious were the concerns arising from this exercise that the surgeon general of the Army agreed to review training conditions at Camp Hale; one officer quipped that "anyone who transfers to combat from Camp Hale is a coward."[291]

Notwithstanding these many challenges, training progressed. Important improvements were made after the February 1943 exercise, including the establishment of the ski school mentioned above. Training continued to improve after the 10th Light Division was activated. The division carried out approximately monthlong Infantry Platoon Combat Firing Proficiency Tests over November and December 1943, carrying out the tests in snow, on rough terrain, and in subzero temperatures.[292] The division's first collective training exercise occurred in November 1943, consisting of a 2,000-foot, 7-mile climb in single-column division movement to a field bivouac, with a truck head for ration and ammunition resupply established by the 126th Engineers 1.5 miles and 1,000 feet below the bivouac area.[293] This exercise revealed significant problems with the division's organization and equipment. Pack animals struggled to cope with icy conditions, impeding the movement of the entire column so that it was eighteen hours before the final elements of the division closed on the bivouac area, and the division's transportation assets were unequal to the challenge of resupplying the division with ammunition in a timely manner.[294] The division commenced collective tactical training in February 1944, initially with a six-week training program in which the troops were in the field from four to seven nights each week.[295] Next followed a grueling, six-week capstone exercise broken into a two-week increment and a three-week increment.[296] D-series, as it was called, "validated the division's ability to conduct large-scale operations in winter and mountain terrain," testing "the individual and collective training of the men and the capabilities of their equipment" by challenging them "to move their personnel and equipment over unforgiving terrain while addressing a series of field problems along the way."[297] The D-series exercise "was the final putting together of all the unit training into a series of six military problems for the whole division . . . in March and early April 1944,"[298] conducted, according to Harris Dusenbery of C Company, 1st Battalion, 86th Infantry, "mostly in the Gore Range at elevations from 9,000 to 12,000 feet."[299] D-series has been characterized as an "agony of cold, with clothes constantly wet and no way to dry them out, with no time for sleep, and no time for more than a bite on the run."[300] "To explain the 'D-Series,'" one participate wrote, "is like explaining a knock-out punch, unless someone else has felt it."[301] Another participant characterized it as

> perhaps the most grueling test ever given to any US Army Division. It was performed under the most adverse and difficult weather conditions; in deep snow, in extreme cold, and with storms and high winds continually hampering individual efficiency. This particular training, which placed exceptional

responsibility on the individual soldier, was essentially the best experience possible for the combat that lay ahead.[302]

Yet another participant reminisced that "to explain the 'D-Series' is like explaining a knockout punch, unless someone else has felt it. 'Soldiers participating in D-series endured temperatures as low as 38°F, "not counting [wind] chill factors."[303] Cold-weather injuries were a major problem, with a hundred frostbite casualties occurring on one occasion in a single night.[304] Harris Dusenbery reported the frostbite phenomenon in his memoir:[*]

> An MP on duty brewed up some coffee and tea for us. In the meantime we took off our parkas and sweaters. Some men removed their shoes and sox to check their feet. One man's toes were a dead white, as white as snow. He had a serious case of frostbite, and his next destination would be the hospital. He was from another company and I never did find out how he got along, but I have heard of similar cases that required weeks of hospitalization. There were other less serious cases, but we did not worry about them.[305]

In total, 9,296 10th Division soldiers began D-series, of whom more than 1,300 were evacuated at one time or another over the course of the exercise, many due to frostbite; more than half returned to duty during the exercise, and 8,673 soldiers completed the exercise.[306] The high rate of injuries notwithstanding,[**] the D-series exercise proved that the men of the 10th Light Division "could endure and operate in harsh conditions for extended periods of time,"[307] and it further demonstrated that the 10th "could sustain combat power" under those conditions, and it "validated their tactics."[308]

---

[*] For a discussion of cold-weather equipment, training, and injuries for US Army troops in the Aleutians and in the 10th Mountain Division at Camp Hale, as well as a discussion of research on cold-weather injuries during the war, see Bruce C. Paton, "Cold, Casualties, and Conquests: The Effects of Cold on Warfare," in *Medical Aspects of Harsh Environments*, 1:313–49.

[**] In 1958, the Army Medical Department published a comprehensive survey of cold-weather injuries among ground forces in the Second World War. Oddly, this work makes no reference to the 10th Mountain Division or to any of its training or combat experiences, including the D-series exercises. It does reference the 87th Mountain Infantry Regiment, but only in the context of the Kiska invasion. Tom F. Whayne and Michael E. DeBakey, *Cold Injury, Ground Type*.

In the years after the Civil War, it was said of the bloody Battle of Shiloh "that the most any Union soldier could say of any later fight was: 'I was worse scared than I was at Shiloh.'"[309] The men of the 10th Mountain Division might have felt something similar about their suffering during the D-series: shortly after the war, Albert H. Jackman captured the harrowing nature of the D-series exercise, and the indelible impression that it made upon the minds of the participants, in *The American Alpine Journal*:

Even 18 months later, after severe combat in the Italian Apennines, mention of the "D" Series brought awe to the voices of the veterans. Cold, snow, refractory mules, sleepless nights, 14,000 ft. peaks, and hazing from the "brass" combined to produce a situation that batters of German 88s and later actions could not make men forget. "It's not as bad as the 'D' Series," they later cried, and believed it.[310]

But while "the division had successfully demonstrated its mastery of tactical and administrative operations under extreme conditions of weather, altitude, and terrain,"[311] the exercises also revealed weaknesses. The Army evaluators overseeing the exercise evaluated the division's performance favorably, but they remained concerned that the 10th needed a more robust logistics capability to better sustain the division in combat, and recommended changes that would have brought the 10th closer to a standard infantry division.[312] Combat reports from Italy seemed to indicate that standard infantry divisions could be adapted to operations in mountain terrain; this, combined with the perceived deficiencies noted above, led Army Ground Forces to recommend conversion of the 10th into a standard division.[313] This Gen. Marshall declined to do; remaining optimistic about "the organization and potential capabilities of the 10th Light Infantry Division," Marshall instead directed that Army Ground Forces develop recommendations on how the 10th "could more effectively perform its mission of combat in high altitudes."[314] Changes were made along these lines. According to the Army Ground Forces' *Study Training for Mountain and Winter Warfare*,

The strength of the division was increased by 2,608 officers and enlisted men, the principal increase being in the infantry regiments. The light infantry battalion had a marked deficiency of fire-power which was remedied by the activation of a heavy weapons company for each battalion. Substantial increases were made in the engineer, signal and medical elements. Organic pack transportation was provided for all combat units of the division, increasing the number of animals from 1,707 to 6,152.[315]

Flatland Interlude:
The 10th Mountain Division at Camp Swift

Despite Gen. Marshall's support for the division and his decision to retain it as an alpine division and against converting it to a standard infantry division, rumors of an impending conversion to standard configuration reached the soldiers of the 10th, dampening spirits.[316] These rumors were seemingly confirmed with the arrival of orders transferring the 10th Division to Camp Swift, Texas,[317] taking the division "from 38 degrees below zero to about 110 degrees above zero."[318] Morale plummeted "because they felt they were a picked body of men who had been selected for their specialized mountain skills and they desired an opportunity to fight as a mountain unit in mountains."[319] As one veteran of this period recalled:

No greater change is possible than from those regions of high winter into the torrid heat and sun-scorched plains of Texas where we've been shipped. Camp Swift. The fool responsible for this couldn't have made a worse foolery. I wish he could be here. That chorus of thousands of curses (none of them fit to print) would deafen him. There's no laughter around here. The 10th has become a sorry outfit.[320]

One disgruntled mountain trooper succinctly stated the state of morale in the 10th at this point, writing in an anonymous postcard from Camp Swift to Minnie Dole: "Emphasized stupidity. A lousy outfit. Two years wasted."[321]

Disaffection in the ranks notwithstanding, the move to Camp Swift was productive. The division arrived at Camp Swift on June 22, 1944, and the recommendations requested by Gen. Marshall, noted above, were submitted a month later on July 22 and approved on September 6.[322] The 10th had been ordered to Camp Swift with the view toward the division's participation in the 1944 Louisiana Maneuvers; in the event, however, the continental United States had been so denuded of troops as units were ordered to Europe that the maneuvers had to be canceled.[323] Cancellation of the Louisiana Maneuvers was a welcome respite that enabled to the division to carry out the reorganization approved on September 6,[324] which required extensive specialized training at the individual and unit levels.[325]

One major focus of the division's efforts during this period was the organization and training of the heavy-weapons companies in each battalion.[326] Cadre for these companies was drawn from within the division itself,[327] while the remaining personnel were provided by Army ground forces and had to be absorbed into the division and into their respective battalions.[328] These soldiers had to be trained on those heavy weapons, which included the heavy .30-caliber machine gun, the M2 .50-caliber machine gun, and the 81 mm mortar,[329] and the battalions, regiments, and division itself had to learn how to keep them supplied.[330] Another major task was the absorption of the vast infusion of mules called for under the new organization structure—an extraordinary and eventful process that began as early as October; maintaining and collecting these mules was to be a major struggle for the division—many of whose members had never been around mules before—from the animals' arrival until they were sent to Oklahoma preparatory to the division's deployment overseas.[331]

The division had largely executed the organizational changes when, on November 6, 1944, the division was redesignated as the 10th Mountain Division[332]—the soldiers' fears of consignment to the status of a standard infantry division had been unfounded. The interlude at Camp Swift,

however, had been important. The soldiers were acclimatized to living and marching in flatlands;[333] useful individual and unit-level training had been accomplished, as in Company C, 86th Infantry, where company commander Charles Smith reports having been able to conduct live-fire maneuver training, and having selected personnel from each platoon trained to call in artillery fire by the division artillery, against a future contingency when forward observers might not be able to reach the company.[334]

Notwithstanding the angst engendered among the men by the movement to Camp Swift, the division's sojourn there proved immensely valuable. As summarized in *A Short History of the 85th, Mountain Infantry Regiment*, training at Camp Swift enabled the division

> to master the problems of "flat-land" fighting; to become acquainted with fire and maneuver in a type of terrain for which nothing at Camp Hale had prepared us. During the training at Camp Swift great emphasis proved to be of utmost value later in combat. These problems were conducted using live ammunition and generally involved units no larger than a squad or platoon. Such consistent importance was attached to the training of these small units—their fire power, maneuverability, and their ability to operate swiftly and independently—that by the end of the training period in Texas, each rifleman had a new concept of his place in his combat-team and of his relationship to the other members of his squad and platoon.[335]

The 10th Mountain Division received its movement readiness dates on November 7, 1944. The three infantry regiments were to be prepared to move sequentially on November 28, December 10, and December 14, with the rest of the division to be prepared to follow on December 23.[336] In the actual event, the 86th Infantry deployed ahead to "the knee" of Italy, with the remainder of the division following in January 1945[337]—at which point its mettle as a mountain division would be put to the test.

Postal cover for the "Ski Troops," 1944. Note the panda on skis—the unofficial emblem of Camp Hale, located at Pando, Colorado. *Author's collection*

The first version of the 10th Mountain Division shoulder sleeve insignia. Note the felt construction, the detailed grips on the handles of the bayonets, and the absence of the mountain tab—all features that would change later. *Author's collection*

Officer's collar insignia of the type that may have been worn by officers of the 85th Infantry Regiment during that regiment's first incarnation in World War I. *Author's collection*

Officers of the 87th Infantry Regiment may have worn insignia like this during that regiment's brief existence during the First World War. *Author's collection*

CHAPTER 3

Operation Cottage: The Invasion of Kiska

On August 15 and 16, 1943, a joint US-Canadian force executed Operation Cottage—the invasion of the remote island of Kiska far out in the Bering Sea, near the end of Alaska's Aleutian Island chain.[1] In a sense, the invasion of Kiska can be thought of as the last echo of "the most dramatic American carrier raid of the period," Army lieutenant colonel James Doolittle's daring raid against Tokyo, Nagoya, Osaka, and Kobe in the Japanese homeland, carried out in sixteen Army B-25 bombers launched from the deck of USS *Hornet*.[2] Although "sarcastically pooh-poohed as not even a 'do-little' but even a 'do-nothing' raid" by Japanese military spokesmen because of the admittedly modest damage the raid inflicted on its targets, the raid nonetheless had a profound impact on the future course of the war in the Pacific by putting a decisive end to the strategic debate within the Japanese navy about the future course of the war, galvanizing the Japanese in their resolve to launch an early attack on Midway Island at the far western end of the Hawaiian chain.[3]

Following Japan's stunning successes at Pearl Harbor and elsewhere in the Pacific, the Japanese navy was confronted with the question of future strategy. At its most fundamental, the question facing them was whether to "go on the defensive and hold what she had won, or should she remain boldly on the offensive in an effort to break the fighting determination of the Allies?"[4] In the event that Japan opted for further offensive action, the question that then presented itself was *where*— should Japan turn and strike out against the British in the west, or should they follow up on their success at Pearl Harbor and strike out to the east and press the attack against the United States?[5] By January 1942, chief of staff of the Japanese Combined Fleet, RAdm. Matome Ugaki, had considered three potential courses of action: an eastward advance toward Hawaii, a westward advance on Australia, or an offensive to seize control of the Indian Ocean from Britain.[6] A move

into the Indian Ocean was ruled out, however, since such a strategy would involve an extensive amphibious operation to seize Ceylon, and the Japanese army refused to consider participating in such an operation on the grounds that it needed to keep forces in readiness closer to home against the possibility of future conflict with the Soviet Union. A sally into the Indian Ocean thus ruled out, Ugaki and the Combined Fleet staff settled on Midway Island as the next objective.[7]

This did not settle the matter, however; while the Combined Fleet was settling on Midway as its next preferred target, the naval general staff in Tokyo had been thinking in terms of an "Australia-first school of strategy" that sought either to occupy parts of Australia or at least cut it off from contact with the United States, in order to prevent its use as a staging area for future attacks against Japan.[8] However, the Japanese army vigorously opposed an invasion of Australia on the grounds that resources existed neither to assemble the ten or more divisions envisioned as necessary for the operation nor to transport them to Australia even if they could be assembled.[9] Furthermore, Adm. Yamamoto made clear his own opposition to the Australia strategy and his insistence upon Midway as the next target; faced with implacable opposition to the Australia-first strategy on two sides, the naval general staff acceded on April 5, 1942, to an attack on Midway.[10]

Even this did not end matters, however, since the Combined Fleet and naval general staffs still disagreed on the timing of the Midway operation, with the Combined Fleet calling for executing in early June, and the naval general staff arguing for a postponement of approximately three weeks. This "haggling over the details of the Midway plan" dragged on into mid-April, with the Naval General Staff "remaining highly skeptical about the whole operation."[11] Doolittle's raid on April 18, however, cut short the debate. As John Keegan notes,

Not only had Doolittle's sixteen B-25s menaced the security of the Emperor, thereby shaming the armed serves, whose ultimate purpose was to die, if necessary, in his defense; *Enterprise* and *Hornet*, which had carried the bombers to their departure point, had found a way through the Pacific perimeter by which the home islands were supposed to be protected from attack.[12]

Stung by the navy's failure to stop Doolittle's aircraft from dropping their ordnance on their targets despite having been warned of *Hornet*'s arrival by the naval picket line screening Japan's coastal flank, Adm. Yamamoto determined never to allow such an occurrence again; this "steeled [the Combined Fleet's] determination to press for an early execution date of the [Midway] operation as originally proposed."[13] Opposition to an early June date disappeared, and on May 5 the Imperial General Headquarters authorized its execution.[14]

The Midway operation, as conceived, had two main objectives: first, to capture Midway as a defensive barrier in the Pacific from which the imperial navy could detect and interdict American thrusts from Hawaii—thereby preventing future attacks on the Japanese homeland, while the second, more significant objective was to draw out the US Pacific Fleet and destroy it in a decisive battle.[15] As a diversionary effort,[16] the Midway plan called for a northern thrust against the Aleutian Islands in an effort to distract the Americans from the Japanese main effort at Midway.[17] Objectives of this diversionary effort were to destroy any US installations located on the islands seized, and to secure the northern flank of the main effort at Midway.[18] In effect, the Japanese hoped to run the US fleet from pillar to post by sending them scurrying to the defense of the Aleutians in response to that diversionary attack, only to have to turn on their heels and rush south to the relief of Midway when the main effort struck, perhaps suffering losses at the hands of Japanese submarines on both legs of the journey.[19]

Unfortunately for the Japanese, their Midway plan of attack would not go according to plan.

The Battle of Midway

Adm. Yamamoto's battle plan for the capture of Midway was a complicated one that would see his fleet divided into eight distinct elements. The battle would begin on June 3, 1942, with a diversionary attack by the Second Carrier Striking Force on Dutch Harbor in the eastern Aleutian Islands, to draw out the US Pacific Fleet from Pearl Harbor, followed up by separate amphibious assaults on the islands of Kiska and Attu in the far western Aleutians.[20] Yamamoto stationed a screening line of sixteen submarines west of Pearl Harbor to interdict and attrit the US fleet as it rushed to the relief of Dutch Harbor.[21] Yamamoto's main effort, the four aircraft carriers and supporting vessels of the First Carrier Striking Force under Adm. Chuichi Nagumo, would strike Midway the next day, on June 5, 1942, and on June 5 the Midway Occupation Force would land 5,000 troops to seize the island.[22] Adm. Yamamoto himself would command from aboard the battleship *Yamato*, one of three battleships, a light carrier, and other vessels composing the main body, standing by in reserve west of Midway.[23]

The attack did not go as planned. Recognizing the possibility of an attack on the Aleutians, Adm. Nimitz dispatched a largely surface fleet, along with USS *Saratoga* and escort carriers, north to cover the islands. When the Japanese raided Dutch Harbor, Nimitz's main striking force, under the command of Adm. Frank Fletcher, declined to take the bait, since on June 3 a US reconnaissance plane had spotted the Midway Occupation Force approaching from the southwest;[24] furthermore, information from intercepted and decrypted Japanese message traffic had given the Americans sufficient confidence to assume some risk in the North Pacific.[25] Nimitz, therefore, intended to concentrate his numerically inferior force to counter the threat to Midway.[26] Aircraft from Midway Island ineffectually attacked the Midway Occupation Force on June 3, doing nothing to impede it.[27] On the morning of June 4, Nagumo attacked Midway with a force of 108 planes; Midway's own land-based planes attempted to counter this thrust, attacking Nagumo's force "in five separate waves"; not a single hit was scored, and most of these planes were destroyed.[28] At

0700, strike forces were launched against Nagumo from USS *Hornet* and USS *Enterprise*; as with the attacks by the land-based aircraft from Midway, these strikes failed to land any significant blows against the Japanese, while suffering heavy losses in men and aircraft.[29] By 10:20 that morning, Adm. Nagumo had ninety-three aircraft ready for action and knew the location of the American carriers with sufficient precision to act; he gave the order to launch when ready.[30] As John Keegan has noted, "At 1025 Nagumo stood poised on the brink of perhaps the greatest naval victory every promised an admiral,"[31] while "the Americans were on the brink of losing the remnants of the Pacific Fleet."[32] But at 10:30 the entire course of the battle changed. At this moment, thirty-seven dive-bombers from USS *Enterprise* appeared atop the Japanese carrier fleet; fortuitously, they arrived to find Nagumo's combat air patrol fighters at low altitude near the surface, having just engaged and destroyed a wave of American torpedo bombers. Nagumo's planes were in the midst of refueling and rearming, the decks of his carriers littered with munitions, crossed by aviation fuel lines, and loaded with fueled aircraft; *Enterprise*'s bombers touched off infernos when they hit the hangar decks of the *Akagi* and the *Kaga*, so laden with flammable and explosive material.[33] But this was not the end of Adm. Nagumo's misfortune, since almost simultaneously with the arrival of *Enterprise*'s bombers, seventeen bombers from USS *Yorktown* arrived and struck the Japanese carrier *Sōryū*, with three bombs landing in the midst of armed and fueled aircraft, turning that vessel into a blazing hell as well.[34] The *Hiryū* was struck by four bombs from planes of *Yorktown* at 1700, sinking soon after.[35] The Battle of Midway ended with Japan's loss of four carriers to the loss of one—*Yorktown*—by the United States.

The Aleutians Campaign

"Yamamoto's vast tenticular plan" for the capture of Midway "had not failed in its entirety," Keegan notes, since "Kiska and Attu, his objectives in the Aleutians, had fallen to his Northern Area Force without loss,"[36] the Japanese having landed about 1,250 troops on each island on June 7 and 8.[37] But these islands were "of the tiniest strategic value."[38] Kiska and Attu would merely be a burden and encumbrance to the Japanese—they would be hazardous to supply, vulnerable to air attack, and difficult to defend against the inevitable American counterattack.

Adm. Yamamoto had entrusted his Aleutians feint—his failed attempt to draw US forces out from Hawaii and away from Midway—to the Second Carrier Striking Force, also known as the Northern Area Fleet, under the command of VAdm. Boshiro Hosogaya. Hosogaya's Northern Area Fleet consisted of two small carriers, four troop transports, six submarines, twelve destroyers, five cruisers, and ancillary support vessels.[39] Against this force was arrayed a largely surface force called Task Force 8, commanded by RAdm. Robert Theobold and consisting of five cruisers, fourteen destroyers, and six submarines, as well as the 11th Air Force under Brig. Gen. William C. Butler, consisting of ninety-five fighters, thirty-four medium bombers, and ten heavy bombers deployed at Cold Bay, Umnak Island, and Elmendorf Airfield, Anchorage; all told, the US had about 45,000 personnel in Alaska.[40]* Adm. Hosogaya launched a modest air strike against Dutch Harbor on the morning of June 3, which was beaten off by effective antiaircraft fire and American fighters from Umnak; the Japanese attacked more effectively the next day, damaging or destroying some infrastructure, killing forty-three Americans and wounding another sixty-four.[41] Adm. Theobold's Task Force 8 remained stationary near Kodiak Island, not making a sortie against the Japanese fleet until June 5, by which time Hosogaya had withdrawn to rejoin Yamamoto following the destruction of the latter's four aircraft carriers at Midway.[42]

Although the Aleutians operation had been a supporting effort by the Japanese, intended to cover the northern flank and draw US forces away from Yamamoto's main effort against Midway, the Japanese opted to continue their occupation of Kiska and Attu even after the withdrawal of the Japanese fleet. Hostile in climate and bereft of

---

* Some of these were mobilized members of the Arkansas National Guard. For an account of their time in the Aleutians, see Donald M. Goldstein and Katherine V. Dillon, *The Williwaw War: The Arkansas National Guard in the Aleutians in World War II*.

resources of almost any kind, there would seem to have been little point in the Japanese continuing to occupy Kiska and Attu after the failure of their Midway gambit. But "having publicized their capture as a military triumph," notwithstanding the absence of any opposition, the Japanese "felt compelled to hold on to them"[43] and so left their occupation forces in possession of the islands after the departure of Yamamoto's fleet. By way of a rationale more substantial than public relations, the commander of the Japanese Northern Army, Lt. Gen. Hideichiro Higuda, cited three objectives for the seizure and retention of the islands:[44]

They wanted to break up any offensive action the Americans might contemplate against Japan by way of the Aleutians, to set up a barrier between the United States and Russia in the event that Russia determined to join the United States in its war against Japan, and to make preparations through the construction of advance airbases for future offensive action.[45]

So the Japanese invaders settled in for the duration, sending off into captivity the Aleut population of the village at Chichagof Harbor—the only settlement on Attu—along with the widow of Foster Jones, the elderly American schoolteacher living there who had killed himself when the Japanese invaded; also captured was the ten-man US Navy weather team found by the Japanese on Kiska when the invaded that island.[46]

American harassment of the Japanese left behind to occupy Attu and Kiska began immediately after Yamamoto's defeat at Midway. On June 11, 1942, a force of five B-24s and five B-17s of the Eleventh Air Force struck Japanese forces at Kiska, and on July 2, 1942, the Eleventh flew bombing and photo missions against Kiska and Attu.[47] On August 30, 1942, 4,500 US troops landed unopposed on the Aleutian Island of Adak, some 200 miles from Kiska; within two weeks an airfield was completed, and the first bombing attack was launched from Adak against Kiska on September

14.[48] Bombing and photographic missions would continue against Attu and Kiska until the recapture of the islands in May and August 1943.[49,50]* Alerted by this bombing of American intentions to reconquer the islands, the Japanese reinforced their garrison on Kiska to 4,000, retaining about 1,000 on Attu.[51] The Americans were reinforcing their strength in the area as well, with total manpower of Alaska Command reaching 94,000 by the beginning of 1943.[52]

The Recapture of Attu

Following the Japanese defeat at Midway, the Aleutian Islands—together with the Kuriles—offered a potential avenue of approach by which to attack Japan,[53] as well as a potential route to Siberia should the USSR enter the war against Japan.[54] While the US ultimately deemed these North Pacific Islands an "unprofitable area in which to undertake a major offensive,"[55]

Japanese possession of Kiska and Attu dealt a significant psychological blow to the American war effort. No enemy force had occupied North American territory since the War of 1812, and news of Japanese presence in the Aleutians threatened both the confidence and morale of the American public.[56]

The US was, therefore, still resolved force the Japanese out of the Aleutians and push back the Japanese perimeter in the northern Pacific[57] and recognized that the sooner this was done, the easier it would be.[58] Accordingly, RAdm. Thomas C. Kinkaid, placed in command in the Aleutians in January 1943, was tasked with reconquering the Aleutians "as soon as ships and men for the task became available."[59]

Preparations to accomplish this task began immediately, with regular bombing and shelling of the Japanese garrisons on Kiska and Attu making the "harsh life of the occupying troops harsher."[60] With the establishment of US air bases on Amchitka and Adak, fighter-escorted, land-based bombers made surface-based communications with their

---

* For a contemporaneous account of the life of US forces on Adak and their mission to harass the Japanese occupiers of Kiska and Attu, see the film *Report from the Aleutians*, directed by John Huston, produced by the US Army Signal Corps and distributed by the Office of War Information, 1943.

Aleutian conquests impossible for the Japanese.[61] Among the events that brought about the almost hermetically sealing off of Kiska and Attu was the Battle of the Komandorski Islands, "the last and longest daylight surface naval battle of fleet warfare,"[62] between a small US force of two cruisers and four destroyers under RAdm. Charles McMorris and a much more powerful opposing Japanese fleet under Adm. Hosogaya, then engaged in escorting a resupply convoy to the Aleutians.[63] The engagement ended when, notwithstanding the superiority of his force, Hosogaya withdrew to Paramushiro Island, just south of Kamchatka; thereafter, all resupply of Kiska and Attu was by submarine only.[64]

The effort to eject the Japanese from the islands began in earnest in December 1942, when 7th Infantry Division was designated for the mission, consisting of two infantry regiments (the 17th and 32nd Infantry), the 50th Engineers, and two battalions of 105 mm howitzers; Alaska Command contributed an additional augmented battalion, held in reserve on Adak Island.[65] The 7th Infantry Division was an untried unit with no combat experience; what's more, prior to its selection for the Aleutians mission it had been training for motorized operations in the California desert—training obviously wholly inappropriate for the task that awaited them; to remedy this, the division was transferred to Fort Ord, California, for three months of training in amphibious operations under the Pacific Fleet, with a group of advisors from Alaska Defense Command on hand to familiarize the leadership of the 7th Division on the unique challenges that awaited them in the Far North.[66]

The 7th Division departed for Alaska by ship on April 24, 1943, arriving six days later on the 30th.[67] Upon arrival in Alaska the 7th Division rapidly discovered that much of their clothing and equipment was unsuitable for the cold, wet, windswept environment of the Aleutian Islands, defects that were remedied in part—but not entirely—by the time of the Attu invasion. Not only did the 7th ID's clothing and equipment

require change when they reached Alaska, but their mission had changed as well. As originally envisioned, the counterattack in the Aleutians would begin on what the US believed was the stronger enemy garrison on Kiska, and then, later, US forces would move to seize Attu. "As the time for the invasion neared," however, "it became apparent that neither adequate shipping nor personnel would not be available for a full-fledged assault on Kiska,"[68] causing Adm. Kinkaid's requests for an early invasion to be repeatedly rebuffed due the unavailability of adequate shipping and manpower; as a result, and at Adm. Kinkaid's request, the decision taken in late March 1943 to initially seize Attu, farther to the west, leaving Kiska for later.[69] This was done at least partly "in the hope that taking of Attu [first] might make Kiska untenable and compel the Japanese to leave it"[70]—a hope that was ultimately fulfilled.[71]

The invasion of Attu, code-named Operation Sandcrab,* began on May 11, 1943, when elements of the 7th Division came ashore, with a northern prong landing west of Holtz Bay on the island's northern shore, and a southern prong landing at Massacre Bay on the southern shore.[72] The Northern Force landed a provisional battalion consisting of the 7th Scout Company and the 7th Division reconnaissance troop at Beach Scarlett, and 1st Battalion of 17th Infantry and 3rd Battalion of 32nd Infantry at Beach Red.[73] The Southern Force landed 3rd Battalion of 17th Infantry and 2nd Battalion of 32nd Infantry at Beach Yellow, and 2nd Battalion of 17th Infantry at Beach Blue, with a smaller landing of a platoon from the 7th Reconnaissance Troop at Alexei Point on the north shore of Massacre Bay.[74] The plan of attack was for Northern and Southern landing forces to link up in the island's interior and then force the Japanese occupiers to the eastern end of the island, where shelling by the surface fleet and air attacks from its carrier would bludgeon them into surrender.[75] This was not to be, however: hunkering down in the island's mountainous terrain, the Japanese resisted for nearly three weeks, until on May 28 the Japanese defenders,

---

* Also called Operation Landcrab in many sources, including in Robert L. Johnson Jr., *Aleutian Campaign, World War II: Historical Study and Current Perspective*; and Del C. Kostka, "Operation Cottage: A Cautionary Tale of Assumption and Perceptual Bias," *Joint Forces Quarterly* 76, no. 1 (2015).

running short on ammunition, launched what amounted to a suicide attack at dawn, flinging themselves upon the Americans and inflicting many casualties, until all but twenty-eight of the Japanese soldiers had been killed or had killed themselves. American casualties were 600 dead and 1,200 wounded.[76]

Attu thus subdued, the stage was set for the final battle of the Aleutians Campaign, the recapture of Kiska, some three months later in August 1943, in which the 87th Infantry would participate.

The 87th Deploys to the Pacific

Planning for the recapture of Kiska was ongoing even before the 7th Infantry Division set sail from California en route to its mission on Attu.[77] At the time, Kiska was "a never-heard-of-before, dinky . . . treeless dot . . . a part of Alaska, but closer to Asia,"[78] endowed with "a perfectly shaped steaming volcano . . . set in a cloud cushion" and "rimmed like a castle with cliff-walled shores, and when occasionally visible, a bright green matting of waist-high tundra and deep lush mosses," and cursed, according to one commentator, with the "world's worst weather."[79]

At first, the general consensus among US planners was to leave the Japanese garrison to weaken and die, since "with Attu in American hands again . . . the US [had] completely severed any vestiges of a Japanese line of communication to Kiska."[80] But Adm. King and his staff advocated an invasion of Kiska to dislodge the Japanese by force; while this approach would require the assembly of an even-larger land force than that employed on Attu, and would further require a large amount of shipping badly need in other areas, maintaining a blockade of Kiska would itself require an immense commitment of naval resources to a mission that battered ships in the harsh seas of the North Pacific and wore hard on their crews; furthermore, these naval units were badly needed elsewhere.[81] The Joint Chiefs of Staff approved the Kiska invasion plan—Operation Cottage—on June 11, 1943.[82]* While detailed planning for the invasion continued, Navy and Army Air Forces prepared the ground

throughout July . . . the US Navy conducted frequent bombardment of Kiska using battleships, cruisers, and destroyers. Major bombardments were conducted on 6 and 22 July, with the latter bombardment group consisting of two battleships, five cruisers, and nine destroyers. The 22 July mission was conducted in coordination with an attack by medium and heavy bombers of the Eleventh Air Force. The results of this mission was [sic] particularly effective owing, in addition to the heavy firepower (the Navy expended 2,793 shells), to the unusually clear weather. Aerial reconnaissance showed extensive damage from this action, however Japanese records indicate the Kiska garrison suffered only fifteen dead, thirteen wounded, and twelve "establishments" badly damaged, the Japanese having industriously dug themselves into the Kiska underground with all of their personnel support facilities operating from these locations, which undoubtedly accounts for the relatively few casualties suffered by the Japanese during their occupation.[83]

The American seizure of Attu also brought another important target within range of American bombers—the Japanese naval base at Paramushiro, at the northern end of the Kuriles, near Kamchatka. Prior to the battle of Attu, US aircraft could not reach and reconnoiter the Paramushiro base; within a month of capturing Attu, the US launched its first aerial bombing and reconnaissance mission over the island.[84]

The 87th Infantry and supporting units received orders in early June 1943 for movement to the West Coast, arriving at Fort Order on June 11, 1943, the same day that the plan for Operation Cottage was approved.[85] At Fort Ord "the ski troops and mountain men" of the 87th Infantry "became virtual Marines."[86] Assigned Marine Corps advisors, over the course of "a couple of weeks" the 87th learned how to descend the rope nets known as "Jacob's ladders" down the sides of a transport ship and

---

* There is some difference of opinion as to the timeline of approval. Benedict states that the plan was "provisionally approved" by the Joint Chiefs of Staff on June 1, 1943, and given "final" approval late that month. H. Bradley Benedict, *Ski Troops in the Mud*, 57.

into an amphibious landing craft, and how to burst out of that same craft, through the turf, and secure a beachhead on the shore.[87] They had to learn much else besides. "Of course we were forced to learn the Navy lingo," recalls Lt. Col. Ross J. Wilson, commander of 1st Battalion, 87th Infantry, "else we would not have been able to communicate with the sea going on arm":

We soon learned starboard from port, the bow from poop and stern. The whistling "Man your battle stations" meant "Get ready to fight." Later on we found out what the Navy called mess was the same as good old army "chow." . . . We manned our own life boats and mastered climbing down a Jacobs [sic] ladder into them . . . at the word "go" everyone clambers over the side of the ship onto the Jacobs ladder and climb down this big net into a landing craft. The landing craft is jumping around in the ocean. . . . The ship is rolling to and fro causing the ladder to be out from the ship maybe 10 to 15 feet. Then the ship rolls the other direction and the ladder bangs the ship's hull, troops and all.[88]

And the soldiers had to negotiate all of this, Wilson reminds us, while "a rifle or mortar tube or machine gun is whacking you over the head all the time, too."[89] This initial training was followed by a week of practice landings at Camp Pendleton, and then on June 27, 1943, the 87th departed Fort Ord for good. Prior to departure the men had been given packing instructions with a "focus on heavy clothing and rainproof gear," thus reinforcing the men's speculation that they were heading for Kiska—speculation confirmed when large terrain models of Kiska Island would be unveiled on ship board three days into their voyage to the island.[90] They would wait a month for their suspicions to be confirmed, however, since although the 87th departed Fort

Ord on June 27, they did not finally sail from San Francisco Harbor until July 29, 1943.[91] The regiment moved in a ten-ship convoy, with the troops loaded on several transports, by battalion: the headquarters and other troops made the transit to Aleutians on the *Doyen*, 1st Battalion embarked on the *J. Franklin Bell*, 2nd Battalion sailed on the *Harris*, and 3rd Battalion on the *Zeilin*.[92]

After a rough crossing (or so it seemed, at least, to the landsmen of the 87th) of "terrible" food and "accommodations [that] were worse," the 87th made landfall at Adak Island on August 9. They would spend only five days acclimatizing to the Aleutians environment: one day offloading the vessels that had brought them there; "three rainy nights in pup tents"[93] conducting physical training, small-unit tactical exercises, and zeroing their weapons; and another day reloading the transport that would take them to their objective—Kiska Island.[94]

Amphibious Task Force 9: The Long Knives

The naval component of the Kiska invasion force would be Task Force 51; the land component would be Amphibious Task Force 9 (ATF-9)—the "long knives," activated on May 4, 1943, under the command of Maj. Gen. Charles H. Corlett and a staff drawn from the Western Defense Command.[95*] Initially, ATF-9 was assigned the 159th Infantry Regiment from the 7th Infantry Division, the 184th Infantry Regiment and the 301st Reconnaissance Troop from the Western Defense Command, as well as various artillery, engineer, and service elements; after the struggle to retake Attu, however, it was realized that two regiments and supporting arms would not be sufficient to overcome what was expected to be a much-larger enemy force on Kiska.[96] ATF-9 was therefore significantly expanded: the 17th Infantry Regiment, also drawn from the 7th Division, but one that had participated in the seizure of Attu, unlike the 159th Infantry, replaced the latter on ATF-9, with the 159th assuming

---

* Oddly, the appellation "ATF" has been interpreted in various ways by various authors. While many sources refer to the unit as I do here, as an "amphibious task force" (see, for example, Benedict, *Ski Troops in the Mud*; and Saul David, *The Force: The Legendary Special Ops Unit and WWII's Mission Impossible*), others interpret "ATF" otherwise, such as "Amphibious Training Force" (see Robert L. Johnson Jr., *Aleutian Campaign, World War II*), "Amphibian Training Force" (Kenneth Finlayson, "Operation Cottage: First Special Service Force, Kiska Campaign." *Veritas* 4, no. 2 [2008]), and even "Amphibious Technical Force" or "Technical Task Force" (Ross Wilson, *History of the First Battalion, 87th Mountain Infantry*).

occupation duties on Attu; the 53rd Infantry Regiment, likely a composite unit assembled from various elements of the Alaska Defense Command, was committed to ATF-9; the elite joint American-Canadian light infantry First Special Service Force brought its 2,300 men to the task force; the 4,800-strong 13th Canadian Infantry Brigade was added; and, finally, the 87th Mountain Infantry joined the task force. Together with ancillary supporting troops, ATF-9 ultimately reached a strength of 34,400 men.[97]

A number of ATF-9's supporting elements had interesting background stories worthy of comment. One of these is, of course, the 87th Mountain Infantry, "undoubtedly included" in ATF-9

not only because it was the best equipped and most accustomed to operate in Aleutian-type adversity, but also because of the regiment's battle-conditioning, battle-testing. Many of its troops had been training for more than a year and were mentally and militarily ready for enemy engagement. Furthermore, in terms of training the 87th was six months to a year ahead of its fellow regiments in the still-growing division at Camp Hale. So it made sense to test the 87th's mettle, while continuing the training at Hale of the 85th and 86th regiments.[98]

Also noteworthy is the First Special Service Force (FSSF). This unit had originally been formed in 1942 for the abortive Operation Plough,[99] where its task would have been to destroy a number of Norwegian hydroelectric dams that not only supplied almost half of Norway's electricity but were also critical to Germany's war effort.[100] Trained in Montana on skiing, mountaineering, and even parachute operations, the FSSF "was at an extremely high state of readiness" when Plough was called off.[101] Desperate to save his unit, the future of which was in doubt now that its intended mission was canceled, the FSSF commander, Col. Robert T. Frederick, traveled to Washington, DC, to lobby for another mission, and other missions were considered, including potential missions in the Russian Caucasus and in New Guinea, and FSSF participation in Operation Husky, the future

invasion of Sicily; ultimately, the invasion of Kiska was decided on.[102]

The Canadian 13th Brigade—the Greenlight Force—also had a colorful background. This brigade contained a substantial contingent of French Canadian conscripts from Quebec who were the subject of some controversy, having been exempted from deployment overseas. This controversy was ultimately resolved on the basis that while conscripts could not be compelled to serve outside North America, Kiska Island was in North America, so that service there was not "overseas" and thus permitted.[103] According to one contemporary observer, they were "the first Canadian conscripts ever sent beyond the borders of the Dominion to fight."[104] The Greenlight Force conducted some amphibious training and some familiarization training with American equipment, clothing, and military commands at Nanaimo Military Reservation.[105] In order to avoid embarrassing mix-ups, Canadian officers pinned American rank insignia on their berets, next to their own, to accommodate those "Americans [who] never could quite learn the Canadian insignia"; more "elaborate precautions" had to be taken to avoid any deadly mix-ups in the field between Americans and French conscripts, some of whom did not speak any English.[106]

The forces composing ATF-9 began assembling at staging areas in the Aleutians, with the First Special Service Force staged on Amchitka Island and the remainder of the maneuver units, save the 87th, at Adak, all of whom were in place by the latter half of July. These units conducted training, including an exercise involving an amphibious landing and three days of maneuvers inland, east of Adak on Great Sitkin Island. The 87th, along with Gen. Corlett and his staff, arrived shortly thereafter.[107]

Firsthand observations on Attu and studies of Kiska led Corlett to adopt an unusual task organization for Operation Cottage. Each of the US infantry regiments and the Canadian 13th Brigade were designated as "tactical groups," and their subordinate battalions were greatly augmented and reorganized as battalion landing groups (BLGs) of 2,000 men each, further subdivided into a "forward combat team" led by the battalion commander that would conduct offensive operations, and a "beach combat team" under a subordinate officer that would see to logistical operations and rear security on the beach and function as a reserve.[108] The forward combat teams were reinforced with a battery of artillery, medical and engineer platoons, and other elements; the beach combat teams were augmented with signal troops, combat engineers, an antiaircraft battery, ordnance, and medical elements.[109]

Fully assembled, ATF-9 consisted of 34,400 troops[110] organized into a Southern Force, a Northern Force, and a Floating Reserve,[111] within which the BLGs were organized into "task groups" (TG). The Southern Force consisted of elements of the First Special Service Force; Task Group 87 consisting of BLGs formed around 2nd Battalion, 87th Infantry; 1st Battalion, 184th Infantry; and 1st Battalion, 53rd Infantry, with TG 17 consisting of BLGs formed around 3rd Battalion, 87th Infantry; 1st Battalion, 17th Infantry; and 3rd Battalion, 17th Infantry. The Northern Force was similarly organized with elements of the FSSF; the Canadian 13th Brigade organized into three BLGs; and TG 184, consisting of BLGs formed around 1st Battalion, 87th Infantry; 2nd Battalion, 184th Infantry; and 3rd Battalion, 184th Infantry. Finally, the Floating Reserve consisted of TG 53, with BLGs formed around 2nd and 3rd Battalions of 53rd Infantry and 2nd Battalion of 17th Infantry, and elements of the FSSF stationed on Amchitka for potential airborne deployment against Kiska.[112]

The Japanese forces were concentrated at the central portion of the island, along the southern shore. Corlett's plan was to mount a naval feint against these positions from the seas to the south of the island at Gertrude, to draw enemy forces away from the landing sites on the northern side of the island; this would be followed by a landing by the Southern Force at Quisling Cove, on the other side of the island from Gertrude Cove on D-day, August 15, 1943;[113] the Northern Force would hit its beach the next day. In each case the FSSF elements would land first to seize key terrain, preparing the way for the BLGs that would follow.[114] Task Force 51 would provide naval gunfire support from positions south and west of Kiska and also provide a screen against any attempted intervention by the Japanese Imperial Navy.[115]

The main assault commenced at 6:21 in the morning on August 15, when the Southern Force landed at their assigned beaches; no resistance was encountered then or as the landings unfolded throughout the day. From this the commanders inferred that the Japanese had relinquished their installations and ensconced themselves on the high ground as they had on Attu, from there to receive the American and Canadian attackers.[116] Others worried that the Japanese were concentrated in position to oppose the landing of the Northern Force,[117] which landed per plan on D+1, with the Canadians on the right and the American units at center and left.[118]

On Kiska the invaders found an extremely well-developed set of installations. The Japanese occupiers had installed power lines fed by several generating plans, a sawmill, a foundry, machine shops, a shortwave-transmitting station and local radio stations for command and entertainment purposes, telephones, a road network, running water,[119] and even a port facility with three midget submarines.[120] What they didn't find were any Japanese. When, by the end of August 17, all the key terrain on Kiska had been secured, including the adjacent Little Kiska Island, the Allied command had to concede what some had long expected—the Japanese had slipped the net and abandoned Kiska prior to the Allied invasion.[121]

The Japanese Withdrawal from Kiska

The Japanese boasted extravagantly about the suicidal sacrifice of their men on Attu. Among their boasts were lavish statements of praise attributed to foreign leaders, such as the following:

When the Incident of the Attu suicidal charge became known all over the world, every country praised their courage . . . the Axis powers was [sic] particularly great. The German Military Attaché wrote: "We . . . wish to express our deepest admiration for the heroic deeds carried out by the Attu Garrison Unit, which fought to the last man." According to the Japanese Ambassador in Russia: Generalissimo Stalin regarded the suicidal charge of the Attu Garrison Unit as the Japanese symbol of Bushido.

He ordered the insertion of this Incident in the primary school textbooks. From the Italian Attaché: "We . . . wish to express our deepest condolences for the heroic deaths of Col. Yamasaki and his men. . . . As long as the nation spirit remains as it is, Japan will emerge victorious."[122]

Of much-greater interest to US and Canadian commanders was the Japanese government's communications to its domestic population, which included fare such as the following:

Kiska is still in our hands. When the nation heard about the courageous suicidal charge of the Attu Garrison Unit, they expressed profound admiration and condolence. This added fuel to the fire of the national spirit and stimulated the production of munitions. In short, the Attu suicidal charge was a tremendous stimulant to the fighting spirit of our nation.[123]

As American and Canadian forces prepared for the next phase in the reconquest of the Aleutians, US intelligence estimated Japanese strength on Kiska at around 10,000 men.[124] Given the example their comrades had set for them on Attu, and given the chest beating of their home government about that slaughter, Allied commanders had good reason to believe that the Japanese garrison on Kiska would follow suit.

Yet, such bombast notwithstanding, there were indications of something amiss on Kiska long before the Southern Force landed on D-day. More than two weeks prior, aerial reconnaissance began to indicate that "routine activities on Kiska appeared to diminish significantly, with bomb damage being left unrepaired and little or no traffic visible in the harbor.[125] Radio traffic had ended on July 28.[126] Beginning to suspect that the Japanese may have evacuated that island, intelligence analysts recommended further aerial reconnaissance and even landing a ground reconnaissance party.[127] Gen. Corlett himself requested a postponement of D-day to assess

indications of a Japanese withdrawal, as well as to train replacements.[128] Even commanders and staffs in the landing battalions began to have their doubts, as reported by Ross Wilson, commander of 1st Battalion, 87th Infantry:

Our information and photos clearly indicated there were no Japs on Kiska. Col. Fredricks, Maj. Nations and Lt. Col. Wilson all volunteered to take a company[-]sized combat patrol; make a night landing and reconnoiter the island and thus confirm our intelligence. The Navy insisted they had blockaded the island, [and] that the Japs could not have escaped.[129]

Adm. Kinkaid, fearing a repetition of the awful slaughter and heavy casualties of the Attu operation, refused all such recommendations and resolved to execute the landings as planned.[130] In later years, Wilson would wistfully remark that "it is impossible for me to believe, even yet, why such a decision was reached," while conceding, in all fairness, that "in defense of the Big Picture plan, the high command was apprehensive that Japs might have set a trap for our Navy and all of us. So, we were in force."[131]

Adm. Kinkaid need not have worried, however, since the Japanese Imperial High Command had ordered the evacuation of Kiska nearly three months earlier, on May 19, 1943.[132] The Japanese evacuation of Kiska was every bit as dramatic a success as the British evacuation from Dunkirk, and comparable in the brilliance and daring of its execution as the Egyptian crossing of the Suez Canal that launched the 1973 Yom Kippur War against Israel.* This withdrawal, executed under the command of VAdm. Shiro Kawase and RAdm. Masatomi Kimura,[133] is worthy of a book in its own right and was in fact the subject of *Retreat from Kiska*, a major Japanese motion picture, in 1965.[134]

As originally planned, the withdrawal of the Kiska garrison was to be accomplished by submarine, but this procedure was abandoned after the loss of three submarines to American destroyers, with only 820 men evacuated to show for the

* For discussion of Egyptian preparations for this operation, see Kenneth M. Pollack, *Arabs at War: Military Effectiveness, 1948–1991*, 98–104.

sacrifice.[135] Instead, a force of eleven surface combatants—two light cruisers and nine destroyers—were dispatched for the mission.[136*] To avoid compromising the operation, coordination between the Japanese navy and the Kiska garrison was not accomplished by radio; instead, Adm. Kawase had staff officers from Kiska exfiltrated by submarine to assist in planning the rescue; these same officers were then reinserted onto the island to brief the garrison on the plan.[137] The Japanese fleet was aided in its mission by a most fortuitous stroke of luck—the remarkable Battle of the Pips. On July 22, 1943, a US Navy PBY identified seven objects—pips—on its radar, tracking them moving eastward for six hours; believing this to be an attempt by the Japanese to reinforce Kiska, Adm. Kinkaid ordered two nearby naval task forces to pursue the targets, even going so far as to order the two destroyers guarding the harbor at Kiska to join the chase.[138] The fleet was about to give up the chase, having failed to make radar contact with the targets themselves, when at 1:00 a.m. on July 26, the battleship *Mississippi* made radar contact with seven targets. The armada opened fire with their 8- and 14-inch guns until the "enemy"—the seven radar pips—changed course and then disappeared. Aerial reconnaissance at daylight revealed no trace of any enemy fleet.[139] The US fleet then withdrew to replenish fuel and ammunition and make repairs, leaving the Kiska harbor unguarded.[140] Seizing the opportunity, Adm. Kimura steamed into Kiska Harbor at 1640 on July 28, 1943. The entire 5,200-man garrison remaining on Kiska** (save for a small rear guard) was removed from the island in a single lift in only fifty-five minutes, using ten landing craft already on the island and thirteen more brought by Kimura's task force.[141] The rear guard destroyed assets, planted booby traps, and engaged US planes with antiaircraft fire, until they themselves were removed from the island by submarine prior to the US assault.[142]

The Cost

Although the landings on Kiska were unopposed, they were not without cost. Ninety-two Allied servicemen were killed in the operation, and 221 wounded.[143] The single biggest loss was endured at sea, when USS *Abner Reed* struck a mine, wounding forty-seven sailors and killing seventy.[144] The landing forces bore losses as well. The Southern Force lost seventeen killed and forty-five wounded or very sick, while the Northern Force suffered four dead Canadians and seventy-six other casualties.[145]

Cold-weather injuries accounted for a significant portion of the Kiska casualties—130, all told, much better than the incidence of cold-weather injuries during the Attu operation, where "twelve hundred cold injuries occurred in twenty-two days."[146] Clothing and equipment provided for the Kiska operation were much improved over those issued for Attu, and the soldiers participating in the Kiska operation received instruction and training materials on how to use the cold- and wet-weather clothing and equipment they had been issued, and how to protect themselves from injury.[147] One source reports that "in spite of the training given them before landing, some of [the Kiska] casualties admitted that they had failed to follow instructions given them and did not remove their shoepacs and socks for several days at a time."[148]

Tragically, another source of casualties on Kiska was friendly fire, which killed twenty-one Allied soldiers.[149***] As one historian reports, "upon landing, the American troops fanned out in the heavy fog, expecting to face enemy resistance at every turn. The columns frequently exchanged fire. . . . As one survivor, Lt. Murphy, later wrote: 'The troops were shooting at anything that moved.'"[150] George F. Earle, a Kiska veteran and historian of both the 87th Infantry and the 10th Mountain Division, describes the ensuing tragedy thus:

> During the night, the inevitable broke out. Units had been located in mistakenly reported positions that, because of the zigzag ridgeline, were invisibly opposition

---

* Note that Benedict states that the force consisted of three cruisers, eleven destroyers, and an oiler. Benedict, *Ski Troops in the Mud*, 64.
** Note that the actual Japanese strength of 6,000 was much less than the 10,000 estimated by US intelligence.
*** Geoffrey Regan, in his book *Blue on Blue: A History of Friendly Fire*, reports twenty-eight Americans killed and fifty "seriously wounded" by friendly fire on Kiska (p. 113).

each other. Fighting erupted and counterfire and counterattack were called for. Eleven of us were killed, killed by us, and we will never forget.[151]*

Benedict described one tragic incident in which a detachment of Headquarters, 3rd Battalion, 87th Infantry, was attacked by another friendly force positioned on higher ground:

Just as the men prepared their last entrenchment in the dead of night (ironic words) on a slope near Link Hill, a machine gun opened fire from above, gunning down at the CP area, with tracer bullets and live ammunition ricocheting over the foxholes . . . some Headquarters personnel began emptying their weapons at unseen targets above. But the machine-gunning persisted, soon accompanied by exploding grenades. . . . Shouts, curses, shots and explosions rent the air in a savage "firefight." And a number of men in the patrols and elsewhere who stood up or crawled at an inopportune time were hit, several mortally wounded.[152]

These tragic mistakes occurred despite the fact that the need for control measures was clearly identified in US Army infantry doctrine before and during World War II, including FM 7-10, *Rifle Company, Rifle Regiment* (1942), and FM 7-5, *Organization and Tactics of Infantry, the Rifle Battalion* (1940).[153] What's more, the danger of fratricide was anticipated as a particular concern in the Aleutians context, as noted in a May 1943 briefing given by Amphibious Branch, G3 Section, Army Ground Forces, on lessons learned from Attu:

We must have some means of identification for patrols. . . . They must have some physical means of signaling to our own troops. . . . They would go up there, get lost, and . . . our own troops here would shoot at them. . . .

It is necessary that we take steps to stop troops shooting at our own flanking patrols.[154]

As one commentator summed the situation up, "The Kiska landing was an embarrassing and costly mistake in several respects, not the least of which was the uncontrolled gunfire of the inexperienced troops.[155]

Return to the Mainland

The 87th Mountain Infantry's brief odyssey in the Pacific continued for a time after the initial reoccupation of Kiska. By August 18, it was clear that no Japanese forces remained on the island; yet, perhaps because Adm. Kinkaid "hated to admit the Japs were gone," the ski troopers of the 87th continued to search for them until at least August 22, "much to Corlett's and the troops disgust."[156] After that, the task of settling in and putting the Allied presence on Kiska on a firm footing commenced in earnest. Troops on Kiska located their baggage and established camps, then relocated their camps, digging tents, installing floors, and scrounging supplies, only to be told to change locations and do it all again—and then again, and again. Supplies were unloaded from ships, in a chaotic manner at first, and later with some semblance of order. Roads constructed by the Japanese were further improved to support all the American vehicular traffic crisscrossing the islands. Wire communication and electricity were contrived for headquarters and soldiers' billets. Soldiers lost track of their gear and "liberated" supplies and equipment from among the detritus of the former Japanese occupiers and the mounds of supplies and equipment piling up on the beaches.** Work details abounded, and range firing, small-unit training, and patrols continued on a small scale.[157]

Happily for the men of the 87th, their cold, wet, fogbound, and windswept life on Kiska was soon to end. By mid-October word reached the 87th of pending redeployment to the United

---

* Earle disagrees with the reported figure of twenty-one noted above, insisting that "from my checking, I am satisfied it was eleven, not fifteen, and certainly not thirty, figures variously given." Earle, *Birth of a Division*, 19.
** For a vivid and lively description of day-to-day life for the soldiers of the 87th and of the other units on Kiska after the reoccupation, see Benedict, *Ski Troopers in the Mud*, 121–60.

States, tentatively set for late October to mid-December.[158] By late November 1943, elements of the regiment were flowing back to the United States,[*] and the 87th was reassembled as a regiment by New Year's Day 1944.[159] Shortly thereafter, the 87th relieved the 90th Infantry at Camp Hale, taking its rightful place in the 10th Light Division (Alpine),[160] soon to complete its training and deploy—after a sojourn in Texas—to join the fight in Europe.

Assessment of the Kiska Mission

Considering the intelligence available at the time, it is easy to fault Adm. Kinkaid for launching the Kiska assault on what was found to be an abandoned island, and Kinkaid and Nimitz (as well as Lt. Gen. DeWitt, commander of the Western Defense Command) were criticized for it,[161] particularly in light of the tragic instances of fratricide that occurred. Adm. Kinkaid had been particularly criticized for the latter, with one commentator characterizing as "somewhat disingenuous" Kinkaid's claim that "of course we had no way of anticipating our men would shoot each other in the fog,"[162] while historian Geoffrey Regen tartly postulates that "Adm. Kinkaid should have known better than to blame it all on the men."[163] George Earle wrote that Kiska "was to be a breathless 'bell ringer' but the bell never rang. Tolled but never rang,"[164] and that the men of the 87th described the embarrassing fiasco of the Japanese slipping out from under the noses of the Navy with an amusing appellation of their own, calling it an "Optical Aleutian."[165]

Nonetheless, Operation Cottage was hardly a worthless exercise. Lt. Col. Wilson of 1st Battalion, 87th Infantry, gives us as the following assessment, a remarkably broad-minded one coming as it does from a man nearly at the point of the spear:

While the whole exercise seemed like and probably was a tactical blunder, we must remember that denying the Japs the Aleutian Island Chain with this great show of force actually did accomplish several things. One, it gave us the first theater[-]wide victory of the war. Two, it gave us the first victory over the enemy ever fought on American soil. Three, it reduced the Jap threat to our northern flank. Four, it scared the hell out of the Japs and caused them to maintain a large combat force (Naval, ground, and air) at or near Paramashiro. This to protect their own northern flank. Five, it did give us a very realistic combat exercise (everyone learned something I hope). Six, it ended the Jap adventure into the western hemisphere. Seven, the strategy then seemed to be to attack Japan to down through the Kuriles from the north.[166]

While Adm. Kinkaid's refusal to accept that the Japanese had evacuated Kiska was an embarrassing failure to grasp the significance of, and to properly exploit, the intelligence available to him, the Kiska operation on the whole represents a very satisfactory tactical success. The American expulsion of the Japanese from the more weakly held Attu effectively dislocated the Japanese position on Kiska. As Robert Leonhard has explained, "Dislocation is the art of rendering the enemy's strength irrelevant. Instead of having to fight or confront the hostile force on its terms, the friendly force avoids any combat in which the enemy can bring his might to bear."[167] This is precisely what the United States achieved, and more: not only did the American seizure of Attu render the much-stronger Japanese garrison on Kiska effectively impotent, but it actually rendered that fortified and well-developed garrison into a positive burden—"a running sore"—for the Japanese.[168]

The Kiska invasion, along with Attu, did not just incur costs; it also produced concrete benefits:

---

[*] Benedict also provides an interesting glimpse of life for the mountain troopers en route from Kiska back to the mainland—in his case, aboard the US Army Transport Ship (USAT) *Chirikof*, with the 1st Battalion, 87th Infantry, 307th Quartermaster, and 229th Engineers. See Benedict, *Ski Troopers in the Mud*, 161–66. USAT *Chirikof* had an interesting history itself. It was laid down as a passenger ship—SS *Lurline*—in 1908 at Newport News, Virginia, being launched on January 11, 1908, and delivered to the Matson Navigation Company in mid-March. It was later purchased by the Alaska Packers Association and rechristened as SS *Chirikof*. The vessel was first charted by the federal government for military service in July 1940, and after a brief interlude back with its owners, it was further charted to the US Army Transportation Corps as USAT *Chirikof*. The vessel was released from federal service and returned to the Alaska Packers Association on March 13, 1946. She was rechristened SS *Radnik* in 1947 and scrapped in 1953. Roland W. Charles, *Troopships of World War II*, 13.

Although the assault of a deserted island was an embarrassment, and Kinkaid was roundly criticized in the American media, the operation did pay dividends in ways not apparent to Kinkaid's detractors. Amphibious warfare techniques were refined after the Kiska landing, and Kinkaid's decision to bypass and isolate heavily defended Kiska by first seizing Attu set a strategic precedent for the successful island-hopping campaign of 1943–1945. Moreover, Japan's foothold in the Aleutians was gone.[169]

A touching epilogue to the Kiska campaign occurred some forty-three years later, in 1986. During the Kiska invasion, 87th Mountain Infantry trooper Sherman M. Smith found a Japanese flag, inscribed with Japanese characters, among the detritus left behind by the Japanese troops when they evacuated. Mr. Sherman kept this flag and displayed it in a place of honor with other memorabilia from his 10th Mountain Division days. One day many years later, a Japanese automotive technician, and the technician's wife, translated some of the Japanese writing on the flag, revealing not only the name of the owner—Karl Kaoru Kasukabe—but also that the flag had been

presented to him by the Chukyo Mountain Climber's Club in 1942, upon the occasion of Mr. Kasukabe's entry into military service. Moved by the unexpected discovery that this flag may have originally belonged to a fellow Alpinist, Smith—who had been contemplating a skiing and mountaineering trip to Japan—resolved to find Mr. Kasukabe and return the flag to him. With the assistance of the Japanese-American Society of the State of Washington and the Japanese Alpine Club, Mr. Sherman located Mr. Kasukabe, as well as Mr. Kasukabe's daughter who living in the United States. The flag was returned to Mr. Kasukabe; a round of events and warm fellowship among former foes, now close friends, ensued in Japan—including, apparently, Mr. Kasukabe being made an associate member of the 10th Mountain Division Association. The source of this information is an odd little book titled *The Aleutians Front Graphics* published by Mr. Kasukabe's company, Commercial Art Center, Nagoya, Japan, in 1986. This interesting volume contains a wealth of articles, photographs, and documents relating to the 87th Infantry, the 10th Mountain Division Association, the Kiska Veteran's Society, the Aleut peoples, the military operations in Kiska, the Chukyo Alpine Society, and other related topics.

Insignia of Amphibious Task Force 9, the "Long Knives," with whom the 87th Mountain Infantry would invade Kiska. *Author's collection*

Allied forces landing at Kiska, seen from ground level. Official US Navy photo. *Author's collection*

Landing on Kiska, August 15, 1943. The caption reads, in part: "United States and Canadian troops swarming ashore from landing barges on a stretch of beach only the northeast coast of Kiska." Official US Navy photo. *Author's collection*

CHAPTER 4

Events in the Mediterranean

A great deal happened in the Mediterranean theater before the arrival of the 10th Mountain Division in Italy. Just as Doolittle's symbolic raid on the Japanese mainland—as physically and conceptually remote from its home and training at Camp Hale as anything could be—nonetheless profoundly shaped the destiny of the 87th Infantry, knocking down the first in a series of dominoes leading inexorably to the regiment's landings on Kiska, so events far afield from Camp Hale, Camp Swift, or even Italy itself would conspire to draw the 10th Mountain Division to battle in that most historic of lands.

Soon after the Japanese attack on Pearl Harbor, the United States and Great Britain agreed on the "Germany first" policy, under which the Allies agreed to concentrate first on subduing Germany and then to turn their full attention to crushing Japan. "In essence," wrote British soldier and historian Maj. Gen. John Strawson, "this strategy was that Japan would be denied the means to wage war while the Allies would concentrate on Germany's defeat, tightening the ring round her by sustaining Russia, strengthening the Middle East and getting hold of the entire North African coast."[1] Within this framework, however, questions remained, not the least of which being to what extent should the Allies expend resources to expand operations in the Mediterranean, as opposed to husbanding them for the anticipated future invasion of France across the English Channel.[2] The American preference, or at least that of Gen. Marshall and the American Joint Chiefs of Staff, was to conserve resources for the Channel crossing, and to strictly eschew any dispersion of effort on any secondary "distraction" or "sideshow" that might detract from that effort.[3] However, both Churchill and Roosevelt were convinced that "an absolute prerequisite to such an invasion was that Russia should be sustained so that the Red Army could continue to engage and weaken the Wehrmacht," and to that end,

Roosevelt had effectively promised Soviet foreign minister Molotov in May 1942 that a second front would be opened against Germany that year; given the strategic and operational realities at the time, if the president's promise to Molotov were to be kept, it would have be by an Allied invasion of North Africa—what was to become known as Operation Torch.[4]

Operation Torch and Operations in North Africa, 1942 and 1943

This "invasion" actually began with British forces already located in North Africa, when on October 23, 1942, the British Eighth Army under Gen. Montgomery attacked at El Alamein, having previously rebuffed an Axis attack; Operation Torch began just over a fortnight later, on November 8, 1942, when a fleet of 400 US and British ships* and 1,000 aircraft landed 107,000 Allied soldiers (including what was to be the first airborne assault by a battalion of US Army paratroopers) in Morocco and Algeria, both still controlled by the French Vichy regime.[5] The invasion force was divided into three elements: the American Western Task Force, which had sailed directly from the United States to its target of Casablanca in French Morocco; the Center Task Force, composed of US Army soldiers transported on British vessels; and the British Eastern Task Force, a mix of British and American troops transported by the Royal Navy, landed at Algiers.[6] Notwithstanding attempted prior coordination with conspirators willing to collaborate in wresting the French colonies from German influence, Vichy troops in French Morocco resisted, resulting in the destruction of thirteen French vessels, the deaths of 15,000 French troops, and many American casualties as well; French troops at Oran, Algeria, resisted as well, while at Algiers, an attempted coup by pro-Ally French officers against Vichy forces aided the Allied landings.[7] Notwithstanding initial French resistance, the French command in North Africa had capitulated by November 11, with the French commander, Adm. Jean François Darlan, eventually ordering the remaining French troops to cooperate with the Allies.[8] Unfortunately, by the time Darlan gave this order, German forces had already secured Tunis, which became the Allies' next objective.[9] In January 1943, Rommel's German and Italian forces took up a defensive position at the Mareth Line, near Tunisia's southern border, while the German general Juergon von Arnim confronted Gen. Eisenhower's forces in the West; with the arrival of the winter rains, the situation settled in to a stalemate that could be broken only when the mud dried in March.[10] The Germans, as it happens, were not willing to wait that long, and Rommel attacked through central Tunisia on February 14, 1943, in what would come to be known as the Battle of Kasserine Pass, in an attempt to cut off and trap the Allies.[11] Despite penetrating the American lines and exposing a number of embarrassing failures and errors by the green American units, the attack was stopped on February 22 with the timely arrival of four battalions of American artillery from Oran, which, in concert with a small force of British tanks, halted Rommel's attack.[12] Concerned about a potential attack by Montgomery's Eighth Army, Rommel then hastily withdrew to meet that threat.[13] Though the German high command refused to accept it at the time, Rommel's failure at Kasserine Pass left the Axis forces in Tunisia in an untenable position, as Allied resupply efforts grew easier while the Axis supply line became increasingly pinched due to Allied interdiction.[14] The Allies resumed the offense by March 17, 1943, when Gen. Patton attacked toward the rear of Rommel's Mareth Line, to be followed up a few days later by the main effort, an attack by Gen. Montgomery; the two armies accomplished a linkup by early April and captured Bizerte and Tunis, bottling up the Axis forces in a peninsula southeast of Tunis, where they capitulated on May 10, 1943.[15]

Operation Husky: the Invasion of Sicily

As had been previously decided at the January 1943 Casablanca conference,[16] the Allies next turned their attention to Sicily, just off the toe of the Italian boot. On July 10, 1943, the joint US-British 15th Army Group, under British general Sir Harold Alexander, landed on southeastern Sicily, with the British Eighth Army under Bernard Montgomery (the main effort) on the right, and the US Seventh Army under Gen. George Patton on the right.[17] The 180,000-man invasion force was transported and supported by what was then the largest amphibious task force ever assembled: "There were no fewer than 180,000 troops and naval forces, which totaled nearly 2,600 vessels, including more than 500 warships, 1,700 landing craft and 200 merchant ships."[18] As in Operation Torch, the amphibious landings of both the 7th and 8th Armies were supported by airborne assaults to the enemy's rear; both were disasters. As one historian of the Italian Campaign put it, the landings were "a fiasco in which the most carefully selected and highly trained soldiers . . . were literally thrown away by inexperienced and inadequately trained aircrews."[19] In the British sector, only twelve of 134 gliders landed in the correct areas; by almost a miracle, a small number of the British glider troops did manage to secure the bridge that was their objective, and hold it until relieved; in the American zone, only one paratrooper landing of the four ordered by Gen. Patton landed in the right place; worse, on two separate nights, aircraft bearing American and British paratroopers were mistaken for enemy planes and fired upon by Allied ships.[20] So poor was the airborne performance and so severe the losses "that for a time some Allied commanders questioned the wisdom of employing this new method of warfare."[21] The seaborne landings also faced problems, including "strong winds, errors of navigation, faulty launching of assault boats, lateness of arrival at the rendezvous—all contributed to the confusion and to troops being landed on the wrong beaches at the wrong time."[22]

---

* At least one of these vessels still exists. USS *Massachusetts* (BB-55) was present, firing over 700 rounds from her 16-inch main armament. Some of these were fired during the course of a gunnery duel in which she scored five hits on the incomplete *Jean Bart*, a French battleship, at its Casablanca mooring, defeating the vessel. *Massachusetts* helped sink five other vessels that day. USS *Massachusetts* is now a museum ship at Battleship Cove, a collection of museum vessels located at Fall River, Massachusetts. See Historic Naval Ships Association, "USS *Massachusetts* (BB-59)"; and Battleship Cove, "USS *Massachusetts* (BB-59)."

These difficulties notwithstanding, the Allies succeeded in getting eight divisions ashore on July 10,[23] "landing about 80,000 men, 300 tanks, 900 guns, and 7,000 vehicles" in the first two days of the operation and capturing the ports of Syracuse, Augusta, and Licata and the airfields at Gela.[24]

Notwithstanding this success, however, the Germans mounted a stout defense, holding Montgomery's Eighth Army in check for three days, until Gen. Alexander authorized Patton to drive for Palermo in the northwestern arm of the Sicilian triangle, which he seized on July 22.[25] Following a conference convened by Gen. Alexander on July 25, Montgomery and Patton executed a coordinated drive on Messina, at the tip of the eastern arm of the Sicily triangle, adjacent to mainland Italy, with Patton's Seventh Army advancing on San Stefano on the northern coast and Nicosia, directly to its south at the intersection of highways 117 and 121, and Montgomery seeking to turn the enemy out of Catania on the eastern shore by capturing Paterno and Adrano in the shadow of Mount Etna, both to Catania's northwest.[26] By August 8, the Allies had captured the towns of San Fratella, Troina, Adrano, and Catania, compromising the Germans' San Fratella (Etna) line and pushing them into the northeastern corner of the Sicilian triangle.[27] At this point Gen. Kesselring made the decision to withdraw from Sicily to preserve the remaining German forces. By the time Patton's Seventh Army entered Messina on August 17, Gen. Hube, the local commander, had successfully extracted 60,000 of his troops from the island, which would be available for action on the Italian mainland.[28]

The human toll of the Sicilian campaign was immense. The Allies suffered approximately 20,000 casualties, while the Axis lost 164,000, of whom 130,000 were Italians, with most of those being captured.[29]* Nonetheless, as Strawson notes, much had been accomplished:

The Allies had achieved great successes and acquired invaluable experience. The handling of great armadas of warships and transports, together with their landing craft; the problems of airborne operations, to say nothing of close air support during amphibious assaults; the logistic requirements of landing supplies across open beaches; the sheer business of directing Anglo-American armies, with all the sensitivities created by prima donna–like commanders in the mould of Montgomery and Patton—all of which were to be exploited in the great enterprise of Overlord, which was still almost a year away.[30]

The Americans, in particular, had grown. As John English observes, "With the invasion and conquest of Sicily, July–August 1943, the American ground forces attained a combat maturity and prestige equal to that of the British."[31] "The American force that fought in Sicily," observed one official US Army history, "was far more sophisticated than that which had gone into battle in North Africa":

New landing craft, some capable of bearing tanks, had made getting ashore much quicker and surer, and the amphibious trucks called DUKWs eased the problem of supply over the beaches. Gone was the Grant tank with its side-mounted gun, lacking wide traverse; in its place was the Sherman with 360-degree power-operated traverse for a turret[-]mounted 75 mm piece. Commanders were alert to avoid a mistake often made in North Africa of parceling out divisions in small increments, and the men were sure of their own ability. Some problems of coordination remained, but they would soon be worked out.[32]

The Activation of Fifth Army

When the 10th Mountain Division finally entered combat in Italy, it was as a part of US Fifth Army under the command of Lt. Gen. Mark W. Clark. The creation of Fifth Army was set in motion on

---

* There are varying casualty estimates. The figures cited here are from John Strawson, *The Italian Campaign*, 121. The Center of Military History's *American Military History*, dated 1989, estimates that the Germans evacuated 40,000 troops from Sicily and suffered 10,000 casualties, with the Italians losing up to 100,000 (mostly captured), with 22,000 Allied losses. *American Military History*, 479.

December 1, 1942, when the War Department wrote to the commanding general, European theater of operations, notifying him that Headquarters, Fifth Army; Headquarters Company, Fifth Army; and Special Troops, Fifth Army would be created in theater from men and material drawn from the Western Task Force, which had sailed from the United States and landed at Casablanca on November 8, 1942, which itself would be disbanded.* Headquarters, European theater of operations, implemented these instructions with the promulgation of General Order No. 67, dated December 12, 1942, constituting 5th Army and allocating it to Allied Force, North Africa.[33]

Lt. Gen. Clark activated his command at one minute past midnight, January 5, 1943, at Oudjda, French Morocco—a fact commemorated to this day in Fifth Army's unit patch, which includes the blue silhouette of a mosque among its elements.[34] I Armored Corps (French Morocco), II Corps (Western Algeria), and XII Air Support Command were its organic subordinate units;[35] the commanding general, European theater, was vested with the authority to assign additional units or resources to Fifth Army at discretion.[36] Upon activation,

Fifth Army was to prepare a well-organized, well-equipped, and mobile striking force with at least one infantry division and one armored division fully trained in amphibious operations. It was to insure [sic], in cooperation with French forces, the integrity of all territory of French Morocco and Algeria west of . . . Orléansville, to act with French civil and military authorities in the preservation of law and order, and to assist in organization, equipping, and training French forces [and] finally, Fifth Army was to prepare plans for and execute special operations.[37]

Fifth Army's first tasking along the latter lines was Gen. Eisenhower's directive to Lt. Gen. Clark to prepare plans for the occupation of Spanish Morocco in the event of hostilities with Spain. Such a contingency never came to pass, however; Fifth Army's "primary task" was to prepare for, and execute, "one of the hardest operations in modern warfare—an amphibious movement in force to land on a defended hostile shore."[38] In addition to the general program of unit training, Fifth Army established eight specialized training centers in North Africa to prepare its units, and those of its French allies, for the future invasion of Italy. The most important of these was the Invasion Training Center established at Port aux Poules, Algeria, where regimental-sized units conducted intensive training, including combined operations with Air Force and naval elements, in preparation for future landings.[39] Others included an Airborne Training Center at Oudjda, French Morocco; a Leadership and Battle Training Center at Slissen, Algeria; a Field Officers Training Center at Chanzy, Algeria; a Tank Destroyer Training Center at Sebdou, Algeria; and Engineer Training, Air Observation Post, and French Training Sections.[40]

As the time for Fifth Army to go into action approached, Gen. Clark redeployed his headquarters 480 miles to Mostagenem, Algeria, with the forward echelon moving by train and the rear echelon by truck, whence he oversaw the completion the Army's training for combat.[41] "The training of Fifth Army ended with an examination in the form of practice landing operations," the official history reports,

carried out by the 36th Division. . . . The 45th Infantry Division in Sicily and the British 10 Corps, which were to be part of

---

* Fifth Army remains with us as an active headquarters today. Although inactivated following the war at Camp Myles Standish, Massachusetts, on October 2, 1945, it was quickly reactivated on June 11, 1946, at Chicago, Illinois (Wilson, *Armies, Corps, Divisions, and Separate Brigades*, 22) as one of six field armies to be activated in the United States. At that time, Fifth Army's function was to reduce Active Component units and installations in its area of responsibility, the north-central United States. It also had the function of providing military capabilities to support civil authorities in times of natural disaster, a function it continues to discharge to this day. From 1950 to 1953, Fifth Army provided trained units and soldiers for deployment to combat operations in Korea, as it did during the Berlin Crisis and during Vietnam. In 1957, it was redesignated Fifth United States Army. In the early 1970s, it moved to Fort Sam Houston, Texas—its current home—and assumed responsibility for fourteen states in the central United States. Fifth Army provided trained and ready units for deployment in support of Desert Shield / Desert Storm and—now expanded to a twenty-one-state area of responsibility—in support of Operations Noble Eagle, Enduring Freedom, and Iraqi Freedom. Fifth Army was redesignated United States Army North on December 19, 2006, when it became the Army Component Command of United States Northern Command. US Army North, "History."

Fifth Army in its first combat operations, had also conducted practice landings. The areas had been especially selected to duplicate or at least to approximate those to be found at Salerno. The example of the 36th Division may be cited. Its ships had been loaded, and everything except the last-minute touches had been given; the troops were embarked on their respective vessels, and the convoy put out to sea, soon to assemble for the dry run, Operation Cowpuncher. The same plans and orders for the invasion were used, wherever practicable, with a simple substitution of geographical names. During the night of 26–27 August the practice operation was conducted against troops of the 34th Division, who had wired the beaches and manned the defenses. The assault troops came ashore in small craft, and a portion of all types of weapons and vehicles were landed. This rehearsal brought out a few changes in manner of loading and unloading, but above all it gave officers and men a feeling of confidence in their ability to carry out the task confronting them."[42]

The Invasion of the Italian Mainland

Gen. Eisenhower had formulated the basic plan for the invasion of mainland Italy as early as August 16, the day prior to the capture of Messina by Allied forces: Gen. Montgomery's Eighth Army—Operation Baytown—would cross the Strait of Messina to the toe of the Italian peninsula between September 1 and 4, 1943, while the US Fifth Army would execute Operation Avalanche—the amphibious invasion of Italy at Salerno—approximately a week later, on or about September 9,[43] the delay being due to a shortage of available shipping, such that some of the vessels that carried Montgomery's forces across from Sicily to the toe would also have to participate in Fifth Army's landing at Salerno.[44]

Operation Baytown commenced at 1:30 on the morning of September 3, 1943, when the British crossed over from Messina to Calabria on the mainland without opposition.[45] "It was soon evident," Marin Blumenson observes, that

early in this phase of the campaign, "the natural obstructions of the terrain and German demolitions would be the main obstacles to an Eighth Army advance."[46]

An early summary of the operations in Italy published by Fifth Army noted that the first chapter of "the Italian Campaign . . . falls into certain convenient phases. They are: the landing at Salerno; the fall of Naples; the crossing of the Volturno; the Winter Line Campaign; the Anzio beachhead; and the May offensive which freed Rome."[47] Although the landings would occur six days later on September 9, the first of these phases—Operation Avalanche—commenced nearly simultaneously with Montgomery's crossing of the Strait of Messina, as the first convoy in support of the operation departed Tripoli for Sicily, carrying part of the British 56th Division, followed by other convoys on successive days through September 6.[48] All the convoys had staged by September 8, at which time they left the waters around Sicily, en route for Salerno,[49] south of Naples at the top of Italy's foot on the western shore. Fifth Army's landings there—the first US forces to land in Europe during World War II—commenced at 3:30 a.m. on September 9, 1943, where they met "a hell of tracers, flares, and shot and shell."[50] The landing force, consisting of the US 36th Division under US VI Corps, followed shortly by the 45th Division and the British 46th and 56th Divisions of the British 10th Corps, was well established and pushing inland by that evening.[51] Despite early success, however, the Germans soon turned the tables dramatically, launching an armored counterattack forcing Fifth Army to give back substantial ground.[52] As Blumenson observed, "Fifth Army found itself at the edge of defeat on the evening of 13 September for one basic reason: the army could not build up the beachhead by water transport as fast as the Germans, for all their difficulties, could reinforce their defenders by land."[53] Nonetheless, "by the morning of 15 September the crisis had passed, and the enemy began to revert to the defensive all along the Fifth Army front."[54] Elements of the 82nd Airborne's 504th Parachute Infantry Regiment had jumped in during the night of September 13–14, reinforcing the 36th Division, and the

British 7th Armoured Division began coming ashore on September 14.[55] According to the official Fifth Army history,

> The reasons for his shift are clear. The British Eighth Army was continuing its advance, though more slowly than expected, and had reached Sapri about 40 miles to the south; the most desperate attacks of the Germans had not driven Fifth Army into the sea; and the build-up of supplies and reinforcements on the beaches was steadily increasing the Fifth Army strength. The 505th Parachute Infantry was dropped behind our lines south of Paestum the night of 14–15 September; and the 325th Glider Regimental Combat Team came in by LCIs on the 15th. The 180th Regimental Combat Team (45th Division), which had landed early on the 14th, went into Army reserve.[56]

Its beachhead at Salerno secure, Fifth Army now turned its attention to "the capture of Naples harbor and the nearby airfields."[57] After a few days of preliminary operations, Fifth Army jumped off on the march to capture Naples on September 23, 1943, with the British 10 Corps advancing on the coast while the American VI Corps, operating inland to the north, pushed the Germans north toward the Volturno River, while Eighth Army advanced northwest on the Adriatic side of the peninsula.[58] British troops reached and bypassed Naples on September 30, continuing on the Volturno, while the US 82nd Airborne Division and Rangers entered Naples on October 1. By October 7, both corps of Fifth Army were firmly established along the Volturno, with Naples in its possession, at the cost of more than 12,000 casualties, including 2,000 dead, 7,000 injured, and 3,500 missing.[59]

At 8:00 p.m. on October 12, 1943, Fifth Army commenced a forced crossing of the Volturno with a 600-gun artillery preparation.[60] Both 10th and VI Corps would attack in zone simultaneously.[61] VI Corps initiated its attack, via US 3rd Division, at 0200.[62] By the morning of the 14th, VI Corps had established three bridges across the river.[63] The 10 Corps had faced greater difficulties in its zone; nonetheless, Fifth Army was successfully across the Volturno by October 14, 1943.[64]

Following its crossing of the Volturno, Fifth Army next began a slow, painful slog through the Winter Line or the "Winter Position, the name they gave the area between the Volturno River and the Gustav Line,"[65] the latter being a defensive line bisecting the Italian peninsula along the northern banks of the Garigliano and Sanra Rivers, including the town of Cassino, over which multiple bloody battles would be fought.[66] Over a period of months, the Allies pushed the Germans successively back until by mid-January 1944, they were in possession of most of the Winter Line and were approaching the leading edge of the Gustav Line. "Yet the Germans had won the battle, even though they had lost the ground," Griess notes, because

> not once had the Allies forced them off a delay line before the time scheduled for its abandonment. During their four-month withdrawal, [the Germans] had accomplished all the classic tasks of a delaying action. The Allies arrived at the defensive position exhausted, punished, harassed, and having consumed much valuable time getting into an unfavorable situation.[67]

On January 22, 1944, Fifth Army's VI Corps executed Operation Shingle, the amphibious landing at the coastal town of Anzio, some 60 miles northwest of the Gustav Line on Italy's west coast.[68] Chester G. Starr describes the scene:

> Promptly at H-Hour, 0200, the first waves of craft nosed onto the beach, and the assault troops swarmed ashore. To their astonishment there was no enemy to greet them. The highly unexpected had happened. We had caught the enemy completely by surprise.[69]

VI Corps executed its landings, seizing the port facilities and its initial objectives unopposed; by the end of the first day, more than 36,000 men and 3,600 vehicles had been brought ashore.[70] The easy going was not to last, however, since from January 28 through February 19, 1944, the Germans brought in reinforcements and fiercely opposed VI Corps in its bridgehead,[71] launching another major attempt to reduce the bridgehead—which would prove to be the last—on February 28, but the offensive soon "died out," with the Germans going over the defensive by March 4.[72]

The cost of Anzio and other actions (including three unsuccessful attempts to breach the German Gustav Line around Cassino) had been high, with Fifth Army suffering 52,130 casualties—a nearly 40 percent increase from the Salerno operations—by March 31, 1944.[73] Thereafter a period of relative calm ensued as the Allies waited for the weather to improve and the ground to dry, and they rested their troops[74] and carried out a "peninsular-wide regrouping" of their forces.[75] A reorganized Fifth Army resumed offensive operations on May 11, 1944, when Operation Diadem commenced at 11:00 p.m. with a 2,000-gun artillery preparation all along its sector from Cassino to the coast.[76] The US II Corps, consisting of the 85th and 88th Infantry Divisions, attacked along the coast,* the three divisions of the French Expeditionary Corps attacked in the center, and British and Canadian forces attacked in the northern portion of Fifth Army's zone.[77] Polish forces of Montgomery's Eighth Army "raised their flag over the monastery ruins" on May 18.[78] VI Corps attacked from the Anzio beachhead on May 23, making contact with II Corps on May 25.[79] Thenceforth, Allied forces would advance across the Peninsula, with the capture of Rome soon to follow. Fifth Army was the first Allied unit to reach the city, with elements of II Corps entering it on June 4, 1944.[80]

Advance to the Gothic Line

The US Fifth Army continued the offensive operations north of Rome on June 5, 1944, with Eighth Army resuming its offensive two days later, on June 7.[81] The Allies pushed forward until August 4, when they reached Florence—270 miles in a little over two months—the Germans having retreated across the Arno and destroyed all the bridges in Florence behind them, except for the Ponte Vecchio, which they blocked with mines and the rubble of destroyed houses on both sides of the river.[82] Eighth Army once again resumed the attack on August 25, along the Adriatic Coast, closing up to the German Gothic Line on August 29, making initial crossings on August 30 and penetrating to the Po Valley by September 21.[83] By this time, Fifth Army had launched its own attack on September 10, 1944, advancing until September 27, when, after Fifth Army captured Monte Battaglia, German counterattacks temporarily halted further advance; Fifth Army resumed the offensive on October 2, capturing Monte Grande Massif and Monte Belmonte, near Bologna, by October 23; on October 27, Fifth Army halted its attack pending diversion of German forces away from its front by Eighth Army, which reached the Ronco by the twenty-fifth of October.[84] In late October, the Allies ran out of artillery ammunition in Italy.[85] By this time the two armies of 15th Army Group "had shot their bolt and Bologna still lay out of reach"; except for one more attack by Eighth Army in December, major fighting in Italy was over for the winter.[86]

---

* For an account of one of the 88th Infantry Division's regiments in the opening of Operation Diadem, see "Santa Maria Infante, 351st Infantry, 11–14 May 1944," in *Small Unit Actions*, 115–73.

Insignia of the 15th Army Group. *Author's collection*

Shoulder sleeve insignia of 5th Army, ca. 1945. *Author's collection*

CHAPTER 5

Operation Encore

On November 6, 1944, the 10th Light Division (Alpine) was redesignated as the 10th Mountain Division.[1] Five days later, on November 11, 1944, the assistant division commander, Col. Robinson E. Duff, traveled from Camp Swift to Washington, DC, where he would be told that the division was to deploy to the Mediterranean theater;[2] the next day, November 12, Brig. Gen. George P. Hays departed from his post in France as commander of the Division Artillery, 2nd Infantry Division, en route to Camp Swift to assume command of the 10th Mountain Division, arriving on Thanksgiving Day 1944.[3] Hays, according to one observer, "fitted the [10th Mountain] like a well-worn and well-loved glove."[4] Hays was a truly distinguished officer. A veteran of the First World War, he had won the Medal of Honor at the Second Battle of the Marne; so far during the Second World War, he had served at Monte Cassino in Italy and then had gone on to command the 2nd Division artillery at Omaha Beach on D-day.[5]

Notwithstanding its rigorous training and the high quality of its personnel, the 10th Mountain initially had a hard time finding a role, because of its organization as a division-sized light infantry formation without organic heavy-weapons companies of its own,* the specialized nature of its training, and its heavy complement of mules.[6] The 10th Mountain Division's reliance on mules would be rather more an asset than a liability in Italy, where the terrain sometimes forced units to rely on pack trains—or even human muscle power—for resupply.** Dr. Klaus Huebner, assistant battalion surgeon with 3rd Battalion, 349th Infantry, 88th Infantry Division, describes his battalion aid station's reliance on mules both in North Africa and Italy.[7] Col. Paul Goodman, in his history of the 92nd Division in Italy, notes that during that division's service in the Coastal

and Serchio sectors, the terrain was so rugged that "a thirty[-]mile trip was necessary in order to pass from two points that were only a little more than ten miles apart on the map." Under these circumstances, the 92nd Division's organic transportation capabilities were insufficient even to keep the unit supplied in static positions on the line, much less during offensive operations; to resolve this, the 92nd Division Mule Pack Battalion was formed on November 17, 1944, commanded by cavalry officer 1Lt. Hugh Hanley, with a complement, at its height, of one officer, fifteen enlisted men, 600 Italians, 173 horses, and 372 mules.[8] In his wartime memoir, Dr. Albert H. Meinke, a battalion surgeon in the 86th Mountain Infantry, recounts another use mules were put to:

> My letters home indicate that during this time we also ate pigeon and rabbit, and a number of times had steak grilled over an open fire in some farmhouse fireplace. What these letters failed to say, however, was that although these steaks were extra choice, they were mule steaks. . . . The division was using mules to supply the far forward areas. . . . Occasionally a mule would be killed in action or so badly wounded that it had to be put down, and whenever this happened to a mule in otherwise good condition, someone would bring us steaks. We never asked any questions, and the fact that they tasted a little like horsemeat didn't bother us either.[9]

The importance of animal transportation to the success of the IV Corps (to which the 10th Mountain would be assigned), Fifth Army, and 10th Mountain Division itself was very well spelled out in the IV Corps History, describing the final

* A shortcoming subsequently remedied by the addition of weapons companies at Camp Swift, as we have seen.
** See, for example, Chester G. Starr, *From Salerno to the Alps: A History of the Fifth Army, 1943–1945*, 34, 69, and 73–75.

drive to penetrate the Apennines and break out into the Po Valley:

No story of this operation could pretend to be complete without mentioning the lowly pack-mule and the important part he played in IV Corps transportation. At the opening of the drive there were five Italian pack companies attached to our divisions; in addition the 10th Mountain had received some 600 mules, which were used by the artillery and the Quartermaster Battalion, both of which were pack outfits but had been motorized when they reached Italy. These animals and the Americans or Italians who led them did an indescribable piece of work in getting food, ammunition and medical supplies to advance elements in the most inaccessible parts of the zone. At times, unorthodox as it may seem, gasoline and oil were actually delivered by those beasts of burden to some of the armored units.[10]*

The division had previously been offered to the 6th Army Group,[11] which had been organized at Corsica on August 1, 1944, for the task of carrying out combined American and Free French operations in southern France, these operations having commenced two weeks later on August 15.[12] The 6th Army Group would see action in the French Riviera, southern France, western France, Germany, Italy, and Austria before war's end.[13] At the time that the 6th Army Group was offered the 10th Mountain Division, that division's arrival in theater was not anticipated until March 1945 due to scarcity of transport for its pack animals, a timetable deemed unacceptable by the

Army group.[14] Ultimately, the division was accepted by the Fifth Army (under the 15th Army Group in Italy), commanded by Lt. Gen. Mark Clark.[15] In his postwar memoir, Clark would give a brief account of how the 10th Mountain came to be deployed in Italy. "The story of how the 10th Mountain Division came to Italy was given to me later by Gen. Marshall," Clark writes:

He had offered it to other theaters, but because it had special equipment instead of the regular infantry requirement, other commanders turned it down. Later, in a conversation with Marshall, one of the commanders indicated that there had been a mistake in regard to the message of refusal and that he would like to have the division. "You're too late," Marshall told him. "I asked Clark if he wanted it, and almost before I could turn around I got a message back to start it moving. I was happy to get any division at that time and, of course, the 10th Mountain was ideally suited for the high Apennines."[16]

In the actual event, the first elements of the 10th Mountain Division would arrive in theater well before March 1945, without its animals: the division's Camp Swift mules had been shipped to Oklahoma on November 13, 1944, preparatory to the division's deployment to Europe,[17] the decision having been taken to temporarily "motorize the division" until animals could be brought over later due to shipping-capacity constraints.[18]

Col. Duff departed Washington, DC, on November 14, 1944. He arrived at Naples, Italy, three days later on November 17, where he began the coordination for the movement of the division

---

* Without minimizing the indispensable contribution made by the mules and their handlers in the Italian Campaign, justice requires acknowledgment that many other logistical and support troops richly deserve a similar recognition of their contribution, and, to its credit, the *History of the IV Corps* gives that recognition, noting that "tribute should be paid here to the omnipresent but generally unsung two-and-a-half-ton 6×6 cargo truck, and to the man who drove it. From the standpoint of dependability for delivery of essential combat supplies through difficult country such as now confronted IV Corps the vehicle was invaluable. The driver, who knew no hours and frequently drove the clock around with only an occasional cat-nap and another cup of coffee, made his contribution to the success of the campaign just as sure as the combat soldier, whose groceries and bullets made up the load." Peter S. Wondolowski, *History of the IV Corps, 1941–1945*, 584–85. The role of these support troops would become only more dangerous as the future unfolded: during the Korean War, S. L. A. Marshall noted the danger facing "the men called to move goods through guerrilla-held country." S. L. A. Marshall, *Commentary on Infantry Operations and Weapons Usage in Korea, Winter of 1950–51*, 69. Following the attacks of 9/11, the Combat Action Badge would be created to recognize the many troops—including logistical support personnel—that would come into contact with the enemy but would not be eligible for award of the Combat Infantryman Badge, and proposals would later be made to extend eligibility back to the Second World War. Kevin Lilley, "CAB for Past Conflicts? 5 Things You Should Know," *Army Times* online, April 4, 2015.

into theater.[19] The division headquarters advanced party arrived in Naples on December 3, 1944, consisting of one field-grade officer and one noncommissioned officer (NCO) each for the G2, G3, and G4.[20] Brig. Gen. Duff established a forward command post at Livorno, Italy, on December 16, from which the advanced party would plan for the reception and training of the division, coordinate the arrival of its elements of the division, and arrange their passage through port and staging areas.[21]

The first major unit of the 10th Mountain Division to move to Europe was the 86th Mountain Infantry Regiment. The regiment cleared Camp Swift on November 28, 1944, traveling by train to Camp Patrick Henry, Virginia, where they arrived on December 2.[22]* The regiment spent seven days receiving orientation on life aboard ship, before finally entraining for Hampton Roads, Virginia, on December 10, arriving at 3:45 a.m. the next day.[23]** The regiment immediately boarded the troopship *SS Argentina* and was underway for Europe by 6:45 a.m.[24]

Described as "one of the best and most active troopships that served in World War II," SS *Argentina* had been built at Newport News Shipbuilding & Drydock Company at Newport News, Virginia, in 1929 and operated under the name *Pennsylvania*[25] by the Panama Pacific Line, before being sold to the US Maritime Commission and renamed SS *Argentina* in 1937.[26] The vessel would make numerous voyages as a troopship, operating as such until 1946, with its final voyage being as a "dependent transport" bringing hundreds of GI "war brides" and their children home from Europe, to be reunited with their now-discharged husbands in New York.[27] The 86th's crossing to Europe was recorded by at least two of the regiment's soldiers. One, David R. Brower, colorfully described the passage thus:

When we boarded our converted luxury liner, the SS *Argentina*, the order was "get in your bunks and stay there until further notice." But the problem at hand still remained how to lower same, when they were ceiling-high, five deep, and there were such slight encumbrances banging around one's neck as steel helmet, rifle, gas mask, pistol belt, pack, and duffel bag. Strong legs and stout hearts plus the ability of some of the men to stand on their heads finally accomplished the order. . . . We were told that we would be fed two meals a day on the trip across. For most of us, during the first days, that was two too many. The safest place to be was on the top deck, where you could get seasick to your heart's content without fear that someone above you was doing likewise. As the days sped by we became acquainted with the big ship, and a few words of the language of the sea. The ship's loudspeaker would inform us to "muster" down in the "galley" for the evening "meal." We frequently patronized the "ship's store," regardless of what it was called, especially with the cigarettes at five cents a pack. . . . Many of the men took advantage of the warm sunshine to lie on the decks wherever there was room. We learned that ordinary soap would not lather in salt water, the importance of strict blackout, the meaning of the word convoy. We watched the ships in our convoys as they changed speed and direction to complicate any submariner's attempt to line up its sights on us. Our ship led the convoy.[28]

Another 86th Infantry veteran who documented the voyage to Italy was the prolific chronicler of the World War II 10th Mountain

---

* Imbrie's *Chronology* says departure from Camp Hale occurred on November 29, 1944, and arrived on December 2. John Imbrie, *Chronology of the 10th Mountain Division during World War II, 6 January 1940–30 November 1945,* 12.
** The men of the 86th learned that they had been authorized to wear the "Mountain" tab the day prior to their departure for Hampton Roads, the news having been published in the unit newspaper, the *Blizzard*, on December 9, 1944, although they would not physically receive the "mountain rockers" until six months later, in May 1945. Imbrie, *Chronology*, 12.

Division, Harris Dusenbery. In a "diary" compiled from "notes, unit records, letters home and memory"[*] after the war, he detailed his experiences during the nearly two weeks on SS *Argentina*. For the men of the 10th Mountain Division, the Atlantic crossing included tedium, drudgery, anxiety, and not a few wonderful sights as well. Dusenbery's trip started with that archetypal military drudge of the mid-twentieth century, KP duty, peeling potatoes[**] and washing pots and pans, punctuated by a first bout of seasickness.[29] There was also a great deal of free time in which to lounge on deck in the unseasonably warm weather, reading—Agatha Christie and a biography of Walt Whitman, for Dusenbery—wearing a life jacket all the while; there were movies in the evening, bands playing on the promenade deck (SS *Argentina* having been an ocean liner before the war), a mimeographed newsletter every day, noontime news announced over the public address system, and watching sunsets from the fantail in the evening.[30]

On December 20, 1944, Dusenbery and his fellows of 86th Infantry got their first indication of their destination when they were informed that they would be passing through the Straits of Gibraltar the following morning; this of course meant a destination in southern France (as had been considered, as we have seen) or Italy, though some imaginative souls talked of a passage through the Suez Canal to Burma.[31] Passing through the strait the next morning, Dusenbery and the rest of the regiment saw the white buildings of Tangier in Africa and Tarifa in Spain in their arid surroundings, and the Rock of Gibraltar itself.[32] SS *Argentina* made landfall on the Italian coast on December 22, 1944;[33] the next morning—December 23, 1944—the 86th Infantry found themselves riding at anchor in the shadow of Mount Vesuvius, in the outer harbor of Naples. The ship weighed anchor and entered the inner harbor, docked, and, over the course of several hours, disembarked the regiment onto a damaged

pier among the strewn wreckage of damaged ships.[34] The 86th Mountain Infantry Regiment had arrived in Italy.

While the 86th was en route across the Atlantic, the rest of the division was preparing to follow. The 85th and 87th regiments traveled by train to Camp Patrick Henry from December 21 through 24, 1944;[35] by Christmas Day they were preparing to board ship for Italy, and by December 29 a division rear command post was operational at Camp Patrick Henry.[36] The division artillery left Camp Swift on Christmas Eve, arriving at Patrick Henry on the twenty-seventh.[37] On January 4, 1945, the 85th and 87th Mountain Infantry Regiments embarked upon USS *West Point* for the trip to Italy.[38][***] The Navy troopship USS *West Point* was built by Newport News Shipbuilding & Drydock Co. in 1940, initially operating in the West Indies as SS *America* before being purchased by the US Navy and renamed *West Point*.[39] *West Point* made over thirty-five voyages before being released from military service on February 22, 1946, having carried 200,000 troops outbound to the combat theaters, and having brought 100,000 home.[40] A fast vessel, *West Point* made the crossing in nine days, sailing unescorted until Gibraltar, reaching her destination on January 13, 1945.[41] One member of the 85th Regiment describes his impressions upon arrival in Italy thus:

> As we came down the gangplank we saw first-hand evidence of unspeakable poverty. Many buildings and harbor facilities bore heavy damage from artillery and bombing. Ships were lying on their sides with the superstructures protruding from the surface of the Bay of Naples. The children were terribly thin and pale with deep dark circles under eyes. They were begging for cigarettes and chocolate, or pimping their sisters. Their clothing was thin and they were shivering from the cold. American Red

---

[*] This is quoted from the flyleaf of Dusenbery's manuscript, *10th Mountain Division, Italian Diary of Harris Dusenbery, Hq. Co. 1st Bn. 86th Mountain Inf. and Riva Ridge Operation, 1st Battalion Journal.* Most of the material in that manuscript, together with additional materials, was subsequently published as Harris Dusenbery, *The North Apennines and Beyond with the 10th Mountain Division.*

[**] KP—"kitchen patrol" or "kitchen police"—is the temporary detailing of soldiers from other duties to temporarily assist the unit mess section.

[***] Ross Wilson reports the departure date from Camp Swift as December 20, 1944. Ross J. Wilson, *History of the First Battalion, 87th Mountain Infantry*, 17.

Cross women brought hot coffee and doughnuts to the docks to welcome us. A few boxes of donuts fell into the sea. Instantly three Italian men jumped into the water, still wearing heavy winter overcoats. They tore the boxes apart, stuffing doughnuts into their mouths, one after the other, while frantically threshing in the frigid water, trying to swim and eat at the same time. From that day forward there were no illusions about the suffering of the Italian people during the German Occupation.[42]

The remainder of the division, consisting of the headquarters, the division artillery (604th, 605th, and 616th Artillery Battalions), the 10th Mountain Reconnaissance Troop, the 110th Signal Company, the 710th Ordnance, a military police platoon, and the Headquarters, Special Troops, embarked on the US Army Transport (USAT) *Meigs* on January 6, 1945.[43] USAT *Meigs* was built in 1943 by Federal Shipbuilding and Drydock Co. of Kearny, New Jersey, and departed on its maiden voyage from Norfolk, Virginia, for Oran and Naples on July 10, 1944; she completed her service as a troopship at San Francisco on January 24, 1946.[44]

Gen. Hays traveled to Italy by air, arriving at Naples two days ahead of the 85th and 87th Regiments on January 11, 1945.[45] Soon after their arrival, elements of the division began moving to Livorno (Leghorn). Most of the 86th Infantry sailed for Livorno aboard the *Sestriere*, a "dirty little"[46] Italian merchant vessel, on December 26, while part of the headquarters moved by truck, all arriving the next day.[47] The 85th and 87th Regiments would follow the 86th to Livorno, some by ground transportation, some aboard the *Sestriere*, and some aboard LCIs,* between January 14 and 16, 1945.[48] The rest of the division landed at Naples on January 18, 1945.[49]

The 10th Mountain Enters the Line

The 86th Mountain Infantry's deployment to Leghorn made it the first element of the 10th Mountain Division to come into enemy contact. Their hurried deployment north was triggered in part by an Axis attack on Christmas Day that had "routed" the US 92nd Division[50] on Fifth Army's "extreme left, operating under direct Army control [and] . . . thinly spread along a front of over 20 miles."[51] Under the weight of this attack, inspired by the German Ardennes offensive, "one regiment of the 92nd 'melted away,'"[52] the 92nd having found itself the only division defending Leghorn, and on a "'rather widely extended over a broad front' . . . divided on opposite sides of the 13-mile mountainous Apuan massif"[53] to boot. It is unfortunate that, as Griess notes, "because this defense was the first major combat action by a Black division in World War II, it received far too much attention in the American press," especially given that "the 92nd had performed no worse than had 106th Division, which had borne the initial onslaught of the Ardennes Offensive and had also 'melted away.'"[54] That the 92nd was a segregated African American division undoubtedly contributed to the morale problems from which it suffered.[55] This is hardly to be wondered at, given the circumstances, as described by 10th Mountain Division veteran Thomas R. Brooks. "Black officers assigned to the 92nd . . . often felt abused," Brooks writes, "seeing only limited potential for advancement. Of the 774 officers in the division as of December 1944, 538 were black"; yet, while it is true that "two of the four artillery battalion commanders and several infantry battalion commanders were black," the fact remains that "most of the top brass was white."[56] In the aftermath, Fifth Army concluded that the 92nd "had not received sufficient training and contained too many category IV and V [low aptitude] personnel."[57] However, the truth probably lies elsewhere, for as Fifth Army commander Lucian B. Truscott would later observe—having succeeded Gen. Clark upon the latter's elevation to command of 15th Army Group—"Command failures . . . usually . . . originate among the higher echelons and are merely reflected downwards."[58]

* Landing Craft, Infantry.

Whatever the causes of 92nd's setback, it was of little strategic consequence, since Gen. Alexander had been apprised of the pending attack by signals intelligence and had reinforced the area with the 8th Indian Division, which held firm, turning back the enemy thrust.[59] It had a large effect on the immediate future of the 86th Mountain Infantry Regiment, however. As Charles Sanders observes,

The gap created in the Allied line by their [the 92nd Division's] retreat meant ostensibly that the only thing between the German Army and the city of Rome to the southeast was the battle-green Eighty-sixth Mountain Regiment. With the Nazis in the midst of staging a stunning, last-gasp offensive in Belgium popularly known as the "Battle of the Bulge," there was immediate concern among the Italian theater commanders that Hitler might launch a similar attack on their front.[60]

To forestall that, "the men of the Eighty-sixth were rushed onto . . . the *Sestriere* and moved from Naples to Livorno [Leghorn]."[61] The 86th Mountain Infantry arrived in sector on January 8, 1945, where they relieved an antiaircraft battalion that had been pressed into service as infantry, holding a 19-mile front. "This was The Gap," recounts David Brower; "We were the relief, and they were very glad to see us."[62] 1st Battalion, 86th Infantry, under Lt. Col. Henry Hampton, was assigned a position under the German guns on Mount Belvedere,[63] "facing the strategic heights of Riva Ridge, from which the Germans could observe [their] every movement"; 2nd Battalion blocked the only north–south road in the sector; and 3rd Battalion acted as regimental reserve and secured the left flank, covered by 25 miles of mountains to the next adjacent friendly unit.[64] On the regiment's right was the Brazilian 1st Infantry Division.[65] The assistant division commander, Brig. Gen. Duff, was appointed commanding general of Task Force 45, some elements of which the 86th had relieved, and 86th then fell under that element's control.[66]

Two days before occupying its position on the line, the 86th Mountain Infantry suffered its first casualties, when on January 6, 1945, a soldier stepped on a German mine near railroad tracks adjacent to the unit's training area; he was killed, as were seven other soldiers, including a Catholic chaplain, when other mines exploded.[67] A patrol of the 86th was ambushed at a bend in road; the German attack was blunted, however, by the failure of their machine gun; it was believed that one enemy had been struck by Browning Automatic Rifle (BAR) fire.[68] Another patrol, this time Company L, 86th Infantry, made contact at Piansinatico on January 19, where effective automatic fire from an estimated platoon-sized enemy element made further advance impossible; the patrol withdrew with the loss of five men (one dead, one missing, three wounded).[69] Another enemy contact, this time involving Company F, 86th Infantry, resulted in one soldier missing and two probable casualties on January 22.[70] On January 25, the Germans attacked a Company L strongpoint and were repulsed.[71] 2nd Battalion, 86th Infantry, attempted a raid in the vicinity of La Serra, only to be forced to withdraw when effective enemy supporting fires made flanking impossible.[72]

While the 86th embarked upon a regular program of patrols and raids in the ensuing days, the rest of the division began to come online;[73] on January 24, 1945, Company L, 86th Infantry, suffered five casualties: one missing, one killed, and three wounded.[74] The 85th and 87th Regiments moved by ship and rail from Naples to Leghorn starting on January 14, with movement of the division complete by the twenty-eighth.[75] By January 20, all three regiments were "on or near the front line between the Serchio Valley and Mt. Belvedere,"[76] and units began rotating on and off the front line shortly thereafter.[77] The division artillery was in supporting position on January 28, 1945.[78]

The 85th Mountain Infantry was assigned to TF 45, along with its brethren in the 86th, on January 19, 1945, with its mission being to "occupy, patrol, and be prepared to defend all Task Force 45 area except that occupied by the 86th Mountain Infantry [and to] continue training under existing conditions to include reconnaissance patrols and raids."[79] 1st Battalion was assigned to a quiet sector on the regiment's left, in contact with the

92nd Division.[80] Nonetheless, Company C made contact with the enemy "in a decisive manner" on January 26, 1945, when it engaged in what the official history describes as "a house fight at Rimessa," suffering one dead—the regiment's first KIA—and one injured while capturing four enemy (two Germans and two Italians) and killing one.[81] The 85th executed another raid in the same area, this time conducted by Company C with the support of elements of Company D, on January 30, with the attacking force making a challenging climb over hard-crusted snow and then cutting steps in order to ascend an exposed slope; the reward was six enemy prisoners, Italians from the San Marco Marine Division.[82] Two officers and eighty-one soldiers of Company B, 85th Infantry, attacked an enemy strongpoint at Berro al Fosso on February 9–10, 1945, killing one enemy soldier and capturing another eleven as well as two MG42 machine guns and 15,000 rounds of ammunition.[83]

2nd Battalion, 85th Mountain Infantry, was assigned a sector on 1st Battalion's right. On February 4–5, 1945, 2nd Battalion executed a raid against enemy positions on Monte Spigolino, marching for six hours through the night to strike the objective at approximately 8:20 a.m., killing two Germans and capturing two more, with a further two enemy probably KIA, with no friendly losses.[84]

3rd Battalion, 85th Mountain Infantry, assumed responsibility for the Cutigliano area from 2nd Battalion of the 86th on January 27.[85] The battalion suffered a setback on the thirtieth when it sent a twenty-two-man patrol to seize prisoners from enemy positions at La Serra;[86] the attacking element found the enemy in "extremely well prepared positions" supported by "interlocking automatic fires,"[87] which split and drove back the patrol, with nine men captured by the enemy and four wounded left behind, with only one enemy wounded and one killed to show for the loss.[88] The 85th sent medics to the scene the next day; two attempts by the rescuers to reach the wounded soldiers were repulsed by enemy machine gun fire despite the fact that the rescuers were clearly displaying red crosses and "carrying the Geneva Convention flag."[89] On February 4, 3rd Battalion attempted a major raid by a reinforced company,

further augmented by two tanks, against enemy elements at Piansinatico—where a patrol of the 86th Regiment had been halted by effective enemy fire about two weeks prior, as noted above.[90] Prevented by automatic fire from closing with the enemy positions, Company K commander Capt. Cooper withdrew to formulate a flank attack; finding that infeasible, he broke off the attack with the loss of two killed and six or seven wounded (successfully evacuated) and no prisoners taken.[91]

The 87th Mountain Infantry entered combat on January 28, 1945, when eighteen of its mortars engaged the enemy from positions behind Company E, 371st Infantry Regiment, 92nd Division; over the next two days, 1st and 3rd Battalions sent out a total of sixty infantrymen as snipers forward of the 371st Infantry, northeast of Seravezza.[92] On February 2, the 2nd Battalion relieved elements of the 86th Infantry in the vicinity of Vidiciatico, after a difficult five-hour march over "mud-coated ice"; the 3rd Battalion was positioned in the vicinity of San Marcello as the regiment's reserve, with its headquarters at the Colonia Montana sanatorium.[93] The 1st Battalion established its command post at Catigliano on February first, but the rest of the battalion did not come forward until four days later, on February 5.[94]

When 1st Battalion, 87th Infantry, finally assumed its position on the line, it found itself holding a 3,500-yard front anchored by mountains on each flank, with a draw containing Catigliano in between.[95] Within two hours of assuming their position, Company B was probed by an enemy patrol from 2nd Company, 4th Mountain Battalion, which was repulsed; the next morning they recovered a wounded German left behind the night before—the 87th's first captured prisoner and the first enemy known to have been wounded by 87th Infantry fires.[96] The next day the Germans mounted a stronger attack of about platoon strength, striking positions identified the previous evening; unfortunately for them, Company B had reconfigured their defense that day so that the enemy hit empty positions; Company B called in artillery fire at 2350, driving the enemy out about an hour later.[97] The 87th suffered no casualties, but they found signs of enemy casualties the next day.[98] A further enemy patrol, this time of eight to ten men, struck Company B at 2130 on February 7, being promptly driven off, only to return again after midnight.[99] The next evening, another small enemy patrol appeared and was brushed aside, followed by enemy machine gun and artillery fire, with a further enemy patrol appearing at dawn the next day; an Italian deserter confirmed later on February 9 that some German casualties had been inflicted on February 7.[100] An enemy patrol returned to this area yet again on February 12, after Company B had been withdrawn and relieved by Company K; two enemy were wounded by friendly mortar fire.[101]

A patrol from Company G was met with machine gun fire, grenades, artillery, and flares on the night of February 7, 1945, but withdrew without loss.[102] Company G retaliated the next night. Positioning themselves atop an escarpment from which they could observe the location where the machine gun fire came from the night before, they waited until two in the morning until they observed three enemy setting up a machine gun there; maneuvering close to the position, the patrol engaged. A firefight ensued, by the end of which the machine gun position had been destroyed by bazooka fire, along with another previously undetected machine gun destroyed with grenades; the patrol suffered one man wounded, who was successfully evacuated.[103] On February 10, an 87th Infantry patrol and an enemy patrol stumbled upon one another in the darkness and exchanged grenades; the enemy retreated to the opposite side of a nearby draw, whence they brought a light machine gun to bear against the Americans, who in turn called for artillery fire, hitting the enemy position.[104] 1st Battalion was then ordered to prepare for yet another attack upon Piansinatico in the hope that the 87th could succeed where its sisters had failed, but the attack was canceled on February 12.[105]

On February 14, a fifty-man patrol composed of elements of Companies G and H set out for the same escarpment described above; this time, however, the patrol was not successful, finding itself confronted with well-placed machine guns atop the escarpment, supported by accurate mortar fire, forcing the Americans to withdraw under cover of artillery support.[106] On February 17, Company G suffered a direct artillery hit on one of its outposts, killing two soldiers—the 87th Mountain Infantry's first fatalities in the European theater.[107]

Mount Belvedere

The Mediterranean theater had been a tumult of activity and change prior to the arrival of the 10th Mountain Division in Italy starting in December 1944, and the organizational changes would continue thereafter. At the execution of Operation Avalanche—the Salerno landing—Fifth Army, under Clark, had consisted of two corps and two separate divisions under Fifth Army Control. The US VI Corps consisted of four US divisions—the 1st Armored Division and the 3rd, 34th, and 45th Infantry Divisions; the British X Corps consisted of three British divisions—the 7th Armored, the 46th Infantry, and the 56th Infantry Divisions; and under Army control were the American 36th Infantry and 82nd Airborne Divisions.[108] By the time the first elements of the 10th Mountain arrived in Italy in late December 1944, Fifth Army had been reorganized into three corps and one separate division. VI Corps had been withdrawn from Italy and allocated to Operation Anvil in southern France, while the 82nd Airborne and British 7th Armored Divisions had been withdrawn for Operation Overlord.[109] Fifth Army's subordinate elements were now 13 Corps, II Corps, IV Corps, and the 92nd Division. The British 13 Corps, consisting of the British 6th Armored Division, the British 1st and 78th Infantry Divisions, and the Indian 8th Division, was on Fifth Army's right at the boundary with the British Eighth Army.[110] The 13 Corps would not stay with Fifth Army long, however, since it would be transferred to Eighth Army that winter.[111] Next in line was the US II Corps, consisting of five American divisions (the 1st Armored and the 34th, 85th, 88th, and 91st Infantry Divisions); then came the American IV Corps, which included the Brazilian 1st Infantry Division, the 6th South African Armored Division, and US Task Force 45.[112] Task Force 45, under command of the 45th Antiaircraft Artillery Brigade, was made up principally of former antiaircraft troops functioning as infantry, including the American 434th, 435th, and 900th Antiaircraft Artillery Automatic Weapons Battalions and the British 39 Light Antiaircraft Regiment (battalion). The 2d Battalion, 370th Infantry (92d Division), was also attached.[113]

The remainder of the 92nd Division, operating independently under Army control, held Fifth Army's left flank along the Mediterranean coast.[114]

The story of Task Force 45 is an interesting one. Once Allied air forces had "wrested command of the air from the Luftwaffe in 1943 and 1944," the US Army's massive antiaircraft artillery (AAA) force became "largely redundant," resulting in the disbandment or inactivation of 258 AAA battalions to free up their personnel as replacements between the beginning of January 1944 and early May 1945, and others were converted to field artillery.[115] Things were managed differently in the Fifth Army area, however. In July 1944, it had been expected that the main effort against the Germans' Gothic Line would be mounted in the central and eastern sectors of the peninsula, with the western sector relegated to "maintaining an active defense and following up any enemy withdrawal."[116] Seeing this comparatively passive role as an opportunity to rest the combat divisions in this sector, he ordered that support troops be brought up online to relieve infantry divisions serving there, with the 34th Infantry Division to be relieved by Task Force 45, formed for this purpose.[117] Created by Fifth Army order on July 26, 1944, the constituent parts of Task Force 45 were Headquarters, 45th Antiaircraft Artillery Brigade; 91st Antiaircraft Group, composed of two antiaircraft battalions, one reconnaissance company from the 894th Tank Destroyer Battalion, and one medical collecting company; the similarly composed 107th

Antiaircraft Artillery Group; the 2nd Armored Group, composed of the British 39th Light Antiaircraft Regiment less one battalion; the 751st Tank Battalion, without its assault guns; one company of the 805th Tank Destroyer Battalion; one antiaircraft battalion; and (initially) 34th Division Artillery.[118] Units were reorganized, infantry equipment was supplied by the 34th Division, and infantry officers were detailed to train the elements of Task Force 45 on its new role, though time for training before they entered the line was short and intermittent, being interrupted and continued along with the units' entry onto and relief from the line.[119]

Although neutral in the early stages of the war, Brazil severed its diplomatic ties with the Axis powers in January 1942 and declared war against Italy and Germany on August 22, 1942,[120] Brazilian president Getulio Dornelles Vargas "believing that [a Brazilian-American] alliance would guarantee Brazil the economic assistance it needed to industrialize its economy and the military weapons necessary to modernize the weak Brazilian military."[121] The 1st Brazilian Infantry Division, known formally as the Brazilian Expeditionary Force or Força Expedicionária Brasileira (FEB)[122]* and colloquially as the *febianos*,[123] "organized . . . as an unambiguous symbol of Brazilian commitment to the allied cause,"[124] began arriving in Italy in July 1944.[125] The FEB was viewed as politically important and sensitive by the Allies, as well. As Lt. Gen. Clark recounts,

> By the end of the first week in August, the first elements of the 25,000-strong Brazilian Expeditionary Forces had arrived in Italy. . . . The performance of the Brazilians was, of course, important politically as well as militarily. Brazil was the only Latin American country to send an expeditionary force to take part in the European war,** and, naturally, we were eager to give them every chance to make a good showing. At the same time . . .

* Also known as the First Expeditionary Infantry Division—Primeira Divisão de Infantaria Expedicionária in Portuguese, or 1st DIE. Derreck T. Calkins, "A Military Force on a Political Mission: The Brazilian Expeditionary Force in World War II," 15.
** But not the only Latin American combatant unit to participate in the war. The Mexican Expeditionary Air Force, the operational element of which was the 201st Squadron, operating Republic P-47 Thunderbolts, participated with American forces in the Pacific theater. See José G. Vega Rivera, *The Mexican Expeditionary Air Force in World War II: The Organization, Training and Operations of the 201st Squadron.*

it was always in our minds that a setback for these troops would have an unhappy political reaction in the Americas.[126*]

When the 10th Mountain Division entered the combat zone, it was deployed in the shadow of Mount Belvedere and related terrain features, forming a part of the Apennine range. The Apennines are a "bow-shaped range" of mountains running the length of the Italian peninsula from Savona at the Mediterranean shore in the northwest, shifting east to the center of the peninsula and bending west again before terminating at Reggio di Calabria in the far south.[127] Mount Belvedere is a mountain of about 1,140 meters in elevation in the Northern Apennines,[128] near the central spine of the Italian peninsula roughly equidistant from Livorno on the Mediterranean coast to the southwest and Bologna to the northeast.[129] Important features nearby include Riva Ridge to the southwest; Mount Gorgolesco, Hill 1088, and Mount Della Torraccia; and Mount Castello to the east, south of Mount Della Torraccia.[130] During previous operations, Fifth Army under Gen. Clark had pushed north along Highway 65 to the east, but because this route ran "through the strongest concentration of Nazi firepower," progress came only "at enormous human cost."[131] When Clark, elevated to commander of the 15th Army Group, proposed a resumption of this costly movement in early 1945,[132] Gen. Truscott was worried that a renewed offensive along Highway 65 "would have been an appalling undertaking . . . with little prospect of success."[133] Instead, Truscott proposed to penetrate the Apennines and break out into the Po Valley by pushing north along Highway 64, "which

had substantially fewer entrenched Nazi positions."[134] Highway 64 was dominated by Mount Belvedere to the northwest,[135] and this terrain feature would have to be in Allied hands if Gen. Truscott's plan was to succeed. Jackman would summarize the situation in 1946:

The Italian front had been stabilized along the crest of the Apennines in October and November 1944. At all points from the Tyrrhenian Sea to the British lines near the Adriatic the enemy held higher ground, and at one place he held a large salient anchored on Mt. Belvedere. From Mt. Belvedere he had observation on Highway 64, one of the two main supply routes of the central Italian front. Until the use of Mt. Belvedere was denied German observers, no allied offensive up Highway 64 could be launched successfully.[136]

Here, however, lay a problem: Mount Belvedere and its environs, including the nearby Mount Castello, had been the focus of three major attacks by Allied forces prior to the 10th Mountain's arrival, all of which had been repulsed. This abysmal record led historian Charles Sanders to characterize them as "The Ridges That Could Not Be Taken."[137] IV Corps issued the order for the first of these attacks on November 18, 1944, directing Task Force 45 to "deny Mt Belvedere Ridge to the enemy, [and] capture and hold Mt Castello–Mt Della Torraccia–Mount Terminale area," and attaching various elements for that purpose.[138] The attack was launched on November 24, 1944.[139] The 435th Antiaircraft Battalion from Task Force 45, as well as a force of 200 partisans

* This was not an idle concern. Many in Brazil opposed the formation of the FEB, considering the "imperialist" United States and Britain a greater threat to Brazilian sovereignty than the Axis powers. Calkins, "A Military Force on a Political Mission," 13. In the years after the war, Brazilian general Nelson de Mello stated that "the hierarchy of the army was Germanophile. There is no debating this" (quoted in Shawn C. Smallman, "The Official Story: The Violent Censorship of Brazilian Veterans, 1945–1954," *Hispanic American Historical Review*, 78, no. 2 [1998]: 233). Mello had been a colonel in command of an infantry regiment in the FEB during the war; see Smallman, "The Official Story," 237; and J. B. Mascarenhas de Moraes, *The Brazilian Expeditionary Force, by Its Commander*, 82, 165, and 176–77. So strongly did some of the Brazilian hierarchy identify with the Germans that when the defense minister, Gen. Eurico Gaspar Dutra, "and his family learned that Paris had fallen to the Germans, they cheered." Smallman, "The Official Story," 234. Additionally, many officers who had chosen to remain in Brazil feared the influence of the FEB. "As the FEB's prestige elevated, many officers began to question their decision to avoid combat and remain in Rio. As the war progressed they became keenly aware that if the FEB succeeded, those officers that filled its ranks would be quickly promoted in the post-war military. Therefore, many within the officer's corps became some of the FEB's greatest detractors during the difficult winter months of 1944–1945 (Calkins, "A Military Force on a Political Mission," 98); for all these reasons, "Anti-FEB and anti-American forces in Brazil depicted the FEB's failures as total defeats," even when these were considered but temporary setbacks by the FEB's American higher command in Italy. Calkins, "A Military Force on a Political Mission," 91.

under "General Armando," attacked Mount Belvedere;[140] 2nd Battalion, 370th Infantry (92nd Division), struck north from Gaggio Montana at the peaks northeast of Belvedere;[141] and the 6th Infantry Regiment of the Brazilian Expeditionary Force attacked Monte Castello to the east.[142] Other supporting elements included the 68th Armored Field Artillery Battalion, the 1106th Engineer Group, the 804th Tank Destroyer Battalion, and the 13th Tank Battalion.[143] Part of the 435th reached the top of Belvedere by the end of the day, while the 370th made progress well up the ridge initially but were driven partway back by a vigorous enemy counteract.[144] On Castello, the Brazilians struggled, facing elements of the seasoned German 232nd Grenadier Division, who enjoyed a "complete view of the [FEB]'s approaches" and caught the Brazilians in "previously established 'interlocking fields of fire'"; the Brazilian regiment was readily repulsed with heavy casualties and forced back to their line of departure by midday.[145] The 435th held on to its gains on Belvedere through the night, however, breaking up a fierce counterattack by men of the German 1st Battalion, 1043rd Infantry, also of the 232nd Division, killing six enemy, wounding ten, and capturing fourteen.[146] The 370th and the Brazilians renewed the attack at 0800 the next day, but the 370th failed to hold beyond Morandella, a point up the slope that they had seized, and surrendered, the previous day; the Brazilians gained ground, but most of them had to relinquish part of their gains for the day in the face of fierce German artillery fire.[147] Devastating German mortar fire forced the Brazilians all the way back to their starting point the next day, while the 370th also gave up ground; Battery C of the 435th attempted a push up the eastern slope of Belvedere but failed.[148] The Allies spent the twenty-seventh preparing for a resumption of the attack, to include reinforcement of the Brazilians.[149] It was not to be. On November 28, 1944, intense German artillery "collapsed" an American strongpoint at Corona, on Belvedere, causing thirty casualties; the Germans then mounted a three-company counterattack, inflicting seventy killed and missing and three tanks destroyed upon Battery D of the 435th, forcing the unit back; Battery B on Belvedere

held on for as long as possible but finally had to withdraw due to a shortage of ammunition; Battery C held on till the next morning but, in danger of being enveloped, had to withdraw itself.[150] The Germans also unsuccessfully attacked the Brazilian 2nd and 3rd Battalions but were turned back.[151]

The Brazilians made their second attempt on Mount Castello on November 29, attacking at 0800 with three battalions abreast following a thirty-minute artillery preparation.[152] They made good progress, making it halfway up the slope by noon, with one battalion nearing the crest, but the Germans had significantly hardened their defenses in the meantime, adding barbed wire, trenches, and mines and additional artillery support.[153] By the end of the day the Brazilians had been driven off the slope and back to their starting line.[154]

The Brazilians did not allow the enemy to rest easy, however, since before long the FEB was planning a third major assault on Mt. Castello. They began a reorganization toward that objective on December 6, 1944.[155] Likely perceiving something in the offing, on December 9 the Germans attempted to disrupt the planned Brazilian attack by strong artillery bombardment, increased patrolling with the aim of returning with prisoners, and a vigorous (if heavy-handed) propaganda effort directed at the Brazilians, firing canisters of leaflets into the Brazilian lines depicting Roosevelt and Churchill as children being prodded along by Stalin, and others "pointedly" asserting "that the European conflict was no concern of the Brazilians who were dying far away from their homes for the benefit of American capitalists."[156] The attack commenced at 0600 on December 12, 1944, following a thirty-minute preparatory barrage by the 424th Field Artillery Group.[157] The official *History of the IV Corps, 1941–1945,* describes the start of the operation:

> The 1st Infantry Regiment delivered the main effort with the 2d and 3d Battalions attacking abreast, the 3d Battalion on the right moving in the general direction of Casellina-Mount Torraccia. Initially the attack made good progress with the enemy

resistance centered mainly against the right battalion. By noon the attacking Brazilian infantrymen had advanced to a general line about midway on the slopes of Mount Torraccia and the 1st Battalion, 11th Infantry advancing on the extreme right flank of the attack had elements not far from the crest of the ridge.[158]

It was not to be, however. "The enemy was determined to keep as long as possible the high ground that gave him observation over Highway 64," and his resistance correspondingly stiffened as the FEB pressed its advance up the slope,[159] forcing the 2nd and 3rd Battalions, once again, back to their starting positions; while other units had had greater success or faced less resistance, the danger of envelopment was too great in light of the withdrawal of the 2nd and 3rd Battalions, and the supporting units were themselves forced to withdraw.[160]

Thus ended the preliminary Allied efforts to seize the Belvedere-Torraccia Massif dominating Highway 64 and effectively blocking the advance into the Po Valley. It had been a bruising battle for all the Allied participants, but it was particularly difficult for the Brazilians, since "while American failures were only considered be temporary setbacks, anti-FEB and anti-American forces in Brazil depicted the FEB's failures as total defeats."[161] But, as the old aphorism goes, reports of the FEB's death had been greatly exaggerated. As the *History of the IV Corps* would later record,

The Brazilians had suffered their first reverses, but like all units who first enter combat, they had learned many lessons and gained valuable experience. The road to ultimate victory was thorny and painful, but the Brazilians who fought at Mount Castello had started down the trail that would eventually lead to success.[162]

And so it would be. In a few short weeks after the failure of the FEB's third assault on December 12, 1944, the 10th Mountain Division would mount a new effort to oust the Germans from Belvedere, and the Brazilians would once more meet their old enemy on Mount Castello; this time both the Americans and Brazilians would prevail.

Operation Encore

Although largely static in the weeks leading up to the 1945 spring offensive in Italy, 15th Army Group conducted three operations aimed at setting the conditions for success in the spring by "obtain[ing] the best possible starting points for the planned spring offensive."[163] On the eastern coast in Eighth Army's sector, Canadian troops attacked to the Senio River, where they destroyed two German bridgeheads before settling in for the rest of the winter.[164] On the opposite coast, in Fifth Army's sector, the 92nd Infantry Division launched Operation Fourth Term in early February.[165] Fourth Term was a weeklong operation in which the 92nd Division pushed north along the Mediterranean coast against both German and Italian forces. The division was to advance into the Serchio Valley on three axes: the 366th Infantry, with supporting tanks, was to cross the Cinquale Canal on the left, near its point of discharge into the Mediterranean; the 371st Infantry was to attack Mount Folgorito on the right; and 370th Infantry would seize the Strettoia Hills.[166] Progress was made initially, especially against Italian units, which "crumbled" in the face of the attack.[167] Progress was also made against German units, but gains were intermittent and temporary as the 92nd and enemy forces traded terrain back and forth, with the important Lama Di Sotta Ridge changing hands five times;[168] when the fighting in the Serchio Valley ended after February 11, the enemy remained in possession of the Lama Di Sotta heights, while the 92nd had netted an advance of about three-quarters of a mile from its original positions.[169]

The most successful operation of the three limited winter attacks, and the most far reaching in its impact on subsequent events, was by far Operation Encore—the 10th Mountain Division's attack on Riva Ridge and Mount Belvedere, and the following final and successful attack by the *febianos* on Mount Castello. Operation Encore, planned for February 1945, was to be "a limited[-] objective attack" intended as a "preliminary move to improve positions before beginning the more extensive spring offensive," with its chief objective being to "secure the high ground dominating a ten-mile section of Highway 64."[170]

During a three-day visit by 10th Mountain Division commander George P. Hays to Fifth Army headquarters from January 8 to 11, 1945, Fifth Army commander Lucian Truscott notified Hays that his plan was to have the 10th Mountain Division "first capture Mt. Belvedere, then proceed by stages to capture all the high ground to a position east of the town of Tolè."[171] This operation would be in part the result of a change in strategy for the spring campaign in the Italian peninsula; namely, the abandonment of "heavily fortified" Bologna as a principal objective in favor of breaking out from the Apennines into the Po Valley itself.[172]

The 10th Mountain received its formal marching orders via Fifth Army Operations Instructions No. 4 on February 16, 1945; according to the *History of the IV Corps*,

> The objectives of the attack were a series of mountain peaks and ridges roughly five miles west of the road and extending from a point opposite Porretta north to a point south and west of Vergato, a distance of approximately eight miles. In German hands these peaks at a general elevation of 3,500 feet afforded complete observation over most of the highway in this area and our positions east of the Reno River. If occupied by our forces, the Germans would not only be denied the use of these valuable observation points, but we would be provided with good positions from which to command the future offensive.[173]

Under this plan, the 10th Mountain Division would first seize "the long[-]disputed Mount Belvedere" and Mount Della Torraccia, and after the 10th Mountain had secured its objectives, the FEB would seize Mount Castello to the east.[174] The attacking forces would then continue forward,

seizing further ridges to the northeast of the original objectives as far as 7 miles north and east of Highway 64.[175] For the conquest of Belvedere and its associated peaks to be secure, however, it would be necessary to eject the Germans from a nearby series of five peaks west of Belvedere, running diagonally for about 4 miles in a northeasterly direction from La Diagio at the southwesternmost extremity, to Mount Mancinello, Mount Serrasiccia, Mount Cappel Buso, and finally Pizzo di Campiano at the northwest terminus of the ridge—all of which would be code-named and go down in history as—Riva Ridge.[176] Pizzo di Campiano, at the northern end of Riva Ridge, at 100 feet higher than Mount Belvedere, "would provide excellent observation on the reverse slopes of the Belvedere-Torraccia ridge; it was therefore considered essential that this ridge be taken and the left flank thus secured before the main assault was launched" against Belvedere.[177] As David Brower observed in his history of the 1st Battalion, 86th Infantry, "Belvedere must fall, and the 10th Mountain must go on from there. But Belvedere could not fall, and stay down, unless Riva Ridge . . . fall first."[178]

The Encore objectives were held by the German 232nd Grenadier Division, with 1044th Grenadier Regiment on Riva Ridge, and 1045th holding the ridgeline from Belvedere to Mount Torroccia; the 1043rd Grenadier Regiment faced the *febianos* from atop Mount Castello, while the 232nd Fusilier Battalion and part of the 4th Independent Mountain Battalion constituted the Germans' reserve.[179]* In support the Germans had concentrated at least ninety-seven guns,** mostly deployed between Belvedere and Mount Castello.[180] The approach to Mount Belvedere consisted in large part of dormant wheat and barley fields; the approaches to all the objectives provided only intermittent concealment in "scattered clumps of stunted, scrubby growth."[181] Owing to the relative quiet around Mount Belvedere since the preceding November, the attacking 10th Mountain troops could look forward to finding

---

* According to *Combat History of the 10th Mountain Division*, "the enemy held in reserve 4 battalions of varying strengths." *Combat History*, 12–13.
** According to *Combat History of the 10th Mountain Division*, "The total number of guns capable of being brought to bear upon our proposed route of attack was 83." *Combat History*, 12.

an enemy more strongly entrenched on the objective peaks than ever, with minefields expected on all likely avenues of approach toward Mount Belvedere and known to exist in the Brazilian sector.[182] Achieving surprise would be vitally important to the success of the attack but, owing to the nature of the terrain, very hard to achieve; stealthy movement, good camouflage, and the cover of darkness would be critical.[183] "Corps artillery commenced the delivery of normal harassing fires" shortly before the attack on Riva Ridge—the kickoff of Operation Encore—"so as not to indicate anything unusual to the enemy,"[184] and to mask the noise of the assaulting troops as they crept up the cliff face, and to encourage the enemy to stay inside their works.[185] The attack on Belvedere would proceed initially without air and artillery support, for fear of alerting the enemy to the attack.[186] They would be available as the operation unfolded, however;[187] to that end, concerned about the 10th Mountain Division's limited organic fire support capabilities, IV Corps commander Crittenberger substantially augmented the division in this area, attaching one tank battalion, two tank destroyer battalions, a battalion of 105 mm howitzers, and a 4.2-inch mortar battalion.[188] Resupply would be challenging. Roads were few, narrow, and often capable of supporting traffic in one direction only; should resupply be necessary, the attackers would be obliged to depend on mule train, Weasel, and jeep.[189] While armored vehicles could, "by very careful and slow driving," maneuver forward in support "in limited numbers," their utility would be sharply limited.[190]

Preparation for the Attack

In the days and weeks leading up to the attack, "Riva Ridge had been scouted out by patrols of expert mountaineers" who "probed for routes up various parts of the ridge,"[191] including assessing the suitability of trails for pack animals.[192] Lt. Col. Henry J. Hampton described one of these patrols in his report on the Riva Ridge attack, written on June 12, 1945. "On 15th of January 1945 a patrol was sent to Campiano [the northernmost peak of Riva Ridge]," consisting of "five expert mountaineers," with the mission of ascertaining

enemy dispositions on the peak and, if possible, of capturing prisoners:[193]

The trail was covered with snow and ice, and in places was rugged and very precipitous. . . . Skis were used, but before the top was reached they were cached and the patrol free[-]climbed to the top. As they neared the top, a dog barked, and a Kraut came out of the trees, looked about, did not see the patrol crouched against the side of a rocky ledge . . . as [the patrol] continued forward up the ledge, the dog barked again. Three Krauts came out, one armed with a slung carbine, the other two unarmed. They moved over towards the ledge where they observed the patrol in column along the ledge . . . [two soldiers] raised their Tommy guns and . . . in English said, "Hands up." The Krauts were both surprised and dazed, whereupon the one with the carbine attempted to unsling the weapon . . . [the two soldiers] let go with a burst from their Tommy guns. The Krauts dropped, a machine gun opened fire, and the patrol rapidly retraced their footsteps . . . with bullets splattering all over the mountain. From then on . . . there was continual improving and digging of old and new positions [on the ridge]. Result of this patrol was that we had one trail over which a small force of well-trained mountain men could advance. More trails were needed if the ridge was to be taken.[194]

Most of 1st Battalion, 86th Mountain Infantry, was withdrawn from the line and transported by truck to Lucca, a mile from the coast; here they learned from a member of the division staff, who produced a model of the objective for the men's inspection, that their objective would be Riva Ridge, the most challenging assault of the Encore attack.[195] Some, including some on the Fifth Army staff, thought the face of Riva Ridge unclimbable by man or beast, and hence immune from being carried by assault—particularly by infantryman encumbered by weapons and equipment.[196] Maj. Gen. Hays thought otherwise; he was convinced that the men of the 10th Mountain had been physically conditioned since arriving in Italy, and he suspected that the Germans would be as convinced as the Fifth Army staff of the impossibility of taking Riva Ridge by storm.[197] As one analyst has observed,

> The southern faces of the mountains in this area were all extremely steep. The northern sides sloped relatively gently down to the Po Valley. Several attempts had been made to seize the heights using the doctrine of the day, bypassing the steep approaches and attacking the heights from the North (rear). These slopes, though much more gradual in their ascent, were heavily mined by the enemy, thereby making the advance of attacking forces very difficult. Attacking forces had sustained severe casualties seizing the heights, only to be pushed back again by determined German counterattacks.[198]

The Germans seem to have believed the face of the ridge to be unclimbable as well. As Charles Wellborn, historian of the 86th Infantry, observed,

> The Germans considered the ridgeline virtually impregnable to any large body of troops because of its natural ruggedness. The steep icy cliffs would have discouraged any "flatland" outfit. Unluckily for the [Germans], the 86th was no flatland outfit. The cliffs . . . were rugged, but to trained rock climbers and mountain men they were far from impassable. Therein lay the American advantage, and the undoing of the surprised Germans, who were to wake up one morning soon with the men of the 86th virtually on top of their positions.[199]

The best chance of success lay in a surprise attack from an unexpected direction: up the face of the ridges—so this is where the 10th Mountain would go. The decision had been made, then, that Riva Ridge would be taken, and 1st Battalion, 86th Infantry, found themselves in a marble quarry near Lucca, where they underwent a

two-week training program, each man receiving a rigorous refresher course in rock climbing, scaling "rock faces [that] were as high as buildings" for hours on end, up and down, then up again, to "harden each man" for the assault climb up the face of Riva Ridge that lay ahead.[200]

The rest of the division was preparing too. Elsewhere in the 86th Infantry, patrols continued, billeting located at the line of departure, and roads leading to the jump-off point cleared.[201] The 85th Regiment learned that its role was to be "the spearhead of the entire operation, with its mission to seize, as initial objectives, both Mte Belvedere and Mte Gorgolesco"; the regimental commander and staff reconnoitered the objective on February 9 and formed a plan,[202] and three days later 85th Mountain Infantry conducted a "Night Field Exercise" east Gavinana,[203] during which the 85th "had a dry run of something to come."[204] After moving by foot and truck to the training area, the men "dug in, pulled guard, and then started out in the wee hours of the morning to attack." Kenyon Cooke, a veteran of Encore, writes: "We attacked a steep, high ridge covered in ice and snow. It was a rugged problem and lasted until an hour or so after daybreak, which found us almost at the top of the ridge."[205] While they may not have been aware of all the details, the men of the 85th felt that this exercise was "a dress rehearsal for an extremely important operation."[206] The 87th Infantry also conducted a practice night exercise for its part in Operation Encore and carried out extensive preparations for the attack, as the battalion commander of 1st Battalion, 87th Infantry describes:

> Since this was to be a surprise night attack, much reconnaissance and planning was required. Anti-personnel mine fields, barbed[-]wire obstacles, etc., were found and marked where possible. In some cases mines were removed and barbed wire cut. Routes through enemy mines and past enemy strong points were found and marked. Cover and directions had all to be predetermined, located and marked. Our practice night attack of a few nights before was to stand us in good stead. The 1st Bn. Hdqs. Companies I & R

Platoon actually located and marked routers through enemy mine fields. They even located many enemy positions.[207]

The 87th made other preparations at the regimental level. Numerous maps and aerial photos of the objective area and plaster models of the terrain were distributed to the battalions.[208] A platoon of military working dogs arrived to support the operation.[209] The regiment was to billet in structures in the town of Vidiciatico on the seventeenth and eighteenth of February; Vidiciatico was already crammed with refugees whose homes on the front lines had been destroyed, so a comprehensive survey of every room in the village had to be made by 1Lt. William C. McGuckin and an Italian-speaking NCO, on the pretext of searching for a fugitive.[210] By means of this subterfuge, and careful planning, every soldier as well as the dogs were successfully lodged during the lead-up to the attack.[211]

Meanwhile, on February 12, 1945, the Brazilian Expeditionary Force received the IV Corps order for its part of the operation, which would be, as expected, the capture of Mount Castello.[212] A conference was held on February 16, attended by 10th Mountain Division commander George Hays, FEB commander Gen. J. B. Mascarenhas de Moraes, Lt. Gen. Crittenberger—IV Corps commander, and William Crane, commander of the IV Corps Artillery, at which final details of the operation were coordinated among the US and Brazilian commanders and the various echelons of command. Gen. Mascarenhas de Moraes and his staff then completed the planning for the Brazilians' role in the attack.[213]

Riva Ridge

Operation Encore would be executed in two phases. In the initial phase, the 3rd Battalion of the 86th Mountain Infantry would scale the 1,500-foot cliffs of Riva Ridge's south face, thus securing the division's left flank during the second phase, an attack on the next day (February 19) by the 85th, the remainder of the 86th, and the 87th Infantry Regiments to seize the Monte Belvedere–Monte della Torraccia hill mass;[214] the Brazilians would then seize Mount Castello.[215]

The 86th Mountain Infantry was commanded by Col. Clarence "Tommy" Tomlinson. Col. Tomlinson was, as 10th Mountain veteran Hal Burton puts it, "no mountaineer," and he "found rock climbing hard going."[216] A Regular, he joined the 86th late, shortly before its departure for Camp Swift, coming from service in the Southwest Pacific; he appears not to have been popular with all of his peers, one of whom "described him disdainfully as a 'soldier of fortune,'" whatever that might mean, but his troops respected him, as recounted by Burton:[217] "He had a tough, swaggering attitude—and a nose both beaklike and squashed—that appealed mightily to his college boy soldiers. What they wanted was a leader; social credentials didn't matter."[218] The 1st of the 86th, which would make the assault, was commanded by Lt. Col. Henry Hampton, an officer "who had meekly learned the arts of roped climbing from enlisted instructors at Camp Hale."[219] He apparently mastered those arts, however, since he would surprise his troops by personally leading a resupply platoon up Riva Ridge over its toughest route, and rapidly too.[220]

In the day or two leading up to Encore, the mountain troopers occupied their assembly areas. Those billeted in structures were required to remain indoors and out of sight during daylight hours.[221] During this time, the troops inspected ropes and pitons in preparation for ascent up Riva Ridge,[222] inspected weapons, issued ammunition, and checked other gear.[223] Others, whose staging areas saw them taking up positions in the open, concealed themselves in wooded areas, where they were ordered to dig in, cover their foxholes with their shelter halves, and refrain from any movement, noise, or light until ordered to attack, a day or more later.[224] The necessity for such stealth was made plain to Company C, 85th Infantry, during their move to the assembly area, as mountain trooper Hugh Evans reports:

We were given the order to pull out that night and move to an appointed bivouac area just under the noses of the Jerries who held our objective. Our movement was made very quickly and successfully early that evening. . . . Immediately after we had pulled out, another unit had moved in, but because they made a little too much noise, the village was shelled. This incident made us move all the more quietly.[225]

Phase I of Operation Encore—the seizure of Riva Ridge—was to be carried out by an augmented battalion of the 86th Infantry. On February 16, 1945, the regiment issued Regimental Field Order 3, which entrusted the Riva Ridge assault to 1st Battalion, 86th Infantry, reinforced, with the mission to secure the objective by 0515, February 19, prior to the attack on Mount Belvedere.[226] The battalion had carefully task-organized for this mission. One question carefully considered was whether, and to what extent, to differentiate between those members of the battalion who had trained at Camp Hale, and those who had not. Lt. Col. Hampton describes the decision-making process on this issue leading up in his report on the operation:

It was originally planned that the assault platoons should be hand-picked men from the Battalion. About 70% of the men in the Battalion had been trained at Camp Hale in the Rocky Mountains. As a result it was decided that there would be no hand picking of assault platoons, but each company commander would designate a platoon from his company as the assault platoon. This was done, and it increased the morale and spirit of the men as they all considered themselves mountaineers, even though they had not all trained in the mountains.... After their two weeks training at Lucca, especially in a quarry, we found the 30% not trained at Camp Hale were fairly good in movement over rough terrain as they were young and desired to be as good as the rest of the mountaineers. Of course if they had had to use skis and snowshoes, it would have been a different story. Skiers and snowshoers are not trained in two weeks.[227]

The challenge facing the 1st Battalion, 86th Infantry, on Riva Ridge was immense. In a letter to Minnie Dole after the attack, one 86th Infantry

lieutenant described his feelings upon learning the magnitude of the task that faced him and his men. "Boy, my memory went back to those bare pine trees we started on back at Fort Lewis," Lt. Ralph Lafferty wrote,

and to the rock climbing on the face over by "B" slope at Hale, and I thanked God for this training when I saw what we faced. Snow wasn't the problem, but, boy, those cliffs. I pity the poor bastards who have to lug machine guns and the heavy equipment.[228]

Company F of the 2nd Battalion, attached for this operation, was to cover the left flank of the attack by occupying La Piagga at the southern end of the ridge.[229] Company F had been augmented with a machine gun platoon from Company H, an 81 mm mortar section, and two litter squads.[230] Company A, less one platoon detached for the Pizzo Campiano assault, was task-organized with a pioneer squad, a forward observer and party, and two litter squads.[231] It was en route to its objective, Mount Mancillo, the penultimate peak at the southern end of Riva Ridge, adjacent to La Piaggo, at 1945 hours.[232] Companies B and C had moved out a few minutes earlier, at 1930 hours, for their objectives—Mount Serrasiccia for Company C, on Company A's right flank; on Company C's right, Company B would seize Mount Cappel Buso.[233] Company B was augmented with a machine gun platoon and two 81 mm mortar sections from Company D, two litter squads, and a forward observer and party; Company C's task organization was similar, except that it received one 81 mm mortar section, three litter squads, and a pioneer squad.[234] At the northern end of Riva Ridge, a separate platoon from Company A, 85th Mountain Infantry, was to seize Pizzo di Campiano;[235] this element had been augmented with two machine guns, two litter squads, and a forward observer and party.[236]

Before the battalion main body crossed the line of departure, a picked force of expert climbers had scaled the ridge to 1,500 feet, hammering in the pitons and laying the ropes ("light lines") that two columns of assaulting troops would need use to ascend the ridge to their objectives;[237] the pitons had been driven into the rock face by using hammers wrapped in cloth to muffle the sound, an expedient that appears to have been effective.[238] The Intelligence and Reconnaissance Platoon had thrown observation posts well out front of the line of departure, all of which had rendered negative reports as the attack had begun.[239]

The 86th achieved almost complete surprise.[240] The first opposition to the assault was not met until after midnight, when at 0030 Company B encountered small-arms fire on Mount Cappel Busso; a skirmish of about an hour's duration ensued; Company B secured its objective by 0210, having killed or captured most of the enemy garrison there.[241] Charles Wellborn describes that action, reporting that two soldiers from Observation Post No. 3

> reported German machine guns, small arms, and mortar fire south of Cappel Buso. The direction of fire was northeast. A minute later, at 0111 . . . OP #2 confirmed the report . . . the whole story began to come in from Company B, 400 yards from their objective. The assault platoon had made contact with the enemy. Now they were engaged in a fierce firefight. The calm was over. . . . In the blackness, Company B moved in on the Germans, who were caught by surprise. The flashes of their rifles and machine guns outlined the top of the ridge and the crackle of fire reverberated down the valley. In an hour it was over. All of the company was on top of Cappel Buso. They had suffered one casualty and the Germans had been forced to withdraw. Expecting the inevitable German counterattack, Company B was digging in.[242]

Company A, supported by Company F, had reached the ridge on Mount Mancinello by 0045 and secured its objective by 3:00 a.m., having benefited greatly from a haze obscuring the lower slopes.[243] Overcoming resistance on Mount Serrasiccia "after a brisk fire fight," Company C had secured its objective by 5:05 a.m.[244] "After a hard nine-hour climb," Company A's detached platoon at the northern end of Riva Ridge secured its objective on Pizzo di Campiano by 5:44 a.m.[245]

Following "a spectacular assault up the sheer face of the cliff,"[246] and "before the light of dawn broke over the embattled area, the 1st Battalion of the 86th Mountain Infantry had secured all of its objectives."[247] In so doing they had achieved nearly total surprise "as the men of the 86th appeared from what the Germans had considered impenetrable terrain."[248] On reaching their objectives, most elements found that "the Krauts had pulled back in their dugouts for the night, not leaving a man in position."[249] As one captured German soldier noted after the assault, "We didn't man the ridge too heavily; we considered in unclimbable!"[250] So thoroughly had the 86th caught the enemy by surprise that it was not until 6:55 a.m. on the morning of the nineteenth that the German artillery began to become active, to which IV Corps counterbattery fire provided an effective reply.[251] As one captured Germany would report in the after years, "We didn't realize you had really big mountains in the United States, and we didn't believe your troops could climb anything quite [as] awkward" as Riva Ridge.[252]

The Germans were not going to passively accept defeat, however; as expected, they soon began their counterattacks to regain the heights of Riva Ridge. Among the German targets was Company A's detached platoon on Pizzo di Compiano. The platoon achieved the summit following a grueling hours-long climb in which they were raked by rifle fire and bombarded by grenades rolled down the slope upon them.[253] The Germans then resolved to throw the platoon, commanded by one Lt. Loose, back off it; the Germans counterattacked, which Loose and his men answered by counterattacks of their own.[254] Lt. Loose's "coolness prevented a disaster"; for it he would be nominated for the Distinguished Service Cross.[255] German artillery began to become effective against them by 10:00 a.m., and the Germans renewed their counterattacks throughout the night of the nineteenth and twentieth of February; having been told that the heights were "to be held at all costs," they held on for thirty-six hours—out of communication, without food or water, and low on ammunition—until relieved on February 21, having killed twenty-six Germans and captured seven, and having at one point called in artillery fire practically on top of themselves to break up a German counterattack.[256] The Germans mounted other counterattacks as well, so much so that two companies of the German 4th Independent Mountain Battalion were virtually annihilated in futile efforts to push the 86th, or parts of it, back off the ridge.[257]

The 1st Battalion, 86th Mountain Infantry, held their hard-won positions on Riva Ridge until the morning of February 22, when the 10th Mountain Reconnaissance Troop and the 10th Mountain Anti-Tank Battalion relieved them.[258] Until that time, the main challenge the 86th faced in holding on to the ridge was logistical. The infantry units on the summits were largely re-supplied by pack trains, Weasels, and human muscle, initially provided by soldiers from Company B, 10th Mountain Quartermaster Battalion, until these soldiers assumed other roles in support of the attack.[259] Casualty evacuation from the ridge was a particular challenge. "Evacuation of the wounded down to the base of the ridge was a herculean task," Minnie Dole wrote, "requiring about five and a half hours to get a man down the face of the ridge."[260] A remarkable feat of logistics engineering was accomplished during this time, when the 126th Engineers constructed an aerial tramway reaching two-thirds up the cliff face on Mount Cappel Buso to assist in resupply and casualty evacuation; on its first day in operation alone, thirty casualties were sent down the ridge and 5 tons of supplies were sent back up.[261] Later, two 75 mm pack howitzers and seven .50-caliber machine guns were transported up and emplaced on Riva Ridge to support the attack on Mount Belvedere.[262] It was an impressive accomplishment, as Lt. Bill McGuckin later observed in another letter to Minnie Dole. "The guys who built the Brooklyn Bridge better come over and see this one," he wrote. "These engineers were terrific. The guys who had to be brought down blessed them."[263]

The Assault on Mount Belvedere

The conquest of Riva Ridge by 1st Battalion, 86th Mountain Infantry, was a spectacular feat of leadership, skill, and valor. But it was only the first act in a longer drama that was to unfold over the next several days; the curtain was to go up on the second act about twenty-four hours later—the assault on Mount Belvedere. "Mount Belvedere—like other Apennine peaks—controlled several of the highways leading north," Curtis Casewit has observed; "It was one of the gates to northern Italy. If Belvedere was taken, US troops could finally smash into the rich plains of the Po River, the larder of Europe."[264]

"While the Germans were occupied with retaking Riva Ridge," one analyst writes, "the remainder of the 10th Mountain Division began its assault of the Belvedere-Torraccia Ridge" during the evening of February 19, 1945.[265] The plan of attack was, in essence, to seize Mount Belvedere and then attack northeast, seizing each of the separate peaks in turn, culminating with the capture of Mount della Torraccia, the north-easternmost peak on the ridge; the *febianos* of the Brazilian Expeditionary Force were to support the attack by seizing Mount Castillo, south of the 10th Mountain's terminal objective.[266] The attack would begin at Belvedere, where two battalions of the 87th Mountain Infantry would attack up the western slope, with 2nd Battalion seizing Polla and Florina, while the 1st Battalion would continue and seize the summit, leaving 3rd Battalion in reserve at Vidiciatico.[267] The 85th Mountain Infantry would attack on the 87th's right, with 3rd Battalion attacking the southeastern slope of Mount Belvedere, while 1st Battalion simultaneously attacked Mount Gorgolesco, immediately northeast.[268] The 1st Battalion would press its attack over the summit and down the northeastern slope, at which point 2nd Battalion, 85th Infantry, would pass through the 3rd Battalion to seize Mount della Torraccia.[269] The 3rd Battalion, 86th Mountain Infantry, would advance along the southeastern slope of the Belvedere–della Torraccia ridge to seize the village of Mazzancana, just southeast of Hill 1053, protecting the right flank of the 85th as it advanced toward Mount della Torraccia; when the 10th Mountain advance reached Hill 1053, the Brazilians would launch their attack on Mount Castello.[270] The 3rd Battalion, 86th, would later resume its advance along the southeastern face of the ridge to Mount della Torraccia.[271] "Reinforcing the fire power of the Division," the *History of the IV Corps* reports, were the 185th Field Artillery Battalion; Company "A," 1125th Armored Field Artillery Battalion; Company "A," 701st Tank Destroyer Battalion, and 4.2-inch mortars of the 84th Chemical Battalion. The 894th Tank Destroyer Battalion and the 751st Tank Battalion provided the armored strength.[272]

The division also received air support from the XXII Tactical Air Command, and the "Rover Joe" system.[273] "Rover Joe" was an innovative aerial fire control system (known to the British as "Rover David" or "Rover Paddy"), first used by the British in North Africa, and by the US Army Air Force beginning at Salerno.[274] Col. Paul Goodman provides this description of the employment of "Rover Joe" by the 92nd Infantry Division during Operation Fourth Term:

In ROVER JOE operations, tactical air liaison detachments were manned by Air Force pilots and radio operations, mounted in ¼-ton trucks equipped with radios capable of operating in the tactical air direction net. Specifically, ROVER JOE controlled forward fighters in a ground liaison team. The team filtered requests for air support from forward units. Its function was to deal with targets which required swift action, either because neutralization of the targets would have an immediate effect on the tactical situation, or because the target was of a fleeting nature. . . . The Regimental S3 would radio the request to ROVER JOE and alert direct-support artillery to mark the target with smoke. Rove Joe would, if all planes were not then engaged, contact the planes overhead . . . and direct the planes accordingly.[275]

A variation on "Rover Joe" was "Horsefly," in which a light aircraft would mark the targets for attack by supporting bombers.[276] Unlike the 86th Infantry's attack on Riva Ridge the night before, however, the 85th and 87th would launch their initial attack on Mount Belvedere without fire support, Maj. Gen. Hays having decided to forego it "in the hope of securing at least tactical surprise in such a night assault."[277] The men had also been ordered to cross the line of departure without rounds in the chambers of their weapons; to avoid compromising their locations, they were initially to refrain from firing their individual weapons, but rather to answer enemy fire with grenades:[278] Gen. Hays's instructions were that "no small[-] arms fire [was] to be permitted by our troops. They could only use hand grenades and bayonets . . . the night attack was not an attack at all. It was simply slipping through and around enemy positions to gain the high ground behind them, so as to deal with the enemy at daybreak."[279] This precaution served a twofold purpose, as 85th Infantry veteran Carl Kerekes recalls:

We were ordered to move out with no ammunition in our weapons. This was done to avoid the possibility of green troops becoming confused and shooting each other in the dark.* If that happened, the element of surprise would be lost and the Germans would realize they were under a massive attack. We were to move forward in teams of two. The first would advance with a fixed bayonet. The second, with his rifle slung over his shoulder, would carry a hand grenade with this finger in the ring.[280]

"After the briefing," Kerekes recalls, "the officers just looked at each other in disbelief. No one said a word."[281]

The 87th began to position for its attack on Belvedere on the night of February 17–18; 1st Battalion moved by truck to Vidiciatico, from there conducting a "grueling" five-hour march of mud, ice, and fog to arrive at its assembly area before dawn, and 3rd Battalion arrived after a long march of its own before dawn on the nineteenth.[282] By 8:00 p.m. on the nineteenth, the companies of the 87th were at or en route to their preattack assembly areas, with machine gun platoons from Company D attached, while the

* As had indeed happened to the 87th on Kiska.

.50-caliber machine guns and 81 mm mortars were under the control of the battalions.[283] All companies crossed the line of departure on time, at 2300. The 1st Battalion moved two companies abreast, Company C on the left and Company B on the right, each with a platoon of machine guns from Company D attached. Company A had been left behind at Quericola, near the base of Mount Belvedere, in reserve, to be prepared to attack Corona on order.[284] The 1st Battalion advanced toward its objectives unopposed until shortly after midnight, when Company B made contact 800 yards from the line of departure, where machine guns and artillery kept the company pinned down for nearly three hours.[285] By half past midnight, Company C had encountered a minefield and was under enemy fire; fortunately, the Intelligence and Reconnaissance (I&R) Platoon, along with a team of military working dogs, had reconnoitered this terrain previously and was able to help the company pick its way through the mines.[286] One of the working dogs—Tarzan—had identified two gun positions during a reconnaissance the previous night.[287] At about a quarter to one in the morning, two soldiers of the I&R Platoon began crawling forward and cutting German wire, but progress was slow; after 2:00 a.m., Company C's 1st Platoon and a part of its 2nd become separated from the main body and spotted four Germans in the light of an enemy flare, who in turn saw them and ran; the scouts killed two by small-arms fire and followed the other two up with grenades thrown over the ridge where the Germans had fled.[288] Shortly after this, six Germans in a dugout, including a lieutenant, surrendered and were sent to the rear, and a local German counterattack was beaten back.[289] Company C reached Corona at 0300; shortly before this, its commander, Capt. Alfred Edwards, had been shot in the leg and had to be evacuated.[290] Company B finally regained forward momentum at 0320; shortly thereafter, Companies B and C

made contact past Corona, 300 yards from the summit.[291] By 0430, Company B was on the summit, having captured the German observation post there, and Company C was at its objective.[292] Company C had bypassed Corona in the interest of reaching its objective; at 0600, Company A was called up from reserve at Vidiciatico to clear the town, killing seven Germans and capturing twenty in the process, at a cost of one dead—Pvt. Lee H. Chew—and four wounded.[293] By daybreak 1st Battalion had captured thirty-five prisoners, but the fight was not over; Company C still had to clear the ridge above Valipiano, which was accomplished after a vigorous fight.[294] Here, Company C faced an act of gratuitous treachery by the Germans. As George Earle recounts,

> Several prisoners emerged, hands in the air, and Sergeant William F. Murphy and some others went forward to make them Prisoners of War. Then the Nazis pulled one of their common tricks—they suddenly hit the ground and other Nazis behind them began firing. Sergeant Murphy of Company D was shot and killed—others were wounded. The soldiers were eliminated to a man. Company C took no further prisoners of war.[295]*

Company B, having also seized its objectives, repulsed two counterattacks that morning, at 0730 and 0930; having been beaten back twice, the Germans now brought intense artillery fire to bear against Company B, which was stopped with the assistance of "Rover Joe."[296]

Meanwhile, 2nd Battalion had crossed the line of departure along with its sister battalion at 2300 on the nineteenth. Shortly after midnight, one platoon of Company G stumbled upon a minefield; although these mines had been exposed by melting snow the previous day, the platoon still suffered ten casualties from two of its squads.[297]

---

* This tragic incident, and Company C's response to it—the resolution to take no more prisoners—provides an object lesson in the reasons for rules of behavior in warfare. *US Army Field Manual 27-10*, July 1956, states that "it is improper to feign surrender so as to secure an advantage over the opposing belligerent thereby." Not all is fair in love and war, and for good reason: "Treacherous or perfidious conduct in war is forbidden because it destroys the basis for a restoration of peace short of the complete annihilation of one belligerent by the other." *FM 27-10*, 22. So it would seem to have been on Mount Belvedere; however the men of Company C, 87th Mountain Infantry, conducted themselves in other fights, on other fields, it appears that this small act of German treachery really did "destroy the basis of for a restoration of peace," on that day, at least.

The platoon continued forward, capturing an enemy mortar position, but the other two platoons were also ensnared in minefields, and the whole of Company G soon began taking automatic weapons fire from Polla; the company then dug in for the remainder of the day, having lost communications with higher headquarters at about 0100.[298] The 126th Engineers moved out at 0330 to help Company G penetrate the German minefields during the night; Company G secured Polla after daybreak, repulsing an attempted counterattack in the process; by shortly after 1030 the company reported its position as 200 yards past Polla.[299] To Company G's left, Company F was struggling as well, making first enemy contact less than an hour and a half after crossing the line of departure, and two hours after that, at 0220, the company was pinned in front of Florio; by an hour later, mortar fire had added to Company F's problems, the company still being immobilized before Florio.[300] Company F's predicament was illustrative of the lessons learned during the Italian Campaign, and reduced to writing by the G-3 staff of the 15th Army Group:

> Troops that . . . permitted themselves to be pinned down were inevitably subjected to deadly mortar and artillery concentrations which very often caused excessive casualties. . . . Our troops had a strong inclination, when fired upon, to dig in without returning the fire, inasmuch as they could see no suitable targets at which to fire. When they did return fire into the hostile area, the German fire either materially decreased or stopped. Some units quickly learned that the proper procedure to take, when fired upon, was to return fire promptly, deploy a force sufficient to overcome the resistance, and keep on going.[301]

"It was shown repeatedly," the 15th Army Group G-3 staff also noted, "that units which pressed their attack vigorously suffered far fewer casualties and were more uniformly successful than those which hesitated or stopped when fired upon."[302] This lesson was not lost on the men of Company F, since as those mortars were falling,

one platoon was flanking the town, and within half an hour—by 0400—Company F was ready to strike, which it did at dawn, securing Florio and all its other objectives, capturing fifty-five Germans and killing three, at the cost of twenty-two casualties among its own men (nineteen injured, three killed).[303] At the time of this assault, 2nd Battalion headquarters had lost contact both with Companies F and G; nonetheless, the objectives were secured and 2nd Battalion consolidated its gains throughout the remainder of the morning.[304] The 2nd Battalion, 87th Mountain Infantry, had had a tough fight on Mount Belvedere and had to rely on aerial and artillery fire support; guns firing from Piazzo Campiano at the northeastern end of Riva Ridge, captured the previous day by the 86th, provided fire support, as did guns in the division rear, and close air support was provided.[305]

On the 87th's right flank was the 85th Mountain Infantry. Just as the leadership of 1/86 had been concerned about the effectiveness of newly integrated men who had not been through the rigorous training of Camp Hale, so too was the leadership of the 85th, and perhaps with greater reason: at Camp Swift, the 85th had been forced to absorb 2,000 fillers without any mountain or winter training.[306] Undoubtedly, all those who had been through the rigorous preparation of Camp Hale agreed with Maj. Gen. Hays, whose assessment follows:

> It's a combination of level of physical fitness and a higher IQ, meaning higher morale. . . . Troops not trained in the mountains have a mental block. There's a terrific advantage when you have troops who know how to handle a mountain. . . . The training at Camp Hale built a comradeship, a sense of reliance on one another, a feeling of cohesion that is immensely important.[307]

The lack of training of these new men was a matter of serious concern to the leaders of the 85th. Burton reports the concerns expressed by one junior officer in a letter home, "expressing anxiety about the fighting qualities of the 85th Infantry."[308] As Burton writes:

The 86th and 87th, with a hard core of skiers and mountaineers, had trained so well at Camp Hale that skiers and non-skiers were thoroughly homogenized. By contrast, the 85th had a much[-]larger percentage of southern draftees, fed in too late to become acclimatized to mountain warfare.* The officer feared that these green recruits would not only be intimidated by the rough mountain terrain but would be physically unable to keep up with the troops who knew how to move and fight in such forbidding country. It wasn't zeal that counted; it was training.[309]

As events would show, however, the 85th's own "hard core of skiers and mountain men" would seem to have brought the new draftees along nicely, since "in the end, the 85th proved itself."[310] As Maj. Gen. Hays noted, "At Swift we had 9,000 trained men in what had been the 10th Light Division. When it became the 10th Mountain Division we took in 3,000 replacements"; yet, he would conclude, "as a matter of fact, before the Italian campaign was over, those replacements were as aggressive as the old-timers."[311]**

The 85th crossed the line of departure at 2300 on February 19; as planned, 3rd Battalion ascended the slopes of Mount Belvedere on the left, while 1st Battalion moved against Mount Gorgolesco on the right, to the northeast.[312] The 3rd Battalion, on Mount Belvedere, first encountered the enemy at

0100, when German forces engaged the battalion with mortars, artillery, machine guns, and grenades—resistance that grew stronger as the battalion continued its advance up the slope.[313] The magnitude of what both the 85th and 87th faced in their assault on Mount Belvedere is well stated by one unnamed chronicler of the 85th Mountain Infantry. "Perhaps it is impossible," he observed,

for anyone to sense the difficulties of such an attack who has not been through one; it is certainly difficult to describe experience of attacking a strong enemy, uphill, in terrain that is wholly unfamiliar, sown with mines, and in a pallid moonlight that silhouetted every figure that ventured across the snow. And when your rifle is unloaded, as ours were, and you move with only a grenade and your bayonet at the ready, it takes a supreme of the will to attack aggressively.[314]

The 85th had this will; 3rd Battalion continued to press forward until the summit was within view at 0410 on the morning of February 21.[315] By this time the battalion had achieved an envelopment of the objective by Companies L and I, but further advance was temporarily delayed by the death of Capt. Walter Luther, Company I commander (the commander of Company L was pinned down by enemy fire and unable to signal his company to resume the attack); the assault was consummated thanks to the initiative of a Company I lieutenant

---

* The officer seems not to have been aware of the same concerns prevalent in 1st Battalion, 86th Mountain Infantry, as they pondered their coming assault on Riva Ridge.

** The effectiveness of individual fillers, and their impact on unit cohesion, seems to be a recurring concern of warfare (at least in the United States). Prior to my own deployment to Iraq, I was in charge of the Mobilization Branch at National Guard Bureau, where the principal task of my staff and me was ensuring that every Army National Guard unit called to active duty left the mobilization station with its full complement of personnel. Generating large numbers of individual fillers was a fact of life. Usually, these vacancies in deploying units were filled by cross-leveling individuals from other units in the same state, conducted by the adjutant general of that state. Invariably, however, the state would be forced to pass some vacancies back to National Guard Bureau for assistance in filling. These would be filled in a variety of ways, from activating platoons or companies from other states as unit "plugs," to calling up ARNG volunteers from across the country to fill vacancies, to involuntarily calling up Individual Ready Reserve soldiers and even, on rarer occasions, by filling vacancies from among the ranks of the active component. The impact of all this on unit cohesion was a constant concern and the subject of much handwringing, as was the impact of late-reporting fillers on the training status of units well advanced into their predeployment collective training. Yet, an examination of nearly every US conflict, and certainly those of the twentieth century, demonstrates that the problem of individual replacements is a permanent fixture in warfare and simply must be accounted for in planning (for a discussion of this phenomenon from the inception of the Army through World War II, see Marvin A. Kreidberg and Merton G. Henry, *History of Military Mobilization in the United States Army, 1775–1945*; and Leonard L. Lerwill, *The Personnel Replacement System in the United States Army*; for an overview of Reserve Component filler and replacement operations during the Afghanistan and Iraq, see Dennis P. Chapman, *Manning Reserve Component Units for Mobilization: Army and Air Force Practice*). The lesson to be gleaned from the experience both of the 10th Mountain Division in World War II and of the Army National Guard in Operations Enduring Freedom and Iraqi Freedom seems to be that given a cadre of well-trained and motivated veterans, a healthy unit culture, and a positive leadership environment, individual fillers—even relatively large numbers of them—can be acculturated and effectively integrated into a unit relatively quickly.

who had sensed that something was amiss and restarted the attack.[316] The 3rd Battalion reported its objective at the summit secure by 0615 but continued to receive heavy indirect fire and casualties from a 120 mm mortar battery farther down the slope of Mount Belvedere.[317]

Meanwhile, 1st Battalion, 85th Infantry, pressed forward against Mount Gorgolesco until 0300, when the battalion came under a powerful protective barrage of mortar fire, laid down by the enemy against what he suspected (quite correctly) to be an American force in its front.[318] Company C, 85th Infantry, veteran Hugh Evans describes the scene:

A tiny whir suddenly rose to a scream and ended in an explosion. We all fell to the ground. They were shelling us! Had they heard us? Did they know where we were? Before we could answer these questions, shells began landing all over the side of the ridge we were ascending. It soon became apparent that the Germans were laying in patterns of artillery fire. The shells would climb up one draw and then ladder down a ridge. They didn't know where we were, but they were shelling all possible avenues of approach to their positions. All we could do was keep moving forward and hope. Soon they had bracketed in on both sides of us. Our area had to be next.[319]

Although this fire took a heavy toll of casualties from the 1st Battalion, and particularly from Company C, the fires slowed but did not altogether stop the battalion's advance: Company C had surrounded the objective on the summit of Mount Gorgolesco by 0440, and twenty minutes later both Companies B and C commenced the assault; the summit was secure by 0610.[320] The majority of the battalion's casualties had been inflicted by mines and indirect fire.[321] Carl Kerekes of Company B describes one casualty-producing encounter with a minefield during this phase of the operation. His platoon had been temporarily pinned down by machine gun fire, and his platoon "spread out and crawled carefully up toward the machine guns," as he explains:

There was no option other than to enter the woods about 150 feet from where the machine guns were still firing. As soon as we entered the woods one of the men hit a trip wire attached to a stick mine. The explosion shattered his leg. He fell among other trip wires each attached to other mines ... before we could assist him another mine exploded.[322]

The 85th Mountain Infantry had achieved its initial objectives by 0730 on February 20, with both battalions still combat effective and capable of further advance.[323] The decision was made, therefore, to commit 1st Battalion's reserve—Company A, suitably reinforced with machine guns and mortars from Company D, to the fight; Company A passed through the positions of the other two companies and assumed the lead, followed in column by Companies B and C (Company K was dispatched from 3rd Battalion to secure the positions vacated on Gorgolesco as 1st Battalion continued its advance).[324] Kerekes helped to guide Company A through its passage lane and into the zone of contact with the enemy. He writes that

Company A came up the trail. Captain Turner had orders to pass through to continue the attack along the ridge. I stopped him before he hit [a] trip wire. Then I and another man kneeled, on each side of the path, we held an M1 rifle across the trail parallel to the wire ... A Company proceeded to step over, one at a time, I kept repeating "step over the wire, step over the wire."[325]

At 10:00 a.m., Company A repulsed a German counterattack and then continued its forward advance along the ridge until coming into contact with a strong German defensive position in a wooded area, oriented so as to serve as an obstacle to just such an attack along the ridgeline as was being mounted by the 85th; this position was neutralized by indirect fire and aerial bombardment.[326] The 1st Battalion continued to press northeast along the ridge, reaching its objective by 1750 hours on February 20. Almost three hours earlier, the regimental commander had ordered 2nd Battalion, 85th Infantry, to move through 1st Battalion as planned, for its attack on Mount della Torraccia; this passage of lines occurred shortly before 1800, with the 2nd Battalion immediately meeting strong resistance.[327] At this point 2nd Battalion was ordered to press forward to a piece of high ground 500 meters along the ridge where it would hunker down for the night, to resume the attack in the morning; Company G captured this position by 2100 and immediately thereafter repulsed a vigorous counterattack by the German 4th Mountain Battalion.[328] Thus, by the end of the day on February 20, 1945, the 85th Mountain Infantry was in possession of Mount Gorgolesco and much of the ridge running to the northeast, with only its final objective— Mount della Torraccia—remaining.[329] The cost in human toll was immense. Once again, Carl Kerekes describes the scene:

> We reached the top of Mount Gorgolesco and looked down upon a scene of horrible death and destruction. We saw what happened the First and Third Platoons during the night. They were caught in fields of fire, which had been carefully prepared by the enemy. . . . There was very little natural cover to provide protection. Bodies of our fallen comrades were lying on the grass all in a row. They were generally in prone positions with rifles to their shoulders. They were all dead. These were men we knew and loved . . . SSg. Irving "Jeep" Savage was lying there with the top of his head blown away. Tragically, his brother Gene from C Company 86 came by that morning and discovered his brother's body.[330]

While the 85th was attacking Mount Gorgolesco and pushing up the ridgeline toward Mount della Torraccia, 3rd Battalion of 86th Infantry was advancing in parallel along the southeastern slope toward the "fortified, battered farm building" known as Mazzancana.[331] The battalion advanced two companies abreast, with Company L "following to the right rear of the 85th," with its ultimate objective being the capture

of the "heavily mined and fortified, castle-shaped house of Mazzancana," which it was to hold at all hazards.[332] Company K was to advance to Company L's right along the lower slopes, clearing all the settlements and inhabited structures along its axis of advance.[333] When the 85th was temporarily stalled between Mount Belvedere and Mount Gorgolesco, Companies L and K were forced to halt and dig in, under heavy indirect fire, to avoid outrunning the 85th, whose flank they were protecting; forward movement by the 85th resumed early the next morning. Company L pushed forward through strong mortar and artillery fire to come abreast of the 85th.[334] Forward movement was extremely difficult in the face of the Germans' carefully planned defenses and extremely accurate artillery; so formidable were the German defenses that they were "surmounted only by skillful leadership and by trained mountain men of high spirit and courage," including "the daring leadership of Maj. Bay, Capt. Baily and the platoon leaders throughout the day."[335] The Germans "fought bitterly as they were driven back across the ridges, David Brower recalls, "exacting a mounting toll of dead and wounded, calling upon heavy artillery and mortar fire, and supporting their shifting defense with automatic weapons, riflemen, and deadly snipers."[336] Despite this fierce resistance, Company L continued make good progress, which ironically redounded to their disadvantage as they outstripped the 85th Regiment on their left flank. Brower records the result, writing that "the Germans were quick to capitalize on this, bringing a murderous crossfire on L's exposed flank, halting further advances."[337] Forward movement was restored by an effective flanking attack by the Americans, while Company K continued to make good progress along the lower slopes; German resistance began to slacken in some instances, and enemy soldiers began to surrender.[338] Around 1300 the advance of the 85th was again halted and Company L was accidentally bombed by an American plane; the Germans exploited these events to launch a counterattack, which was repelled after an hour's hard fighting. After this attack was defeated, Company L turned and fell upon its objective, Mazzancana, where only four enemy soldiers remained, who surrendered.[339] Companies K and L consolidated on the objective, established a perimeter, and settled in for a long, cold night.[340] Thus ended the first two days of fighting for the Belvedere–Della Torraccia hill mass.

The 2nd Battalion, 85th Infantry, had halted for the night at 2100 on the evening February 20. At about 0430 the next day, the battalion came under intense enemy artillery fire, aggravated by the fact that surrounding trees caused the German shells to explode in the treetops, spraying shrapnel directly down onto the soldiers below in their foxholes, and over the course of the night, 2nd Battalion had to fight off five enemy counterattacks.[341] The battalion was scheduled to resume the attack at 0600 on the twenty-first, but by this time the excessive losses over the past two days, aggravated by the fact that the battalion had been cut off from resupply overnight, had left 2nd Battalion in such a wretched state that the battalion commander reported the unit as unfit to continue the attack; he was promptly overruled by Maj. Gen. Hays, who ordered him to renew the attack "and to continue until his battalion was expended," which commenced at 1300.[342] Strong enemy resistance prevented the battalion from reaching Mount della Torraccia, forcing it to stop again for yet another night, followed, again, by a resumption of the attack—again unsuccessful—at 0700 on February 22.[343] By this time the 2nd Battalion had endured almost 90 percent of the 85th Infantry Regiment's soldiers killed in the operation and nearly 70 percent of the wounded; nonetheless, 2nd Battalion continued to press on toward della Torraccia on the twenty-third, until the exhausted unit was finally relieved by 3rd Battalion, 86th Mountain Infantry—called forward from Mazzancana—on the afternoon of February 23.[344] One important member of the 85th—2nd Battalion's surgeon, Morton E. Levitan—had a remarkable encounter over the course of the regiment's drive up the ridgeline. Out searching for the wounded, Levitan walked right into a detachment of Germans, Burton reports; made prisoner, "he was introduced to a very proper German officer by his captors," who

asked him, "Do you know who is really responsible for this war? . . . the Jews."[345] To this, Levitan replied, "But I'm Jewish," which naturally "stopped the conversation for a bit."[346]*

"The 2d Battalion of the 85th was scheduled to take Della Torraccia," one NCO of Company I, 3rd Battalion, 86th Infantry, later recorded, "but they had been moving a long way and were in no condition to complete an attack on the mountain. I Company men who relieved them will verify the beating they had taken."[347] The task was given to 3rd Battalion, 86th Infantry, which began its movement at 0500 on February 24; the battalion crossed the line of departure at 0700, two companies abreast (Company I on the right, Company K on the left, and Company L in reserve).[348] The soldiers of Company I crossed the line of departure under the cover of numerous light and heavy machine guns firing in support, which the Germans answered almost immediately. SSgt. Richard Emerson described the scene:

This was to be the first combat for these men, and it proved to be a very thorough initiation. . . . At 0645 the preparation began and at 0700 Lt. Wilde blew the whistle. With one stroke all the light and heavy machine guns opened up and the second and third platoons went over the top. A few seconds later the Germans pressed their triggers and the party was on. . . . From then on it was fire and movement and a lot of praying . . . it was close-in fighting and very tricky for both sides."[349]

TSgt. Cross of Company K, 3rd of the 86th, describes the attack on della Torraccia from his company's perspective. "It was hardly light when we organized the company and formed up for the jump-off," he writes:

With the terrifying ferocity of a 20-minute artillery preparation still pounding in our ears, K Company moved out. . . . We had been told the objective was 700 yards ahead, but I'm sure if we had realized what those

---

* Levitan ended the war a prisoner, from which he was liberated by Allied forces at a prison camp in Moosberg, Germany. Hal Burton, *The Ski Troops*, 162.

700 yards held in store for us it would have taken greater force than patriotism, self-pride, and intestinal fortitude to maintain our forward impetus. . . . Dashing madly, loaded with ammo and rations and an M3 "grease gun," I followed the platoon up another hedgerow. Shells began falling on us like a New England hailstorm. It seemed that the bastards could see every man, the way they sniped with 75s and 105s.[350]

Company I secured its objectives at Hill 991, Le Borre, Hill 983, and the ridges north and northeast of the mountain, while Company K had conquered the western slope of Mount della Torraccia by 1430, by which time, TSgt. Cross reports, "Jerry decided we were there to stay. Or rather, Jerry concluded we were there to stay. We had decided it" [emphasis is original].[351]

The 3rd Battalion, 86th Mountain Infantry, had secured della Torraccia, but the Germans had not yet conceded the ground to them. At 1620 they counterattacked until 1850, when the German attack culminated temporarily.[352] During this lull the battalion dug in. Owing to the nature of the terrain and resources available, the battalion found itself defending a frontage of 4,000 to 5,000 meters, such that it was necessary to organize the defense on the basis of mutually supporting, individual strongpoints.[353] These strongpoints were organized around elements of machine guns and BARs, ranging in size from section to platoon depending on terrain, with riflemen attached for security; the approaches were covered by direct fire, mines, wire, flares, and mortars or artillery, and mortars and artillery were registered as soon as possible.[354] The battalion's extensive preparations were put to the test almost immediately; the Germans hit 3rd Battalion's positions at about 2230 with an immense artillery preparation of 1,000 to 2,000 rounds of 155 mm, 105 mm, and 75 mm artillery, followed at 2400 by a ground assault consisting of a company-sized diversionary attack on the battalion's center while two other companies carried out the main attack on the 3rd of the 86th's left flank.[355] This force was immediately struck by 60 mm mortar fire from the local area; within two minutes the battalion concentrated the fire

of a battalion of artillery and six 81 mm mortars on the main attack, and a barrage poured on the enemy, now fixed in position, for twenty-five minutes until both attacking company commanders surrendered their units after heavy casualties.[356] This yielded fifty-six prisoners and numerous enemy dead and wounded.[357] The counterattack had been beaten without the need of employing the 86th's reserves.[358] Mount della Torraccia had been taken: "The final objective had been secured and successfully defended."[359]

While the 85th and 86th were fighting for Mount della Torraccia, the Brazilian Expeditionary Force struck again at its old nemesis, the German forces holding Mount Castello. With air support from their own aircraft, the *febianos* launched their attack from positions north and east of Mazzancana at 0530 on February 21, capturing the hills adjacent to Mount Castello by 0730.[360] The Brazilians attacked with two battalions: 1st Battalion, 1st Infantry Regiment, under Maj. Uzeda; and 3rd Battalion, 1st Infantry Regiment—the Franklin Battalion.[361] The Brazilian infantry launched its main effort against the mountain at 1200, with Maj. Uzeda's battalion attacking in a northeasterly direction and the Franklin Battalion north, both battalions moving on converging axes.[362] At the same time, the Ramagem Battalion—2nd Battalion, 11th Infantry—moved against the town of Abetaia, while the 6th Infantry Battalion secured the FEB's right flank.[363] German resistance began to weaken by 1720.[364] By 1745, the first of Maj. Uzeda's men had reached the summit; the Franklin Battalion arrived shortly thereafter, at 1845. By 2040, February 21, 1945, the Brazilians had secured Mount Castello;[365] the FEB continued clearing isolated pockets of enemy holdouts through February 23.[366] The Brazilians pushed north and northeast in Bellavista on February 24, capturing Hill 958 and La Serra; this the Germans would not abide, launching three counterattacks.[367] All of these the Brazilians defeated, with only one causing serious concern, this one being a counteract against La Serra by infiltrating German troops who had surrounded the position by 0830, only to be driven away by the Brazilians within an hour.[368]

Maj. Gen. Mascarenhas de Moraes described the aftermath of the battle: "Dozens of corpses, many of them even bearing the infernal machines of destruction, lay there as evidence of the prolonged bloody struggle and as proof of the consummate criminality of the forces which had garrisoned the sinister hill."[369] The capture of Mount Castello was a cathartic event for the Brazilians, who had tried and failed to capture it three times before. As Maj. Gen. Mascarenhas de Moraes further reflected, years after the war,

With the capture of this hill the Brazilian Expeditionary Force wrote the most thrilling chapter of its life. By resisting for 3 months the onslaught of Allied arms, Monte Castello had been given the buildup as the citadel of assumed German invincibility. . . . For the Brazilians, on the other hand, it signified the bloody forge of our aggressiveness. . . . It marked the beginning of a series of victories which elevated Brazil's name and the prestige of our Army.[370]

The End of the Beginning

Operation Encore had ended as an unqualified triumph. Historian W. G. F. Jackson summarized the accomplishment of the 10th Mountain Division and the 1st Brazilian Division thus:

10 (US) Mountain Division supported by 1 Brazilian Division executed a brilliant operation, clearing several very high peaks including roping a whole battalion up the precipitous 3,000-foot Riva Ridge. So successful were they that the Germans hastily committed 29 Panzer Grenadier Division to stabilize this part of their front.[371]*

Gen. Clark also characterized the 10th Mountain's attack on Riva Ridge and Mount Belvedere as "brilliant" in his postwar memoir *Calculated Risk*, noting that the attack triggered the collapse of the 232nd Grenadier Division's defense.[372] But both Jackson and Clark also note that the capture of the Mount Belvedere–della Torraccia massif was not an end in itself; Operation Encore was a preliminary action intended to set the conditions for future, more-expansive operations in which the 10th Mountain Division would participate, establishing the IV Corps' start line for the Allied spring offensive into the Po Valley.[373]

---

* It will in no way diminish Jackson's compliment to note that he embellishes slightly, in that only part of 1st Battalion, 86th Infantry, had to ascend Riva Ridge by rope, and that the heights were actually about 1,500 feet, rather than 3,000.

Hello! Boys of 86th and 85th!

Welcome to Europe and to the Italian Front!

Hope you like it?

Though there may be some doubt because you might find things not too comfortable around here.

No, this isn't the time when it was just pleasant and fashionable "Go to Italy for the Winter". *Cooks* got the tickets and arranged everything. Then off on the *"Southern Route"* to Europe = for a cruise in the Mediterranean.

THEN SUNNY ITALY = with fine hotels, good food and lots of fun. = Altogether: A swell time and the best of it: Whenever you didn't like it anymore or had enough of it, you could just take the next boat back for home.

Well, well if *this* isn't different! This time you picked...

Obverse of a German propaganda leaflet "welcoming" the 85th and 86th Mountain Infantry to Italy. *Author's collection*

THE WRONG TOURIST AGENCY!

There is just a bit too much "conducting" on *this* trip.

No choice where to go and where to stay. No sights, no comforts, no smartly dressed girls –

NOTHING!

But a fine chance of getting killed and just be buried and forgotten.

Or (if you're lucky) to finish up in a prisoner's camp to be amongst those who survive this mess and get back home as soon as the war is over!

It was a long way from *Camp Hale* to *Mount Belvedere* and *Abetone!* You will find out that it will be even longer to get back – if you ever do get back.

You know the Italians say:

"See Naples and die!"

Well, you did see Naples and the rest will also be yours, unless...

AF - 36 - 2/45

Reverse of a German propaganda leaflet "welcoming" the 85th and 86th Mountain Infantry to Italy. *Author's collection*

Evolving 10th Mountain Division shoulder sleeve insignia. *Left to right:* Early design of felt construction and detailed bayonet grips, without the mountain tab; early design with detailed bayonet grips, but of woven construction and with a separate mountain tab added; a revised design with simplified bayonet grips and separate mountain tab; and finally, a less common variation with the less detailed bayonet grips and factory-attached mountain tab. *Author's collection*

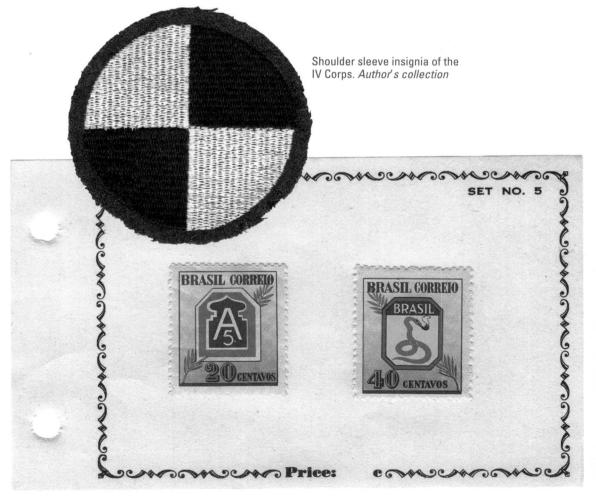

Shoulder sleeve insignia of the IV Corps. *Author's collection*

Pair of Brazilian commemorative stamps, honoring the Brazilian Expeditionary Force and Fifth Army. *Author's collection*

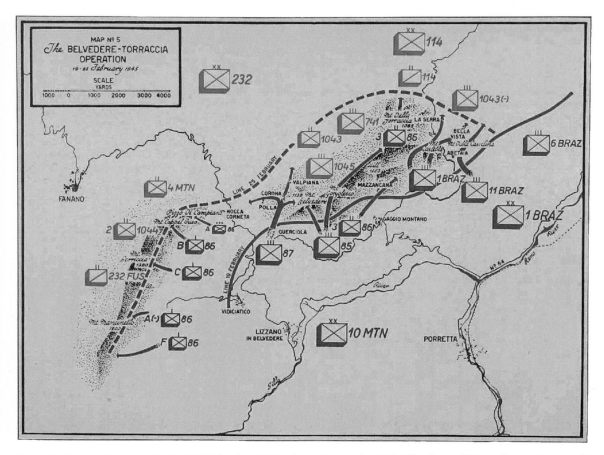

Operation Encore, February 19–25, 1945. *Map No. 5, Fifth Army History, Part VIII: "The Second Winter," opposite page 85*

CHAPTER 6

The Final Campaign: From The Apennines to the Alps

The conquest of Riva Ridge and the Belvedere–Mt. Torraccia massif was only the first of two phases of the IV Corps' limited offensive operations during the winter of 1945. The second phase had been scheduled to launch on March 1 but was postponed for two days due to inclement weather, until March 3, 1945.[1] As with the Riva Ridge–Mount Belvedere phase, this was to be a two-division operation by the 10th Mountain Division and the Brazilian 1st Infantry Division; this time, however, the attack would precede two divisions abreast, with 10th Mountain Division on the left and the FEB on the right.[2] The 10th Mountain's axis of advance would take it across a rugged 4-mile stretch of mountainous terrain, while the *febianos* on the right would advance northeastward toward the Castelnuovo ridge, parallel to Highway 64.[3]

Maj. Gen. Hays initially committed two regiments abreast, with the 86th Mountain Infantry attacking in the west to seize a series of hills and peaks, the principal targets being Mount Terminale and Mount Grande d'Aiano, while the 87th attacked in the eastern zone, with its objectives being Mount della Vedetta, Mount Acidola, Mount della Croce, and Castel d'Aiano, among others; initially the 87th was also to press the attack to the northeast against Mount della Spe and Mount della Castellana, but in the event the 85th Mountain Infantry would seize these objectives.[4] Additionally, in a supporting attack east of Mount Castellana, the 10th Antitank Battalion and the 10th Reconnaissance Troop would attack Hills 781

and 715, respectively, on Mount Valbura.[5] The 751st Tank Battalion and the 701st Tank Destroyer Battalion (3-inch self-propelled guns) supported the division's attack.[6] Company B of the 126th Engineers would be attached to the 86th, Company C would support the 87th by clearing obstacles along its axis of advance, and Company A / 126th Engineers would support the 85th Mountain Infantry when that regiment was called forward.[7] The operation would be initiated by an artillery preparatory fire, after which the 616th Field Artillery would be in direct support of the 87th Mountain Infantry, the 605th Field Artillery would support the 86th, and the 604th would be paired with the 85th when committed.[8] Opposing the 10th Mountain were two battalions from the German 1045th Regiment and two from the 1043rd, with elements of the 144th Reconnaissance Battalion, the 721st Regiment, and the Mittenwald Training Battalion.[9]

This "Second Attack"[10] finally began with the artillery preparatory barrage at 0630 by division and corps artillery.[11] The 87th Mountain Infantry launched its part in the attack—what George F. Earle calls the "Battle of Castel d'Aiano"[12]—at 0700 on March 3, when 3rd Battalion of 87th Infantry crossed the line of departure, in column of companies, with Company K in the lead.[13] Earle notes the difference between Phase 2 and the Phase 1 attack on Mount Belvedere:[*]

---

[*] At this point a brief orientation on the organization of the World War II infantry battalion and regiment may be useful. The following excerpt from the 70th Infantry Division Association website provides a good overview: "Three infantry rifle companies, a headquarters & headquarters company, and a heavy weapons company together made up the infantry battalion. The headquarters & headquarters company was referred to by that name, or as 'HHC.' The other companies of the battalion, however, were known as the 'letter companies.' Identification of the 'letter companies' ran consecutively through the three battalions of the infantry regiment: 1st Battalion contained A, B, and C Companies (rifle companies) and D Company (heavy weapons); 2nd Battalion contained E, F, and G Companies (rifle companies) and H Company (heavy weapons); 3rd Battalion contained I, K, and L Companies (rifle companies) and M Company (heavy weapons). The letter J was not used, as it could be confused with the letter 'I' when handwritten." The website goes on to state that while regiments within the same Army Reserve division were always consecutively numbered, and regiments within National Guard divisions were sometimes consecutively numbered, "through a very complex and convoluted regimental assignment system, the regiments of a Regular Army division in WWII were never consecutively numbered." The 10th Mountain Division provides an obvious exception, given its regiments being numbered 85, 86, and 87 (although they were not activated in that numerical order). See Lt. Col. (USA, Ret.) Hugh Foster, "The Infantry Organization for Combat."

The Battle of Belvedere in February had been a night attack. All objectives of the 87th were taken before dawn on the 20th. From then until the relief at the end of the month, the fighting had been defensive. On the other hand, the Battle of Castel d'Aiano was a deadly struggle in sunlight, from bunker to bunker, hill to hill, objective to objective, for three bloody days. It was accomplished against prepared positions and heavily mined areas, in the roughest kind of terrain and under heavy enemy artillery fire.[14]

Company L followed hard on K's heels, crossing the line of departure at 0717 and immediately coming under heavy indirect fire, as did 2nd Battalion of 87th Infantry behind them.[15] The initial objective for Company K was Hill 997, which effectively blocked the regiment's forward advance.[16] With Hill 997 secure, Company L would then attack Objective C to the northeast, a short ridgeline consisting of two summits, denoted "Charlie 1" and "Charlie 2," separated from Hill 997 by a short saddle.[17]

Company K moved to envelop the enemy, with 2nd Platoon attacking up the slope near the adjacent road, while 3rd Platoon attacked Hill 997's eastern flank, taking fire from enemy positions located in a the adjoining saddle as they ascended the hill to the higher slope.[18] The 2nd Platoon reached a position near the slope, where they were forced to ground by a strong enemy position with clear fields of fire on the hilltop; this resistance was overcome by a single NCO—SSgt. Edmund Bennett, "a famous cross-country skier"—who crawled forward under cover of a stone wall toward the enemy position, capturing three enemy soldiers and causing two more to flee.[19] Bennett then set up a machine gun abandoned by the enemy on the crest of Hill 997, and turned it on the enemy, killing or injuring several as they fled, and capturing another eight.[20] Hill 997 was largely secure by 0830, but resistance from the farm located in the saddle between it and Charlie 1 continued to delay the movement of Company L against the Charlie 1 ridgeline.[21] Some Germans firing from a haystack were killed when the hay was set alight

by American tracer fire; Company L was finally able to bypass resistance in the saddle and continue on against the east slope of Charlie 1.[22] Later, two squads from 1st Platoon, Company K, cleared out the farm buildings in the saddle, continuing up the western slope of Charlie 1 to suppress the rifle and machine gun positions harassing friendly forces on Hill 997 that L Company had bypassed as it advanced.[23] K Company suffered heavy casualties during this phase of the attack and encountered another instance of German treachery when a US medic ran out from cover under the protection of his Red Cross in plan display; Earle describes the event:

> T/5 William R. Conner . . . did heroic work. Under the heavy fire, he moved openly about to get quickly to the wounded men. He spotted one man lying wounded out in front less than fifty yards from an enemy position. . . . Putting his Red Cross flag on a stick, he dashed out to the wounded man's side. He stuck the flag in the ground and in full view was giving aid, when he was shot and killed by a German sniper in cold blood and in under disregard for the Red Cross flag, which the German himself depends on so often.[24]

In fact, the Germans would rely on the protection of the Red Cross Flag after 0900 that very morning during Company L's attack.[25] Company L had crossed the line of departure at 0717, shortly after Company K, with the initial mission to seize Objective Charlie and the follow-on mission to secure Objective Easy, both of which formed part of a ridge known collectively as Mount della Vedetta.[26] Company L met resistance almost immediately from the enemy troops ensconced at the farm in the saddle northeast of Hill 997, including from the soldiers incinerated under the haystack mentioned above.[27] Company L used mortars to silence one of two enemy machine guns firing from the farmhouse in the saddle; the other was silenced by Pfc. Ralph Mattson, who singlehandedly charged with his Browning Automatic Rifle, killing the enemy machine gun crew.[28] By 0920, Company L's 1st Platoon had reached the right flank of Charlie

1. By 1030, they, 2nd Platoon, and the weapons platoon had reached Charlie 2, having bypassed Charlie 1 and scaled Charlie 2 from the east; enemy troops who had been bypassed on the western slope of Objective Charlie attempted a counterattack, which was repulsed.[29] At this point, 2nd Battalion, 87th Infantry, had come up into positions previously occupied by 3rd Battalion, while Company I was following in Company L's wake.[30] By the time the counterattack was turned back, Lt. Col. Works, commander of 3rd Battalion, having learned that the 86th Infantry—attacking on the left—had made sufficient progress to secure his left rear, brought Company K forward from Hill 997 to relieve L on Objective Charlie and ordered Company L to attack and seize Hill 998, Objective Easy.[31] Company L had seized its objectives on "Easy" by 1100, with large numbers of German prisoners "coming out from their overrun positions . . . confused and surprised by the attack";[32] by 1130, 3rd Battalion had taken all its initial objectives and was atop Hill 998, overlooking the Petra Colora road.[33] Company L lost five soldiers killed and twenty wounded in these actions, while losses in these actions were twenty wounded and six killed in Company K.[34] Company I commenced its passage of lines with Company L at 1315 and advanced toward Pietra Colora, which concealed an enemy command posted defended by a force of about thirty Germans.[35] 2nd Platoon attacked the enemy position from the rear, thus bypassing the enemy obstacles, and carried out its assault hard behind a very effective artillery preparation, thus enabling the platoon to overcome the defending force of about equivalent size with only a single minor casualty (though further casualties were sustained as a result of enemy indirect fire after the capture of the town).[36]

The 2nd Battalion, 87th Infantry, was to attack Objective I, a hill northeast of a road junction on the Pietra Colora road on the left side of the regiment's zone, but at 1145 the division commander modified 2nd Battalion's mission to establishing a roadblock at a crossroads later known as "Shrapnel Junction" before moving on to Objective I.[37] The battalion was to jump off from Mount della Vedetta and was ready to by 1400

but was pinned down by artillery fire from Crocette de Sotto to the east, this fire being neutralized by counterbattery fire and aerial bombardment after 1500.[38] At 1505 the division commander ordered the 86th Infantry to clear objectives Fox and George, which dominated Objective I.[39] 2nd Battalion started movement in column with Company E in the lead at 1700; two platoons pushed across the Pietra Colona road and into the town of Canavaccia.[40] Communications had been severed for a time, and when the breaks in the wire were found and repaired, Company E received orders to move back to the west side of the Pietra Colona road for the night, since the 86th had not advanced far enough to secure its flank, leaving Company E's position in Canavaccia exposed and vulnerable to encirclement.[41] By the end of the day on March 3, the 87th had cleared the area up to and established roadblocks on the Pietra Colona road and captured the town; the plan for March 4 was a three-battalion attack with 1st and 2nd Battalions attacking abreast to the north while 3rd Battalion attacked Mount della Croce to the east.[42]

In the eastern zone of the division attack, the commander of the 86th Infantry, Col. Tomlinson, had briefed the battalion commanders on their units' respective roles in the upcoming mission on February 28, only to have the attack repeatedly postponed; the delays were put to good use, however, for the purpose of aggressive reconnaissance and patrolling in preparation for the attack, and the regiment requisitioned 185 replacements for losses incurred during Encore (but the division G1 could promise only fifty-five).[43] In the division's western zone of attack, the 86th Infantry attacked on March 3, with two battalions abreast—1st Battalion on the right, and 2nd Battalion on the right.[44] The 3rd Battalion would initially be in reserve but later pass around 2nd Battalion to Objective G, Campo del Sol, on the Pietra Colora road.[45]

The 86th's attack began at 0640 on March 3, with a twenty-minute artillery barrage.[46] The regiment crossed the line of departure at 0700* as planned, with 1st Battalion on the left, while

* Wondolowski says 0800 (Wondolowski, *History of the IV Corps*, 525), but Wellborn says 0700 (see Charles Wellborn, *History of the 86th Mountain Infantry in Italy*, 21). Given the context, it appears that the IV Corps history is in error on this point.

2nd Battalion advanced on in, right across Mount Terminale.[47] The 1st Battalion immediately had to contend with artillery and mortars, enemy minefields, and resistance by enemy ground troops;[48] "the first phase of combat operations had taught the 86th a vital lesson," however, which was to "never let the Germans pin you down. Keep moving. Once pinned down, you are an easy target for Jerry artillery, [so] despite a hail of fire, the companies moved up"; so the advance continued.[49] They bypassed Hill 1011 at 0728 and by 0830 were advancing on Monteforte and the adjacent Hill 956, receiving extensive air support as "Rover Joe filled the skies above with planes which bombed and strafed Monteforte in advance of the attacking troops"; after clearing Hill 956, the battalion secured Objective Able—Hill 928—at 1052.[50] Meanwhile on the right, 2nd Battalion sent Company G against Hills 952 and 953, the latter being due west of Terminale, while Company E, supported by a heavy-weapons platoon from Company H, attacked eastern Mount Terminale, getting halfway up the slope by 0747.[51] The leading elements reached the top by 0800, with three platoons on the objective twenty-seven minutes later; Mount Terminale was secured by 0840.[52] Company F, the battalion reserve, was moved up to secure Terminale, while Companies E and G moved on to their next target, Objective Dog at Hill 921.[53] The 2nd Battalion faced a major obstacle, however, in the town of Iola at the northern base of Terminale, where Company E faced fierce hand-to-hand combat, fighting house to house to clear the town, as one observer reports:[54]

Supported by the direct-fire of tank destroyers, the battalion battled through the streets and cleared houses which had been turned into strong points by the Germans; the village was finally cleared about noon. Among the prisoners taken at Iola were the commanding officers and most of the staff of the 2d Battalion, 721st Light Regiment. The action of the 86th Mountain Infantry in the first five hours

of the attack virtually destroyed this enemy battalion and inflicted heavy losses on other elements of the 721st Light Regiment.[55]

Nor was Company F spared a bloodletting, even in reserve. Louise Borden, in her unusual free-verse biography of Pete Seibert, a platoon sergeant in Company F,[56] describes his severe wounding by mortar fire during his company's movement to secure Mount Terminale:

Pete Seibert checked on his men, his platoon of brothers, and called their names with instructions. Suddenly, a mortar blast shattered a nearby tree and Pete was thrown to the ground, hit by shards of wood and torn by shrapnel, that tore through his helmet, split open his nose, and knocked out some of his teeth. His left arm was almost cut in half at the elbow, and his right leg was sliced open. In a cloud of pain and blood, Pete tried to stand but fell back. Shocked faces passed above him, and he heard voices.[57]*

At 1745, 3/86, formerly in regimental reserve, conducted a passage of lines through 2nd Battalion and occupied Objective G, consisting of the town of Compo del Sole on the Pietra Colora road and Hills 864 and 869 to the west,[58] an area that, according to Brower, "lent itself admirably to a text-book defensive organization,"[59] where 3rd Battalion stopped for the night.[60]

The Brazilian Expeditionary Force launched a diversionary effort on the far right of the IV Corps on March 3, in support of the 10th Mountain Division's attack.[61] Its Ramagem Battalion (2nd Battalion, 11th Infantry Regiment) occupied its objectives on the Ca Di Giansimone–Narecchie–Rocco Pitigliana line by 1415; the Silvino Battalion (3rd Battalion, 6th Infantry Regiment) moved out at 1100, capturing territory in the vicinity of Rocca Pitiglia later that day, and by dusk on March 4 occupied Santa Maria Villiana and later Hill 882 and 822; the *febianos* assumed all 10th

---

* Pete Seibert survived his wounds. After many months of rehabilitation, he returned to skiing, eventually qualifying for the US Ski Team and helping to found the ski resort at Vail, Colorado. Louise Borden, *Ski Soldier: A World War II Biography*, 148 and 157; and "Pete Seibert of 10th Mountain Division," World War II in Color, February 28, 2016.

Mountain positions east of Pietra Colora on March 4 as well.[62]

The attack resumed on March 5, with regiments moving at approximately 0800, following the customary artillery preparation.[63] The 1st Battalion, 86th Infantry, attacked Sassamolare, "a tough nut to crack," at 0805, with Companies B and C abreast, A in reserve, and tanks in direct support.[64*] The 1st Battalion had four platoons atop Hill 892 by 0950.[65] By noon, 1/86 had cleared Sassamolare and continued the attack north to Mount Grande d'Aiano, beginning the final assault by 1315 and clearing it in just over two hours.[66] This being the limit of advance for the time being, 1st Battalion immediately began establishing a defense on the objective.[67]

The 87th Infantry attacked with two battalions on line, 2nd Battalion on the left and 1st Battalion on the right, crossing the line of departure—the Pietra Colora road—at 0800.[68] The 1st Battalion, tasked with the capture of Mount Acidola and Bacucco, also known as "Love," started movement from Stancadora for a passage of lines through 3/87 at Mount della Vedetta before crossing the line of departure at 0800, with Company A in the lead.[69] The battalion secured Acidola by 0930; tragically, Pfc. Joe C. Miller was killed in this operation. Miller had been the unofficial cartoonist of the regiment, producing many entertaining images, some of which appeared in the regimental paper, the *Blizzard*.[70**] Company B, meanwhile, passed through Company A en route to its objective, Bacucco.[71] About 400 yards from the objective, seven Germans emerged from a house, using some Italian women as human shields; when Company B continued to advance, the enemy retreated into the house, waving white flags, save one who ran and was shot.[72] A number of Germans at various points surrendered before Bacucco was secured at around noon.[73] The 2nd Battalion, 87th Infantry, crossed the line of

departure at 0800, with the mission of capturing Objective K, consisting of Hill 926 and the Madna di Brasa, with E Company in the lead and G following.[74] Company E captured Hill 926 with two platoons in a flanking action around 1500; at approximately 1600, Company G then captured both Madna di Brasa and Hill K 20 to its north.[75] The 3rd Battalion of 87th Infantry crossed the line of departure three hours later than the other two battalions, at 1100; Company I had scaled Mount della Croce and seized its initial objective by 1200.[76] The company then proceeded to its next and final objective for the day, Hill 882, "a knob off to the east on a shoulder of the mountain"; 3rd Battalion then set up its battalion command post in Petra Colora.[77]

The 85th Mountain Infantry joined the battle on the morning of March 5, for the first time during the follow-up to Encore,[78] when it crossed the line of departure at 0800, 1st and 2nd Battalions abreast, with 1/85 to capture Mount della Spe (Hills 899, 920, and 935) in the north, and 2/85 to seize Mount della Castellana, Mount Sinistro, and Mount Spicchione to the south—both objectives being well east of the 86th's and 87th's operational areas.[79] The 1st Battalion crossed the line of departure in column of companies with Company A in the lead; by 1100, Company A had occupied Hill 916 but was delayed four hours on the approach from there to Hill 899—the first target on Mount della Spe—"by a murderous artillery, mortar, and hand grenade concentration," costing the company seventeen casualties.[80] Company A reached Hill 916 that afternoon, conducting a passage of lines with Company B at 1500; by 1830, Mount della Spe was in American hands despite "resistance [that had] stiffened enormously in the last minutes of the attack."[81] The 2nd Battalion, 85th Infantry, moved out at 0800; Company E initially attempted to cross Tora—a feature en route to Mount della

---

* This material is from the unpublished *History of the 86th Mtn Inf Regt 10th Mtn Div* (typescript, no date), an undated and unsigned manuscript typed on onionskin, six pages in length. Though unsigned, one candidate for authorship would be the prolific Harris Dusenbery. This deduction is based on three facts: first, Dusenbery was a passionate and prolific chronicler of the history of the 86th Mountain Infantry and of the 10th Mountain Division, his other works being cited in this book; second, Dusenbery was assigned to the staff of the 1st Battalion, 86th Infantry, and would presumably have had access to the big-picture information necessary to write such an overview; and finally, the typescript omits a discussion of the Riva Ridge operation, instead alluding to it as "ably described by Lt. Col. HAMPTON in his report" (page 1), a report that Dusenbery included in toto in his book *North Apennines and Beyond*.
** Ross Wilson, in his *History of the First Battalion, 87th Mountain Infantry*, writes that it took Company A, 1/87, until 1030 to capture Mount Acidola (page 29).

Castellana—but, upon meeting resistance, withdrew to Canolle below and bypassed Tora to attack up the west slope of Castellana, which was largely secured by 1500.[82] Company F now changed its direction of attack toward Mount Spicchione, assisting with the clearance of Castellana's summit along the way.[83] Company G probed Tora at 0200 the next day and, detecting no enemy, attacked the position, with Company H in support, at 0600, meeting only light resistance; Company G then captured Monte Sinistro, while elements of Company E captured Monte Spicchione.[84] The 2nd Battalion, 85th Regiment, had captured all of its objectives by noon on March 6.[85]

The 87th resumed operations on March 5, with 1st Battalion's attack on Castel D'Aiano.[86] Division had originally wanted 1st Battalion to attack this objective on March 4, but Lt. Col. Wilson, the battalion commander, had requested a delay due to shortages of food and ammunition and the need to rest his men, which had been granted.[87] Hence the attack was set for 0630, but the attack was postponed until 1400, by which time the 85th had secured Mount della Spe, on the 87th's right.[88] The operation began with Company C, which faced "a 'rocky road' to Hill 813. It was an open slope all the way and easily observed all the way," and "the enemy artillery and mortar fire was intense with good observation"; Company C was stopped by this fire short of the objective but was able to capture it after dark with friendly artillery support.[89] During the course of this attack, two German soldiers were fired on by their comrades while attempting to surrender, one American being killed while attempting to take charge of the prisoners.[90] Meanwhile, Company A, which had followed Company C in column across the objective, turned right and moved against Castel D'Aiano, assisted in their advance by partisans who guided them through minefields into the town.[91] After the company had captured the eastern part of the town, a strong German artillery barrage cut part of the company off from contact with the company command group; Capt. Klemme, Company A's commander, reestablished control by "enveloping the enemy"—that is, by circling around the town to enter from another direction, reestablishing control, and securing the town.[92] This concluded

the 1st Battalion of 87th Infantry's operations for the day, the battalion suffering seven dead and nine wounded.[93] Overall, the 87th Mountain Infantry had lost thirty-nine killed and 116 wounded, captured 600 enemy, and cut a gash into his territory 2,000 to 3,000 yards wide and 6,000 yards deep.[94] Elsewhere on March 5, the 10th Antitank Battalion and the 10th Reconnaissance Troop had occupied their positions at Hills 781 and 715, respectively, on Mount Valbura.[95] To their right, the Brazilian Division attacked to capture Soprasasso (subdued by 2nd Battalion, 6th Infantry Regiment, that day), and Castelnuovo, which was captured by 3rd Company, 1st Battalion, with 6th Infantry Regiment under the command of Capt. Aldenor Maia.[96] As recorded in the Fifth Army History,

In conjunction with the attack of the 85th Mountain Infantry [on March 5, 1945] the 1st and 2d Battalions, 6th Brazilian Infantry, moved northeast to outflank the town of Castelnuovo from the west, finally penetrating into the village at 1910, following an intense shelling of German positions in the vicinity. On the right of the 6th Brazilian Infantry and just west of Highway 64 the 11th Brazilian Infantry advanced east of Castelnuovo and pushed forward nearly 1 mile beyond it into positions which overlooked Vergato.[97]

"The long-expected counter-attacks finally materialized during the night of 5–6 March," the *History of the IV Corps* reports:

Directed against our most forward positions on Mount della Spe. Elements of the 15th Panzer Grenadier Regiment launched one attack before midnight, followed with others at 0030, 0130 and 0440, but failed to drive the 1st Battalion, 85th Infantry, off the peak, although one German group penetrated to such close range that bayonets came into play. After the fourth attempt failed, the enemy ceased this effort to re-take the position and relied on heavy artillery fire to harass the American positions.[98]

Over the course of the three-day battle, the 10th Mountain Division occupied more than 35 square miles of enemy-held territory and took 1,200 prisoners.[99]

Preliminary Operations before the Spring Offensive

The Italian front was largely quiet for the rest of March 1945. With only routine patrolling to tax them, the regiments and battalions were able to attend to administrative matters such as receiving replacements, training, and absorbing the lessons learned during the previous battles and preparing to apply them in the inevitable spring campaign.[100] They were able to enjoy the many accolades that came pouring in from mothers and fathers, from the press, and from their commanders, for their brilliant and courageous exploits during Operation Encore; they were able to relish their newfound elite status, not as "glamorous . . . ski troops" but as tough "Mountain Infantry," and they were able to find satisfaction in "the most meaningful decoration for them, the blue and silver Combat Infantryman's Badge, which almost every man in the regiment was now entitled to wear."[101] And last but certainly not least, the 10th Mountain Division had the opportunity to begin rotations, by battalion, through Campo Tizzoro and Montecatini, where battalions would receive three days of rest.[102] "Monticatini, a former mountain resort," George Earle observed,

was an amazing surprise to the men of the regiment, with night clubs, shows, wine, women, and song; hot water, even rest for those who wished it. It was an unexpected relief to the men from the constant shell fire, and the confining existence in a foxhole.[103]

This was, of course, merely a "respite or 'calm before the storm,'" as Ross Wilson called it.[104] The Germans still had thirty divisions in northern Italy according to Lt. Gen. Clark—"twenty-five German and five Italian Fascist."[105*] While many of these formations had taken serious casualties

during previous combat, and most "were under-strength in front line soldiers" or even, in the case of the 232nd Reserve Division, "made up largely of older men and convalescents," they were still a formidable enemy.[106] Axis forces, under the overall command of Gen. Heinrich von Vietinghoff's Army Group C, consisted of the Fourteenth Army under Lt. Gen. Joachim Lemelsen facing Lt. Gen. Truscott's US Fifth Army in the west, with his most powerful element, the XIV Panzer Corps, south of Bologna arrayed against the US II Corps, and the 10th Army under Lt. Gen. Traugott Herr was facing the British Eighth Army under Lt. Gen. Sir Richard L. McCreery.[107] Herr's defenses

were in considerable depth to protect Bologna from an attack coming from the southeast. They were based upon a series of river lines, beginning with the Senio, then the Santerno, the Sillaro, a switch position along the Sellustra, and, finally, the so-called Genghis Khan Line, based on the Idice River and anchored in the east in the flooded plain west of the Comacchio Lagoon.[108]

While the soldiers of the 10th Mountain were enjoying their well-deserved rest, plans were being finalized for the culminating offensive against the Axis powers in Italy. As Field Marshal Harold Alexander, now supreme Allied commander in the Mediterranean, would report after the war,

We were no longer thinking merely of the capture of Bologna, nor, indeed of any objective on the ground, but of more wide-sweeping movement which would encircle as many of the Germans as possible between the converging blows of the two armies.[109]

One reason for this focus on entrapping as many enemy as possible, as reported by Gen. Clark (now 15th Army Group commander), was that by the spring of 1945, word began to reach the

---

* Reported numbers of German divisions vary. The number thirty cited here is from Gen. Clark's memoir, *Calculated Risk*. Jackson estimates the number of divisions as twenty-three (see W. G. F. Jackson, *The Battle for Italy*, table 9, page 343), while Fisher puts the number at twenty-six (see *Cassino to the Alps*, page 441).

Allies of a "Southern Redoubt," or as Fisher calls it, a "National Redoubt,"[110] into which "Hitler and the survivors of his legions might fall back into an Alpine defense zone extending from Salzburg and Klagenfurt in the east to the Swiss frontier in the west,"[111] and in this "vast mountain stronghold they might hold out indefinitely."[112] Although British intelligence "remained skeptical of the redoubt's existence," as Fisher points out, "No commander could afford to ignore the possibility."[113] To prevent this, Gen. Clark observed, "The task of the Allied armies in Italy was clear: destroy the enemy armies in the Po Valley before they could withdraw to the Alps and prolong the war."[114]

The 15th Army Group's Spring Offensive would be known as Operation Grapeshot.[115] Under Gen. Clark's plan as announced on March 18, 1945, with "detailed orders" following on March 24, this would be accomplished in three phases: The first phase would consist of a diversionary attack by Eighth Army in the east—Operation Buckland—crossing the Senio and then establishing bridgeheads over the Santerno, during which they would have priority for air support; once Eighth Army was across the Santerno, Fifth Army would launch Operation Craftsman—15th Army Group's main effort —penetrating into the Po Valley to either "capture or isolate Bologna," at the discretion of the Fifth Army commander, Gen. Truscott, with the "emphasis . . . on encircling major enemy forces south of the Po" River.[116] This would mark the commencement of Phase II, which "envisioned a breakthrough by either or both armies to encircle German forces south of the Po, Eighth Army blocking the enemy at Ferrara and Bondera and Fifth Army joining it at either of these two towns."[117] In the third phase, the 15th Army Group would cross the Po River and engage enemy forces at the Adige River, which, it was hoped, would not be strongly defended given that a large portion of the enemy's force would have been trapped and cut off between the pincers of the two Allied armies.[118]

Both sides made good use of the comparative calm in Italy during the winter of 1944–45. For their part, "the enemy had fortified his positions in his usual diligent fashion," purposely inundating swaths of land to obstruct the movement of mechanized forces and constructing a series of defensive lines through northern Italy back to the Alps.[119] But the Allies had profited from the relative pause too. "The winter halt had improved the Allied situation in Italy," Brooks observes. "Battle-worn divisions were rested and restored, replenished and reinforced, and their morale was high."[120] The Allies dominated the skies and outnumbered the Germans by a two-to-one ratio in artillery and three to one in armored vehicles; Fifth Army enjoyed a 7,000-man "overage" in its maneuver divisions and had on hand "21,000 officers and enlisted replacements, 2,000 black soldiers for the 92nd Division, 5,000 for the Brazilian Expeditionary Force and 1,200 Nissei for the Japanese-American 442nd Infantry Regiment," not to mention 50,000 well-supplied and well-supported partisans operating behind German lines.[121] The 15th Army Group was ready to resume the offensive.

Before executing Operation Grapeshot on April 9, 1945 (it had originally been planned for April 10 but was accelerated by a day),[122] 15th Army Group executed some preliminary operations. Eighth Army would carry out commando operations on Lake Comacchio from April 1 to 7, 1945.[123] These attacks aimed at small bits of territory on Lake Comacchio on the Adriatic coast. In Operation Roast, British commandos crossed the lake by boat to seize the spit that separated Lake Comacchio from the Adriatic Sea, the object being "to deny the enemy the opportunity to observe Eighth Army's right flank," while other commandos captured islands in the lake.[124] In the Fifth Army sector from April 5 to 10, 1945, elements of the 92nd Division would attack on the Italian west coast to seize the town of Massa and then continue toward the town of La Spezia, where a port and former naval base were located.[125] According to Starr, "It was considered possible, but not probable" that this diversion might goad the Germans into committing some portion of their reserve, consisting of the 29th and 90th Panzer Grenadier Divisions; whether it succeeded in accomplishing this or not, it was hoped that the 92nd Division's attack would tie down the enemy's 148th Grenadier and Italia Bersaglieri Divisions deployed in this sector.[126]

The 442nd Regimental Combat Team was attached to the 92nd for this operation, which attacked with 3rd Battalion and 100th Battalion on the right and 3rd Battalion, 370th Infantry, on the left.[127] The 473rd began the attack initially in division reserve, but after several days of fighting, it was Company B, 473rd Infantry, that first entered Massa itself.[128] From there the 92nd Division pressed on to capture La Spezia, which was entered by a reinforced 92nd Reconnaissance Troop on April 23 and fully occupied the next day.[129]

The Spring Offensive

The Spring Offensive—Operation Grapeshot—began on April 9, 1945, when "Eighth Army launched a powerful, stunning blow from the east coast,"[130] as Gen. Clark writes:

> Rested, revitalized and ready for the kill, the Eighth Army swarmed against the Sernio River line in a drive toward Argenta and Bologna, with V Corps, the Polish Corps, the New Zealanders, and Indian Divisions in the lead. At first the going was steady, but slow, because a fast network of rivers and canals aided the German defense. As the fighting progressed, however, the British 56th Division launched a daring and carefully planned amphibious attack across Lake Comacchio . . . other units landed on the south shore of the lake and still others walked along a narrow bank between the lake and the land which the Germans had flooded. By the 11th, the Senio and Santerno lines had crumbled and Bastia was caught in a pincers from the east and south. In the next two days, heavy fighting and steady progress had broken a third river line—the Sillaro—and the flooded route to Bologna was almost opened.[131]

Fifth Army's Role: Operation Craftsman

Fifth Army would launch Operation Craftsman—"the last great battle of the Fifth Army in Italy"—on April 14, 1945.[132] The II and IV Corps would attack abreast, with the main effort initially in the IV Corps area astride Highway 64, previously cleared of enemy domination by the 10th Mountain Division and the Brazilian Expeditionary Force during the bloody fighting of Operation Encore, thus freeing IV Corps from the necessity of moving along Highway 65 to the west and allowing it to bypass strong enemy defenses to the south of Bologna.[133] The drive to the Alps would be a challenging operation, in part due to the diversity of the terrain over which Fifth Army would fight: initially Fifth Army would have to clear 15 miles of mountains remaining before the Po Valley was reached, presenting "a slugging match all too familiar to the men of the Army."[134] Once through mountains, however, Fifth Army would have to quickly transition to a fast-paced push across flatlands. As Starr observed, "Whereas distances throughout much of the drive up the Peninsula had been measured in yards, distances in the northern part of the country [would be] calculated in scores of miles."[135] Even once Fifth Army broke out into the flatlands, the terrain would continue to present a challenge, however, since the Po River watershed contained numerous rivers—the Po itself and its tributaries—that would impede the Army's advance.[136]

The Fifth Army attack would be organized by lines—Green, Brown, and Black. The 10th Mountain Division would attack in the initial, Green Phase, during which "only IV Corps would attack, sending the Brazilian, 10th Mountain, and 1st Armored Divisions northeast along the ridge west of Highway 64 so as to bring the IV Corps' front up even with that of II Corps," in part to cover II Corps construction of bridges at Vergato and to assist II Corps' attack at Mount Sole.[137] During the Black and Brown Phases, II Corps would join the attack; once Fifth Army forces neared Praduro in the final phase, 1st Armored Division and the 6th South African Armoured Division would be relieved and fall under Fifth Army control as an armored striking force to "push into the Po Valley and seize the Panaro River Line."[138] At this point, "the 10th Mountain Division . . . was to turn due north and drive over the dwindling hills, with the 85th Division under II Corps on its right," while the Brazilian 1st Infantry Division held "their defensive positions, reconnoitered, and prepared to follow up any enemy withdrawals" on Corps orders.[139] As for prospects thereafter, *History of the IV Corps* observes that

> since its arrival at the Arno River, IV Corps had looked forward to the day when it might be designated as the main effort of Fifth Army[,] but after reading the Array plan it was apparent that again this was not to be the case. Despite the secondary part which IV Corps was to play, there was, however, the strong possibility that the situation might develop that would allow the 10th Mountain Division to stop its mountain hopping and strike due north for a break-through into the Po Valley. If this occasion should arise, perhaps the Army Commander might see fit to exploit this advantage and tear wider the gap by directing his main effort there.[140]

10th Mountain Division in Operation Craftsman

The 10th Mountain Division would be the IV Corps' main effort during the opening phase of Operation Craftsman.[141] It would attack along the high ground west of Highway 64, while the BEF secured its left flank and prepared to advance on Corps order, and the 1st Armored Division attacked on the 10th's right at the corps boundary.[142] IV Corps had four battalions of nondivisional armored vehicles available, consisting of two tank destroyer battalions—the 701st and 894th—and two tank battalions—the 751st Tank Battalion and a portion of the 760th Tank Battalion; a portion of this mechanized force would be attached to the 10th Mountain Division during the Phase Line Green attack.[143]

IV Corps went to great lengths to ensure that the 10th Mountain Division was well rested, supplied, and equipped for its upcoming mission. Immediately after the termination of the second phase of Encore on March 5, an extensive program of unit rotation and relief was implemented for the 10th Mountain; to facilitate this, 1st Battalion, 365th Infantry, had been attached to the division to occupy a portion of the line, later replaced first by elements of the BEF and then by the 371st Infantry, which 1/365IN joined.[144] On April 10–11,

elements of the 1st Armored Division relieved elements of the 10th Mountain Division's right flank, and another battalion was relieved on the right flank between April 11 and 13.[145] The result of these movements was that every battalion of the 10th Mountain Division could "have a few days of combined rest and training in a rear area, followed by a period in reserve" prior to the launch of Operation Craftsman, a period of recuperation that the *History of the IV Corps* likened to "the conditioning of a race horse."[146] Other preparations were being made as well. "Special ammunition allocations were received from Army to provide increased artillery fires for the 10th Mountain Division and the BEF," *History of the IV Corps* reports,[147] while "ordnance personnel worked in shifts to repair all ordnance equipment of battalions of the 10th Mountain Division while they were in rest areas," and "vehicles were inspected and those found to be in bad need of repair were replaced."[148] In the month of March, IV Corps received 2,870 replacements, enabling every infantry battalion to be filled above its authorized strength in anticipation of the upcoming attack.[149]

In the IV Corps sector the enemy had concentrated the bulk of his strength opposite the 10th Mountain and the 1st Armored Division from Montese to Vergato, consisting of the 114th Light Division and the 232nd, 94th, and 334th Grenadier Divisions, totaling sixteen line and nine reserve infantry battalions.[150] While not as strongly emplaced as those facing the II Corps, enemy forces in the IV Corps area nonetheless occupied a "strong belt emplacements machine gun nests and bunkers" located in mutually supporting strongpoints on "commanding heights," reinforced with antitank weapons and with machine guns covering all approaches to the summits, and with all high-speed avenues of approach such as creek beds, trails, ravines, and roads being mined; bunkers were reinforced with barbed wire and linked together by communications trenches, and stone houses were used as fortifications.[151] The enemy opposite IV Corps was supported by an estimated 285 artillery pieces, hundreds of mortars, and tanks.[152]

As the date for the kickoff of Operation Craftsman approached, IV Corps was arrayed with the 1st Armored Division on the right flank between the Reno River and the eastern slope of Mount della Spe; the 10th Mountain Division held the center of the corps sector from the 1st Armored Division to just west of Montese, where it met the Brazilian right flank, with the Brazilian Division sector extending nearly to Mount Belvedere, where the 371st and 365th Infantry Regiments held the left:[153]

After the preliminary operations around Massa and Lake Comacchio described above, and following a "stupendous air-artillery preparation," Eighth Army launched Operation Buckland—its portion of Grape-shot—on the night of April 9.[154] Preparation for the launch of Fifth Army's Operation Craftsman was to begin on D+3—April 12, 1945—with a complex program of aerial reconnaissance and bombardment—but this was delayed until April 14 due to weather constraints.[155] Finally, at 0830 on that day, a massive, 40[-]minute[-]long bombing campaign hit the Germans, followed by artillery preparation from 0910—0945; then, at 0945 on April 14, 1945, the 10th Mountain Division attacked— the Spring Offensive was on for Fifth Army.[156]

10th Mountain Division Attacks

As set forth in its Field Order No. 4, dated April 4, 1945, the 10th Mountain Division's scheme of maneuver was to be an attack of two regiments abreast—85th on the left and the 87th on the right—launched from the salient captured in March, with the 86th following in the 87th's wake to "mop up the right half of the objective assigned" to that regiment.[157] The 85th was to "seize occupy and defend" Hills 883, 913, 915, and 909, covering the division's left flank in the 85th's zone while "maintain[ing] contact with the BEF on the left and the 87th Mountain Infantry on the right."[158] The 87th was ordered to "seize, occupy and defend the left (north) of the Division in the zone of action, and prepare to displace, defend and mop up additional

areas to the northeast when passed through by the 86th Mountain Infantry in the attack."[159] The 86th was tasked with "mop[ping] up the area between the 87th Mountain Infantry on the left and the 1st Armored Division on the right," and to "be prepared to attack . . . Casa di Bello and seize, organize and defend these areas."[160] The 10th Mountain Anti-Tank Battalion would be held in reserve during the first phase of the attack.[161]

The 10th Mountain would face new challenges during the initial phase of the offensive. One of these was a flood of refugees. Prior to the commencement of the Spring Offensive, the Germans had issued evacuation orders to clear the civilian population out of the combat zone. An example of these was quoted by George Earle in his *History of the 87th Mountain Infantry, Italy, 1945*:

Your district may become a battle area within the next weeks. In order to save your life and your property, it is in your interest to evacuate this district up to the line of Semalano di Sopramonte, Righetti, Montetorte, and find safety north of this line. . . . The area has to be evacuated by the 5th of April at 1900. *Whoever shall be found in this area after that date will be shot as a spy without challenge.*[162] [emphasis added]

Although this order directed Italians to move north, many chose to go south, bringing into Allied lines "milling herds of cattle, pigs, goats, chickens, horses, and donkeys; and hundreds of Italians with their pitiful collections loaded on all manner of wagons and carts, or being carried on their backs," so that for "days, truckload after truckload of livestock and civilians were shipped to the rear to be handled by [the Allied military government]."[163]

Much-bigger challenges than this faced the division going into the Spring Offensive. One was terrain, as Earle vividly describes:

The difficulties of cracking the initial line cannot be over-emphasized. The first and most obvious difficulty was with terrain. The hills were steeper than any the regiment had fought on. Their sides were lightly wooded with chestnut trees, although in many places were bare, rocky cliffs, outcroppings, and boulders. In places, gentler slopes and tops, fields were cleared and small clusters of farm buildings were built in against the mountain sides. Between the mounts were deep, wooded draws with precipitous sides, difficult to cross. The valleys, although cultivated, were gouged out in a deep network of draws with small fields between them. The location and formation of the band of hills was jumbled and without apparent geographical pattern, so that individual hills and locations were difficult to identify.[164]

Another challenge facing the 10th Mountain was the loss or reduction in the element of surprise, once again illuminatingly articulated by Earle:

In addition to the terrain obstacle, the other difficulty was loss of surprise. The German, this time, knew what was facing him across the line. At Belvedere, the 86th had amazed him by scaling the cliffs; the 87th and 85th confounded him by attacking in the dark. On della Vedetta in March, the German was taken aback by the speed and direction of attack. But what would be the surprise in April? The jump-off salient pointed at his center like an arrow. . . . Therefore the usual advantage of the mountain attack, surprising an enemy when he depended too heavily on natural obstacles, could not be realized. The enemy expected to be attacked right where the attack came. Knowing that the rugged terrain had not yet slowed down the mountain troops, he built up a complete defense with elaborate fire plans.[165]

But the 10th Mountain also had one intangible, yet valuable, advantage in the form of a larger-than-life reputation growing in the minds of their adversaries. When the 10th Mountain Division had begun flowing into Italy at the end of 1945, the Germans might have scoffed at them as "mountain division" in name only. By the time of the Spring Offensive, that had changed. The 10th Mountain had been "the only unit that had been able to punch a hole in his lines all winter,"[166] and that had made an impression, as indicated by what the Germans were telling their own troops, and themselves, about the 10th:

Among the prisoners taken on the first day [of the Spring Offensive] . . . was one who carried a diary. In it was recorded a warning that the 10th Mountain Division was about to attack and would not take prisoners. This sort of enemy propaganda had become customary since Monte Belvedere.[167]

While such hyperbole may have inspired some Germans to "fanatical resistance," it also seems likely that it demoralized many others.[168] It is also clear that however much the German high command may have wanted their own troops to see the men of the 10th Mountain as merciless brutes, on the basis of captured enemy documents, the German command itself took the 10th Mountain very seriously indeed. The enemy knew the men of the 10th Mountain really "were mountain troops," as Earle reports:

He also, rightly or wrongly, believed them to be [a] "hand-picked," "elite corps," made up of, to use his own words, "physically superior soldiers, sports personalities, and young men from wealthy or politically significant American families."[169]*

---

* While not true of every member of the 10th Mountain Division, the German description contains a lot of truth nonetheless, including regarding the manner in which many of them were recruited, the social and economic classes from which many of those early recruits came, and the athletic and physical prowess of many of them, so that it may in truth be said that the men of the 10th Mountain Division of World War II really were an "elite corps" of light infantry.

First Day of the Offensive

On April 14, 1945, following "thirty-five minutes of the most intensive artillery and mortar fires any of [them] had ever seen [against] Hills 909, 883, 913, and 860," as well as incendiary bombs dropped by P-47s,[170*] the 85th Mountain Infantry attacked on the division's left, to the northwest, two battalions abreast, with 3rd Battalion on the left and 2nd Battalion on the right.[171] The 2nd Battalion met comparatively light resistance, but 3rd Battalion, pushing into the Pra del Bianco Basin toward Hill 883 ("actually the Southwest nose of Hill 913"), met stiff resistance.[172] As the battalion crossed the open terrain near Pra del Bianco, it encountered extremely dense and extensive minefields[173] and was engaged by heavy machine gun and mortar fire, forcing the battalion to deploy and assume firing positions, greatly slowing its progress.[174] The 2nd Battalion was soon able to come to its aid, however, seizing Hill 860, from which heavy weapons could engage the enemy in front of 3rd Battalion.[175] Company L reached Hill 854 by 1100 and was moving onto Hill 913 by 1130; a small element of Company L seized the summit of Hill 913 and defended it against strong enemy resistance until relieved by the rest of Companies L and K at 1430, though strong enemy fire continued; the cost of seizing Hill 913 was immense, with Company L reporting only twenty-eight effectives left from the summit.[176] Company I had initially been ordered to attack Hill 883 and reached within 200 yards of it by 1100, but the minefield was so strong and resistance was so fierce that the company was ordered to withdraw, follow Company L to Hill 913, and attack Hill 883 from there.[177] Hill 883 would ultimately be captured by 1st Battalion.[178] Initially, 1st Battalion had been assigned a supporting role, providing fire support to 2nd and 3rd Battalions from positions around Castel d'Aiano, and securing the division's left flank; its mortar platoon fired more than 2,000 rounds, the tubes getting so hot that the propellant charge for one round was ignited by the heat of the tube itself rather than the firing

pin.[179] Finally, Company A, 1st Battalion, reinforced by a platoon of heavy machine guns from Company D, was ordered to seize Hill 883; by that time, the enemy had evacuated and the only opposition Company A faced was deadly and effective sniper fire throughout the night.[180]

The 2nd Battalion, 85th Infantry, attacked at 0945 against Hill 860 on the left, which was easily reached by Company E, and Hill 909 on the right, which was attacked by Company G.[181] Company G's mission would prove to be one of the most important of the day for the division, because on it depended the success of the 87th Mountain Infantry on the right.[182] The 1st Battalion of 87th Infantry was held up by strong resistance in front of Torri Iussi; to break this resistance, Company A 1/87 passed through Company E, 85th, on Hill 860 to strike the enemy in front of the 87th on the flank; the 87th's attack could not be assured of success, however, until Company G occupied Hill 909, thus depriving the enemy of it as a vantage point for observation.[183] By 1155, Company G was at the base of Hill 860 but was enduring a "punishing shelling" by the enemy; within thirty-five minutes the company had nearly reached the summit, which was captured during the afternoon with the assistance of machine gun fire delivered by Company H at long range from Monte della Spe, and with support from Company E; Company F then joined G on the objective.[184] Only a single member of the 85th Mountain Infantry—Pfc. John D. McGrath—would be nominated for the Medal of Honor during the war, and it was for this action, where Pfc. McGrath "personally knocked out three machine gun nests and . . . killed, wounded, and put to route over fifty Germans."[185]

On the division's far right, the 2nd Battalion, 86th Infantry, moved out behind the 87th to capture Hill 868 and Rocco Rocca Roffeno.[186] The battalion captured Hill 868 by 1620,[187**] and Rocca Roffeno by 1648.[188] The battalion then established defensive positions for the night, coordinating with the 87th Infantry on the 86th's left.[189]

* Not without mishap, unfortunately, since two bombs went astray—one hitting the command post of 2nd Battalion, 87th Infantry, and another that set the 85th Mountain Infantry's ammunition dump alight. See Wilson, *History of the First Battalion, 87th Mountain Infantry*, 34; and Earle, *History 87th Mountain Infantry*, 58. Wilson observes that the air support in this instance was under division control and performed better under battalion control.
** Though, as discussed below, this hill would have to be retaken by the 87th later in the day.

In the center, the 87th Mountain Infantry attacked from Mount della Spe,[190] 1st Battalion on the left and 2nd Battalion on the right.[191] In what was to be its "toughest battle of all," 1st Battalion, 87th Infantry, was ordered to seize the town of Torri Iussi and then follow on to seize Hill 903, proceeding in column of companies with Company B in the lead.[192] Company B detailed a platoon to silence enemy machine guns on Hill 860 in support of Company A, which would pass through Company B and attach Torri Iussi.[193] The town was fortified and required "bitter house-to-house fighting" to clear it; from there, Company A was to continue its attack to the regiment's key objective for the day, Hill 903.[194] Company A had begun to ascend Hill 903 on the left, and 2nd Battalion was ordered to bypass Torri Iussi and seize Hill 903, the regimental headquarters apparently being unaware of Company A's progress.[195] The 2nd Battalion gave the mission to Company F, but in the event, the two company commanders—Capt. Klemme of Company A and Capt. Kennett of Company F—met at Torri Iussi and coordinated their attack, seizing Hill 903 together.[196] By nightfall, 1st Battalion had Company A on Hill 903, Company B on Hill 860, and Company C in reserve in Torri Iussi, covering the regiment's left flank; from this position, 1st Battalion prepared for future operations.[197] The 2nd Battalion, 87th Infantry, was ordered to take Mount Pigna upon the securing of Hill 903, but between that objective and Pigna lay Hill 868, occupied by members of German 334th Infantry Division, and from which enemy machine guns had been able to engage the flank and rear of the 87th.[198] Two companies—F and G—were dispatched to deal with Hill 868 at 1900; Company G attacked the Strada, a village on the southern slope of the hill, while Company F advanced along the ridge north of Strada; the hill was taken by Company F.[199] The attack on Mount Pigna was postponed until April 15, at which point the 2nd Battalion established a defensive near Strada.[200]

Continuing the Drive to the Po Valley

The next day, April 15, 1945, 2nd Battalion of 86th Mountain Infantry was tasked with capturing Hill 840.[201] Following a thirty-five-minute artillery preparation, Company E crossed the line of departure, heading in a northeasterly direction at 0710 and encountering a wide array of booby traps, conventional and improvised, along the way.[202] After passing through Lamare and Amore (entered at 0950) en route, Company E occupied Hill 840 by 1207, having captured along the way a German company commander who declared that "all we have left now is our honor, so don't expect me to give any military information";[203] Company E then moved east to take Hill 860.[204] Company G took Hill 775 at 1650.[205] Company F, which had originally been tasked with taking Hill 787, was diverted en route to Hill 804.[206]* At 0640 a preparatory fire began, including artillery, tanks, and tank destroyers, and at 0700, 2nd Battalion of 87th Mountain Infantry crossed the line of departure for its attack on Mount Pigna, delayed from the night before; the mountain was taken by 0810.[207] From there, 1st Battalion of 87th Mountain Infantry moved against and captured Mount Le Coste,[208] while 2nd Battalion attacked and seized Mount Croci by dark.[209]**

From April 16 through 18, the 85th Mountain Infantry was given the task of securing the division rear area, while the 86th and 87th Regiments continued the advance in a cycle of "hurried pursuit of the enemy punctuated with strong but temporary resistance."[210] On April 16, 2nd Battalion of 87th Mountain Infantry seized Mount Croce (not to be confused with Croci of the day prior) at 1305; the 3rd Battalion, 87th, then continued the attack toward Mount Mosca, with the mission of seizing the high ground between Mounts Croce and Mosca to facilitate a further attack to the north by 3rd Battalion, 86th Mountain Infantry.[211] Mount Mosca was finally taken after a laborious fight against a tenacious enemy along the ridgeline, at 1415, but it took until 1600 to clear all resistance from the

---

* There is a discrepancy among various sources on the date upon which this action occurred. Wellborn reports this action as having taken place on April 14; however, Lockwood (*Mountaineers*), Brooks (*The War North of Rome, June 1944–May 1945*), and the *Combat History*, taken together, seem to indicate it occurred on April 15.
** Here again is a discrepancy among between sources: Lockwood states that 3rd Battalion, 87th Mountain Infantry, aided in the attack on Mount Croci (Lockwood, *Mountaineers*, 30), while the *Combat History* states that it joined in the attack on Mount Le Coste (*Combat History*, 50).

area.[212] The enemy then attempted a series of ten counterattacks by infiltration, all of which failed.[213] The 2/87 then proceeded to exploit the gains thus secured by attacking toward Tolè, which lay 4 miles northeast of Mount della Spe.[214] The capture of Tolè secured the rear of the 86th Mountain Infantry.[215] At 0800, Maj. Gen. Hays "ordered the regiment to attack as soon as possible, since the 87th had surprised elements of the 94th Division and was now on that unit's flank. The 86th was ordered to attack if possible before the enemy could bring up reserves."[216] The regiment crossed the line of departure at about 1115.[217] It encountered serious resistance by enemy infantry, two self-propelled 88 mm guns, and a tank near Checkpoints #29 and #30 (Monzuno), which was silenced by friendly air support; the advance continued and Checkpoint #29 was captured at 1750, while Monzuno fell to 3rd Battalion of the 86th at 1945 hours.[218] Tanks and tank destroyers had provided valuable assistance to the infantry in capturing Checkpoint # 30 by providing support from firing positions in the vicinity of Checkpoint #29.[219]

The attack continued on April 17, with the 87th Mountain Infantry capturing Mount Ferra at 1905 and Mount S. Prospero at 2105.[220] By this point the division had advanced into an area of good roads and less challenging terrain, so that armored vehicles could advance with the infantry and even transport ground troops; direct fire from tanks provided valuable assistance to Company F, 87th Infantry, in the capture of Mount Ferra.[221] At the same time, the increasing pace of the advance required the division artillery to displace forward to keep the leading elements of the division within supporting range.[222] The 86th Mountain Infantry also continued its attack this day, crossing the line of departure at 0730 and capturing the town of Montepastore by 0945, with 2nd Battalion passing through the town toward Bianello and 3rd Battalion bypassing it and moving toward Checkpoint #35, Mount Moscoso, capturing it by 0845; by 1800, 2nd Battalion had captured Mount Tramonico and Pgio Castelanso.[223]

The 86th and 87th Regiments continued the attack on April 18, with the 3rd Battalion, 86th, crossing the line of departure at 0930, supported

by tanks, taking Sulmonte at 1245 against light resistance and continuing the advance to Hill 487 by 1830; at the same time, 2nd and 3rd Battalions met stronger resistance from enemy dug in on higher ground.[224] The 87th Mountain Infantry was delayed in resuming the attack until late morning, when the 85th Regiment had completed its relief of the 87th; the 87th then advanced in a column of battalions, with 1st Battalion in the lead, 2nd in the center, and 3rd in the rear.[225] The 3rd Battalion, 87th Infantry, was ordered to clear as far north as the Samoggia River, reaching the high ground above Savigno, situated on the river, by 1100; 1st Battalion captured Merlano and advanced toward Mongiorgio and Sulmonte.[226] The BEF relieved the 85th Mountain Infantry on this day, freeing that regiment up for further operations.[227]

April 19 was an important day since it set the stage for the final breakout into the Po Valley. The 85th Mountain Infantry resumed the offensive, conducting a passage of lines with the 87th and attacking into the Lavino River valley, turning the left flank of the German 90th Panzer Division against strong resistance and artillery support, which was silenced by friendly counterbattery fire.[228] The 87th Infantry resumed the advance it had begun the day before: 1st Battalion, 87th Mountain Infantry, resumed the offensive against Mongiorgio and supported the British 178th Medium Royal Artillery; the German defense of the town was strong, and the 87th was required to fight house to house before the town was finally secured.[229] The 3/87 captured Sylvestri, Il Piggio, and, after overcoming a strong delaying action, San Pietrio and Paldi Musico, and Mount Avezzano by the end of the day.[230]

By the end of day on April 19, 1945, the 10th Mountain Division had reached the very edge of the Po Valley; "By evening," Theodore Lockwood writes, "the 85th held the last ridge of the Apennine Mountains. There were no more mountains. The enemy had lost control of the Apennines entirely."[231]

Events had proceeded apace elsewhere across Italy. The Eighth Army had attacked on April 9, following a "terrific bombardment"[232] by 825 heavy, 234 medium, and 740 fighter bombers.[233] At 1920 the Eighth Army's Polish Corps and V

Corps attacked at 1920 to cross the Senio River, supported by 975 artillery pieces.[234] By the end of the day on the tenth, the Eighth Army had penetrated 2 miles across the Senio on a 15-mile front.[235] On the eleventh, New Zealand Forces crossed the Santerno, and Eighth Army forces began LTV-borne* amphibious crossings of flooded areas south of Lake Camaccio.[236] The LTV was a lightly armed and armored, tracked, amphibious vehicle propelled by tracks both on land and water, capable of negotiating muddy riverbanks. It had been developed in the United States for use in the Florida Everglades, before being adapted for military use by the US Marine Corps and deployed in the Pacific.[237] Known as the Buffalo elsewhere in Europe, the LTV was code-named "Fantail" in Italy as a deception effort to conceal their presence in that theater from the Germans.[238] Eighth Army continued the advance on April 12, with three divisions securing bridges over the Santerno.[239] Progress continued, but slowly, on April 13 and 14, as New Zealand troops crossed the Sillaro River, subsequently holding their bridgehead against enemy counterattacks.[240] On April 15, two Eighth Army Corps—XIII and 2 Polish—established bridgeheads across the Sillaro River on a wide front, with the Poles repelling strong counterattacks, capturing Bastia.[241] Eighth Army continued its attack across the Sillaro River on the sixteenth, as the 11th and 169th Brigades reached the Marina Canal and put forward elements across it; the town of Argenta was surrounded.[242] Eighth Army pushed the enemy back to defenses on the Gaiana River and the Quaderna Canal on April 17; on the eighteenth, the Indian 10th Division approached the Idice River, while the New Zealand Division crossed the Gaiana River and pushed the 9th New Zealand Brigade and the 43rd Indian Lorried (Motorized) Infantry Brigade to the Quaderna River.[243] On the nineteenth the New Zealand Division crossed the Quaderna, overran Budrio, and pressed 1 mile across the Idice River; the 10th Indian Division finally reached the Idice and crossed it on the twentieth, pushing 2 miles inland on the twenty-first.[244] Polish troops crossed the Idice on the

twentieth and entered Bologna on the twenty-first, linking up with Fifth Army units there that had entered the city from the south.[245]

While the 10th Mountain Division had been fighting its way across the Apennines, troops had been active elsewhere in the Fifth Army area, both within the II and IV Corps. II Corps began its attack on April 14, following a massive aerial preparatory bombardment by 830 heavy bombers, 258 medium bombers, and 120 fighter bombers; the aerial bombardment continued the next day and was followed by II Corps' first ground attacks, consisting of an intense artillery bombardment at 2230.[246] Thirty minutes later, the US 88th Infantry Division and the South African 6th Armoured Division attacked, followed at 0300 on the sixteenth by the US 91st and 34th Divisions, supported on their right by the Italian Legnano Group.[247] By daylight on April 16, the South Africans had taken Mount Sole, east of Highway 64; nearby were two critical objectives—Monterumici and Mount Adone, which had for months been used as observation points by the Germans from which to call down artillery fire as they observed Allied movements.[248] The operation to clear the enemy off these features began on April 16, with yet another complex aerial bombardment by fighters and medium and heavy bombers against Mount Adone.[249] The 88th Division captured Monterumici on April 17, and the 91st Division captured Mount Adone on the eighteenth.[250] On April 19, the 88th Division shifted to the left of the 6th South African Armoured Division, and both units attacked down the Reno River valley, each pushing elements across the river that day, while the 91st Division assumed the 88th's former sector.[251] The 34th Division then captured the Cevizzano and Gargognano Ridges, which controlled the Idice River valley after a bitter fight.[252]

In the IV Corps area, 1st Armored Division was given the task of clearing Highway 64 on the west of the Reno River—an important task, given that this once-secondary highway would serve as the main supply route for the Fifth Army in the Po Valley.[253] Its units began to advance in the

* Landing Vehicle, Tracked.

late afternoon of April 14, with the 81st Cavalry Reconnaissance Squadron attacking toward Vergato at 1750.[254] Securing Vergato would be a bitter house-to-house struggle that would drag on from the evening of the fourteenth to the morning of the sixteenth.[255] The 81st would then push on to the village of Africa and continue the advance 5 miles along Highway 64 by the seventeenth.[256] Meanwhile, 1st Armored Division's main effort was along the hills overlooking Highway 64 on the left,[257] capturing Suzzano on April 15 with the 14th Armored Infantry Battalion, supported by the 13th Tank Battalion, with the 11th Armored Infantry Battalion following.[258] The division would push 8 miles to Phase Line Brown by April 17.[259] The 14th Armored Infantry Battalion then occupied Mount Pero to the east on April 16, while the 6th and 11th Armored advanced toward Mount Mosca (recently captured by the 10th Mountain), and thence on the seventeenth to Mount d'Avigo (6th Armored Infantry) and Mount Milano (11th Armored Infantry).[260] On April 16 and 17, the 85th Division was called up from Army reserve and committed to the IV Corps sector, relieving the 1st Armored Division and assuming the right-hand portion of the 10th Mountain Division's sector, completing these reliefs on the eighteenth.[261] The 1st Armored Division was ordered to concentrate in the vicinity of Tolè preparatory to future operations, behind the 10th Mountain Division.[262] While it had always been planned to bring the 85th Division forward in this manner, it had originally been envisioned that the 85th Division would operate under II Corps control; given the hard fight facing the II Corps on Highway 65 and the strong momentum of the IV Corps at that time, the decision was made that "the momentum of the IV Corps could best be maintained by a unified command in its fight on Highway 65."[263] The 85th Division was assigned a narrow sector initially, but the Fifth Army commander, Gen. Truscott, soon ordered it to send a force to cut across the front of II Corps' 88th and 6th South African Armored Divisions to seize the Bologna suburb of Casalecchio, cutting off the enemy retreat along Highway 64; the 85th reached the town on April 19.[264] Although the 85th Division elements

encountered a sharp fight a mile west of Casalecchio, the division suffered only eighty-eight casualties from April 18 to 20.[265]

At this point, Fifth Army was poised to achieve a major milestone—the long-anticipated breakout into the Po Valley. Writing after the war in 1948, Fifth Army historian Chester Starr summed up the situation as it stood on April 20, 1945, thus:

> At dark on the 20th IV Corps had three divisions coming out of the hills and onto the plain, the 85th Division just west of Bologna, the 10th Mountain Division about Ponte Samoggia, and the 1st Armored Division south thereof. The advance so far had been speedy for hill fighting; ahead lay possibilities of even swifter maneuver. Through the gap which had been opened up by the 10th Mountain Division and kept open by the units on its flanks, our troops might dash to the Po. The fact that II Corps had smashed through the defenses south of Bologna meant that the pursuit of the retreating enemy would take place on a large scale with all the major forces of the Fifth Army involved in the coordinated but flexible push.[266]

Breakout into the Po Valley

At the beginning of the final drive across the Apennines to break out into the Po Valley, IV Corps fretted that it had yet again been allocated the role of a supporting effort. But events had dictated a change of plan, and by virtue of the rapidity of the 10th Mountain Division's advance across the mountains, IV Corps had become, in effect, the main effort. By the end of the day on April 19, 1945, the 10th Mountain Division's 85th Mountain Infantry Regiment sat atop the "last ridge" of the Apennines.[267] The next day—April 20—would be a momentous one for the Allied forces fighting in Italy. This final drive to the Po Valley had been hard fought and expensive, costing the Division 401 wounded and eighty-four killed in action.[268] But this sacrifice had brought the war in Italy to a decisive point and to a change in the nature of the ground over which the 10th Mountain would fight. It would now leave the mountains and push out into fighting on flatlands, as the division had trained for at Camp Swift. As the 15th Army Group would later report,

> The 20th was the day on which the approaching victory first appeared clearly in the distance. For days the Fifth Army had been fighting over rugged, heavily mined, strongly fortified terrain west and south of Bologna. On the 17th and 18th, Mt. Adone and Mt. Rumici, dominating the approaches to the city, had been taken by the 91st and 88th Divisions. Then, on the 20th, the 10th Mountain Division and the 1st Armored cut Highway 9 between Bologna and Mode; and the 85th Division . . . cut it again.[269]

On April 20, 1945, the 10th Mountain Division became the first US unit to break out of the Apennines and penetrate the Po Valley, "increas[ing] the speed of advance by putting the infantry aboard tanks, jeeps and trucks as it debouched into" the valley after a week of continuous offensive action.[270] The division attacked three regiments abreast, aiming for Ponte Samoggia, at the intersection of the Samoggia River and Highway 9.[271] The 86th Mountain Infantry would attack in the center, the 85th would attack on the division's right flank, and the 87th Mountain Infantry would attack on the left.[272]

At 1:15 in the morning on April 20, Maj. Gen. Hays ordered the 85th Regiment to send a rifle company into the Po Valley "without delay," with the mission of cutting the first highway in the valley to Bologna, thus completing its encirclement.[273] This mission was given to Company A under Lt. Coggins, whose 3rd Platoon would be the first element of the 10th Mountain Division to enter the Po Valley, at 8:30 a.m. in the vicinity of Viacava, his mission being accomplished by 0900.[274] The main body of the regiment crossed the line of departure at 0730, forcing back an enemy delaying action on the division's right.[275] The 1st and 2nd Battalions of the 85th seized road junctions and set up roadblocks in the valley throughout the day, with "the entire Regiment . . . several thousand

yards within the Po Valley" by dark; the 85th had linked up with the 86th Infantry by 2100 and reached Highway 9 by midnight.[276]

Although the 85th was the first regiment of the 10th Mountain Division to enter the Po Valley, the most successful push of the day was by the 86th Regiment in the division's center. Preparation for the final push had begun by April 19, when the 86th was rested for the planned attack into the Po Valley on April 20; the transition away from mountain to flatland fighting had begun by this point, when the regiment was equipped with trucks to make it a "mobile reserve for the division," while the mules, heretofore completely indispensable, "having outlived their usefulness, were sent to the rear."[277] By 1500 on April 19, the 86th received its orders for the April 20 drive into the Po Valley: the 86th would move to the left flank of the 85th Mountain Infantry and attack in a northwesterly direction to cut Highway 9; 1st and 3rd Battalions, abreast with the 2nd Battalion in reserve, echeloned to the right behind 1st Battalion.[278]

The 86th began its preparatory movement at 1800 on the nineteenth, bivouacking for the night shortly after 2100.[279] The battalion commanders received their final instructions at 0300 on April 20; the regiment would conduct a passage of lines through the 85th Mountain Infantry and attack due north, with the 1st Battalion on the right and 3rd Battalion on the left as planned, and each battalion receiving a battalion of tank destroyers and a battalion of tanks in direct support.[280] The 86th Regiment's attack, initially set to begin at 0700 on the twentieth, started at 0830 with Ponte Samoggia as its objective, the start having been delayed to give the troops the chance of a little rest.[281] Companies A and C captured road junctions by 0900, and the lead elements of 1st Battalion penetrated the valley at 1050.[282]* The 3rd Battalion crossed the line of departure as scheduled and advanced 1,300 yards in thirty minutes, unopposed, while 2nd Battalion followed in 1st Battalion's wake.[283] Throughout the attack, infantry would race forward to seize and hold key intersections until armor support arrived, and the process would repeat itself.[284] The 1st Battalion cut Highway 9—the main supply

---

* Wellborn writes that "the 1st Battalion moved into the valley at noon." Wellborn, *History of the 86th Mountain Infantry in Italy*, 39.

route for German forces in Bologna—at 1500,[*] with Company A reaching Martignone by 1634; by 1530, 3rd Battalion had cut Highway 9 as well.[285] The entire regiment, three battalions on line, was just south of Highway 9 by 1900, and 3rd Battalion captured the regimental objective, Ponte Samoggia, by 2000.[286] The 86th Mountain Infantry Regiment "advance[d] . . . like wildfire" into the Po Valley on April 20.[287] Resistance on the valley floor was light, and "whenever [the 86th] did meet small pockets of resistance they immediately wiped out the Germans with the aid of supporting armor,"[288] which often served as transportation for the infantry as they raced ahead.[289] Quite understandably, "the doughboys had taken a great liking to these moving cannons" by the time the day was over.[290] "The magnitude of the breakthrough was difficult to comprehend," Wellborn notes:

The enemy line had been wrecked. After the first stages of the attack there had been little opposition. The 1st Battalion had advanced 13 miles in 5 hours. Companies A and B had each taken 85 prisoners, besides field guns and truckloads of equipment. . . . During the day, the 3rd Battalion had hit nothing more formidable than occasional enemy artillery . . . Company K alone had taken 138 prisoners and four field guns.[291]

The swiftness of the 86th Mountain Infantry's advance completely overwhelmed and devastated the defending Germans, both morally and physically, as Wellborn further recounts:

Germans, left behind in the rush to retreat, were eager to surrender. Pfc. Raymond Alpert of Company B started back to the division stockade with one prisoner and ended up with sixteen. The others "just accumulated" as he walked along. One prisoner who spoke English was quite willing to talk. He had been with an artillery outfit. When the Yanks broke into the valley,

the German artillerymen were told they were now infantry. They were taken completely by surprise, amazed at the rapidity of the American advance."[92]

The local Italians, by contrast, exhibited a markedly different attitude, cheering the American GIs at every crossroads, throwing flowers, giving them gifts of "wine, eggs, milk, and bread."[293] By the time the 86th Mountain Infantry stopped for the night, 3rd Battalion was hunkered down in a defense at Ponte Samoggia, and the other two battalions occupied Highway 9 from the Samoggia river crossing to a point 3 miles away to the southeast.[294]

In contrast to the rapid advance of the 86th and 85th Regiments on the division's center and right flank, respectively, the 87th Mountain Infantry faced stiff resistance from the 90th Panzer Grenadier Division opposing them throughout the twentieth.[295] The 87th received its orders for the day at 0100, which directed that "87th Mt. Inf will continue mission of mopping up previously designated areas."[296] More specifically, 2nd Battalion was ordered, not later than 0800 on April 20, to "advance north to Pradalbino and continue north mopping up on a broad front to a position south of the main road (Route No. 9) through Crespellano," and there establish a defensive position as the division reserve, while 1st and 3rd Battalions were to rest in place and await orders.[297] Company G of 2nd Battalion was ordered to seize the town of Tomba in order to secure the battalion's right flank; it departed on its attack at 0645 and attacked with three platoons, 3rd Platoon fixing the entrance to the town while 1st and 3rd Platoons moved against the flanks. Both platoons succeeded in penetrating the town, against resistance, and prisoners were taken, despite the company taking the heaviest artillery barrage it had ever received, the shock of the concussion dazing many men.[298] By 1130, 2nd Battalion was taking heavy mortar and artillery fire, hampering its advance.[299] Before Company G could complete the capture of the town, however, the rapid progress being made by the other regiments into the valley caused Maj. Gen. Hays to order the 87th to expedite

---

[*] Lockwood states that Company A, 1st Battalion, 86th Infantry, cut Highway 9 at 1430. Lockwood, *Mountaineers*, 37.

its movement toward the valley, and at 1500, Company G was told to break contact with the enemy in Tomba, bypass the town, and move toward the valley.[300] The 2nd Battalion was to bypass Mount Avezzano, which it accomplished by 1135, and attack Pradalbino;[301] in support of this, Company E was to traverse Mount Avezzano and attack C. Marchese.[302] However, when they reached the town, only five American artillery rounds were fired at it instead of the eight-minute planned barrage; although the company engaged the enemy in the town with direct fire, an attack was not feasible without a stronger preparatory barrage than a meager five rounds. While awaiting further support, Company G received word that Company F had captured Pradalbino and was ordered to bypass C. Marchese and rendezvous with the battalion at Pradalbino, which they did by 1800.[303] The battalion resumed its advance toward the Po Valley at 1830, with Company G reaching C. Vazuolo by 2030, where it stopped for the night.[304] Company F, as previously noted, had been given the primary task of capturing Pradalbino, which they reached at 1430 with limited resistance, and at 1600, Company F was ordered forward to establish a roadblock at Muffa in Po Valley, but strong resistance prevented the company not merely from reaching Muffa, but from even consolidating during daylight; only after dark was the company able to reassemble.[305] Company F was treated to a remarkable sight from its forced perch in the hills, however, as Earle reports: "From the high ground could be seen the enemy retreating out of the mountains and out on the plain columns of 10th Division troops were visible."[306]

The 3rd Battalion, 87th Infantry, set up a defensive perimeter near Martignone, "on the last gentle slope" before the valley floor, while 2nd Battalion set up on that same "last slope" farther west; 1st Battalion set up its defense for the night in the Po Valley itself, "out on the strangely flat valley floor," which it had reached by 2310.[307] Although the 87th had not penetrated as deep into the valley as the other two battalions of the regiment had, its fight on April 20 was important nonetheless, by covering the left flank of the 86th as it made its brilliant thrust out onto the valley floor.[308]

Pursuit in the Flatlands

By the end of the day on April 20, 1945, three divisions of the IV had penetrated through the Apennines and reached the floor of the Po Valley—the 85th Division, the 10th Mountain Division, and the 1st Armored Division south thereof, with even more rapid movement ahead in prospect.[309]

On April 19, 1945, as the Fifth Army was securing its Operation Craftsman Phase Line Black objectives and contemplating a debouchment out into the Po Valley, Fifth Army issued Operations Instructions No. 9, which would spell out in broad outline of operations in the immediate future: Fifth Army would continue to press the attack, with the goals of capturing or cutting off Bologna and destroying the German army south of the Po River; IV Corps' particular tasks were to advance to the Panaro and seize the river line west of Camposanto; be prepared to cross the Panaro, proceed to the Po River, and seize to Ostiglia-Borgoforte line; and provide one infantry regiment to be held by Fifth Army in reserve.[310] Gen. Truscott's concept of how he expected the tactical units of Fifth Army to proceed was made clear in a directive that he issued both to corps and division commanders on April 21, as reported by the *History of the IV Corps*:

At 1110, 21 April, the Army commander sent a directive to Corps and Division Commanders stating that a strong pursuit was indicated and a maximum use of transportation would be made; artillery and tanks were to carry infantry, and organic transportation on good roads would be loaded to capacity. When any opportunities came to pursue or cut off the enemy, unit commanders would utilize every possible means of getting fighting personnel, guns, and ammunition forward. The emphasis was placed on speed and more speed; for the first time in the Italian campaign we had an enemy falling back over terrain suitable for swift pursuit. The Germans were short of vehicles and gasoline and as a result they were retreating slowly across an open valley with a superb network of roads and they had to cross the unfordable Po River. The slow, persistent tempo of mountain fighting was to be transformed into a headlong dash to reach the Po in order to pick off the Heinies as the tried to cross.[311]

Task Force Duff

The IV Corps commander, Gen. Willis Crittenberger, issued orders for the pursuit across the Po Valley on April 20, 1945. The scheme of maneuver was simple and straightforward: the IV Corps would attack with 1st Armored Division on the left of the corps' main body, the reinforced 10th Mountain in the center, and the 85th Division (less one regiment) on the right; on the far left coastal sector, two regiments—the 365th and 371st Infantry—would pursue the retreating enemy; and to 1st Armored Division's west, the 1st Infantry Division, Brazilian Expeditionary Force, was to "was to reconnoiter aggressively and to follow anew withdrawals."[312]

To implement his higher commander's intent and to carry out the 10th Mountain Division's role in the pursuit, at Maj. Gen. Hays's direction the division issued Field Message No. 16 at 0200 on April 21, directing the creation of Task Force Duff under the command of the 10th Mountain Division assistant division commander, Brig. Gen. Robinson E. Duff.[313] The "hard-hitting fast-moving" TF Duff would consist of 2nd Battalion, 86th Mountain Infantry Regiment; Company D, 751st Tank Battalion; Company B, 126th Engineers; one platoon of Tank Destroyers from the 701st Tank Destroyer Battalion; the 91st Armored Reconnaissance Squadron;[314] a signal platoon; and 1st Battalion, 87th Mountain Infantry, in reserve.[315] TF Duff's mission would be to advance by vehicle to Bomporto and secure the crossing over the Panaro River, 13 miles from Ponte Samoggia.[316] It was critically important that TF Duff reach and seize its objective rapidly, since the Panaro was deemed unfordable and failure to secure a crossing would be a great impediment to reaching the Po River and cutting off the enemy retreat there.[317]

TF Duff crossed the line of departure at Ponte Samoggia at 0630, with the armored-forces column advancing with "lightning speed," destroying small pockets of resistance as encountered.[318] The advance continued throughout the day; although towns were bypassed whenever possible, scattered enemy left behind continued to harass our forces along the route of march.[319] Communication was a challenge throughout the attack as the mobile column, deprived of wire communications by the rate of advance, had to rely entirely on radio, which was not always reliable, and the task force was often out of contact with higher headquarters.[320] The handling of prisoners proved an interesting challenge, since the advancing task force could spare neither the men nor the time to escort them to the rear; instead, the prisoners were ordered to simply march along the road toward the American rear in parallel to the advancing column, to be picked up later by follow-on forces advancing in Task Force Duff's wake.[321] Task Force Duff secured the bridge at Bomporto by 1600, taking sixty prisoners who were sent to the rear.[322] Upon arrival, the bridge was found to be wired for demolition. Since it was vital that the bridge be taken intact, the 126th Engineers immediately began the task of disarming the charges; the Germans, for their part, gave the task force the parting gift of an artillery barrage of more than half an hour's duration.[323]

The rest of the 10th Mountain Division would catch up with Task Force Duff at the Bomporto Bridge by midnight, but there would be little rest for anyone; on corps orders, Maj. Gen. Hays ordered Task Force Duff to move 25 miles the next day, April 22, to attack and seize San Benedetto Po on the south bank of the Po River.[324] The advance to the town is described in *History of the IV Corps*:

At dawn on the 22d of April, the Task Force once again moved out with tanks and tank destroyers leading the column. Shortly after leaving Bomporto the column became divided because of a German bazooka team which had waited in hiding and allowed half of the column to pass before it fired on one of the tanks in the center of the Force. This disorganized the column to some extent, but the infantry wasted no time in detrucking and wiping out the pocket after which the rapid chase continued. The advance was astoundingly swift; save for this one halt mentioned, the column sped almost straight to its objective without interruption.[325]

Task Force Duff secured San Benedetto Po by 1800, and by 2300 the rest of the division had caught up and was at the Po River; the bewildered enemy found here either readily surrendered to the Americans or were rounded up by local Italian partisans and turned over to US forces.[326] Tragically, Brig. Gen. Duff himself was seriously wounded by an antitank mine an hour or so before reaching San Benedetto Po and rendered hors de combat.[327]

The rest of the 10th Mountain Division had been hard at work throughout Brig. Gen. Duff's lightning push to the Po River, following TF Duff's wake and neutralizing the pockets of resistance it had bypassed along the way.[328] "In a struggle to keep up with one of the fastest drives of the war," Imbrie writes, "German trucks, cars, horses, wagons, carts, bicycles, motorcycles, and Italian Fiats [were] pressed into service to ease aching backs and tired feet."[329] Troops of 1st Battalion, 86th Mountain Infantry, "took to the fields and a weird procession travelled cross country," one battalion history records; "Doughboys on captured Kraut horses and abandoned horse-drawn caissons and carts prompted [one officer] to remark 'It looks like Coxey's Army.'"[330]*

A chaotic environment awaited the infantry of the 10th Mountain as they were carried out into the Po Valley in their motley convoys. "Now, we entered the flat plains of the Po," Robert Woody of the 85th writes:

There was little or no resistance. We walked or rode anything we could commandeer—horses, bicycles... We moved day and night, leapfrogging, wading through canals, wobbling through newly plowed fields. We'd stop briefly, dig in. Then the word would come: "Saddle up." We were on the move.[331]

"Wrecked German vehicles, from horse-drawn weapons carriers to half-tracks, were strewn by the roadside," remembered Kenyon Cooke of Company C, 85th Infantry; "Here and there were dead horses and Germans."[332] At 0330 on April 22, Cooke and his company were awakened after two hours of sleep for a "merry chase ... all over the damned place" following up Task Force Duff's advance, and a lot more scenes of carnage, chaos, and tumult."[333] "Every now and then a dead German would be sprawled by the road," Cooke recalls, and "Partisans were riding everywhere in captured cars and trucks—waiving rifles, wearing Italian colors for arm bands. ... People waved and cheered from the streets and villages; large groups of German prisoners sulked in town squares and church yards."[334] On April 22, 3rd Battalion, 85th Mountain Infantry, was ordered to relieve 2/86 as the infantry component of Task Force Duff, linking up with the task force at Bomporto and driving hard toward the Po River, which 3/85 reached at 0545, April 23.[335] Meanwhile Company E, 2/85, was tasked with clearing the enemy out of the town of Carpi, previously bypassed by advancing friendly forces, while the remainder of the battalion continued to Novi, where it stopped for the night; 1st Battalion passed through 2nd Battalion, reaching Camatta on April 23, followed closely by the 2nd Battalion, bringing the regiment to the shores of the Po.[336]

In the 86th Mountain Infantry Regiment, 1st and 3rd Battalions continued their advance as 2nd Battalion moved forward with Task Force Duff. The two battalions were to attack abreast on an azimuth of 350 degrees initially, then 335 degrees, to capture a bridge at Bomporto.[337] The regiment moved out on the attack at approximately 1100, closing the 17-mile gap to Bomporto by 1730, the regimental command post relocating there at 2020.[338] The 3/86 had captured more than 300 prisoners by 1500, sending these back to the rear under guard of the British 337 Artillery Regiment.[339] The 1st Battalion halted at Ravarino for the night

---

* While unfamiliar to contemporary readers, the comparison to Coxey's Army provides a vivid illustration of just what these advancing mountain troops must have looked like on April 21 and 22, 1945. Coxey's "army" was an 1894 protest march on Washington, DC, led by Ohio businessman Jacob Coxey following a massive economic crash the year before. *Smithsonian Magazine* described the march as "a 'ragamuffin pageant' of unemployed workers, spiritualists, women dressed as goddesses, thoroughbred collies and bulldogs . . . waving peace flags and . . . religious banners." Jon Grinspan, "How a Ragtag Band of Reformers Organized the First Protest March on Washington, DC," *Smithsonian Magazine* online, May 1, 2014. See also Donald L. McMurry, *Coxey's Army.*

but would shortly be sent across the Panaro to relieve 2nd Battalion, accomplishing this by 0130 on the twenty-second; 3rd Battalion halted at Casoni.[340] The advance continued on April 22, as the battalions were shuttled forward, intermittently walking and riding.[341] As the regiment moved swiftly forward, large contingents of the enemy were bypassed, resulting in occasional firefights along the route; most amounted to little, but 1st Battalion was hit by a powerful ambush around 1950, when a German force of infantry and tanks struck the convoy at a crossroads, destroying a number of vehicles and scattering the convoy in an encounter lasting four hours.[342] An improvised firing line was formed and many exposed vehicles were successfully extricated before the enemy infantry was driven off by mortars and the tanks withdrew.[343] The regiment halted after a 13-mile push, Company K having captured 20,000 gallons of wine, and all three battalions established defensive positions at Varagna (1st Battalion) and Moglia (2nd and 3rd).[344]

The 87th Mountain Infantry Regiment continued its advance on April 21 and 22 as well, receiving its orders from division at 0400 on April 21; the 87th would move on the division's left flank, led by a platoon of tank destroyers and 3rd Battalion at the head of the column, followed by the regimental headquarters and 1st Battalion supported by tank destroyers, and 2nd Battalion securing the division's flank and rear on the march.[345] As Earle notes, "Even the march cadence was indicated: 104 steps per minute with a fifteen-minute break the first hour, and ten minutes per hour thereafter, so that the troops would not become exhausted by too rapid marching."[346] Minor engagements occurred along 3rd Battalion's march at the head of the column, with companies bypassing those engaged to keep the advance moving and using the fire from tank destroyers to neutralize resistance.[347] At the town of Manzolino, Company I encountered two enemy tanks, soon joined by a third; after a sharp engagement in which the 3rd Battalion suffered a number of casualties,[348] two of the German tanks left the town, while one remained behind, soon abandoned by its crew though undamaged.[349] The supporting tank destroyer crews had

performed abysmally, refusing to engage the enemy tanks for fear of "disclos[ing] their position"; they had been equally shy in the face of the enemy on the approach march.[350] By the time the engagement was over, seven enemy tanks had been spotted and eight Germans captured before the company was ordered to "pull out and bypass."[351] Company L had earlier bypassed I and K and, leading the battalion, been caught unawares by a German artillery field artillery battalion retreating over a bridge at Navicello; the tank destroyers engaged, followed by machine gun fire, and the tank destroyers followed the retreating enemy across the bridge and continued to engage.[352] 1st Platoon of Company L then ambushed another retreating artillery column, killing fifty enemy; tragedy found the men of Company L as well, however, when a captured American plane in German service bombed the company, who had thought it to be a friendly aircraft.[353] A major, four-hour-long engagement involving the entire 3rd Battalion began when Company L reached Bastiglia. Crossing the bridge over the canal running through the town at 2330, the battalion encountered a large body of Germans lounging about, completely unaware that the war had reached their doorstep, so utterly oblivious that they mistook the approaching 3rd Battalion for friendly forces.[354] Company L promptly disabused them of their mistake, and a fierce, chaotic, and dreadfully confusing battle for the town ensued, with firing in all directions.[355] The fight was a seesaw affair in which the Americans would surge forward under the support of tank destroyers, only to be driven back by volleys of *Panzerfaust* (bazooka) fire; the effectiveness of the men of 3/87 was degraded as the killing fatigue of the relentless and rapid race across the Po Valley began to tell, while that of the enemy was equally degraded by the shock and disorganization caused by their having been taken by surprise.[356] Eventually, Company I withdrew from the town at 0330 and bypassed it, moving around to the north and forward toward a bridge over the Secchia River, the regimental objective; at 0400 the companies still fighting for the town were ordered to disengage, pull back over the canal, and bivouac, which was accomplished by 0430, the troops almost dead with exhaustion; Company I, en route to the Secchia, was told to halt for the night.[357] Despite the shocking chaos of this battle, the 3rd Battalion had suffered surprisingly few casualties—three from Company L and one from the battalion headquarters; the Germans, by contrast, had suffered mounds of casualties: "Two and a half truckloads of German dead were carted away in the morning," and 3rd Battalion captured two German 88s and half-tracks.[358]

The 1st Battalion, 87th Mountain Infantry, had a strange encounter of its own as it was held up behind 3rd Battalion during the Battle of Bastiglia. To the amazement of everyone, a freight train came barreling down the train tracks cutting across the battalion column, from which enemy began firing at the men of the 1st Battalion; finally the train itself was fired upon and stopped—literally cutting 1st Battalion in half, until the last four cars were uncoupled and pushed back down the tracks to reopen the road.[359] The 2nd Battalion, for its part, conducted a largely uneventful march on the twenty-first, with only minor enemy contact. On the twenty-second, 1/87 was to be mounted in trucks and follow Task Force Duff, while 2nd and 3rd Battalions would be shuttled on the march by the trucks of the 616th Field Artillery Battalion.[360] The 1st Battalion reached the Po River by midnight, capturing German vehicles and their occupants along the way that blundered into 1st Battalion's column on the march; 2nd Battalion entrucked at 1600 after Company G suffered grievously from four German artillery rounds that landed among them as they finished a meal and prepared to move out; the company marched and rode to Bastiglia, arriving before sunset.[361] The 3rd Battalion, after two false starts earlier in the day, began its march to the Po at 1700; after passing through jubilant celebrations of their arrival at Limidi and Capri, the battalion was picked up by trucks at 2000, before finally stopping at San Benedetto Po; "The trucks roared off in the dust without lights at twenty-five to forty miles per hour," as Earle recalls:

The road was a narrow ribbon of Allied Territory, stretching mile after mile deeper into German terrain; Task Force Duff had led the column; however, there was nothing but enemy on either side of the long procession of vehicles. Step off the road and one was in Kraut land. Occasionally a stray burp gun would fire toward the road to emphasize this, but mostly the Germans hugged their dugouts for the night and surrendered quietly in the morning.[362]

The 87th Mountain Infantry Regiment would play a leading role next day: On April 23, 1945, the 10th Mountain Division would conduct an opposed crossing of the Po River, with the 87th in the lead. The crossing was to be executed by the 126th Engineers and conducted by boat, the necessary equipment—fifty M2 assault boats spaced at 10-yard intervals along the shore—arriving early on the twenty-third; each boat was crewed by three engineers and could carry thirteen infantrymen and were propelled across the river by oar.[363] A pontoon bridge would be built later.[364] The 1st Battalion, 87th Infantry, would be the first element across the Po in this first-ever river crossing by the 10th Mountain Division; the battalion was in position by 0945.[365] During 1st Battalion's crossing, 2nd Battalion would extend the regiment's defensive line to the right, and 3rd Battalion was alerted to be prepared to provide fire support to the crossing elements.[366] Companies A and B moved out onto the water at 1200.[367] The enemy had positioned 20 mm antiaircraft guns and 88s on the river within range and engaged the soldiers on the shore, this being aggravated by the presence of friendly tank destroyers and self-propelled guns nearby, which further attracted enemy fire.[368] During the crossing the enemy would hit the 87th with two one-hour-long barrages, from their 20 mm guns and 88s as well as direct fire from three points along the opposition shore, all of which were effectively silenced by friendly counterfire.[369] While many casualties were suffered on the members of the regiment waiting on the south shore, the troops in the assault boats "miraculously threaded their way through the M.G. [machine gun] bursts and huge splashes caused by the artillery misses," suffering no casualties.[370] The 1st and 3rd Platoons of Company A, 1st Battalion, were the first wave across the river, in four boats, whose occupants were ordered to fix bayonets.[371] "Others had crossed the Po" before, George Earle notes, but these mountain troopers of "the first wave were the first Allied soldiers to *fight* their way across the great river" (emphasis added); the first soldier ashore was reported to have been TSgt. George W. Hur:[372]

> Hitler, himself, was probably notified that American infantrymen were across the Po on the 23rd of April. And where the Mountain Infantry has reached, there no enemy has ever held forth again. The footprints of the 87th on the sandbars, and up the grassy north bank of the Po, were that day marked on the maps of the world.[373]

"The first wave cleaned out snipers, M.G. nests and spiked any big guns," Wilson reports;[374] by 1300, 1st Battalion had reported the beachhead on the north side of the Po secure and that the follow-on elements could safely cross.[375] The 1st Battalion secured its objectives on the north side of the Po by 1500 as the 2nd Battalion followed them across the river, close behind, beginning the process of expanding the bridgehead.[376] The 3/87 then followed, but having difficulty getting the 126th Engineers to return the boats to the south shore, 3/87 had to pilot themselves across and shuttle the boats back on their own.[377] The 87th Mountain Infantry was across the river and in defensive positions by 1745.[378] The 85th Mountain Infantry was hot on their heels, commencing its own crossing east of the 87th at Camatta late in the afternoon of the twenty-third, completing it by 1800.[379] The 3rd Battalion, 85th Mountain Infantry, crossed first, establishing its beachhead by 1830, followed by 1st Battalion at 2000 and 2nd Battalion overnight.[380]

The 86th Mountain Infantry Regiment had closed at San Benedetto Po at 1200 on April 23, and the regimental command post displaced there by 1245, here to serve as the division reserve while the bridgehead was secured on the north side of the Po.[381] The regiment prepared to begin its crossing at 1900, having then been relieved by the 10th Anti-Tank Battalion.[382] Advanced

parties departed at 2000 and 2045 to establish a forward command post, but the battalions did not get across until the morning of the twenty-fourth, with 3rd Battalion leading at 0630, followed by 2nd Battalion at 0830 and 1st Battalion at 1000.[383]

Task Force Darby

April 24, 1945, was spent bringing supplies and equipment across the Po, expanding the beachhead, patrolling aggressively, and, in the case of the 87th Mountain Infantry, receiving enough replacements to bring the regiment to full strength.[384] That afternoon, a new mobile striking element—Task Force Darby—was formed under the command of a former Ranger commander, Col. William O. Darby. Darby had joined the 10th Mountain Division to succeed Brig. Gen. Duff after the latter had been evacuated.[385] Task Force Duff was to rapidly advance on Verona to block Brenner Pass as an escape route for the retreating Germans.[386] Assigned to the task force were the 13th Tank Battalion (detailed to the 10th Mountain Division from the 1st Armored Division); the 86th Mountain Infantry Regiment ("completely motorized, utilizing captured German vehicles"); Company B, 751st Tank Battalion; Company B, 701st Tank Destroyer Battalion; the 605th Field Artillery Battalion; the 1125th Armored Field Artillery Battalion; the 616th Field Artillery Battalion; and parts of the 126th Engineers.[387]

Task Force Darby's start was delayed while bridges capable of supporting armored vehicles were constructed across the Po at San Benedetto.[388] While this was happening, 1st Battalion, 85th Mountain Infantry, set out on foot to clear the road network leading north from the beachhead in preparation for Task Force Darby's movement, and to seize the enemy-held airport at Villafranca.[389] The 1st Battalion set out at 0100 on the twenty-fifth, seizing its initial objective—the town of San Lucia—by 0800; the battalion continued north after an hour's rest, setting up company-sized roadblocks with Companies A and B at road junctions, which constituted the next objective.[390] En route to Villafranca, Company C disposed of another enemy force, and then, at the town, machine gunners of Company D engaged two

German vehicles that had entered the city, found the Americans there, and tried to escape; sixty Germans surrendered and several were killed.[391] Forward elements of 1st Battalion reached the Villafranca Airport by 0945, and the battalion had secured it by 1700.[392] Several enemy vehicles were caught at roadblocks established by 1/85 at the northern end of Villafranca that night; by far the most noteworthy, however, was the prize that literally fell into the battalion's hands at the airport itself, when an enemy aircraft landed in the midst of the Americans occupying the facility.[393] *History of the IV Corps* describes the episode:

A German aviator circled the airfield and landed his Messerschmitt at the Villafranca airfield, thinking it was still in German hands, only to be greeted by the snub nose of a Tommy Gun staring him in the face, held by an American GI who drawled, "Step down, brother[,] this is old[-]home week!"[394]*

The same source succinctly stated the magnitude of the 1st Battalion of 85th Mountain Infantry's accomplishment that day, observing that

the field, although damaged, was not beyond repair. With no assurance of immediate support, these men had marched almost twenty miles, most of that during darkness, through strange country. The daring of this advance was the climax of the entire drive by the Division.[395]

Bridging across the Po sufficient to support armor artillery was complete by about 1200 on April 25,[396] and Task Force Darby moved out after 1612.[397] The task force linked up with the 85th Mountain Infantry at Villafranca that evening, departing from there by 2045 for Verona,[398] reaching it by 0600, with 2nd Battalion, 86th Mountain Infantry, entering the suburbs of the city by 0820; very little enemy contact was had, elements of the 88th Division having entered the

city previously but finding the bridges over the Adige River in the area destroyed or badly damaged.[399] The 2nd and 3rd Battalions, 86th Mountain Infantry, assisted in clearing the town, while 1st Battalion was tasked to cross the Adige River in tandem with armored forces.[400] Companies A and C crossed the river starting at 1100 for the town of Bussolenge, "Co A [riding] in on these battle-wagons," clearing the town by 1645.[401] From Bussolenge, 1st Battalion of 86th Infantry deployed to Fornace with 1/85, and 2/86 was called up from Verona to Bussolenge, while 3/86 remained in Verona until relieved by the 85th Division.[402]

The Battle along Lake Garde

The 87th Mountain Infantry Regiment continued its advance on the April 26. Having had no word on the availability of transportation from the 86th Mountain Infantry, the 87th's regimental commander, David Fowler, "force marched" the regiment across the Adige via the Govornolo Bridge, 2nd Battalion leading, then 1st Battalion, then 3rd Battalion.[403] On the evening of April 26–27, 1945, the 10th Mountain Division was redirected toward a new objective, as described in *A Short History of the 85th Mountain Infantry Regiment*:

Rather than continue as before on the road to Verona and the north, we were to swing sharply to the northwest, heading for Lake Garda and eventually the city of Trento. Thus the last possible escape route of the enemy would be sealed. The various regiments were to alternate as Division spearhead for eight-hour periods, with the relief moving up by motors, and passing through the attacking organization. The 87th started for Lake Garda on the 27th; the 85th was to pass through them that evening and be relieved, in turn, by the 86th Regiment in the early hours of the 28th.[404]

The 87th issued its orders at 0300 on April 27, by radio and telephone; 3rd Battalion would lead

* Sources disagree on the details of the capture of this aircraft. *A Short History of the 85th Mountain Infantry Regiment* describes the plane as a Focke-Wolf Fw 190 and states that "the pilot escaped in the excitement" (page 55); Lockwood agrees that the plane was a Focke-Wolf, but reports that the "bewildered German pilot . . . recalled the scene most vividly. He landed to be greeted and captured by an American sentry." Lockwood, *Mountaineers*, 48.

the column, departing at 0800; 1st and 2nd Battalions would join the march behind 3rd Battalion on the eastern shore of Lake Garda at Lazise.[405] The regiment encountered no effective opposition until the town of Garda, where a strong force of German paratroopers and SS troops with 20 mm, 40 mm, and 88 mm guns in support was lying in wait for the Americans, resisting stubbornly until 1st and 2nd Battalions outflanked the enemy force to the right.[406] The 87th encountered further resistance at Torre de Benaco.[407] The 2nd Battalion, 85th Mountain Infantry, relieved the 87th as spearhead for the division at 2000, moving 18 miles in four hours to the resort town of Malcesine by midnight, stopping there until relieved by the 86th Mountain Infantry at 0200 on April 28; by 0700, 2nd Battalion of the 86th was passing through the 85th, followed by 3rd Battalion, then 1st Battalion.[408] By this point, German resistance was beginning to stiffen. As the 86th advanced along the coastal road on the eastern shore of Lake Garda, the terrain became increasingly challenging, as Brower reports:

> At Navene we found that the shoreline of Italy's largest lake was beginning to get rugged; gray granite cliffs and steep brushy slopes dropped sharply to the black, very deep, rough water, and rose more than seven thousand feet to the snow-covered bordering peaks.[409]

The terrain was becoming so rugged, in fact, that "along the east shore it became increasingly difficult for a highway to cling to the mountainside";[410] so difficult that beginning about a mile north of Navene, the highway passed through a series of six tunnels en route to the towns of Riva and Torbole at the northwestern and northeastern corners of the lake, respectively.[411] It was at these tunnels that the Germans planned to make a stand. A force of regular infantry stiffened by a picked group of SS and paratrooper reinforcements had stayed behind to delay the American advance and buy time for German forces farther north to reorganize their defenses, by blowing portions of the tunnels and covering the exits with infantry and self-propelled guns.[412] "The situation was not a happy one," Brower recalls.

We were committed to attack along Garda's east shore, where the ruggedness of the terrain multiplied the strength of each defending enemy soldier by ten. The highway, our main avenue of approach, was entirely too much an avenue for enemy defensive fires and demolition.[413]

The 2nd Battalion, 86th Mountain Infantry, reached the first of these tunnels at 0845; as they did, the Germans partly demolished the tunnel with the explosives previously prepared for that purpose.[414] "An attempt was made to send Company K around the tunnels on the ridge to the east," Wellborn reports, "but the terrain proved so formidable that progress was extremely difficult and slow."[415] Wishing to avoid a murderous direct attack along the coastal highway, a flanking attack through the mountains was considered but discarded. Notwithstanding the 10th Mountain Division's specialized mountain training, a movement through the heights along Lake Garda's shore would require specialized equipment that the 10th Mountain Division troops did not have with them at the front but rather was likely still in storage back at Naples.[416] Time was another consideration. A single man properly equipped and clothed and without a load could have traversed the route through the heights to Torbole in seventeen hours. But it would take much longer for a battalion to traverse that route—and that would be after the appropriate equipment had been brought forward and mules provided to transport the artillery and other equipment, and then there was the fact that the 10th Mountain had endured many casualties during the campaign, including "too many of the original mountain men."[417] "As in most of the Po campaign," one chronicler of 1/86 recorded, "our movements were so rapid that we were running out of maps faster than they could be supplied and we guessed our way most of the time."[418] It was imperative that this rapid rate of advance be sustained so as to prevent the retreating forces either from regrouping and making a stand in the Po Valley or escaping into the Alps—taking the time necessary to fit out the troops for an Alpine attack was out of the question, So an indirect attack across the adjacent mountains was not a viable option. But whether "through fortune [or] foresight," another option was available: an amphibious assault.[419] During the Po River crossing, a force of DUKWs—"ducks"—had been attached to the division to assist in the crossing and had been carrying loads for the 10th Mountain since.[420] The DUKW was an amphibious hybrid—a six-wheeled, all-wheel-drive truck built on a boat hull that could traverse land or water.[421] At 1235, division directed that the 86th would use these DUKWs to outflank the blown tunnel by water.[422] The attack began at 1410, when Company G took to the water in seven DUKWs, supported by tank destroyers and 105 mm howitzers; the Germans resisted vigorously, firing on the DUKWs with 88 mm guns, sending up 50-foot-tall geysers but destroying no boats.[423] The assault was successful, by-passing tunnels 1 through 3, and by 1530 the first four tunnels had been cleared, but the Germans had destroyed the road between tunnels 4 and 5; the remainder of the regiment would follow by water.[424] They had also rigged tunnel 5 for demolition, but their charges blew prematurely, splashing the enemy soldiers themselves throughout the tunnel and bringing part of the rock roof down, leaving a grisly scene of destruction and gore for the men of the 86th advancing through that tunnel.[425]

The 87th Infantry continued its advance on April 28, although marred by some confusion. Intent on preventing the retreating Germans from reaching the Brenner Pass northeast of Lake Garda, and through it a temporary sanctuary in Austria, on the morning of April 28 the division commander ordered the 86th Mountain Infantry Regiment to dispatch a battalion to cross the ridge near Navene and outflank the town of Torbole, at the northeastern corner of Lake Garda, and he ordered the 87th to send a battalion to take Mori, well to Torbole's east.[426] The 2nd Battalion was then awaiting orders at the northern Verona suburb of Pesina and could proceed by road through Spiazzi to Mori, but there were two concerns: first, the enemy disposition between Pesina, Spiazzi, and Mori was unknown, and, if present in force along this route, the enemy could seriously hamper the 2nd Battalion's movement;

second, and probably more important, were rumors that an important bridge in the vicinity of Spiazzi had been destroyed by the enemy.[427] If true, 2nd Battalion could still reach Mori by crossing the mountain ridge near P. di Naoli, but it would have to leave its motor transport behind; since the regiment's Alpini Mule Pack Company had not rejoined the regiment since it debouched in the Po Valley, the 2nd Battalion would be left without resupply capability.[428] To ameliorate these concerns, Col. Fowler resolved on a two-battalion operation: 2nd Battalion would indeed approach Mori over the ridgeline, but 1st Battalion would ensure on open supply line for the 2nd by clearing through Spiazzi.[429] The 2nd Battalion departed Pesina by truck at 1330, arriving at the trailhead where they would disembark from and move across the ridge at 1700.[430] Just as they commenced their overland march, Col. Fowler received orders to report to the division command post at once, where he was told that the division commander had changed his mind and wanted the 87th's battalions recalled and positioned closer to the northern end of Lake Garda.[431] By this time, however, 2nd Battalion was out of radio communication, and 1st Battalion could not be recalled from its mission until 2nd Battalion was en route back; until confirmation was received that 2nd Battalion had received the change of mission, 1st Battalion would have to press its attack on Spiazzi.[432] The 1st Battalion left Garda by truck, riding to Caprino, where they dismounted the trucks and planned the attack on Spiazzi.[433] Company B would remain in reserve with a company of medium tanks, which, due to the blown bridge alluded to above, would not be able to proceed all the way to Spiazzi, and elements of Company D; Company A would execute a direct attack on Spiazzi, while Company C moved around the left flank and seized the high ground behind the town, both to block the enemy's retreat and as the assault position from which it would join the attack.[434] Both companies were in position by 0300 on April 29, and the attack began with Company A at 0330, and a fierce battle developed in the town, killing scores of Germans, with friendly casualties as well.[435] Company C joined the attack from behind Spiazzi at 0900, catching the enemy completely by surprise; German resistance collapsed, netting 1st Battalion forty to fifty prisoners in addition to the approximately fifty enemy killed.[436] The 2nd Battalion finally received word at 1000 hours on the twenty-ninth to abandon the march to Mori and return.[437]

The 86th Infantry resumed its slog along the coastal highway and through its tunnels shortly after midnight on April 29; at 0440 that day, 1st Battalion began moving toward Nago on the regiment's right while 3rd Battalion resumed its advance through the tunnels.[438] By 1000, the head of 3rd Battalion had cleared the sixth tunnel without incident while the rear, with part of the headquarters of 2nd Battalion, was transiting tunnel 5, near the exit; at this point, a German strongpoint across Lake Garda, having directed observation of the two regiments leaving tunnel 5, fired three shells at them and scored a "lucky hit," wreaking havoc.[439] One of the shots entered the tunnel and exploded about 50 feet inside, killing seven, wounding forty-four, and at least temporarily stunning everyone in the area.[440]

By 1230 on the twenty-ninth, 3rd Battalion's patrols had reached Torbole, but 1st Battalion was still 1,000 yards away from Nago, and the cost of the progress made even this far had been high: both battalion commanders had been wounded and evacuated—both 1st and 2nd Battalions were now commanded by *captains*.[441] The Germans bitterly contested both towns with infantry and armor; nonetheless, 3rd Battalion occupied Torbole by 2214, although 1st Battalion was still just short of its objective.[442] At 0055 the enemy launched a strong counterattack; 3rd Battalion held fast in Torbole, while 1st Battalion withdrew 1,700 meters to high ground and held there.[443] On the morning of the thirtieth a patrol found that the enemy had evacuated Nago, and 1st Battalion occupied the town; 2nd Battalion was also able to occupy Riva.[444] Tragedy stalked the 86th that day, however, striking at 1750, when a German shell killed MSgt. John T. Evans and mortally wounded the assistant division commander, Col. Darby, who died forty-five minutes later; the regimental commander was lightly wounded as was one other officer.[445]

On April 29, the 85th Mountain Infantry Regiment commenced an amphibious operation across Lake Garde. On that day 1Lt. Eugene S. Hames, platoon leader of 1st Platoon, Company K, received instructions from the 3rd Battalion S2* that he was to take ten men across Lake Garda to "capture and occupy" Mussolini's villa located there.[446] As Lt. Hames and his men were preparing for their mission, Col. Darby arrived and, not liking what he heard when the mission was described to him, countermanded the order; instead, a task force consisting of the entirety of Company K, plus reinforcements, would make the crossing.[447] Company K pushed off the eastern shore at 0130 the next morning (April 30) in twelve DUKWs, occupying the town of Gargano (and Mussolini's villa) upon arrival and commencing patrols shortly thereafter.[448] Company L pushed off at 1745, landing on the western shore and occupying the town of Campione del Garda by 1936.[449] Company I crossed the lake at 0430 on May 1; the 85th moved up the highway on the west side of the lake, establishing contact with the 86th at Riva.[450]

German Capitulation in Italy

While the 10th Mountain was fighting its bloody battles around Lake Garda, negotiations for the surrender of Axis forces in Italy were underway. One step in this direction occurred when Lt. Gen. Max Joseph Pemsel, the German chief of staff of the enemy Ligurian army, presented himself on April 28 to the IV Corps to negotiate the surrender of his staff; an extended interview with Gen. Crittenberger ensued, in which Pemsel equivocated as to the extent of his authority, sought information on Allied dispositions, asked for aid in contacting his units, and generally played for time.[451] Of special interest to this study is the colloquy between Pemsel and Crittenberger about the status and fate of the German 34th Division:

> Pemsel: My main worry is the 34th Division. That is what I want to save.
> Crittenberger: That is also my objective and the whole American Fifth Army

---

* Intelligence officer.

for today. That is the remaining formed unit of the German Army in front of the IV Corps.

Pemsel: It is not very good. It is especially bad as the division is in a mountain defense and they have never fought in such a situation.

Crittenberger: Will it stand up with our 10th Mountain Division[,] which has spearheaded this drive from Belvedere?

Pemsel: The 10th Mountain Division is certainly much more better. I was General of the Mountain troops myself, and I am sure of this.

Crittenberger: The 34th Division will have to meet the 10th Mountain Division before it gets out of Italy."

Pemsel: I realize that as far as the fighting goes in the south, it is over.[452]

Finally, on April 29, Gen. Pemsel signed an order on behalf of Marshal Graziani, the Italian supreme commander of the Ligurian army (then out of contact with his troops), directing the surrender of all elements of that army to Allied forces (but not to the partisans), and a further order directed specifically at enemy forces in the city of Milan, to the same effect.[453] Unfortunately, not every commander in the Ligurian army was prepared to honor these orders. On April 30, Gen. Schlemmer, commanding general of the German LXXV Army Corps, replied by letter that "the arrangements made by Major General Pensel are not recognized by me as commanding general of the LXXV Army Corp[s], inasmuch as I consider myself bound by my oath until the death of the Führer," further implying that while he would not surrender, he would also not engage in offensive operations if his units were not themselves molested.[454] Also on April 28, emissaries representing both Gen. Heinrich von Vietinghoff, German supreme commander in Italy, and SS general Karl Wolff arrived at 15th Army Group Headquarters and the next at day, April 29, 1945, at 1400, signed a surrender agreement at the Royal Palace at Caserta, under which all German troops in Italy, and several Austrian provinces or parts thereof, were to cease resistance

by 1200 on May 2, 1945.[455] The surrender orders were to be broadcast to the German troops by German radio on May 2, and Allied forces were to continue the offensive until that happened; only when Allied forces began intercepting German transmissions ordering the surrender did the offensive stop.[456] The recalcitrant Gen. Schlemmer surrendered on this date, signing the same text that Gen. Pemsel had previously signed, his scruples about his oath to the Führer perhaps satisfied by his having received word of Hitler's suicide the day before.[457] Hostilities ended in the rest of Europe a few days later, on May 8, 1945.

It was a great victory for Allied forces everywhere, but it was an especially great victory for the 10th Mountain Division, which had contributed mightily to the outcome. The division had been the only Allied unit able to punch a hole in the German line of defense, capturing Mount Belvedere when no one else could, and setting the stage for its penetration of the Apennines and into the Po Valley. Although the 10th Mountain Division began the Spring Offensive as the main effort in the IV Corps, the IV Corps itself was a supporting effort in the larger Fifth Army "Operation Craftsman." In the actual event, the 10th Mountain would prove the spearhead of the entire Fifth Army, carrying out

one of the most spectacular and unbelievable advances of the war. The 10th Mountain Division, trained and equipped primarily for mountain warfare, had actually outfought and out-raced all other units in the successful effort to drive the enemy back to the wall and at the same time seal all the escape routes for hundreds of thousands of Germans in North Italy.[458]

The 10th Mountain Division proved itself to be exactly the "elite corps" that its enemies had imagined it to be.

Occupation Duty

After the German capitulation, the 10th Mountain Division embarked upon a period of occupation duty in Germany and Austria. Initially, on May 3, the division was ordered to form two task forces built around infantry battalions and augmented with armor and artillery, which were to place themselves astride passes leading from Italy to Austria to prevent exfiltration of German forces through them.[459] Later. Company F, 85th Mountain Infantry, was detailed to guard the headquarters of Gen. Vietinghoff.[460] For a short time the 10th Mountain Division was charged with the security of the huge prisoner-of-war camp at Ghedi, where Fifth Army was concentrating that portion of the Axis prisoners for which it was responsible, but was relieved of this duty on May 18, when the division was attached to II Corps for movement to Udine in the British Eighth Army sector,[461] where they would cope with a political problem: Tito's partisans. The postwar position of Tito and Communist forces in Yugoslavia had long been a concern of the British, which had influenced British strategic thinking throughout the campaign in Italy, as Fisher describes:

> Thinking in terms of the post-war balance of power in Europe, the British continued to focus much of their attention on northeastern Italy [and] . . . thwarting long-held Yugoslav ambitions to acquire territory along Italy's northeastern frontier. The Italian ports of Trieste, Fiume, and Pola lay within the region coveted by Marshal Tito and his communist-oriented partisans, and the British were determined to keep the ports out of communist hands lest they become naval bases from which a Soviet fleet might dominate the Adriatic.[462]

The capitulation of German forces in Italy now gave rise to just the eventuality that the British had dreaded—a play by Tito's partisans to secure control of some or all of these territories—when his forces occupied Trieste.[463] To counter this and retain control of Trieste, a large force was transferred from the Fifth Army to the Eighth Army area under the control of II Corps: the 10th Mountain and 91st Divisions were deployed, and a five-day supply of ammunition for two infantry divisions, two tank battalions, two 155 mm howitzer battalions, and one 155 mm gun battalion—5,300 tons in all—was moved to Udine.[464] On May 1, Gen. Clark had recorded in his diary Gen. Alexander's assessment that Tito would not object to 15th Army Group's occupation of Trieste and other port facilities in the area, and even that Tito would put his troops under Allied command.[465] Such an assessment was wildly optimistic, to say the least, and the Yugoslavs protested so vigorously as the Allies moved east on May 22–23 that the 85th Division was alerted.[466] Upon arrival at Udine the three regiments were formed into regimental combat teams, each with a platoon of tanks, a field artillery battalion, and medical and engineering elements attached, and assigned a zone of operations, in which the regiment's mission would be "to prevent any additional western movement of Yugoslav forces and civilians by peaceful means."[467] Notwithstanding the presence of various armed groups and lingering tensions, this period passed largely uneventfully.[468]

The 10th Mountain Division would remain in Italy until July 14, 1945, when it would be ordered back to the United States in preparation for the planned invasion of Kyushu, the southernmost of Japan's three main home islands, with the division departing Italy in stages from July 26 through August 2, 1945.[469]

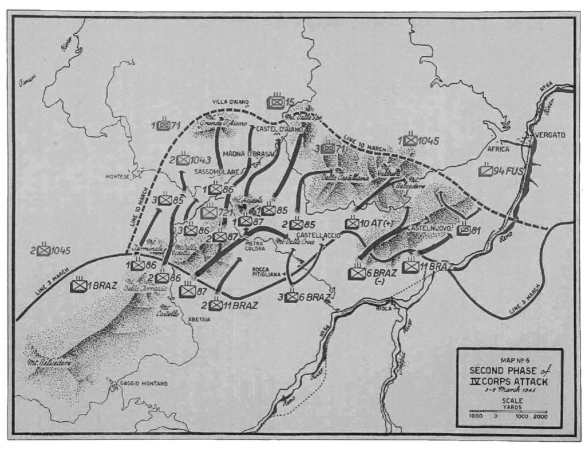

Second phase of IV Corps Attack, March 3–9, 1945. *Map No. 6, Fifth Army History, Part VIII: "The Second Winter," opposite page 89*

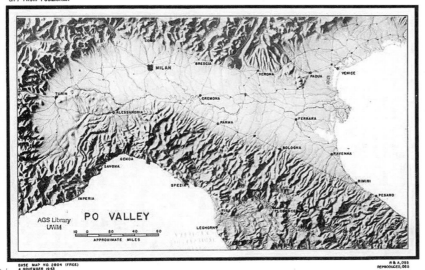

OSS map of the Po Valley, November 4, 1943. *Central Intelligence Agency, via Twitter. https://twitter.com/CIA/status/796843917056602112/photo/2*

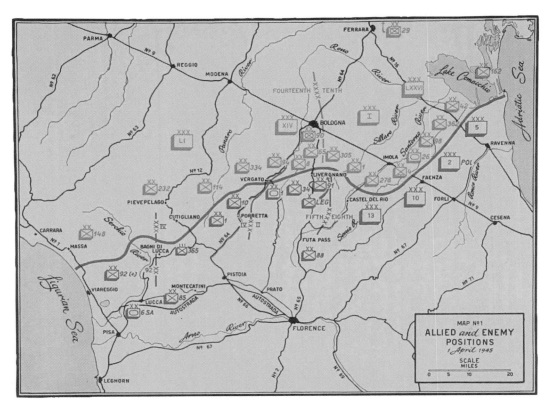

Allied and enemy positions, April 1, 1945. *Map No. 1, Fifth Army History, Part IX, "Race to the Alps,"
opposite page 12*

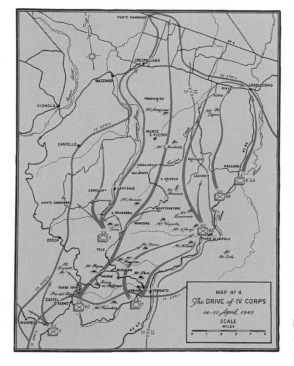

Drive of IV Corps, April 14–20, 1945.
*Map No. 4, Fifth Army History, Part IX,
"Race to the Alps," opposite page 63*

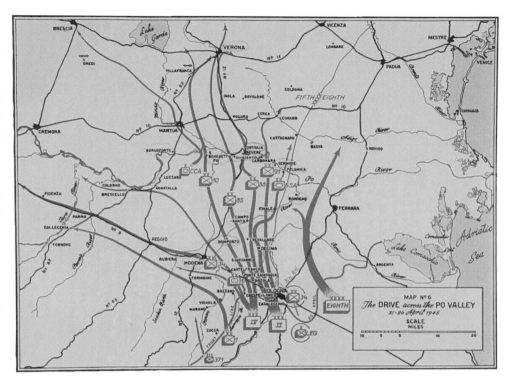

Drive across the Po Valley. *Map No. 6, Fifth Army History, Part IX, "Race to the Alps," opposite page 118*

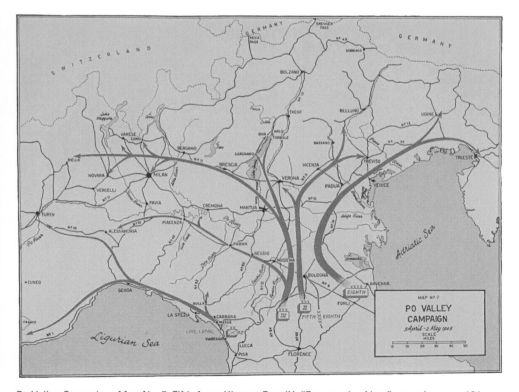

Po Valley Campaign. *Map No. 7, Fifth Army History, Part IX, "Race to the Alps," opposite page 124*

Fifth Army in Italy, September 9, 1943–May 2, 1945. *Map No. 8, Fifth Army History, Part IX, "Race to the Alps," opposite page 137*

R E S T R I C T E D

HEADQUARTERS IV CORPS
APO 304   U S Army

GENERAL ORDERS   30 August 1945
NUMBER   54

1. 15 July 1945 marked the termination of operations of IV Corps
after 401 days of continuous operations in Italy. The accomplishments
of IV Corps in the Italian Campaign stand as a memorial to a great
organization and are in keeping with the heritage it received from
former wars.

2. IV Corps entered combat in Italy on 11 June 1944 with the
same tenacity of purpose and the same grim determination that led to
distinction and battle honors during World War I. On 11 June 1944,
north of Rome, IV Corps began a rapid and systematic pursuit and
destruction of the German Wehrmacht in western Italy and did not cease
its efforts until all German forces in northwest Italy had been destroyed
or had surrendered in hopeless confusion.

3. From 11 June to 9 September 1944 the Rome Arno Campaign provided a test of quick, accurate decisions, speed, and maneuverability.
German forces were routed from their prepared positions and withdrew in
disorder to temporary refuge in the well-prepared and naturally strong
Gothic Line defensive positions in the Apennines. IV Corps had liberated 11,600 square miles of Italian soil. Enemy casualties and the mass
of destroyed and abandoned German equipment were mute evidence of the
power and determination of this offensive.

4. From 10 September 1944 to 4 April 1945 the North Apennines
Campaign was a test of strength and power of IV Corps against the
German Gothic Line defenses, naturally strong on dominating terrain
and made stronger by concrete and wire, and against the rigors of
winter in the Apennine Mountains. IV Corps breached the Gothic Line,
pushed through the Apennines to the north fringe of the mountains, and
prepared for the final blow which would silence the German Wehrmacht
in Italy for all time.

5. On 5 April 1945 IV Corps opened the Po Valley Campaign, which
was its last and which ended on 2 May 1945 with the surrender of all
German and Italian Republican forces in northwest Italy. From the
jump-off positions which had been systematically occupied during the
winter IV Corps breached the German defenses, debouched into the Po
Valley, and rendered the entire German defenses opposite Fifth Army
untenable. The German forces dazed by IV Corps speed, retreated in
hopeless confusion to the north. IV Corps troops raced to the Po River,
forced a crossing, and continued rapidly to the north and west. Possible
escape routes for the trapped German forces were quickly cut and secured
and a methodical cleaning up of all the German forces remaining in northwest Italy was begun. On 29 April the 1st Ligurian Army surrendered

R E S T R I C T E D

Lt. Gen. Crittenberger's order congratulating IV Corps on the end of hostilities. *Author's collection*

R E S T R I C T E D

to IV Corps, and on 2 May the surrender of the 75th German Corps accounted
for the destruction or surrender of all German and Italian Republican
armies in northwest Italy. Remnants of 23 German Divisions were captured.
170,000 Prisoners of War, including 21 General Officers passed through
IV Corps prisoner of war cages.

6. During the 401 days of continuous operations 246,366 troops,
including American, British, South African, Indian, Brazilian, and Italian
served with IV Corps, and liberated 24,580 square miles of Italian soil
including more than 600 cities and towns. IV Corps was the first American
Corps to enter the Po Valley, first to cross the Po River, and first to
receive the surrender of a German Army.

7. The history of IV Corps is a history of determined men who fought
with a unity of purpose and with great mutual understanding to secure a
peace which, God willing, will endure.

WILLIS D. CRITTENBERGER
Lieutenant General, U. S. Army
Commanding

- 2 -

R E S T R I C T E D

The reverse side of Gen. Crittenberger's order. *Author's collection*

HEADQUARTERS 15th ARMY GROUP

To the Soldiers
OF THE 15th ARMY GROUP

With a full and grateful heart I hail and congratulate you in this hour of complete victory over the German enemy, and join with you in thanks to Almighty God.

Yours has been a long, hard fight — the longest in this war of any Allied troops fighting on the Continent of Europe. You men of the Fifth and Eighth Armies have brought that fight to a successful conclusion by recent brilliant offensive operations which shattered the German forces opposing you. Their surrender was the inevitable course left to them, they had nothing more to fight with in Italy.

You have demonstrated something new and remarkable in the annals of organized warfare: You have shown that a huge fighting force composed of units from many countries with diverse languages and customs, inspired, as you have always been, with a devotion to the cause of freedom, can become an effective and harmonious fighting team.

This teamwork which has carried us to victory has included in full measure the supporting arms which have worked with us throughout the campaign. The services that have supplied us have overcome unbelievable obstacles and have kept us constantly armed, equipped, and fed. The magnificent support which we have always had from the Allied air and naval forces in this theater has written a new page in the history of cooperative combat action.

Our exultation in this moment is blended with sorrow as we pay tribute to the heroic Allied soldiers who have fallen in battle in order that this victory might be achieved. The entire world will forever honor their memory.

The war is not over. The German military machine has been completely crushed by the splendid campaigns waged by you and your colleagues of the Western and Russian fronts. There remains the all important task of inflicting a similar complete defeat on our remaining enemy — Japan. Each one of us in the 15th Army Group must continue without pause to give the full measure of effort to that task wherever we may be called upon to serve.

I am intensely proud of you all and of the honor which I have had of commanding such invincible troops. My thanks go to each of you for your capable, aggressive, and loyal service which has produced this great victory.

Men of the 15th Army Group, I know you will face the task ahead with the same magnificent, generous and indomitable spirit you have shown in this long campaign. Forward, to final Victory. God bless you all.

May 1945

Mark W. Clark

General, USA Commanding

Gen. Mark Clark's congratulatory letter to 15th Army Group upon defeat of Germany. *Author's collection*

CHAPTER 7

The 10th Mountain Division after the War

With the end of the war in Germany, demobilization began in Europe. In early September 1944, the War Department released to the press its "War Department Demobilization Plan after Defeat of Germany."[1] Under this plan, demobilization would be conducted on two tracks—by individual and by unit. Individual soldiers would be issued an "Adjusted Service Rating Card" with a score that would determine their order of demobilization, determined on the basis of the soldier's time in service, his time overseas, combat service as reflected in Bronze Service Stars (also known as "battle participation stars"), and the number of children under eighteen years of age that the soldier had.[2] The second track would be by unit, with units divided into categories—those needed for occupation duty in Europe, those needed for future operations in the Pacific, and those deemed "surplus" that would be returned to the United States and demobilized; soldiers would be cross-leveled between units in the various categories, so that soldiers with the highest number of points would be assigned to the "surplus" units and redeployed to the United States with them.[3] "After the surrender of Germany," this plan began to be executed, with the Pentagon "demobilizing the veterans with the highest number of points; and after securing the required number of European occupation troops from personnel with fewer points, it [would] redeploy the freshest troops from Europe to the Pacific Theater."[4]

Some 10th Mountain Division troops were demobilized apart from their units, as in the case of one Sgt. Sposato of B Company, 85th Mountain Infantry, who, eligible for early release on the basis of his points, was unceremoniously given twenty minutes to pack his things and transferred to the 85th Division, returning to the United States for discharge two months later.[5] Most, however, flowed back to the United States with the 10th Mountain Division, then slated for participation in the anticipated invasion of Japan. First to depart was the

86th Mountain Infantry, which left from Livorno aboard SS *Westbrook Victory* on July 26, arriving at Newport News on August 7, 1945.[6] *Westbrook Victory* was one of ninety-seven Victory ships converted for service as troopships.[7] The 604th Field Artillery sailed from Livorno on July 28 aboard *Blue Ridge*, arriving at Newport News on August 9, 1945.[8] The 85th Mountain Infantry sailed from Naples on July 31 aboard SS *Marine Fox*, a troopship constructed in 1945, arriving at New York Harbor on August 11.[9] Finally, the 87th Mountain Infantry and the remainder of the division departed Naples on August 2 aboard *Mount Vernon*, a passenger liner built in 1933 as *Washington* for US Lines and rechristened as *Mount Vernon* by the Navy in 1942; the 87th arrived at Newport News on August 11.[10] The men of the division received thirty-day furloughs upon arrival back in the United States,[11] during which Japan capitulated and the war was over. Following their furloughs the men were to report to Camp Carson, Colorado, with the advanced party arriving by September 12.[12] The demobilization process began immediately, with the soldiers having eighty-five points being discharged; the units of the division were functioning again by September 20, though shortly after that, many leaves and passes began to be granted, with a skeleton staff on hand in the units to handle administrative matters.[13] In mid-October 1945, word came that the 10th Mountain Division would be inactivated, inaugurating "the dreary business of closing up shop" in which "low-point men were transferred to the 2nd Division at, of all places, Camp Swift [and] the pace of discharge rose,"[14] until finally, on November 30, 1945, the 10th Mountain Division was inactivated at Camp Carson.[15]

The men of the 10th Mountain Division went on to varied fates after the war, some gaining renown in other fields. Not everyone associated with the division had an easy road afterward, including the man who might well be called its father, Minnie Dole. Although the War Department subsidized the activities of the National Ski Patrol System on the division's behalf, Minnie Dole received no salary for his work; instead, he lived on a $7,500 drawing account from the insurance company Flynn, Harris, and Conroy—an account overdrawn by $10,000 at the end of the war.[16] Dole had to liquidate $5,000 from his savings and borrow another $5,000 to repay the debt.[17] In later years Dole worked as a hospital fundraiser and as an executive recruiter.[18] Dole might have taken some satisfaction, however, in the impact that the division he nurtured would have on the sport of skiing, which he loved, since 10th Mountain Division veterans would play a key role in the promotion of American skiing. 10th Mountain Division veterans Friedl Pfeiffer, Percy Rideout, and John Litchfield returned to Aspen, Colorado, after the war and founded a skiing school on Ajax Mountain, beginning work on the project in 1945 and officially opening in January, 1947.[19] Pfeiffer and 10th Mountain veterans formed the Aspen Skiing Corporation (ASC) and, with the backing of Chicago entrepreneur Walter Paepcke,[20] set about the business of building Aspen into the thriving ski resort that it would become. At the same time, 10th Mountain veteran Larry Jump would form Arapahoe Basin, Inc., which, unlike Aspen—which sought to appeal to wealthy vacationers from across the country—"catered almost exclusively to middle[-]class skiers within driving distance of the mountain."[21] 10th Mountain veterans Pete Siebert and Bob Parker promoted skiing at Vail, while 10th Mountain veterans Ed Link and Roe Duke Watson promoted the sport in the Cascades near Fort Lewis and Mount Rainier; Jack Murphy and Arthur G. Draper of the 86th Mountain Infantry Regiment established facilities at Sugarbush Valley, Vermont, and Whiteface Mountain, New York, respectively.[22] Every year, millions of Americans take to the slopes, oblivious to the debt that they owe to the men of the 10th Mountain Division, not only for their freedom but for the recreation as well.

The New 10th Infantry Division, 1948–1958

The Regular Army rapidly contracted following the end of the Second World War, from eighty-nine divisions on active duty on VE-day to sixteen divisions on active duty by the summer of 1946; the 10th Mountain Division, having been inactivated the previous fall, was not among them.[23] As divisions were dropped from the active duty rolls, a contentious tussle ensued among division commanders, active duty members, and veterans as to what divisions would be retained on active duty.[24] Ultimately, the adjutant general of the Army canvassed senior commanders throughout the Army for their views on the subject and produced a recommendation that divisions 1–10 and 24–25 be allocated to the Regular Army for infantry divisions, 82 and 101 for Airborne Divisions, and 1–4 for Armored Divisions, which was implemented.[25] The 10th Mountain would be redesignated as the 10th Infantry Division and would, with the 25th Infantry Division and the 82nd Airborne Division, be allotted to the Regular Army from the now-defunct Army of the United States (10th and 25th) and Organized Reserve (82nd), to which they had previously formally belonged.[26] However, while now a permanent part of the Regular Army's allotment of divisions, the 10th Infantry Division remained on an inactive status.

A change was on the horizon, however, in the form of the Army's arrangements for the training of new recruits. In the summer of 1947 the Army began denominating its recruit-training centers as active divisions, with the first four such—the 3rd Armored and 4th, 5th, and 9th Infantry Divisions—being activated as training centers in July 1947; the experiment was deemed a success, since "the cadres who trained the recruits responded favorably to the use of divisions as of building esprit since they wore the divisional shoulder sleeve insignia, and the recruits were inspired by the accomplishments of historic units."[27] In July 1948, the program was expanded, with four more "divisional" training centers being activated.[28] Eventually, a total of twelve training divisions would be activated in the Regular Army, though they would not all serve at the same time; five—3rd Armored, 4th Infantry, 8th Infantry, 10th Infantry, and 101st Airborne—would eventually be reorganized as combat divisions, with the 6th and 69th Divisions being activated as training divisions to replace two of them. [29] The practice of denominating Army training centers by active-duty divisions would not become a permanent feature of the Army institutional training program. By July 1955, there were seven functioning training centers, only five of which bore divisional designations, and the continued practice of divisional training centers was in doubt, since "for some time the divisional designations had confused the general public, government officials, and the trainees."[30] All the divisional training centers would be either reorganized or inactivated by 1956, and their functions assumed by branch replacement centers.[31]

Among the divisional training centers activated in 1948 was the 10th Infantry Division.[32] As it did during World War II, the 10th Division wore the "blue powder keg-like" patch with two scarlet bayonets, crossed to form a Roman numeral "10," but the patch was now shorn of the "mountain tab."[33] The 10th Infantry Division was reactivated at Fort Riley, Kansas, on July 1, 1948.[34] The division "marked a home-coming" when, the next month, it "returned to Camp Funston [adjacent to Fort Riley] for its third activation"* under the commanding general, Maj. Gen. Lester J. Whitlock.[35] Maj. Gen. Whitlock had begun his military career as a private with the Ohio National Guard in 1916, subsequently earning his commission in France as a second lieutenant in the field artillery in 1918.[36] During the Second World War, he served in Australia; as G-4, Southwest Pacific Area; as deputy chief of staff, US Armed Forces Pacific at Manila; and, after the war, as deputy chief of staff, general headquarters, Supreme Commander Allied Powers, Tokyo.[37] In a remarkable historical coincidence, the 10th Division had been reactivated at Camp Funston almost thirty years to the day after the original 10th Division had been organized at this same installation under the famous Leonard Wood.[38] The 10th Division was not reactivated as a maneuver division at this

time; rather, the division, along with the 85th, 86th, and 87th Infantry Regiments,[39] was activated as a training center, "assigned the mission of processing and training soldiers for service both within the continental United States and overseas"[40] for "the first great peace-time Army in the history of the United States."[41] The division's primary mission was providing basic training to inductees, to shape the individual recruit "into an aggressive, fighting infantryman with confidence in his weapons and equipment; the ability to use them; and the will to close with and destroy the enemy."[42] One of the many soldiers to pass through Camp Funston under the tutelage of the 10th Division during this period was Donald G. Bartling, who was inducted on January 12, 1951, and was assigned to Company D, 87th Infantry, for training at Camp Funston.[43] Bartling describes a hectic environment during his basic training, during which "it was apparent early on that there was a monstrous amount of learning that we needed to do in a relatively short time," and that "acceptance of that premise made the actual learning process much more palatable."[44] The focus of training during the first few weeks at Camp Funston was what one would expect in a basic training unit. Bartling and his comrades were expected to "learn to take and follow orders and respect for authority," understand the responsibilities of citizenship, learn to respect and behave properly around others, and, most importantly, "learn about and the use of the infantry weapons—M1 Rifle, M1 and M2 Carbine, Browning Automatic Rifle (BAR), light .30-cal. Machine Gun, 60 and 81 mm Mortars, Recoilless Rifle, 3.5 Bazooka, Grenades, .45-cal. Pistol, and .45-cal. Grease Gun."[45]** Bartling's first two months of training—January and February 1951—were spent on individual training in garrison; in March, his unit embarked upon its first bivouac, a six-day exercise during which Bartling and his comrades would be exposed to both rain and snow; training

---

* This particular reference is one of the few since the activation of the 10th Light Division (Alpine) in 1943 in which the Army has recognized the existence of the first 10th Division formed during World War I, and the service of the men who served in it. Another example is the 1952 yearbook for Company I, 86th Infantry, which acknowledges that "10th Division was first activated at Camp Funston when it trained men for combat in World War I," before being "deactivated in 1919 following the Armistice [and] remained inactive until 1943." *10th Infantry Division, Fort Riley, Kansas, 1952, Company I 86th Infantry*, 1952, 6.

** Officially known as the M3 Submachine Gun. See *Field Manual 23-41, Submachineguns, Caliber .45 M3 and M3A1*, Headquarters, Department of the Army, June 1974.

culminated in tactical exercises ("field problems") conducted with live ammunition, including an attack on a hill supported by live mortar fire, and an "infiltration fire" course simulating maneuver through a town during which the trainees engaged "pop-up targets" with live ammunition.[46]

The division operated a leadership school for prospective NCOs designated as the 25th Field Artillery Battalion, which began operating in 1949,[47] and a "Common Specialist School" for supply clerks, automotive mechanics, and clerk-typists designated as the 35th Field Artillery Battalion, also organized in 1949.[48] Upon completion of basic training around the beginning of May 1951, Bartling attended the 25th Artillery Leadership School.[49] He describes a rigorous course of instruction that was less regimented than his basic-training experience, with greater privacy and better accommodations, but required intensive individual study on the part of the students, with eighteen-to-twenty-hour days being common;[50] of more than 100 candidates that began the training, only sixty graduated.[51]

On July 10, 1951, the division had to cope with a natural disaster as flooding by the Kansas River forced the evacuation of all personnel and all the equipment that could be moved from Camp Funston to hills to the north.[52] This occurred toward the end of Donald Bartling's Leaders Course class with the 25th Field Artillery; he describes the experience thus:

About a week was needed for us to process and leave for our next duty stations. We had not completed that when the flooding rivers became so high that though we had orders to leave, we could not do so as the roads were flooded. Everyone took their turns filling and carrying sandbags to build the dikes higher. It came to the point that we used pillow cases and mattress covers as sandbags. The effort to save Camp Funston came to an end when the water came over the top of the sand-bags, and we were forced to pack up our field packs and head for the hills north of Highway

40. We formed up in "formation" and were marched past the "weapons room"; each man was given as many weapons as he could carry to take with us to our temporary camp. It was not advisable to leave these weapons exposed to looters that were operating in the flooded towns along the flooded rivers.[53]

Despite substantial damage to the physical plant of the installation, all the damage had been repaired by the first quarter of 1952.[54]

The division's mission both diversified and grew in importance in the summer of 1950 with the start of the Korean War. Initially, the 10th Infantry Division served as a source of cadre and specialized personnel to help fill out a number of "hurriedly activated training units" preparing to join the battle in Korea, in addition to its primary mission of training recruits from the Fifth Army area, Fifth Army having been reactivated in 1946 to draw down the active-duty force, build up the reserve components, and, later, provide both trained units and individual replacements—both new recruits and retrained enlisted reserve corps soldiers recalled to active duty—to the forces fighting in Korea, a task all the more challenging in light of the resumption of Selective Service.[55]

The 10th Division enjoyed several prosperous years during its role as a training center, and aside from the flood, they appear to have been pleasant ones. Writing to his future sister-in-law late on a Sunday morning in 1953, one soldier assigned to Company E, 85th Infantry Regiment, in 1953 depicts life with the 10th Division as one of busy days during the week and sometimes busy evenings, but with plenty of downtime, especially on weekends, and plenty of amenities to enjoy during that downtime.[56] Dances and music, bowling at the service club, bingo,* a tavern, the PX, and church, as well as first-run movies available on post before they opened at his hometown of Buffalo, are among the distractions and amusements available.[57]

By the time the 10th Division terminated its training mission in 1954 preparatory to its

---

* In an interesting sign of just how times have changed in sixty-seven years, the prizes given out during these bingo games were, according to our correspondent, cigarettes.

participation in Operation Gyroscope (discussed below), the 10th Infantry Division had trained 125,000 individual soldiers, and its leadership school had produced 13,000 graduates.[58]

Operation Gyroscope

In 1954, the program that would ultimately become Operation Gyroscope was proposed.[59] Touted by the Army as "a new look about going overseas today,"[60] Operation Gyroscope was an attempt to address the concern of the chief of Army Field Forces, Lt. Gen. John E. Dahlquist, and Army deputy chief of staff for personnel (G1), Maj. Gen. Robert N. Young, that the then-current individual replacement system "required the Army to maintain a large manpower overhead as a substantial percentage of its soldiers were always in transit"; a system of unit rotation, it was hoped, would be cheaper to operate rather than of individual replacements.[61] The Army also hoped for a broad array of other substantial benefits. It was hoped that the system of unit rather than individual rotation would improve morale by eliminating the long family separations previously attendant with overseas assignments, even when the soldier's family ultimately joined him abroad; it was hoped that a unit rotation system would facilitate keeping soldiers in their units for longer periods and thus enhance esprit de corps, and it was hoped that draftees would have a better view of unit than individual rotation, thus improving public support for the Army.[62] The Army expected to improve combat efficiency by retaining trained personnel in their units longer, enhancing teamwork as soldiers stayed together longer, to improve the overall utilization of scarce manpower resources, and to amass valuable experience in the mass movement of large units.[63] Finally, the Army hoped to improve general fiscal savings via savings on transportation achieved through economies of scale of mass movements, reduced recruiting and training costs by improved retention, and improved maintenance of equipment spurred by periodic preparation of major end items for transfer to incoming units.[64]

Under the Gyroscope program, US- and overseas-based divisions would simultaneously replace one another in their respective duty stations. Maintaining operational readiness was of paramount importance. In order to minimize any adverse impact on the readiness of the rotating units, each division would deploy in three increments of one regiment each, two months apart, so that the entire move would be completed in six months; the division headquarters would move with the second, or middle, increment.[65] The overseas tour for the replacement unit was expected to be thirty-three months, plus two months of travel time, so that many soldiers would be able to complete their entire term of service (less basic training) with the division overseas.[66] Rotating units were to arrive at 110% of authorized strength;[67] all soldiers were to have completed basic and advanced individual training prior to arrival at the rotational station, and units were to conduct a minimum of two weeks of tactical training each at the squad, section, platoon, and company levels.[68] Transportation efficiency was to be maximized in order to minimize operational disruption, as again noted in the Army's interim report:

> To cut transfer time to a minimum and reduce costs accordingly, incoming units would be moved directly from ship to train upon arrival. Vessels and rail transportation provided for the incoming increment would also be utilized by the outgoing increment. Returnees would depart within four to six hours after the arrival of their replacements, and ships would not be delayed in the harbor for more than four days.[69]

Training at echelons of battalion and higher would occur overseas; at a minimum, each battalion was to carry out a "reinforced battalion" field-training exercise by the second week after arrival in Germany.[70]

The Gyroscope program was announced to the public via press release in September 1954; the next month the 10th Division's participation became official, when the secretary of the Army announced his approval of the concept, which would begin in July 1955, with the first rotations being the exchange of the 10th Infantry Division at Fort Riley and the 1st Infantry Division in

Germany, and the 3rd Armored Cavalry Regiment at Fort Meade, Maryland, and the 2nd Armored Cavalry Regiment, also in Europe.[71] Performance expectations were high for the units arriving in Germany; as noted in *Operation Gyroscope in the United States Army, Europe*, each rotating unit

would assume its mission immediately upon arrival in Europe and would have to be trained to the point of operational effectiveness prior to moving overseas. Therefore, during the last six months in the United States each rotating increment would be at full strength, plus overstrength to allow for attrition, and would be engaged in training the personnel it was to take overseas.[72]

This would pose a formidable challenge, since while denominated as an "infantry" division, the 10th Division was configured to operate a training center primarily focused on providing initial entry training to new recruits. The 8th Infantry Division, another training division unit that would replace the 9th Infantry Division in Germany under Operation Gyroscope, as well as the 3rd Armored Division, which would replace the 4th Infantry Division, would have to juggle their training missions simultaneously with preparing to deploy to Germany as operational divisions.[73*] For the 10th Infantry Division, however, the Army took a much more radical approach. In June 1954, a few months prior to the announcement that the 10th Division would participate in Gyroscope, the secretary of the Army took the decision to release to state control four Army National Guard infantry divisions—the 28th, 31st, 37th, and 43rd—each of which would be replaced in the active-duty force structure by a reactivated Regular Army division.[74] The 10th Infantry Division was designated as the unit that would replace the 37th Division as an operational

unit, and the transition would take place at the 10th Division's then-current duty station of Camp Funston / Fort Riley, Kansas.[75] This change would be effectuated by moving the 37th Division from Camp (now Fort) Polk, Louisiana, where it was on active duty, to Kansas in May 1954.[76] The 37th Infantry Division was an Ohio Army National Guard unit that had been called to federal service on January 15, 1952.[77] By the time the 37th began arriving at Camp Funston and Camp Forsyth (subposts of Fort Riley) in May 1954, the 10th Infantry Division's strength had been reduced to zero; when the 37th Division reverted to state control on June 15, 1954,[**] many of its personnel remained on active duty, providing the human material around which the new, operational 10th Infantry Division would be built.[78] A noteworthy example of the individuals and units that would transition from the 37th Division to the 10th Division was Col. C. J. Van Sickle, executive officer of the 147th Infantry. Van Sickle had entered the Army as a platoon leader in the 3rd Infantry Regiment at Fort Snelling, Minnesota, in 1937; he later served as a battalion commander with the 20th Infantry Regiment and as an infantry battalion commander in the Pacific theater during World War II and, after the war, taught ROTC. In 1950 he was assigned as executive officer, 147th Infantry Regiment, with the 37th Division at Fort Polk; in July 1954 he became the G3, 10th Infantry Division; and on February 10, 1956, he assumed command of the 86th Infantry Regiment at Schweinfurt, Germany—the 86th itself having been re-formed from personnel of the 147th Infantry Regiment when that unit was released from federal service back to state control.[79]

The 37th Division itself had a distinguished history prior to its being used as raw material for the rebuilding of the 10th Division, having been called to federal service for both the First and Second World Wars. In fact, at least one member

---

[*] For a brief account of the 8th Infantry Division's Operation Gyroscope experience, see Carl Wiese, field ed., *8th Infantry Division: Gyroscope 1956*, 9.

[**] The 37th Infantry Division no longer exists in that form, but it continues to exist as a unit in the Ohio Army National Guard in another form. On February 15, 1968, it was reorganized and redesignated as Headquarters, 73d Brigade, 38th Infantry Division; on September 1, 1993, it was reorganized and redesignated as Headquarters, 37th Brigade, 28th Infantry Division; on September 1, 1994, it was redesignated as Headquarters, 37th Brigade, 38th Infantry Division; and finally, on September 1, 2007, it was relieved from assignment to the 38th Infantry Division and took its current form, being reorganized and redesignated as Headquarters, 37th Infantry Brigade Combat Team. See "Headquarters, 37th Infantry Brigade Combat Team (Buckeye)," Center of Military History, May 19, 2017.

of the division—Brig. Gen. Kenneth Cooper, division artillery commander—would take part in all three of these activations, having enlisted in the 37th Division upon its organization in 1917.[80] The 37th Division was alerted for its third tour of active duty on September 12, 1951, with a courtesy call by the secretary of the Army to Ohio governor Frank J. Lausche, officially confirmed later that day, that the division would enter federal service on January 15, 1952; in the interim, 3,100 of the division's officers and NCOs were called to active duty to attend Army service schools.[81] The division and unit staffs had worked out detailed training programs by December 1951, and from January 15 to 25, 1952, twenty-five trains carried the 37th Division to Camp Polk.[82] Unlike current practice, where the states aggressively cross-level personnel from other units to bring their alerted units to full strength prior to their mobilization dates,* the assigned strength of the 37th Division was frozen on its alert date, leaving it badly understrength when it entered active duty.[83] To remedy this, 4,000 veterans of overseas service—many from Korea—were assigned to the 37th at Camp Polk, and in February and March another 3,000 personnel arrived from training and replacement centers, finally bringing the division to full strength.[84] The 37th Division underwent a comprehensive training program upon arrival at Fort Polk:** the first sixteen weeks were devoted to individual training, followed by thirteen weeks of unit training from squad through regimental level, two weeks for Regimental Combat Team training exercises, and two weeks for division-level training; the division passed a four-day Army Training Test and completed its initial training cycle on September 13, 1952.[85] Despite this aggressive training program, however, the 37th Division would itself never deploy to combat in Korea. As early as March 1952, reports appeared in the media that the 37th Division would, instead, supply individual replacements to fill vacancies in units already fighting overseas in Korea—reports

confirmed by Gen. Mark Clark on April 17, 1952, during a visit to the 37th at Camp Polk.[86] Officers began departing for overseas units that month, and by October 1952, more than half of the 37th Division's officer complement had been ordered overseas; the first overseas levy for enlisted specialists—170 soldiers—arrived in July, followed by levies in August (1,040), September (700), and October (2,000), most of whom would be assigned to Far Eastern Command, a euphemism that, without doubt, meant Korea for the great majority of the soldiers affected.[87] The demand for combat replacements in Korea impacted the 37th Division in another way as well, when the 148th Infantry Regiment, the 136th Field Artillery Battalion, and the 112th Engineer Battalion were constituted as the 148th Regimental Combat Team and assigned the mission of conducting basic training for inductees, the first increment of whom arrived at Camp Polk on October 8, 1952.[88]

By July 1955, a year after its reconfiguration as an operational division and absorption of the remnants of the 37th Infantry Division, the 10th Infantry Division had trained 12,000 newly assigned personnel for the unit's operational mission in Germany.[89] Other preparations began with the division's transformation in July 1954 as well. Guidebooks and pamphlets were prepared in both Kansas and Germany to assist the soldiers and families who would be arriving in Germany, and at Fort Riley, various training courses were established for military personnel in preparation for the move; special courses in the German language were organized for the troops and their dependents, and even road signs in the area were supplemented with German signs to familiarize the rotating personnel with German traffic practices.[90]

On January 5, 1955, a 10th Division planning group arrived in Germany and, over the course of more than two weeks, reviewed shipping and transportation schedules for personnel and equipment, transfer of property between the rotating units, uniform requirements, military

---

* For a detailed examination of modern cross-leveling practices, see Dennis P. Chapman, *Manning Reserve Component Units for Mobilization: Army and Air Force Practice*, 2009.
** As an exception, the 137th Antiaircraft Artillery (Automatic Weapons) (AAA AW) Battalion conducted its individual and unit-level tactical training at Fort Bliss, Texas, joining the remainder of the division at Camp Polk on August 11, 1952. Although the armed forces had been formally desegregated in 1948, the 137th AAA AW had been formed in the Ohio National Guard in 1947 and was still a largely African American unit at time the 37th Division was called up. *Pictorial History of the Thirty-Seventh*, 14, 381–96.

personnel policies and facilities for dependent support, pay and finance activities, security clearance requirements, training programs, ammunition and training areas required, and other matters.[91]* In the spring of 1955, a major rehearsal of the Gyroscope concept was undertaken via the movement of a single battalion, as described in the Army's interim report:

> To test Gyroscope plans, in the spring of 1955 the 216th Field Artillery Battalion was moved as a unit in a "Little Gyroscope" from the United States to the Darmstadt area of West Germany. Fifty-four wives and 102 children accompanied the military personnel of the unit on board the USNS *Patch*. When the ship docked at Bremerhaven on 25 March 1955, the unit, including dependents, moved directly to waiting trains. Within 24 hours all personnel were at their new posts. Each dependent family was met at the Darmstadt railroad station by a member of the 760th Field Artillery Battalion and was driven in the host's automobile to its new home. The apartments had been prepared for the new occupants; each kitchen was filled with provisions calculated to last for three days, beds had been made, individual commissary accounts had been opened and post exchange and class VI cards were distributed immediately.[92]

This test having been deemed a success, preparations for the movement of the 10th Division continued. On May 9, 1955, the 10th Division dispatched a liaison officer to Germany to assist in preparations for the movement of the division, and on May 26 the first serial of the advanced party—ninety-one personnel—arrived by air at Rhine-Maine Airbase, Frankfurt, before departing the next day for Würzburg.[93] The remainder of the advanced party arrived by June 1, for a total of sixty officers, 123 enlisted soldiers and NCOs, 285 dependents, and three dogs; after in-briefing and orientation, the members of the advanced party assumed the jobs of the personnel they

were replacing, those soldiers having already left Würzburg en route to the United States during the first half of May.[94]

The first rotational increment of the division's deployment consisted of the 86th Infantry Regiment; its first serial—1,494 officers, enlisted men, and dependents—arrived by sea at Bremerhaven on July 11, 1955, and their counterparts from the 1st Infantry Division boarded the same ship for the return trip to the United States three days later.[95] The second serial arrived on July 17 at Bremerhaven.[96] The lead elements of the 10th Infantry Division's second deployment increment made landfall in Germany on September 2, 1955, with their counterparts departing by sea nine days later, on September 11; the arrival of the second increment was complete—and the divisional change of command ceremony occurred—on September 27, 1955, at which point the 10th Infantry Division "was officially in charge."[97] In total, 1,492 military personnel and dependents of the third and final rotational increment—the 85th Infantry Regiment—arrived in Germany on November 13, and five days later, on November 18, 1955, the 10th Infantry Division's 41st Engineer Battalion relieved its 1st Infantry Division counterpart, thus completing the initial iteration of Operation Gyroscope within a five-month period.[98]

To accomplish this rotation, believed to have been among the Army's largest peacetime moves, required four Military Sea Transportation Service vessels and 150 transatlantic flights.[99] Upon arrival in Germany, the 10th Division's headquarters was stationed at the Bavarian city of Würzburg, southeast of Frankfurt, with most of the division's separate companies, while the remainder of the division was distributed at various other locations, generally within 75 miles of Würzburg:[100] the 85th Infantry was stationed at Bamberg by November 29, 1955; the 86th Infantry was stationed at Schweinfurt;[101] the 87th was at Aschaffenburg.[102] The division artillery headquarters was at Würzburg, while the 40th Field Artillery Battalion was located to the east at Aschaffenburg, the 35th Field Artillery was

---

* For an overall timeline of the *Gyroscope* program through April 1957, see David A. Lane, Robert Gumerove, and Elizabeth W. Holtzworth. *Operation Gyroscope in the United States Army, Europe*, 51–52.

northeast at Schweinfurt, the 85th FA was southeast at Kitzingen, and the 25th FA and 43rd Antiaircraft Artillery Battalion were located well to the east, north of Nuremberg at Bamberg and Erlangen, respectively.[103]

In terms of administration and logistics, this first iteration of Operation Gyroscope was an unequivocal success—the 10th Infantry Division had arrived in Germany and assumed the mission of the 1st Infantry Division on time and as planned. As the interim report on Operation Gyroscope noted,

> Certainly one area of positive military achievement was in directing mass movements. There can be no doubt that from the first exchange the technical aspects of the operation were handled extremely well and provided much valuable experience. Gyroscope moves generally went according to schedule; in many ways they facilitated the tasks of the transportation and other technical services. Although the interchange of unlike units imposed an undue workload on some supply activities, the exchange of like units caused no great difficulty.[104]

As valuable as this exercise was, enhanced technical experience was not the only dividend that the Army hoped for from Gyroscope. Again quoting the interim report, "Operation Gyroscope planners envisioned three areas—morale, military efficiency, and monetary savings—in which the program would be of particular value."[105] How did the program stack up against these expectations?

In many was well, or at least so it appeared to the authors of the Army's 1957 report on the program. In terms of morale, some benefits were noted. Soldiers' family lives were improved by the increased prevalence of concurrent travel of dependents with their military sponsors, thus avoiding the months' long family separation that often occurred with typical overseas reassignments.[106] Operation Gyroscope also seems to have enhanced unit cohesion and esprit de corps among the participating soldiers, as attested by a majority of the enlisted and officer personnel queried on the subject.[107] There was a discordant

note, however, with respect to unit discipline. While "offenses against Germans committed by personnel of incoming units did not exceed or were fewer than those of the replaced units," there was a sharp disparity between the rotating units in the number of courts-martial imposed: while the 1st Division had convened 1,630 during the one-year period ending in September 1955, the 10th Division convened 2,558 courts-martial during the corresponding period ending in 1956, while the 11th Airborne Division suffered an even-higher negative disparity with the unit it replaced—the 5th Infantry Division—in the number of courts-martial imposed.[108] "The increased number of courts-martial of new Gyroscope units in the command was attributed to the shortage in experienced NCOs," the Army's assessment of Gyroscope notes, "which was in turn caused by the shortage of family housing in Germany—as well as to all the difficulties inherent in placing great numbers of men in a new and strange environment."[109]

In terms of other military considerations, the results of Operation Gyroscope were mixed. The valuable technical experience accrued from the mass movement of large formations has already been noted. Another clear benefit of the program was in the efficient use of personnel, since "unit rotation and packet replacements, by decreasing the number of casual assignments and the man-hours required to process casuals, tended toward better utilization of manpower"; however, improvement in the retention of experienced manpower—for which the Army had high hopes in the Gyroscope program—was variable, with the key determinant being the availability of family housing at the overseas duty station.[110] Of more concern was the impact of Operation Gyroscope on unit readiness. Analysis of Gyroscope rotations revealed a tendency to yield reduced combat readiness at three distinct points during the rotational cycle, with the first, predictably, being the first few months immediately following the arrival of the incoming unit at the overseas station, attributed to insufficient training in the United States before departure for Germany.[111] A second interval of reduced readiness occurred midway through the unit's overseas tour as replacement cohorts arrived, until those new unit members could be fully integrated into the unit and trained to standards.[112] The final period of reduced readiness occurred at the end of the rotational cycle, as the unit looked forward to redeployment to the United States; as personnel began to be transferred out, advanced parties departed for the United States ahead of the main body, and the unit began to turn its attentions to administrative matters relating to the Gyroscope[113] rotation itself rather than to combat readiness.

The 10th Infantry Division completed its rotational cycle and redeployed to the United States under Operation Gyroscope in 1958, being replaced in Germany by the 3rd Infantry Division; that same year, the 4th Armored Division also replaced the 2nd Armored Division in Germany under the Gyroscope program.[114] These would be the last Gyroscope division-sized rotations.[115] Smaller units continued to rotate under Gyroscope for a short time thereafter, it having previously

been observed that rotations of units of battalion size and below under the Gyroscope model had a much less adverse impact on readiness, these lower-echelon formations being more readily integrated into existing command structures and achieving the required readiness posture at the overseas station more quickly, and few logistical and personnel problems were encountered.[116]

The smaller level rotations did not continue for long, however. The Army formally terminated Gyroscope on September 1, 1959.[117] The commanding general of US Army Europe, Gen. Clyde D. Eddleman, had concluded that an individual replacement system would better serve US forces in Europe.[118] While Operation Gyroscope had netted some fiscal benefits by maximizing the efficient use of transportation assets and improved morale, the Army finally concluded that on balance, "the scheme did not save money or improve readiness," and it was discontinued.[119]

10th Infantry Division morale patch with unofficial "Germany" scroll. *Author's collection*

Distinctive unit insignia, 85th Infantry Regiment. *Author's collection*

Distinctive unit insignia, 86th Infantry Regiment. *Author's collection*

Distinctive unit insignia 87th Infantry Regiment. *Author's collection*

Obsolete insignia of the 10th Infantry Division headquarters. Made in Germany by Fritz Buttner & Sohn. *Author's collection*

Obsolete insignia of the 10th Division Artillery. *Author's collection*

Obsolete insignia of the 10th Signal Company. Made in Germany by Fritz Buttner & Sohn. *Author's collection*

Postwar officer's branch insignia, 86th Infantry Regiment.
Author's collection

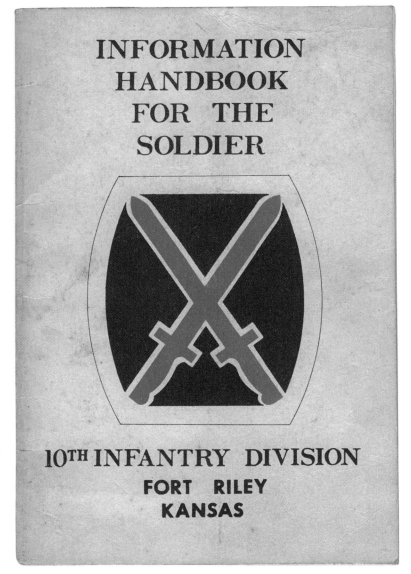

Information Handbook for 10th
Infantry Division soldiers during the
unit's incarnation as a training
division at Fort Riley, Kansas.
Author's collection

CHAPTER 8

The 87th Infantry Regiment

Under Operation Gyroscope, it was envisioned that units would return to their original duty stations when they rotated back to the United States from their overseas postings. In the case of the 10th Infantry Division, this would have meant rotation from Germany back to Fort Riley, Kansas. However, by the end of 1956 the Army had come to the conclusion that operational requirements necessitated the moving of 10th Division to Fort Benning, Georgia.[1] Concerned about the promises made to the soldiers of the division that they would return to Fort Riley, a formal survey was undertaken to ascertain the views of the soldiers who would be affected, which revealed that only fifteen soldiers had arranged their personal affairs on the basis of the assumption of a return to Fort Riley, and a large number of solders were found to prefer a return to Georgia, which would put them closer to family on the East Coast.[2] This established, the few intent upon a return to Fort Riley were given the option of reassignment there, and in 1958 the 3rd Division relieved the 10th Division in Germany, and the 10th Division moved to Fort Benning, Georgia.[3]

Upon arrival at Fort Benning in 1958, the immediate postwar chapter of the 10th Mountain Division's history came to a close, as the division was deactivated on June 14 of that year.[4] But while the 10th Infantry Division became dormant, the story of its oldest regiment—the 87th Infantry— would continue, under the colors of the 2nd Infantry Division. The 2nd Infantry Division was a venerable organization, having been first organized on October 26, 1917, at Bourmont, France, for service with the American Expeditionary Force.[5] The 2nd Infantry Division went on to serve in Europe during the Second World War

and then in the Korean War.[6] The 2nd Division initially remained in Korea following the armistice on the Korean peninsula, since President Eisenhower had been reluctant to withdraw forces from Korea, given the tenuous nature of the peace there.[7] However, in 1953 the administration announced that it would return two of the seven American divisions in Korea—the 40th and 45th—to the United States.[8] In 1954, three more American divisions—the 25th, 2nd, and 3rd Infantry Divisions—returned to the United States; in the case of the 2nd and 3rd, the divisions' assigned strength was reduced almost to zero, and these hollowed-out formations fell in on Army National Guard divisions stateside, which they replaced in a manner similar to the way the 10th Division replaced the 37th leading up to Operation Gyroscope. The 2nd Infantry Division replaced the 44th Division at Fort Lewis, Washington, arriving in October 1954.[9] The 18,000 soldiers assigned to the 44th Division were transferred to the newly arrived 2nd Infantry Division, with the 44th Division's colors cased, and that division returned to state control.[10] The 2nd did not remain long at Fort Lewis, however, rotating to Alaska under Operation Gyroscope in August 1956, replacing the 71st Infantry Division, which inactivated.[11] The 2nd Division's odyssey continued in November 1957, when it was reduced to zero strength and transferred to control of the Department of the Army, until June 14, 1958, when it was reorganized at Fort Benning, Georgia, from the personnel and equipment of the 10th Infantry Division there.[12] With this reorganization, the 85th and 86th Infantry Regiments passed out of existence, never again to appear in the Army's force structure.[*] The 87th

---

[*] The 85th Infantry actually has made a reappearance, albeit in a different form. In 2007 and 2008, the Army and Marine Corps organized special units for the management and care of injured, ill, or wounded personnel. As of the end of September 2011, the Army had organized twenty-nine warrior transition units (WTU), managing 10,000 soldiers. In most cases, these units were designated warrior transition battalions or brigades. However, the leadership at Fort Drum, New York, took a different approach for the WTU associated with the 10th Mountain Division. At Fort Drum the WTU was designated 3rd Battalion, 85th Mountain Infantry Regiment Warrior Transition Battalion. See *Semiannual Report to Congress, April 1, 2011–September 30, 2011* (DoD Inspector General, 2011), 39.

Infantry, however, would endure, with 1st and 2nd Battalions continuing as part of the newly reorganized 2nd Infantry Division as the 1st and 2nd Battle Groups, 87th Infantry.[13*]

Combat Arms Regimental System

On July 1, 1957, the 87th Infantry Regiment was relieved from assignment to the 10th Infantry Division and reorganized as a "parent regiment" under the Army's then newly implemented Combat Arms Regimental System (CARS).[14] The practical impact on the personnel of the 87th Infantry serving with the 10th Infantry Division in Germany was negligible, however, since concurrently with the regiment's reorganization as a parent unit, the elements serving in Germany were reorganized and redesignated as 1st Battle Group, 87th Infantry, under the 10th Division.[15] The implementation of CARS would have significant practical effects going forward, however, since it would mark the end of the regiment as a tactical echelon on the battlefield, except for Armored Cavalry regiments.[16]

The rationale underlying CARS was the preservation of heritage and tradition, as explained by the Center of Military History:[*]

Before the adoption of the CARS, there was no satisfactory means of maintaining the active life of the combat arms organizations. Whenever the nation entered periods of military retrenchment, units were invariably broken up, reorganized, consolidated, or disbanded. During periods of mobilization, large numbers of new units were created. Changes in weapons and techniques of warfare produced new types of units to replace the old ones. As a result, soldiers frequently served in organizations with little or no history, while units with long combat records remained inactive.[17]

The impetus for CARS came from the adoption of the pentomic division structure, which replaced regiments with battle groups, leading to the concern that "replacing infantry regiments

with anonymous battle groups" would "destroy all [the] traditions," as well as the history and lineage, of the Army's regiments, effectively cutting the Army off from its past in a significant way.[18] Secretary of the Army Wilber M. Brucker approved CARS on January 24, 1957, to address this situation.[19] While the regiment would largely disappear from the Army as a tactical unit, it would continue to serve as the repository of the history and traditions of the Army's various tactical units—a process facilitated by the fact that under the CARS program, the regiments would be untouched by the turmoil of periodic organizational changes driven by doctrinal, policy, or even fiscal considerations; in other words, the regiment "could serve as a permanent vehicle for perpetuating unit lineage, honors, and customs without restricting future organizational trends."[20]

As implemented, the regimental headquarters would revert to the control of Headquarters, Department of the Army, while special companies such as Service, Mortars, and Medical would be disbanded. The organic maneuver companies—in the case of an infantry regiment, A–M (J not used), as well as the headquarters and headquarters companies (HHC) of each of the three line battalions of the regiment—would form the basis for each new battle group (later battalion) formed under the regiment: Company A would be reorganized as 1st Battalion, Company B as 2nd Battalion (for Regular Army regiments, 1st and 2nd Battalions would be earmarked for active-duty service), and Company C would form 3rd Battalion (for Regular Army regiments, 3rd Battalion would be earmarked for Army Reserve service), while Companies D–M, as well as the HHCs of the original line battalions, would provide the basis for units as needed; the subordinate elements of each of these reorganized units would be newly constituted when the unit was activated.[21]

The 87th Infantry Regiment itself was reorganized in Germany as 1st Battle Group, 87th Infantry, on July 7, 1957, under the pentomic division concept.[22] Company A, 87th Infantry Regiment, was reorganized and redesignated as HHC, 1st

---

[*] The battle group structure will be discussed under the pentomic division concept, below.
[**] CARS has subsequently been replaced by the US Army Regimental System. See Army Regulation 870-21, *The US Army Regimental System*, Headquarters, Department of the Army, April 13, 2017.

Battle Group, 87th Infantry, on July 1, 1957, and subsequently reorganized and redesignated as 1st Battalion, 87th Infantry; Company B went through a similar sequence as 2nd Battalion, 87th Infantry.[23] Company D, 87th Infantry, was constituted on November 15, 1942, inactivated and relieved from the 10th Infantry Division on July 1, 1957, and concurrently redesignated as Headquarters Company, 4th Battle Group, 87th Infantry. It was redesignated Company D, 87th Infantry, on March 23, 1966, and activated for service in Vietnam on June 1, 1966, at Fort Lewis, Washington; Company C underwent a similar sequence of events.[24]

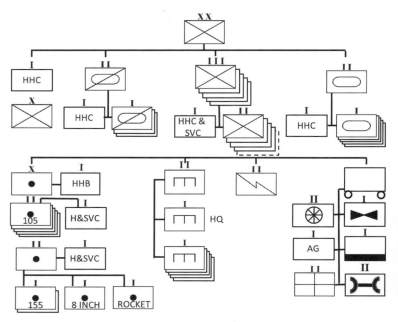

Organization of the pentomic division, excluding 1959 revisions. *From House, Toward Combined Arms Warfare, page 156*

The Pentomic Division

In July 1957, the 87th Infantry Regiment, still under the 10th Infantry Division in Germany, was reorganized as the 1st Battle Group, 87th Infantry, under the pentomic concept. With the introduction of nuclear weapons into the battlefield environment, Army planners believed that to be effective in the new nuclear environment:

Tactical units had to be sufficiently small so that they would not present a lucrative target, sufficiently balanced between the arms so that they could defend themselves when isolated, and sufficiently self-supporting that they could fight without vulnerable logistical tails.[25]

Combat in this new environment would be "cellular rather than linear," and rapid passage of information among echelons of command would be at a premium.[26] Because of this, Army planners sought to flatten the command structure of the division with fewer command echelons, and to facilitate greater physical dispersion between tactical units.[27] Field tests conducted by the Army in 1954 indicated that improved communications capabilities

had rendered feasible a division span of control greater than the traditional three regiments, to an "optimum number" of five.[28] The result was the pentomic division, the name being a "Madison Avenue adjective" contrived for public-relations purposes to "add glamor to ground combat in the era of massive retaliation."[29] The term was nonetheless apt, describing a combat division of five subordinate maneuver units designed to fight and survive on the nuclear battlefield. These battle groups were "relatively self-contained and semi-independent [infantry] units containing many of the support elements previously found in the regimental combat team," but smaller, while still being "larger than the established triangular battalion."[30]

The 87th Infantry under the 2nd Division

Though it would be reorganized as a battle group in July 1957, the 87th Infantry would not function in that configuration for long, because as soon as the 2nd Division was reactivated in 1958, it began functioning as a training division, providing basic and advanced individual training for new recruits, a return to the 87th Infantry's role from its Camp Funston days prior to rotating to Germany.[31] This continued for three years, until

August 1961, when the 2nd Infantry Division was alerted for assignment to the Army's Strategic Army Corps, with a corresponding mission of "engaging in a continuous training program to build and maintain an effective combat capability"; a corresponding "build-up of men and equipment, along with an intensive combat-readiness program, was initiated" to make this mission a reality.[32] The Strategic Army Corps began in 1956, when the chief of staff of the Army "directed the development of a task force in the continental United States that would be prepared for deployment to any part of the world under conditions short of general war, i.e. limited war."[33] Originally designated the "Strategic Army Force," the name was changed to "Strategic Army Corps" (STRAC) in 1957.[34] As originally constituted, the STRAC consisted of three divisions—the 101st Airborne at Fort Campbell, Kentucky; the 4th Infantry Division at Fort Lewis, Washington; and the 82nd Airborne at Fort Bragg, North Carolina.[35] By August 1963, the STRAC consisted of the 1st, 2nd, and 4th Infantry Divisions, as well as the 82nd and 101st Airborne Divisions.[36] As a part of the STRAC, the 2nd ID and the 87th Infantry with it were expected to be "ready to move if called upon to any part of the globe," in whole or in part, to deal with "brushfire trouble spots ... before they spread."[37] As such, the 2nd Infantry Division and the 1st Battle Group, 87th Infantry, with it embarked upon an intensive training program, conducting a four-day division exercise in November 1961 and with units conducting tactical field training from the squad through battle group level four days per week throughout the winter; divisional elements conducted two logistical exercises at Fort McClellan, Alabama.[38] The 2nd Division's status as part of the STRAC became effective on February 15, 1962, and the following April the division deployed Fort Stewart, Georgia, for Exercise Seneca Spear.[39] This was followed in May of that year by Exercise Quick Quick, in which five of the 2nd Division's battle groups trained on amphibious warfare on a rotational basis, and later the 87th Infantry conducted a ten-day exercise in guerrilla warfare in the Chattahoochee National Forest in Georgia.[40]

Back to Germany: The 87th Infantry with the 8th Infantry Division

The year 1963 saw the end of yet another era in the history of the 87th Infantry, and the dawn of another, with the assignment of 1st and 2nd Battalions, 87th Infantry, to the 8th Infantry Division in Germany. As previously noted, 1st Battle Group, 87th Infantry, had been assigned to the 2nd Infantry Division when that organization replaced the 10th Infantry Division in the force upon the latter's redeployment from Germany under Operation Gyroscope. The 2nd Battalion, 87th Infantry, returned to life on January 25, 1963, when it was redesignated as Headquarters and Headquarters Company, 2nd Battalion, 87th Infantry (from 2nd Battle Group, 87th Infantry, which designation it had assumed concurrently with its inactivation pursuant to the implementation of the pentomic division concept in the 10th Infantry Division in 1957).[41] The battalion was reactivated on February 15, 1963, at Fort Benning under the 2nd Infantry Division.[42] Both 1st and 2nd Battalions then deployed back to Germany as part of Rotaplan, a program of temporary rotations of units between Europe and the United States.[43] On September 4, 1963, both battalions were relieved of assignment to the 2nd Infantry Division and assigned to the 8th Infantry Division in Germany.[44] Rotations under Rotaplan were originally intended to last six months, but in the case of the 87th Infantry, the move would be permanent: neither battalion would ever return to Fort Benning.[45]

The 87th Infantry would serve under 8th ID in yet another configuration—this time, as set forth in the Reorganized Objectives Army Division (ROAD) concept.[46] The impetus for ROAD came from Vice Chief of Staff Clyde D. Eddleman, when, on December 16, 1960, he directed the commanding general of Continental Army Command (CONARC) to prepare a division model to replace the pentomic division concept for the years 1961–1965.[47] In addition to the standard infantry and armored divisions, Eddleman directed the development of a new mechanized-division model consisting of "armored infantry units that had the mobility and survivability needed for the nuclear battlefield"; he further ordered consideration as to whether the Army should retain the battle group or revert to battalions, and whether the new division structure should include an intermediate command echelon between the battalions or battle groups and the division headquarters.[48] CONARC produced its study, "Reorganization Objective Army Divisions (1961–1965)," in less than three months.[49] While the pentomic division had focused heavily on combat on the nuclear battlefield, the ROAD planners sought a divisional structure consistent with the new doctrine of "flexible response," which could operate effectively in any combat scenario from "low intensity" counterinsurgency operations to conflict characterized by mechanized and armored warfare, all the way to fighting on a nuclear battlefield if need be.[50] ROAD envisioned a modular approach wherein all types of divisions would share a common basic structure, "to which a varying number of basic combat maneuver battalions could be attached,"[51] with divisions being defined largely by the number of each type of battalion that was included in its organic structure, with the basic structure of an armor division consisting of six armor battalions and five mechanized infantry battalions, and that of a mechanized infantry division being somewhat reversed, with seven mechanized infantry and three armor battalions.[52] This was by no means written in stone, however, since a basic assumption of the ROAD division was that it could be task-organized, with varying numbers of battalions and companies of different types being cross-attached or task-organized for specific missions.[53] Experience had shown the battle group to be a cumbersome element to manage in some respects, such as being too large for some missions but too small for others; additionally, the battle group imposed an overly large span of control on the commander as he sought to control a wide variety of subordinate elements of various types; another consideration was career progression for infantry officers, with the battle group structure significantly constraining the percentage of officers that would receive command and executive officer assignments. Finally, there was concern that concentration of so much of its capability in the individual battle groups rendered the divisions inordinately vulnerable to excessive attrition if faced with nuclear fires, with the loss of a single battle group amounting to 20 percent of the division's combat power.[54] To address these problems, the Army would revert to the smaller battalion, rather than the sprawling and complex battle group, as the basic maneuver unit within the division.[55] Another innovation of the ROAD division was the insertion of the brigade as the intermediate command echelon between the battalions and the division.[56] For armor divisions, this would be a relatively familiar arrangement, being very similar to the combat commands employed in armored divisions during the Second World War, and being designed to "control a varying number of combat and combat support elements," as opposed to the old infantry regiments that consisted of a fixed number of battalions and companies in a homogeneous structure.[57] Finally, the ROAD division ushered in what would be a defining feature of the United States Army at home and as deployed in Europe—the mechanization of the infantry, with maneuver elements from squad on up mounted in the "fully tracked, lightly armored" M113 personnel carrier, which "provided a high degree of cross-country mobility, protection from small arms and fragmentation, and substantial protection from the effects of nuclear weapons."[58]

The ROAD concept was approved by the chief of staff of the Army shortly after its presentation to the Department of the Army in March 1961 and was publicly announced by the president the following May, with reorganization to begin less than a year later, in April 1962.[59] Implementation of ROAD across the Army would be delayed by the need to devote resources to responding to events in Berlin and Cuba, but reorganization was complete throughout the Army by May 1964.[60] The 8th Infantry Division was reorganized effective April 1963, a few months prior to the reassignment of 1st and 2nd Battalions, 87th Infantry, to the division the following September, so that it was in this configuration that the 87th Infantry would serve in Europe.[61]

The 1st Battalion, 87th Infantry, was organized as a mechanized infantry battalion under 2nd Brigade, 8th ID, and stationed at Smith Barracks,

Baumholder, Germany.[62] The 1-87IN would continue in active service in Germany without interruption until October 1, 1983, when it was relieved from assignment to 8th Infantry Division and inactivated.[63] The 2nd Battalion, 87th Infantry, was initially stationed at Sullivan Barracks, Mannheim, Germany, with 1st Brigade, 8th ID.[64] The 2-87IN was inactivated on May 1, 1966, and reactivated (again in Germany, under 3rd Brigade, 8th Infantry Division) on August 31, 1973, at Lee Barracks at Mainz-Gonsenheim, Germany.[65] The 2-87IN was relieved from assignment to 8th Infantry Division and inactivated again on June 16, 1986.[66]

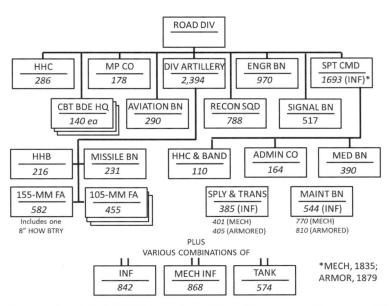

Organization of the ROAD Division. *From Wilson,* Maneuver and Firepower, *299*

The 87th Infantry in Vietnam

It was not just battalion-sized elements of the 87th Infantry that were periodically activated and inactivated under the Combat Arms Regimental System. In two instances, separate companies—C and D—were activated, both for service as rifle security companies in Vietnam. Company C was activated at Fort Lewis, Washington, on June 1, 1966,[67] initially for service with the 92nd Military Police Battalion in Vietnam, providing security at Ton Son Nhut Airbase.[68] The 92nd MP Battalion itself was first activated in France in 1945 and then inactivated in Belgium in 1946; it was reactivated in 1950 for service in Korea, inactivated again in 1953, and then reactivated 1961 at Fort Bragg, North Carolina, for service in Vietnam, where it was inactivated once again on February 5, 1970.[69] Company C was later transferred to Long Binh under the control of the US Army Support Command, Saigon.[70] Company C received Meritorious Unit Citations for 1966–1967 (Saigon Area) and 1967–1968 (Vietnam) before being inactivated.[71]

Company D was activated on June 1, 1966,[72] and would serve two tours in Vietnam.[73] For the first tour, the company traveled by sea to Vietnam

aboard the *General Simon B. Buckner*, making the crossing in twenty-three days.[74] On arrival it was attached as a rifle security company to the 18th Military Police Brigade—one of seven infantry companies to fulfill that role with the brigade during the war, tasked with responsibility for certain physical security functions, allowing more military police to perform their proper function in the field.[75] Company D's command arrangements were complicated: attached to the 18th MP Brigade upon arrival in country, it was further attached to the 89th MP Group operationally, while the 95th MP Battalion provided logistical and administrative support; Company D itself initially supported the 720th Military Police Battalion, by relieving that unit of its responsibilities for Cogido dock and barge facilities, the US Army Vietnam stockade, and the Petroleum, Oil and Lubricant (POL) offloading facility at the Dong Nai River.[76] In 1967, Company D formed a mortar platoon that provided fire support for the 720th MP Battalion.[77] From August to October 1968, Company D's mission further expanded when it augmented Company B, 720th Military Police, at village outposts and on ambush patrols.[78] Company D received Meritorious Unit Commendations for 1967 and 1968 and was inactivated in Vietnam on November 8, 1969.[79]

The company arrived in Vietnam for its second tour on June 30, 1971, providing security for the installations of the 26th General Support Group at Ton May, and departed the country for the last time on April 30, 1972.[80]

That Company D and the other infantry security companies made an important contribution to the success of the 18th Military Police Brigade was attested to in an operational assessment in March 1970:

As of 30 September 1969, D Company, 52 Infantry[,] and D Company, 87th Infantry[,] were reduced to zero strength. These two 18th MP Brigade units provided supplementary physical security personnel and equipment for the protection of three critical logistical sites, namely the Long Birth Ammunition Supply Depot, Cogido Ammunition Discharge Point, and Dong Nai POL Pumping Station. Adjustments were made by the 18th MP Brigade to provide as much support as possible from other of their resources to reduce the impact on 1st Logistical Command units to the minimum possible. The loss of direct support infantry security forces and their constant understrength position has required that mission[-]oriented personnel have had to be diverted from their primary duties to perform guard duties necessary to operate logistical facilities. Consequently, the command's ability to satisfy its logistical function has diminished. By and large the geographical dimensions and security requirements of these sites have changed very little. Critical logistical facilities should be authorized a dedicated force of sufficient size to preclude the need to divert skilled technicians from their primary mission. This security force should be an authorized/integral part of logistics elements of battalion and larger size."[81]

Task Force Wildcat: The 5th Battalion, 87th Infantry, in Operation Just Cause

The 87th Infantry's next battle would occur at a place almost as remote from the mountains of its birth as Vietnam itself—the Isthmus of Panama. On December 20, 1989, only a few weeks after the opening of the Berlin Wall and only a few months before the commencement of Operation Desert Shield / Desert Storm,[82] US Forces executed Operation Just Cause, the invasion of Panama and the overthrow of the regime of the Panamanian "Maximum Leader," Gen. Manuel Noriega.[*] Among the attacking forces was 5th Battalion, 87th Infantry—Task Force Wildcat. The 5-87IN began as Company E, 87th Infantry; on July 1, 1957, Company E was redesignated as Headquarters and Headquarters Company, 5th Battle Group, 87th Infantry, simultaneously with its relief from assignment to 10th Infantry Division.[83] It was reorganized and redesignated as Headquarters and Headquarters Company, 5th Battalion, 87th Infantry, with subordinate elements simultaneously constituted, on May 1, 1987, and assigned to the 193rd Infantry Brigade in Panama.[84] As often occurs, 5-87IN was formed from raw material provided from another organization—in this case by reflagging the 1st Battalion, 187th, as 5th Battalion, 87th Infantry.[85]

Operation Just Cause was a massive and carefully coordinated attack. Striking twenty-one "major points of attack" across central Panama from Fort Cimarron on the Atlantic side to Coco Solo Naval Station on the Pacific, the US invasion force consisted of approximately 26,000 troops, roughly 13,000 of which were already located in Panama, with the remainder deploying from the United States.[86] Facing them was the Panamanian Defense Force (PDF), with a strength of about 12,800, of whom about 4,000 were combat troops, as well as up to eighteen so-called Dignity Battalions, paramilitary units loyal to Noriega.[87]

Conflict with Panama had been a long time in coming. Panama had been at least nominally allied with the US since at least the overthrow of President Arnulfo Arias after just eleven days in office in 1968, by a junta led by Col. Omar Torrijos,

[*] Noriega had been named "Maximum Leader" by the legislature on December 15, 1989. See William Harrison Huff IV, "The United States 1989 Military Intervention in Panama: A Just Cause?," 19–20.

who shortly thereafter consolidated his power and pushed aside Maj. Boris Martínez, who had actually led the coup.[88] This was Arias's third term as president and the third to be terminated by military intervention. Arias had first been elected president in 1940, when he showed himself to be "a fascist and a populist" and "an open admirer of Hitler and Mussolini."[89] He had previously been overthrown by the Panamanian Guardia Nacional (as the PDF was previously known) in 1941, and again in 1951, after having been re-elected in 1949; the senior leadership of the Guardia Nacional resolved to overthrow him a third time after he had after threatened to "purge the Guardia" during this 1968 run for president.[90] Given Panama's geographical position and the existence of the Panama Canal, it was inevitable that Panama would have close ties to the United States, irrespective of the views of Arias and others. Nonetheless, "the United States had a poor relationship with the Guardia Nacional"—and it would get much worse.[91] Future "Maximum Leader" Noriega had assisted Torrijos in consolidating power following the 1968 coup but was "viewed as a most unattractive ally" by US forces in Panama owing to Noriega's "brutal behavior," only kept "in check" by Torrijos—so much so that Gen. Frederick Woerner, commander of US Southern Command, viewed a rise of Noriega to power as "the worst scenario."[92] Trouble was on the horizon, however, with Torrijos's August 1981 death in a plane crash; Noriega consolidated control of the PDF two years later, and "the checks on [him] disintegrated."[93] US concerns about Noriega began to grow by 1985, when national security advisor John M. Poindexter and Assistant Secretary of State for Inter-American Affairs Elliot Abrams spoke out about Noriega's involvement with drug smuggling, and in November of that year the United States stopped military aid to Panama following an attack on our embassy; on February 5, 1988, Noriega and others were indicted in US District Court on drug charges.[94] Other provocations followed, including harassment of Americans in Panama; Noriega's nullification of national elections in May 1989; the declaration of a "state of war" with the United States by Panama in December 15, 1989; the

killing of a US officer and wounding of two others by PDF forces that same month; and the arrest and brutal abuse of a US Navy officer and his wife who witnessed the shootings.[95] The treatment of the Navy lieutenant and his wife was particularly shameful; as described by a Joint Staff study of the Panama invasion, the

> junior US naval officer and his wife were brought to a police station for questioning. Interrogators kicked the officer in the groin, hit him in the mouth, and pointed a gun at his head. Other PDF members forced his wife to stand against a wall while they groped her; she collapsed.[96]

These shootings and arrests were the last straw; President Bush ordered execution of Operation Blue Spoon—soon to be renamed Just Cause—on December 17, 1989.[97] "The mission of Operation Just Cause," as summarized by one scholar, "included five distinct tasks":

> To safeguard lives; protect the Canal; establish democracy; neutralize the Panamanian Defense Force (PDF); and bring Noriega to justice. The enemy included Noriega and the entire PDF, which became the rationalization for the degree of force applied by the US.[98]

In part to pave the way for the establishment of a legitimate civilian government, the chairman of the Joint Chiefs of Staff, Colin Powell, insisted that the United States go in to Panama with overwhelming force, to ensure that US forces would "capture or drive out the entire leadership" of the PDF.[99] Application of "hammerhead military force" would also ensure the rapid destruction of the PDF, thereby preventing it from seizing American hostages, hardening its defensive positions, or carrying out its doctrinal plan of retreating into the jungle and carrying out a guerrilla campaign against the invading US forces.[100] To counter this, US forces struck Panama in a massive, coordinated attack by four separate assaulting task forces. Task Force Atlantic, led by 3rd Brigade, 7th Infantry Division, with two infantry battalions (one from Fort Ord,

California, and one from Fort Bragg, North Carolina), together with other supporting forces, would attack a sector stretching from the Atlantic entrance to the Panama Canal southeast past Cerro Tigre.[101] Task Force Semper Fi, consisting of the elements of the 6th Marine Expeditionary Battalion and supporting forces, struck at the Pacific coast on the western side of the canal, with the primary mission being "to occupy the approaches to the Bridge of the Americas, a vital choke point along the main roads for PDF forces fleeing Rio Hato with possible intent of reinforcing" the Panamanian military headquarters at the Comandancia.[102] Task Force 82nd, also known as Task Force (TF) Pacific, consisting of 1st Brigade of 82nd Airborne Division and other units, struck objectives on Panama's Pacific coast from southeastern Panama City and eastward.[103] Special-operations forces participating included the 75th Ranger Regiment and 3rd Battalion, 7th Special Forces Group.[104]

Although it had the smallest geographical area, covering the eastern half of Panama City, most of Fort Clayton, Albrook Air Force Base, and a triangular-shaped area between TF Atlantic and TF 82nd, the final ground maneuver element, TF Bayonet, arguably had the toughest mission.[105] As the Joint Staff study states,

> Task Force BAYONET faced perhaps the greatest challenge on D Day. Supported by four Sheridan armored reconnaissance and assault vehicles and helicopter gunships, three battalions (5-87th Infantry, 1-508th Infantry [Airborne], and 4-6th Infantry [Mechanized]) at 0100 moved through the sprawling urban area of Panama City to capture Fort Amador, seize the Comandancia, and protect the US embassy.[106]

The core of TF Bayonet was the 193rd Infantry Brigade and its two organic battalions, 5th Battalion of 87th Infantry and 1st Battalion of 508th Infantry, as well as 4th Battalion of 6th Infantry from Fort Polk, which had been deployed to Panama the

previous May as part of ongoing training exercises and was attached to TF Bayonet for the operation.[107] Other TF Bayonet elements included one platoon each from 3rd Battalion, 73rd Armor (Fort Bragg), and Company D, 2nd Light Armored Infantry Battalion (USMC); the 59th Engineer Company; and the 519th MP Battalion, including companies from Fort Meade, Maryland; Fort Lee, Virginia; and Fort Benning, Georgia.[108]

As an organic element within the 193rd Infantry Brigade, 5th Battalion, 87th Infantry, participated in the Panama invasion as TF Wildcat, under the command of TF Bayonet, and consisted of the battalion headquarters company, its three organic light infantry companies, and Company A, 4th Battalion, 6th Infantry (Mechanized).[109] As one of the units permanently assigned to Panama participating in the attack, 5-87IN enjoyed the profound advantage of having been able to fight on ground with which it was intimately familiar and had already trained, and that training began early. As recounted by TF Wildcat commander Lt. Col. William H. Huff III,[*] 5-87IN's training had traditionally focused on jungle operations but had undergone a radical transformation during the months leading up to the invasion:

> Jungle warfare used to be our big emphasis, but that was before the political situation changed. MOUT[**] operations were not part of our wartime mission, but they are now. In July of 1989, we reoriented our Mission Essential Task List to include Military Operations in Urban Terrain. We concentrated previously on jungle operations. Now we are going into specifically two tasks: attack of a built-up area and defense of a built-up area.[110]

This shift in focus required a fair amount of improvisation. Not having a proper MOUT training facility of its own, Lt. Col. Huff "used an old coast artillery bunker complex to train his troops in basic room-clearing techniques," moving from individual to "squad, and eventually platoon, dry-fire

---

[*] Lt. Col. Huff seems to be the father of William Harrison Huff IV, author of the thesis from which this quote is taken; per his vita attached to that thesis, the younger Huff was visiting his father and the rest of the family from college in the US over the Christmas holidays when the invasion took place.
[**] Military Operations in Urban Terrain.

run-throughs of objectives" using blank ammunition and the Army's Multiple Integrated Laser Engagement System (MILES) simulators, before culminating in complex company-level live-fire training scenarios on mock urban sites integrating artillery, engineer, and mechanized infantry support.[111] These sophisticated exercises also included simulated noncombatants, which, if engaged, required the entire unit to repeat the scenario.[112] TF Wildcat also participated in several of the small "Sand Flea" exercises that Gen. Thurman had initiated after succeeding Gen. Woerner in command of SOUTHCOM; ostensibly deemed "freedom of movement" exercises intended to exercise the US forces' treaty rights to traverse the area, they were in reality "very important intelligence[-]gathering missions, as leaders could document the enemy's reaction patterns and conduct reconnaissance of actual objectives."[113] Sand Flea operations carried out by 5-87IN included convoys, "simulated air assaults" in urban areas, and movements in the vicinity of PDF locations, sometimes becoming "armed standoffs between US and PDF forces that came precariously close to actual firefights."[114] As described by one participant,

These short operations, most lasting no more than a single day, were carefully designed to test the Panamanian responses to various US troop movements. Most of the operations dealt with moving fully loaded combat troops into areas that US forces normally did not go. Other combat units were on standby if something had gone wrong. Most missions ended in nothing more than words and gestures being directed toward the US forces. Rarely were they returned in kind from our better[-] disciplined soldiers, but the information gained by the US about the command and control the PDF displayed was crucial.[115]

Training increased in intensity to the point that by November 1989, the battalion was on a seven-day-per-week training schedule, with multiple Sand Flea operations each week.[116] The value of this meticulous training and detail on the ground reconnaissance would become obvious during the battle to come. As one enlisted member of TF Wildcat would reflect years later,

Apparently, the Department of Defense had been planning an invasion for some time, and a detailed plan for this invasion had been disseminated down to the leader level. Since US forces had freedom of maneuver throughout the country and because they knew their planned objectives for an impending invasion, leaders within the Brigade could actually walk the ground they would later fight to seize. Within both battalions, leaders as far down as squad leaders knew the location of the platoon objectives.[117]

Matters came to a head in December 1989, and at 4:30 p.m. on December 19, Lt. Col. Huff briefed his commanders on TF Wildcat's mission, which was "to conduct operations to protect US lives, property, and vital Panama Canal facilities by fixing and neutralizing PDF units in Area of Operation ANTIETAM," while giving PDF forces "every possible chance to surrender."[118] TF Wildcat crossed the line of departure at 12:30 a.m. on December 20, with the attached Company A, 4-6IN, and Company A, 5-87IN (the latter dismounted), leaving from the Curundu Housing Area, while Companies B and C departed for their objectives in a convoy of 2.5-ton trucks hardened with sandbags for this mission.[119] The 5-87IN's mission was to seize and secure certain key locations and establish roadblocks to prevent enemy reinforcement of the area.[120] Company A, 5-87IN, "was to fix and, on order, seize the Panamanian Engineer Battalion Compound to prevent the reinforcement of the Brigade Task Force's main objective: La Comandancia."[121] Company B was to neutralize enemy forces located at the Departamento Nacional de Investigaciones (DENI)* facility in Balboa while protecting the housing facility there and a nearby electrical substation.[122] Company C was to seize the headquarters of the Dirección Nacional de Tránsito Terrestre (DNTT),** a Panamanian police entity, and the Ancón DENI station.[123] Finally, the mechanized troops of Company

---

* National Department of Investigations. See Huff, "The United States 1989 Military Intervention in Panama: A Just Cause?," 75.
** National Directorate of Land Transit. See Huff, "The United States 1989 Military Intervention in Panama: A Just Cause?," 75.

A, 4-6IN, were to establish roadblocks to prevent enemy reinforcement of the Comandancia.[124]

Company A, 5-87IN, had occupied positions overlooking the Engineer Battalion Compound from the east, northeast, and northwest by 12:45 a.m. and, in accordance with the rules of engagement, began making demands by loudspeaker for the PDF forces there to surrender.[125] When the PDF answered with small-arms fire, Company C engaged in "firepower demonstrations" against the buildings to educate the enemy as to what they were facing,[126] as described by Capt. Stacy Elliott, then a platoon leader participating in the attack:

Once we were set in positions around the buildings, the company-attached loudspeaker team started with the requests for surrender. The PDF inside the compound answered with automatic fire. The 1st Platoon then conducted a firepower demonstration, consisting of 100 rounds from each of their three M60s and one round from each of the two 90 mm recoilless rifles. The company mortars, "Thumper," would add in three or four 60 mm HE rounds from a direct lay position on Crystal Hill. After each of these demonstrations, we would again call for the PDF to surrender.[127]

This process continued for several hours, resulting in the surrender of a few enemy soldiers but no sign that the bulk of the fighters ensconced in the facility intended to give themselves up, until at 5:45 a.m. the battalion commander ordered Company A to seize the compound.[128] With 1st Platoon providing suppressive fire, 2nd and 3rd Platoons cleared the compound of enemy soldiers, moving successively from building to building until the compound was reported as secure at 1:00 p.m. on December 20.[129]

Company B commander Capt. Marc Conley divided his unit into three elements to accomplish three distinct tasks assigned to his unit: 1st Platoon protected the Balboa housing area and the civilian families residing there; 3rd Platoon secured the critical Panama Canal Commission (PCC) facilities in the company's area of operations and prevented reinforcement of the Balboa DENI

station, which was assaulted by 2nd Platoon.[130] The 3rd Platoon's mission was not as innocuous as it sounded: it encountered a complex, squad-sized ambush en route to its objective, which it destroyed before securing the PCC, an electrical substation in the area, and the Panamanian Maritime Bureau, as well as securing TF Bayonet's Tactical Operations Center. By 12:45 a.m., 2nd Platoon had encircled the Balboa DENI, establishing support by fire positions in a restaurant, a nearby library, the local YMCA, and a church; as with Company A, attempts to persuade the enemy to surrender by loudspeaker broadcast and firepower demonstrations failed, and the battalion commander ordered Company B to clear the objective by force, which it did with the aid of an AC-130 Spectre Gunship—a C-130 transport specially configured to provide devastating fire support to US ground elements; the objective was secured by 4:45 a.m.[131]

Capt. Scott Smith participated in Company C's attack as an enlisted soldier, serving as squad automatic rifleman in 2nd Platoon.[132] He describes his company's mission this way:

The company was assigned two objectives: the DNTT and the Ancón DENI. The DNTT was a large Panamanian police complex, located on the very western edge of Panama City. The backside of the complex bordered Albrook Air Force Base. An American household goods warehouse bordered the western edge. A short distance to the northeast was a dangerous, high-crime neighborhood known as Hollywood. Across the street from the DNTT was Ancón Hill, which was a large military[-]style housing area that was the home to employees of the Panama Canal Commission. . . . About a mile closer to Panama City was the other company objective known as the Ancón DENI station; it was a large police station just on the very edge of downtown Panama City. . . . The company was task organized with two platoons to seize the DNTT and one platoon to seize the Ancón DENI. The two platoons at the DNTT had an attached team from the 4/6 Mechanized Infantry. This team would secure the rear of the compound and provide some direct fire support.[133]

The Company C commander, Capt. Don Currie, assigned his main effort—the attack on the DNTT—to 2nd Platoon, which would establish a support by fire position across a highway south of the objective, in support of 3rd Platoon, which would conduct the assault; the task of seizing the Ancón DENI fell to 1st Platoon.[134] The DNTT strike force moved to its objective 2.5-ton trucks reinforced with sandbags, while 1st Platoon moved to its attack position to seize the DENI, somewhat comically, in a school bus from the motor pool.[135] As with Companies A and B, Company C attempted to persuade the defenders at the DNTT compound to surrender,[136] as Capt. Smith described after the war:

Shortly after we were in position, someone from the HQ element began to speak over a bullhorn in Spanish, telling the officers inside to immediately exit the building and that they would not be harmed. If they did not comply, the speaker warned, the United States military would treat them as enemy. After repeatedly warning the occupants, to no avail, the platoon was ordered to begin firing at the building in a show of force. The entire platoon opened fire for one minute. The warning was issued several times again. The new warnings yielded the same results: nothing. An M113 from the attached 4/6 Mech unit soon took up position on the road above us. After repeated warnings with no results, the show of force was escalated; this time 60 mm mortars and the .50-caliber machine gun rounds began to rain down on the objective. The .50-caliber tracers bounced around the cars in front of the building as the bullets left 6-inch pockmarks in the walls.[137]

Although these efforts coaxed a few enemy personnel to surrender, they were largely as in-effective as those of Companies A and B had been, and Lt. Col. Huff gave the order to seize the DNTT facility at 3:30 a.m.; the objective was

secured by 9:00 a.m.[138] Meanwhile, 1st Platoon encountered significant resistance as it occupied its positions overlooking the Ancón DENI and was reinforced by a section of mechanized infantry from A/4-6IN; the platoon leader, Lt. Dwayne Spurlock, received the order to assault the objective at 3:30 a.m., which was accomplished within an hour and fifteen minutes.[139]

As to the one company of mechanized infantry attached to TF Wildcat, one scholar has described its role thus:

Huff gave his only mechanized company, Alpha, 4-6 IN (M), the mission of establishing a series of five roadblocks to prevent the reinforcement of La Comandancia from Balboa or Ancón, which tied into Task Force GATOR's left flank. The mechanized company left the Curundu housing area and moved along Gaillard Highway towards Ancón, establishing the roadblocks as it moved. As one of the platoons was positioning its vehicles, it received sniper fire that killed one soldier. It suppressed the sniper and continued the mission. The company encountered little resistance, but its mission was vital to the success of TF BAYONET's main effort on La Comandancia, the center of gravity within Just Cause.[140]

The 5th Battalion, 87th Infantry, played a vital role in securing victory in Operation Just Cause. TF Wildcat was fortunate in having the distinction of being one of very few units in US military history to have the opportunity to train, maneuver, and gather intelligence during the preparation for combat on the very ground on which it would later fight. This provided 5-87IN a distinct advantage over its PDF opponents, notwithstanding the fact that they too were fighting on home turf. Capt. Smith recounts just what a remarkable state of affairs this was. Describing his platoon's arrival at its support by fire position, he recalled that

we jumped down the embankment that separated the road from the railroad tracks below and immediately took up positions behind the tracks. Team leaders and squad leaders made minor adjustments to weapon systems and personnel to match the configuration used in the CALFEX.* The platoon had rehearsed this very occupation repeatedly without the soldiers knowing why. Leaders had enforced the repetitiveness to allow the smooth occupation of the support by fire position. I don't know if I was the only one who felt a sense of deja vu, but it was overwhelming. I asked my acting squad leader, Sgt. Henry Vangas, if I had been here before. He slapped me on the helmet and reminded me we had come here three weeks earlier to get my Panamanian driver's license. Immediately, I understood the entire train-up and how everything we had done in training had led up to this exact moment.[141]

This detailed training was of immense value to the men of TF Wildcat, as recounted by another soldier who participated in the battalion's mission. "When we get a new 18[-] or 19-year-old kid in here, you can watch their eyes get big when you hand them live rounds the first time," he remembered, "but, after a while, it becomes a normal way of life. You start to accept that every time you get sent out, it could be for the real thing."[142] The value of the training was also reflected in the outcome of the battle: TF Wildcat suffered only one killed in action—the Company A, 4-6IN, soldier killed by a sniper—and ten wounded over the course of three days of fighting during the invasion; by contrast, it captured 185 enemy personnel, killed fifty, wounded sixteen, and captured three enemy V300 armored vehicles.[143]** Following the cessation of combat operations, 5-87IN participated in civil affairs activities to support the Panamanian population on an interim basis and assisted in the establishment of the Panamanian Public Forces, the police entity that replaced the PDF.[144] From midsummer to early

fall 1990, the battalion transferred to Panama's Pacific coast, where it assumed a mission focused on security of the canal and protecting US lives and property, while remaining ready to support the Panamanian government and to respond to contingencies in the region.[145] Unfortunately, 5-87IN would soon be called upon to provide such support in response to the attempted coup launched by Col. Eduardo Herrera, former PDF officer who served as the second of the four Panamanian chiefs of police immediately following Operation Just Cause.[146] Unable to accept the fall of Noriega's regime despite his appointment to the new police, Herrera had been jailed, until December 4, 1990, when he "conducted a spectacular escape by helicopter" from prison and, with the aid of fifty policemen, succeeded in taking control of the headquarters of the Panamanian National Police (PNP), attempting to exploit the anniversary of Operation Just Cause to foment an uprising against the government of President Guillermo Endara.[147] President Endara requested US assistance, and 5th Battalion, 87th Infantry, participated in the suppression of the coup, with Herrera and his supporters being taken into custody within a day of US involvement.[148]

In 1994 and 1995, 5-87IN was called upon to secure and house 2,500 Cuban migrants during Operation Safe Haven at one of four camps constructed for the purpose at Empire Range in Panama, and in December 1994, three of the battalion's companies conducted an air assault to suppress rioting at two of these camps, as well as other operations in support of US forces operating the camps.[149]

The 5-87IN was relieved from assignment to the 193rd Infantry Brigade on July 15, 1994, in anticipation of the inactivation of the latter the following October.[150]*** In 1997, the 518th Engineer Company was attached to 5-87IN with the deactivation of its parent, the 536th Engineer Battalion.[151] 5th Battalion, 87th Infantry, inactivated in Panama in 1999.[152]

---

* Combined Arms Live-Fire Exercise.
** The V300 was a six-wheeled light armored vehicle manufactured by Cadillac Gage Textron. See Stephen A. Rel and Randy Stoehr, *Front End Analysis of Armored Vehicles for the Chemically and Biologically Protected Shelter*, 5.
*** Originally constituted in 1921, the 193rd Infantry Brigade had been activated in Panama on August 8, 1962; it was inactivated in Panama on October 14, 1994. It was then transferred to US Army Training and Doctrine Command in 2007 and activated at Fort Jackson, South Carolina. See Headquarters, 193rd Infantry Brigade Lineage, Center of Military History, 2007.

Challenge coin of 5th Battalion, 87th Infantry, Panama. *Author's collection*

Soldiers from Company B, 5th Battalion, 87th Infantry Regiment, board an M939 5-ton truck for transportation to a riot control training session. Fort Clayton, Panama, September 1, 1989. *US National Archives, via US National Archives Public Domain Archive*

A US Army M113 armored personnel carrier guards a street near the destroyed Panamanian Defense Force headquarters building during the second day of Operation Just Cause. Panama City, Panama, December 21, 1989. *Department of Defense photo by PH1(SW) J. Elliott via US National Archives Public Domain Archive, https://picryl.com/, https://nara.getarchive.net*

Soldiers from Company B, 5th Battalion, 87th Infantry Regiment, stay spread out during a tactical training march to Fort Clayton. *Department of Defense photo, 09/01/1989, Fort Clayton, Panama, via US National Archives Public Domain Archive, https://picryl.com/, https://nara.getarchive.net*

A member of the 5th Battalion, 87th Infantry Brigade, armed with an M 249 squad automatic weapon equipped with multiple integrated laser engagement systems (MILES), participates in exercise Fuerzas Unidas Peru '87. *Department of Defense photo, 09/08/1987, Pisco Airbase, Peru, photo by Sgt. Gildow, via US National Archives Public Domain Archive, https://picryl.com/, https://nara.getarchive.net*

The 3rd Battalion, 87th Infantry, during the Gulf War

The 1990 Persian Gulf War was a remarkable conflict in many respects, not least of which because of the heavy reliance on reserve component units called to active duty and deployed rapidly after activation. According to the Association of the United States Army, 140,000 reserve component members were ordered to active duty, many of whom deployed to Saudi Arabia and participated in combat operations there, while many others served to backfill Active Component units in the United States or Europe that had themselves deployed to the Persian Gulf.[153] Notwithstanding the massive employment of the Army National Guard and Army Reserves during the war, controversy arose within the

Army over the notable absence of reserve-component combat maneuver units in the Gulf. Particularly acrimonious was dispute over the Army's employment, or lack thereof, of three Army National Guard roundout brigades mobilized but never deployed—48th Infantry Brigade (Mechanized), Georgia Army National Guard; 256th Infantry Brigade (Mechanized), Louisiana Army National Guard; and 155th Armor Brigade, Mississippi Army National Guard.[154] Under the Roundout program, selected reserve component brigades and battalions were paired with Active Component divisions to provide force structure missing from the Active Component unit's authorized complement; as such, "Each roundout unit represented a significant portion of a parent division's actual combat power."[155]* The three

* The 10th Mountain Division, having by then been reactivated in 1985, had its own Roundout brigade, the 27th Infantry Brigade (Light), New York Army National Guard (Information Paper, Subject: Major Army National Guard Units, NGB-ARF-I, 14 August 1992, in John P. Lewis, *The Army National Guard: Meeting the Needs of the National Military Strategy*, appendix A).

Army National Guard brigades mentioned above were designated as the Roundout brigades for the 24th Infantry Division, the 5th Infantry Division, and the 1st Cavalry Division, respectively (although when mobilized, 155th Brigade was then attached to the 4th Infantry Division).[156] Neither the 5th nor 4th Infantry Divisions deployed to the Persian Gulf, thus accounting for the decision not to deploy the ARNG brigades attached to them, the 256th Infantry Brigade and the 155th Armor Brigade.[157] But the 24th Infantry Division did deploy, prior to the activation of its Roundout unit, Georgia's 48th Infantry Brigade, and the Army's decision not to deploy the 48th to the Gulf despite the latter's having been "validated as combat ready" was the subject of particularly bitter recriminations between the Army National Guard and the Active Army.[158]* The controversy over the 48th Infantry Brigade served as a proxy for resentment of the larger fact that despite the vast extent of reserve component participation in the Persian Gulf War, not a single reserve-component combat maneuver unit—that is, infantry or armor—deployed to the Gulf.

In fact, only a single "reserve component combat maneuver unit" deployed outside the United States during the Gulf War at all; that unit was the Army Reserve's 3rd Battalion, 87th Infantry Regiment.[159]** At the beginning of the Gulf War, 3-87IN was a US Army Reserve infantry battalion stationed in Colorado, one of two separate infantry battalions then extant in the Army Reserve, the other being the 100th Battalion, 442nd Infantry Regiment, descendant of the famous unit composed of Japanese American Nissei that had performed brilliantly in Europe during World War II.[160] The CAPSTONE mission*** of 3rd Battalion, 87th Infantry—that is, the wartime mission allocated to it during peacetime planning, and on which it was to focus its peacetime training

program—was to assist the Active Army's 193rd Infantry Brigade in providing physical security against sabotage and other attacks in the Panama Canal Zone, and 3-87IN had trained for this mission by attending US Army Jungle School in Panama in 1987, by sending personnel to train in Guatemala in 1988, and by carrying out a battalion exercise in Florida in 1989.[161] By one of those ironic twists of history, another element of the regiment—5th Battalion, 87th Infantry— was an Active Component battalion assigned to the 193rd at this time and actually conducted an evaluation of the 3-87IN in 1990, pronouncing the 3rd Battalion to be "a truly competent sister battalion."[162]

The 3rd Battalion, 87th Infantry, would carry out its force protection mission during the Gulf War, but not in Panama. Rather, the coming of war in the Persian Gulf would see the battalion return once again to the regiment's old stomping ground of Germany. On November 8, 1990, President George H. W. Bush announced that the United States would deploy additional forces to Saudi Arabia in preparation for the possibility of an offensive to eject Iraqi forces from Kuwait. Many of these units deployed from Germany, including the mighty VII Corps, two armored divisions, one army and one cavalry brigade, and two field artillery brigades, as well as engineer, military police, military intelligence, combat aviation, and signal brigades.[163] All told, 87,000 soldiers deployed from Germany to Saudi Arabia, leaving a gaping hole both in operational and force protection capabilities in Europe; to compensate for this, 9,088 reserve component soldiers were activated and sent to Europe—3,508 from the Army National Guard and 2,588 from the Army Reserve.[164] Some of these units, though based in Europe, were intended to support the war fight in the Middle East, but ten military police companies,

---

* I remember these recriminations well; many in the Army National Guard firmly believed that the 48th Infantry Brigade had been ready to deploy, and only the self-serving bias of the Active Army prevented it; many in the active component felt otherwise, as evinced by an anonymous letter that circulated in the years following the Gulf War, shown to me by my own battalion commander (I was in the ARNG then myself), citing numerous alleged irregularities in the training, administration, conduct, and discipline of the 48th Brigade, before and after mobilization, to justify the decision.

** The reader will recall that under the Combat Arms Regimental System, Company C of each parent regiment was designated as the parent element for a potential reserve component 3rd Battalion of the regiment.

*** For an overview of CAPSTONE and other attempts by the Army to integrate reserve component units into wartime contingency plans, see Dennis P. Chapman, *Planning for Employment of the Reserve Components: Army Practice, Past and Present.*

two Army National Guard engineer battalions, and 3rd Battalion, 87th Infantry, provided support to US forces in Europe itself.[165]

The mission of 3-87IN would be in support of V Corps; although the V Corps headquarters had not deployed to Saudi Arabia, many of its soldiers had, including the entire 3rd Infantry Division and a number of smaller units.[166] Several thousand of these soldiers had deployed from around Frankfurt, a part of Germany with a particularly high terrorist threat, where attacks against American soldiers, including against two generals, had occurred and where threats against Americans continued to be reported.[167] Concerned about the threat to vulnerable facilities and military dependents left in the area after US troops had deployed to Southwest Asia, the V Corps chief of staff, Brig. Gen. James R. Harding, sought additional forces to fill the security void; initially the gap was filled by the 3rd Battalion, 12th Infantry, an 8th Infantry Division stationed in Baumholder, initially tasked with the Frankfurt security mission as an interim measure until additional forces from the reserve component arrived.[168] Among the forces V Corps received to offset deployments to Saudi Arabia were two military police companies—the 323rd MP Company, ARNG, from Toledo, Ohio, and the 340th MP Company, USAR, from Jamaica, New York; these units did not solve V Corps' security problem, however. V Corps' 18th Military Police Brigade had deployed four of its companies to Southwest Asia and therefore required all the efforts of these two reserve component MP companies for its law enforcement mission.[169] Given the high demand for MP units in the combat theater and elsewhere to perform their law enforcement role, V Corps requested a light infantry battalion for the security mission, since such a unit would have sufficient personnel but would not be encumbered by an excessive amount of heavy equipment.[170] Both the active component and the Army National Guard wanted this mission for one of their units, but the Army Reserve succeeded in securing it for 3-87IN, because "it met all the criteria and was best in terms of reported personnel readiness and availability—an important measure because there were too few

[personnel] fillers to meet all demands for them."[171]

The 3rd Battalion, 87th Infantry, was activated on January 17, 1991, at Fort Carson, Colorado, where it spent twenty days preparing for deployment, departing for Germany on February 5.[172] As reported by a study commissioned by the Office of the Chief, Army Reserve (OCAR), "On the eve of Desert Storm, the 3/87th was eager to go to war and the members of the battalion considered themselves to be well trained and ready to deploy to fulfill their Panama mission—or any other infantry mission,"[173] but "the troops were upset by not being sent into combat in Southwest Asia. The word that the battalion would be going instead to Germany led to a great deal of disappointment, particularly among the IRR fillers who had volunteered for combat duty."[174] The mobilization and deployment of 3-87IN at Fort Carson, during its initial reception in Germany and during the execution of its operational mission, was marked by significant mistrust and misunderstanding between the reserve component unit and its Active Component counterparts, but this dissipated to a large extent during the course of 3-87IN's deployment as the unit itself improved and as its Active Component higher headquarters gained confidence in it; as such, the experience of 3-87IN can be viewed as something of a microcosm of the experience of reserve component mobilizations during the Gulf War generally.

At Fort Carson, 3-87IN underwent administrative processing and predeployment training under the supervision of the US Army garrison at Fort Carson, an entity responsible for the operation of Fort Carson's physical plant and support infrastructure (as distinct from the deployable military units stationed there), and Readiness Group Denver, an Active Component entity responsible for advising and assisting reserve component units in the area.[175] This predeployment period was strained by uncertainty in the minds of the garrison and the readiness group about the nature of 3-87IN's mobilization mission, interpersonal friction between the readiness group and the 3-87IN command, and the perception on the part of many in 3-87IN that much of the training was redundant, since the battalion had already trained for a force protection mission similar to the task it would perform in Germany, pursuant to training for its Panama CAPSTONE mission.[176] The interpersonal friction between the readiness group and the 3-87IN commander was of long standing and predated the unit's alert and mobilization;[177] on the other hand, the confusion about 3-87IN's mission in Germany was largely the fault of the Fort Carson garrison and the readiness group themselves: The 18th MP Brigade had sent a liaison officer to Fort Carson to assist in the 3-87IN's preparations, but

> Fort Carson and MAT* personnel were reluctant to accept the word from the gaining command about the unit's mission. The 18th MP Brigade Liaison Officer, Captain Simmons, sat in on the daily TRRMs** and described the circumstances in Germany, the 18th MP Brigade, and the forthcoming mission of the battalion. However, this information direct from the 18th MP Brigade had little impact on the mobilization processors at Fort Carson because Captain Simmons was outside of the "correct" channels. As the Fort Carson people put it: "The unit had communications with the gaining overseas command before departure from Fort Carson. However, no clear mission guidance was provided, just general type of information was discussed. The overseas gaining command, no matter how good their intentions, had no command responsibility for the unit at that point, and any mission guidance should have come from FORSCOM [US Army Forces Command] through Fort Carson." For their part, the 18th MP Brigade staff was frustrated by their inability to influence what was happening at Fort Carson and by the lack of definite information on the condition and state of training of the battalion and what equipment they would bring to Germany.[178]

Although 3-87IN received excellent logistical support from Fort Carson during its stay there,[179] this period was marred by starkly different perceptions on the part of the 3-87IN, on the one hand, and its Active Component trainers, on the other hand. The readiness group and garrison commanders complained that "the 3/87th did have difficulty getting its units to the right places at the right times and was not good at paying attention to detail" and that "the battalion had poor internal organization and did not seem to function well."[180] Needless to say, the members of the unit themselves did not agree with this view. The 3-87IN had a high sense of esprit de corps and "'regarded itself as a really good unit that was treated poorly in the mobilization process.' Few members of the battalion agree with the outside opinion that the battalion was in poor condition."[181] Both interpersonal friction between the 3-87IN command and the readiness group, and the larger controversy over the decision not to deploy reserve component infantry and armor units to Saudi Arabia, fed into this sense of mutual mistrust. As the OCAR report found,

> This insistence by the Readiness Group that the battalion could not be validated for combat was taken by some members of the unit as an expression of a Regular Army determination not to let RC combat units succeed. Citing the example of the three National Guard Roundout brigades, some Reservists found it credible that there would be such a policy. [One reserve component chaplain] relates that he and another 3/87th officer were told by an officer from the Readiness Group Denver that the 3/87th would "never go to Saudi Arabia" because the Army was not going to allow RC combat units to look good. Allegedly, the members of the Readiness Group were told this by a brigadier general.

---

* The Mobilization Assistance Team (MAT) operated under the leadership of the commander, Readiness Group Denver, and "had primary responsibility for evaluating and providing training assistance to all ANG and Army Reserve units (including the 3/87th). The duties of the MAT were to review the battalion's condition upon activation, set up a training program to remedy defects, monitor progress through the training, and recommend to the garrison commander when the battalion was ready to deploy." John R. Brinkerhoff, John Seitz, and Ted Silva, *Countering the Terrorist Threat: The 3rd Battalion, 87th Infantry*, 13.
** "The basic management event used at Fort Carson to monitor the progress and problems of mobilizing units was the Training and Readiness Meeting (TRRM) held at 1600 hours daily," chaired by the garrison commander and attended by the Readiness Group Denver commander. Brinkerhoff et al., *Countering the Terrorist Threat*, 13.

The importance of this incident is that competent, dedicated Reservists believe that this might have been the Army policy.[182]

On the basis of this author's experience in both the Regular Army and the Army National Guard, it seems likely that there was some truth in the perceptions of both sides of this controversy. As the OCAR study put it, "A neutral observer thought that both of these organizations were wrong, and that [3-87IN] needed to 'calm down' and go along more willingly, while [the readiness group] should not have gotten upset.' As [the garrison commander] pointed out, the 3/87th was fairly typical of most of the RC units that mobilized through Fort Carson."[183] What is clear, however, is that whatever their differences, everyone involved in preparing 3rd Battalion, 87th Infantry, for deployment acted in good faith and did their best to get the unit ready.

In this they were successful: 3-87IN left Fort Carson on February 5, 1991, arriving at Frankfurt Airport on two 747 aircraft—the first at 1645 and the second at 2130—on February 6.[184] In Germany, 3-87IN would serve under the command and control of the 18th Military Police Brigade. The 18th MP Brigade had been first activated in 1966 and deployed to Vietnam to control all nondivisional military police assets in that country; it was inactivated in 1973, later to be reactivated and assigned to V Corps in Germany.[185] Unfortunately, when 3rd Battalion, 87th Infantry, arrived at Frankfurt, they and their hosts in the 18th MP Brigade found themselves, initially at least, repeating some of the difficulties encountered at Fort Carson, for which both sides were in part responsible. The 3-87IN got off to a bad start from the beginning, when the battalion commander, met on the ramp by the 18th MP Brigade commander, had difficulty providing a correct head count of personnel and weapons. The OCAR report describes the situation:

In response to a question about the number of troops and weapons on hand, Lt. Col. O'Neil was unable to give a prompt answer and had to ask for the company commanders to give him an oral report on the spot.

During the ensuing confusion, one of the company commanders gave an incorrect answer and was corrected. The troops waited for over two hours on the cold and windy airfield while all personnel and weapons were accurately accounted for to standard.[186]

While this gaffe may have left the 18th MP Brigade with a bad first impression of 3-87IN, poor coordination and discontinuities on the Active Component side equally tainted the 3-87IN's impression of their hosts. One example is the matter of billeting the incoming 3-87IN troops. The 18th MP Brigade staff worked hard to provide proper support for the 3-87IN and in most respects succeeded, as credited by the personnel of 3-87IN themselves,[187] but on the matter of billeting, significant problems arose. The first was the location of the barracks themselves: sufficient space was not available in the Frankfurt area, so the battalion had to be billeted at Ray Barracks, 18 miles away, making 3-87IN "commuters during their stay in Germany."[188] This was the least of the problems with the barracks, however: the most serious issue was gaining access to them in the first place. "Even after the approval was obtained to utilize Ray Barracks," the OCAR report notes, "gaining possession of the buildings proved to be difficult. The units that had deployed to Southwest Asia had left instructions that their barracks and property were not to be disturbed in their absence."[189] Even after authorization to use the barracks had been obtained, the 3-87IN advanced party found it so difficult to locate the rear detachment NCOs left behind by the owning units that "in desperation" they "broke into the barracks to gain access for the 3/87th" so that they could inventory contents and prepare for the arrival of the main body.[190] Once inside, they found property belonging to the deployed soldiers still unpacked and the facilities in "poor condition," and even after this was addressed, serious problems remained.[191] The 3-87IN was unable to secure adequate weapons racks, especially for pistols, and could not gain access to the office space, conference rooms, or dayrooms in the building, forcing the commander and staff to get by with improvised offices; furthermore, the unit was not provided adequate administrative equipment, since the permanent-party units had locked up all their computers and typewriters, as well as TVs and morale and recreation items, forcing 3-87IN to get by with a "few old items loaned to them by the Giessen Military Community" for office equipment, "while the troops were unable to use any of the morale, welfare, and recreation equipment locked away by the departed units."[192]

Once finally ensconced in the barracks, 3-87IN commenced with in-theater training to prepare for its mission. Initially this was to consist of a three-part training program, with Part I covering Force Protection, and Part II consisting of training relating to 3-87IN's secondary reaction force mission; Part III was to consist of unit training based on 3-87IN's wartime METL* (which closely mirrored its mission in Germany), but this phase of training was never conducted.[193] The force protection portion of the training program consumed 145 hours broken up into several categories, as follows: twenty hours was spent orienting the unit to service in Germany, "information needed by the 3/87th personnel to operate effectively in the local environment"; Force Protection proper required nineteen hours, covering the terrorist threat as well as "USAREUR Security Program, guard procedures, search procedures, recognition of explosive devices, use of military working dogs, weapon and ammunition control, use of force, and crime prevention"; and individual soldier skills included components such as first-aid, nuclear, biological, and chemical skills as well as communications and physical training; and the single largest component of Phase I, qualification on the M16 rifle, the M1911 .45 pistol, and the M60 machine gun, required seventy-eight hours.[194]

As previously noted, in addition to its primary force protection mission, 3-87IN had a secondary mission to provide a "ready reaction force" for Germany and the rest of the US Army, Europe. As described in the OCAR report,

The requirement was to have a company ready for immediate movement anywhere in Germany, and a platoon prepared to move anywhere in Europe. These units were held on standby in Ray Barracks, ready if necessary to be picked up by helicopters and flown to the location of an incident. The housing area had been selected partially because it had a helipad, and the companies had trained in airmobile operations to prepare themselves for this mission.[195]

In Phase II, 3-87IN trained for this mission, spending forty-eight hours on reaction force planning, air mobile operations, security augmentation operations, sustainment, and relief of mission.[196]

The in-theater training received by the 3-87IN provided additional cause for frustration among the members of the battalion, but it was also the turning point in the battalion's relationship with its higher headquarters in Europe, since it stimulated a growing sensing of confidence among the latter in 3-87IN's capabilities.

One reason that the 3-87IN found the training frustrating was that much of it duplicated what the unit had conducted at Fort Carson. As the OCAR report notes, "Unfortunately, the 18th MP Brigade did not know much about the condition or training status of the 3/87th until the unit actually arrived, and so some of the training repeated what had already been done at Fort Carson"; while 3-87IN viewed itself as already trained and proficient on the force protection mission: "The approach of the 18th MP Brigade, as perceived by the senior enlisted personnel of the 3/87th, was that the battalion 'knew nothing' and was an untrained unit that had to start from scratch."[197] In this, the 18th MP Brigade probably had the better of the argument; had the members of 3-87IN had more experience with previous mobilizations, as all reserve component units now do, they likely would have recognized that repetitive training of this sort is simply part and parcel of Army life generally and of the mobilization and deployment process in particular, and not a reflection either upon

---

* METL stands for Mission Essential Task List, defined as "a compilation of collective mission essential tasks which must be successfully performed if an organization is to accomplish its wartime mission(s)." See FM 25-100, *Training the Force*, Department of the Army, 1988, glossary-5.

themselves or their wartime command in Germany. As the OCAR report observed, it was

> noted that while there was some grumbling at the outset about having to fire again on the range, the battalion did it and did it well. What the Reservists perceived as unnecessary training was perceived by the 18th MP Brigade staff as prudent preparation for their important mission of security for the Frankfurt Area.[198]

In other respects, however, the 18th MP Brigade could have handled 3-87IN's training in a more tactful manner and thus avoided some of the friction that arose. One example is the air mobile training portion of the program. As related in the OCAR report,

> Airmobile training was scheduled to prepare the battalion for its rapid[-]response mission. Captain Robert S. Scott, the Battalion Assistant S3, prepared a training plan based on the latest Army doctrine and his experience in planning airmobile training and operations while on active duty with the 25th Infantry Division. However, when his plan was presented by the 18th MP Brigade Operations Officer to the Brigade Commander, he . . . substituted his own plan. Captain Scott and the other leaders of the 3/87th took this as a sign that the Brigade Commander would not accept their knowledge and experience.[199]

The greatest source of friction between 3-87IN and the 18th MP Brigade was conduct of the so-called Warfighters, a group of officers and NCOs assigned by the 18th MP Brigade to assist 3-87IN with its in-theater training program, as described by the OCAR report:

> The "Warfighters" [were] a group of five Captains and five Sergeants First Class or Staff Sergeants of the 18th Military Police Brigade, specially selected for their appearance, physical fitness, leadership, knowledge of training, and professional standards. A team of one officer and one NCO [was] satellited with each company to perform duties as host, liaison, advisor, external evaluation, and, for certain key subjects, principal instructor. Among other functions, the "'Warfighters' [were to] assist units in preparing unit trainers to present instruction, . . . serve as external evaluators for all training sessions, . . . closely monitor safety in all activities, and . . . submit daily progress reports to the Brigade Headquarters."[200]

As is to be expected, the Warfighters were instructed that "training [was to be] managed through the 3/87th chain of command," but many 3-87IN leaders felt that the Warfighters exceeded the brigade commander's mandate and interfered with the 3-87IN's own chain of command, and it would seem that the behavior of some of the Warfighters fully justified this feeling, since "the MP officers and NCOs did try to run the infantry units, driving the first sergeants and NCOs wild by making corrections at formations and giving orders freely"; at least one 3-87IN first sergeant felt that the Warfighters treated him like a "Private E8."[201] Eventually, in some cases after frank discussions instigated by 3-87IN leaders with their Warfighter counterparts, the Warfighters eased off and "reverted to a more helpful stance."[202]*

---

* That the Warfighters assisted the 3-87IN in accomplishing its in-theater training is clear, but they could have done so at a lower cost in personal trust had they taken a more tactful approach. One example of a better approach is that taken by Michael Lee Lanning following the completion of his company command tour in Vietnam. In part because of the high standard of training that he had established in his own company, he was tasked with setting up a program of "refresher" training for the other companies as they rotated in and out of the field. Understanding the proprietary sense that all infantry leaders have over their units, be it a squad or a company—a sense of pride and ownership fully felt by the leadership of 3-87IN—Lanning structured his training to include training events and tasks designed to make it more palatable to the proud infantryman going through it; he ensured that all training and instruction passed through the unit's organic chain of command, and he structured the training program so as to be capable of self-execution by the training unit itself. While 3-87IN, being new to its theater of operations in Germany, was not in entirely the same situation as the companies that Lanning was tasked with training, it had exactly the same sense of pride as any other unit, and, at the very least, the chain of command ought to have been treated as sacrosanct. As Lanning himself wrote about his refresher training, "Although the ranges were under my control, I made sure that instructions to the troops were given through the company commander and his chain of command. I provided facilities and ammunition, but I was careful not to infringe on the commander's turf. I had not forgotten my resentment toward anyone besides the battalion commander telling my troops what to do." See Michael Lee Lanning, *Vietnam, 1969–1970: A Company Commander's Journal*, 225, 247, 257–60, 293.

The training period also had a positive impact on the relationship between 3-87IN and the chain of command in Germany, however, since it gave the latter the opportunity to observe the progress the battalion was making and the overall capability of the unit. An important moment occurred when Maj. Gen. Garner observed Company B, 3-87IN, running a rifle range; he later remarked that he had been so surprised at the quality of Company B's work that he thought that they had run the range better than an Active Component unit would have.[203] Despite frustration among members of 3-87IN at the repetitive nature of some of the training and their resentment of the Warfighters' heavy-handed behavior, 3-87IN won the confidence of their higher headquarters. As the OCAR report notes,

The actual response of the Active Army personnel in Germany to the 3/87th training was genuine delight at how well the Reservists did. General Harding noticed the improvement in the way the battalion operated. Initially, he had supervised the battalion's activities closely, but as he gained confidence in the unit, he turned his attention to other, more pressing matters.[204]

The 3-87IN assumed its force protection mission on March 1, 1991. The units rotated between the physical-security mission (conducted by two companies at a time), the rapid-reaction mission (one company), and "time off" (one company), with the units in the latter two statuses conducting training; the headquarters and headquarters company (HHC) provided support to the battalion throughout.[205] The battalion's core task was its force protection mission, in which it guarded five secure areas that rotated among the units weekly, with the soldiers working twelve-hour shifts with two to three days off per month.[206] Initially 3-87IN inherited positions built by their predecessors of the 3rd Battalion, 12th Infantry, but 3-87IN improved them substantially.[207] As the OCAR report described it,

The essence of the mission was to provide fixed site security for facilities and housing areas by standing guard at fighting positions, patrolling barbed wire and other fences, and controlling access to the secured areas by checking identification and conducting vehicle and individual searches as required.[208]

The 3-87IN successfully executed its force protection mission and was never called upon to carry out its rapid-reaction function; as summarized by the OCAR report,

The force protection mission of the 3/87th was carried out successfully but not uneventfully. There were numerous instances requiring increased vigilance, but there were no terrorist attacks—perhaps due to the visible presence of the infantry soldiers defending the Army's facilities and families.[209]

Sadly, it was some of the very families that the men of the 3-87IN were assigned to protect that gave rise of the more regrettable aspects of the unit's deployment, since, surprisingly, some members of the local American community resented rather than appreciated the 3-87IN's presence. As related by the OCAR report, "At first, the wives of the 1st Brigade, 3rd Armored Division[,] resented having the 3/87th occupy the barracks and offices of their husbands who were serving in Southwest Asia," and some particularly unpleasant dependents of deployed troops actually "screamed at them and harassed" members of 3-87IN.[210] Happily, this tawdry state of affairs did not persist, as the community grew to appreciate 3-87IN, in part viewing them as an improvement over the 3-12IN infantry that had preceded them, who "had left a bad taste in some people's mouths."[211] In time the relationship between 3-87IN and the local community warmed to the point that

many dependents showed their appreciation by bringing food and drink to the troops, and throwing parties for them. The dependents were well aware of the terrorist threat and welcomed the presence of the 3/87th, saying that they liked seeing soldiers marching in formation and that hearing cadence counts was "music to our ears."[212]

The 3-87IN's mission in Germany lasted eighty-four days, with the battalion arriving back at Fort Carson on May 1, 1991, where "demobilization processing . . . proceeded rapidly but not smoothly," since as is always the case, "The troops wanted out and were generally not content to go along with the desire of the authorities at Fort Carson for an orderly process."[213]* The battalion was released from active duty on May 15, 1991, after having served 120 days.[214]

The 4th Battalion, 87th Infantry, in Haiti: Operation Uphold Democracy

As with the 3rd and 5th Battalions, 4th Battalion of 87th Infantry was one of the elements of the regiment that not only existed apart from the 10th Mountain Division, but whose separate existence overlapped the earlier years of the modern 10th Mountain Division's existence. On June 16, 1986, Company D, 87th Infantry Regiment (previously inactivated following service in Vietnam), was reorganized and redesignated HHC, 4th Battalion, 87th Infantry, and the new battalion was activated and assigned to the 25th Infantry Division, with which it would serve until being inactivated on July 15, 1995.[215] Unlike 3rd and 5th Battalions, however, 4-87IN has the distinction of not only having served in an expeditionary capacity in the same theater of operations as the modern 10th Mountain Division itself—Haiti during Operation Uphold Democracy—but having actually relieved another 87th Infantry unit—2nd Battalion, 87th Infantry, 10th Mountain Division—when assuming that mission.[216]

Often when activating and inactivating units, the Army simply reflags existing formations—an existing unit sheds one designation and assumes another without significant change in personnel. Not so with 4-87IN: when this battalion was activated as a light infantry battalion in 1986, it was assembled as a cohort unit, with many of the unit leaders reporting first, then undergoing training themselves, including the Army's Light

Leaders Course at Fort Benning, Georgia, to be joined later by the junior enlisted soldiers, who completed their initial entry training in the Army contemporaneously and reported to 4th Battalion as a group, or cohort.[217] As with many light infantry units, 4-87IN commenced a rigorous training-and-deployment schedule, including exercises in locales such as Australia; Japan; Fort Hunter Liggett, California; and the Jungle Operations Training Center in Panama.[218] The 4-87IN's most noteworthy adventure, however, was the battalion's deployment to the island nation of Haiti as part of Operation Uphold Democracy.

US forces entered Haiti on September 19, 1994, pursuant to UN Security Council Resolution 940, adopted July 31 of that year, to restore deposed Haitian president Jean-Bertrand Aristide to power.[219]** The initial entry and operations in Haiti were conducted by the 10th Mountain Division,*** but in early December 1994 the 25th Infantry Division received a warning order that it would relieve the 10th Mountain Division in Haiti.[220] The 3rd Brigade, 25th Infantry Division, including 4-87IN, was tasked to relieve with 10th Mountain Division's 2nd Brigade at Cap-Haitien, Haiti, the relief to occur in January 1995.[221] Maj. Bruce E. Stanley has left as an interesting description of 4-87IN's tour in Haiti from his vantage point as officer in Company C, 4-87IN, during that deployment.[222]

Preparation for the deployment began immediately upon alert, when 3rd Brigade, 25th Infantry Division, established a planning cell consisting of the battalion executive officer and the Company B and C commanders from 4-87IN, tasked with developing a predeployment training plan based in part on lessons gathered from the 10th Mountain Division's experience there.[223] The resulting plan focused on dealing with what the brigade commander viewed as the most significant threat 25th ID would face in Haiti—"one armed individual, in one room of a building, with one or more noncombatants in the building with him

---

* As anyone who has ever redeployed from an overseas mission can attest, this impatience is felt by every soldier at every demobilization station; what's more, if the experience of the US Army following World War II is any indication, this chaffing at the time it takes to complete demobilization and get back home can fairly said to be universal. See R. Alton Lee, "The Army 'Mutiny' of 1946."

** The background and larger context of Operation Uphold Democracy is deferred to the treatment of the 10th Mountain Division's participation in that expedition. For now, we simply examine 4-87IN's deployment there.

*** Discussed in chapter 9.

at night"—as well as the mission-critical tasks of close quarters combat (CQC), "presence patrols, fixed site security, convoy operations, and check-point operations," and the rules of engagement (ROE) for the deployment.[224] Company C, 4-87IN, began its predeployment training on December 8, 1994, its advanced party consisting of the company executive officer, supply sergeant, com-munications sergeant, company drivers, and the armorer deployed on January 3, 1995, and the main body arrived in Haiti on January 17, 1995.[225] The 4-87IN relieved sister battalion 2-87IN at Camp Catamount in Haiti's second city, Cap-Haitien, northern Haiti, assuming operational control on January 21, 1999.[226] Per Maj. Stanley, TF 4-87IN would be based at Camp Catamount along with

> a platoon of engineers, a platoon of MP's, a postal unit, a CA and PSYOP unit, an Armed Forces radio station, a small Army Airforce Exchange Service (AAFES) post exchange, the Brown and Root contractors, and the AT&T telephone contractor. Brown and Root operated and maintained the camp infrastructure. They provided base maintenance, fuel, laundry and bath facilities, a mess hall, and garbage disposal. Each function they performed reduced the requirements for the unit. AT&T provided a long[-]distance telephone service in the camp with about twenty phones available. The Post Exchange carried snacks, books and magazines, sodas, and toiletries, and some Uphold Democracy souvenir items.[227]

Missions conducted on a recurrent basis by TF 4-87IN included security of Camp Catamount, urban presence patrols, and "out[-]of[-]sector missions," rotated by company weekly.[228] Per Maj. Stanley,

> The base camp security mission required the company to conduct sustained operations for 24 hours a day, for seven days [and] included the security of the base camp, the

airfield, the fuel point and the camp entrance. The scope of the mission included occupation of guard positions, with a minimum of two soldiers per position. The platoons conducted the guard mission in six-hour shifts with six hours on and twelve hours off. The company noncommissioned officers planned and executed this mission. The platoon sergeant was the sergeant of the guard.[229]

Additionally, the company on base security detail provided a platoon for the battalion quick-reaction force (QRF) and conducted the weapons buyback program.[230] The platoon QRF consisted of "one rifle platoon, a medical section, a combat engineer team, one psychological op-erations team, a field grade officer from the battalion, and a battalion communications team"; it was billeted in living quarters adjacent to the battalion TOC,* with vehicles loaded, and was ready to deploy on ten minutes' notice.[231] TF 4-87IN alerted its QRF five times during the deployment to Haiti.[232] The Weapons Buy Back Program would be implemented by an officer and a small security detail. As described by Stanley,

> The intent of the program was to reduce or eliminate the number of weapons the Haitians possessed. The dates and times of the buy back were broadcast to the Haitians over the radio and by the psychological[-] operations broadcasts in Cap-Haitien. During the three months in Cap-Haitien the battalion paid $12,500 for nine MI rifles, three M14 rifles, four shotguns, 19 pistols, and 32 CS hand grenades while in Haiti. The weapons were operational even though obvious recent operator maintenance was lacking on all the weapons. The success of the program is unknown since it was voluntary."[233]

One of TF 4-87IN's key tasks in Cap-Haitien was the conduct of presence patrols through the city, which sought to deter violence, provide stability, and foster confidence among the populace that they were secure; during its tenure in Haiti, 4-87IN

---

* Tactical Operations Center.

conducted 242 mounted and 345 dismounted presence patrols.[234] Maj. Stanley describes the typical routine for units on presence patrol duty:

A typical day for a platoon during the patrolling week included an early breakfast, a morning patrol followed by physical training, personal hygiene, a lunch break and preparation time for the afternoon patrol. Following the afternoon patrol the platoon [ate] dinner and prepare[d] for the night patrol. Each patrol lasted between two and four hours. The start times of the patrols varied every day so no patrol ever started or ended the same time. With two platoons patrolling and one platoon on QRF, the company conducted a minimum of four daylight patrols and two night patrols every day.[235]

During out-of-sector missions, 4-87IN would "leave the Cap Haitien area, get out into the country of Haiti and interact with the local Haitian people."[236] On these missions, TF 4-87IN would assess local economic and security conditions (including assessing local jails to ascertain the number of prisoners, their condition, and the how they were being treated by the new Haitian police), provide security for specific events, broadcast messages from the Haitian government, and make the US presence felt.[237] During its participation in Operation Uphold Democracy, TF 4-87IN "conducted eleven out[-]of[-]sector patrols to Gonaives, Port de Paix, Liberte/Ferrier/Ouanaminthe, Saint Raphael / Don Don, Magasin, Le Borgne, two to Fort Liberte, Hinch, Capotilee, and Gros Morne."[238] The 4-87IN units encountered strange things on some of these patrols, including dead bodies and voodoo rituals. On one occasion, a platoon from Company C of 4-87IN patrolling on the outskirts of Cap-Haitien observed a stack of bodies at the local cemetery; "Regarding this as a less than normal occurrence," the platoon secured the area and reported the information.[239] As Stanley reports,

The platoon observed about a dozen bodies each with a variety of injuries to their bodies. Once the report was forwarded to battalion and brigade the confusion and requests for

information began. The brigade headquarters began requesting a variety of detailed information about the number of bodies, the type of injuries, and details about the bodies such as approximate age, race, and sex. Answering these questions required the platoon to possibly move the bodies for a more accurate report. In the meantime the brigade contacted the local police . . . and reported the platoon's find. . . . The platoon did well by reacting quickly to cordon off and secure the area and reporting quickly. Unfortunately for them they had to wait for about three hours in the midday heat with a dozen bodies while the local police and their monitors responded to the report. Additionally, they had to endure a series of unfortunate requests for information from brigade that required them to examine the bodies closer than anyone wanted to.[240]

As strange a sight as it was, however, the matter turned out to be a false alarm: when the local gravedigger arrived, the platoon learned that the bodies were unclaimed corpses from the local hospital delivered to the cemetery "for a pauper's burial."[241] Another strange force encountered by members of TF 4-87IN was the Haitian custom of voodoo. Again, Stanley provides an example:

Voodoo was something the company was briefed on prior to deploying to Haiti. The expectation that the company would encounter any type of voodoo was very low or non-existent. Most of C Company didn't really understand voodoo. Lt. Powel, the platoon leader of 2nd Platoon, was conducting a presence patrol in AO St. Louis. During the conduct of the patrol the owners of a radio station informed him that a voodoo ceremony site was found in an adjacent field. Upon further investigation he found three voodoo symbols in the field. The radio station operators were nervous because they saw the site as a threat to them. They were in the process of purchasing the field that was adjacent to the land on which the radio station was located. Allegedly, another person claimed ownership of the land. Upon further investigation the platoon was unable to determine who had placed the voodoo symbols in the field. Additionally, the specific ownership of the field could not be determined. The radio station did request additional US presence and asked if the military could provide security to their property. This request was forwarded to brigade but declined.[242]

The 4-87IN's remarkable mission in Haiti ended in March 1995, relieved by a Pakistani battalion in Haiti under UN auspices.[243]

Challenge coin commemorating the deployment of 4th Battalion, 87th Infantry, 25th Infantry Division, for the Multinational Force and Observers Mission in the Sinai desert, Egypt, from August 1991 to February 1992, obverse. *Author's collection*

Another 4-87IN challenge coin, obverse. *Author's collection*

Reverse of a challenge coin commemorating the deployment of 4th Battalion, 87th Infantry, 25th Infantry Division, for the Multinational Force and Observers Mission in the Sinai desert, Egypt, from August 1991 to February 1992, obverse. *Author's collection*

Reverse of another 4-87IN challenge coin. *Author's collection*

Soldiers from Company A, 4th Battalion, 87th Infantry, 25th Infantry Division, Schofield Barracks, Oahu, Hawaii, walk through the river Esthere Bambou on the morning of March 3, 1995. They are walking to the pickup zone, wearing their backpacks with bedrolls and M85 Kevlar-lined helmets, and carrying M16A2 rifles and M249 squad automatic weapons (SAW), so they can be flown to Cap Haitien. They have just completed their mission of patrolling Le Borgne, Haiti, and surrounding smaller towns, to deter violence and maintain a safe and secure environment, in support of Operation Uphold Democracy. *Department of Defense photo, March 3, 1995, Le Borgne, Haiti; photo by Spc. Kyle Davis (USA) via US National Archives Public Domain Archive, https://picryl.com/, https://nara.getarchive.net*

Soldiers from Company A, 4th Battalion 87th Infantry, 25th Infantry Division, Schofield Barracks, Oahu, Hawaii, approach and board a CH-47 Chinook helicopter on the morning of March 3, 1995, after conducting a company-size patrol of Le Borgne and its outlying smaller villages to deter violence and maintain a safe and secure environment in support of Operation Uphold Democracy. *Department of Defense photo, March 3, 1995, Le Borgne, Haiti; photo by Spc. Kyle Davis (USA) via US National Archives Public Domain Archive, https://picryl.com/, https://nara.getarchive.net*

Soldiers from Company B, 5th Battalion, 87th Infantry Regiment, wait for transportation to a riot control training session, Fort Clayton, Panama. *Department of Defense photo, September 1, 1989, via US National Archives Public Domain Archive, https://picryl.com/, https://nara.getarchive.net*

CHAPTER 9

The Modern 10th Mountain Division

The ROAD division, on the basis of Army studies beginning in the late 1950s and implemented from 1962 to 1964, persisted as the Army's basic organizational structure, with updates, throughout the 1970s.[1] However, work on the Army's next-generation division structure had begun by the middle of that decade. Stimulated in part by the course of the 1973 Yom Kippur War between Israel and an Arab coalition, the US Army developed the "Active Defense" tactical doctrine; this, as well as emerging technological developments, led the US Army Training and Doctrine Command (TRADOC) to launch the Division Restructuring Study (DRS) in 1975, which produced a new heavy-division design by March 1977.[2] A test of the new structure, based on the DRS model, was initiated in 1979, using one brigade of the 1st Cavalry Division at Fort Hood as the test bed; the results were found unsatisfactory, however, and even before the test was completed, TRADOC commander Donn A. Starry began work on a new concept based on tactical ideas that would eventually become the AirLand Battle concept and displace the Active Defense doctrine in 1982.[3]* This became the Division-86 initiative, "so named because 1986 was as far out as [the army] could project the threat.[4] Chief of staff of the Army, Gen. Edward C. Meyer, approved the Division-86 Heavy Division model in October 1979; at the same time, he directed TRADOC to develop standard models for airborne, air mobile, and standard-infantry divisions, now classed together as "light divisions."[5]

Throughout the 1970s, Department of Defense (DoD) policy focused nearly all Army modernization efforts on meeting the Soviet threat to NATO in Europe, and as a consequence, little thought was given to contingency operations elsewhere in the world; the department's nearly total focus was deployment of heavy forces to reinforce Europe, and so strong was this impulse that as late as 1979, DoD policy "envisaged mechanizing all the remaining active light infantry divisions exclusive of one airborne and one air assault division."[6] However, events in 1979, including the Soviet invasion of Afghanistan and the Iran hostage crisis, finally awoke the Carter administration to the importance of flexible forces, including light infantry divisions, capable of rapid deployment to cope with unexpected contingencies.[7] With that, Gen. Meyer was able to tamp down the pressure for further mechanization, and in late August 1979 it was announced that the light-division concept was to be studied within the framework of the Division-86 initiative, with the 9th Infantry Division at Fort Lewis, Washington, designated as a test bed and "organizational model for the effort."[8] Late the next month, Generals Starry and Meyer agreed on the basic mission of the future light infantry division: "The light division," they announced, "should be able to deploy rapidly to reinforce forward forces in NATO. It would also conduct worldwide contingency operations to destroy enemy forces and to control land areas, including population and resources," reflecting Gen. Starry's view that notwithstanding the primary threat posed by the USSR, "the magnitude of the threat to NATO had not lessened the Army's requirement to respond to contingencies worldwide,"[9] and that

the Army had to be prepared to field strategically responsive, flexible, sustainable light divisions for an array of contingencies. These divisions would have to seize beachheads and airheads, repel counterattacks, and ready the area of operations for arrival of heavy forces [while being] flexible enough to reinforce in Europe.[10]

---

* AirLand Battle doctrine envisaged "nonlinear battles which attack enemy forces throughout their depth with fire and maneuver" and "require[d] the coordinated action of all available military forces in pursuit of a single objective." FM 100-5, *Operations*, Department of the Army, 1982, 1–5.

In terms of tactical capabilities, the new light infantry divisions were to be able to "attack or defend to delay or disrupt enemy armored forces, or to destroy light enemy forces" on mixed or open terrain; to be able to attack, defend, and seize and hold objectives against mechanized or dismounted forces in "close terrain"; and to be able to be able "to conduct rear area and urban operations and to delay or disrupt enemy operations."[11] Concept development proceeded apace throughout 1980, with several design models being developed: on January 15 of that year, planners presented Gen. Starry with an 18,000-man light infantry division model, which he rejected as too heavy.[12] Later that month a 14,000-man planning model was approved as the basis for further work; further refinements were presented in April 1980, in the form of a proposed 15,593-man light division, which was rejected by the chief of staff of the Army as too manpower intensive; on April 30 that year, Gen. Starry directed consideration of a 12,000-man model; on August 1 a third proposal was rejected.[13] Finally, in September 1980, Gen. Starry relaxed the 14,000-man cap, approving a 17,773-man concept for purposes of planning and testing.[14] Plans also advanced for the use of the 9th Infantry Division as the "high technology test bed" (HTTB) for development of the light infantry concept, with a 15,977-soldier "High Technology Light Division" (HTLD) division model being approved in April 1982 for testing, later growing to 17,742.[15]

Both the Division-86 and HTLD concepts were brought to an abrupt halt, however, when Gen. Meyer's successor, Gen. John A. Wickham, initiated the Army of Excellence initiative in 1983.[16] Drawing lessons from the US invasion of Grenada, the British experience in the Falkland Islands, and Israeli operations in Lebanon, Gen. Wickham concluded that "credible forces did not have to be heavy forces"; this, combined with his belief that the Army could not afford light divisions organized under the Division-86 or HTLD models, led Wickham to order the development of a 10,000-soldier model for light infantry divisions.[17] Under Gen. Wickham's guidance, "the new light division should be significantly lighter than Infantry Division 86" and the HTLD division;

further, it would "not be expected to be self-sustaining."[18] Rather,

The division would need to be firepower-intensive, applicable to the low-intensity realm but not designed for that option alone. It should embody only minimum support, requiring corps support for much of its combat service support requirements [and] would always deploy with support from corps.[19]

In August 1983, Gen. Wickham provided further guidance on the Army of Excellence concept. With respect to the light infantry division design,[20]

General Wickham directed TRADOC to continue work on a 10,000-man structure with a high infantry component—50 percent—oriented primarily to contingencies in the Pacific, Latin America, and Africa. The division would be oriented only secondarily for use in NATO Europe and Southwest Asia, when augmented and used in terrain suited to its light capabilities such as urban and forested areas. The division would also be designed for preventing escalation of low[-]intensity conflicts, and for supplementing heavy forces. Gen. Wickham's . . . directive to TRADOC was to create design options that would "form the nucleus of a hard-hitting, high esprit, elite light force serving as the cornerstone of global flexible response in conjunction with air assault and airborne forces."[21]

These proposals were to be ready by October 1983, and he approved the 10,000-man light infantry division concept presented to him at that time.[22] The result was the Army of Excellence light infantry division of 10,220 soldiers initially, later increased to 10,791 with the addition of a military intelligence battalion and additional support personnel.[23] The 7th Infantry Division was designated for conversion to the new light model and designated as the test force tasked with evaluating the concept and resolving the organizational, training, operational, and equipment issues that would inevitably emerge.[24] In addition to the conversion of the 7th Infantry Division, the 25th Infantry Division at Schofield Barracks, Hawaii, was designated for conversion, and the 6th Infantry Division (Fort Richardson, Alaska) and 10th Mountain Division (Fort Drum, New York) were to be activated as light infantry divisions.[25] Two of these divisions—the 7th and 25th—would be organized without resort to reserve-component Roundout units, whereas the 6th and 10th would require round-out augmentation, the 10th receiving an Army National Guard round-out brigade, and the 6th receiving Roundout elements from both the Army National Guard and Army Reserve.[26] The 7th Infantry Division was to commence conversion first, in 1984.[27]

On September 11, 1984, the Defense Department announced that the 10th Mountain Division was to be reactivated in 1985 as the Active Army's seventeenth division and stationed at Fort Drum, New York.[28] The previous April, Gen. Wickham had published a white paper on the light infantry division concept, setting forth his intention to man each of the divisions at 100% authorized strength; nonetheless, when the 10th Mountain Division's activation and stationing was announced, it was to be with only two Active Component brigades, with the third brigade being supplied as a Roundout unit from the reserve components.[29] Fiscal and political considerations undoubtedly played a major role in the 10th Mountain Division's stationing decision as well as the decision to organize it as a two-brigade formation with RC Roundout. As to stationing, New York State and its congressional delegation had lobbied for one of the new light infantry divisions to be activated there, and the adjutant general of the New York National Guard had pressed the matter directly with Gen. Wickham.[30]

The acceptance of Roundout elements rather than fully manned Active Component divisions for the 6th Infantry and 10th Mountain Divisions was a significant retreat from the stance on readiness taken by Gen. Wickham in his 1984 white paper, since "the resulting substitution of a Roundout brigade from the New York National Guard meant that the complete division would never be able to achieve a short-notice, rapid[-] deployment capability"[31] (emphasis added). But it paid dividends in other ways, both in terms of offering the opportunity for enhanced congressional support and fiscally: the active-duty authorizations that would have been utilized in standing up the 10th Mountain Division's third brigade were able to be applied to creating a second brigade—in addition to the already extant 172nd Brigade in Alaska—for the new 6th Infantry Division to be formed there; thus, by making use of reserve-component Roundout elements, the Army was able to form two new light infantry divisions, essentially, for the price of one.[32] As its Roundout brigade, the 10th Mountain Division was assigned the New York Army National Guard's 27th Infantry Brigade.[33] The 27th Infantry Brigade was originally constituted as the 27th Division and called into federal service on July 15, 1917, serving in France during World War I; it was again called into federal service on October 15, 1940, and subsequently served in the Pacific theater during the Second World War. After numerous reorganizations, it was finally converted to the 27th Brigade, 50th Armored Division, in 1968.[34] The 27th Brigade was subsequently reactivated as the 10th Mountain Division's Roundout brigade, in which capacity it served from 1986 to 1992.[35*]

Given the physical realities of Fort Drum in 1985, the facilities at Fort Drum, then extant, could support only a single brigade; accordingly,

---

* The 27th Infantry Brigade was subsequently redesignated as one of the Army National Guard's enhanced separate brigades; following a tour of duty in Iraq in 2006, it was reorganized as a brigade combat team. It is now a subordinate echelon of the New York Army National Guard's 42nd Division. John J. McGrath, *The Brigade: A History, Its Organization and Equipment in the US Army*, 232; and "HQ, 27th Infantry Brigade Combat Team, NYARNG."

initially only 1st Brigade, 10th Mountain Division, was activated at Fort Drum, while 2nd Brigade was activated at Fort Benning, Georgia, and transitioned to Fort Drum only after installation construction was completed in October 1988.[36] Fort Drum is located in the "North Country" of upstate New York, near Canada. It lies about 13 miles northeast of Watertown, the largest city in the area; approximately 25 miles east of the old Madison Barracks at Sackets Harbor, on the shore of Lake Ontario, approximately 30 miles south of the famous Thousand Islands region of the St. Lawrence River; about 62 miles southeast by road from Kingston, Ontario; and about a five-hour drive north of New York City. The United States Army and the military forces of New York State have a long history in the region. A detachment of soldiers were posted in the area in 1809 to enforce the 1808 Embargo Act, which proscribed trade with Canada.[37] At the outbreak of the War of 1812, Fort Volunteer, a hastily constructed earthen fortification, was established in the area, shortly to be superseded by a new blockhouse, fortifications, and barracks for 2,000 soldiers, named Fort Pike for Gen. Zebulon M. Pike.[38] Madison Barracks was established at Sackets Harbor in 1816, with initial construction completed by 1819, being intermittently occupied through 1945 and playing a part in every major war between, hosting artillery, infantry, and recruit-training units at various times.[39] During its long tenure as a military installation, Madison Barracks was home to a number of luminaries of American history, including Ulysses S. Grant, who served there as a lieutenant in the 4th Infantry following the Mexican War;[40] Dr. Samuel Guthrie, inventor of the percussion system of ignition for firearms, and one of the first discoverers of chloroform;[41] and the future Gen. Mark W. Clark, who would have such a great impact on the 10th Mountain Division's campaign in Italy and was born at Madison Barracks in 1896.[42]

The history of Fort Drum proper began at least as early as 1907. In that year, Col. Philip Reade, commander of the 23rd US Infantry, then stationed at Madison Barracks, concluded that the facilities there were unequal to the requirements for military training on modern weapons.[43] Reade worked with leaders in the local community, and an area near the tiny hamlet of Felts Mills, adjacent to the Black River, was selected for training, and the New York National Guard established Camp Hughes there as a training encampment from August 31 to September 7 of that year.[44] The following year, Brig. Gen. Frederick Dent Grant, son of former US president Ulysses S. Grant, trained 10,000 troops in the area—2,000 Regular Army soldiers and 8,000 militiamen—at a site known as Pine Plains; this location was purchased for permanent use as a training facility the next year, and the future Fort Drum was born.[45] A major US Army exercise was conducted here in 1935, with 36,500 soldiers from the northeastern United States participating.[46] Such was the scale of the exercise that additional land had been leased for the purpose, with the government purchasing another 9,000 acres to expand the site thereafter.[47] By the Second World War the area had become known as Pine Camp, and it was vastly expanded to support the war effort: an additional 75,000 acres of land was purchased, displacing 525 families and obliterating five whole villages while greatly reducing the size of others; the 3,000 extant structures thus abandoned were replaced by a "city" of 800 buildings built to sustain training of units at the post, including 4th Armored Division, the 45th Infantry Division, and the 5th Armored Division, as well as the housing of enemy prisoners of war.[48*] Following the war, Pine Camp was renamed Camp Drum in 1951 after Lt. Gen. Hugh A. Drum, a World War II First Army commander; it was redesignated Fort Drum in 1974, when a permanent-party garrison was assigned to the

---

* Notwithstanding the value of Pine Camp to the war effort, the displacement of many families engendered bitterness, some still persisting upon the reactivation of the 10th Mountain Division. As the division's *Historical Review for 1984–1986* notes, although "good for the war effort," this expansion "left long-lasting, and in some cases, extremely bitter feelings toward the government because of the loss of family lands. These feelings existed even if the reimbursement was at a 'fair market value.' At the time of the World War II expansion, many of the displaced families—in some cases whole communities—left the area. However, many returned during the following decades to take up residence in the towns and villages which had survived basically unmolested by government actions. A considerable number of these people were still on-hand in the fall of 1984, with their memories of real or perceived injuries." Edwin P. Stouffer, *Fort Drum / 10th Mountain Division Bi-annual Historical Review for October 1, 1984–September 30, 1986*, 1.

post, including the 76th Engineer Battalion, which inactivated in 1985.[49]

In December 1984, the division commander designee, Maj. Gen. William S. Carpenter Jr., arrived with a planning cell of twenty to assume command of Fort Drum and oversee the activation of the division.[50] The division was formally activated on February 13, 1985, and the 10th Military Police Company was activated the following month.[51] In June, the 10th Supply and Transportation Battalion activated, becoming the revived 10th Mountain Division's first battalion-sized entity, and in September the 710th Maintenance Battalion and the 41st Engineer Battalion were activated, the latter tracing its lineage to the original 10th Mountain Division's 126th Engineer Company of the Second World War.[52]

The division took a major step forward on October 2, 1985, when the division's 2nd Brigade was constituted and activated at Fort Benning, with Col. Michael T. Plummer commanding.[53] The 1st Brigade, the lineal descendant of the original Mountain Training Center at Camp Hale,

Colorado, was activated at Fort Drum on April 2, 1986, in preparation for the arrival of COHORT troops to form the brigade's maneuver battalions.[54] The first of these battalions—1st Battalion, 22nd Infantry—activated at Fort Drum on May 1, 1986.[55] The following month, the personnel that would form 1st Battalion, 7th Field Artillery, as well as the 1-22IN's sister battalion—2nd Battalion, 22nd Infantry—began arriving at Fort Drum, and those units activated.[56]* Unit activations continued in 1987, with 10th Division Artillery Headquarters; the 2nd Battalion, 7th Field Artillery (Light); the 1st Battalion, 87th Infantry (Light); the 10th Signal Battalion; the 247th Transportation Aviation Maintenance Company; and the 121st Combat Aviation Company all activating.[57] Unit activations continued in 1988 and 1989. The 2nd Battalion, 87th Infantry—relieved from assignment to the 8th Infantry Division in Germany and inactivated on June 16, 1986—was activated at Fort Drum on May 2, 1988, and assigned to 2nd Brigade, 10th Mountain Division.[58] The 10th Aviation Brigade and its subordinate elements

10th Mountain Division Reactivated at Fort Drum

The division, inactive for 30 years, is the active Army's 17th and the first added since 1975. Although designated a mountain division, it will be organized as light infantry. Originally formed in 1943, it saw World War II service in Italy.*

LRC

A commemorative postal cover recognizing the reactivation of the 10th Mountain Division, 1985. *Author's collection*

---

* The 1-22IN is no longer part of the 10th Mountain Division, having been reassigned to the 4th Infantry Division on December 16, 2004. *Lineage and Honors, 1st Battalion, 22nd Infantry Regiment*, Center of Military History, 2009.

AOE LIGHT INFANTRY DIVISION
October 1986

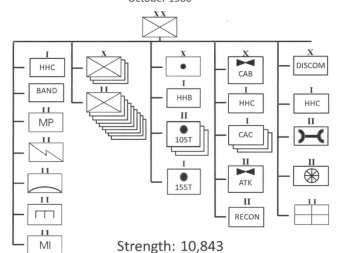

The Army of Excellence Light Infantry Division, October 1, 1986. *Adapted from John L. Romjue, The Army of Excellence: The Development of the 1980s Army, page 175*

Strength: 10,843

A soldier from 2nd Battalion, 87th Infantry, 10th Mountain Division (Light Infantry), shouts to members of this squad during Army Training and Evaluation Program (ARTEP) maneuvers. The soldiers are wearing multiple integrated laser engagement system (MILES) gear. Fort Drum, New York, December 1, 1988. *Via US National Archives Public Domain Archive, https://picryl.com/, https://nara.getarchive.net*

10TH MTN DIV (LI) AND FORT DRUM PAMPHLET 600-5

25 OCTOBER 1991

MOUNTAIN

10TH MOUNTAIN DIVISION (LI)

BASIC STANDARDS

10th Mountain Division (LI) Basic Standards, October 25, 1991. *Author's collection*

2-25 Aviation, 3-25 Aviation, and 3-17 Cavalry; 110th Military Intelligence Battalion; 3rd Battalion, 62nd Air Defense Artillery; 59th Chemical Company; and 312th Aviation Detachment also activated in 1988.[59] Finally, 2nd Brigade relocated from Fort Benning to Fort Drum during this year, bringing with it 2nd and 3rd Battalions, 14th Infantry Regiment, to join 2-87IN, already activated there.[60]

The 10th Mountain Division Becomes an Operational Division

The 10th Mountain Division reached full strength, with its full complement of subordinate units activated, in 1989.[61] Many organizational changes would occur in the future, according to the vicissitudes of war and the federal budgeting process. The 3rd Brigade Combat Team, 10th Mountain Division, was activated at Fort Drum on September 16, 2004, and 4th Brigade Combat Team, 10th Mountain Division, was activated on January 16, 2005, at Fort Polk, Louisiana.[62] Upon its initial activation, 3rd Brigade consisted of 1st Battalion, 32nd Infantry; 2nd Battalion, 87th Infantry; 3rd Squadron, 71st Cavalry; 4th Battalion, 25th Field Artillery; 3rd Brigade Special Troops Battalion (BSTB); and the 710th Brigade Support Battalion (BSB).[63*] Although 4th Brigade devoted all of 2005 to "organizing, manning, equipping, and training the Brigade to execute and sustain combat operations," it was actually deemed "available for deployment" by July 15, 2005.[64] Upon initial activation, 4th Brigade consisted of 2nd Battalion, 4th Infantry; 2nd Battalion, 30th Infantry; 3rd Squadron, 89th Cavalry; 5th Battalion, 25th Field Artillery; 4th BSTB; and the 94th BSB.[65] Unfortunately, the division was to undergo a contraction in August 2014, when 3rd Brigade inactivated its elements at Fort Drum or

transferred them to other organizations and moved its colors to Fort Polk, where 4th Brigade cased its colors and was redesignated as 3rd Brigade; although 4th Brigade's existence was short, it was distinguished, having deployed over 6,000 soldiers overseas in support of the global war on terror and another 300 in support of relief operations following the devastating Hurricane Katrina in 2005.[66] In September 2016, 3rd Brigade was designated to participate in the Army's three-year pilot Associated Unit Program, which associated selected active- and reserve-component units in order to enhance the readiness of the latter.[67**] Under this program, 3rd Brigade Combat Team, 10th Mountain Division, retained its designation but became associated with the 36th Infantry Division, Texas Army National Guard, with 3rd Brigade wearing the "Texas T" of the 36th; a decision on whether to continue the association was to be made in September 2019.[68***]

As would be expected, during its initial period as a fully operational entity the 10th Mountain's focus was developing the capabilities and readiness of the division itself. Nonetheless, operational deployments began even before the division was fully formed, with the deployment of the 511th Military Police Company—part of the US Army garrison at Fort Drum after being transferred from Fort Dix, New Jersey, in September 1987—in support of Joint Task Force Bravo, a US military task force stationed in Honduras, and in the spring or early summer of 1990 the division was notified that it would participate in the Reforger '90 exercise in Germany.[69] The 10th Mountain Division did not participate in Operations Desert Shield and Desert Storm, but approximately 1,200 members of the division did, the majority of whom—nearly 1,000—were members of the 548th Supply and Services Battalion,[70****] a part

---

* The 2-87IN had previously been assigned to 2nd Brigade, 10th Mountain Division, and was subsequently reassigned to that brigade, where it remains assigned today. The 1st Battalion, 32nd Infantry, is now assigned to 1st Brigade Combat Team, 10th Mountain Division. See "1st Brigade Combat Team," *US Army Fort Drum*; and "2nd Brigade Combat Team," *US Army Fort Drum*.

** For an overview of previous active- and reserve-component association efforts, see Chapman, *Planning for Employment of the Reserve Components*.

*** The 36th Infantry Division was originally formed at Camp Bowie, Texas, on July 18, 1917, and deployed to France in July and August 1918, returning to the United States, and was released from active duty on July 20, 1919. The division served under 5th Army in the Italian Campaign during the Second World War. It was deactivated in 1963 and reactivated as the 36th Brigade, 49th Armored Division, in 1973, and on May 1, 2004, the 49th Division was reorganized as the 36th Infantry Division. See "36th Infantry Division, the 'Texas' Division," *Texas Military Forces Museum*.

**** The 548th is now designated as the 548th Combat Sustainment Support Battalion, assigned to the 10th Sustainment Brigade, 10th Mountain Division (see "10th Sustainment Brigade").

of the US Army garrison at Fort Drum that had been relocated there from Fort McClellan, Alabama, in August 1987.[71] The 548th S&S spent 200 days in theater during operations Desert Shield and Desert Storm under 1st COSCOM, supporting the 24th Infantry Division.[72] The battalion occupied its attack position at Ash Shu'bah, Saudi Arabia, on February 2 1991, where it remained until the beginning of the ground war on February 24, 1991; the battalion entered Iraq shortly thereafter, establishing a base between Basra and Nasiriya at Al Zuba airfield.[73] The 548th redeployed to Fort Drum on April 15, 1991.[74]

Hurricane Andrew

The division's first major operation after becoming fully operational was, ironically, not a truly military mission at all, but rather a major deployment from Fort Drum to South Florida to assist in the recovery effort following Hurricane Andrew, a devastating Category 5 storm that struck Florida on August 24, 1992, leaving a 35-mile trail of devastation across a wide swath Miami-Dade, Broward, and Monroe Counties.[75*] With sustained winds of 165 miles per hour, causing $26.5 billion in damage, Andrew was the second-costliest hurricane in American history, second only to Hurricane Katrina in August 2005.[76] As one source has summarized the situation,

> On 24 August 1992, Hurricane Andrew, a category four [later 5] hurricane, crashed through southern Florida, devastating the town of Homestead, Homestead Air Force Base, Florida City, and the surrounding areas; it continued its path through the Gulf of Mexico making final landfall in Louisiana. Andrew, one of the three most devastating hurricanes to hit the United States in the twentieth century, doomed the southern Florida coast with winds exceeding 160 miles per hour, carving a 3 5-mile path of destruction south of Miami. It destroyed approximately 65,000 homes,

leaving survivors without water, electricity, or telephone service. Furthermore, heavy debris blocked most lines of communication, making food delivery and emergency medical services (ambulance and fire services) difficult. It was considered the most damaging hurricane on record [up to that point] in terms of property damage.[77]

Hurricane Andrew damaged 80,000 businesses, interrupted telephone services for 140,000 people, left more than 1.4 million customers without electrical power, rendered the "majority of water sources . . . non-potable," killed twenty-six people, and, according to the *Miami Herald*, indirectly killed eighty-two others.[78**] Handling natural disasters and other disturbances is first and foremost a state responsibility under our federal system, but following "Hurricane Andrew, the amount of damage was so widespread and devastating that the State of Florida required extensive assistance."[79] The situation in Florida was so desperate, and the response so sluggish, that Dade County Office of Emergency Management director Kate Hale implored the nation for help, exclaiming, "Where the hell is the cavalry on this one? We need food. We need water. We need people. For God's sake, where are they?"[80] "The 'cavalry' was about to arrive," as one commentator has observed; in part responding to Hale's plea, President Bush established a task force under the direction of the secretary of the Department of Transportation and directed the Department of Defense to participate; the military element of this response—Joint Task Force (JTF) Andrew—was formed on August 28, 1992, just four days after Andrew's landfall.[81]

Under the command of 2nd US Army commanding general Samuel E. Ebbeson, JTF Andrew was a sprawling enterprise.[82] With 24,000 service members deployed from the 10th Mountain Division, 82nd Airborne Division, the United States Marine Corps, the US Air Force, US Army Materiel Command, and even a Canadian element,

---

* Andrew had originally been classed a Category 4 storm, but it was recategorized as a Category 5 storm in 2002. See Chris Landsea, "Hurricane Andrew's Upgrade," Atlantic Oceanographic and Meteorological Laboratory, Hurricane Research Division, 2002.
** For a visual record of the massive devastation wrought by Hurricane Andrew, see Roman Lyskowski and Steve Rice, eds., *The Big One: Hurricane Andrew*.

the Hurricane Andrew relief effort that included JTF Andrew was the largest federal emergency response to that date.[83]

According to the Forces Command (FORSCOM) Hurricane Andrew after-action review, JTF Andrew's mission was to "provide humanitarian support by establishing field feeding sites, storage/distribution warehousing, cargo transfer operations, local/line haul transportation operations, and other logistical support to the local population," with these services to be provided in three phases:[84] During Phase I, the "relief phase," JTF Andrew would address those needs necessary to sustain and support daily life: "food and water, shelter, medical supplies and services, sanitation, and transportation"; in the second or "recovery" phase, the joint task force would continue the sustainment effort while assisting the civil authorities in reestablishing public services; and in the final or "reconstitution" phase, JTF Andrew would continue the foregoing while reducing its presence and redeploying military forces to their various home stations.[85]

Elements of the 82nd Airborne Division began to move to Florida on August 29, 1992, completing their deployment the next day.[86] On August 31, elements of the 10th Mountain Division began movement to Florida, and on September 5 two of its brigades entered the area of operations.[87] Once fully deployed, JTF Andrew's Army forces (ARFOR) element consisted of Headquarters, XVIII Airborne Corps; Task Force All American, consisting of the Assault Command Post of the 82nd Airborne Division; Task Force Falcon (2nd Brigade, 82nd Airborne Division); Task Force 27 (Engineers); part of the 519th Military Police Battalion; portions of the XVIII Airborne Corps Support Group (provisional); and Task Force Mountain, consisting of 10th Mountain Division, the 937th Engineer Group, the 841st Engineer Battalion, the 503rd Military Police Battalion, the 507th Corps Support Group, the 18th Aviation Brigade, the 20th Engineer Brigade, the 16th Military Police Brigade, and the 35th Signal Brigade.[88] Other ARFOR elements included the 1st Corps Support Command, the 361st Civil Affairs Brigade, the 1st Psychological Operations Battalion, the 18th Personnel Services Group,

the 18th Corps Finance Group, a provisional logistics support group from United States Army Materiel Command, AMC Depot Command, and the 80th Ordnance Battalion.[89]

Of the nearly 24,000 military personnel deployed to South Florida, approximately 12,000 were Army personnel; of these, about 6,000 were from the 10th Mountain Division.[90] On August 30, Gen. Ebbeson designated XVIII Airborne Corps as the headquarters of the JTF ARFOR; on September 15, 1992, the 10th Mountain Division—Task Force Mountain—assumed operational control of Task Force All American, and on September 27, it assumed the ARFOR mission from XVIII Airborne Corps.[91] The mission of JTF Andrew in South Florida generally, and that of the 10th Mountain Division in particular, was a complex, as described by the then 10th Mountain Division commander, Maj. Gen. S. L. Arnold:

Division personnel worked closely with representatives of the Federal Emergency Management Agency (FEMA) and the Department of Transportation, with members of the Red Cross, the United Way, and the Salvation Army, and with tens of thousands of individual volunteers, all of whom were committed to helping the citizens of southern Florida recover from the hurricane. When the division became the operational headquarters for all active and reserve Army units providing relief services in the operation (the ARFOR) near the conclusion of the operation, total assigned and attached strength exceeded 12,000.[92]

The relief effort was immense, as the *FORSCOM JTF Andrew After Action Report* demonstrates:

Relief operations involved over 24,000 US soldiers, sailors, airmen, marines, and Canadian Forces deployed to Florida in the largest peacetime CONUS deployment. Forces successfully completed 99 FEMA taskings during the period 24 August to 15 October. Forces cleared six million cubic yards of debris; constructed and operated four life support centers; established and operated three depots and a donated[-] goods reception point to receive, store, and dispense humanitarian goods; provided 67,000 civilians with medical care; and repaired 98 schools.[93]

JTF Andrew units established and operated more than fifty mobile kitchens (MKTs), which served an aggregate of more than 900,000 meals to the local population, and they established four life support centers (LSCs), which provided an average 2,400 victims per day with food and water, shelter, sanitation, medical services, and childcare.[94] In addition to the treatment of civilian patients, military personnel assigned to JTF Andrew also provided "veterinary care to large and small animals, water sampling support, preventative [sic] medicine, vector control, psychiatric crisis intervention, and medical logistics and organizational support."[95] Military aircraft assigned to JTF Andrew flew more than 1,000 sorties, delivering over 19,231 tons of cargo, JTF Andrew erected more than 1,000 tents, and where necessary to keep relief supplies moving, JTF Andrew military police established traffic control points and directed traffic, freeing up Florida National Guard personnel for other law enforcement functions.[96]

By clogging communications arteries and presenting other hazards, the vast amount of debris left in Andrew's wake represented a major threat to health and safety—one that JTF Andrew helped a great deal to alleviate:

Hurricane Andrew left an estimated 42 million cubic yards of debris. Most roads were blocked and most structures were destroyed. Broken telephone and power poles hanging by power lines, partially uprooted trees, and unstable structures threatened public safety. Piles of leaves, garbage, and other debris blocked drains and sewers. Debris also provided breeding places for insects and rodents capable of carrying disease. Initially, Florida Army National Guard (FLARNG) engineers cleared debris. The US Army Corps of Engineers (USACE), Jacksonville District[,]

began letting contracts for debris removal. However, the magnitude of the amount of debris overwhelmed their efforts.[97]

The units of the 10th Mountain and 82nd Airborne that initially reached the area of operations were poorly equipped for the task of debris removal, lacking heavy equipment, but by deploying quickly they were able to initiate the effort until heavier units could arrive, augmenting their equipment in the meantime with purchased and leased chain saws, dump trucks, bucket loaders, etc. until relieved of the task by contractors hired for that purpose by the US Army Corps of Engineers, which took place by September 18; after this, military units engaged in debris removal were able to shift their focus to more-important humanitarian projects.[98] "The military's initial debris-hauling effort was critical to the mission's success because it enabled mega-contractors and residents to enter areas and begin their clean-up efforts," but by mid-September, that effort had shifted from nearly all the debris-hauling effort being conducted by military personnel to a mere 6 percent of it being executed by them.[99]

The combat units deployed to Florida played a critical role in the disaster recovery effort by

establish[ing] contact with the disaster victims, moving throughout the disaster area, in many cases going door-to-door, and making contact with disaster victims and local officials to determine community and neighborhood needs. These soldiers determined requirements, provided information on location of LSCs and MKTs, delivered emergency supplies, and provided emergency labor and first aid.[100]

As the FORSCOM AAR observes,

The challenge to determine "what was required where" was solved by having DRB personnel from the 82d Airborne and 10th Mountain Divisions canvass communities and neighborhoods on their needs and requirements. Units established command posts in communities and went door-to-door to determine requirements. By establishing company[-]size areas of responsibilities (AOR), units became knowledgeable of local needs. Going door-to-door allowed units to determine community requirements for life support. The flow of this information up through the chain of command allowed both military and civilian decision makers to make decisions on resource allocation based on facts. As conditions changed, decision makers had timely information [on] how to reallocate resources. By going door-to-door soldiers were also able to provide information to hurricane victims on locations of life support centers, mobile kitchen trailers (MKT), medical aid stations, and other essential information. In some cases, soldiers provided first aid. In other cases, soldiers aided elderly and infirmed people to make emergency repairs to their homes that otherwise would not have been accomplished.[101]

The personnel of JTF Andrew also made another less tangible contribution in fostering increased sense of security and hope among the population:

A major benefit of having a highly visible presence in the communities and neighborhoods is the imparting in the disaster victims that their government had not abandoned them. Due to the initial, slow response by all levels of government, many communities felt abandoned. The presence of soldiers in their Battle Dress Uniforms (BDU) going door-to-door and living in their communities showed them they were not abandoned. An additional benefit was the deterring effect on looters. While law enforcement was not a mission, a visible military presence had a deterring effect on crime.[102]

Yet, however beneficial these psychological effects on the people of South Florida may have been, it also presented JTF Andrew with a dilemma: not only was law enforcement not the

joint task force's mission, but the active-duty military personnel were actually prohibited by federal law from engaging in civilian law enforcement.[103] Active duty forces were sent to Florida under the auspices of 42 US Code § 5121 et. seq., commonly known as the Stafford Act.[104] Under the Stafford Act, federal military forces may be deployed within the United States for purposes of consequence management following a natural or man-made catastrophe when there has been a presidential declaration of emergency and where the governor of the state or territory has requested federal assistance; once so requested, Department of Defense assets can be deployed to assist in the recovery under the auspices of the Federal Emergency Management Agency (FEMA).[105] However, even when federal military forces are deployed pursuant to the Stafford Act, they remain subject to the strictures of 18 US Code § 1385, more commonly known as the Posse Comitatus Act, which prohibits enforcement of state and federal criminal statutes by the military authorities under most circumstances.[106] Thus, with the exception of JTF Andrew providing physical security for its own facilities and providing traffic control "where such activity was in furtherance of a military purpose [such as] facilitating the movement of military convoy traffic," all expressly law enforcement and physical-security duties were performed by sworn civilian law enforcement personnel or by the Florida National Guard.[107]

The 10th Mountain Division and the rest of JTF Andrew made an immense contribution to the recovery of South Florida in a remarkably short time. The 10th Mountain began its deployment on August 31, 1992; the division assumed operational control of Task Force All American on September 15 and assumed the ARFOR mission for the JTF on September 27.[108] JTF Andrew began winding down on September 14, when the first military units were released from recovery operations for redeployment; recovery operations were terminated by October 15, and the last elements of the joint task force redeployed by October 20.[109] Little did the members of the 10th Mountain Division know that their next challenge was waiting for them, right around the corner.

Pvt. Robert W. Hopkins from HHC 1/87th Infantry Regiment checks identification cards of local residents whose possessions were lost as a result of Hurricane Andrew. Homestead Goulds Park, September 17, 1992. *DoD photo by Sgt. Kevin Thomas, via US National Archives Public Domain Archive, https://picryl.com/, https://nara.getarchive.net*

Spc. Jarrod H. Choate from HHC 1/87th Infantry Regiment gives out supplies to local civilians whose possessions were torn away from them by Hurricane Andrew. Homestead Goulds Park, September 17, 1992. *DoD photo by Sgt. Kevin Thomas, via US National Archives Public Domain Archive, https://picryl.com/, https://nara.getarchive.net*

An aerial view of devastation caused by Hurricane Andrew. Homestead Goulds Park, August 1, 1992. *Department of Defense photo by Sgt. 1st Class Otero, via US National Archives Public Domain Archive, https://picryl.com/, https://nara. getarchive.net*

Somalia: Operation Restore Hope

The 10th Mountain Division would not have long to rest after its mission with JTF Andrew. Within about ninety days of the arrival of the division's leading elements in Florida, the first elements of the 10th Mountain Division would depart again for the most exotic and remote destination the division had ever seen—the arid plains of the Somali Democratic Republic on the Horn of Africa.[110]

The events that brought the light infantry troopers of the 10th Mountain Division from the frigid North Country around Fort Drum to the East African heat were the culmination of a long, eventful, and tragic history. Somalia lies on the Horn of Africa, a peninsula jutting out from Africa's eastern shore into the Indian Ocean. Somalia is shaped roughly like a boomerang: overlaid atop a map of the United States, the boomerang's longer southern blade would extend from the Florida Panhandle all the way to its apex

at a point north of Albany, New York, while the shorter northern blade would extend westward from there to Detroit, Michigan.[111] Somalia is bounded on the north by the Gulf of Aden, on the south and east by the Indian Ocean, on the west by Ethiopia, and on the southwest by Kenya.[112] Known by the ancient Egyptians as the Land of Punt and to medieval Arabs as the land of the Berberi, what is now Somalia had long been visited by Greek, Chinese, and Arab traders.[113] By the dawn of the colonial period, Somalia had developed into a largely pastoral and nomadic culture, punctuated by scattered urban settlements on the coast and elsewhere and dominated by the Islamic faith.[114] Somalia soon found itself divided among several powers. Most of the southern "blade" of the boomerang, from the Gulf of Aden in the north to Kismayo in the south, and from the coast inland to Ethiopia, formed Italian Somaliland, bounded on the south by a section of Somali territory forming part of Kenya; the remainder of the northern "blade" of the boomerang was governed by the United Kingdom as British Somaliland, directly bounded on its north by French Somaliland on the Gulf of Aden; to the west, a large population of Somalis resided in the Ogaden region of Ethiopia.[115]

The colonial period came to an end for most of Somalia when British Somaliland and Italian Somaliland become independent and on July 1, 1960, merged, becoming the Republic of Somalia.[116] French Somaliland remained separate, becoming the independent state of Djibouti in 1977.[117] Despite the growing pains of merging the two different colonial administrations, the newly born republic functioned well until October 15, 1969, when Somali president Abdirashid Ali Shermarke was murdered by one of his own guards, apparently as "an individual act, not part of a plot or conspiracy."[118] Whatever the killer's motive, the assassination produced an inflection point in Somali history—one that was to have tragic repercussions in future decades—when just days after the killing, a Somali army officer, Gen. Mohamed Siad Barre, launched what he termed the "October Revolution," a "bloodless coup" that installed him as president and ended Somalia's experiment in democracy, inaugurating the Somali Democratic Republic.[119] "An expert in the art of dividing and ruling since his early days as an intelligence officer under the Italian Fascists,"[120] Siad Barre skillfully maintained power for more than twenty years; nonetheless, the first cracks had begun to appear by the 1980s, following Siad Barre's humiliating defeat at the hands of Ethiopia in the Ogaden War, instigated by Siad Barre from 1977 to 1978, which killed 8,000 Somali soldiers and damaged the country's economy and finances.[121] Notwithstanding Siad Barre's repressive measures, the Ogaden defeat spurred opposition to his regime and aggravated one of the most self-destructive aspects of Somali culture—its stubborn balkanization along tribal or clan lines. Despite the fact that Somalia is homogeneous culturally, ethnically, linguistically, and religiously, the principal focus of identity for individual Somalis has historically been their clan, which "militates against the evolution

and endurance of a stable, centralized state"; though "exacerbated by Siad Barre's exploitation of interclan rivalries, institutional instability is actually woven into the fabric of Somali society" in the form of Somali clan allegiance.[122]

Historically, the Samaal clans were associated with a nomadic and pastoral way of life, while the Saab clans were traditionally more associated with a more sedentary way of life.[123] This dichotomy is a major feature of Somali culture, since Somali society is derived from these two major lineages, then further divided into six major clan families; each of these clan families is further divided into clans, and the clans are further divided into subclans or lineages.[124] The dominant lineage is said to descend from a common ancestor known as Samaal and accounts for as much as 85 percent of Somalia's population; the Darod, Dir, Hawiye, and Isaaq clan families claim descent from Samaal.[125] The smaller of the major lineages claims descent from Saab, consisting of the Digil and Rahanweyn clan families.[126] This deeply ingrained societal fragmentation began to manifest itself immediately as opposition to Siad Barre's regime began to cluster around clan-based organizations. These included the Somali Salvation Democratic Front, or SSDF (Majeerteen clan); the Somali National Movement, or SNM (Isaaq); the Somali Patriotic Movement, or SPM (Ogaden clan); the United Somali Congress, or USC (Hawiye); the Somali Democratic Alliance, or SDA (Gadabursi clan); the Somali National Alliance, or SNA (Habr Gidr); and the Somali Democratic Movement, or SDM (Rahanweyn clan).[127]

The Somali Civil War began in the early 1980s in the wake of Siad Barre's Ogaden defeat; as the war progressed, the situation spiraled out of control until Siad Barre's regime finally collapsed in 1991, driving him and his coterie into exile.[128] His departure merely accelerated, rather than ameliorated, Somalia's descent into anarchy, since regardless of the form of government in effect at any given time, Somali society has always been subject, to a greater or lesser degree, to internecine clan conflict.* "The meaning of segmentation" in Somali society, notes the US Army's official study of Somalia,

---

* For an interesting fictional account of such violence during the British colonial period in Somalia, see J. A. Golding's novel *Shifta*.

is captured in an Arab Bedouin saying: My full brother and I against our half-brother, my brother and I against my father, my father's household against my uncle's household, our two households (my uncles and mine) against the rest of our immediate kin, the immediate kin against non-immediate members of my clan, my clan against other clans, and finally, my nation and I against the world.[129]

Given such an all-pervasive and atomistic world view, it is almost inevitable that Siad Barre's flight resulted not in the formation of a new government and new political institutions, but rather in a descent to a vicious, interminable civil war among and between Somalia's clans.[130]

Famine and United Nations Intervention

The situation in Somalia rapidly deteriorated after Siad Barre's defeat; not only did the various clans and their front organizations return to Somalia's time-honored practice of mutual conflict, but they now did so with unprecedented ferocity, since "Siad Barre's large inventory of weapons which he had acquired by playing East against West during the Cold War were now available to the clans."[131] As the Joint Staff History Office observed in its official history on the Somalia relief effort,

Somalia as a nation and as a cohesive society had dissolved. Then an unusually severe drought struck. Food became a form of currency and marauding gangs seized this "money." In mid-December 1991, the first relief supplies from abroad reached war-torn Mogadishu. Within thirty days, however, the International Committee of the Red Cross (ICRC) warned that starvation threatened hundreds of thousands of refugees living in camps south of the capital.[132]

Despite the efforts of more than thirty non-governmental organizations that attempted to stem this humanitarian catastrophe, the situation continued to deteriorate; in response, UN secretary-general Boutros Boutros-Ghali urged action,

and the Security Council passed Resolution 751 on April 24, 1992, directing the secretary-general to send fifty observers to monitor a tenuous ceasefire in Mogadishu and agreeing "in principle" to the establishment of a UN security force in Somalia at the appropriate time. The first observers arrived on July 23, and on August 4, Secretary-General Boutros-Ghali announced that Pakistan would provide 500 soldiers to guard relief supplies, marking the beginning of the United Nations in Somalia effort (UNOSOM I); the United States launched Operation Provide Relief shortly thereafter, on August 15, 1992.[133] The Operation Provide Relief mission was to "provide military assistance in support of emergency humanitarian relief to Kenya and Somalia"; to accomplish this, the United States deployed twelve aircraft—eight C-130s and four C-141s—to airfields at Wajir and Mombasa, Kenya.[134] From the start of the operation until the transition to Operation Restore Hope on December 9, 1992, US forces averaged twenty aircraft sorties and 150 metric tons of supplies delivered daily, 28,000 metric tons in total.[135] Despite this effort, Somalia continued to collapse: by November 1992, the country had no functioning government or security services, and 500,000 people had starved to death while another four million were in danger of malnutrition.[136] On August 24, the Security Council approved Resolution 775, enacting Secretary-General Boutros-Ghali's proposal to deploy a force of 3,500 troops, with 750 to be deployed in each of four "security zones."[137] These efforts soon proved not just insufficient but abortive. While the airlift did appear to be improving matters in Somalia's interior, "conditions remained dire in Mogadishu," and maintenance of the airlift by civilian aircraft only would be prohibitively expensive once the military airlift ended, so that the Agency for International Development (AID) would be forced to curtail its civilian airlift from seven aircraft to two by February 25, 1993.[138] Greatly aggravating the situation was the prevailing state of anarchy on the ground. Northwestern Somalia declared itself the independent state of Somaliland, while the region directly to its east declared itself the autonomous state of Puntland.[139] On September 14, 1992, Pakistani troops began arriving at the

Mogadishu airport but refused either to move out from the airport or provide security for relief convoys (only on November 10 were the Pakistanis finally able to establish a perimeter); at the interior cities of Baidoa and Beledweyne,* armed gangs disrupted the relief effort and the US was forced to suspend aid deliveries to those locations. Aideed and "provisional president" Ali Mahdi, each leading rival factions, fought each other in the vicinity of Mogadishu, and in the south, Siad Barre's son-in-law, Gen. Hersi Morgan, led his troops against his rival Omar Jess, who was seeking control of the port city of Kismayo.[140] By November 16, UN special envoy Ismet Kittani reported that

> humanitarian supplies had become the basis of an otherwise non-existent economy. Somali "authorities" at all levels competed for anything of value; threats and killings often decided the outcome. Large sums were being extorted from private relief agencies; perhaps no more than twenty percent of relief supplies actually reached the needy. In Mogadishu, where the five hundred lightly armed Pakistanis still were virtual hostages of the warlords, the airport had come under heavy fire on 13 November and "provisional president" Mahdi's men prevented ships from docking.[141]

Faced with this witches' brew of anarchy, civil war, and a massive humanitarian disaster, on November 29, Secretary-General Boutros-Ghali proposed five possible courses of action to the Security Council; despite having rejected US feelers about a greater American role only ten days earlier, Boutros-Ghali made clear that of the five options, he considered only one feasible: "Have UN members, with the Security Council's authorization, conduct a country-wide operation that would create the conditions necessary to ensure the delivery of relief supplies."[142] In response, the UN Security Council approved Resolution 794 on December 3, 1992, authorizing member states to "use all necessary means to

establish as soon as possible a secure environment for humanitarian relief operations in Somalia."[143] The US contribution toward the implementation of this resolution, executed from December 9, 1992, through May 4, 1993, would be known as Operation Restore Hope.[144]

Operation Restore Hope

To implement Resolution 794, the United States formed a unified task force (UNITAF) under Lt. Gen. Robert B. Johnston, with most of the headquarters coming from the I Marine Expeditionary Force at Camp Pendleton, California.[145] On December 9, Navy SEALs went ashore in Somalia, only to be met there by media camera crews, while 1,300 US Marines moved by helicopter to Mogadishu airport.[146] Initially, US forces met a permissive environment with warlords agreeing to cooperate and moving their technicals (pickup trucks with machine guns mounted on them) either into secure cantonment sites or to caches outside Mogadishu.[147] The Army component of UNITAF—Task Force Mountain—was built around elements of the 10th Mountain Division, which had been alerted for the mission on November 30, initially under the 10th Mountain Division assistant division commander, Brig. Gen. Lawson Magruder, and later under the 10th Mountain commanding general, Maj. Gen. Steven Arnold; TF Mountain would reach 10,000 soldiers at its largest.[148] The core of Task Force Mountain was 2nd Brigade of 10th Mountain Division, with two infantry battalions, 2nd Battalion of 87th Infantry, and 3rd Battalion of 14th Infantry.[149] Other elements included the 10th Division Artillery (Task Force Kismayo); the 10th Aviation Brigade, consisting of Task Force 5-158 Aviation, 3-17 reconnaissance squadron, and two aviation maintenance companies; the 10th Division Support Command, with the 210th Forward Support Battalion, 710th Maintenance Battalion, the 200th Supply Detachment, and the 59th Chemical Company; the 10th Signal Battalion; the 110th Military Intelligence Battalion; elements of the 4th Psychological Operations Group; the 41st Engineer Battalion; the 10th Military Police

---

* Also known as Belet Uen and Beletweyn.

Company; the 511th Military Police Company; the 548th Supply and Services Battalion; the 36th Engineer Group; the 720th MP Battalion, with two companies; and various division elements.[150] Once in country, UNITAF forces fanned out across the southern portion of Somalia, with Marine forces principally responsible for humanitarian relief sectors (HRS) centering on Mogadishu, Gialalassi, Beledweyne, Oddur, and Bardera. The ARFOR, led by the 10th Mountain Division, assumed responsibility for HRS Baidoa (in the center of the UNITAF area of operations), HRS Baledogle (north and west of Mogadishu), HRS Marka (south of Mogadishu along the coast and encompassing a large portion of the Shabeelle River valley), and HRS Kismayo, encompassing the southernmost section of the country from just east of the Jubba River to the Kenyan border and the coastline between the two.[151]

Elements of the 10th Mountain Division began departing Fort Drum by December 11, with the first elements arriving in Somalia on December 13, and the bulk of the movement occurring between December 23, 1992, and January 6, 1993.[152] The division headquarters would be at Mogadishu, while 3-14IN would deploy directly from Fort Drum to the main airport in their sector at Kismayo, a port city near Somalia's southernmost tip about 250 miles from Mogadishu, along with the 10th Division Artillery headquarters.[153] The 2nd Brigade, 10th Mountain Division, including 2nd Battalion, 87th Infantry, entered Somalia at Baledogle airfield, abandoned by the Soviets in 1977, located about midway between Mogadishu and Baidoa[154] and still strewn with unexploded munitions, the airframes of derelict fighter plans stripped down to their skeletons, and other debris. The 2-87IN (with Company A, 1-87IN, attached in lieu of its organic Company C, which had deployed to the Joint Readiness Training Center at Fort Polk, Louisiana, prior to the alert) would stay at Baledogle until December 31.[155] The 2-87IN received its first operational mission at this time, conducting a lengthy 250-mile air assault with two companies in late December to secure the airfield at Beledwayne ahead of the 1st Canadian Parachute Regiment, which would operate in that area.[156] The entry

into Beledweyne was unopposed, with the only complication being the raucous local residents excited at the spectacle of the major US air movement into the area, and the US and Canadian brigade commanders, along with State Department and CIA representatives, were able to make contact with the local personages; the Canadian regiment arrived via C-130s of the Royal Canadian Air Force the next day, and 2-87IN returned to Baledogle.[157] During the battalion's short stay at Beledweyne, however, confirmation had come of 2-87IN's next mission, a movement to the coastal town of Marka, about 60 miles south of Mogadishu.[158] The 2-87IN deployed to Marka by air on January 1, 1993, and would remain based there throughout the rest of its deployment in Somalia.[159] In Marka the battalion had three principal tasks: securing the small port there, guarding the checkpoint into the town where persons entering Marka would be required to temporarily surrender their weapons until departing, and conducting local patrols.[160] Marka also served as a base of operations from which the battalion conducted operations throughout the lower Shebele valley, including air mobile operations to Afgoi, north of Mogadishu; Kurtenwary, south of Marka; and as far south as Kismayo. Major ground operations were conducted at Quorleey, north of Marka; Brava, midway to Kismayo; and Jelib, near the juncture of the Shebelle and Jubba Rivers, north of Kismayo.[161] The 2-87IN had a comparatively uneventful stay in Somalia, being relieved by 1-22IN in April 1993.[162] Tragically, more-dramatic events lay ahead.

UNOSOM II

Operations Restore Hope concluded on May 4, 1993, with the commencement of UNOSOM II.[163] On March 26, 1993, the UN Security Council had adopted Resolution 814, which extended the mandate of UNOSOM II until October 31, 1993, unless sooner extended, and charged Lt. Gen. Cevik Bir of Turkey, whom Secretary-General Boutros-Ghali had appointed as UNOSOM II commander, with "responsibility for the consolidation, expansion, and maintenance of a secure environment throughout Somalia," heavily emphasizing disarmament.[164] Under this ambitious mandate, "for the first time in UN history, a force would be armed under chapter VII of the UN Charter to restore peace, law, and order, including disarming of Somali militias and holding those responsible for violence individually accountable"; even more ambitious, "Resolution [814] further established as an objective the rehabilitation of the country's political institutions and economy."[165] As one retrospective on America's involvement in Somalia observed, with the advent of UNOSOM II "the focus now changed from 'stopping the dying' to rebuilding Somali national institutions, infrastructure, and political consciousness," even as the focus of effort in achieving these ambitious objectives shifted "from the United States to the UN and from overwhelming military force to the smallest possible American military footprint."[166] Initially under UNOSOM II, twenty-nine nations were to contribute 29,732 soldiers, including only 4,200 from the US, of whom 1,100 would be combat troops or "trigger pullers"; from mid-March to early June 1993, US forces in Somalia fell from 17,000 to 4,200, and greater commitments from the international community notwithstanding, only 17,200 troops from twenty-one nations were present on the ground when UNOSOM II commenced on May 3.[167] A major US contribution to the new mission would be the quick-reaction force (QRF) for the coalition, a mission that had begun previously under UNITAF with 2nd (Commando) Brigade, then 1st (Warrior) Brigade, both of the 10th Mountain Division; under UNOSOM II the QRF would consist of a military police platoon, an aviation task force of six OH-58A and four AH-1W aircraft, a forward support battalion, and the QRF's principal fighting element, a single infantry battalion from the 10th Mountain Division.[168] US forces continued to rotate in and out of Somalia, and by August the QRF head-quarters mission had devolved upon the 10th Aviation Brigade (Falcon Brigade), 2nd Battalion, 14th Infantry, as the ground component (both of the 10th Mountain Division).[169]

Unfortunately, the dramatic reduction of forces in Somalia coincided not only with the major expansion of the UN mission from famine relief to nation building, but with increasingly sharp conflict between the coalition and the Aideed's forces.[170] Conditions in Somalia began to deteriorate as soon as the UN coalition began to draw down. On May 6, 1993, a force of about 150 Somalis fired upon members of the Belgian parachute battalion at Kismayo, wounding one.[171] On June 3, fighters of Aideed's Somali National Alliance (SNA)—a front for the Habr Gidr, a subclan of the Hawiye—ambushed a Pakistani force inspecting a weapons storage facility, killing twenty-three or twenty-four soldiers and wounding fifty-nine.[172] The shocking massacre outraged the international community, and on June 6 the UN Security Council authorized the "arrest and detention for prosecution, trial, and punishment" of those responsible for the attack.[173] US forces attacked targets throughout Mogadishu, including ammunition storage areas and a radio station, and launched a major raid with significant loss of life against the "Abdi House" in an effort to capture SNA leaders.[174] On August 8, four US Army military police soldiers were killed when their vehicle was destroyed by a command-detonated bomb, and two further attacks in August wounded ten more soldiers.[175] A major escalation occurred with the deployment of a Joint Special Operations Task Force (JSOTF), code-named Task Force Ranger, to Somalia later that month. Task Force Ranger was a formidable force built around US Army Rangers, as well as

a detachment from the Army's famed Delta Force, and an aviation element from the 160th Special Operations Aviation Regiment (SOAR), equipped with MH60 Black Hawk utility helicopters and MH6 and AH6 "Little Bird" light helicopters [and] small numbers of communicators, Air Force combat controllers and pararescue Airmen, and SEALs.[176]

Task Force Ranger immediately embarked upon an aggressive campaign against SNA leadership, beginning with the first raid on August 30 and followed in rapid succession by five more operations in September.[177] Although "spotty intelligence" often meant that the raids did not yield the capture of the high-level leadership targets promised,[178] they were always brilliant tactical successes, with one tragic exception: the disastrous Battle of the Black Sea.

Task Force Ranger
and the Battle of the Black Sea

Commonly known as "Black Hawk Down," due to Mark Bowden's book of the same title, what Somalis called the Battle of the Black Sea began on October 3, 1993, as a raid on Mogadishu's Olympic Hotel to capture a number of Aideed lieutenants reported to be there at that time.[179] Prior to this operation, Task Force Ranger had carried off a number of raids following a similar template: "an insertion by MH60 and MH6 helicopters, with Rangers forming an outer perimeter and Delta operators conducting the actual prisoner snatch, supported by a ground convoy to extract detainees and covered by AH6s aloft."[180]

Although intended to confront the target with "complete surprise coupled with overwhelming force," the repeated operational pattern carried the risk that Somali fighters might adapt their tactics to counter ours, of which they were much more capable than US forces had credited them, as one commentator observed:

Although poorly equipped and undisciplined to American eyes, many [Somali fighters] were hardened by years of combat. Their ability to mass quickly and fight in large numbers with determination and courage had been amply demonstrated in the days and weeks preceding the October 3 raid. The local SNA commander, Col. Sharif Hassan Giumale, had trained for 3 years in Russia and later in Italy, fought in the Ogaden against Ethiopia, and commanded a brigade in the SNA [Somali National Army] before joining Aideed during the civil war.[181]

In fact, Aideed's forces adapted rapidly. Task Force Ranger had assembled in Mogadishu by August 28, 1993, and had gone into action promptly thereafter. Yet, within less than a month, Aideed's fighters had become increasingly willing to engage Task Force Ranger with small arms and rockets, and as early as September 21, in response to the

raid near Digfer Hospital that had captured Aideed financier Osman Atto, they began the tactic of employing massed volleys of rocket-propelled grenades (RPGs) against Task Force Ranger elements—a tactic that would prove deadly in the days ahead.[182]

Task Force Ranger launched its seventh raid to capture two Aideed lieutenants on October 3, 1993, against the Olympic Hotel near the Bakara Market in the Black Sea district, an impoverished area in Mogadishu and an Aideed stronghold.[183] The attack force departed the Mogadishu airport at 3:30 p.m., with 110 personnel moving by helicopter and another fifty by ground convoy, reaching the target by 3:42 and establishing blocking positions while the assault force searched for the target personnel.[184] Twenty-four Somalis were rapidly detained and loaded on vehicles for the trip back to the airport, but things quickly went awry from there, starting when an MH-16 helicopter was struck by an RPG and crashed three blocks from the objective.[185] A six-man element of Rangers from the blocking force as well as two helicopters immediately responded to the scene; the first to arrive—an MH6 assault helicopter—successfully extracted and evacuated two injured soldiers from the crash site.[186] Next the rangers arrived on foot, followed by the second helicopter, an MH-60 Black Hawk helicopter with a fifteen-man combat search-and-rescue (CSAR) force aboard; the CSAR team disembarked, but as the last two members were on the way down, the helicopter was struck by RPG fire, forcing the aircraft to limp back to the airport after the two remaining rescuers reached the ground.[187] Now two more MH-60s were struck by rocket fire; one successfully reached the airport, but the other crashed south of the original crash site, less than a mile away, and was quickly set upon by a Somali mob that killed all aboard despite a valiant resistance, save one of the pilots, who was captured; two of the defenders, MSgt. Gary Gordon and Sfc. Randall Shughart, posthumously received the Medal of Honor for their part in the battle. The assault and blocking forces then deployed by foot to the first crash site, taking casualties en route, where they established defensive positions.[188] Meanwhile, the ground convoy containing the detainees, as well as a Task

Force Ranger relief convoy sent to try to reach the second crash site, were both forced by enemy fire to return to the airport.[189]

At this point the 10th Mountain Division QRF under the Falcon Brigade became engaged. At 4:55 p.m., Company C, 2nd Battalion, 14th Infantry, departed for the airport, arriving at Task Force Ranger headquarters at 5:25; leaving from there, they were then ambushed at 5:50 p.m. en route to the second crash site at the K4 traffic circle in Mogadishu.[190] The directing of Company C through that traffic circle was an unfortunate decision, since K4 "was the gateway to Aideed territory and his followers surrounded it."[191] Not only that, but Aideed's followers there were well organized. As Falcon Brigade commander Lawrence Casper recounts,

> Although UN intelligence estimates had placed the SNA militia strength at 950–1000, there were thousands of Habr Gidr SNA sympathizers in southern Mogadishu who were organized by neighborhoods and city blocks to prevent any penetration of their safe haven. These sectors represented SNA military districts manned by a duty officer at all times.[192]

Even worse for the 10th Mountain Division QRF, the locals were very adept at exploiting the urban terrain around them, as well as their numerical advantage, as Lawrence further recounts:

> The Somalis were adept at the emplacement of obstacles, and known to employ everything from burning tires to derelict CONEX containers. Their tactic was elementary: allow the enemy force to proceed far enough down the street until it confronted an impassable obstacle, then quickly obstruct the enemy's rear to trap the force.[193]

Once this was accomplished, the Somalis could then employ what was "termed the swarm effect, which had been experienced before during clashes between UN forces and Somalis on the city streets," when "Somalis, coming from surrounding neighborhoods, would swarm around their victims, eventually overwhelming them."[194]

The 2-14IN's QRF company—Company C—quickly encountered stiff resistance, including heavy fire from both sides of the street, as well as "plunging fire from second[-] and third[-]story rooftops."[195] Faced with this situation—a "thin-skinned" force, "too small and outgunned," and with enemy RPGs "in abundance," it soon became obvious that C/2-14 Infantry was "not going to penetrate the force securing the streets leading to the crash from the direction of K4 circle."[196] Shortly thereafter, Company C was withdrawn to the airport to prepare for another effort.[197]

Over a period of several hours, a multinational rescue plan was pieced together, consisting of American infantry transported in Malaysian armored personnel carriers, surviving members of Task Force Ranger and other US personnel, and Pakistani armor.[198] Under this plan, the rescue force centered on 2-14IN would consolidate at the Mogadishu New Port on the Indian Ocean and approach the crash sites and trapped Task Force Ranger personnel via a circuitous route east along Via Roma and Via Londra, where the force would turn left at Via Jen Daaud, where it would initially pass through an area dominated by the Abgal subclan of the Hawiye—supporters of Aideed rival Ali Mahdi Mohammed—and proceed north to National Street, at which point the convoy would proceed west on National Street to a point near the original Task Force Ranger objective and roughly midpoint between the north and south crash sites; from there, Company A, 2-14IN, would proceed north to the first crash site and Company C would proceed south to the second crash site, while Company B would remain in reserve.[199] Although longer than a more direct route along Tanzania Street, the selected route would reduce (though not eliminate) the amount of time that the rescue force had to traverse hostile territory dominated by Aideed supporters.[200]

The Pakistani tanks arrived at the New Port at 6:30 p.m.; 2-14IN completed its consolidation there thirty-five minutes later, linking up with the Pakistani and Malaysian forces at 9:30 p.m. After an hour and forty minutes of coordination, the rescue force of more than sixty vehicles departed New Port at 11:10 p.m.[201] Supported overhead by AH-1 Cobra attack helicopters, OH-58As, and command and control elements carried aloft in Black Hawks, the convoy moved out "in fits and starts"; the Pakistani tanks led the convoy as far as the Pakistani position at Strongpoint 69.[202] The convoy proceeded without opposition until it passed Pakistani-manned checkpoint 207, about 200 meters west of Via Jen Daaud; checkpoint 207 "marked the beginning of Habr Gidr territory and represented the separation between" fiercely hostile Aideed supporters and "the indifferent" followers of Ali Mahdi.[203] The convoy was immediately set upon by a storm of hostile fire, such that soldiers inside the Malaysian APCs (armored personnel carriers) would later compare it to "being in a tin shack during a heavy rain"; others would call it the "Bullet Car Wash."[204] Matters were immediately complicated when two Malaysian vehicles carrying 2nd Platoon, Company A, 2-14th Infantry, turned south 200 meters east of the point where the rescue convoy was to break off for the respective crash sites; one of the APCs was struck by an RPG, wounding the driver, while the second vehicle was struck in the engine compartment and disabled.[205] The platoon dismounted the vehicles, set up a defensive position in a nearby building, and fought for their lives until relieved by their sister platoon, 1st Platoon, Company A, 2-14IN, four hours later.[206]

After a fierce fight supported by rockets and gunfire from the orbiting American helicopters, the Malaysian vehicles carrying Company A, 2-14IN, augmented by Task Force Ranger and special-operations personnel, turned north on Shalalawi Street, passing the Olympic Hotel, until penetrating the northern crash site at 0155; they would hold this position until dawn as they struggled to free the body of the pilot encased in the wreckage.[207] Company A (less 2nd Platoon, fighting separately from the rest of the company after the unfortunate wrong turn) succeeded in reaching the southern crash at 2:30 a.m. but found no sign of the crew or passengers; shortly thereafter they effected a linkup with the "lost" 2nd Platoon.[208] Back at the northern crash site, extricating the remains of CWO Clifton Wolcott from his wrecked

aircraft proved a challenge, since even an electric saw brought along for the purpose proved unequal to the task; ultimately his remains were pulled from the wreckage via a cargo strap wrapped around his body and attached to a Humvee.[209]

With the recovery of Wolcott's body, the relief force and the members of Task Force Ranger whom they were sent to rescue were free to withdraw. But on this dangerous night, even the return to base was fraught with danger. Rather than returning immediately to New Port or the Mogadishu airport, the force would extract instead to the so-called Pakistani Stadium northeast of the northern crash site.[210] The harrowing trip there would become known as the Mogadishu Mile. Beginning at 5:42 a.m. on October 4, 1993, the allied force moved south along Shalalawi Street back to National Street, where they headed east—survivors on foot, casualties mounted in vehicles, all supported by the orbiting gunships.[211] As the force began moving down National Street, Aideed's militiamen resumed their attack with renewed fury, having reorganized along the street in preparation for this eventuality; dismounted soldiers scrambled into the relative shelter of APCs and Humvees, and the overcrowded vehicles "raced through the gauntlet of fire toward Checkpoint 207" and the edge of Aideed territory.[212] Once ground forces were clear of the enemy, Cobra gunships demolished the two Malaysian Condor APCs that had made the erroneous turn south, firing a total of eight TOW missiles, "rendering them useless."[213]

The October 3–4 Battle of the Black Sea was a deadly affair. Task Force Ranger alone suffered sixteen killed and fifty-seven wounded; they would lose one more killed and twelve wounded two days later from a mortar attack on the Mogadishu airport.[214] The 10th Mountain Division's 2-14IN suffered two killed and twenty-two wounded; two Malaysian soldiers were killed and seven wounded, while the Pakistanis had two wounded, and estimates of Somali casualties ranged from 500 to 1,500.[215]

Following the Battle of the Black Sea, the United States substantially strengthened its presence in Somalia. A mechanized infantry company with a platoon of tanks attached was dispatched from the 24th Infantry Division at Fort Stewart, Georgia, as well as a marine expeditionary unit, additional special-operations forces, and more AC-130 gunships.[216] The Falcon Brigade QRF was also significantly augmented, with the 10th Mountain Division's 2nd Battalion, 22nd Infantry, being brought from Fort Drum, as well as 1st Battalion, 64th Armor, and additional support assets.[217] Nonetheless, US policy shifted dramatically after the battle. On October 6, the Clinton administration dropped the effort to capture Aideed and directed the withdrawal of all US forces by March 31, 1994; on March 3, 1995, Operation United Shield completed the withdrawal of remaining UN personnel.[218]

America's involvement in Somalia remains controversial, especially after the heavy casualties of October 3–4, 1993. The failure of the UN effort to foster national reconciliation and broker a political settlement, aggravated by the rise of the radical Islamic Courts Union and its militant wing, Al Shabaab,* has fostered a popular consensus that the US intervention in Somalia was a failure. But this conception is unjust. It is certainly true that UNOSOM II, sometimes known as Operation Continue Hope—the United Nations' "nation building" effort to "bring together all the clans and political entities" in Somalia—did end in failure.[219] But the preceding phase of US and UN involvement—Operation Restore Hope—very successfully achieved its more limited objective of "breaking the cycle of starvation in Somalia by ensuring that humanitarian relief operations could be conducted without interference."[220]

The detritus of civil war—abandoned munitions near a former Somali army training facility at Baledogle Air Base, December 1992. *Photo by author*

* See "Al-Shabaab (Al-Shabab), The Supreme Islamic Courts Union (ICU)," GlobalSecurity.org.

A tangible legacy of Siad Barre's disastrous regime—the derelict wreck of an aircraft at Baledogle Air Base, December 1992. *Photo by author*

The control tower at Baledogle, with soldiers of 2nd Battalion, 87th Infantry, visible in the foreground, December 1992. *Photo by author*

Another view of Baledogle's control tower, this time taken from a Black Hawk helicopter transporting 2nd Battalion, 87th Infantry, from Baledogle to Marka. *Photo by author*

Base camp of Company B, 2nd Battalion, 87th Infantry, at a former Somali army training facility at Baledogle Air Base, December 1992. *Photo by author*

TO THE SOLDIERS OF
TF CONDOR

Your performance during the first 30 days of Operation Condor Guardian has been outstanding. There has been no equivalent operation for U.S. forces in over 20 years. You are demonstrating once again the unique versatility, flexibility and discipline of well trained, highly motivated light fighters. You are the lead elements of a changed American security doctrine that seeks to change the face of fighting for liberty by defending the rights of mankind to the same sense of hope our nation enjoys. Though we have seen much death and destruction, this is still a humanitarian mission; maintain the edge you have shown in force protection and compassion.

We must continue to relate to the Somali people in a positive manner. They are not a population we subdued, they are people we are here to save. The somali people are tired of suffering and look to UNITAF elements to improve overall security situation in order to begin the long road to normalcy. We are getting a great deal of information from the Somali people on the movements and actions of the hostile forces and bandits that continue to take advantage of the helpless. While this means our operation will be more dangerous, and we will be more vulnerable, we must continue the positive interaction we have developed with the people of Marka.

As we continue to squeeze the bandits out and work with the emerging local governments, we will see an increase in attempts to show our operations in a negative light. The ROE has not changed.

-Control your aggressive tendencies. The vast majority of the population only deserve to be treated with dignity and respect.

-Understand the tactical environment so that you are familiar with the potential trouble spots. Approach with caution. Your chain of command will lead you when the potential is higher for direct hostile fire.

-Engage targets discriminately. Fire on anyone who raises a weapon or attacks you with intent to injure (knife). Fire on anyone who attempting to steal a sensitive item. Detain anyone with a visible weapon and confiscate the weapon.

Vary operations. Patrol times, start points-routes-end points, size of patrols, and method of patrol. Remember this is a hostile situation!

-At check points, show courtesy. Smile as you search. Ask the driver to show you where the weapons are and inform you if he has registration forms for the weapons. If he volunteers to show you the weapons and register them, tell him he can return to the check point when he concludes his business in Marka and claim the weapon.

Keep up the good work. We will be continuing our stabilization operations in the lower Shabelle River Region with more extended overnight missions. As the U.S. forces withdraw, the hostile forces may grow bolder and we will surely be involved in more dangerous, direct action missions. As you corresponded with your loved ones, remind them you are skilled in your task and will do well, but false hopes of return before prior to mid-April would be unfair to them. Again, you are demonstrating great Lightfighter skills. Drive on!

CONDOR SFX

Letter by the 2nd Battalion, 87th Infantry, commander, Lt. Col. James E. Sikes Jr., to his soldiers, issued after the battalion's move from Baledogle to Marka. *Author's collection*

WAXAANU XAGAN UNIMID IN AANU DIFAACNO DADCA IDIN CAAWINAYA.

HA HOR-ISTAAGINA WADADA !

Ciidankayagu wuxuu-xagan ujoogaa inay difaacaan dadka idin caawinaya. Ha dhax galina inaba-ha ahaate. Ha hor-istaagina wadada! Waxaanu isticmaalidoonaa hubkayaga si-aanu u-difaacno dadka idin caawinaya.

A flyer distributed by US forces to the local Somali population during Operation Restore Hope. *Author's collection*

Capt. Wes Bickford, commander, Company B, 2nd Battalion, 87th Infantry, at the port of Marka, 1993.
Photo by author

Confiscated Somali weapons at checkpoint Condor in Marka, Somalia. They are mostly small arms and crew weapons that are lined up against the wall of a building. The weapons were taken by the 2/87th Infantry Regiment, 10th Mountain Division, Fort Drum, New York, and await shipment to Mogadishu. This mission is in direct support of Operation Restore Hope. Marka, Somalia, January 1993. *Department of Defense photo by Sgt. Daniel Hart, via US National Archives Public Domain Archive, https:// picryl.com/, https://naragetar-chive.net*

Haiti: Operation Uphold Democracy

The deployment in January 1995 of the 25th Infantry Division's 4th Battalion, 87th Infantry, to Haiti during Operation Uphold Democracy is discussed in chapter 8; also noted there is that 4-87IN was preceded in Haiti by its sister battalion, 2nd Battalion, 87th Infantry, of the 10th Mountain Division, which deployed to Haiti during the initial phase of the American intervention there.

Haiti occupies the western portion of the island of Hispaniola, its border with the Dominican Republic, which occupies the eastern portion of the island, running on a north–south axis from the northern to the southern coasts; the country is in the shape, roughly, of the letter "U" tipped over on its left side, with one peninsula jutting west out into the Caribbean in the north, and another, longer peninsula, also extending west, in the south.[221] The division of the island between a Spanish-speaking culture in the east and a French-Creole-speaking culture in the west dates to the 1697 Treaty of Ryswick, which divided the island between France and the declining colonial power of Spain; under French rule, Saint-Domingue, as Haiti was originally known, grew into "the most productive colony in the Western Hemisphere, if not the world."[222] It was not to last, however, since a major slave rebellion in 1791 set off the Haitian Revolution, a tumultuous period of violence, political intrigue, and foreign intervention

that finally culminated in Haitian independence on January 1, 1804.[223] Poorly prepared for independence and "shunned" by the international community,[224] Haiti embarked upon a century and a half of military rule, brutal despotism, corruption, economic coercion (sometimes resembling the slavery abolished during the revolution), and racial animosity between the Black and mulatto communities of the country (the white colonial majority having been killed or driven out over the course of the revolution and subsequent establishment of independence).[225]

The events that would ultimately lead to the 1994 US intervention in Haiti—Operation Uphold Democracy—actually began decades earlier with the election of François Duvalier (the infamous "Papa Doc") as president of Haiti in September 1957.[226] Notwithstanding the democratic exercise that put him in office, Papa Doc proceeded to rule in the tradition of his predecessors, establishing a dictatorial and repressive regime. Despite a constitutional provision that he himself promulgated, barring his serving more than one term, he ran for reelection in 1961, winning a landslide "victory" of 1,320,748 votes to zero, and in 1964 he declared himself president for life—as had seven of his predecessors.[227] Holding on to power by violence (killing an estimated 30,000 Haitians during his rule), by driving opponents into exile through emigration, and by "limited patronage,"

Duvalier remained in office until his death in 1971, designating his son Jean-Claude Duvalier—"Baby Doc"—as his successor.[228] Baby Doc continued his father's kleptocratic rule; popular discontent began to emerge in 1983 and spread in 1984, and by 1985–86, protests had spread to six major cities.[229] In January 1986, the Reagan administration began to pressure Baby Doc to leave Haiti; shortly thereafter, under pressure from members of his own military, he departed the country on February 7, 1986.[230] Duvalier was succeeded in office by Lt. Gen. Henry Namphy, who was in turn overthrown by Lt. Gen. Prosper Avril; although Avril scheduled elections for 1990, he detained or expelled his political opponents instead and declared Haiti to be in a "state of siege."[231] A new round of popular demonstrations erupted in March 1990, driving Avril from the country, with Maj. Gen. Hérard Abraham leading a coup that forced Avril from power and led to the installation of Haitian Supreme Court justice Ertha Pascal-Trouillot as interim president.[232] Elections were held on December 16, 1990, won by Catholic priest Jean-Bertrand Aristide with 67 percent of the vote.[233] Despite an abortive attempted coup seeking to obstruct the transition, Aristide assumed office on February 7, 1991.[234] Although Aristide moved to implement reforms, his success in the months after taking office was mixed, as John R. Ballard notes:

> Overall, the results of Aristide's administration through September 1991 were hard to judge. He had introduced measures to improve revenues, counter smuggling, promote tourism, and create tax incentives to encourage investment in the private sector but had not completed enough of his program to assure the elites that he posed no real threat to them, in view of his commitment to the masses. He had also failed to demonstrate to outsiders that he was committed to the democratic process. . . . Aristide did not speak out against mob violence, he did not prevent the arrest of his opponents on vague charges, and perhaps most fatal to his chances for success, he antagonized both the military and the rich.

Equally damning, he failed to build any form of political rapport with his legislature, including alienating members of his own Lavalas support group.[235]

The result was a predictable return to "the traditional Haitian response to reform: a conservative coup" led by Lt. Gen. Raoul Cedras and Chief of Police Michel François—the latter ironically elevated from lieutenant colonel to become chief of the Army staff by Aristide when the latter forced the retirement of most of his generals upon taking office—on September 30, 1991, driving Aristide into exile, initially in Venezuela.[236]

Unfortunately for Gen. Cedras, however, this time the world was not willing to quietly acquiesce as Haiti's traditional mode of power politics played out. After about twenty-one months of diplomatic and international pressure, Cedras signed the Governor's Island Agreement, providing for the return of Aristide to Haiti by October 30, 1991, along with UN forces to train the military and police and help repair the country's damaged infrastructure; in exchange, the participants in the 1991 coup would receive amnesty and Cedras would be allowed to retire.[237] It soon became apparent, however, that Cedras had no intention of implementing the accord but, rather, was simply buying time in which to eliminate dissidents and consolidate his own power.[238] Cedras's obstruction reached a crescendo with the arrival of USS *Harlan County* in Port-au-Prince in the early hours of October 11, 1993, carrying members of the Haiti Assistance Group (HAG) to begin their mission of aiding Aristide's return.[239] Rather than permit the HAG to land, the Cedras regime and its supporters physically obstructed *Harlan County* from docking at its berth and entered upon an unrelenting round of hostile and threatening actions against the ship.[240] Finally, in the early afternoon of Tuesday, October 12, *Harlan County*'s commanding officer, concluding that the situation in Port-au-Prince was not the permissive environment that he had been told to expect, determined to withdraw his vessel from Haitian waters and steamed for Guantánamo Bay, Cuba.[241]

Despite this embarrassing retreat, pressure continued on Cedras to leave power. In December, representatives of the United States, Canada, Venezuela, and France traveled to Haiti to persuade Cedras to leave power by January 15, 1994.[242] Meanwhile, events took a decisive turn behind the scenes in the United States; if Cedras believed that he had forced the US to back down, he was sorely mistaken, since shortly after the *Harlan County* "debacle,"* US military planners shifted their planning focus for Haiti from preparing for a noncombatant evacuation (NEO) to planning for a forced entry into the country.[243] As Robert Baumann has observed,

> The stage was set for Operation Uphold Democracy. At the National Command Authority's direction, US Atlantic Command initiated joint planning based on two clear options. According to Operations Plan (OPLAN) 2370, the XVIII Airborne Corps operated as Joint Task Force (JTF) 180 with the mandate to execute a violent seizure of key sites in Port-au-Prince in order to wrest authority from the illegal junta. The second option, expressed in OPLAN 2380, formed JTF 190 around the 10th Mountain Division . . . to conduct a permissive entry into Haiti, based either on acquiescence by the Cedras regime or a handover of control from JTF 180 in the aftermath of a forcible entry. In the meantime, just to be on the safe side, 10th MD (L) planners prepared for the contingency that a permissive entry might be less than completely permissive. In short, JTF 190 had a "takedown option" of its own, if needed.[244]

The continuing obstinacy of the Cedras regime pushed the Clinton administration toward the forcible-entry option; finally, the administration set September 19, 1994, as the date that US forces would invade and forcibly remove Cedras from power if he had not capitulated by that time.[245] As D-day for the invasion neared, President Clinton dispatched Jimmy Carter, Gen. Colin Powell, and Senator Sam Nunn to Haiti to negotiate a settlement, talks that continued to the very day

scheduled for the assault; finally, on September 19, 1994, as elements of the 82nd Airborne were in flight en route for the attack, a spy alerted Gen. Cedras that US military aircraft were leaving Pope Air Force Base in North Carolina; only then did Cedras and his government capitulate.[246] Fortuitous as it was, this sudden change in plan from forced entry by the 82nd Airborne to permissive entry by the 10th Mountain Division disrupted logistical and transportation arrangements and created some early challenges in terms of living arrangements for US forces once they arrived, since the 10th Mountain Division had expected to assume control of the various logistical assets and facilities that were to have been previously established by the forcible-entry forces about a week after the invasion; instead, the 10th Mountain Division would itself be the lead element.[247]

Although its timeline was accelerated and some of the expected preparations in country had not been accomplished, the 10th Mountain Division was still well prepared when the order came; as noted above, even in the forced-entry scenario, the 10th Mountain Division had been expected to relieve the initial invasion force in place within about a week of the latter's entry into the country. To that end, elements of the 10th Mountain Division had begun to prepare for deployment to Haiti since being alerted to the possibility the previous July.[248] Once in country, the division headquarters not only would command the division but would serve as the headquarters for Joint Task Force 190, exercising command and control over all operations in country, requiring a major provisional reorganization and effectively doubling the size of division headquarters.[249]

Training for deployment to Haiti began in early August for 1st Brigade and the 10th Aviation Brigade, with August 31 being the target for completion.[250] There was good reason for haste, since the initial insertion would be precedent setting: 1st Brigade would be inserted into Haiti by the 10th Aviation Brigade from the deck of USS *Dwight D. Eisenhower*, traversing the open sea from the carrier to the airport at Port-au-Prince. Preparation

---

* As Kretchik characterizes it; see Walter E. Kretchik, Robert F. Baumann, and John T. Fishel, *Invasion, Intervention, "Intervasion": A Concise History of the US Army in Operation Uphold Democracy*, 35.

for this amphibious air assault was an immense task. The 10th Aviation had to establish its own ground school at Fort Drum for the initial phase of learning carrier operations, with the outline of a carrier deck painted on the airfield to facilitate training; two naval aviators were dispatched to Fort Drum to certify the Army pilot's training.[251] The challenge was formidable, as 10th Aviation Brigade commander Lawrence Casper attests:

It was a monumental task, because we were confronted with the task of training in excess of 120 aviators for both day and night deck qualifications. At times it appeared as if we didn't have enough time in a 24-hour period. Although confronted with a new set of visual cues associated with shipboard operations, the army aviator's real challenge was assimilating the navy jargon. Terms like *port beam* and *starboard bow*, traffic patterns like Charlie, Delta, and Alpha, and ship-to-pilot and pilot-to-ship signals became second nature to many pilots.[252]

The Black Hawk helicopters had to be fitted with extended-range tanks, and the crews had to complete associated mandatory training and flight orientation with them; water survival was another key task, given the lengthy stretch of open sea the aircraft would traverse en route to Haiti, including drown-proofing and training on egress from a downed aircraft.[253] The final phase of the training would be flight operations from the deck of an actual aircraft carrier underway—USS *Theodore Roosevelt*—which began on August 16 and continued day and night for four days.[254] On September 12, 1994, USS *Eisenhower* began embarking the 1st Brigade and the 10th Aviation Brigade, and the next day, September 13, the carrier and its Army tenants set sail for Haiti.[255] The 1st Brigade's maneuver battalions—1-22IN, 2-22IN, and 1-87IN—began training for Haiti, along with the Aviation Brigade, in August.[256] Training for most of 2nd Brigade geared up in September. The 2-14IN, less than ten months back from Somalia and the fierce Battle of the Black Sea, scrapped its Expert Infantryman Badge test scheduled for that month and focused entirely

on preparation for deployment to Haiti.[257] The 3-14IN had been training the cadets of the US Military Academy at West Point prior to the Haiti mission, having spent May 1994 preparing for Operation Black Knight, as the West Point support mission was called, and spent June, July, and half of August executing the mission; following a two-week block of leave, 3-14IN started its training cycle for the deployment at the beginning of September.[258] The 2-87IN had deployed to the Jungle Operations Training Center (JOTC) in May and transitioned to preparation for the Haiti mission upon its return to Fort Drum in June.[259]

The aircraft of the 10th Aviation Brigade, bearing infantrymen of 2nd Battalion, 22nd Infantry, 1st Brigade Combat Team (BCT), 10th Mountain Division, touched down at Port-au-Prince Airport shortly after 9:30 a.m. on September 19, 1994, near the local police barracks and the passenger terminal.[260] The 1st Battalion, 87th Infantry, followed, being inserted at Port-au-Prince's port facility.[261] By the end of the first day, 10th Aviation Brigade brought 1,622 infantrymen ashore and transported fifty-five loads of cargo by sling load from USS *Eisenhower*, conducting 225 sorties all told, securing the airport, the port, and government and communications facilities in Haiti's two main cities of Port-au-Prince and Cap-Haitien.[262]

From its initial objectives at the airport and port, 1st BCT would consolidate at Bowen Field, the former headquarters of the Haitian Air Force, whence it would commence operations.[263] The 1st Battalion, 87th Infantry, seized munitions caches in Port-au-Prince during raids against the Formora ketchup factory, the local publishing house, and the Acura warehouse on October 5; less than a week later it was tasked with the security of the presidential palace and the presidential residence, and from October 17 the battalion was tasked with security of the airfield complex being utilized by coalition forces.[264] The 1st Battalion, 22nd Infantry, established the most successful of many weapons buyback programs at the Bowen Airfield; it carried out a joint patrol with Bangladesh forces on November 11 and conducted an out-of-sector stability operation at the town of Jacmel on Haiti's southern coast.[265] The 2-22IN was initially tasked with establishing a quick-reaction force (QRF) with security of the airfield and the surrounding area; as the months wore on, the battalion executed cordon-and-search operations in the vicinity of Port-au-Prince against suspected weapons caches belonging to the Front for the Advancement and Progress of Haiti (FRAPH), a paramilitary group that supported the Cedras regime and opposed the return of President Aristide, and later secured thirteen government buildings in preparation for Aristide's return in early October.[266] The 2-22IN provided security and established a joint task force / strike force in support of Aristide's return to Haiti on October 15, 1994, and assumed responsibility for security of the National Palace two days later, on October 17, then assuming responsibility for security of the local stadium, the parliament, the mayor's house, and President Aristide's residence on October 19, as well as patrolling responsibilities—functions the battalion retained until late November.[267]

The 2nd Brigade Combat Team, 10th Mountain Division, began flowing into Haiti shortly after the initial forces landed; by D-5 they began to arrive at Cap-Haitien, Haiti's second city, where they would be established by the end of September and would be responsible for the security of the northern portion of the country, an area of some 14,000 square kilometers.[268] While there, 2nd BCT's 2nd Battalion, 87th Infantry, headed a 1,000-soldier task force—Task Force 2-87IN, including a mechanized infantry element and a Guatemalan contingent.[269] TF 2-87 would execute more than 2,000 operations over an area of 160,000 square kilometers; these included 2,000 patrols, thirty-three out-of-sector missions, twenty-one QRF operations, eighteen site security missions, and eight major reliefs in place.[270]

The 2nd Battalion of 14th Infantry arrived in Port-au-Prince on September 21, 1994; after initially being tasked with assisting with the security of the airport there, the battalion rejoined 2nd BCT in northern Haiti after being relieved at the airport by 1st Brigade.[271] The 2-14IN would spend about six weeks in Cap-Haitien, conducting patrols over an area of approximately 3,000 square kilometers; providing security at the local airfield, the United Nations food storage facility, and the

power plant; and conducting show-of-force missions at various locations, including the towns of Le Borgne, Petit Bourg, Port Margot, Limbe, Limonade, Plaisance, Ennery, Acul du Nord, Plain du Nord, St. Suzzane, Caracol, Trou du Nord, Quanaminthe, and La Citadelle.[272] In one such operation, Company A of 2-14IN captured more than forty "anti-Aristide conspirators" at Gran Rivier du Nord.[273] The 2-14IN completed its mission and redeployed to Fort Drum on November 18, 1994.[274]

The 2nd Brigade's 3rd Battalion, 14th Infantry (less its Company A, which remained at Fort Drum to receive a COHORT contingent of soldiers completing initial entry training), arrived in Haiti on September 24 and also had an eventful deployment, during which it operated apart from the rest of the brigade in Port-au-Prince.[275] The first two days were spent drawing the battalion's vehicles the Port-au-Prince port facility and establishing a lodgment at the Port-au-Prince airport, with Company B billeted at Air Haiti's cargo terminal while the Headquarters and Headquarters Company (HHC) and Company C took up residence in the passenger terminal.[276] The battalion then deployed a HMMWV-mounted section from the antitank platoon to the US embassy; shortly thereafter the battalion embarked upon its first operational mission to secure the Port-au-Prince City Hall and the National Parliament building, facilitating the reconvening of Haiti's democratic institutions for the first time after a three-year hiatus.[277] The battalion then occupied a new tent-city lodgment in the Port-au-Prince airfield.[278] On October 7, Company C executed the battalion's first cordon-and-search mission against a target designated Objective Muffler, with Bradley fighting vehicles in support, resulting in the seizure of a small amount of marijuana.[279] The battalion conducted a 150-man operation the next day, October 8, against the home of FRAPH official JoJo Chamberlain; though Chamberlain himself eluded capture, the raid yielded a treasure trove of intelligence including names, addresses, and photographs of many key FRAPH members.[280] From October 9 to 13, Company B was tasked with the security of the Ministry of Public Works while Company C secured the home of Gen. Cedras's mother; HHC prepared for President Aristide's return, with the antitank platoon conducting reconnaissance of potential staging areas for the QRF. October 14 through 16 saw the battalion engaged in preparations for and the execution of President Aristide's return to Haiti; on the day of the president's return, Company C was stationed adjacent to the presidential palace, while Company B executed patrols on the higher ground overlooking the airport, and HHC secured a portion of the airport itself.[281] The 3-14IN redeployed to Fort Drum on November 12, 1994, save for a small trail party charged with preparing the battalion's vehicles for shipment back to Fort Drum.[282]

The 10th Mountain Division's performance in Haiti has been criticized by some, notably Dr. Robert Baumann and Dr. John Fishel. In their view,

> In its execution of the mission, the 10th Mountain Division took limited account of recent experience but perhaps lost perspective in the process. Conscious and unconscious reference to the experience of Somalia, where during the UNOSOM II phase the division provided the brigade that acted as the quick[-]reaction force for the UN, raised a false analogy for what the

division faced in Haiti. As the situation in Somalia deteriorated, the 10th adopted a siege mentality, and it brought that mentality with it to the planning and execution of Uphold Democracy. An analogy more relevant to the Haitian scenario was the posture of the 10th in Somalia during its initial deployment under Maj. Gen. Steve Arnold in the first phase of the operation. As the ARFOR in Operation Restore Hope, the 10th had enjoyed a high degree of success in a relatively low-threat environment. In Haiti, the contrast between the behavior of the 10th's units in Port-au-Prince and 2 BCT in Cap Haitien points to the way in which different leaders interpret similar experiences . . . and establish different command climates, with attendant consequences in terms of attaining military and political objectives.[283]

Baumann and Fishel further allege that "the variety of problems encountered by the 10th Mountain Division early in the operation convinced Army leadership that replacing the 10th at the earliest opportunity would be appropriate. Thus, plans were made to have the 25th Infantry Division relieve the 10th."[284] After having received an earlier

Challenge coin, 2nd Brigade, 10th Mountain Division, ca. 1994, obverse. *Author's collection*

Challenge coin, 2nd Brigade, 10th Mountain Division, ca. 1994, reverse. *Author's collection*

warning order orally, the 25th Division was formally alerted for the mission on December 4, 1994, with orders to begin movement of 3,500 soldiers three weeks later, on the day after Christmas.[285] As already noted, 2-14IN and 3-14IN redeployed to Fort Drum in early to mid-November; 2-87IN and 1st BCT remained in Haiti until relieved by elements of the 25th Infantry Division. The 10th Mountain Division command group returned to Fort Drum in January 1995, with the bulk of 1st Brigade headquarters and its three maneuver battalions returning later that month.[286]

Notwithstanding the criticism leveled by Baumann and Fishel, the 10th Mountain Division

accomplished a great deal in Haiti. In addition to the operational missions described above, the division cooperated with approximately 400 charitable organizations operating in Haiti, coordinated with humanitarian organizations for the importation of food supplies into the country, worked with ministerial advisory teams assisting Haiti's revived democratic government to carry out technical assessments of the situation on the ground and formulate long-term development strategies, and facilitated Operation Light Switch to restart sixteen electrical power plants across the country.[287]

USS *Dwight D. Eisenhower* (CVN-69) departs from her home port of Norfolk bound for the Caribbean in support of Operation Uphold Democracy. Large harbor tugs assist the nuclear-powered aircraft carrier into the channel, Norfolk, Virginia. *Department of Defense photo by PH1 Reymundo Arellano (USN) via US National Archives Public Domain Archive, https://picryl.com/, https://nara. getarchive.net*

A UH-60 Black Hawk (Blackhawk) helicopter from the 3-25 Assault Helicopter Battalion takes off from the deck of the aircraft carrier USS *Eisenhower* (CVN-69), taking the first wave of combat troops ashore in Haiti, September 19, 1994. More Black Hawks (Blackhawks)are in line waiting for takeoff (USS *Dwight D Eisenhower* (CVN 69), September 19, 1994. *Department of Defense photo by PH1 Martin Maddock (US Navy photo via US National Archives Public Domain Archive, https://picryl.com/, https://nara. getarchive.net)*

Soldiers from the various battalions of the 10th Mountain Division, Fort Drum, New York, are lifted on Elevator #2 to the flight deck for a dress rehearsal on the deck of USS *Eisenhower*, preparing to enter Haiti, September 16, 1994. *Department of Defense photo by PH2 Ken Riley via US National Archives Public Domain Archive, https://picryl.com/, https://nara.getarchive.net*

Two soldiers of Company A, 2-87 Infantry, 10th Mountain Division, enter an outside door while two other soldiers, armed with an M16A2 rifle and an M249 squad automatic weapon (SAW), squat on the sidewalk to provide security for the weapons search in Cap-Haitian. US military troops are in Haiti to preserve law and order and to restore the democratic government. Cap-Haitien, Haiti, August 10, 1994. *Department of Defense photo by Spc. Jean-Marc Schaible, US Army, via National Archives, via US National Archives Public Domain Archive, https://picryl.com/, https://nara. getarchive.net*

Soldiers of Company A, 2-87 Infantry, 10th Mountain Division, armed with M16A2 rifles and M249 squad automatic weapons (SAW), aim toward an open window as they climb an outside staircase to raid a building in Cap-Haitian. The facility was suspected of containing a cache of weapons. US military troops are in Haiti to preserve law and order and to restore the democratic government. Cap-Hatien, Haiti, October 8, 1994. *Department of Defense photo by Spc. Jean-Marc Schaible, US Army, via US National Archives Public Domain Archive, https://picryl.com/, https://nara. getarchive.net*

A soldier from the 511th Military Police Company, Fort Drum, New York, talks to a Haitian man while on patrol during Operation Uphold Democracy. Cap-Hatien, Haiti, September 1, 1994. *Department of Defense photo by TSGT Val Gempis (USAF), via US National Archives Public Domain Archive, https:// picryl.com/, https://nara.getarchive. net*

Sfc. Philip Mims, US Army, from Bravo Company, 2nd Battalion, 22nd Light Infantry Brigade, Fort Drum, New York, leads a group of soldiers armed with M16 rifles in civil disturbance training while in transit to Haiti on board USS *Dwight D. Eisenhower* (CVN-69), in support of Operation Uphold Democracy. A UH-60 Black Hawk helicopter can be seen in the background. On the deck of *Eisenhower* preparing to enter Haiti, September 15, 1994. *Department of Defense photo by PH1 Martin Maddock, USN, via US National Archives Public Domain Archive, https://picryl.com/, https://nara.getarchive. net*

High-Mobility Multipurpose Wheeled Vehicles (HMMWV) from the 10th Mountain Division form a line on the tarmac at the Port-au-Prince International Airport during Operation Uphold Democracy. They have just driven off the C-5A Galaxy aircraft in the background. Port-au-Prince, Haiti. *Department of Defense photo by A1C Sean Worrell (USAF), USN, via US National Archives Public Domain Archive,https://picryl. com/, https://nara.getarchive.net*

US Army soldiers from Charlie Company, 2nd Battalion, 22nd Light Infantry Brigade, Fort Drum, New York, simulate assault tactics on board USS *Dwight D. Eisenhower* (CVN 69) in support of Operation Uphold Democracy. The soldiers are armed with an M60 machine gun and M16 rifles. On the deck of *Eisenhower* preparing to enter Haiti, September 15, 1994. *Department of Defense photo by PH1 Martin Maddock, USN, via US National Archives Public Domain Archive, https://picryl.com/, https://nara.getarchive.net*

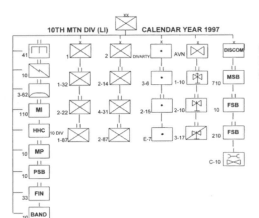

Organization of the 10th Mountain Division, 1997. *From* Annual Historical Review 10th Mountain Division (LI), Calendar Year 1997 (10th Mountain Division [LI], *G3 Plans, 1998), page 4*

The Global War on Terrorism

A high operational tempo (OPTEMPO) packed full of training events and operational deployments awaited the 10th Mountain Division in 2001. At the beginning of the year, the division was planning for three major operational deployments: 1st Battalion, 87th Infantry, would support the summer training program for the cadets of the United States Military Academy at West Point; 2nd Battalion, 87th Infantry, was to execute rotation 41 of the Multinational Force and Observers mission in the Sinai Desert, enforcing the Camp David Agreement between Israel and Egypt; 2nd Battalion, 22nd Infantry, was to deploy to Bosnia in support of rotation 10 of the Stabilization Force (SFOR) mission there; and 2nd Battalion, 14th Infantry, was to deploy to Kosovo for rotation 3B of the peacekeeping mission in that ethnic Albanian, breakaway province of Serbia.[288] Each of these missions would see these respective battalions task-organized with supporting elements from other organizations and put through a rigorous and comprehensive training regime in preparation for deployment, in addition to the normally aggressive peacetime training cycle executed by the division and its subordinate elements every year. Yet, the burdens upon the 10th Mountain Division, like that of the rest of the Army and indeed the nation, would grow exponentially with the outrageous terrorist attacks against the United States on September 11, 2001.

In the immediate aftermath of the attacks, the 10th Mountain had to continue its ongoing preparations for those portions of its previously assigned missions that remained to be executed, but it now had additional, new priorities. These included deployment of elements of 2nd Brigade's 4th Battalion, 31st Infantry, to secure critical infrastructure in the United States and Fort Drum itself under Operation Noble Eagle, and preparation for possible deployment of other units overseas in support of combat operations in Afghanistan—Operation Enduring Freedom.[289]

First to deploy in response to the 9/11 attacks was Company C, 4th Battalion, 31st Infantry: the Polar Bears. The 31st Infantry was first organized in August 1916 as a Regular Army unit in the Philippines; it would deploy to Siberia in 1918 and

1919, following World War I, before returning to the Philippines, where it would remain until surrendering to the Japanese 14th Army on April 9, 1942.[290] The 31st was reorganized in Korea on January 19, 1946, as part of the 7th Infantry Division, seeing combat throughout the Korean War, ultimately being inactivated on July 1, 1957.[291] The battalion was reactivated in 1965 under the 196th Infantry Brigade and subsequently was reassigned to the 23rd Infantry Division in 1969, participating in the Tet Counteroffensive of 1969 and other campaigns and being relieved from this assignment in 1971.[292] From October 1991 to February 1995, Company D, 31st Infantry, served with Training and Doctrine Command; finally, on April 16, 1996, the battalion as a whole was reactivated and assigned to the 10th Mountain Division.[293]

On September 23, 2001, Company C, 4th Battalion, 31st Infantry, deployed via Black Hawk helicopter on four hours' notice to Aberdeen Proving Ground, Maryland, where it would spend six weeks securing sensitive facilities under Operation Noble Eagle, until relieved by Army National Guard forces.[294] From September through November, 4-31IN formed the center of the provisional Task Force Polar Bear, a combined arms task force organized to respond to terrorist attacks in the northeastern United States, consisting of elements of HHC 4-31IN, Company B of 41st Engineer Battalion, Company B of 2-15 Field Artillery, and Companies B and C of 3-62 Air Defense Artillery.[295] Other parts of the battalion deployed to Kuwait and Qatar to secure coalition forces at Camp Doha, in Kuwait, and As-Sayliyah, in Qatar.[296]

The first 10th Mountain Division organization to deploy in support of combat operations after 9/11 was 1st Battalion, 87th Infantry, whose lead elements arrived in Uzbekistan on October 5, initially to provide base security and provide the quick-reaction force (QRF) for coalition forces stationed at the Karashi-Khanabad Airbase (K2), but "the battalion's mission would evolve into much more as the ground campaign developed."[297] Over the course of its seven-month deployment, 1-87IN would send elements to Bagram and Mazar-e Sharif in Afghanistan—the first conventional forces deployed into Afghanistan—where it would engage in extensive combat operations under 3rd Brigade, 101st Airborne Division, Task Force Rakkasan, including Operation Anaconda.[298]

The 1-87IN was quickly followed by the 2nd Brigade headquarters—Task Force Commando—which deployed to K2 with a company from 4-31IN on December 21, 2001, to provide command and control over operations in the vicinity of Mazar-e Sharif and detainee-screening operations at Sheberghan Prison.[299] The 2nd Brigade transitioned to Bagram in February and supported the 10th Mountain Division headquarters, which had assumed the role of Combined Forces Land Component Command (CFLCC) (Forward) in planning for Operation Anaconda, executed from March 2 to 19, 2002, against Al-Qaeda and Taliban forces in the rugged Sha-i-Koht valley of eastern Afghanistan.[300] During Anaconda, 2nd Brigade would execute Operations Harpoon and Glock, commanding a joint and multinational force for this operation, including Companies A and C, 4-31IN; 3rd Princess Patricia's Canadian Light Infantry (PPCLI); United States Marine Corps aviation assets; and other forces.[301] The 2nd Brigade headquarters and 4-31IN redeployed to Fort Drum in April 2002.[302]

May 2003 saw the deployment of 80 percent of the 10th Mountain Division staff to Afghanistan to assume the role of Combined Joint Task Force 180 (CJTF-180), which had previously been filled by Headquarters, XVIII Airborne Corps, in which capacity the division would serve until April 2004.[303] The reduction of CJTF-180 from a corps- to a division-sized headquarters was partly motivated by a desire to "avoid redundancy and thus operate with greater efficiency" by "'flattening out' the command organizations in OEF by integrating the operational-level responsibilities, normally handled by corps-level headquarters, into a tactical-level division headquarters."[304] It is clear, however, that the decision also reflected "the desire to conserve manpower and other resources," United States Central Command (CENTCOM) being "under enormous pressure not to overcommit resources to Afghanistan to make sure everything possible was available for Iraq."[305]

Shortly after the division headquarters assumed the CJTF-180 mission, 1st Brigade Combat Team—Task Force Warrior—and the 10th Aviation Brigade deployed to Afghanistan for combat operations, serving under CJTF-180 from August through the following February.[306] Task Force Warrior was task-organized for the mission, with subordinate elements including 1-87IN, 2-87IN, 2-22IN, 3-17CAV, 3-6FA, and 10th Forward Support Battalion from 10th Mountain Division, as well as 1-501 Parachute Infantry (PIR) and C/159th Aviation.[307] The 1-87IN was based at forward operating bases (FOB) Orgun-e, Shkin, and other points along the Afghan-Pakistani border; 3-17CAV was based at FOB Gardez; 2-22IN provided QRF forces for southern Afghanistan out of Kandahar Airfield while 2-87IN did the same for northern Afghanistan, operating out of Bagram Airfield and Asadabad; 1-501 PIR operated from FOB Salerno near Khost; and 3-6FA deployed throughout 1st Brigade's area to support all the maneuver elements.[308] The 1st Brigade also operated with a substantial international component. This included an 800-man Italian airborne battalion—Task Force Nibbio II—operating out of FOB Salerno, a 250-man French force dubbed Task Group Arés, and 400 soldiers of the Romanian 151st Infantry Battalion—the "Black Wolves"—providing security for civil affairs and convoy operations out of Kandahar Airfield.[309] "Combat operations and contact with the enemy were routine events for Task Force Warrior during this deployment, including numerous mounted and dismounted patrols, small-scale cordon-and-search operations, and providing security for humanitarian and Provincial Reconstruction Team (PRT) missions."[310] CJTF-180 and Task Force Warrior also carried out larger operations. One such was Operation Mountain Viper, launched in August 2003 against what was suspected to be "a large number of Taliban fighters" in Zabol Province, north of Deh Chopan.[311] The operation commenced with Afghan forces and Coalition Special Operations personnel inserting and reconnoitering the objective areas; once enemy forces were located, 2nd Battalion, 22nd Infantry, was inserted with its three infantry companies, a civil affairs element, linguist teams, and psychological-operations personnel.[312] Combat began on August 30, when 2-22IN closed with their objectives on foot; instead of dispersing upon contact as expected, Taliban forces in the area opted to make a stand.[313] Persisting in the attack, 2-22IN penetrated further into enemy territory, attacking a suspected Taliban headquarters ensconced in a cave complex in early September, killing 150–200 Taliban fighters.[314] CJTF-180 conducted at least three other large-scale operations during 1st Brigade's rotation, including Mountain Avalanche in December 2003, Mountain Blizzard the next month, and, finally, Operation Mountain Storm, the last major operation that Task Force Warrior would carry out before returning to Fort Drum in April 2004.[315] The aim of Operation Mountain Storm was to "set the right security conditions for the [Afghan] presidential elections scheduled for late 2004" by disrupting the Taliban line of communications between Kandahar and Pakistan in Oruzgan Province; 2-22IN, two Afghan National Army battalions, and 2,000 Marines of the 22nd Marine Expeditionary Unit participated, with 2-22IN alone conducting five air assaults and more than a dozen cordon-and-search operations in and around Kandahar.[316]

The 1st Brigade's 1st Battalion, 31st Infantry, would not accompany the brigade to Afghanistan but would instead deploy to Iraq as motorized infantry in September, mounted fifty-four HMMWVs, initially attached to 1st Brigade, 82nd ABN Division, then to 1st Brigade, 1st Infantry Division, and finally to the 1st Marine Expeditionary Force (MEF).[317]

The 2nd Brigade headquarters would also deploy to Afghanistan in May 2003, but with a very different mission: instead of conducting command and control of maneuver elements, 2nd BCT would deploy with parts of 4-31IN and elements of 210th Forward Support Battalion (FSB) to form Combined Joint Task Force (CJTF) Phoenix to train the new Afghan army.[318] CJTF Phoenix would fall under the control of the Office of Military Cooperation–Afghanistan (OMC-A), commanded by Maj. Gen. Karl Eikenberry.[319]* MG Eikenberry directed CJTF Phoenix to task-organize itself into mobile training teams (MTTs) and embedded trainer teams (ETTs); under this arrangement, the MTTs would conduct the initial training of Afghan troops at the Kabul Military Training Center (KMTC), after which the MTTs would be succeeded by the ETTs, small elements of ten to fifteen soldiers who would live with their Afghan National Army (ANA) counterparts and "mentor them during actual operations."[320] Trainers from 4-31IN conducted live-fire training in August with ANA mortar, recoilless-rifle, and reconnaissance platoons, and platoon and company live-fire exercises; the following month 4-31IN assisted the ANA in movement of troops by C-130 aircraft from Kabul International Airport to Qalat, Afghanistan.[321] In October, 4-31IN relinquished a portion of its training mission to a team of Canadian trainers, with the Americans thus relieved, turning their attention to the training of the headquarters, Afghan National Army 1st Brigade, while others accompanied their counterparts on operations in Qalat.[322] In November 2003, 2nd Brigade and their Afghan counterparts began planning for the security of the upcoming Loya Jirga that would approve a new constitution for Afghanistan, while other 2nd Brigade trainers deployed with their ANA counterparts from Kabul to Mazar-e Sharif to support the disarmament, demobilization, and reintegration of Afghan militia forces, and still others accompanied their Afghan counterparts to Khost for operations in the Afghan border areas.[323] The 2nd Brigade was relieved of the CJTF Phoenix mission in December 2003 by the 45th enhanced Separate Brigade (eSB), Oklahoma Army National Guard.[324]

While the brigade headquarters was performing the CJTF Phoenix mission, the remainder of the brigade was scattered to the four winds. Company C, 4-31IN IN, deployed to Djibouti on the Horn of Africa, immediately adjacent to Somalia on the West African coast, while Company B deployed to Iraq, as did 2-14IN.[325] The 2-14IN entered Iraq at Bashur Airfield in Iraq's autonomous Kurdistan region, from which it conducted a ground attack convoy (a "GAC")** 50 kilometers southwest to the Kurdistan region's capital, Erbil.[326] From there,

---

* MG Eikenberry had himself served in 2nd Brigade, 10th Mountain Division, in the early 1990s, as the battalion commander of 2-87IN.
** The *10th Mountain Division Annual Historical Summary* for 2003 characterizes the movement this way (at page 115), but this is rather a misnomer. Iraqi Kurdistan was and is friendly territory effectively governed and secured by local Kurdish security forces and was completely free of Iraqi army forces, who had been unable to penetrate the Kurdistan region since the end of the 1991 Gulf War. The Kurds of Iraq were very happy to see the Americans arrive and continue to regard us as allies today. For further discussion, see Dennis P. Chapman, *Security Forces of the Kurdistan Regional Government*; and Dennis P. Chapman, "Our Ambivalent Iraqi-Kurdistan Policy," *Small Wars Journal*, June 13, 2010.

Company A and the mortar platoon participated in operations from April 10 to 19, 2003, to seize Mosul, Kirkuk, and the Bashur and Kharbaz oil fields.[327] Company C, 2-14IN, deployed to Baghdad for operations there, while 2-87IN deployed to Afghanistan with 1st BCT, as already noted.[328]

The year 2004 would be a remarkable and tumultuous one for the 10th Mountain Division, filled not only with continued combat deployments but also with a major reorganization of the division and its subordinate units and the activation of a 3rd Brigade. The division headquarters completed its deployment in command of CJTF-180 in Afghanistan in April 2004.[329] From January through May, 2-14 Infantry (augmented by A/4-31 Infantry) served as the Operation Noble Eagle QRF for Installation Management Region 5, while the 642nd Engineer Company (CSE) deployed to Douglas, Arizona, to construct a barrier along the US southern border.[330] As noted previously, 3rd Brigade, 10th Mountain Division—the Spartan Brigade—was officially activated in mid-September 2004, marking a 50 percent increase in the division's ground combat power once the activation of the brigade was fully implemented; 3rd Brigade's focus throughout the year would be on manning, equipping, and training the brigade and its newly assigned subordinate elements to achieve combat readiness.[331]

The 1st Brigade—Task Force Warrior—having deployed to Kandahar, Afghanistan, in August 2003, was relieved by 3rd Brigade, 25th Infantry Division, in April 2004 and returned to Fort Drum in May; 1-32IN, while still in Iraq, was transferred from 1st Brigade to the newly formed 3rd Brigade on August 20, ahead of the battalion's redeployment to Fort Drum in September 2004.[332] The 1st Brigade would begin the transition to the new infantry brigade combat team / unit of action (IBCT/UA) configuration on August 20, 2004.[333]

The 2nd Brigade, meanwhile, would take the 10th Mountain Division in a new direction as the first of the division's brigade combat teams to deploy to Iraq, being alerted for the mission on May 2, 2004.[334] The 2nd Brigade would deploy as a brigade task force consisting of the brigade headquarters and its headquarters company; two of its organic battalions (2-14IN and 4-31IN); 1-41IN (a Fort Riley–based mechanized infantry

heavy task force); "habitually attached units" from 2nd Battalion, 15th Field Artillery; 210th Forward Support Battalion; Company D, 110th Military Intelligence Battalion; Company B, 10th Signal Battalion; and, finally, Companies A and B, 1st Battalion, 509th Airborne Infantry—the Opposing Force (OPFOR) unit from the Joint Readiness Training Center (JRTC)—which would replace Company C of 2-14IN and Company B of 4-31IN, both of which had returned to Fort Drum from other deployments shortly before the brigade's alert.[335] Also alerted to deploy with the brigade was the 58th Combat Engineer Company (an OPFOR unit from the National Training Center [NTC] at Fort Irwin, California); Company B, 27th Engineers, from Fort Bragg, North Carolina; and one platoon of the 463rd Military Police Company of Fort Leonard Wood, Missouri.[336]

The 2nd Brigade's advanced party departed for theater on June 7, 2004, the main body following five days later on June 12; by June 25, the brigade combat team had consolidated at Camp Buehring, Kuwait, where it would acclimate to the harsh desert climate (temperatures reached 125 degrees Fahrenheit while the brigade was there) and complete all the training and certifications required prior to entry into the theater of combat operations—Iraq.[337] Perhaps the most significant task that the BCT had to accomplish in Kuwait was the temporary conversion from light to motorized infantry, drawing 200 "up-armored" HMMWVs and other equipment left behind by the 2nd Armored Cavalry Regiment (Light).[338] The brigade began its 710-kilometer road movement into Iraq on July 11, 2004, moving along Route Tampa in multiple convoys, each of which completed the movement in three days, from Convoy Support Center (CSC) Navistar in Kuwait with stops at CSC Kenworth and CSC Scania, culminating in the arrival at Camp Liberty near Baghdad, with 2nd Brigade Combat Team (BCT) "distinguishing itself as the first and only BCT to complete the [movement] with no loss of personnel or equipment" as of that time.[339]

Once in Iraq, 2nd Brigade operated under the command of the 1st Cavalry Division, assuming responsibility for the "rural Western Baghdad" area of operations on August 12, with its subordinate elements arrayed as follows: 2nd Battalion, 14th Infantry (with Company B of 1-41IN attached), was assigned an operational area south of the Baghdad International Airport (BIAP); 4th Battalion, 31st Infantry, assumed responsibility for Saba-al-Bore and environs in the north; 1st Battalion, 41st Infantry (with Company B, 2nd Battalion, 14th Infantry, attached), operated in the area west of Baghdad; and 2nd Battalion, 15th Field Artillery, operated north of Abu Ghraib.[340] The 2nd Brigade's initial mission was to suppress and interdict any enemy man-portable air defense systems (MANPAD) mortars, or portable rocket systems in support of the 1st Cavalry Division, which enabled the resumption of civil air traffic at Baghdad International Airport on August 14, 2014.[341]

The 1-41IN was detached to 1st Brigade, 1st Cavalry Division, for operations against the forces of Moqtada al-Sadr in Sadr City, Baghdad, during September and October; Company B, 2-14IN, having previously been task-organized to 1-41IN, remained with that battalion and "fought in the high[-]intensity combat against the Mahdi Militia," remaining under the control of 1st Cavalry Division's 1st BCT for the subsequent stability operations thereafter.[342] Late October 2004 saw a major redeployment of 2nd Brigade from the rural districts west of Baghdad into Baghdad's urban western districts to backfill 2nd BCT, 1st Cavalry Division—the Black Jack Brigade—which was transferred to the tactical control of the 1st Marine Expeditionary Force for Operation Al Fajr, the liberation of Fallujah from the insurgent groups that had taken control of the city, with the initial mission of securing bridges and other points of access south and east of Fallujah to contain the insurgents ensconced there.[343] The actual breach of the city walls and assault would begin in the evening of November 8, 2004.[344] The 2nd BCT, 10th Mountain Division, was remissioned to "fill the void left by Blackjack BCT's departure," assuming responsibility for Ghazaliyah, Khadamiyah, and Monsour districts; the eastern portion of Abu Ghraib; and that segment of Route Irish connecting Baghdad International Airport

with the International Zone in the city of Baghdad itself.[345] Initially, 2nd Brigade received control of a number of additional formations to accomplish this new mission, including 1st Battalion, 5th Infantry; 2nd Battalion, 13th Armor; 2nd Squadron, 7th Cavalry; the 91st Engineer Battalion; 2nd Battalion, 82nd Field Artillery; 4th Battalion, 5th Air Defense Artillery; the 127th Military Police Company; the 303rd Iraqi Army Battalion;[*] and an Estonian infantry platoon.[346] While the 91st Engineers and 4-5 ADA would remain with 2nd Brigade for the duration, several of these units—2-12 Armor, 2-7 Cavalry, 1-5 Infantry, and 2-82 Field Artillery—would be associated with the brigade for only a short time, moving to Fallujah themselves in late October 2004.[347]

Those elements remaining under 2nd BCT's control after the departure of all other forces to Fallujah were deployed operations as follows: 2-14IN assumed control of eastern Abu Ghraib, 4-31IN assumed control of Khadamiyah in Northwest Baghdad, 2-15FA and 58th Combat Engineer Company were tasked with responsibility for the Monsour district, 4-5ADA was tasked with security of Route Irish, and the 91st Engineer Battalion maintained its position in Ameriyah and Ghazaliyah.[348] In February 2005, 1st Battalion, 41st Infantry, would return to 2nd BCT control and relieve the 91st Engineers in Ghazaliyah; 1st Battalion, 69th Infantry, New York Army National Guard, would be assigned to 2nd Brigade to assume responsibility for the security of Route Irish when the 91st Engineers and 4-5 ADA returned to Fort Hood.[349]

One of the most momentous events in the relatively short life of the Republic of Iraq occurred on January 30, 2005, when Iraqi citizens went to the polls to elect a Transitional National Assembly, which would prepare the way for the drafting of a new constitution and for the election of a permanent government in the months to follow.[350] Election security was primarily the responsibility of Iraq's own nascent security forces, but US and other coalition forces inevitably played a key role in establishing an environment secure enough to hold an election and in ensuring that the election

---

[*] Subsequently reflagged as 2nd Battalion, 1st Brigade, 6th Iraqi Army Division (Brandon J. Iker, *10th Mountain Division Light Infantry Annual Historical Summary, 1 January 2004–31 December 2004*, 150).

was successfully carried out.[351] The 2nd Brigade, 10th Mountain Division, would play its part, ramping up security efforts such as Operation Commando Freeze, in which 745 suspected insurgents were taken into custody.[352] Despite five suicide attacks in 2nd BCT's sector, the election "proceeded unhindered as a result of the brigade's intensive and successful security efforts."[353] In the weeks following the election, 2nd Brigade would participate in Operation Flying Eagle / Warning Track, 3rd Infantry Division's effort to secure the formation of the transitional government and the seating of the Transitional National Assembly.[354]

Shortly after the election, Company C of 2-14IN and Company B of 4-31IN rejoined their parent battalions in Iraq, with B/4-31 operating in Khadamiyah and C/2-14IN deploying to eastern Abu Ghraib.[355] That same month, February 11–21, 2nd Brigade and the Iraqi 303rd Battalion carried out intensive operations to secure the Khadamiyah Shrine in western Baghdad during a Shia religious pilgrimage.[356] The 2nd Brigade provided further security for Shia religious observances from March 25 to April 1, 2005, protecting the massive pilgrimage from Khadamiyah to Najaf commemorating the death of Imam Hussain.[357]

Mid-April 2005 saw a major change in 2nd Brigade's mission, as it transitioned its area of operations to the rural areas south and west of Baghdad, some of which the brigade had occupied prior to 1st Cavalry Division's mission in Fallujah. The brigade would retain responsibility for eastern Abu Ghraib, where 2-14IN would continue to operate; TF 1-41 assumed responsibility for both western Abu Ghraib and the external security of the coalition detention center there; and 2-15FA assumed responsibility for the area north of Abu Ghraib.[358] Operations in the new AO included Operation Commando Squeeze Play, in which 2nd Brigade supported Iraqi 6th Division operations resulting in the capture of more than 440 insurgents, and later Operation Commando Squeeze Play South in the Mahmudiya district and Latifiyah, 20 miles south of Baghdad.[359] Squeeze Play South was a massive, four-day operation in which 2nd Brigade assumed control of the US 2nd Battalion, 70th Armor and 3rd Squadron, 3rd Cavalry Regiment; 4th Brigade,

6th Iraqi Army Division; 1st Brigade, Iraqi Intervention Force; 2nd Brigade Iraqi Ministry of Interior (MOI) commandos; and the Iraqi 4th Public Order Brigade. This operation resulted in the capture of 366 insurgents and a more than tenfold reduction in insurgent attacks.[360] Following Squeeze Play South, 2nd Brigade transferred authority over its area of operations to the 48th Brigade Combat Team, Georgia Army National Guard, on June 17 2005.[361] The Commando Brigade redeployed to Fort Drum four days later, on June 21, 2005.[362]

The 2nd Brigade carried out other functions in addition to security and combat operations during this period. One such was the establishment of a brigade internment facility (BIF) operated by twenty-four volunteers under the command of a captain, securing seventy prisoners per day on average, with a maximum of 169.[363] Another important mission was the training and development of the Iraq security forces that would eventually succeed US forces in securing the country. The 2nd Brigade contributed to this effort by "training, advising, and mentoring" the 303rd Iraqi Army Battalion, forming a thirty-six-soldier commando advisory group (CAG) for the effort; the CAG—augmented with a small medical detachment, a communications support team, and a perimeter security detail—would live, work, and fight alongside the 303rd at its base, Forward Operating Base (FOB) Hawk.[364] The 2nd Brigade made substantial progress in the training and development of Iraqi security forces, as the 2004 *Division Annual Historical Summary* reports:

Two of the crowning achievements which will ultimately lead to the long[-]term stability of Iraq were the development of the 303rd IA Battalion and the 3rd Muthana Brigade, 6th IA Division. The 303rd, later renamed 2/1/6 IA[,] progressed from a unit able to execute only squad[-] and platoon[-]level operations to a competent, hard-charging battalion which was feared by the enemy. 2/1/6 IA conducted hundreds of patrols throughout Ameriyah, notorious for AIF [enemy] operations and cells, rounding up dozens of AIF planners, facilitators and operators. Eventually, 2/1/6 IA was assigned to defend Haifa Street, a road made infamous by the QJBR and Ansar al Sunna terror cell attacks. Within a matter of weeks, 2/1/6 had regained the street[,] bringing stability to the area. The second achievement was the [Iraqi army's] 3rd Muthana Brigade's occupation of FOB Constitution in the heart of Abu Ghraib. Again, introduction of a competent, disciplined unit brought stability to an area high in enemy contact. These accomplishments were made possible by the Commando Advisory Group.[365]

The 2nd Brigade was also active in civil-military operations, including governance, essential services, and economic development.[366] The brigade worked closely with local governing counsels and sought to restore critical infrastructure such as water service, electrical power, sewage, and trash removal in Al Mansour, Abu Ghraib, Kadhimiya, Mahmudiya, and Saba Al Bor districts, executing 308 projects valued at more than $50 million and monitoring another seventy-one projects funded by other entities, valued at nearly $75 million.[367] Another important area of effort was restoration of the agricultural sector in the rural areas west of Baghdad, with 2nd BCT providing thirty pumps and twenty generators to provide improved irrigation capacity and delivering 300 tons of barley and wheat seed and 100 tons of fertilizer.[368]

The 2nd Brigade's efforts in the civil-military arena were challenging, since insurgents vigorously resisted US-sponsored development efforts, as Wright et al. report:

In some places, the insurgents mounted a concerted campaign to deter all coalition rebuilding plans. In 2004, for example, insurgent forces launched a coordinated effort to end all rebuilding in the town of Abu Ghraib. . . . The 2nd Battalion, 14th Infantry (2-14IN) [of the] 2nd Brigade, 10th Mountain Division, had begun work with contractors on a number of local

projects designed to improve the quality of life and economic prospects for the citizens of Abu Ghraib. In August 2004, 2-14 IN invested $72,000 in renovating a local business center; but only 3 days after the facility opened, an insurgent group blew it up. Maj. John Allred, executive officer of 2-14IN[,] told an American journalist at the time, "Anything we're involved with, [the insurgents] want to see it fail. Anyone involved with us they want to kill."[369]

The Commando Brigade departed Iraq having conducted a vigorous campaign in Baghdad and its environs, as summarized by the brigade's *Annual Historical Summary* for 2005:

The Commando AO of Western Baghdad had the highest concentration of casualties in Iraq and had the largest number of enemy contacts. Throughout the deployment 2nd BCT conducted over 66,000 combat patrols, captured 1,905 detainees, experienced 645 IEDs detonated, 413 IEDs discovered, 316 mortar attacks, 148 rocket attacks, 65 IDF attacks of undetermined type/caliber, 537 small[-]arms fire attacks, 128 rocket[-]propelled grenade attacks, 136 coordinated attacks, 14 surface-to-air missile attacks, 165 attacks against local nationals, seven suicide bomber attacks, 56 vehicle borne improvised explosive devices detonated, 21 vehicle[-]carried improvised explosive devices detonated, 3 Vehicle[-]Born[e] IEDs (VBIED) and 4 Vehicle[-]Concealed IEDs (VCIEDs) discovered.[370]

Almost as soon as 2nd Brigade had returned to Fort Drum from Iraq, the 10th Mountain Division dispatched 1st Brigade there in August 2005, for a deployment that would end with the return of the brigade one year later in August 2006.[371]

The 1st Brigade Combat Team (1 BCT) relieved the 256th enhanced Separate Brigade (eSB), Louisiana Army National Guard, on September 10, 2005, and immediately embarked upon counterinsurgency operations and continued efforts to equip and train Iraqi security forces, with the principal objective being to facilitate the success of the next two rounds of Iraqi elections: the Constitutional Referendum in October 2005, and the election of a new national government just a few months later in December.[372] With respect to the former, 1st BCT executed, under the aegis of the US Army's 3rd Infantry Division, Operation Free Speech, a four-phase operation to set the conditions for a successful Constitutional Referendum on October 15.[373] The first phase consisted of intelligence preparation of the battlefield, in which the brigade staff gathered and analyzed intelligence on enemy forces and used that intelligence to develop targets for further operations; in the second phase, the brigade carried out "spoiling attacks focused at disrupting and interdicting AIF* activity prior to the referendum"; the third phase would encompass the security of the balloting itself, with the "hardening of Polling Sites and District Election Offices" and the provision of quick-reaction forces to deal with any contingencies; and in the final recovery phase the BCT would remove the nearly 3,800 pieces of barrier material previously installed to secure the voting.[374] The 1st Brigade continued to support the Iraqi political process during November and December, carrying out offensive operations in support of the December 2005 national elections. One significant mission was Operation Hail Storm, consisting of cordon-and-search operations against eleven battalion-sized objectives: 2nd Battalion, 22nd Infantry, kicked

off Hail Storm on November 30, with a mission against Objective Sherman in Area of Operations (AO) Courage, followed up by operations against Objective Sedgwick; 1st Squadron, 11th Armored Cavalry Regiment, operating in AO Bengal under 1st Brigade, 10th Mountain Division, carried out operations against Objectives Meade, McClellan, Moore, and Fulda Gap; and 1st Battalion, 87th Infantry, conducted executive operations against Objectives Chamberlain, Warren, Pope, Burnside, Reynolds, and Hancock, as well as executing Operations Bear Trap I, Bear Trap II, Squirrel Hunter I, and Squirrel Hunter II to secure Corps Main Supply Routes (MSR).[375] To counter enemy improvised-explosive-device (IED) and indirect-fire operations in AO Courage, 2nd Battalion 22nd Infantry, carried out Operations Hunter, Archer, and Clam Shell and, from November 11 to 13, 2005, executed Operation Round Up against five company-sized objectives to disrupt enemy activity in eastern Abu Ghraib.[376] On seven occasions, 1st Brigade deployed the Division Ready Reaction Force Platoon (DRRF) from Charlie Company, 1st Battalion, 121st Infantry Regiment, 48th Brigade of the Georgia Army National Guard (GAANG), "to disrupt AIF activity [and] provide battle field circulation and additional combat power."[377] Another important focus during this period was on the development of Iraqi security forces in the brigade's area of operations, as the brigade transitioned responsibility for Area of Operations Summit and Scimitar to Iraqi forces.[378]

---

* "AIF" stands for "Anti-Iraqi Forces," the euphemism used by coalition forces to refer to the insurgency as the struggle wore on.

Spc. Clint Beaty and William Gordon, combat engineers, attached to Company B, 1st Battalion, 32nd Infantry Regiment, 10th Mountain Division, carefully tape a highly explosive M7 blasting cap to detonation cord near rock they are removing from a helicopter landing zone at an outpost in the Nuristan Province. Arranas, Afghanistan, September 1, 2006. *Photo by Spc. Eric Jungels, US Central Command Public Affairs*

Soldiers from Company B, 1st Battalion, 32nd Infantry Regiment, 10th Mountain Division, await orders to move out on a nighttime patrol designed to interrupt movement of enemy fighters in the Nuristan Province. Arranas, Afghanistan, September 1, 2006. *Photo by Spc. Eric Jungels, US Central Command Public Affairs*

From front to rear: 1Sgt. Jamie Nakano, Sgt. Daniel Wilder, and Spc. Michael Davis, Soldiers from Company B, 1st Battalion, 32nd Infantry Regiment, 10th Mountain Division, negotiate the mountainous terrain of the Nuristan Province while on patrol. Arranas, Afghanistan, September 1, 2006. *Photo by Spc. Eric Jungels, US Central Command Public Affairs*

Spc. Rufino Persaud, a native of Jacksonville, Florida, watches over the Afghan countryside while fellow members of Headquarters and Headquarters Company, 1st Battalion, 32nd Infantry Regiment, speak with members of the Afghan border police, at an Afghan border patrol outpost, June 30, 2009. The 10th Mountain Division soldiers work closely with their ABP counterparts in order to help stop illegal activity along the border with Pakistan. June 30, 2009. *Photo by Sgt. Matthew Moeller, 5th Mobile Public Affairs Detachment*

A Pakistani detainee explains his plight as a Taliban member to 10th Mountain Division soldiers, in the prison at Sherberghan, Afghanistan, during Operation Enduring Freedom. Sherberghan, Afghanistan, December 31, 2001. *Department of Defense photo by SSgt. Cecilio M. Ricardo, USAF via US National Archives Public Domain Archive, https://picryl.com/, https://nara.getarchive.net*

In their Tactical Vehicle System (TVS) vehicle, soldiers from the 10th Mountain Division, Fort Drum, New York, arrive at an undisclosed location in support of Operation Enduring Freedom, on October 10, 2001. *Department of Defense photo by SSgt. Cecilio M. Ricardo Jr., USAF, via US National Archives Public Domain Archive, https://picryl.com/, https://nara.getarchive.net*

First Lieutenant Ochman, US Army, platoon leader of 2nd Platoon Alpha Company, 3rd Battalion Special Troops Brigade, 10th Mountain, exits a room he has just searched during an investigation of local residences in the village of Stonaga, Afghanistan, on April 19, 2006. Paktia, Afghanistan, April 20, 2006. *Department of Defense photo by Spc. Christopher Barnhart, via US National Archives Public Domain Archive, https://picryl.com/, https://nara.getarchive.net*

US Army corporal Powell from 3rd Platoon Alpha Company, 3rd Battalion Special Troops Brigade, 10th Mountain, holds up pieces of carrying devices for mortar rounds that he found while searching a building in Kandu, Afghanistan, on April 17, 2006. The soldiers of Company A were searching for materials used in the manufacturing of IEDs. Paktia, Afghanistan, April 17, 2006. *Department of Defense photo by Spc. Christopher Barnhart, USA, via US National Archives Public Domain Archive, https://picryl.com/, https://nara.getarchive.net*

PFC Matthew J. Mongiove, US Army, 4th Brigade, 10th Mountain Division, scans the area through the sight of an M249 Squad Automatic Weapon (SAW) while providing security for the Canadian Military Police Mobile Training Team (MTT) at Kandahar Air Field, Afghanistan, on May 16, 2006, during Operation Enduring Freedom. Kandahar Airfield, Afghanistan, May 16, 2006. *Department of Defense photo by SGT André Reynolds, USA, via US National Archives Public Domain Archive, https://picryl.com/, https://nara.getarchive.net*

US Army soldiers assigned to the 10th Mountain Division rest in an open field due to lack of quarters after spending over sixteen hours on their feet in-processing, digging defensive positions, and setting up entry control points, at an undisclosed location in support of Operation Enduring Freedom. Undisclosed location, May 16, 2006. *Department of Defense photo by Sgt. André Reynolds, via US National Archives Public Domain Archive, https://picryl.com/, https://nara.getarchive.net*

US Army captain Brad Frey, 10th Mountain Division (Light Infantry), examines and treats a severely malnourished Afghani infant during a one-day Coalition Medical/Dental Civil Affairs Project (MEDCAP) humanitarian mission to the village of Najoy, Kandahar Province, Afghanistan (AFG), during Operation Enduring Freedom. Kandahar, Afghanistan, April 24, 2004. *Department of Defense photo by GYSGT Keith A. Milks, via US National Archives Public Domain Archive, https://picryl.com/, https://nara.getarchive.net*

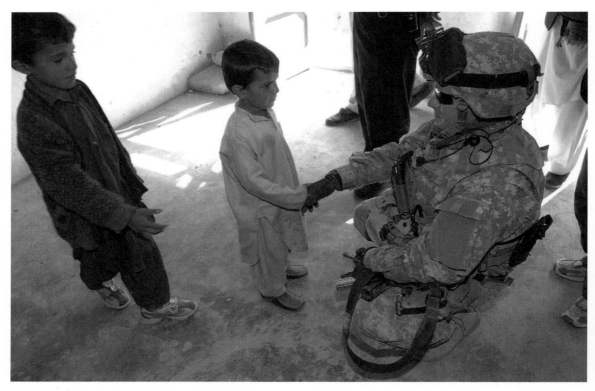

US Army first lieutenant Douchkoff (*right, kneeling*), platoon leader, 3rd Platoon, Alpha Company, 10th Mountain Division, greets two Afghani boys in Kandu, Oruzgan Province, Afghanistan, while delivering clothes for the local children during Operation Enduring Freedom. Oruzgan, Afghanistan, April 17, 2006. *Department of Defense photo by Spc. Christopher Barnhart, USA via US National Archives Public Domain Archive, https://picryl.com/, https://nara.getarchive.net*

US Army soldiers from the 10th Mountain Division (Light Infantry), Forward Support Battalion, Fort Drum, New York, surveying the area for any possible threats as US and Romanian troops from Kandahar Army Airfield, Afghanistan, conduct a combined medical assistance mission at the village of Loy Karezak during Operation Enduring Freedom. Kandahar, Afghanistan, October 8, 2003. *Department of Defense photo by Spc. Gul A. Alisan, USA, via US National Archives Public Domain Archive, https://picryl.com/, https://naragetarchive.net*

A 2nd Brigade combat team, 10th Mountain Division, soldier observes a soldier from 2nd Battalion, 1st Iraqi Army Brigade, pull security during a cordon search in Baghdad. Baghdad, Iraq March 28, 2005. *Courtesy of Photo 10th Mountain Division*

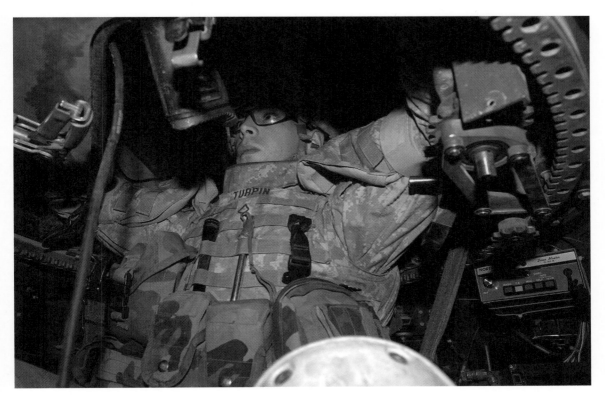

PFC Justin Turpin, US Army, Company B, 1st Battalion, 87th Infantry Regiment, 10th Mountain Division, sits in a vehicle turret observing other 1-87IN Soldiers setting up traffic control point barriers on Routes 49 and 50 in Baghdad, Baghdad Province, Iraq, to assist Iraqi police and Iraqi army personnel in controlling the area during Operation Iraqi Freedom. Baghdad, Iraq, March 29, 2006. *Department of Defense photo by Ssgt. Kevin L Moses Sr., USA, via US National Archives Public Domain Archive, https://picryl.com/, https://nara.getarchive.net*

US Army sergeant Antwan Williams (*left*), PFC Mike O'Connell, and Spc. Okino Leiba, all from 4th Battalion, 31st Infantry Regiment, 10th Mountain Division, communicate on a field radio while conducting security operations on March 17, 2007, behind a hill in the Hittite ruins in Baghdad Province, Iraq, during a search for weapons caches in the area while deployed in support of Operation Iraqi Freedom. Baghdad, Iraq, March 17, 2007. *Department of Defense photo by SGT Tierney P. Nowland, USA, via US National Archives Public Domain Archive, https://picryl.com/, https://nara.getarchive. net*

Soldiers with 1st Battalion, 87th Infantry Regiment, 1st Brigade Combat Team, 10th Mountain Division, take time to chat with Iraqi children while patrolling in the neighborhood of Ameriyah in western Baghdad. Baghdad, Iraq, May 11, 2006. *Photo by Spc. Jason Jordan, 1st Brigade Combat Team, 10th Mountain Division*

Cpl. Jason Rodriguez of 1st Brigade, 10th Mountain Division, prepares to depart for a reconnaissance patrol supporting the brigade's senior leadership assessment of the security situation on Iraq's historic election day. Baghdad, Iraq, December 15, 2005. *Photo courtesy of 1st Brigade Combat Team, 10th Mountain Division*

Soldiers with the personal security detachment of 1st Brigade, 10th Mountain Division, receive a convoy briefing before departing on a reconnaissance patrol supporting the brigade's senior leadership assessment of the security situation on Iraq's historic election day. Baghdad, Iraq, December 15, 2005. *Photo courtesy of 1st Brigade Combat Team, 10th Mountain Division*

US Army soldiers from 1st Battalion, 87th Infantry Regiment, and Iraqi soldiers from 2nd Battalion, 1st Iraqi Army Division, conducted joint patrols in the city of Ameriyah, Iraq, on May 6, 2006. Baghdad, Iraq, May 6, 2006. *Department of Defense photo by Ssgt. Kevin L. Moses Sr., USA, via US National Archives Public Domain Archive, https://picryl.com/, https://nara.getarchive.net*

Implementation of the Modular Design Concept

At the same time the 10th Mountain Division was coping with repeated deployments to Iraq, Afghanistan, and peacekeeping operations throughout the world, it was also going through major organizational changes. One aspect of that change was the activation of two new brigade combat teams—3rd Brigade at Fort Drum and 4th Brigade at Fort Polk, mentioned previously.[379] The second major organizational change that the division had to implement was *modularity*.[380] Throughout most of the twentieth century, the basic tactical unit of the Army—that is, "the lowest level capable of conducting autonomous, combined arms operations for a set amount of time"—was the division; under the modular reorganization, the brigade combat team would be the basic tactical unit of the Army.[381] Among the considerations supporting the transformation

were that "existing and emerging technologies enable smaller combat formations to dominate the same battlespace that had previously required much larger units"; that the organizational structure promised "greater flexibility, strategic responsiveness (deployability), increased operational tempo, and increased lethality"; and that the concept would provide for "more of the basic building-block unit of combat power."[382] As described in a 2012 RAND Corporation study:

> In the move to the brigade-centric force structure, or modularity, the Army replaced its division-centric force structure with a force whose constituent building blocks are brigades and brigade combat teams (BCTs). BCTs were rebuilt by making proportionate combat, combat support, and combat service support, formerly provided by the host division, organic to

the BCTs' organization. In the process, the Army reduced the number of combat brigade types in its force structure, from some 17 individual types to three: infantry BCTs, heavy BCTs, and Stryker BCTs. The move to modularity provided the Army with a greater number of smaller, very capable force packages, making it easier to sustain the protracted operations in Iraq and Afghanistan.[383]

A key aspect of the modularity concept was the augmentation of brigades to make them much more robust and self-sufficient.[384] Under the traditional organizational model, combat brigades consisted largely of subordinate combat battalions, relying on their parent division or higher headquarters for much of their intelligence, logistics, and fire support and for planning capabilities. Modular brigades, however, would have much of this capability organically, including a reconnaissance, surveillance, and target acquisition (RSTA) squadron; an artillery battalion and brigade special troops and support battalions; and "a larger and more capable headquarters staff (that is also organic) . . . [that] allows the brigade to do the bulk of its own planning for complex operations . . . [that] typically had to be done at higher-echelon headquarters in the pre-modular force."[385] The result is a larger number of brigade combat teams in the Army that are more self-sufficient and possess greater combat power, better situational awareness, and more joint capability than brigades of the previous generation.[386]

Completing the transition to modularity, however, was a massive effort, planning for which began in January 2003; the division *formally* converted to the new structure on August 20, 2004.[387] But a vast amount of work lay ahead before this titular conversion became a reality on the ground. To facilitate this effort, an "ad hoc staff section" was formed under the assistant chief of staff, G37, in the form of the Modularity Coordination Center (MCC), with a staff of twenty-nine headed by a lieutenant colonel, charged with monitoring and synchronizing the transformation process across the division.[388]

While 2nd Brigade was forced to implement this transformation in parallel with its preparation for deployment to Iraq, the remainder of the division was able to focus on carrying out what has been characterized as "the largest[-]scale reorganization since World War II."[389] Illustrative of the magnitude of the division's reorganization is that of 1st Brigade. Although the number of infantry battalions was reduced from three to two, with 1-87IN and 2-22IN staying with the brigade and 1-32IN departing, its overall span of control expanded from three battalions to six as it gained 3rd Battalion, 6th Field Artillery; 1st Squadron, 71st Cavalry (a RSTA squadron); a brigade support battalion (formerly the 210th Forward Support Battalion); and a brigade special troops battalion, with organic military police, signal, engineer, and chemical recce capabilities. None of these capabilities had previously been organic to the brigade.[390] The 2nd Brigade would undergo a similar transformation, which would have to compete for its attention with the brigade's preparations for another rotation in Iraq.[391] The 3rd and 4th Brigades were organized under the new structure as they came online. Between transitioning to the modular structure and expansion to four brigades, 10th Mountain Division saw more than a 55 percent increase in authorized strength from its previous light infantry configuration, a nearly 94 percent increase in tactical vehicles, a nearly 78 percent increase in weapons and mounts, almost a 58 percent increase in night vision equipment, and more than a 79 percent increase in radios.[392] These gains would retract somewhat with the deactivation of 4th Brigade in February 2015, but the 10th Mountain Division nonetheless retained a substantial increase in combat power even then.[393]

Shoulder sleeve insignia of the modern 10th Mountain Division. *Clockwise from the top*: (1) the full-color patch worn on the sleeve of the former Class A uniform and the current Army Green Service uniform; (2) the subdued patch worn on the Army's Battle Dress Uniform (BDU) from 1981 to 2008; (3) the tan-and-brown patch worn on the Army's Desert Battle Dress ("chocolate chip") uniform from the mid-1970s until 1995, and the Desert Combat Uniform (DCU) from 1991 to 2008; and (4) and the patch worn on the Army Combat Uniform (ACU) in the universal camouflage pattern, which entered service in 2005, and has since been replaced by the operational camouflage pattern (not shown). *Author's collection*

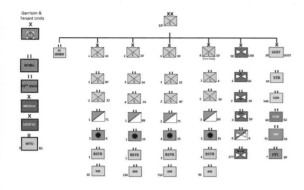

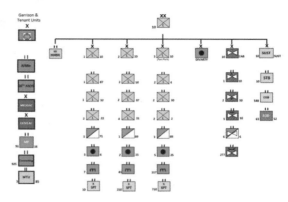

10th Mountain Division transformation to the modular design structure as of January 2014. Note the inclusion of the now-inactive 4th BCT. *From 1Lt. (P) Michael C. Loveland,* 10th Mountain Division (Light Infantry) Annual Command History 2014 & 2015, *10th Mountain Division (Light Infantry), 2016, figure 1.E.2.iii.A, page 36*

10th Mountain Division structure after December 2015, following the inactivation of the 4th Brigade and reconstitution of the Division Artillery headquarters. *From 1Lt. (P) Michael C. Loveland,* 10th Mountain Division (Light Infantry) Annual Command History 2014 & 2015, *10th Mountain Division (Light Infantry), 2016, figure 1.E.2.iii.A, page 36*

Obverse of a challenge coin of the provisional 3rd Battalion, 85th Mountain Infantry Regiment Warrior Transition Battalion, organized by the 10th Mountain Division to serve as its associated Warrior Transition Unit. Note that the crest displayed on the coin is the unofficial crest used by the 85th Mountain Infantry Regiment during World War II, rather than the official crest approved by the Army after the war on August 21, 1951. *Author's collection*

Challenge coin of the provisional 3rd Battalion, 85th Mountain Infantry Regiment Warrior Transition Battalion, 10th Mountain Division (reverse). *Author's collection*

CONCLUSION

The story of the 10th Mountain Division continues beyond 2005, where my narrative ends. The division has continued to participate in America's wars and military operations around the world: US forces remain engaged in Afghanistan, and notwithstanding the US withdrawal from Iraq completed on December 18, 2011,[1] the US was obliged to return forces to Iraq beginning on June 15, 2014, in response to the massive offensive of the Islamic State in Iraq and Syria (ISIS) that summer;[2] the US relinquished the military base at Taji, Iraq, back to the Iraqi government control only on August 23, 2020.[3] But the historical record of these struggles remains incomplete. The US Army's official history of the Afghanistan War (*A Different Kind of War: The United States Army in Operation Enduring Freedom*) covers only the period through September 2005, while the Army's two-volume official history of Iraq (*On Point* and *On Point II*) is similarly limited, extending only through January 2005. Even the 10th Mountain Division's own Annual Historical Summaries, which provide such a wealth of information on the division's participation in the Iraq and Afghanistan campaigns, are limited, with the volumes from 2008 to 2011 and 2016 forward unavailable as of this writing. In light of these limitations, a truly comprehensive account of the 10th Mountain Division's participation in these conflicts will likely have to wait for a comprehensive account of the conflicts themselves. But even if the Army's historical record of these campaigns was more complete and more readily available now, constraints of time and space would make a thoroughgoing review of the 10th Mountain Division's service in Iraq and Afghanistan infeasible here, and the same can be said about a comprehensive review of the many other missions conducted by elements of the modern 10th Mountain Division, such as deployments to the Balkans and to the Sinai Desert in support the Multinational Force and Observers mission there, rotations to the Joint Readiness Training Center and the National Training Center, and innumerable other operational and training deployments.

What is clear, however, is that the history of the 10th Mountain Division can be viewed as something of a proxy for the history of the Army generally and of the division as a tactical unit of the Army in particular during the twentieth and twenty-first centuries. This is particularly true if we include in our account, as I have, the history of the 10th Mountain Division's predecessor division of the same number formed during World War I, and the history of the 87th Infantry Regiment apart from the 10th Mountain, both at Kiska and during the Cold War period.

Looked at in this way, the 10th Mountain Division, by which I mean the US Army's 10th Division in all its various permutations and designations, is represented in every aspect of the US Army's history for more than a century past, from the first emergence of divisions as a permanent tactical formation and echelon of command in the US Army during World War I; through the pentomic and ROAD divisions, Division 86, and the Modular Division; in total war; and in regional contingencies, peacekeeping, stabilization missions, and humanitarian operations. At times the 10th Mountain Division has been at the tip of the spear in major campaigns; at other times it has played a supporting role in the institutional training base back home.

But however and wherever it has served, the 10th Mountain Division is the embodiment of America's enterprising spirit of ingenuity, tenacity, courage, and devotion to duty. It is, in an important sense, the story of the United States Army itself—and what a magnificent story it is.

ENDNOTES

Chapter 1

1. John B. Wilson, *Armies, Corps, Divisions, and Separate Brigades*, Army Lineage series (Washington, DC: Center of Military History, 1993), 259.
2. *Order of Battle of the United States Land Forces in the World War, Zone of the Interior: Territorial Departments, Tactical Divisions Organized in 1918, Posts, Camps, and Stations*, vol. 3, part 2 (Washington, DC: Center of Military History, 1993), 644.
3. Steven E. Clay, *US Army Order of Battle, 1919–1941*, vol. 1, *The Arms: Major Commands and Infantry Organizations* (Fort Leavenworth, KS: Combat Studies Institute Press, 2010), 8 (stating that the 10th through 20th Divisions and other specified organizations are not among those still on the roles of the Army).
4. Ibid., 305.
5. *Order of Battle of the United States Land Forces in the World War, Zone of the Interior*, 644.
6. Ibid.
7. Clay, *US Army Order of Battle, 1919–1941*, 1:7.
8. Ibid.
9. Ibid.
10. Ibid.
11. Ibid., 7 and 8.
12. Ibid., 8.
13. John B. Wilson, *Maneuver and Firepower: The Evolution of Divisions and Separate Brigades*, Army Lineage series ((Washington, DC: Center of Military History, 1998), 37.
14. Clay, *US Army Order of Battle, 1919–1941*, 1:8.
15. *American Military History*, Army Historical Series (Washington, DC: Center of Military History, 1989), 374.
16. Ibid.
17. Wilson, *Maneuver and Firepower*, 65.
18. Ibid.
19. Wilson, *Maneuver and Firepower*, 66; and *Order of Battle of the United States Land Forces in the World War, Zone of the Interior*, 644.
20. Leonard P. Ayres, *The War with German: A Statistical Summary*, 2nd ed., Department of the Army (Washington, DC: Government Printing Office, 1919), 26.
21. *American Military History*, 374; and Wilson, *Maneuver and Firepower*, 55.
22. *Brief Histories of Divisions, US Army, 1917–1918* (US Army War Plans Division, General Staff, 1921), 10.
23. Ibid.; and *Order of Battle of the United States Land Forces in the World War*, 645.
24. George Paul Kion, "Army Town Kansas: The History of a World War I Camp Town" (abstract of thesis, Kansas State University of Agriculture and Applied Science, 1960), 1.
25. W. F. Pride, *The History of Fort Riley* (n.p., 1926), 277, 278.
26. *Brief Histories of Divisions, US Army, 1917–1918*, 10.
27. Colin M. Fleming, *Leonard Wood, Operational Artist or Scheming Careerist?* (Fort Leavenworth, KS: School of Advanced Military Studies, 2012), 50.
28. Robert J. Sperberg, *Major General Leonard Wood: A Study of Leadership in an Army of Transition* (Carlisle Barracks, PA: US Army War College, 1992), 13.
29. Ibid., 36, 110.
30. Nelson Miles, *Serving the Republic* (New York: Harper & Brothers, 1911), 224.
31. Sperberg, *Major General Leonard Wood*, 37.
32. Ibid., 111.
33. Ibid., 47.
34. Ibid., 50–53.
35. Ibid., 53, 55; and Fleming, *Leonard Wood, Operational Artist or Scheming Careerist?*, 9–27.
36. Edward M. Coffman, *The Regulars: The American Army, 1898–1941* (Cambridge, MA: Belknap Press of Harvard University Press, 2004), 52.
37. Sperberg, *Major General Leonard Wood*, 57.
38. Fleming, *Leonard Wood, Operational Artist or Scheming Careerist?*, 27–44.

39. Sperberg, *Major General Leonard Wood*, 84, quoting James E. Hewes Jr., *From Root to McNamara: Army Organization and Administration, 1900–1963* (Washington, DC: Center of Military History, 1975), 14.

40. Sperberg, *Major General Leonard Wood*, ii.

41. Ibid., 106.

42. Eric B. Setzekorn, *Joining the Great War, April 1917–April 1918*, CMH Pub. 77-3 (Washington, DC: Center of Military History, 2017), 18.

43. Coffman, *The Regulars*, 204; and Sperberg, *Major General Leonard Wood*, 100.

44. *Brief Histories of Divisions, US Army, 1917–1918*, 77; and Sperberg, *Major General Leonard Wood*, 89.

45. Sperberg, *Major General Leonard Wood*, 90.

46. Ibid.

47. Ibid.

48. Coffman, *The Regulars*, 208.

49. Sperberg, *Major General Leonard Wood*, 100.

50. Ibid., 97.

51. Ibid., 100, quoting Donald Smyth, *Pershing: General of the Armies* (Bloomington, Indiana University Press, 1986), 85.

52. Sperberg, *Major General Leonard Wood*, 100–101.

53. C. J. Masseck, *Official Brief History, 89th Division USA, 1917–1918–1919* (G-2, 89th Division, 1919), 3–4.

54. Hermann Hagedorn, *Leonard Wood: A Biography*, vol. 2 (New York: Harper & Brothers, 1931), 313.

55. Ibid., 307.

56. Ibid., 308.

57. Ibid.

58. Ibid.

59. *Order of Battle of the United States Land Forces in the World War, Zone of the Interior*, 644.

60. Hagedorn, *Leonard Wood*, 312.

61. Ibid.

62. Ibid., 308.

63. Ibid.

64. Ibid., 309.

65. Ibid., 309–10.

66. Ibid., 310.

67. Naomi Ngadiman, "A Historical Review of the Influenza Outbreaks within Military Settings and Understanding the Viral Spread of the 1918 Influenza Pandemic" (Atlanta: Georgia State University School of Public Health Capstone Project, 2018), 14.

68. Bill Bynum, "Stories of an Influenza Pandemic," *The Lancet* 373 (March 14, 2009): 886.

69. John M. Barry, "The Site of Origin of the 1918 Influenza Pandemic and Its Public Health Implications," *Journal of Translational Medicine* 2, no. 3 (2004): 2.

70. Ngadiman, "A Historical Review of the Influenza Outbreaks within Military Settings and Understanding the Viral Spread of the 1918 Influenza Pandemic," 14.

71. Ibid., 30; and *Brief Histories of Divisions*, 19.

72. Hagedorn, *Leonard Wood*, 314.

73. Ayres, *The War with Germany*, 127, diagram .

74. Hagedorn, *Leonard Wood*, 314.

75. Ngadiman, "A Historical Review of the Influenza Outbreaks within Military Settings and Understanding the Viral Spread of the 1918 Influenza Pandemic," 30.

76. William Page Johnson II, "Where Honor Is Due: Fairfax County Casualties of World War I; A Requiem," *Fare Facs Gazette* 15, no. 1 (Winter 2018): 18.

77. *Order of Battle of the United States Land Forces in the World War, Zone of the Interior*, 644.

78. Ibid.

79. Ibid.

80. Clay, *US Army Order of Battle, 1919–1941*, 1:305.

81. John J. McGrath, *The Brigade: A History, Its Organization and Equipment in the US Army* (Fort Leavenworth, KS: Combat Studies Institute Press, 2004), 166.

82. Clay, *US Army Order of Battle, 1919–1941*, 1:305–06.

83. *The Army Lineage Book*, vol. 2, *Infantry* (Washington, DC: Department of the Army, 1953), 179–83.

84. James A. Sawicki, *Infantry Regiments of the US Army* (Dumfries, VA: Wyvern, 1982), 168–69.

85. *The Army Lineage Book*, 2:121–22; and Sawicki, *Infantry Regiments of the US Army*, 92–93.

86. Sawicki, *Infantry Regiments of the US Army*, 172.

87. Wilson, *Maneuver and Firepower*, 99.

88. "World War I: Birth of the Modern Army Division" (Washington, DC: Center of Military History), https://history.army.mil/html/book-shelves/resmat/wwi/wwi_bomad/index.html, retrieved April 12, 2020.

89. *Brief Histories of Divisions, US Army, 1917–1918*; and *Order of Battle of the United States Land Forces in the World War*.

90. *Lineage and Honors, 5th Battalion, 20th Infantry (Sykes' Regulars)* (Washington, DC: Department of the Army, August 19, 2014); *Lineage and Honors, 1st Battalion, 41st Infantry* (Washington, DC: Department of the Army, October 26, 2014); and *Lineage and Honors, 3rd Battalion, 41st Infantry* (Washington, DC: Department of the Army, March 18, 2011).

91. Rosemary Sutcliff, *The Eagle of the of the Ninth* (Oxford: Oxford University Press, 1954).

92. Headquarters Tenth Division, Discharge Orders, Charles Miller, Headquarters Company, 41st Infantry, Camp Funston, Kansas, February 20, 1919.

Chapter 2

1. "Armies on Skiis," *Mid-Week Pictorial* 41, no. 3 (March 2, 1935), 17.

2. Justin J. Chabalko, *Forging the 10th Mountain Division for War, 1940–1945: How Innovation Created a Highly Adaptive Formation* (Fort Leavenworth, KS: US Army Command and General Staff College, 2017), 21.

3. Ibid.; see also George F. Earle, *Birth of a Division* (Syracuse, NY: Signature, 1993), 1.

4. Thomas E. Griess, ed., *The Second World War: Europe and the Mediterranean* (Wayne, NJ: Avery, 1984), 27.

5. Jouni Keravuori, *The Russo-Finnish War, 1939–1940: A Study in Leadership, Training, and Esprit-de-Corps* (Carlisle Barracks, PA: US Army War College, 1985), III-4.

6. H. B. Elliston, *Finland Fights* (Boston: Little, Brown, 1940), 174–201.

7. Russell D. Harris, *The Finnish Campaigns: Failure of Soviet Operational Art in World War II* (Quantico, VA: USMC Command and Staff College, 2013), 8.

8. Ibid.

9. Ibid.

10. Ibid., 8–11.

11. John A. English, *On Infantry* (New York: Praeger, 1984), 91.

12. Keravuori, *The Russo-Finnish War, 1939–1940*, V-8.

13. English, *On Infantry*, 91.

14. Keravuori, *The Russo-Finnish War, 1939–1940*, V-8.

15. Ibid., V-10.

16. Sperberg, *Major General Leonard Wood*, 49.

17. Ibid., 47.

18. Keravuori, *The Russo-Finnish War, 1939–1940*, V-5.

19. Chabalko, *Forging the 10th Mountain Division for War, 1940–1945*, 21.

20. Thomas P. Govan, *Training for Mountain and Winter Warfare*, Army Ground Forces Study 23 (Washington, DC: Historical Section, Army Ground Forces, 1946b), 3.

21. English, *On Infantry*, 91.

22. D. Fedotoff White, *The Growth of the Red Army* (Princeton, NJ: Princeton University Press, 1944), vii.

23. English, *On Infantry*, 91–92.

24. Harris, *The Finnish Campaigns*, 1.

25. Govan, *Training for Mountain and Winter Warfare*, 5.

26. *The Soviet-Finnish War, 1939–1940 / The Campaign in Norway, 1940* (West Point, NY: US Military Academy, Department of Military Art and Engineering, 1948), 29.

27. Karl Rommetveit, *Narvik 1940: Five-Nation War in the High North*, Forsvarsstudier 8/1991 (Oslo, Norway: Institutt für Forsvarsstudier, 1991), 110.

28. Govan, *Training for Mountain and Winter Warfare*, 5.

29. Ibid.

30. Ibid.

31. Ibid.

32. Ibid.

33. Ibid.

34. Ibid.

35. Mylon Ollila, "Finland in Crisis: Finnish Relations with the Western Democracies, 1939–1941" (MA thesis, University of Waterloo, 2012), 1.

36. Ibid., 19.
37. Charles Minot Dole, *Adventures in Skiing* (New York: Franklin Watts, 1965), 90.
38. Ibid.
39. Ibid., 91.
40. "Re-creation through Recreation: Chapter III, World War II and the 10th Mountain Division," www.heritageaspen.org/recre3.html, retrieved July 2, 2008.
41. "Charles Minot 'Minnie' Dole," National Ski Patrol Eastern Division, https://www.nspeast.org/minnie-dole-hof.html, accessed February 8, 2020.
42. "Minnie Dole Biography," New England Ski History, https://newenglandskihistory.com/biographies/doleminnie.php, retrieved February 8, 2020.
43. Ibid.
44. "Charles Minot 'Minnie' Dole."
45. Dole, Charles Minot, chairman, Editorial Board, *The National Ski Patrol System Manual* (New York: National Ski Patrol System, 1941), 3.
46. Ibid.
47. John C. Jay, *The History of the Mountain Training Center*, Army Ground Forces Study 24 (Washington, DC: Historical Section, Army Ground Forces, 1948), 1.
48. Dole, *Adventures in Skiing*, 94.
49. Ibid.
50. Ibid., 95.
51. Jay, *The History of the Mountain Training Center*, 1.
52. Frank Harper, *Night Climb: The Story of the Skiing 10th* (New York and London: Longmans, Green, 1946), 80.
53. Jay, *The History of the Mountain Training Center*, 1.
54. Dole, *Adventures in Skiing*, 96–97.
55. Ibid.
56. Harper, *Night Climb*, 82; and Dole, *Adventures in Skiing*, 98–100.
57. Jay, *The History of the Mountain Training Center*, 1.
58. Harper, *Night Climb*, 82.
59. Ibid.
60. Chabalko, *Forging the 10th Mountain Division for War, 1940–1945*, 28.
61. Dole, *Adventures in Skiing*, 101–02.
62. Chabalko, *Forging the 10th Mountain Division for War, 1940–1945*, 29.
63. Burton, *The Ski Troops* (New York: Simon and Schuster, 1971), 185.
64. Jay, *The History of the Mountain Training Center*, 1.
65. Ibid.
66. Ibid., 3.
67. Ibid.
68. Ibid.
69. Ibid.; see also Dole, *Adventures in Skiing*, 106.
70. Jay, *The History of the Mountain Training Center*, 5.
71. Ibid.
72. Ibid., 4.
73. Ibid.
74. Ibid., 3.
75. Ibid.
76. Ibid.
77. Ibid.
78. Ibid., 4.
79. Ibid.
80. Ibid., 4–5.
81. Ibid., 5.
82. Ibid.
83. Ibid.
84. Ibid., 4.
85. "Army's New Ski Patrol Practices on the Snowy Slopes of Mt. Rainier," *Life*, January 20, 1941, 78.
86. Ibid.
87. *Biennial Report of the Chief of Staff of the United States Army, July 1, 1939–June 30, 1941* (Washington, DC: Government Printing Office, 1941), 17.
88. "Army's New Ski Patrol Practices on the Snowy Slopes of Mt. Rainier."
89. Dole, *Adventures in Skiing*, 106–07.
90. Govan, *Training for Mountain and Winter Warfare*, 5.
91. Jay, *The History of the Mountain Training Center*, 6.
92. Ibid.
93. Ibid., 7.
94. Harper, *Night Climb*, 84.
95. Dole, *Adventures in Skiing*, 104.
96. Ibid.

97. Ibid.

98. Ibid., 85.

99. Ibid.

100. Jay, *The History of the Mountain Training Center*, 7.

101. Ibid.; see also Dole, *Adventures in Skiing*, 106.

102. Harper, *Night Climb*, 85.

103. Ibid.

104. Ibid., 85–86.

105. Jay, *The History of the Mountain Training Center*, 8.

106. Ibid.

107. Ibid., 9.

108. Dole, *Adventures in Skiing*, 107.

109. Jay, *The History of the Mountain Training Center*, 9.

110. Ibid., 9.

111. Govan, *Training for Mountain and Winter Warfare*, 6.

112. Chabalko, *Forging the 10th Mountain Division for War, 1940–1945*, 29–30.

113. Govan, *Training for Mountain and Winter Warfare*, 6.

114. Ibid.

115. Jay, *The History of the Mountain Training Center*, 11.

116. Ibid.

117. Chabalko, *Forging the 10th Mountain Division for War, 1940–1945*, 31.

118. Govan, *Training for Mountain and Winter Warfare*, 7.

119. Ibid.

120. Ibid.

121. Jack A. Benson, "Skiing at Camp Hale: Mountain Troops during World War II," *Western Historical Quarterly*, April 1984, 165.

122. Ibid.

123. Govan, *Training for Mountain and Winter Warfare*, 12.

124. Dan Archibald, Adam Smith, Sunny Adams, and Manroop Chawla, *Military Training Lands Historic Context Training Village, Mock Sites, and Large Scale Operations Areas*, ERDC/CERI, TR-10-10 (Champaign, IL: US Army Corps of Engineers Engineer Research and Development Center, March 2010), 180; and Govan, *Training for Mountain and Winter Warfare*, 16.

125. Govan, *Training for Mountain and Winter Warfare*, 16.

126. *Order of Battle of the United States Land Forces in the World War, Zone of the Interior*, 658; and Sawicki, *Infantry Regiments of the US Army*, 188.

127. *Brief Histories of Divisions*, 28.

128. *Order of Battle of the United States Land Forces in the World War, Zone of the Interior*, 659.

129. Ayres, *The War with Germany*, 26.

130. *Order of Battle of the United States Land Forces in the World War, Zone of the Interior*, 659.

131. Ibid., 659; and *Brief Histories of Divisions*, 28.

132. *Brief Histories of Divisions*, 28.

133. Sawicki, *Infantry Regiments of the US Army*, 188.

134. Ibid., 189.

135. George F. Earle, *History of the 87th Mountain Infantry, Italy 1945* (Denver, CO: Bradford-Robinson, 1945), 6.

136. Ibid.

137. Kenneth Finlayson, "Operation Cottage: First Special Service Force, Kiska Campaign," *Veritas* 4, no. 2 (2008)

138. Dole, *Adventures in Skiing*, 107.

139. Ibid., 108.

140. Harper, *Night Climb*, 89.

141. Dole, *Adventures in Skiing*, 108.

142. Jay, *The History of the Mountain Training Center*, 12.

143. Earle, *History of the 87th Mountain Infantry, Italy 1945*, 6.

144. Harper, *Night Climb*, 89–90.

145. Ibid., 90.

146. Jay, *The History of the Mountain Training Center*, 16.

147. Ibid.

148. Ibid.

149. Chabalko, *Forging the 10th Mountain Division for War, 1940–1945*, 64.

150. Jay, *The History of the Mountain Training Center*, 21.

151. Ibid.

152. Ibid.

153. Dole, *Adventures in Skiing*, 117.

154. Archibald et al., *Military Training Lands Historic Context Training Village*, 190.
155. Chabalko, *Forging the 10th Mountain Division for War, 1940–1945*, 68–69.
156. Dole, *Adventures in Skiing*, 116.
157. Ibid.
158. Jay, *The History of the Mountain Training Center*, 12.
159. Dole, *Adventures in Skiing*, 119.
160. John Imbrie and Hugh W. Evans, eds., *Good Times and Bad Times: A History of C Company, 85th Mountain Infantry Regiment, 10th Mountain Division* (Quechee, VT: Vermont Heritage, 1995), 188.
161. Ibid.
162. Rene L. Coquoz, *The Invisible Men on Skis* (Boulder, CO: Johnson, 1970),10.
163. Jay, *The History of the Mountain Training Center*, 31.
164. Harper, *Night Climb*, 126.
165. Thomas P. Govan, *History of the Tenth Light Division*, Alpine Study 26 (Washington, DC: Historical Section, Army Ground Forces, 1946a), 8.
166. Chabalko, *Forging the 10th Mountain Division for War, 1940–1945*, 60.
167. Ibid.
168. Benson, "Skiing at Camp Hale," 165.
169. Archibald et al., *Military Training Lands Historic Context Training Village*, 180.
170. Benson, "Skiing at Camp Hale," 165.
171. Ibid.
172. Ibid., 165–66.
173. Ibid., 166.
174. Chabalko, *Forging the 10th Mountain Division for War, 1940–1945*, 60.
175. Bell I. Wiley, *Training in the Ground Army, 1942–1945*, Study XI (Washington, DC: Historical Section, Army Ground Forces, 1948), 7.
176. Harper, *Night Climb*, 95.
177. Ibid., 95–96.
178. Jay, *The History of the Mountain Training Center*, 22.
179. Dole, *Adventures in Skiing*, 116.
180. Jay, *The History of the Mountain Training Center*, 23.
181. Dole, *Adventures in Skiing*, 119.
182. Ibid., 120.
183. Ibid.
184. Coquoz, *The Invisible Men on Skis*, 12.
185. Ibid., 21.
186. Ibid., 23.
187. Dole, *Adventures in Skiing*, 116–17; and Jay, *The History of the Mountain Training Center*, 30.
188. Earle, *History of the 87th Mountain Infantry, Italy 1945*, 6.
189. Ibid.
190. Govan, *History of the Tenth Light Division*, 8.
191. Chabalko, *Forging the 10th Mountain Division for War, 1940–1945*, 60.
192. Govan, *History of the Tenth Light Division*, 38.
193. Ross J. Wilson, *History of the First Battalion, 87th Mountain Infantry* (n.p., 1991), 3–4.
194. Benson, "Skiing at Camp Hale," 166.
195. Ibid.
196. Ibid., 168.
197. Ibid., 170.
198. Earle, *History of the 87th Mountain Infantry, Italy 1945*, 6.
199. Ibid.
200. Ibid.
201. Ibid.; see also Archibald et al., *Military Training Lands Historic Context Training Village*, 182–99.
202. Earle, *History of the 87th Mountain Infantry, Italy 1945*, 6.
203. H. Bradley Benedict, *Ski Troops in the Mud; Kiska Island Recaptured; A Saga of the North Pacific Campaign in the Aleutian Islands in World War II, with Special Emphasis on Its Culmination Led by the Forerunners of the 10th Mountain Division* (Littleton, CO: H. B. & J. C. Benedict, 1990), 47.
204. Nathan A. Marzoli, "The Best Substitute": US Army Low-Mountain Training in the Blue Ridge and Allegheny Mountains, 1943–1944," Army History PB 20-19-4, no. 113 (Fall 2019): 9.
205. Ibid.
206. Govan, *Training for Mountain and Winter Warfare*, 10.
207. Marzoli, "The Best Substitute," 9.

208. Ibid., 11.
209. Ibid.
210. Jay, *The History of the Mountain Training Center*, 113.
211. Ibid.
212. Ibid.
213. Sawicki, *Infantry Regiments of the US Army*, 187.
214. Govan, *Training for Mountain and Winter Warfare*, 9.
215. *The Army Lineage Book*, 2:269.
216. Govan, *History of the Tenth Light Division*, 1.
217. Govan, *Training for Mountain and Winter Warfare*, 11.
218. Ibid.
219. Earle, *Birth of a Division*, 7.
220. Govan, *History of the Tenth Light Division*, 5
221. Earle, *Birth of a Division*, 7.
222. Sawicki, *Infantry Regiments of the US Army*, 186.
223. *The Army Lineage Book*, 2:267.
224. *A Short History of the 85th Mountain Infantry Regiment* (n.p., November, 1945), 1.
225. Govan, *History of the Tenth Light Division*, 1.
226. Imbrie and Evans, *Good Times and Bad Times*, 24.
227. Ibid., 199.
228. *The Army Lineage Book*, 2:274.
229. Govan, *History of the Tenth Light Division*, 1.
230. John K. Mahon and Romana Danysh, *Infantry*, part I, *Regular Army*, Army Lineage series (Washington, DC: Center of Military History, 1972), 42–43.
231. Ibid., 43.
232. Sawicki, *Infantry Regiments of the US Army*, 186–87.
233. Ibid.; and *Order of Battle of the United States Land Forces in the World War, Zone of the Interior*, 657.
234. *The Army Lineage Book*, 2:267–69.
235. *Order of Battle of the United States Land Forces in the World War, Zone of the Interior*, 660; and *The Army Lineage Book*, 2:274.
236. Ibid.
237. Sawicki, *Infantry Regiments of the US Army*, 187–90.
238. Ibid., 192.
239. Govan, *Training for Mountain and Winter Warfare*, 12; and Dole, *Adventures in Skiing*, 117.
240. Govan, *History of the Tenth Light Division*, 2.
241. Ibid., 1.
242. Wilson, *History of the First Battalion, 87th Mountain Infantry*, 3.
243. Govan, *History of the Tenth Light Division*, 1
244. Ibid.
245. "'The Weasel': The Studebaker M29 Cargo Carrier," Center of Military History, https://history.army.mil/museums/artifacts/0010_the-WeaselM29.html, retrieved March 3, 2020.
246. David Doyle, *M29 Weasel Track Cargo Carrier & Variants: Rare Photographs from Wartime Archives*, Images of War (Barnsley, UK: Pen and Sword Military, 2019), viii; see also Scott R. McMichael, *A Historical Perspective on Light Infantry*, Research Survey 6 (Fort Leavenworth, KS: Combat Studies Institute Press, 1987), 169.
247. Jeff Woods, *Studebaker M29 Weasel* (London: ISO, 1985), 4.
248. Henry Hemming, *The Ingenious Mr. Pyke: Inventor, Fugitive, Spy* (New York: Public Affairs, 2015), 5.
249. Woods, *Studebaker M29 Weasel*, 4.
250. Ibid., 13.
251. Finlayson, "Operation Cottage," 3.
252. Doyle, *M29 Weasel Track Cargo Carrier & Variants*, viii–ix.
253. "M-29 Weasel."
254. Imbrie and Evans, *Good Times and Bad Times*, 188.
255. Philip R. Kern, "The Studebaker M29 Weasel, Part II," *Military Vehicles* 43 (May 1994): 7.
257. Ibid., 8.
258. Ibid.
259. "The Weasel," Center of Military History.
260. Ibid.
261. Studebaker, *The Weasel: Snow, Mud and Deep Water Operations, US M-29* (Studebaker, January 1944; reprint, Andover, NJ: Portrayal, n.d.), 12–13.

262. Ibid., 14–17.
263. "The Weasel," Center of Military History.
264. In his little Camp Hale memoir, 10th Mountain veteran Harris Dusenbery describes his evacuation to an "enemy" command post after being "captured" by opposing forces during the 86th Infantry's D-series exercises toward the end of 10th Mountain's training at Camp Hail. This interesting volume also contains many sketch illustrations made by Wilson P. Ware, S-2 (intelligence officer) of 1st Battalion, 86th Infantry, of their Camp Hale training, including several depicting the Weasel in action. Harris Dusenbery, *Ski the High Trail: World War II Ski Troopers in the High Colorado Rockies*, illustrated by Wilson P. Ware (Portland, OR: Binford & Mort, 1991), xi, 15, 48, 82, 142, and 145.
265. "The Weasel," Center of Military History.
266. Hemming, *The Ingenious Mr. Pyke*, 383.
267. Robert E. Mac Hugh, ed., 38th *Regimental Combat Team Mountain and Winter Warfare, Annual 1947–1948 APHOREC (Army PHOtographic RECord)* (Pueblo, CO: O'Brien, 1948), 221.
268. Ibid.
269. Govan, *History of the Tenth Light Division*, 1.
270. Ibid.
271. Ibid., 2.
272. Ibid.
273. Ibid., 3
274. Ibid.
275. Ibid., 4.
276. Ibid.
277. Ibid.
278. Ibid.
279. Wilson, *History of the First Battalion, 87th Mountain Infantry*, 5.
280. Robert L. Palmer, Bell I. Wiley, and William R. Keast, *The Army Ground Forces: The Procurement and Training of Ground Combat Troops* (Washington, DC: Historical Division, Department of the Army, 1948), 76.
281. Ibid., 178.
282. Ibid., 80.
283. Ibid., 208.
284. Ibid., 474.
285. Ibid., 474.
286. Govan, *History of the Tenth Light Division*, 4.
287. Ibid.
288. Benson, "Skiing at Camp Hale," 167.
289. Ibid.
290. Ibid.
291. Ibid., 168.
292. Govan, *History of the Tenth Light Division*, 7.
293. Ibid.
294. Ibid.; see also Chabalko, *Forging the 10th Mountain Division for War, 1940–1945*, 85.
295. Chabalko, *Forging the 10th Mountain Division for War, 1940–1945*, 86.
296. Govan, *History of the Tenth Light Division*, 7.
297. Chabalko, *Forging the 10th Mountain Division for War, 1940–1945*, 86.
298. Dusenbery, *Ski the High Trail*, xi.
299. Ibid.
300. Imbrie and Evans, *Good Times and Bad Times*, 6.
301. Earle, *Birth of a Division*, 23.
302. *A Short History of the 85th Mountain Infantry Regiment*, 2.
303. Wilson, *History of the First Battalion, 87th Mountain Infantry*, 17.
304. Ibid.
305. Dusenbery, *Ski the High Trail*, 80–81.
306. Chabalko, *Forging the 10th Mountain Division for War, 1940–1945*, 86.
307. Ibid.
308. Ibid., 87.
309. Bruce Catton, "Grant at Shiloh," American Heritage 11, no. 2 (February 1960), https://www.americanheritage.com/grant-shiloh#7, retrieved October 24, 2020.
310. Albert H. Jackman, "The Tenth Mountain Division," *American Alpine Journal*, Special War Number, 1946 (reprint edition, 1991), 16.
311. Govan, *Training for Mountain and Winter Warfare*, 13.
312. Chabalko, *Forging the 10th Mountain Division for War, 1940–1945*, 87.
313. Govan, *Training for Mountain and Winter Warfare*, 13.
314. Ibid.
315. Ibid.

316. Ibid.

317. Ibid.

318. Wilson, *History of the First Battalion, 87th Mountain Infantry*, 17.

319. Govan, *Training for Mountain and Winter Warfare*, 13.

320. Harper, *Night Climb*, 164–65.

321. Dole, *Adventures in Skiing*, 126.

322. Govan, *Training for Mountain and Winter Warfare*, 13.

323. Ibid., 13–14.

324. Ibid., 14.

325. *A Short History of the 85th Mountain Infantry Regiment*, 2; and Govan, *Training for Mountain and Winter Warfare*, 13, 14.

326. *A Short History of the 85th Mountain Infantry Regiment*, 2.

327. Imbrie and Evans, *Good Times and Bad Times*, 223–24.

328. Govan, *Training for Mountain and Winter Warfare*, 14.

329. Imbrie and Evans, *Good Times and Bad Times*, 8; and *A Short History of the 85th Mountain Infantry Regiment*, 2.

330. *A Short History of the 85th Mountain Infantry Regiment*, 2.

331. Imbrie and Evans, *Good Times and Bad Times*, 219–22.

332. Govan, *Training for Mountain and Winter Warfare*, 14.

333. Imbrie and Evans, *Good Times and Bad Times*, 185, 202.

334. Ibid., 33.

335. *A Short History of the 85th Mountain Infantry Regiment*, 3.

336. Govan, *Training for Mountain and Winter Warfare*, 14.

337. Ibid.

Chapter 3

1. *Aleutian Islands*, CMH Pub. 72-6 (Washington, DC: Center of Military History, 1992), 8, 23.

2. Thomas E. Griess, ed., *The Second World War: Asia and the Pacific* (Wayne, NJ: Avery, 1984), 96–97.

3. Mitsuo Fuchida and Masatake Okumiya, *Midway: The Battle That Doomed Japan, the Japanese Navy's Story* (Annapolis, MD: Naval Institute Press, 1955), 70–72.

4. Ibid., 55.

5. Ibid.

6. Ibid., 56–58.

7. Ibid., 58–59.

8. Ibid., 59–60.

9. Ibid., 60.

10. Ibid., 64–65.

11. Ibid., 66.

12. John Keegan, *The Price of Admiralty* (New York: Viking, 1989),183.

13. Fuchida and Okumiya, *Midway*, 71.

14. Ibid., 72.

15. Ibid., 76.

16. *American Military History*, 439; and Del C. Kostka, "Operation Cottage: A Cautionary Tale of Assumption and Perceptual Bias," *Joint Forces Quarterly* 76, no. 1 (2015): 94.

17. James F. Dunnigan and Albert A. Nofi, *Victory at Sea: World War II in the Pacific* (New York: William Morrow, 1995), 26.

18. Fuchida and Okumiya, *Midway*, 79; and Earle, *Birth of a Division*, 1.

19. Dunnigan and Nofi, *Victory at Sea*, 26.

20. E. B. Potter, ed., *Sea Power: A Naval History* (Annapolis, MD: Naval Institute Press, 1981), 296; and Keegan, *The Price of Admiralty*, 187.

21. Ibid.; and Dunnigan and Nofi, *Victory at Sea*, 26.

22. Potter, *Sea Power*, 296; and Keegan, *The Price of Admiralty*, 187.

23. Ibid.

24. Dunnigan and Nofi, *Victory at Sea*, 26–27; and Potter, *Sea Power*, 298.

25. Robert L. Johnson Jr., *Aleutian Campaign, World War II: Historical Study and Current Perspective* (Fort Leavenworth, KS: Command and General Staff College, 1992), 13.

26. Dunnigan and Nofi, *Victory at Sea*, 26.

27. Potter, *Sea Power*, 298.

28. Ibid.

29. Dunnigan and Nofi, *Victory at Sea*, 28.

30. Keegan, *The Price of Admiralty*, 204.

31. Ibid.

32. Kenneth J. Hagan, *This People's Navy: The Making of American Sea Power* (New York: Free Press, 1992), 313.

33. Dunnigan and Nofi, *Victory at Sea*, 28.

34. Ibid., 28–29.

35. Ibid., 29.

36. Keegan, *The Price of Admiralty*, 209.

37. Johnson, *Aleutian Campaign, World War II*, 17.

38. Ibid.

39. *Aleutian Islands*, 5.

40. Ibid., 6.

41. Ibid., 6–7.

42. Ibid., 7, 9.

43. Potter, *Sea Power*, 310.

44. *The Capture of Attu: Tales of World War II in Alaska, as Told by the Men Who Fought There* (Edmonds, WA; Alaska Northwest, 1984), 5.

45. Ibid.

46. Ibid., 4–5; and Johnson, *Aleutian Campaign, World War II*, 18.

47. Kit C. Carter and Robert Mueller, *US Army Air Forces in World War II Combat Chronology, 1941–1945* (Washington, DC: Center for Air Force History, 1991).

48. *Aleutian Islands*, 12.

49. Kit C. Carter and Robert Mueller, *US Army Air Forces in World War II Combat Chronology, 1941–1945*.

50. Ibid.

51. *Aleutian Islands*, 12.

52. Ibid.

53. *American Military History*, 506.

54. Potter, *Sea Power*, 310.

55. *American Military History*, 506.

56. Kostka, "Operation Cottage," 94.

57. Ibid.

58. *Aleutian Islands*, 10.

59. Potter, *Sea Power*, 310.

60. Ibid.

61. Ibid.

62. *Aleutian Islands*, 12.

63. Potter, *Sea Power*, 310.

64. Ibid.

65. *The Capture of Attu*, 10.

66. Ibid.

67. Ibid.

68. *World War II in Alaska: A Historic and Resources Management Plan* (Anchorage, AK: Army Corps of Engineers, Alaska District, 1987), 2-50.

69. Potter, *Sea Power*, 310–11; *The Capture of Attu*, 12; and *World War II in Alaska*, 2-50.

70. *The Capture of Attu*, 12.

71. *American Military History*, 506.

72. *Aleutian Islands*, 17–19; and *The Capture of Attu*, 12–13.

73. Ibid.

74. *Aleutian Islands*, 17–19; and *The Capture of Attu*, 12–16.

75. Potter, *Sea Power*, 310.

76. Ibid., 310–11.

77. *World War II in Alaska*, 2-53; Johnson, *Aleutian Campaign, World War II*, 152; and Benedict, *Ski Troops in the Mud*, 57.

78. Earle, *Birth of a Division*, 5.

79. Ibid.

80. Johnson, *Aleutian Campaign, World War II*, 152.

81. Ibid., 154.

82. Ibid.

83. Ibid., 155.

84. Howard Handleman, *Bridge to Victory: The Story of the Reconquest of the Aleutians* (New York: Random House, 1943), 236–40.

85. Benedict, *Ski Troops in the Mud*, 51; and Wilson, *History of the First Battalion, 87th Mountain Infantry*, 7.

86. Benedict, *Ski Troops in the Mud*, 51.

87. Ibid.

88. Wilson, *History of the First Battalion, 87th Mountain Infantry*, 7.

89. Ibid.

90. Wilson, *History of the First Battalion, 87th Mountain Infantry*, 9; Benedict, *Ski Troops in the Mud*, 51; and Harper, *Night Climb*, 140.

91. Wilson, *History of the First Battalion, 87th Mountain Infantry*, 9; and Benedict, *Ski Troops in the Mud*, 51.

92. Benedict, *Ski Troops in the Mud*, 51.

93. Ibid., 53.

94. Ibid.; and Wilson, *History of the First Battalion, 87th Mountain Infantry*, 9.

95. Benedict, *Ski Troops in the Mud*, 57; Johnson, *Aleutian Campaign, World War II*, 154–55, 162; Finlayson, *Leonard Wood*; and Handleman, *Bridge to Victory*, 259.

96. Benedict, *Ski Troops in the Mud*, 58.

97. Ibid., 58–59; Finlayson, *Leonard Wood*, 1; and Johnson, *Aleutian Campaign, World War II*, 162–63.

98. Benedict, *Ski Troops in the Mud*, 59.

99. Hemming, *The Ingenious Mr. Pyke*, 382.

100. Finlayson, *Leonard Wood*, 1.

101. Ibid., 3.

102. Ibid.

103. Benedict, *Ski Troops in the Mud*, 58; and Desmond Morton, *A Military History of Canada* (Edmonton, AB: Hurtig, 1985), 189.

104. Handleman, *Bridge to Victory*, 243.

105. Benedict, *Ski Troops in the Mud*, 59.

106. Handleman, *Bridge to Victory*, 244–45.

107. Benedict, *Ski Troops in the Mud*, 59.

108. Ibid., 61–62; and Wilson, *History of the First Battalion, 87th Mountain Infantry*, 10.

109. Benedict, *Ski Troops in the Mud*, 62.

110. Johnson, *Aleutian Campaign, World War II*, 163.

111. Ibid., 166.

112. Benedict, *Ski Troops in the Mud*, 69.

113. Handleman, *Bridge to Victory*, 254.

114. Benedict, *Ski Troops in the Mud*, 67–68; Finlayson, "Operation Cottage"; and Johnson, *Aleutian Campaign, World War II*, 163.

115. Johnson, *Aleutian Campaign, World War II*, 163; and Finlayson, "Operation Cottage."

116. Johnson, *Aleutian Campaign, World War II*, 168.

117. Handleman, *Bridge to Victory*, 255.

118. Ibid., 258; and Benedict, *Ski Troops in the Mud*, 68.

119. Benedict, *Ski Troops in the Mud*, 72.

120. Finlayson, "Operation Cottage."

121. Johnson, *Aleutian Campaign, World War II*, 168.

122. Ibid., 150–51.

123. Ibid., 150.

124. Kostka, 96–97.

125. Ibid., 97.

126. Ibid.

127. Ibid.

128. Johnson, *Aleutian Campaign, World War II*, 167.

129. Wilson, *History of the First Battalion, 87th Mountain Infantry*, 10.

130. Kostka, "Operation Cottage," 97.

131. Wilson, *History of the First Battalion, 87th Mountain Infantry*, 10.

132. Kostka, "Operation Cottage," 97.

133. Johnson, *Aleutian Campaign, World War II*, 158; and Benedict, *Ski Troops in the Mud*, 63.

134. *Taiheiyô kiseki no sakusen: Kisuka* ("Miraculous military operation in the Pacific Ocean"), also known as *Retreat from Kiska*.

135. Johnson, *Aleutian Campaign, World War II*, 158.

136. Ibid., 159.

137. Ibid.

138. Benedict, *Ski Troops in the Mud*, 64.

139. Ibid.

140. Ibid., 65.

141. Ibid., 159, 161–62.

142. Kostka, "Operation Cottage," 98.

143. Ibid., 97.

144. Ibid.

145. Benedict, *Ski Troops in the Mud*, 87.

146. Tom F. Whayne and Michael E. DeBakey, *Cold Injury, Ground Type* (Washington, DC: US Army Medical Department, Office of the Surgeon General, 1958), 98–99.

147. Ibid., 98.

148. Ibid.

149. Johnson, *Aleutian Campaign, World War II*, 168.

150. Geoffrey Regan, *Blue on Blue: A History of Friendly Fire* (New York: Avon Books, 1995), 113.

151. Earle, *Birth of a Division*, 19.

152. Benedict, *Ski Troops in the Mud*, 82.

153. William B. Garrett III, *Fratricide: Doctrine's Role in Reducing Friendly Fire* (Fort Leavenworth, KS: School of Advanced Military Studies, 1993), 9.

154. Ibid., 9–10.

155. Charles R. Shrader, *Amicide: The Problem of Friendly Fire in Modern War* (Fort Leavenworth, KS: Combat Studies Institute Press, 1982), 91.

156. Wilson, *History of the First Battalion, 87th Mountain Infantry*, 14.

157. Ibid.

158. Benedict, *Ski Troops in the Mud*, 150.

159. Wilson, *History of the First Battalion, 87th Mountain Infantry*, 16.

160. Ibid.

161. Kostka, "Operation Cottage," 97; and Johnson, *Aleutian Campaign, World War II*, 168.

162. Shrader, *Amicide*, 91.

163. Regan, *Blue on Blue*, 113.

164. Earle, *Birth of a Division*, 8.

165. Ibid., 22.

166. Wilson, *History of the First Battalion, 87th Mountain Infantry*, 14.

167. Robert Leonhard, *The Art of Maneuver: Maneuver-Warfare Theory and Airland Battle* (Novato, CA: Presidio, 1994), 66–67.

168. Finlayson, "Operation Cottage," 1.

169. Kostka, "Operation Cottage," 97.

Chapter 4

1. John Strawson, *The Italian Campaign* (New York: Carroll & Graf, 1988), 68.

2. Ibid., 69.

3. Ibid., 70–71.

4. Ibid., 70–72; and *American Military History*, 473.

5. *American Military History*, 476; and Griess, *The Second World War: Europe and the Mediterranean*, 172.

6. Chester G. Starr, *From Salerno to the Alps: A History of the Fifth Army, 1943–1945* (Washington, DC: Infantry Journal Press, 1948), 2; and Griess, *The Second World War: Europe and the Mediterranean*, 172.

7. Robert Aron, *The Vichy Regime, 1940–44* (London: Putnam, 1958), 399–400.

8. Starr, *From Salerno to the Alps*, 2; and Griess, *The Second World War: Europe and the Mediterranean*, 172.

9. Griess, *The Second World War: Europe and the Mediterranean*, 173.

10. Ibid.; and *American Military History*, 476–77.

11. *American Military History*, 477; and Griess, *The Second World War: Europe and the Mediterranean*, 173–75.

12. Ibid.

13. *American Military History*, 477.

14. Griess, *The Second World War: Europe and the Mediterranean*, 176–78.

15. *American Military History*, 477; and Thomas E. Griess, ed., *Atlas for the Second World War: Europe and the Mediterranean* (Wayne, NJ: Avery, 1985), map 42b.

16. Strawson, *The Italian Campaign*, 100–102; and *American Military History*, 478.

17. *American Military History*, 478.

18. Strawson, *The Italian Campaign*, 108.

19. Ibid., 109, quoting General Sir William Jackson.

20. Strawson, *The Italian Campaign*, 109–10; and *American Military History*, 479.

21. *American Military History*, 479.

22. Strawson, *The Italian Campaign*, 110.

23. Ibid.

24. Ibid., 113.

25. Ibid.

26. Ibid., 120; and Griess, *Atlas for the Second World War: Europe and the Mediterranean*, 46.

27. Strawson, *The Italian Campaign*, 121; and Griess, *Atlas for the Second World War: Europe and the Mediterranean*, 46.

28. Strawson, *The Italian Campaign*, 121.

29. Ibid.

30. Ibid.

31. English, *On Infantry*, 136.

32. *American Military History*, 479–80.

33. *Fifth Army History*, part 1, *From Activation to the Fall of Naples* (Headquarters, Fifth Army, 1945), 1–2.

34. Wilson, *Armies, Corps, Divisions, and Separate Brigades*, 21; and Starr, *From Salerno to the Alps*, 2.

35. Starr, *From Salerno to the Alps*, 2–3.

36. *Fifth Army History*, 1:1.

37. Starr, *From Salerno to the Alps*, 3.

38. Ibid., 3–4; and *Fifth Army History*, 1:5.

39. *Fifth Army History*, 1:6; and Starr, *From Salerno to the Alps*, 4.

40. *Fifth Army History*, 1:5–11.

41. Ibid., 12.

42. Ibid., 13.

43. W. G. F. Jackson, *The Battle for Italy* (New York: Harper & Row, 1967), 87–88.

44. Martin Blumenson, *Salerno to Cassino* (Washington, DC: Center of Military History, 1993), 23.

45. Ibid., 52–53; and Jackson, *The Battle for Italy*, 94.

46. Blumenson, *Salerno to Cassino*, 53; see also Jackson, *The Battle for Italy*, 102.

47. *Road to Rome* (Fifth Army, 1945), n.p.

48. Blumenson, *Salerno to Cassino*, 53–54.

49. Ibid., 54.

50. *Road to Rome*, n.p.

51. Ibid.

52. Blumenson, *Salerno to Cassino*, 128.

53. Ibid., 118.

54. *Fifth Army History*, part 1, chapter IV, "Invasion of Italy," 41.

55. Ibid., 40–41.

56. Ibid., 41.

57. Starr, *From Salerno to the Alps*, 33; and *Fifth Army History*, part 1, chapter V, "The Drive on Naples," 43.

58. Starr, *From Salerno to the Alps*, 34; *Road to Rome*, 7; and Griess, *Atlas for the Second World War: Europe and the Mediterranean*, 48.

59. Blumenson, *Salerno to Cassino*, 166.

60. *Road to Rome*, 14.

61. Starr, *From Salerno to the Alps*, 40.

62. Ibid., 41.

63. Ibid., 45.

64. Ibid., 47.

65. Griess, *The Second World War: Europe and the Mediterranean*, 236; and Griess, *Atlas for the Second World War: Europe and the Mediterranean*, 48.

66. Griess, *The Second World War: Europe and the Mediterranean*, 48.

67. Ibid., 238.

68. *Road to Rome*, 27; and Griess, *Atlas for the Second World War: Europe and the Mediterranean*, 48.

69. Starr, *From Salerno to the Alps*, 129.

70. Ibid.

71. *Road to Rome*, 33.

72. Starr, *From Salerno to the Alps*, 161–65.

73. Ibid., 176; *Griess, The Second World War: Europe and the Mediterranean*, 242; and Blumenson, *Salerno to Cassino*, 448.

74. Blumenson, *Salerno to Cassino*, 448.

75. Starr, *From Salerno to the Alps*, 176.

76. *Road to Rome*, 37; and Jackson, *The Battle for Italy*, 230–32.

77. *Road to Rome*, 39–42; Jackson, *The Battle for Italy*, 232; and Griess, *Atlas for the Second World War: Europe and the Mediterranean*, 50.

78. Griess, *The Second World War: Europe and the Mediterranean*, 245.

79. *Road to Rome*, 44–45.

80. *Road to Rome*, 48; Starr, *From Salerno to the Alps*, 263; and Jackson, *The Battle for Italy*, 245–46.

81. Jackson, *The Battle for Italy*, 249–50.

82. Ibid., 260; and Griess, *The Second World War: Europe and the Mediterranean*, 245.

83. Jackson, *The Battle for Italy*, 269–77; and Griess, *The Second World War: Europe and the Mediterranean*, 246.

84. Jackson, *The Battle for Italy*, 276, 280–81.

85. Griess, *The Second World War: Europe and the Mediterranean*, 247.

86. Jackson, *The Battle for Italy*, 281; and Griess, *The Second World War: Europe and the Mediterranean*, 247.

Chapter 5

1. John Imbrie, *Chronology of the 10th Mountain Division during World War II, 6 January 1940–30 November 1945* (Houghton, NY: National Association of the 10th Mountain Division, 2004), 11.

2. *Combat History of the 10th Mountain Division, 1944–1945* (from the files of the US Army Infantry School Library, Fort Benning, GA; privately published by Earl E. Clark, 1977), 1.

3. Ibid.; and Imbrie, *Chronology of the 10th Mountain Division during World War II, 6 January 1940–30 November 1945*, 11.

4. Thomas R. Brooks, *The War North of Rome, June 1944–May 1945* (Edison, NJ: Castle Books, 2001), 352.

5. Ibid.

6. Ibid., 351.

7. Klaus H. Huebner, *Long Walk through War: A Combat Doctor's Diary* (College Station: Texas A&M University Press, 1987), 18, 69.

8. Paul Goodman, *A Fragment of Victory: The 92nd Infantry Division in World War II* (Nashville: Battery, 1993), 80–81.

9. Albert H. Meinke Jr., *Mountain Troops and Medics: Wartime Stories of a Frontline Surgeon in the U.S. Ski Troops* (Kewadin, MI: Rucksack, 1993), 146–47.

10. Peter S. Wondolowski, *History of the IV Corps, 1941–1945* (IV Corps Headquarters, 1945), 585.

11. McMichael, *A Historical Perspective on Light Infantry*, 204.

12. "History: 6th Army Group," 70th Infantry Division Association, https://www.trailblazer-sww2.org/history_6thgroup.htm, accessed April 4, 2020.

13. Ibid.

14. McMichael, *A Historical Perspective on Light Infantry*, 204.

15. *Combat History of the 10th Mountain Division, 1944–1945*, 2; Starr, *From Salerno to the Alps*, 6; and Brooks, *The War North of Rome*, 351.

16. Mark W. Clark, *Calculated Risk* (New York: Harper & Brothers, 1950), 417.

17. Imbrie and Evans, *Good Times and Bad Times*, 9.

18. *Combat History of the 10th Mountain Division, 1944–1945*, 1–2.

19. Ibid, 1; and Imbrie, *Chronology of the 10th Mountain Division during World War II, 6 January 1940–30 November 1945*, 11.

20. *Combat History of the 10th Mountain Division, 1944–1945*, 2; and Imbrie, *Chronology of the 10th Mountain Division during World War II, 6 January 1940–30 November 1945*, 12.

21. Ibid.

22. *Combat History of the 10th Mountain Division, 1944–1945*, 2.

23. Ibid., 2–3.

24. Ibid., 3; and Imbrie, *Chronology of the 10th Mountain Division during World War II, 6 January 1940–30 November 1945*, 12.

25. Roland W. Charles, *Troopships of World War II* (Washington, DC: Army Transportation Association, 1947), 157.

26. Ibid.; and "SS Argentina," http://www.moore-mccormack.com/SS-Argentina-1938/SS-Argentina-1938-Timeline.htm, retrieved April 4, 2020.

27. Charles, *Troopships of World War II*, 157; and "War Brides," https://jhgraham.com/2017/10/08/war-brides/, retrieved April 4, 2020.

28. David R. Brower, *Remount Blue: The Combat Story of the 3rd Battalion, 86th Mountain Infantry*, (originally published in 1948; reprinted, Chicago: Barajima Books, 2020), 1.

29. Harris Dusenbery, *The North Apennines and Beyond with the 10th Mountain Division* (Portland, OR: Binford & Mort, 1998), 5–6.

30. Ibid., 6–8.

31. Ibid., 8.

32. Ibid., 9.

33. Ibid., 11; and Imbrie, *Chronology of the 10th Mountain Division during World War II, 6 January 1940–30 November 1945*,12.

34. Dusenbery, *The North Apennines and Beyond with the 10th Mountain Division*, 11–12; and *Combat History of the 10th Mountain Division, 1944–1945*, 3.

35. Imbrie, *Chronology of the 10th Mountain Division during World War II, 6 January 1940–30 November 1945*, 12,

36. *Combat History of the 10th Mountain Division, 1944–1945*, 4.

37. Imbrie, *Chronology of the 10th Mountain Division during World War II, 6 January 1940–30 November 1945*,12.

38. Ibid.; *Combat History of the 10th Mountain Division, 1944–1945*, 4; Wilson, *History of the First Battalion, 87th Mountain Infantry*, 17; and Carl D. Kerekes, *Recollections: Company B, 85th Regiment, 10th Mountain Division, US Army, WWII; The Italian Campaign, Ski Troops [sic] at War* (n.p., 1998), 7.

39. Charles, *Troopships of World War II*, 146.

40. Ibid.

41. *A Short History of the 85th Mountain Infantry Regiment*, 5; Imbrie, *Chronology of the 10th Mountain Division during World War II, 6 January 1940–30 November 1945*, 12; Wilson, *History of the First Battalion, 87th Mountain Infantry*, 4, 18; and *Combat History of the 10th Mountain Division, 1944–1945*, 4.

42. Kerekes, *Recollections, Company B*, 8.

43. *Combat History of the 10th Mountain Division, 1944–1945*, 4; Wilson, *History of the First Battalion, 87th Mountain Infantry*, 4; and Imbrie, *Chronology of the 10th Mountain Division during World War II, 6 January 1940–30 November 1945*, 12.

44. Charles, *Troopships of World War II*, 106.

45. *Combat History of the 10th Mountain Division, 1944–1945*, 4.

46. Earle, *History of the 87th Mountain Infantry, Italy 1945*, 10.

47. Brower, *Remount Blue*, 4; and *Combat History of the 10th Mountain Division, 1944–1945*, 3.

48. *Combat History of the 10th Mountain Division, 1944–1945*, 4; Earle, *History of the 87th Mountain Infantry, Italy 1945*, 9–10; and Imbrie, *Chronology of the 10th Mountain Division during World War II, 6 January 1940–30 November 1945*, 14.

49. *Combat History of the 10th Mountain Division, 1944–1945*, 4.

50. Charles J. Sanders, *The Boys of Winter: Life and Death in the Ski Troops during the Second World War* (Boulder: University of Colorado Press, 2005), 118.

51. *Fifth Army History*, part 8, *The Second Winter*, 5.

52. Griess, *The Second World War: Europe and the Mediterranean*, 247.

53. Brooks, *The War North of Rome*, 324.

54. Griess, *The Second World War: Europe and the Mediterranean*, 247.

55. Sanders, *The Boys of Winter*, 118.

56. Brooks, *The War North of Rome*, 345.

57. Griess, *The Second World War: Europe and the Mediterranean*, 247.

58. Brooks, *The War North of Rome*, 345.

59. Griess, *The Second World War: Europe and the Mediterranean*, 247.

60. Sanders, *The Boys of Winter*, 118.

61. Ibid.

62. Brower, *Remount Blue*, 7.

63. *Combat History of the 10th Mountain Division, 1944–1945*, 5.

64. Ibid.; and Imbrie, *Chronology of the 10th Mountain Division during World War II, 6 January 1940–30 November 1945*, 13.

65. Imbrie, *Chronology of the 10th Mountain Division during World War II, 6 January 1940–30 November 1945*, 13.

66. *Combat History of the 10th Mountain Division, 1944–1945*, 3–4.

67. Ibid., 3.

68. Ibid., 6.

69. Ibid., 6–7.

70. Ibid., 7.

71. Ibid.

72. Ibid., 10.

73. Ibid., 5–8.

74. Ibid., 7.

75. Ibid., 4–5.

76. Imbrie, *Chronology of the 10th Mountain Division during World War II, 6 January 1940–30 November 1945*, 14.

77. *Combat History of the 10th Mountain Division, 1944–1945*, 6–11.

78. Ibid., 8.

79. *A Short History of the 85th Mountain Infantry Regiment*, 6.

80. Ibid.

81. *Combat History of the 10th Mountain Division, 1944–1945*, 7; and *A Short History of the 85th Mountain Infantry Regiment*, 7.

82. *A Short History of the 85th Mountain Infantry Regiment*, 7; and *Combat History of the 10th Mountain Division, 1944–1945*, 8.

83. *A Short History of the 85th Mountain Infantry Regiment*, 7; and *Combat History of the 10th Mountain Division, 1944–1945*, 11.

84. *A Short History of the 85th Mountain Infantry Regiment*, 7; and *Combat History of the 10th Mountain Division, 1944–1945*, 10.

85. *A Short History of the 85th Mountain Infantry Regiment*, 7.

86. *A Short History of the 85th Mountain Infantry Regiment*, 8; and *Combat History of the 10th Mountain Division, 1944–1945*, 8.

87. *A Short History of the 85th Mountain Infantry Regiment*, 8.

88. Ibid.

89. Ibid.

90. *A Short History of the 85th Mountain Infantry Regiment*, 8; and *Combat History of the 10th Mountain Division, 1944–1945*, 10.

91. Ibid.

92. Earle, *History of the 87th Mountain Infantry, Italy 1945*, 11.

93. Ibid.

94. Ibid.

95. Wilson, *History of the First Battalion, 87th Mountain Infantry*, 19.

96. Ibid., 20; and Earle, *History of the 87th Mountain Infantry, Italy 1945*, 14.

97. Ibid.

98. Earle, *History of the 87th Mountain Infantry, Italy 1945*, 14.

99. Ibid., 15.

100. Ibid.

101. Ibid., 16.

102. Ibid., 14.

103. Ibid.

104. Ibid.

105. Wilson, *History of the First Battalion, 87th Mountain Infantry*, 21.

106. Earle, *History of the 87th Mountain Infantry, Italy 1945*, 13.

107. Ibid., 14.

108. Jackson, *The Battle for Italy*, 334.

109. Ibid., 154, 258.

110. Ibid., 342; and *Fifth Army History*, part 8, *The Second Winter*, 6.

111. Jackson, *The Battle for Italy*, 301.

112. Ibid., 342; and *Fifth Army History*, 8:5.

113. *Fifth Army History*, 8:5–6.

114. Jackson, *The Battle for Italy*, 342; and *Fifth Army History*, 8:5.

115. Rich Anderson, "The United States Army in World War II," Military History Online.

116. Curry N. Vaughan, Robert E. Neiman Jr., Vasco J. Fenili, et al., *Mud, Mountains and Armor: The 1st Armored Division from Rome to the Alps* (Fort Knox, KY: Armored School Officers Advanced Course, 1949), xxxvi.

117. Ibid.; and Starr, *From Salerno to the Alps*, 294.

118. Vaughan et al., *Mud, Mountains and Armor*, xxxvi–xxxvii; and Brooks, *The War North of Rome*, 137.

119. Vaughan et al., *Mud, Mountains and Armor*, xxxvii–xxxviii.

120. Derreck T. Calkins, "A Military Force on a Political Mission: The Brazilian Expeditionary Force in World War II" (Georgia Southern University Electronic Theses and Dissertations, 2011, https://digitalcommons.georgiasouthern.edu/etd/600, retrieved April 18, 2020), 12.

121. Ibid., 13.

122. Ibid., 11.

123. Ibid., 40.

124. Ibid., 14.

125. Ibid., 15.

126. Clark, *Calculated Risk*, 391.

127. John P. Bethel, general ed., "Apennines," in *Webster's Geographical Dictionary* (New York: Merriam, 1959), 53–54.

128. "Mount Belvedere," Musea Diffuso dela Linea Gotica Montese, http://www.lineagoticamontese.eu/en/the-trails/monte-belvedere/72-mount-belvedere.html, retrieved April 18, 2020.

129. *Mapcarta*, https://mapcarta.com/N3025050852.

130. Dwight D. Oland, *North Apennines*, CMH Pub. 72-34 (Washington, DC: Center of Military History, n.d.); and Imbrie, *Chronology of the 10th Mountain Division during World War II, 6 January 1940–30 November 1945*, 15.

131. Sanders, *The Boys of Winter*, 128–29.

132. Ibid., 128.

133. Ibid., 129.

134. Ibid.

135. Wondolowski, *History of the IV Corps, 1941–1945*, 406; Sanders, *The Boys of Winter*, 129; and "69 anos da tomada de Monte Castelo," http://www.defesanet.com.br/ecos/noticia/14284/69-anos-da-tomada-de-Monte-Castelo/, retrieved April 18, 2020.

136. Jackman, "The 10th Mountain Division," 17.

137. Sanders, *The Boys of Winter*, 128; and Imbrie, *Chronology of the 10th Mountain Division during World War II, 6 January 1940–30 November 1945*, 12.

138. Wondolowski, *History of the IV Corps, 1941–1945*, 406.

139. Brooks, *The War North of Rome*, 306.

140. Ibid.; Calkins, "A Military Force on a Political Mission," 89; and "Mount Belvedere."

141. Brooks, *The War North of Rome*, 306.

142. Ibid.; and Calkins, "A Military Force on a Political Mission," 89.

143. Brooks, *The War North of Rome*, 306.

144. Ibid.

145. Ibid.; and Calkins, "A Military Force on a Political Mission," 89.

146. Brooks, *The War North of Rome*, 306–07.

147. Ibid., 307; and Calkins, "A Military Force on a Political Mission," 89.

148. Brooks, *The War North of Rome*, 307.

149. Ibid.

150. Wondolowski, *History of the IV Corps, 1941–1945*, 411; and Brooks, *The War North of Rome*, 307.

151. Wondolowski, *History of the IV Corps, 1941–1945*, 413; and Brooks, *The War North of Rome*, 308.

152. Ibid.; and Imbrie, *Chronology of the 10th Mountain Division during World War II, 6 January 1940–30 November 1945*, 12.

153. Brooks, *The War North of Rome*, 308–09.

154. Wondolowski, *History of the IV Corps, 1941–1945*, 436–37; and Brooks, *The War North of Rome*, 309.

155. Wondolowski, *History of the IV Corps, 1941–1945*, 435.

156. Ibid., 435–36.

157. Ibid., 437.

158. Ibid.

159. Ibid., 438.

160. Ibid., 437.

161. Calkins, "A Military Force on a Political Mission," 91.

162. Wondolowski, *History of the IV Corps, 1941–1945*, 414.

163. Oland, *North Apennines*, 28.

164. Ibid.

165. Ibid.

166. Goodman, *A Fragment of Victory*, 86.

167. Ibid., 89.

168. Wondolowski, *History of the IV Corps, 1941–1945*, 497.

169. Starr, *From Salerno to the Alps*, 383; Goodman, *A Fragment of Victory*, 87–90; and Wondolowski, *History of the IV Corps, 1941–1945*, 493–97.

170. Wondolowski, *History of the IV Corps, 1941–1945*, 506; see also *Fifth Army History*, 8:78.

171. Imbrie, *Chronology of the 10th Mountain Division during World War II, 6 January 1940–30 November 1945*, 13; see also Harper, *Night Climb*, 22.

172. Oland, *North Apennines*, 29.

173. Wondolowski, *History of the IV Corps, 1941–1945*, 506–07.

174. Ibid., 507; and Calkins, "A Military Force on a Political Mission," 105.

175. Wondolowski, *History of the IV Corps, 1941–1945*, 507; see also *Fifth Army History*, 8:79.

176. Imbrie, *Chronology of the 10th Mountain Division during World War II, 6 January 1940–30 November 1945*, 15; and Wondolowski, *History of the IV Corps, 1941–1945*, 507; see also *Fifth Army History*, 8:79.

177. Wondolowski, *History of the IV Corps, 1941–1945*, 508; see also *Fifth Army History*, 8:79.

178. Brower, *Remount Blue*, 13.

179. Wondolowski, *History of the IV Corps, 1941–1945*, 509.

180. Ibid.

181. Curtis W. Casewit, *Mountain Troopers: The Story of the Tenth Mountain Division* (New York: Thomas Y. Crowell, 1972), 79.

182. *Combat History of the 10th Mountain Division, 1944–1945*, 13.

183. Wondolowski, *History of the IV Corps, 1941–1945*, 508.

184. Ibid., 512.

185. Melvin E. Richmond, *Combat Operations in Mountainous Terrain: Are the US Army Light Infantry Divisions Preparing Properly?* (Fort Leavenworth, KS: US Army Command and General Staff College, 1987), 56.

186. Casewit, *Mountain Troopers*, 61–62.

187. Earle, *History of the 87th Mountain Infantry, Italy 1945*, 19.

188. Ernest F. Fisher Jr., *Cassino to the Alps* (Washington, DC: Center of Military History, 1993), 428.

189. Wondolowski, *History of the IV Corps, 1941–1945*, 509; and Fisher, *Cassino to the Alps*, 428.

190. Ibid.; and *Combat History of the 10th Mountain Division, 1944–1945*, 13.

191. Brower, *Remount Blue*, 13.

192. Harris Dusenbery, *10th Mountain Division Italian Diary of Harris Dusenbery Hq. Co. 1st Bn. 86th Mountain Infantry and Riva Ridge Operation 1st Battalion Journal* (typescript, n.d.), n.p.

193. Dusenbery, *The North Apennines and Beyond with the 10th Mountain Division*, 181.

194. Ibid., 181–82.

195. Casewit, *Mountain Troopers*, 61.

196. Harper, *Night Climb*, 24–27.

197. Ibid., 27.

198. Richmond, *Combat Operations in Mountainous Terrain*, 53.

199. Charles Wellborn, *History of the 86th Mountain Infantry in Italy* (originally published in 1945, digitized and edited by Barbara Imbrie, 2004, www.skitrooper.org/86.htm, retrieved April 19, 2020), 7.

200. Casewit, *Mountain Troopers*, 62.

201. Dusenbery, *The North Apennines and Beyond with the 10th Mountain Division*, 48–49; and Brower, *Remount Blue*, 13.

202. *A Short History of the 85th Mountain Infantry Regiment*, 12–13.

203. Ibid., 10.

204. Imbrie and Evans, *Good Times and Bad Times*, 54.

205. Ibid.

206. *A Short History of the 85th Mountain Infantry Regiment*, 10.

207. Wilson, *History of the First Battalion, 87th Mountain Infantry*, 21–22.

208. Earle, *History of the 87th Mountain Infantry, Italy 1945*, 17.

209. Ibid., 18.

210. Ibid.

211. Ibid.

212. J. B. Mascarenhas de Moraes, *The Brazilian Expeditionary Force, by Its Commander* (Washington, DC: US Government Printing Office, 1966), 108.

213. Ibid., 109.

214. Fisher, *Cassino to the Alps*, 429; and Wondolowski, *History of the IV Corps, 1941–1945*, 512–13, 515–16.

215. Mascarenhas de Moraes, *The Brazilian Expeditionary Force*, 111.

216. Burton, *The Ski Troops*, 152.

217. Ibid.

218. Ibid.

219. Ibid., 156.

220. Ibid.

221. Dusenbery, *The North Apennines and Beyond with the 10th Mountain Division*, 49.

222. Casewit, *Mountain Troopers*, 63.

223. Wellborn, *History of the 86th Mountain Infantry in Italy*, 7.

224. Kerekes, *Recollections: Company B*, 18.

225. Imbrie and Evans, *Good Times and Bad Times*, 46.

226. Wellborn, *History of the 86th Mountain Infantry in Italy*, 7.

227. Dusenbery, *The North Apennines and Beyond with the 10th Mountain Division*, 185–86.

228. Dole, *Adventures in Skiing*, 130.

229. Wondolowski, *History of the IV Corps, 1941–1945*, 513; and Imbrie, *Chronology of the 10th Mountain Division during World War II, 6 January 1940–30 November 1945*, 15.

230. Dusenbery, *The North Apennines and Beyond with the 10th Mountain Division*, 187.

231. Ibid.

232. *Combat History of the 10th Mountain Division, 1944–1945*, 16.

233. Ibid.; and Wellborn, *History of the 86th Mountain Infantry in Italy*, 9.

234. Dusenbery, *The North Apennines and Beyond with the 10th Mountain Division*, 186.

235. *Combat History of the 10th Mountain Division, 1944–1945*, 16; and Wondolowski, *History of the IV Corps, 1941–1945*, 513.

236. Dusenbery, *The North Apennines and Beyond with the 10th Mountain Division*, 186.

237. *Combat History of the 10th Mountain Division, 1944–1945*, 16; Richmond, *Combat Operations in Mountainous Terrain*, 54; and Wellborn, *History of the 86th Mountain Infantry in Italy*, 9.

238. Dusenbery, *The North Apennines and Beyond with the 10th Mountain Division*, 185.

239. *Combat History of the 10th Mountain Division, 1944–1945*; Richmond, *Combat Operations in Mountainous Terrain*, 54; and Wellborn, *History of the 86th Mountain Infantry in Italy*, 9.

240. *Fifth Army History*, 8:80.

241. Ibid.; and *Combat History of the 10th Mountain Division, 1944–1945*, 16.

242. Wellborn, *History of the 86th Mountain Infantry in Italy*, 10.

243. *Fifth Army History*, 8:80; and *Combat History of the 10th Mountain Division, 1944–1945*, 16.

244. Wondolowski, *History of the IV Corps, 1941–1945*, 514.

245. Ibid.; and *Combat History of the 10th Mountain Division, 1944–1945*, 16.

246. *Fifth Army History*, 8:80.

247. Wondolowski, *History of the IV Corps, 1941–1945*, 514.

248. Richmond, *Combat Operations in Mountainous Terrain*, 57–58.

249. Dusenbery, *North Apennines and Beyond with the 10th Mountain Division*, 193.

250. Dole, *Adventures in Skiing*, 131.

251. Wondolowski, *History of the IV Corps, 1941–1945*, 514.
252. Burton, *The Ski Troops*, 153.
253. Ibid., 155.
254. *Combat History of the 10th Mountain Division, 1944–1945*, 16.
255. Burton, *The Ski Troops*, 155.
256. *Combat History of the 10th Mountain Division, 1944–1945*, 16–17; and Burton, *The Ski Troops*, 155–56.
257. Wondolowski, *History of the IV Corps, 1941–1945*, 514–15.
258. Ibid., 515.
259. *Combat History of the 10th Mountain Division, 1944–1945*, 17.
260. Dole, *Adventures in Skiing*, 131.
261. *Combat History of the 10th Mountain Division, 1944–1945*, 15; and *Fifth Army History*, 8:81; see also Burton, *The Ski Troops*, 156.
262. Wondolowski, *History of the IV Corps, 1941–1945*, 515.
263. Dole, *Adventures in Skiing*, 131.
264. Casewit, *Mountain Troopers*, 69.
265. Richmond, *Combat Operations in Mountainous Terrain*, 58.
266. Imbrie, *Chronology of the 10th Mountain Division during World War II, 6 January 1940–30 November 1945*, 15; and Oland, *North Apennines*, 28.
267. Earle, *History of the 87th Mountain Infantry, Italy 1945*, 18.
268. *A Short History of the 85th Mountain Infantry Regiment*, 13.
269. Ibid.
270. Wondolowski, *History of the IV Corps, 1941–1945*, 515–16 and map 5.
271. Imbrie, *Chronology of the 10th Mountain Division during World War II, 6 January 1940–30 November 1945*, 16.
272. Wondolowski, *History of the IV Corps, 1941–1945*, 515.
273. *Fifth Army History*, 8:81.
274. Matthew G. St. Clair, *The Twelfth US Air Force: Tactical and Operational Innovations in the Mediterranean Theater of Operations, 1943–1944* (Maxwell Air Force Base, AL: School of Advanced Air and Space Studies, 2007), 41.
275. Goodman, *A Fragment of History*, 87.
276. Ibid.
277. *Fifth Division History*, 8:81; and Sanders, *The Boys of Winter*, 134.
278. Sanders, *The Boys of Winter*, 134.
279. Brooks, *The War North of Rome*, 354.
280. Kerekes, *Recollections: Company B*, 19.
281. Ibid.
282. Earle, *History of the 87th Mountain Infantry, Italy 1945*, 19.
283. Ibid., 20.
284. Wilson, *History of the First Battalion, 87th Mountain Infantry*, 22.
285. Earle, *History of the 87th Mountain Infantry, Italy 1945*, 20.
286. Ibid.
287. Ibid.
288. Ibid.
289. Ibid.
290. Ibid.
291. Ibid.
292. Ibid., 21; Wilson, *History of the First Battalion, 87th Mountain Infantry*, 23.
293. Earle, *History of the 87th Mountain Infantry, Italy 1945*, 21.
294. Ibid.
295. Ibid.
296. Ibid.
297. *Combat History of the 10th Mountain Division, 1944–1945*, 17; and Earle, *History of the 87th Mountain Infantry, Italy 1945*, 21.
298. Casewit, *Mountain Troopers*, 76; and Earle, *History of the 87th Mountain Infantry, Italy 1945*, 22.
299. Earle, *History of the 87th Mountain Infantry, Italy 1945*, 22.
300. Ibid.
301. 15th Army Group, *A Military Encyclopedia Based on Operations in the Italian Campaigns, 1943–1945* (n.p., 1945), 169.
302. Ibid.
303. Earle, *History of the 87th Mountain Infantry, Italy 1945*, 22.
304. Ibid.
305. Ibid.
306. Burton, *The Ski Troops*, 162.
307. Ibid.
308. Ibid.
309. Ibid.

310. Ibid.
311. Ibid.
312. *A Short History of the 85th Mountain Infantry Regiment*,14.
313. Ibid.
314. Ibid.
315. Ibid.
316. Ibid., 16.
317. Ibid.
318. Ibid.
319. Imbrie and Evans, *Good Times and Bad Times*, 48.
320. *A Short History of the 85th Mountain Infantry Regiment*, 16.
321. Ibid.
322. Kerekes, *Recollections: Company B*, 24.
323. *A Short History of the 85th Mountain Infantry Regiment*, 16.
324. Ibid., 17; and Kerekes, *Recollections: Company B*, 30.
325. Kerekes, *Recollections: Company B*, 25.
326. *A Short History of the 85th Mountain Infantry Regiment*, 17; and Kerekes, *Recollections: Company B*, 25.
327. *A Short History of the 85th Mountain Infantry Regiment*, 18.
328. Ibid.
329. Ibid.
330. Kerekes, *Recollections: Company B*, 26.
331. Brower, *Remount Blue*, 15.
332. Ibid., 15–16.
333. Ibid., 15.
334. Ibid.
335. Ibid.
336. Ibid., 16.
337. Ibid.
338. Ibid.
339. Ibid.
340. Ibid.
341. Ibid., 20.
342. Ibid., 21.
343. Ibid.
344. Ibid., 22.
345. Burton, *The Ski Troops*, 161.
346. Ibid.
347. Brower, *Remount Blue*, 17.
348. Ibid.; and *Combat History of the 10th Mountain Division, 1944–1945*, 23.
349. Brower, *Remount Blue*, 16.
350. Ibid., 19–20.
351. Ibid., 21; and *Combat History of the 10th Mountain Division, 1944–1945*, 23.
352. *Combat History of the 10th Mountain Division, 1944–1945*, 23–24.
353. Brower, *Remount Blue*, 33.
354. Ibid.
355. Ibid., 35.
356. Ibid.
357. Ibid.
358. Ibid., 36.
359. *Combat History of the 10th Mountain Division, 1944–1945*, 24.
360. Mascarenhas de Moraes, *The Brazilian Expeditionary Force*, 113–14; and Wondolowski, *History of the IV Corps, 1941–1945*, 520.
361. Mascarenhas de Moraes, *The Brazilian Expeditionary Force*, 115; and Wondolowski, *History of the IV Corps, 1941–1945*, 520.
362. Wondolowski, *History of the IV Corps, 1941–1945*, 520.
363. Mascarenhas de Moraes, *The Brazilian Expeditionary Force*, 115; and Wondolowski, *History of the IV Corps, 1941–1945*, 520.
364. Mascarenhas de Moraes, *The Brazilian Expeditionary Force*, 115.
365. Wondolowski, *History of the IV Corps, 1941–1945*, 520.
366. *15th Army Group History, 16 December 1944–2 May 1945* (Nashville: Battery, 1989), 66.
367. Ibid.
368. Ibid.
369. Mascarenhas de Moraes, *The Brazilian Expeditionary Force*, 115.
370. Ibid., 116.
371. Jackson, *The Battle for Italy*, 299.
372. Clark, *Calculated Risk*, 417–18.
373. Ibid., 418; and Jackson, *The Battle for Italy*, 299.

Chapter 6

1. *History of the IV Corps*, 524.
2. Ibid.
3. Ibid.
4. Ibid., 524–25; *Fifth Army History*, 8:85; and *Chronology of the 10th Mountain Division during World War II, 6 January 1940–30 November 1945*, 18.

5. Imbrie, *Chronology of the 10th Mountain Division during World War II, 6 January 1940–30 November 1945*, 18.

6. *History of the IV Corps*, 525.

7. *Combat History of the 10th Mountain Division, 1944–1945*, 29.

8. Ibid.

9. Ibid.

10. Earle, *History of the 87th Mountain Infantry, Italy 1945*, 32.

11. *Combat History of the 10th Mountain Division, 1944–1945*, 29.

12. Earle, *History of the 87th Mountain Infantry, Italy 1945*, 32.

13. Ibid., 35.

14. Ibid., 32.

15. *Combat History of the 10th Mountain Division, 1944–1945*, 30.

16. Earle, *History of the 87th Mountain Infantry, Italy 1945*, 36; and Imbrie, *Chronology of the 10th Mountain Division during World War II, 6 January 1940–30 November 1945*, 18.

17. Earle, *History of the 87th Mountain Infantry, Italy 1945*, 35–37; *Combat History of the 10th Mountain Division, 1944–1945*, 30; and Imbrie, *Chronology of the 10th Mountain Division during World War II, 6 January 1940–30 November 1945*, 18.

18. Earle, *History of the 87th Mountain Infantry, Italy 1945*, 36.

19. Ibid.

20. Ibid.

21. Ibid.

22. Ibid.

23. Ibid., 36–37.

24. Ibid., 37.

25. Ibid., 38.

26. Ibid., 35–41.

27. Ibid., 37–38.

28. Ibid., 38.

29. Ibid., 38–39.

30. Ibid., 39.

31. Ibid., 39.

32. Ibid.

33. Ibid.; and Imbrie, *Chronology of the 10th Mountain Division during World War II, 6 January 1940–30 November 1945*, 18.

34. Earle, *History of the 87th Mountain Infantry, Italy 1945*, 44.

35. Ibid., 41.

36. Ibid.

37. Ibid.

38. Ibid., 41–42.

39. Ibid., 42.

40. Ibid.

41. Ibid.

42. Ibid.

43. Wellborn, *History of the 86th Mountain Infantry in Italy*, 19–20.

44. Imbrie, *Chronology of the 10th Mountain Division during World War II, 6 January 1940–30 November 1945*, 18.

45. Wellborn, *History of the 86th Mountain Infantry in Italy*, 20.

46. Ibid.

47. Wondolowski, *History of the IV Corps, 1941–1945*, 525; and Imbrie, *Chronology of the 10th Mountain Division during World War II, 6 January 1940–30 November 1945*, 18.

48. Wondolowski, *History of the IV Corps, 1941–1945*, 525.

49. Wellborn, *History of the 86th Mountain Infantry in Italy*, 21.

50. Ibid.; and Imbrie, *Chronology of the 10th Mountain Division during World War II, 6 January 1940–30 November 1945*, 18.

51. Wondolowski, *History of the IV Corps, 1941–1945*, 525; Wellborn, *History of the 86th Mountain Infantry in Italy*, 21; and Imbrie, *Chronology of the 10th Mountain Division during World War II, 6 January 1940–30 November 1945*, 18.

52. Wondolowski, *History of the IV Corps, 1941–1945*, 525; and Wellborn, *History of the 86th Mountain Infantry in Italy*, 21.

53. Wellborn, *History of the 86th Mountain Infantry in Italy*, 21.

54. Ibid., 22; and Imbrie, *Chronology of the 10th Mountain Division during World War II, 6 January 1940–30 November 1945*, 18.

55. Wondolowski, *History of the IV Corps, 1941–1945*, 525–26.

56. "Pete Seibert of 10th Mountain Division," World War II in Color, February 28, 2016, http://ww2colorfarbe.blogspot.com/2016/02/pete-seibert-of-10th-mountain-division.html, retrieved May 11, 2020.

57. Louise Borden, *Ski Soldier: A World War II Biography* (Honesdale, PA: Calkins Creek, 2017), 118.

58. Wondolowski, *History of the IV Corps, 1941–1945*, 525–26; *Combat History of the 10th Mountain Division, 1944–1945*, 31; and Imbrie, *Chronology of the 10th Mountain Division during World War II, 6 January 1940–30 November 1945*, 18.

59. Brower, *Remount Blue*, 38.

60. Wondolowski, *History of the IV Corps, 1941–1945*, 526.

61. Ibid., 529.

62. Ibid.; and Mascarenhas de Moraes, *The Brazilian Expeditionary Force*, 122–23.

63. Wondolowski, *History of the IV Corps, 1941–1945*, 526.

64. *History of the 86th Mtn Inf Regt 10th Mtn Div* (typescript, n.p., n.d., est. 1945), 2.

65. *Combat History of the 10th Mountain Division, 1944–1945*, 32.

66. Wondolowski, *History of the IV Corps, 1941–1945*, 526–27.

67. Ibid., 527.

68. Earle, *History of the 87th Mountain Infantry, Italy 1945*, 42–43.

69. Ibid., 43; and Wilson, *History of the 1st Battalion, 87th Mountain Infantry*, 29.

70. Earle, *History of the 87th Mountain Infantry, Italy 1945*, 43; and Wilson, *History of the First Battalion, 87th Mountain Infantry*, 29–30.

71. Wilson, *History of the First Battalion, 87th Mountain Infantry*, 30.

72. Earle, *History of the 87th Mountain Infantry, Italy 1945*, 43.

73. Ibid.

74. Ibid.; and *Combat History of the 10th Mountain Division, 1944–1945*, 32–33.

75. Earle, *History of the 87th Mountain Infantry, Italy 1945*, 43–44.

76. Ibid.

77. Ibid., 45.

78. *Combat History of the 10th Mountain Division, 1944–1945*, 33.

79. *A Short History of the 85th Mountain Infantry Regiment*, 26; and Imbrie, *Chronology of the 10th Mountain Division during World War II, 6 January 1940–30 November 1945*, 18.

80. *A Short History of the 85th Mountain Infantry Regiment*, 28.

81. Ibid.

82. *A Short History of the 85th Mountain Infantry Regiment*, 26; and Imbrie, *Chronology of the 10th Mountain Division during World War II, 6 January 1940–30 November 1945*, 18.

83. *A Short History of the 85th Mountain Infantry Regiment*, 26.

84. Ibid., 26–28.

85. Ibid., 28.

86. Earle, *History of the 87th Mountain Infantry, Italy 1945*, 45.

87. Wilson, *History of the First Battalion, 87th Mountain Infantry*, 30.

88. Ibid.

89. Ibid.

90. Earle, *History of the 87th Mountain Infantry, Italy 1945*, 45.

91. Ibid., 46.

92. Wilson, *History of the First Battalion, 87th Mountain Infantry*, 30; and Earle, *History of the 87th Mountain Infantry, Italy 1945*, 46–47.

93. Earle, *History of the 87th Mountain Infantry, Italy 1945*, 47.

94. Ibid.

95. *Combat History of the 10th Mountain Division, 1944–1945*, 34; and Imbrie, *Chronology of the 10th Mountain Division during World War II, 6 January 1940–30 November 1945*, 18.

96. Mascarenhas de Moraes, *The Brazilian Expeditionary Force*, 125–27.

97. *Fifth Army History*, 8:88.

98. Wondolowski, *History of the IV Corps, 1941–1945*, 529.

99. Ibid.

100. Wilson, *History of the First Battalion, 87th Mountain Infantry*, 31.

101. Wellborn, *History of the 86th Mountain Infantry in Italy*, 18.

102. *Combat History of the 10th Mountain Division, 1944–1945*, 35.

103. Earle, *History of the 87th Mountain Infantry, Italy 1945*, 50.

104. Wilson, *History of the First Battalion, 87th Mountain Infantry*, 31.

105. Clark, *Calculated Risk*, 426; see also *Finito! The Po Valley Campaign, 1945* (Headquarters, 15th Army Group, Italy, 1945), 7.

106. Fisher, *Cassino to the Alps*, 442.
107. Ibid.
108. Ibid.
109. Ibid., 445; and Brooks, *The War North of Rome*, 361.
110. Clark, *Calculated Risk*, 426; and Fisher, *Cassino to the Alps*, 443.
111. Fisher, *Cassino to the Alps*, 443.
112. Clark, *Calculated Risk*, 426.
113. Fisher, *Cassino to the Alps*, 443.
114. Clark, *Calculated Risk*, 426.
115. Richard Doherty, *Victory in Italy: 15th Army Group's Final Campaign, 1945* (Havertown, PA: Pen & Sword Military, 2014), 76.
116. Ibid.; Fisher, *Cassino to the Alps*, 448; and Starr, *From Salerno to the Alps*, 388–89.
117. Starr, *From Salerno to the Alps*, 388.
118. Fisher, *Cassino to the Alps*, 448.
119. Doherty, *Victory in Italy*, 53.
120. Brooks, *The War North of Rome*, 362.
121. Ibid.
122. Ibid., 361.
123. *15th Army Group History, 16 December 1944–2 May 1945*, 99.
124. Ibid., 99–100; and Doherty, *Victory in Italy*, 77, 94.
125. Clark, *Calculated Risk*, 429; and Starr, *From Salerno to the Alps*, 391.
126. Starr, *From Salerno to the Alps*, 391.
127. Roberts, 120.
128. Ibid., 136; and *Fifth Army History*, 9:37.
129. Roberts, 138–44.
130. Clark, *Calculated Risk*, 429.
131. Ibid., 429–30.
132. *19 Days: From the Apennines to the Alps* (Fifth Army, 1945), 37–38.
133. Starr, *From Salerno to the Alps*, 391.
134. Ibid., 389.
135. Ibid., 389–90.
136. Ibid., 390.
137. Ibid., 392.
138. Ibid.
139. Wondolowski, *History of the IV Corps, 1941–1945*, 539.
140. Ibid., 539–40.
141. Ibid., 540.
142. Ibid.
143. Ibid., 540–41.
144. Ibid., 542.
145. Ibid.
146. Ibid., 542; see also Earle, *History of the 87th Mountain Infantry, Italy 1945*, 53.
147. Wondolowski, *History of the IV Corps, 1941–1945*, 543.
148. Ibid.
149. Ibid.
150. Ibid., 548–49.
151. Ibid., 550–51.
152. Ibid., 551.
153. Ibid., 542.
154. Ibid., 558.
155. Ibid., 559–61.
156. Ibid.,
157. *Combat History of the 10th Mountain Division, 1944–1945*, 47; and Earle, *History of the 87th Mountain Infantry, Italy 1945*, 54.
158. Ibid., 47; and Imbrie, *Chronology of the 10th Mountain Division during World War II, 6 January 1940–30 November 1945*, 19.
159. *Combat History of the 10th Mountain Division, 1944–1945*, 47.
160. Ibid.
161. Ibid.
162. Earle, *History of the 87th Mountain Infantry, Italy 1945*, 54.
163. Ibid.
164. Ibid.
165. Ibid.
166. Ibid.
167. *A Short History of the 85th Mountain Infantry Regiment*, 43.
168. Ibid.
169. Earle, *History of the 87th Mountain Infantry, Italy 1945*, 54.
170. *A Short History of the 85th Mountain Infantry Regiment*, 36.
171. Theodore Lockwood, ed., *Mountaineers* (Artcraft / 10th Mountain Alumni Association, ca. 1945), 27–28.
172. *A Short History of the 85th Mountain Infantry Regiment*, 37.
173. Ibid.
174. Lockwood, *Mountaineers*, 28.
175. Ibid.
176. *A Short History of the 85th Mountain Infantry Regiment*, 38.

177. Ibid., 40.
178. Ibid., 41.
179. Ibid., 40.
180. Ibid., 41.
181. Ibid.
182. Ibid.
183. Ibid.
184. Ibid.
185. Ibid.
186. Wellborn, *History of the 86th Mountain Infantry in Italy*, 33; and *Combat History of the 10th Mountain Division, 1944–1945*, 48.
187. Earle, *History of the 87th Mountain Infantry, Italy 1945*, 65.
188. *Combat History of the 10th Mountain Division, 1944–1945*, 48.
189. Wellborn, *History of the 86th Mountain Infantry in Italy*, 34.
190. Imbrie, *Chronology of the 10th Mountain Division during World War II, 6 January 1940–30 November 1945*, 19.
191. Wilson, *History of the First Battalion, 87th Mountain Infantry*, 34–35.
192. Ibid., 34.
193. Ibid.
194. *Combat History of the 10th Mountain Division, 1944–1945*, 48.
195. Ibid.; Wilson, *History of the First Battalion, 87th Mountain Infantry*, 34; and Earle, *History of the 87th Mountain Infantry, Italy 1945*, 64–65.
196. Wilson, *History of the First Battalion, 87th Mountain Infantry*, 34–35.
197. Ibid., 36.
198. Earle, *History of the 87th Mountain Infantry, Italy 1945*, 68.
199. Ibid., 65–67.
200. *Combat History of the 10th Mountain Division, 1944–1945*, 49.
201. Ibid.; and Lockwood, *Mountaineers*, 29.
202. Wellborn, *History of the 86th Mountain Infantry in Italy*, 34.
203. Ibid.; and Brooks, *The War North of Rome*, 374.
204. Wellborn, *History of the 86th Mountain Infantry in Italy*, 34.
205. Ibid.
206. Ibid.
207. Lockwood, *Mountaineers*, 29; *Combat History of the 10th Mountain Division, 1944–1945*, 49; and Earle, *History of the 87th Mountain Infantry, Italy 1945*, 69.
208. Lockwood, *Mountaineers*, 30.
209. Ibid.; and *Combat History of the 10th Mountain Division, 1944–1945*, 50.
210. *A Short History of the 85th Mountain Infantry Regiment*, 46.
211. *Combat History of the 10th Mountain Division, 1944–1945*, 51.
212. Ibid.
213. Ibid.
214. Ibid.; and Imbrie, *Chronology of the 10th Mountain Division during World War II, 6 January 1940–30 November 1945*, 20.
215. *Combat History of the 10th Mountain Division, 1944–1945*, 52.
216. Wellborn, *History of the 86th Mountain Infantry in Italy*, 35.
217. *Combat History of the 10th Mountain Division, 1944–1945*, 52.
218. Ibid.; and Wellborn, *History of the 86th Mountain Infantry in Italy*, 35–36.
219. *Combat History of the 10th Mountain Division, 1944–1945*, 52.
220. Ibid., 53.
221. Ibid.
222. Ibid.
223. Ibid.
224. Ibid., 54.
225. Ibid.
226. Earle, *History of the 87th Mountain Infantry, Italy 1945*, 95–97.
227. *Combat History of the 10th Mountain Division, 1944–1945*, 54.
228. Lockwood, *Mountaineers*, 34–35.
229. Ibid., 35.
230. Ibid.
231. Ibid.
232. *Finito!*, 13.
233. *15th Army Group History*, 103.
234. Ibid., 103–04.
235. Ibid., 104.
236. *Finito!*, 14.
237. Doherty, *Victory in Italy*, 43.
238. Ibid.
239. *15th Army Group History*, 105.

240. Ibid., 107–08; and *Finito!*, 14.

241. *15th Army Group History*, 107.

242. Ibid., 114.

243. Ibid., 115.

244. Ibid.

245. Ibid.

246. Starr, *From Salerno to the Alps*, 412; and *19 Days*, 42.

247. *19 Days*, 42.

248. Ibid., 43.

249. Ibid.

250. Ibid.

251. Ibid., 46.

252. Ibid., 46, 50.

253. Wondolowski, *History of the IV Corps, 1941–1945*, 571.

254. Ibid., 573–74.

255. Starr, *From Salerno to the Alps*, 403.

256. Wondolowski, *History of the IV Corps, 1941–1945*, 573–74.

257. Ibid., 574.

258. *19 Days*, 41; and Starr, *From Salerno to the Alps*, 403.

259. Wondolowski, *History of the IV Corps, 1941–1945*, 575.

260. Starr, *From Salerno to the Alps*, 403.

261. Ibid., 405.

262. Ibid., 408; and Wondolowski, *History of the IV Corps, 1941–1945*, 583.

263. Jackson, *The Battle for Italy*, 310; and Starr, *From Salerno to the Alps*, 405.

264. Starr, *From Salerno to the Alps*, 408; and *19 Days*, 51.

265. Starr, *From Salerno to the Alps*, 408.

266. Ibid., 409.

267. Lockwood, *Mountaineers*, 34–35.

268. Imbrie, *Chronology of the 10th Mountain Division during World War II, 6 January 1940–30 November 1945*, 22.

269. *Finito!*, 15.

270. Wondolowski, *History of the IV Corps, 1941–1945*, 587–88.

271. Ibid., 588.

272. Imbrie, *Chronology of the 10th Mountain Division during World War II, 6 January 1940–30 November 1945*, 22; Lockwood, *Mountaineers*, 36; and *Combat History of the 10th Mountain Division, 1944–1945*, 58.

273. *A Short History of the 85th Mountain Infantry Regiment*, 49.

274. Lockwood, *Mountaineers*, 37; *A Short History of the 85th Mountain Infantry Regiment*, 49; and Imbrie, *Chronology of the 10th Mountain Division during World War II, 6 January 1940–30 November 1945*, 22.

275. Wondolowski, *History of the IV Corps, 1941–1945*, 589; and *Combat History of the 10th Mountain Division, 1944–1945*, 58.

276. Ibid.; Lockwood, *Mountaineers*, 37; and *A Short History of the 85th Mountain Infantry Regiment*, 49.

277. Wellborn, *History of the 86th Mountain Infantry in Italy*, 38–39.

278. Ibid., 39.

279. Ibid.

280. Ibid.

281. Ibid., 39; and *Combat History of the 10th Mountain Division, 1944–1945*, 57.

282. *Combat History of the 10th Mountain Division, 1944–1945*, 57.

283. Wellborn, *History of the 86th Mountain Infantry in Italy*, 39.

284. *Combat History of the 10th Mountain Division, 1944–1945*, 57.

285. Ibid.; and Wellborn, *History of the 86th Mountain Infantry in Italy*, 39–40.

286. *Combat History of the 10th Mountain Division, 1944–1945*, 57.

287. Wellborn, *History of the 86th Mountain Infantry in Italy*, 39.

288. *Combat History of the 10th Mountain Division, 1944–1945*, 57; and Wondolowski, *History of the IV Corps, 1941–1945*, 588.

289. Lockwood, *Mountaineers*, 37.

290. *History of 1st Bn 86th Mtn Inf Regt 10th Div*, 3.

291. Wellborn, *History of the 86th Mountain Infantry in Italy*, 40.

292. Ibid.

293. Ibid.

294. Wondolowski, *History of the IV Corps, 1941–1945*, 588.

295. *15th Army Group History*, 117.

296. Earle, *History of the 87th Mountain Infantry, Italy 1945*, 107.

297. Ibid.

298. Ibid.
299. *Combat History of the 10th Mountain Division, 1944–1945*, 57.
300. Earle, *History of the 87th Mountain Infantry, Italy 1945*, 107.
301. *Combat History of the 10th Mountain Division, 1944–1945*, 57.
302. Earle, *History of the 87th Mountain Infantry, Italy 1945*, 108.
303. Ibid.
304. Ibid.
305. Ibid., 108–09.
306. Ibid., 109.
307. Ibid., 111; and Wondolowski, *History of the IV Corps, 1941–1945*, 589.
308. *Combat History of the 10th Mountain Division, 1944–1945*, 57; Wondolowski, *History of the IV Corps, 1941–1945*, 589; and *Fifth Army History*, part 9, "Race to the Alps," 56.
309. *Fifth Army History*, part 9, "Race to the Alps," 61.
310. Wondolowski, *History of the IV Corps, 1941–1945*, 589.
311. Ibid., 598.
312. Ibid., 599.
313. Ibid., 600; and *Combat History of the 10th Mountain Division, 1944–1945*, 58.
314. Ibid.; and Imbrie, *Chronology of the 10th Mountain Division during World War II, 6 January 1940–30 November 1945*, 22.
315. Imbrie, *Chronology of the 10th Mountain Division during World War II, 6 January 1940–30 November 1945*, 22.
316. Wondolowski, *History of the IV Corps, 1941–1945*, 600; and *Combat History of the 10th Mountain Division, 1944–1945*, 58.
317. Wondolowski, *History of the IV Corps, 1941–1945*, 599–600.
318. *Combat History of the 10th Mountain Division, 1944–1945*, 58; and Wondolowski, *History of the IV Corps, 1941–1945*, 600.
319. Ibid.
320. *Combat History of the 10th Mountain Division, 1944–1945*, 59; and Wondolowski, *History of the IV Corps, 1941–1945*, 600.
321. Ibid.
322. *Combat History of the 10th Mountain Division, 1944–1945*, 59.
323. Ibid.
324. Wondolowski, *History of the IV Corps, 1941–1945*, 601.
325. Ibid.
326. Ibid., 601–02.
327. Ibid., 602; and *Combat History of the 10th Mountain Division, 1944–1945*, 59.
328. *Combat History of the 10th Mountain Division, 1944–1945*, 59.
329. Imbrie, *Chronology of the 10th Mountain Division during World War II, 6 January 1940–30 November 1945*, 22–23; *History of the 85th Mountain Infantry*, 52; and Imbrie and Evans, *Good Times and Bad Times*, 15.
330. *History of 1st Bn 86th Mtn Inf Regt 10th Mtn Div*, 3.
331. Imbrie and Evans, *Good Times and Bad Times*, 154.
332. Ibid., 93.
333. Ibid., 94.
334. Ibid.
335. *A Short History of the 85th Mountain Infantry Regiment*, 52
336. Ibid., 53.
337. Wellborn, *History of the 86th Mountain Infantry in Italy*, 40.
338. Ibid., 40–41; and *History of 1st Bn 86th Mtn Inf Regt 10th Mtn Div*, 3.
339. Wellborn, *History of the 86th Mountain Infantry in Italy*, 41.
340. Ibid.; and *History of 1st Bn 86th Mtn Inf Regt 10th Mtn Div*, 3–4.
341. Wellborn, *History of the 86th Mountain Infantry in Italy*, 41–42.
342. Ibid., 42.
343. Ibid.
344. Ibid.
345. Earle, *History of the 87th Mountain Infantry, Italy 1945*, 111.
346. Ibid.
347. Ibid., 112–13.
348. Ibid., 113–14.
349. Ibid., 114.
350. Ibid.
351. Ibid., 115.
352. Ibid.
353. Ibid.
354. Ibid.

355. Ibid., 115–17.
356. Ibid.
357. Ibid., 116–17.
358. Ibid, 116.
359. Ibid., 118.
360. Ibid., 119.
361. Ibid., 120.
362. Ibid., 121.
363. *Combat History of the 10th Mountain Division, 1944–1945*, 60.
364. Ibid.
365. Ibid.
366. Ibid.; and Wilson, *History of the First Battalion, 87th Mountain Infantry*, 57.
367. *Combat History of the 10th Mountain Division, 1944–1945*, 60.
368. Wilson, *History of the First Battalion, 87th Mountain Infantry*, 58.
369. *Combat History of the 10th Mountain Division, 1944–1945*, 60.
370. Ibid.; and Wilson, *History of the First Battalion, 87th Mountain Infantry*, 59.
371. Earle, *History of the 87th Mountain Infantry, Italy 1945*, 123.
372. Ibid.
373. Ibid.
374. Wilson, *History of the First Battalion, 87th Mountain Infantry*, 59.
375. *Combat History of the 10th Mountain Division, 1944–1945*, 60.
376. Ibid.; and Wilson, *History of the First Battalion, 87th Mountain Infantry*, 60.
377. Wilson, *History of the First Battalion, 87th Mountain Infantry*, 60.
378. *Combat History of the 10th Mountain Division, 1944–1945*, 61.
379. Ibid.; and *A Short History of the 85th Mountain Infantry Regiment*, 54.
380. *A Short History of the 85th Mountain Infantry Regiment*, 54.
381. Wellborn, *History of the 86th Mountain Infantry in Italy*, 42.
382. Ibid.
383. Ibid.
384. Ibid., 54; and *Combat History of the 10th Mountain Division, 1944–1945*, 62.
385. *A Short History of the 85th Mountain Infantry Regiment*, 57; *Combat History of the 10th Mountain Division, 1944–1945*, 61; and Wondolowski, *History of the IV Corps, 1941–1945*, 625.
386. *Combat History of the 10th Mountain Division, 1944–1945*, 61.
387. Wondolowski, *History of the IV Corps, 1941–1945*, 625–626; *Combat History of the 10th Mountain Division, 1944–1945*, 62; and Wellborn, *History of the 86th Mountain Infantry in Italy*, 43.
388. Wondolowski, *History of the IV Corps, 1941–1945*, 626.
389. *A Short History of the 85th Mountain Infantry Regiment*, 55.
390. Ibid.
391. Ibid.
392. Ibid.; *Combat History of the 10th Mountain Division, 1944–1945*, 63; and Wondolowski, *History of the IV Corps, 1941–1945*, 626.
393. *A Short History of the 85th Mountain Infantry Regiment*, 55.
394. Wondolowski, *History of the IV Corps, 1941–1945*, 626.
395. Ibid.
396. *Combat History of the 10th Mountain Division, 1944–1945*, 63.
397. Wellborn, *History of the 86th Mountain Infantry in Italy*, 43.
398. Ibid.; and *Combat History of the 10th Mountain Division, 1944–1945*, 63.
399. Ibid.; and Wondolowski, *History of the IV Corps, 1941–1945*, 620.
400. *History of 1st Bn 86th Mtn Inf Regt 10th Mtn Div*, 4.
401. Ibid.; and Wellborn, *History of the 86th Mountain Infantry in Italy*, 43.
402. Wellborn, *History of the 86th Mountain Infantry in Italy*, 43.
403. Earle, *History of the 87th Mountain Infantry, Italy 1945*, 134; and Wilson, *History of the First Battalion, 87th Mountain Infantry*, 62.
404. *A Short History of the 85th Mountain Infantry Regiment*, 57.
405. Earle, *History of the 87th Mountain Infantry, Italy 1945*, 135.

406. Ibid.; Wilson, *History of the First Battalion, 87th Mountain Infantry*, 63; and Lockwood, *Mountaineers*, 51.

407. Lockwood, *Mountaineers*, 51.

408. Ibid.; *A Short History of the 85th Mountain Infantry*, 57; and *Combat History of the 10th Mountain Division, 1944–1945*, 66.

409. Brower, *Remount Blue*, 83.

410. Ibid.

411. Ibid.; and Lockwood, *Mountaineers*, 52.

412. Lockwood, *Mountaineers*, 53.

413. Brower, *Remount Blue*, 83.

414. Wellborn, *History of the 86th Mountain Infantry in Italy*, 44.

415. Ibid.

416. Brower, *Remount Blue*, 83–84.

417. Ibid., 83–85.

418. *History of 1st Bn 86th Mtn Inf Regt 10th Mtn Div*, 4.

419. Brower, *Remount Blue*, 85.

420. Lockwood, *Mountaineers*, 53.

421. Becky Little, "Duck Boats Offered a Unique Solution to a World War II Problem," History.com, August 30, 2018, https://www.history.com/news/duck-boats-world-war-ii-d-day, retrieved May 30, 2020.

422. Wellborn, *History of the 86th Mountain Infantry in Italy*, 44.

423. Ibid.; Lockwood, *Mountaineers*, 53; and Brower, *Remount Blue*, 85–86.

424. Lockwood, *Mountaineers*, 53–56; and Wellborn, *History of the 86th Mountain Infantry in Italy*, 44.

425. Wellborn, *History of the 86th Mountain Infantry in Italy*, 44; and Brower, *Remount Blue*, 87.

426. Earle, *History of the 87th Mountain Infantry, Italy 1945*, 140.

427. Ibid.

428. Ibid.

429. Ibid.

430. Ibid.

431. Ibid.

432. Ibid.

433. Wilson, *History of the First Battalion, 87th Mountain Infantry*, 63.

434. Ibid.

435. Ibid., 64–65; and Earle, *History of the 87th Mountain Infantry, Italy 1945*, 142.

436. Ibid.

437. Earle, *History of the 87th Mountain Infantry, Italy 1945*, 144.

438. Wellborn, *History of the 86th Mountain Infantry in Italy*, 44; and *History of 1st Bn 86th Mtn Inf Regt 10th Mtn Div*, 5.

439. Wellborn, *History of the 86th Mountain Infantry in Italy*, 45.

440. Brower, *Remount Blue*, 88–89.

441. Wellborn, *History of the 86th Mountain Infantry in Italy*, 45.

442. Ibid.

443. Ibid.

444. Ibid.

445. Ibid., 46.

446. Eugene S. Hames, "We Captured Mussolini's Villa," 1 [76] (in Kerekes, *Recollections: Company B*, immediately following page 75).

447. Ibid., 2 [76].

448. *Combat History of the 10th Mountain Division, 1944–1945*, 68.

449. Ibid.

450. Ibid., 68–69.

451. Wondolowski, *History of the IV Corps, 1941–1945*, 648–60.

452. Ibid., 656–57.

453. Ibid., 661–62.

454. Ibid., 663.

455. *Finito!*, 62; and *19 Days*, 86.

456. *19 Days*, 88.

457. Wondolowski, *History of the IV Corps, 1941–1945*, 684.

458. *A Short History of the 85th Mountain Infantry Regiment*, 58–59.

459. *Combat History of the 10th Mountain Division, 1944–1945*, 71.

460. Ibid., 72.

461. *Fifth Army History*, 9:132–33.

462. Fisher, *Cassino to the Alps*, 444.

463. Clark, *Calculated Risk*, 443; and Earle, *History of the 87th Mountain Infantry, Italy 1945*, 148.

464. Starr, *From Salerno to the Alps*, 440; and *Fifth Army History*, 9:134.

465. Clark, *Calculated Risk*, 442.

466. Starr, *From Salerno to the Alps*, 440.

467. *Combat History of the 10th Mountain Division, 1944–1945*, 76; and Imbrie, *Chronology of the 10th Mountain Division during World War II, 6 January 1940–30 November 1945*, 27.

468. Ibid.

469. Imbrie, *Chronology of the 10th Mountain Division during World War II, 6 January 1940–30 November 1945*, 27.

Chapter 7

1. John C. Sparrow, *History of Personnel Demobilization in the United States Army*, Department of the Army Pamphlet 20-210 (Washington, DC: Department of the Army, July 1952), 302–05.

2. Ibid., 303.

3. Ibid., 303–04.

4. R. Alton Lee, "The Army 'Mutiny' of 1946," *Journal of American History* 53, no. 3 (December 1966): 557.

5. Kerekes, *Recollections: Company B*, 72.

6. Imbrie, *Chronology of the 10th Mountain Division during World War II, 6 January 1940–30 November 1945*, 27; and Wellborn, *History of the 86th Mountain Infantry in Italy*, 52.

7. Charles, *Troopships of World War II*, 356–57.

8. Imbrie, *Chronology of the 10th Mountain Division during World War II, 6 January 1940–30 November 1945*, 27.

9. Ibid.; and Charles, *Troopships of World War II*, 208.

10. Charles, *Troopships of World War II*, 135; and Imbrie, *Chronology of the 10th Mountain Division during World War II, 6 January 1940–30 November 1945*, 27.

11. Imbrie, *Chronology of the 10th Mountain Division during World War II, 6 January 1940–30 November 1945*, 27.

12. Ibid., 28; and Wellborn, *History of the 86th Mountain Infantry in Italy*, 110.

13. Wellborn, *History of the 86th Mountain Infantry in Italy*, 110–11.

14. Ibid., 111.

15. Wilson, *Armies, Corps, Divisions, and Separate Brigades*, 259.

16. Burton, *The Ski Troops*, 185.

17. Ibid.

18. Ibid., 185–86.

19. David M. Leach, "The Impact of the Tenth Mountain Division on the Development of a Modern Ski Industry in Colorado and Vermont: 1930–1965" (student thesis, Middlebury College, 2005), 65.

20. Ibid., 67–70.

21. Ibid., 70–71.

22. Ibid., 75–77; Sanders, *The Boys of Winter*, 200; and Burton, *The Ski Troops*, 187.

23. Wilson, *Maneuver and Firepower*, 207–09.

24. Ibid., 212–13.

25. Ibid., 213.

26. Ibid.

27. Ibid., 222.

28. Ibid.

29. Ibid., 245.

30. Ibid., 254.

31. Ibid.

32. Ibid., 222.

33. Wilson, *Armies, Corps, Divisions, and Separate Brigades*, 259.

34. Ibid.

35. *Fort Riley, Kansas* (n.p., ca. 1951), 40.

36. *Company K, 87th Infantry, 10th Infantry Division, Fort Riley, Kansas*, 3.

37. Ibid.

38. *Brief Histories of Divisions, 1917–1918*, 19.

39. *Company K, 87th Infantry; 10th Infantry Division, Fort Riley, Kansas, 1953; Company M, 85th Infantry; 10th Infantry Division, Fort Riley, Kansas, 1952; Company I, 86th Infantry.*

40. *Information Handbook for the Soldiers: 10th Infantry Division, Fort Riley, Kansas* (Fort Riley, KS, ca. 1952), 4.

41. *Fort Riley, Kansas*, 40.

42. *Information Handbook for the Soldiers: 10th Infantry Division, Fort Riley, Kansas*, 6.

43. Donald G. Bartling, *For Country: My Little Bit, Twenty-One Months of Service* (La Vergne, TN: PageTurner Press and Media, 2018), 1, 5.

44. Ibid., 5.

45. Ibid., 6.

46. Ibid., 7–9.

47. *Information Handbook for the Soldiers: 10th Infantry Division, Fort Riley, Kansas*, 5–7.

48. Ibid., 5.

49. Bartling, *For Country*, 11.

50. Ibid., 12–19.

51. Ibid., 19.

52. *Information Handbook for the Soldiers: 10th Infantry Division, Fort Riley, Kansas*, 5–7; and *10th Infantry Division: 1957* (Dallas: Taylor, 1957), 8.

53. Bartling, *For Country*, 21–22.
54. *Information Handbook for the Soldiers: 10th Infantry Division, Fort Riley, Kansas*, 5–7; and *10th Infantry Division: 1957*, 8.
55. *Information Handbook for the Soldiers: 10th Infantry Division, Fort Riley, Kansas*, 5; and US Army North, "History," https://www.arnorth.army.mil/about/pages/history.aspx, retrieved April 7, 2020.
56. [Private] Robert E. Hubert, Co. E, 85th Infantry Regiment, 10th Mountain Division, personal letter dated February 1, 1953.
57. Ibid.
58. *10th Infantry Division: 1957*, 9.
59. David A. Lane, Robert Gumerove, and Elizabeth W. Holtzworth, *Operation Gyroscope in the United States Army, Europe* (Washington, DC: US Army Current History Branch, Historical Division, 1957), i.
60. Stuart Queen, narr., "Operation Gyroscope," in *The Big Picture* (Army Signal Corps Pictorial Center, ca. 1955).
61. Wilson, *Maneuver and Firepower*, 252.
62. Lane et al., *Operation Gyroscope in the United States Army, Europe*, 2–3.
63. Ibid., 3–4.
64. Ibid., 4–5.
65. Ibid., 6.
66. Ibid.
67. Ibid., 18.
68. Ibid., 46.
69. Ibid., 12.
70. Ibid., 21, 46.
71. Ibid.; and *The Crusader: 86th Inf Regt, 1955–56* (n.p., 1956), 9.
72. Lane et al., *Operation Gyroscope in the United States Army, Europe*, 6.
73. Ibid., 39; and Wilson, *Maneuver and Firepower*, 253.
74. Wilson, *Maneuver and Firepower*, 250–51.
75. Ibid., 251.
76. *The Crusader*, 9.
77. *Headquarters, 37th Infantry Brigade Combat Team (Buckeye)* (Washington, DC: Center of Military History, 2017).
78. Ibid.; *10th Infantry Division: 1957*, 9; Wilson, *Maneuver and Firepower*, 251; and *The Crusader*, 9.
79. *The Crusader*, 4, 9.
80. Richard R. Riehm, *Pictorial History: Thirty-Seventh Infantry Division, Camp Polk, Louisiana, 1952* (Columbus, OH: F. J. Heer, 1952), 14.
81. Ibid., 13.
82. Ibid., 14.
83. Ibid.
84. Ibid.
85. Ibid., 14, 399.
86. Ibid., 14.
87. Ibid.
88. Ibid., 399.
89. *10th Infantry Division: 1957*, 10
90. Lane et al., *Operation Gyroscope in the United States Army, Europe*, 26–27.
91. Ibid., 27.
92. Ibid., 14–15.
93. Ibid., 27.
94. Ibid., 28.
95. Ibid.
96. Ibid.
97. Ibid., 28.
98. Ibid.
99. *10th Infantry Division: 1957*, 10.
100. Ibid., 8
101. Ibid., 73.
102. Ibid., 102.
103. Ibid., 130–31.
104. Lane et al., *Operation Gyroscope in the United States Army, Europe*, 46.
105. Ibid., 44.
106. Ibid.
107. Ibid., 44–45.
108. Ibid., 45.
109. Ibid.
110. Ibid., 46.
111. Ibid., 46–47.
112. Ibid., 48.
113. Ibid.
114. Wilson, *Maneuver and Firepower*, 253.
115. Ibid.
116. Ibid.; and Lane et al., *Operation Gyroscope in the United States Army, Europe*, 48–49.
117. Wilson, *Maneuver and Firepower*, 253.
118. Ibid.
119. Ibid.; and Lane et al., *Operation Gyroscope in the United States Army, Europe*, 48.

Chapter 8

1. Lane et al., *Operation Gyroscope in the United States Army, Europe*, 45.
2. Ibid.
3. Ibid.; and Wilson, *Maneuver and Firepower*, 253, 279.
4. *Lineage and Honors, Headquarters and Headquarters Battalion, 10th Mountain Division* (Washington, DC: Center of Military History, updated October 26, 2015), https://history.army.mil/html/forcestruc/lineages/branches/div/010mdhqtbn.htm, retrieved July 24, 2021.
5. Wilson, *Armies, Corps, Divisions, and Separate Brigades*, 160.
6. Ibid.
7. Wilson, *Maneuver and Firepower*, 250.
8. Ibid.
9. Ibid., 251; and *2nd Battalion, 9th Infantry* (Army & Navy Publishing, n.d.), 46.
10. Wilson, *Maneuver and Firepower*, 250; and *2nd Infantry Division, Company A, First Battle Group, Eighty-Seventh Infantry* (Albert Love, n.d.), 23.
11. Ibid., 25; Wilson, *Maneuver and Firepower*, 253; and *2nd Battalion, 9th Infantry*, 46.
12. *2nd Infantry Division, Company A, First Battle Group, Eighty-Seventh Infantry*, 24; and *2nd Battalion, 9th Infantry*, 47.
13. Mahon and Danysh, *Infantry*, part 1, *Regular Army*, 767–68; and *2nd Infantry Division, Company A, First Battle Group, Eighty-Seventh Infantry*, 41–42.
14. Mahon and Danysh, *Infantry*, part 1, *Regular Army*, 766.
15. Ibid.
16. Wilson, *Maneuver and Firepower*, 281.
17. *The Combat Arms Regimental System: Questions and Answers* (Washington, DC: Center of Military History, 1978), 3–4.
18. Wilson, *Maneuver and Firepower*, 281.
19. Ibid.
20. Mahon and Danysh, *Infantry*, part 1, *Regular Army*, 96.
21. *The Combat Arms Regimental System: Questions and Answers*, 9.
22. *2nd Infantry Division, Company A, First Battle Group, Eighty-Seventh Infantry*, 41.
23. Mahon and Danysh, *Infantry*, part 1, *Regular Army*, 767–68.
24. Ibid., 769–71.
25. Jonathan M. House, *Toward Combined Arms Warfare: A Survey of 20th-Century Tactics, Doctrine, and Organization* (Fort Leavenworth, KS: Combat Studies Institute, 1984), 154.
26. Ibid.; and Robert A. Doughty, *The Evolution of US Army Tactical Doctrine, 1946–76* (Fort Leavenworth, KS: Combat Studies Institute, 1979), 16.
27. House, *Toward Combined Arms Warfare*, 154.
28. Doughty, *The Evolution of US Army Tactical Doctrine, 1946–76*, 16.
29. Ibid.; and House, *Toward Combined Arms Warfare*, 155.
30. Doughty, *The Evolution of US Army Tactical Doctrine, 1946–76*, 17; and House, *Toward Combined Arms Warfare*, 155.
31. *2nd Battalion, 9th Infantry*, 47.
32. Ibid.; and "2d Infantry Division," *Army Information Digest*, August 1962, 28.
33. "Strategic Army Corps (STRAC) and Strategic Army Forces (STRAF)," *Army Information* 355-201-1 (August 1961): 133.
34. Ibid.
35. Ibid.
36. "2d Infantry Division," 27–28 and 32–33.
37. Stuart Queen, narr., "Strategic Army Corps (STRAC) Fourth," in *The Big Picture* (Army Pictorial Services, ca. 1960).
38. *2nd Battalion, 9th Infantry*, 47.
39. Ibid.
40. Ibid., 48.
41. *Lineage and Honors, 2nd Battalion, 87th Infantry* (Washington, DC: Center of Military History, 2015), https://history.army.mil/html/forcestruc/lineages/branches/inf/0087in002bn.htm, retrieved August 10, 2020.
43. Ibid.; *2nd Battalion, 9th Infantry*, 48–49; and *Lineage and Honors, 1st Battalion, 87th Infantry* (Washington, DC: Center of Military History, 2015), https://history.army.mil/html/forcestruc/lineages/branches/inf/0087in001bn.htm, retrieved August 10, 2020.
45. Ibid.; and *2nd Battalion, 9th Infantry*, 48–49.
46. *2nd Battalion, 9th Infantry*, 48–49.
47. Wilson, *Maneuver and Firepower*, 293.
48. Ibid.
49. Ibid., 296.

50. House, *Toward Combined Arms Warfare*, 158.

51. Doughty, *The Evolution of US Army Tactical Doctrine, 1946–76*, 21.

52. Ibid.

53. Ibid., 21–22.

54. Wilson, *Maneuver and Firepower*, 297.

55. Ibid.

56. Doughty, *The Evolution of US Army Tactical Doctrine, 1946–76*, 21.

57. House, *Toward Combined Arms Warfare*, 158.

58. Doughty, *The Evolution of US Army Tactical Doctrine, 1946–76*, 23.

59. Ibid., 21.

60. Wilson, *Maneuver and Firepower*, 305–08.

61. Ibid., 310.

62. McGrath, *The Brigade*, 188; and US Army in Germany, "8th Infantry Division (Mech)," https://usarmygermany.com/Sont.htm?https&&&usarmygermany.com/Units/8th%20Inf%20Div/USAREUR_8th%20Inf%20Div.htm, retrieved July 8, 2020.

63. *Lineage and Honors, 1st Battalion, 87th Infantry*.

64. McGrath, *The Brigade*, 188; and US Army in Germany, "8th Infantry Division (Mech)."

65. McGrath, *The Brigade*, 188; *Lineage and Honors, 2nd Battalion, 87th Infantry*; and US Army in Germany, "Locations of 8th Infantry Division (M), Based on Station List for 1974," https://usarmygermany.com/Sont.htm?https&&&usarmygermany.com/Units/8th%20Inf%20Div/USAREUR_8th%20Inf%20Div.htm, retrieved July 8, 2020.

66. *Lineage and Honors, 2nd Battalion, 87th Infantry*.

67. Mahon and Danysh, *Infantry*, part 1, *Regular Army*, 769.

68. Shelby L., Stanton, *Vietnam Order of Battle* (New York: Galahad Books, 1986), 154.

69. *Headquarters and Headquarters Detachment, 92d Military Police Battalion Lineage* (Washington, DC: Center of Military History, 2006), https://history.army.mil/html/forcestruc/lineages/branches/mp/0092mpbn.htm, retrieved August 7, 2020.

70. Stanton, *Vietnam Order of Battle*, 154.

71. Mahon and Danysh, *Infantry*, part 1, *Regular Army*, 769.

72. Ibid.

73. Stanton, *Vietnam Order of Battle*, 155.

74. Pete Cullen and Larry May, *The Trip to Vietnam on the Buckner*, http://alphaassociation.homestead.com/files/index1.htm, retrieved July 10, 2020.

75. Thomas Terry Watson, *History of the 720th Military Police Battalion*, book II, vol. 1, *Vietnam Journal*, ed. Robert P. Schmitz (Alpharetta, GA: Booklogix, 2013), 98.

76. Ibid.

77. Ibid.

78. Ibid.

79. Mahon and Danysh, *Infantry*, part 1, *Regular Army*, 770.

80. Stanton, *Vietnam Order of Battle*, 155.

81. *Operational Report: Lessons Learned, Headquarters, 1st Logistical Command, Period Ending 31 October 1969* (Washington, DC: Department of the Army, December 18, 1969), 117.

82. R. Cody Phillips, *Operation Just Cause: The Incursion into Panama*, CMH Pub. 70-85-1 (Washington, DC: Center of Military History, 2004), 3, 44.

83. *History of the 5th Battalion, 87th Infantry (Light)* (Washington, DC: US Army, n.d.), copy available at the US Army Heritage and Education Center Library, Carlisle Barracks, PA, 5.

84. Ibid.

85. Ibid., 23.

86. Phillips, 6–7, 18–19.

87. Ronald H. Cole, *Operation Just Cause: The Planning and Execution of Joint Operations in Panama, February 1988–January 1990* (Washington, DC: Joint History Office of the Chairman of the Joint Chiefs of Staff, 1995), 37.

88. Thomas Donnelly, Margaret Roth, and Caleb Baker, *Operation Just Cause: The Storming of Panama* (New York: Lexington Books, 1991), 2, 4–5.

89. Ibid., 4.

90. Ibid., 4–5.

91. Ibid., 4.

92. Ibid., 5.

93. Ibid., 6.

94. David E. Johnson, Adam Grissom, and Olga Oliker, *In the Middle of the Fight: An Assessment of Medium-Armored Forces in Past Military Operations* (Santa Monica, CA: RAND Arroyo Center, 2008), 98.

95. Ibid., 98–100.

96. Cole, *Operation Just Cause*, 27.

97. Ibid., 29–30.

98. William Harrison Huff IV, "The United States 1989 Military Intervention in Panama: A Just Cause? (MA thesis, Louisiana State University, 2002), 24.

99. Bob Woodward, *The Commanders* (New York: Simon and Schuster, 1991),133.

100. Donnelly et al., *Operation Just Cause*, 99; and Timothy D. Bloechl, *Operation JUST CAUSE: An Application of Operational Art?* (Fort Leavenworth, KS: School of Advanced Military Studies, 1993), 17, 24, 30–31, 33, 37, 39.

101. Phillips, *Operation Just Cause*, 6–7; Cole, *Operation Just Cause*, 39; and *Operation Just Cause: XVIII Airborne Corps and Joint Task Force South* (Fort Bragg, NC: History Office, XVIII Airborne Corps and Joint Task Force South, n.d., https://history.army.mil/documents/panama/taskorg.htm, retrieved July 25, 2020), 2.

102. Phillips, *Operation Just Cause*, 6–7; Cole, *Operation Just Cause*, 40; and *Operation Just Cause: XVIII Airborne Corps and Joint Task Force South*, 2.

103. Phillips, *Operation Just Cause*, 6–7; Cole, *Operation Just Cause*, 41; and *Operation Just Cause: XVIII Airborne Corps and Joint Task Force South*, 3.

104. *Operation Just Cause: XVIII Airborne Corps and Joint Task Force South*, 4.

105. Phillips, *Operation Just Cause*, 6–7; and Cole, *Operation Just Cause*, 40.

106. Cole, *Operation Just Cause*, 40.

107. *Operation Just Cause: XVIII Airborne Corps and Joint Task Force South*, 2; and Johnson et al., *In the Middle of the Fight*, 104.

108. *Operation Just Cause: XVIII Airborne Corps and Joint Task Force South*, 2.

109. Huff, "The United States 1989 Military Intervention in Panama," 52; and Scott Smith, *Operation in Panama* (Fort Benning, GA: US Army Infantry School, n.d.), 1.

110. Ibid., 51.

111. Ibid.

112. Ibid.

113. Ibid.

114. Ibid., 52.

115. Stacy Elliott, *Operation Just Cause, 3rd Platoon, A Co, "JAGUARS," 5-87 INF* (Fort Benning, GA: US Army Infantry School, 1992), 5.

116. Huff, "The United States 1989 Military Intervention in Panama," 51–52.

117. Smith, *Operation in Panama*, 1.

118. Huff, "The United States 1989 Military Intervention in Panama," 52.

119. Ibid., 53; and Smith, *Operation in Panama*, 3, 5–6.

120. Huff, "The United States 1989 Military Intervention in Panama," 52.

121. Ibid.

122. Ibid.; and *Panamanian Defense Force Order of Battle: Operation Just Cause* (Fort Bragg, NC: History Office, XVIII Airborne Corps and Joint Task Force South, n.d., https://history.army.mil/documents/panama/pdfob.htm, retrieved July 26, 2020), 2.

123. Smith, *Operation in Panama*, 4; and Huff, "The United States 1989 Military Intervention in Panama," 52–53.

124. Huff, "The United States 1989 Military Intervention in Panama," 53.

125. Ibid.

126. Ibid.

127. Elliott, *Operation Just Cause, 3rd Platoon, A Co, "JAGUARS,"* 12.

128. Ibid., 12–14; and Huff, "The United States 1989 Military Intervention in Panama," 54.

129. Huff, "The United States 1989 Military Intervention in Panama," 54; and Elliott, *Operation Just Cause, 3rd Platoon, A Co, "JAGUARS,"* 14–19.

130. Huff, "The United States 1989 Military Intervention in Panama," 54–55.

131. Ibid., 55.

132. Smith, *Operation in Panama*, 1.

133. Ibid., 4–5.

134. Huff, "The United States 1989 Military Intervention in Panama," 55.

135. Smith, *Operation in Panama*, 5–6.

136. Huff, "The United States 1989 Military Intervention in Panama," 56.
137. Smith, *Operation in Panama*, 7–8.
138. Huff, "The United States 1989 Military Intervention in Panama," 56.
139. Ibid.
140. Ibid.
141. Smith, *Operation in Panama*, 7.
142. Huff, "The United States 1989 Military Intervention in Panama," 57–58.
143. *History of the 5th Battalion, 87th Infantry (Light)*, 26.
144. Ibid.
145. Ibid.
146. Ibid., 29.
147. Ibid.
148. Ibid.
149. Ibid., 32.
150. Ibid., 4; and *Headquarters, 193d Infantry Brigade Lineage* (Washington, DC: Center of Military History, 2007), https://history.army.mil/html/forcestruc/lineages/branches/div/193infbde.htm, retrieved August 7, 2020.
151. *History of the 5th Battalion, 87th Infantry (Light)*, 35.
152. Ibid., 38.
153. Association of the United States Army, *Special Report: The US Army in Operation Desert Storm, an Overview* (Arlington, VA: AUSA Institute of Land Warfare, 1991), 10.
154. *Army National Guard After Action Report (2 August 1990–28 February 1991), Operation Desert Shield Operation Desert Storm* (Arlington, VA: National Guard Bureau, 1991), 7.
155. John P. Lewis. *The Army National Guard: Meeting the Needs of the National Military Strategy* (Fort Leavenworth, KS: School of Advanced Military Studies, 1993), 25.
156. *Army National Guard After Action Report*, 7.
157. Ibid.
158. Ibid.; and Lewis, *The Army National Guard*, 26.
159. *FM 100-17, Mobilization, Deployment, Redeployment, Demobilization* (Washington, DC: Department of the Army, 1992), 3-10.
160. John R. Brinkerhoff, John Seitz, and Ted Silva, *Countering the Terrorist Threat: The 3rd Battalion, 87th Infantry* (Washington, DC: Office of the Chief, Army Reserve, 1993), 6.

161. Ibid.
162. Ibid.
163. Ibid., 2.
164. Ibid.
165. Ibid., 3.
166. Ibid., 3–4.
167. Ibid., 4.
168. Ibid., 4–5.
169. Ibid., 5.
170. Ibid.
171. Ibid., 5–6.
172. Ibid., 12.
173. Ibid., 6.
174. Ibid., 18.
175. Ibid., 12–13.
176. Ibid., 13, 17, 20.
177. Ibid.
178. Ibid., 15.
179. Ibid., 16.
180. Ibid., 17.
181. Ibid., 17–18.
182. Ibid., 19.
183. Ibid., 20.
184. Ibid., 1.
185. *US Army, Europe & Seventh Army Fact File, History: 18th Military Police Brigade* (USAREUR and Seventh Army Public Affairs, 2007).
186. Brinkerhoff et al., *Countering the Terrorist Threat*, 22.
187. Ibid.
188. Ibid., 21.
189. Ibid.
190. Ibid., 22.
191. Ibid.
192. Ibid., 22.
193. Ibid., 23, 41n81.
194. Ibid., 24.
195. Ibid., 29.
196. Ibid., 24.
197. Ibid., 23–24.
198. Ibid., 27.
199. Ibid., 25.
200. Ibid.
201. Ibid., 25–26.
202. Ibid., 26.
203. Ibid., 27.
204. Ibid.
205. Ibid., 28.

206. Ibid., 28.
207. Ibid.
208. Ibid.
209. Ibid., 29.
210. Ibid., 31.
211. Ibid.
212. Ibid.
213. Ibid., 32.
214. Ibid.
215. "Infantry—25th Infantry Division Association," https://www.25thida.org/units/infantry, page 25, retrieved June 1, 2020.
216. Bruce E. Stanley, *Military Operations Other Than War: One Soldier's Story* (Fort Leavenworth, KS: US Army Command and General Staff College Press, 1999), 34.
217. Harry Blanco Comacho, interviewed by Dennis Chan and Tito Sablan, Library of Congress American Folklife Center, Veteran's History Project.
218. Ibid.
219. John R. Ballard, *Upholding Democracy: The United States Campaign in Haiti, 1994–1997* (Westport, CT: Praeger, 1998), 39–56, 106–14, 241.
220. Walter E. Kretchik, Robert F. Baumann, and John T. Fishel, *Invasion, Intervention, "Intervasion": A Concise History of the US Army in Operation Uphold Democracy* (Fort Leavenworth, KS: US Army Command and General Staff College Press, 1998), 78–79, 134–35, 145.
221. Stanley, *Military Operations Other Than War*, 16.
222. Ibid., 2.
223. Ibid., 18; and Kretchik et al., *Invasion, Intervention, "Intervasion,"* 135.
224. Stanley, *Military Operations Other Than War*, 19, 25.
225. Ibid., 21, 33.
226. Ibid., 34.
227. Ibid., 33–34.
228. Ibid., 34.
229. Ibid., 40.
230. Ibid., 34–35, 40.
231. Ibid., 40–41.
232. Ibid., 41.
233. Ibid.
234. Ibid., 41–42.
235. Ibid.
236. Ibid., 35.
237. Ibid., 35–39.
238. Ibid., 39.
239. Ibid., 45.
240. Ibid.
241. Ibid., 46.
242. Ibid., 47–48.
243. Ibid., 50.

Chapter 9
1. John L. Romjue, *The Army of Excellence: The Development of the 1980s Army* (Fort Monroe, VA: US Army Training and Doctrine Command, 1993), 4.
2. Wilson, *Maneuver and Firepower*, 379–81.
3. Ibid., 383–84.
4. Ibid., 384.
5. Ibid., 384, 390.
6. John L. Romjue, *A History of Army 86, Volume II: The Development of the Light Division, the Corps, and Echelons above Corps, November 1979–December 1980* (Fort Monroe, VA: US Army Training and Doctrine Command, 1982), 25.
7. Ibid.
8. Ibid., 26.
9. Ibid.
10. Ibid., 26–27.
11. Ibid., 29–30.
12. Ibid., 33.
13. Ibid., 34, 36–41, 46–47.
14. Romjue, *The Army of Excellence*, 16.
15. Ibid., 16–18.
16. Ibid., 18, 23; and Wilson, *Maneuver and Firepower*, 391.
17. Wilson, *Maneuver and Firepower*, 391; and Romjue, *The Army of Excellence*, 24–25, 30–31.
18. Romjue, *The Army of Excellence*, 30.
19. Ibid.
20. Ibid., 35.
21. Ibid., 36.
22. Ibid., 37, 52.
23. Wilson, *Maneuver and Firepower*, 392–95.
24. Romjue, *The Army of Excellence*, 52.
25. Wilson, *Maneuver and Firepower*, 395.
26. Romjue, *The Army of Excellence*, 56.
27. Wilson, *Maneuver and Firepower*, 395.

28. Romjue, *The Army of Excellence*, 69.

29. Ibid., 59, 69–70.

30. Ibid., 70; and Robert Allen Zirkle, *Communities Rule: Intra-service Politics in the United States Army* (Cambridge: Massachusetts Institute of Technology, 2008), 258.

31. Zirkle, *Communities Rule*, 258.

32. Ibid.

33. Ibid.; and Wilson, *Maneuver and Firepower*, 395.

34. "27th Infantry Brigade Combat Team," GlobalSecurity.org, https://www.globalsecurity.org/military/agency/army/27in-bde.htm, retrieved August 8, 2020; and "27th Brigade Combat Team History, https://web.archive.org/web/20181210213302/http://ny.ng.mil/27bct/Pages/History.aspx, retrieved August 8, 2020.

35. McGrath, *The Brigade*, 232.

36. Ibid., 188; Romjue, *The Army of Excellence*, 71; and Zirkle, *Communities Rule*, 258.

37. "Sackets Harbor Forts," American Forts, https://www.northamericanforts.com/East/New_York/Sackets_Harbor/Sackets_Harbor.html, retrieved August 9, 2020.

38. "Fort Pike," New York State Military Museum, https://dmna.ny.gov/forts/fortsM_P/pikeFort.htm, retrieved August 9, 2020.

39. Charles J. Sullivan, *Army Posts & Towns: The Baedeker of the Army* (New York: Free Press, 1926), 75; and "Madison Barracks," New York State Military Museum, https://dmna.ny.gov/forts/fortsM_P/madisonBarracks.htm, retrieved August 9, 2020.

40. Jean Edward Smith, *Grant* (New York: Simon and Schuster, 2001), 74–75, 76, 90.

41. Joseph G. E. Hopkins, ed., *Concise Dictionary of American Biography* (New York: Charles Scribner's Sons, 1964), 380; and "Historical Madison Barracks," https://madisonbarracks.com/historical-madison-barracks/, retrieved August 9, 2020.

42. Duane Colt Denfeld, "Clark, General Mark Wayne (1896–1984)," https://www.historylink.org/File/9004, retrieved August 8, 2020.

43. "History," US Army, Fort Drum, https://home.army.mil/drum/index.php/about/history, retrieved August 9, 2020.

44. Ibid.

45. *Fort Drum Economic Statement Economic Impact Statement Fiscal Year 2000* (Washington, DC: US Army, 2000), 1.

46. Ibid.

47. Ibid.

48. Ibid., 1–2.

49. Ibid.

50. Edwin P. Stouffer, *Fort Drum / 10th Mountain Division Bi-annual Historical Review for October 1, 1984–September 30, 1986* (Washington, DC: US Army, 1987), 3.

51. Ibid., 4–5; and *Lineage and Honors, Headquarters and Headquarters Battalion, 10th Mountain Division.*

52. Stouffer, *Fort Drum / 10th Mountain Division Bi-annual Historical Review*, 6–7; and *Lineage and Honors, 41st Engineer Battalion* (Washington, DC: Center of Military History, 2018), https://history.army.mil/html/forcestruc/lineages/branches/eng/0041enbn.htm, retrieved August 9, 2020.

53. Stouffer, *Fort Drum / 10th Mountain Division Bi-annual Historical Review*, 7; and *Lineage and Honors, Headquarters, 2nd Brigade Combat Team, 10th Mountain Division (Commandos)* (Washington, DC: Center of Military History, 2013), https://history.army.mil/html/forcestruc/lineages/branches/div/010md2bct.htm, retrieved August 9, 2020.

54. Stouffer, *Fort Drum / 10th Mountain Division Bi-annual Historical Review*, 9; and *Lineage and Honors, Headquarters and Headquarters Company, 1st Brigade Combat Team* (Washington, DC: Center of Military History, 2016), https://history.army.mil/html/forcestruc/lineages/branches/div/010md1bct.htm, retrieved August 9, 2020.

55. Stouffer, *Fort Drum / 10th Mountain Division Bi-annual Historical Review*, 10; and *Lineage and Honors, 1st Battalion, 22nd Infantry Regiment* (Washington, DC: Center of Military History, 2009), https://history.army.mil/html/forcestruc/lineages/branches/inf/0022in001bn.htm, retrieved August 9, 2020.

56. Stouffer, *Fort Drum / 10th Mountain Division Bi-annual Historical Review*, 12; *Lineage and Honors, 2nd Battalion, 22nd Infantry Regiment* (Washington, DC: Center of Military History,

2016), https://history.army.mil/html/forcestruc/lineages/branches/inf/0022in002bn.htm, retrieved August 9, 2020; and *Lineage and Honors, 1st Battalion, 7th Field Artillery* (Washington, DC: Center of Military History, 2012), https://history.army.mil/html/forcestruc/lineages/branches/fa/0007fa01bn.htm, retrieved August 9, 2020.

57. *Annual Historical Review, 10th Mountain Division (LI), Fiscal Year 1987* (10th Mountain Division, G-3 Plans, 1988), 14, 17; *Lineage and Honors, 2nd Battalion, 7th Field Artillery Regiment* (Washington, DC: Center of Military History, 2012), https://history.army.mil/html/forcestruc/lineages/branches/fa/0007fa01bn.htm, retrieved August 10, 2020; *Lineage and Honors, 1st Battalion, 87th Infantry Regiment* (Washington, DC: Center of Military History, 2012), https://history.army.mil/html/forcestruc/lineages/branches/inf/0087in001bn.htm, retrieved August 10, 2020; and *Lineage and Honors Information, 10th Signal Battalion* (Washington, DC: Center of Military History, 1995), https://history.army.mil/html/forcestruc/lineages/branches/sc/0010scbn.htm, retrieved August 10, 2020.

58. Judith M. DeSantis, *Fort Drum / 10th Mountain Division Public Affairs Office Annual Historical Review, 1 October 1987–30 September 1988* (Washington, DC: US Army, 1989), 3; and *Lineage and Honors, 2nd Battalion, 87th Infantry Regiment*.

59. *Annual Historical Review, 10th Mountain Division (LI), Fiscal Year 1987*, 4, figures 1-1 and 1-2; *Lineage and Honors, Headquarters and Headquarters Company, Combat Aviation Brigade, 10th Mountain Division* (Washington, DC: Center of Military History, 2018), https://history.army.mil/html/forcestruc/lineages/branches/div/010mdCAB.htm, retrieved August 10, 2020; *Lineage and Honors Information, 3rd Squadron, 17th Cavalry Lineage* (Washington, DC: Center of Military History, 1996), https://history.army.mil/html/forcestruc/lineages/branches/armor-cav/017cv003sq.htm, retrieved August 10, 2020; *Lineage and Honors, 2nd Battalion, 25th Aviation Regiment* (Washington, DC: Center of Military History, 2018), https://

history.army.mil/html/forcestruc/lineages/branches/av/025av002bn.htm, retrieved August 10, 2020; *Lineage and Honors, 3rd Battalion, 25th Aviation Regiment* (Washington, DC: Center of Military History, 2011), https://history.army.mil/html/forcestruc/lineages/branches/av/025av003bn.htm, retrieved August 10, 2020; and *Lineage and Honors, 59th Chemical Company* (Washington, DC: Center of Military History, 2011), https://history.army.mil/html/forcestruc/lineages/branches/chem/059cmco.htm, retrieved August 10, 2020.

60. *Annual Historical Review, 10th Mountain Division (LI), Fiscal Year 1989* (10th Mountain Division, G-3 Plans, 1990), figures 1-1 and 1-2 and page V-1.

61. *Fort Drum Economic Statement Economic Impact Statement Fiscal Year 2000*, 5.

62. *Lineage and Honors, Headquarters, 3rd Brigade Combat Team, 10th Mountain Division* (Washington, DC: Center of Military History, 2011), https://history.army.mil/html/forcestruc/lineages/branches/div/010md3bct.htm, retrieved August 15, 2020; and *Lineage and Honors Information, Headquarters, 4th Brigade Combat Team, 10th Mountain Division (Patriot Brigade)* (Washington, DC: Center of Military History, 2007), https://history.army.mil/html/forcestruc/lineages/branches/div/010md4bct.htm, retrieved August 15, 2020.

63. Brandon J. Iker, *10th Mountain Division Light Infantry Annual Historical Summary, 1 January 2004—31 December 2004* (10th Mountain Division Light Infantry G3, 2005), 158–60.

64. Douglas R. Cubbison, *10th Mountain Division (Light Infantry) Annual Historical Summary, 1 January 2005–31 December 2005* (10th Mountain Division Command Historian, 2006), 22.

65. Ibid., 124.

66. "3rd Brigade Combat Team," US Army, Fort Drum; and "10th Mountain Division's 4th Brigade Transforms to 3rd Brigade," *Beauregard Daily News*, February 28, 2015.

67. "Army May Keep Program for Active, Guard Units," *Association of the United States Army*, August 6, 2019.

68. "3rd Brigade Combat Team," US Army, Fort Drum, https://home.army.mil/drum/index.

php/units-tenants/3rd-BCT, retrieved August 15, 2020.

69. DeSantis, *Fort Drum / 10th Mountain Division Public Affairs Office Annual Historical Review*, 6; *Annual Historical Review, 10th Mountain Division (LI), Fiscal Year 1989*, figure III-1 and page V-2; and *Annual Historical Review, 10th Mountain Division (LI), Fiscal Year 1987*, 5.

70. *Fort Drum Economic Statement Economic Impact Statement Fiscal Year 2000*, 5.

71. *Annual Historical Review, 10th Mountain Division (LI), Fiscal Year 1987*, 5; and *Annual Historical Review, 10th Mountain Division (LI), Fiscal Year 1988*, figure III-1.

72. "548th Combat Sustainment Support Battalion," GlobalSecurity.org, https://www.globalsecurity.org/military/agency/army/548csb.htm, retrieved August 12, 2020.

73. Ibid.

74. Ibid.

75. Sierra Sarkis, "The 25th Anniversary of Hurricane Andrew," *Atlantic Oceanographic and Meteorological Laboratory*, https://www.aoml.noaa.gov/keynotes/keynotes_0817_andrew25.html, retrieved August 12, 2020; *Forces Command Hurricane Andrew Response After Action Report*, part 2 (Forces Command, n.d.), 17; and Ramon Valle, *Is a Deployable Joint Task Force Augmentation Cell (DJTFAC) a Viable Tool for U.S. Northern Command during Consequence Management Operations?* (Fort Leavenworth, KS: School of Advanced Military Studies, 2003), 34.

76. Sarkis, "The 25th Anniversary of Hurricane Andrew."

77. Valle, *Is a Deployable Joint Task Force Augmentation Cell (DJTFAC) a Viable Tool for U.S. Northern Command during Consequence Management Operations?*, 34.

78. Dave Wellons, *Doctrine for Domestic Disaster Response Activities* (Fort Leavenworth, KS: School of Advanced Military Studies, 2000), 18; and Jacob Middleton, *Calling the Cavalry: Disaster Relief and the American Military* (Maxwell Air Force Base, AL: School of Advanced Air and Space Studies, 2011), 30, citing the *Miami Herald*, January 31, 1993.

79. Wellons, *Doctrine for Domestic Disaster Response Activities*, 18.

80. A. G. Smart, *Military Support to Domestic Disaster Relief: Doctrine for Operating in the Wake of the Enemy?* (Fort Leavenworth, KS: School of Advanced Military Studies, 1993), 23.

81. Wellons, *Doctrine for Domestic Disaster Response Activities*, 19.

82. Eugene R. Woolridge III, *Challenges and Considerations for Employing Military Chaplains in the Homeland in Support of US Northern Command* (Carlisle Barracks, PA: US Army War College, 2005), 9.

83. Wellons, *Doctrine for Domestic Disaster Response Activities*, 19.

84. *Joint Task Force Andrew After Action Report (AAR)*, vol. 1 (Forces Command, n.d.), 3.

85. Ibid., 4.

86. Smart, *Military Support to Domestic Disaster Relief*, 47.

87. Ibid.

88. *Forces Command Hurricane Andrew Response After Action Report*, 2:19–20.

89. Ibid., 2:20.

90. S. L. Arnold and David T. Stahl, "A Power Projection Army in Operations Other Than War," *Parameters*, Winter 1993, 4–5.

91. Smart, *Military Support to Domestic Disaster Relief*, 47.

92. Arnold and Stahl, "A Power Projection Army in Operations Other Than War," 5.

93. *Forces Command Hurricane Andrew Response After Action Report*, part 1 (Forces Command, n.d.), 4.

94. *Forces Command Hurricane Andrew Response After Action Report*, 2:22–23.

95. Ibid., 23.

96. Ibid.; and Gay M. McGillis, *Organizing NORTHCOM for Success: A Theater Special Operations Command* (Fort Leavenworth, KS: School of Advanced Military Studies, 2003), 24.

97. *Forces Command Hurricane Andrew Response After Action Report*, 2:24.

98. Ibid.

99. Robert M. Ralston and Douglas L. Horn, "Engineers Respond to Operations Other Than War," Engineer 23 PB 5-93-2 (April 1993): 13.

100. *Forces Command Hurricane Andrew Response After Action Report*, 2:23.

101. Ibid., 27–28.

102. Ibid., 28.

103. Thomas R. Lujan, *Legal Aspects of Domestic Deployment of the Army* (Carlisle Barracks, PA: US Army War College, 1996), 3.

104. Ibid., 2.

105. Ibid., 3.

106. Ibid., 3–4; and *Forces Command Hurricane Andrew Response After Action Report*, 2:12–13.

107. Ibid.

108. Smart, *Military Support to Domestic Disaster Relief*, 47.

109. *Forces Command Hurricane Andrew Response After Action Report*, 2:17–18.

110. Arnold and Stahl, "A Power Projection Army in Operations Other Than War," 4.

111. Helen Chapin Metz, ed., *Somalia: A Country Study* (Washington, DC: Headquarters, Department of the Army, 1993), xiii.

112. Ibid., xx.

113. Ibid., xxi, 3.

114. Ibid., 3.

115. Ibid., xxi, 12.

116. Margaret Castagno, *Historical Dictionary of Somalia* (Lanham, MD: Scarecrow, 1975), xiii.

117. "Djibouti," in *The World Factbook* (Central Intelligence Agency, 2020), https://www.cia.gov/library/publications/the-world-factbook/geos/dj.html, retrieved August 15, 2020.

118. Castagno, *Historical Dictionary of Somalia*, xiv.

119. Ibid.

120. Metz, *Somalia: A Country Study*, 92.

121. Ibid., xxvi.

122. Ibid., xxi, 94.

123. Castagno, *Historical Dictionary of Somalia*, 34.

124. Ibid., 34, 261.

125. Ibid., 34, 136.

126. Ibid., 133.

127. Metz, *Somalia: A Country Study*, xxviii–xxix, 50–51; and Lawrence E. Casper, *Falcon Brigade:*

Combat and Command in Somalia and Haiti (Boulder, CO: Lynne Rienner, 2001), 18.

128. Ibid., 92–93.

129. Ibid., 93–94.

130. Ibid., 94.

131. James O. Tubbs, *Beyond Gunboat Diplomacy: Forceful Applications of Airpower in Peace Enforcement Operations* (Maxwell Air Force Base, AL: Air University Press, 1997), 31.

132. Walter S. Poole, *The Effort to Save Somalia, August 1992–March 1994* (Washington, DC: Joint History Office, 2005), 6.

133. Ibid., 7–8; Christopher L. Baggott, *A Leap into the Darkness: Crisis Action Planning for Operation Restore Hope* (Fort Leavenworth, KS: School of Advanced Military Studies, 1997), 9; and Kenneth Allard, *Somalia Operations: Lessons Learned* (Washington, DC: National Defense University Press, 1995), 15.

134. Allard, *Somalia Operations*, 14.

135. Ibid., 15.

136. Baggott, *A Leap into the Darkness*, 9.

137. Poole, *The Effort to Save Somalia, August 1992–March 1994*, 10, 18.

138. Ibid., 16, 19–20.

139. Ibid., 6; Brad Poore, "Somaliland: Shackled to a Failed State," *Stanford Journal of International Law* 45 (2009): 117; and Markus V. Höhne, "Political Identity, Emerging State Structures and Conflict in Northern Somalia," *Journal of Modern African Studies* 44, no. 3 (2006): 397–414.

140. Poole, *The Effort to Save Somalia, August 1992–March 1994*, 6, 11, 16–17; and Metz, *Somalia: A Country Study*, xxix;

141. Poole, *The Effort to Save Somalia, August 1992–March 1994*, 16.

142. Ibid., 17, 21.

143. Ibid., 22.

144. Allard, *Somalia Operations*, 15.

145. Richard W. Stewart, *The United States Army in Somalia, 1992–1994* (Washington, DC: Center of Military History, 2002), 9.

146. Ibid., 9.

147. Ibid.

148. Ibid., 10; and Arnold and Stahl, "A Power Projection Army in Operations Other Than War," 8.

149. Arnold and Stahl, "A Power Projection Army in Operations Other Than War," 9.
150. Ibid.
151. Stewart, *The United States Army in Somalia, 1992–1994*, 11–12.
152. Poole, *The Effort to Save Somalia, August 1992–March 1994*, 25; and Martin Stanton, *Somalia on $5.00 a Day: A Soldier's Story* (Novato, CA: Presidio, 2001), 71, 77.
153. Stewart, *The United States Army in Somalia, 1992–1994*, 11; and Stanton, *Somalia on $5.00 a Day*, 105.
154. Stanton, *Somalia on $5.00 a Day*, 84.
155. Ibid., 73, 81.
156. Ibid., 99.
157. Ibid., 102–03.
158. Ibid., 103.
159. Ibid., 123.
160. Ibid., 140.
161. Ibid., 111.
162. Ibid., 266–67.
163. Allard, *Somalia Operations*, 15.
164. Poole, *The Effort to Save Somalia, August 1992–March 1994*, 36–37.
165. Casper, *Falcon Brigade*, 11.
166. R. D. Hooker Jr., "Hard Day's Night: A Retrospective on the American Intervention in Somalia," *Joint Forces Quarterly* 54, no. 3 (2009), 129.
167. Ibid., 130; and James C. Dixon Jr., *United Nations Operation in Somalia II: United Nations Unity of Effort and United States Unity of Command* (Carlisle Barracks, PA: US Army War College, 1996), 65.
168. Dixon, *United Nations Operation in Somalia II*, 78–79, 137.
169. Ibid., 81; Stewart, *The United States Army in Somalia, 1992–1994*, 21; and Stanton, *Somalia on $5.00 a Day*, 73.
170. Hooker, "Hard Day's Night," 130.
171. Dixon, *United Nations Operation in Somalia II*, 87.
172. Casper, *Falcon Brigade*, 31; and Hooker, "Hard Day's Night," 131.
173. Hooker, "Hard Day's Night," 131.
174. Ibid.
175. Casper, *Falcon Brigade*, 32; and Hooker, "Hard Day's Night," 131.
176. Stewart, *The United States Army in Somalia, 1992–1994*, 19; and Hooker, "Hard Day's Night," 131.
177. Ibid.
178. Ibid., 131–32.
179. Ibid., 133.
180. Ibid., 131.
181. Ibid., 134.
182. Stewart, *The United States Army in Somalia, 1992–1994*, 18.
183. Ibid., 19; and Hooker, "Hard Day's Night," 133.
184. Ibid.
185. Stewart, *The United States Army in Somalia, 1992–1994*, 19.
186. Ibid.
187. Ibid., 19–21.
188. Ibid., 21.
189. Ibid.
190. Ibid.; and Casper, *Falcon Brigade*, 41, 62.
191. Casper, *Falcon Brigade*, 44.
192. Ibid., 45.
193. Ibid.
194. Ibid., 40.
195. Ibid., 46.
196. Ibid.
197. Ibid., 48.
198. Hooker, "Hard Day's Night," 134.
199. Casper, *Falcon Brigade*, 53–55, 59–64.
200. Ibid., 53–54.
201. Ibid., 59, 63; and Stewart, *The United States Army in Somalia, 1992–1994*, 22.
202. Stewart, *The United States Army in Somalia, 1992–1994*, 22; and Casper, *Falcon Brigade*, 56.
203. Casper, *Falcon Brigade*, 67
204. Ibid., 68.
205. Stewart, *The United States Army in Somalia, 1992–1994*, 22–23; and Casper, *Falcon Brigade*, 67–68.
206. Casper, *Falcon Brigade*, 68.
207. Stewart, *The United States Army in Somalia, 1992–1994*, 23.
208. Ibid., and Casper, *Falcon Brigade*, 63.
209. Ibid., 83.
210. Stewart, *The United States Army in Somalia, 1992–1994*, 23; and Casper, *Falcon Brigade*, 83.
211. Stewart, *The United States Army in Somalia, 1992–1994*, 23; and Casper, *Falcon Brigade*, 85.

212. Casper, *Falcon Brigade*, 85–86.
213. Ibid., 86.
214. Stewart, *The United States Army in Somalia, 1992–1994*, 23.
215. Ibid.
216. Ibid., 24.
217. Ibid.; and Dixon, *United Nations Operation in Somalia II*, 139.
218. Stewart, *The United States Army in Somalia, 1992–1994*, 24–25.
219. Ibid., 25.
220. Arnold and Stahl, "A Power Projection Army in Operations Other Than War," 6–7.
221. Richard A. Haggerty, ed., *Dominican Republic and Haiti: Country Studies* (Washington, DC: US Army, 1991), 194.
222. Ibid., xvii.
223. Ibid., 207–13.
224. Ibid., xviii.
225. Ibid., 207–32.
226. Ibid., 231.
227. Ibid., 232.
228. Ibid., 234.
229. Ibid., 236–37.
230. Ibid., 237–38.
231. Ibid., xix.
232. Ibid., xx.; and Ballard, *Upholding Democracy*, 44.
233. Haggerty, *Dominican Republic and Haiti*, xxiv; and Ballard, *Upholding Democracy*, 46.
234. Haggerty, *Dominican Republic and Haiti*, xxiv.
235. Ballard, *Upholding Democracy*, 48–49.
236. Ibid., 46; and Kretchik et al., *Invasion, Intervention, "Intervasion,"* 20, 27.
237. Kretchik et al., *Invasion, Intervention, "Intervasion,"* 34.
238. Ibid., 33–34.
239. Ibid., 38.
240. Ibid., 39–41.
241. Riehm, "The USS *Harlan County* Affair."
242. Kretchik et al., *Invasion, Intervention, "Intervasion,"* 43.
243. Ibid.
244. Robert F. Baumann, "Operation Uphold Democracy: Power under Control," *Military Review* 77 (July–August 1997).
245. Ibid.

246. Ibid.
247. Ibid.
248. Casper, *Falcon Brigade*, 151; and *Annual Historical Review, 10th Mountain Division (LI), Calendar Year 1994* (10th Mountain Division G-3 Plans, 1995), i.
249. *Annual Historical Review, 10th Mountain Division (LI), Calendar Year 1994*, 24–25.
250. Casper, *Falcon Brigade*, 167; and *Annual Historical Review, 10th Mountain Division (LI), Calendar Year 1994*, 55, 81.
251. Casper, *Falcon Brigade*, 168; and Ballard, *Upholding Democracy*, 188.
252. Casper, *Falcon Brigade*, 168.
253. Ibid., 168–69.
254. Ibid., 170–74.
255. Ballard, *Upholding Democracy*, 93; and *Annual Historical Review, 10th Mountain Division (LI), Calendar Year 1994*, 82.
256. *Annual Historical Review, 10th Mountain Division (LI), Calendar Year 1994*, 55.
257. Ibid., 59.
258. Ibid., 67.
259. Ibid., 72.
260. Casper, *Falcon Brigade*, 205–06.
261. Ibid., 208.
262. Ibid., 208–09.
263. Ballard, *Upholding Democracy*, 110.
264. *Annual Historical Review, 10th Mountain Division (LI), Calendar Year 1994*, 57.
265. Ibid.
266. Ibid., 56; and Kretchik et al., *Invasion, Intervention, "Intervasion,"* 39.
267. *Annual Historical Review, 10th Mountain Division (LI), Calendar Year 1994*, 56; and Ballard, *Upholding Democracy*, 125.
268. Ballard, *Upholding Democracy*, 114, 118; and *Annual Historical Review, 10th Mountain Division (LI), Calendar Year 1994*, 59, 64.
269. *Annual Historical Review, 10th Mountain Division (LI), Calendar Year 1994*, 71.
270. Ibid.
271. Ibid., 64.
272. Ibid.
273. Ibid.
274. Ibid.
275. Ibid., 64, 67.
276. Ibid., 68.

277. Ibid.

278. Ibid.

279. Ibid.

280. Ibid., 68–69.

281. Ibid., 69.

282. Ibid., 67, 69.

283. Kretchik et al., *Invasion, Intervention, "Intervasion,"* 143.

284. Ibid., 145.

285. Ibid., 135.

286. *Annual Historical Review, 10th Mountain Division (LI), Calendar Year 1995* (10th Mountain Division G-3 Plans, 1996), 3-A, 67.

287. *Annual Historical Review, 10th Mountain Division (LI), Calendar Year 1994*, 32.

288. Steve Lively, *Annual Historical Summary, 10th Mountain Division Light Infantry, 1 January 2001–31 December 2002* [*sic*; should be 2001] (10th Mountain Division Light Infantry G3, 2002), 28.

289. Ibid., 2.

290. *Lineage and Honors, 4th Battalion, 31st Infantry Regiment (The Polar Bears)* (Washington, DC: Department of the Army, 2018), https://history.army.mil/html/forcestruc/lineages/branches/inf/0031in004bn.htm, retrieved September 20, 2020.

291. Ibid.

292. Ibid.

293. Ibid.

294. Lively, *Annual Historical Summary, 10th Mountain Division Light Infantry, 1 January 2001–31 December 2002* [*sic*; 2001], 75.

295. Ibid.

296. Ibid.

297. Donald P. Wright, James R. Bird, Steven E. Clay, et al., *A Different Kind of War: The United States Army in Operation Enduring Freedom, 2001–2005* (Fort Leavenworth, KS: Combat Studies Institute Press, 2010), 62.

298. Ibid., 67, 331; Lively, *Annual Historical Summary, 10th Mountain Division Light Infantry, 1 January 2001–31 December 2002* [*sic*; 2001], 67; and Steve Lively, *Annual Historical Summary, 10th Mountain Division Light Infantry, 1 January 2002–31 December 2002* (10th Mountain Division Light Infantry, 2003), 82.

299. Lively, *Annual Historical Summary, 10th Mountain Division Light Infantry, 1 January 2001–31 December 2002* [*sic*; 2001], 75; and Wright et al., *A Different Kind of War*, 166.

300. Lively, *Annual Historical Summary, 10th Mountain Division Light Infantry, 1 January 2002–31 December 2002* [*sic*; 2001], 88; and Wright et al., *A Different Kind of War*, 331, 339.

301. Lively, *Annual Historical Summary, 10th Mountain Division Light Infantry, 1 January 2001–31 December 2002* [*sic*; 2001], 88.

302. Ibid.

303. Wright et al., *A Different Kind of War*, 333; and Joseph M. Burkhardt, *Annual Historical Summary, 10th Mountain Division Light Infantry, 1 January 2003–31 December 2003* (10th Mountain Division Light Infantry G3, 2003), 5.

304. Wright et al., *A Different Kind of War*, 238.

305. Ibid.

306. Burkhardt, *Annual Historical Summary, 10th Mountain Division Light Infantry, 1 January 2003–31 December 2003*, 5.

307. Wright et al., *A Different Kind of War*, 334; and Burkhardt, *Annual Historical Summary, 10th Mountain Division Light Infantry, 1 January 2003–31 December 2003*, 108–09.

308. Wright et al., *A Different Kind of War*, 248–49.

309. Ibid., 249.

310. Ibid., 250.

311. Ibid., 252.

312. Ibid., 253.

313. Ibid.

314. Ibid.

315. Ibid.

316. Ibid.

317. Burkhardt, *Annual Historical Summary, 10th Mountain Division Light Infantry, 1 January 2003–31 December 2003*, 5, 108.

318. Ibid., 116; and Wright et al., *A Different Kind of War*, 232–33.

319. Wright et al., *A Different Kind of War*, 232–33, 332.

320. Ibid., 233, 346.

321. Burkhardt, *Annual Historical Summary, 10th Mountain Division Light Infantry, 1 January 2003–31 December 2003*, 116.

322. Ibid.

323. Ibid.

324. Ibid., 117; and Wright et al., *A Different Kind of War*, 332.

325. Burkhardt, *Annual Historical Summary, 10th Mountain Division Light Infantry, 1 January 2003–31 December 2003*, 116–17.

326. Ibid., 115.

327. Ibid., 116.

328. Ibid.

329. Iker, *10th Mountain Division Light Infantry Annual Historical Summary, 1 January 2004–31 December 2004*, 12.

330. Ibid.

331. Ibid., 12, 158–63.

332. Ibid., 140.

333. Iker, 10.

334. Ibid., 148.

335. Ibid., 148–49.

336. Ibid., 149.

337. Ibid.

338. Ibid.

339. Ibid.

340. Ibid., 149–50.

341. Ibid., 150.

342. Ibid.

343. Ibid.; and Donald P. Wright and Timothy R. Reese, *On Point II: Transition to the New Campaign; The United States Army in Operation Iraqi Freedom, May 2003–January 2005* (Fort Leavenworth, KS: Combat Studies Institute, 2008), 344–49.

344. Wright and Reese, *On Point II*, 344–45.

345. Iker, *10th Mountain Division Light Infantry Annual Historical Summary, 1 January 2004–31 December 2004*, 150.

346. Ibid.

347. Ibid.

348. Ibid.

349. Ibid.

350. "Iraqi Elections: January 30, 2005" (US Department of State, Bureau of Public Affairs, 2005), https://2001-2009.state.gov/documents/organization/41314.pdf, retrieved September 29, 2020; and "Rebuilding Iraq: US Assistance for the January 2005 Elections" (US Government Accountability Office, 2005), https://www.gao.gov/new.items/d05932r.pdf, retrieved September 29, 2005.

351. "Rebuilding Iraq: US Assistance for the January 2005 Elections," 8.

352. Douglas R. Cubbison, *10th Mountain Division (Light Infantry), Annual Command History, 1 January 2006–31 December 2006* (10th Mountain Division, 2007), 111.

353. Ibid.

354. Ibid., 112.

355. Ibid., 111.

356. Ibid.

357. Ibid., 111–12.

358. Ibid., 112.

359. Ibid.

360. Ibid.

361. Ibid., 113.

362. Ibid.

363. Iker, 150.

364. Ibid.

365. Ibid., 153.

366. Ibid., 150.

367. Ibid., 150–51.

368. Ibid.

369. Wright and Reese, *On Point II*, 389.

370. Cubbison, *10th Mountain Division (Light Infantry), Annual Command History, 1 January 2006–31 December 2006*, 113.

371. Ibid., 23; and Cubbison, *10th Mountain Division (Light Infantry), Annual Command History, 1 January 2006–31 December 2006*, 21, 33.

372. Cubbison, *10th Mountain Division (Light Infantry), Annual Command History, 1 January 2006–31 December 2006*, 82.

373. Ibid.

374. Ibid.

375. Ibid., 85–86.

376. Ibid.

377. Ibid., 86.

378. Ibid., 85.

379. Burkhardt, *Annual Historical Summary, 10th Mountain Division Light Infantry, 1 January 2003–31 December 2003*, 41; Iker, *10th Mountain Division Light Infantry Annual Historical Summary, 1 January 2004–31 December 2004*, 158–65; and Cubbison, *10th Mountain Division (Light Infantry), Annual Command History, 1 January 2006–31 December 2006*, 115–31.

380. Stuart E. Johnson, John E. Peters, Karin E. Kitchen, Aaron Martin, and Jordan R. Fischbach, *A Review of the Army's Modular Force Structure* (Santa Monica, CA: RAND Arroyo Center, 2012), iii.

381. Ibid.; and Thomas F. Talley, *Is Reorganization of the Army under the Unit-of-Action and Unit-of-Employment Concept Consistent with the Army's Identity?* (Fort Leavenworth, KS: US Army Command and General Staff College, 2004), 85.

382. Talley, *Is Reorganization of the Army under the Unit-of-Action and Unit-of-Employment Concept Consistent with the Army's Identity?*, 85.

383. Johnson et al., *A Review of the Army's Modular Force Structure*, iii.

384. Ibid., 21.

385. Ibid., 21, 26.

386. Ibid., 26–28.

387. Burkhardt, *Annual Historical Summary, 10th Mountain Division Light Infantry, 1 January 2003–31 December 2003*, 41; and Iker, *10th Mountain Division Light Infantry Annual Historical Summary, 1 January 2004–31 December 2004*, 13.

388. Iker, *10th Mountain Division Light Infantry Annual Historical Summary, 1 January 2004–31 December 2004*, 13, 45, 50–51.

389. Ibid., 49.

390. Ibid., 140–41.

391. Ibid., 149.

392. Cubbison, *10th Mountain Division (Light Infantry), Annual Command History, 1 January 2006–31 December 2006*, 38.

393. "10th Mountain Division's 4th Brigade Transforms to 3rd Brigade," *Beauregard Daily News*, February 28, 2015, https://www.beauregarddailynews.net/article/20150228/NEWS/150229708, retrieved August 9, 2020.

Conclusion

1. "US Troops Complete Their Withdrawal from Iraq," *Herald Sun News*, December 18, 2011, https://web.archive.org/web/20140304204059/http://www.heraldsun.com.au/news/breaking-news/us-troops-complete-their-withdrawal-from-iraq/story-e6frf7jx-1226225154019, retrieved October 4, 2020.

2. Jim Garamone, "DoD Authorizes War on Terror Award for Inherent Resolve Ops," *DOD News*.

3. "Camp Taji Handover: A Significant Milestone and New Phase in Ensuring the Enduring Defeat of Daesh," Global Coalition, August 26, 2020, https://theglobalcoalition.org/en/camp-taji-handover/, retrieved October 4, 2020.

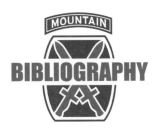

Aleutian Islands. CMH Pub. 72-6. Washington, DC: Center of Military History, 1992.

Allard, Kenneth. *Somalia Operations: Lessons Learned*. Washington, DC: National Defense University Press, 1995.

"Al-Shabaab (Al-Shabab), the Supreme Islamic Courts Union (ICU)." GlobalSecurity.org. https://www.globalsecurity.org/military/world/para/al-shabaab.htm, retrieved August 23, 2020.

American Military History. Army Historical Series. Washington, DC: Center of Military History, 1989.

Anderson, Rich. "The United States Army in World War II." Military History Online. https://www.militaryhistoryonline.com/WWII/USArmy, retrieved April 18, 2020.

Annual Historical Review, 10th Mountain Division (LI), Fiscal Year 1987. 10th Mountain Division, G-3 Plans, 1988.

Annual Historical Review, 10th Mountain Division (LI), Fiscal Year 1989. 10th Mountain Division, G-3 Plans, 1990.

Annual Historical Review, 10th Mountain Division (LI), Calendar Year 1994. 10th Mountain Division G-3 Plans, 1995.

Annual Historical Review, 10th Mountain Division (LI), Calendar Year 1995. 10th Mountain Division G-3 Plans, 1996.

Annual Historical Review, 10th Mountain Division (LI), Calendar Year 1997. 10th Mountain Division (LI), G3 Plans, 1998.

Archibald, Dan, Adam Smith, Sunny Adams, and Manroop Chawla. *Military Training Lands Historic Context Training Village, Mock Sites, and Large Scale Operations Areas*. ERDC/CERL TR-10-10. Champaign, IL: US Army Corps of Engineers Engineer Research and Development Center, March 2010.

"Armies on Skiis." *Mid-Week Pictorial* 41, no. 3 (March 2, 1935).

The Army Lineage Book. Vol. 2, *Infantry*. Washington, DC: Department of the Army, 1953.

"Army May Keep Program for Active, Guard Units." Association of the United States Army, August 6, 2019. https://www.ausa.org/news/army-may-keep-program-active-guard-units, retrieved August 15, 2020.

Army National Guard After Action Report (2 August 1990–28 February 1991), Operation Desert Shield Operation Desert Storm. Arlington, VA: National Guard Bureau, 1991.

Army Regulation 870–21. In *The US Army Regimental System*. Headquarters, Department of the Army, April 13, 2017.

"Army's New Ski Patrol Practices on the Snowy Slopes of Mt. Rainier." *Life*, January 20, 1941.

Arnold, S. L., and David T. Stahl. "A Power Projection Army in Operations Other Than War." *Parameters*, Winter 1993–94.

Aron, Robert. *The Vichy Regime, 1940–44*. London: Putnam, 1958.

Association of the United States Army. *Special Report: The US Army in Operation Desert Storm, an Overview*. Arlington, VA: AUSA Institute of Land Warfare, 1991.

Ayres, Leonard P. *The War with Germany: A Statistical Summary*. 2nd ed. Department of the Army, Washington, DC: Government Printing Office, 1919.

Baggott, Christopher L. *A Leap into the Darkness: Crisis Action Planning for Operation Restore Hope*. Fort Leavenworth, KS: School of Advanced Military Studies, 1997.

Ballard, John R. *Upholding Democracy: The United States Campaign in Haiti, 1994–1997*. Westport, CT: Praeger, 1998.

Barry, John M. "The Site of Origin of the 1918 Influenza Pandemic and Its Public Health Implications." *Journal of Translational Medicine* 2, no. 3 (2004): 2.

Bartling, Donald G. *For Country: My Little Bit, Twenty-One Months of Service*. La Vergne, TN: PageTurner Press and Media, 2018.

Battleship Cove. "USS *Massachusetts* (BB-59)." https://www.battleshipcove.org/uss-massa-chusetts-bb59, retrieved April 11, 2020.

Baumann, Robert F. "Operation Uphold Democracy: Power under Control." *Military Review* 77 (July–August 1997), file:///C:/Users/Dennis/Downloads/427.pdf, retrieved September 13, 2020.

Benedict, H. Bradley. *Ski Troops in the Mud: Kiska Island Recaptured; A Saga of the North Pacific Campaign in the Aleutian Islands in World War II, with Special Emphasis on Its Culmination Led by the Forerunners of the 10th Mountain Division*. Littleton, CO: H. B. & J. C. Benedict, 1990.

Benson, Jack A. "Skiing at Camp Hale: Mountain Troops during World War II." *Western Historical Quarterly*, April 1984, 163–74.

Bethel, John P., general ed. "Apennines." *Webster's Geographical Dictionary*. New York: Merriam, 1959.

Biennial Report of the Chief of Staff of the United States Army, July 1, 1939–June 30, 1941. Washington, DC: Government Printing Office, 1941.

Bloechl, Timothy D. *Operation JUST CAUSE: An Application of Operational Art?* Fort Leavenworth, KS: School of Advanced Military Studies, 1993.

Blumenson, Martin. *Salerno to Cassino*. Washington, DC: Center of Military History, 1993.

Borden, Louise. *Ski Soldier: A World War II Biography*. Honesdale, PA: Calkins Creek, 2017.

Brief Histories of Divisions, US Army, 1917–1918. US Army War Plans Division, General Staff, 1921.

Brinkerhoff, John R., John Seitz, and Ted Silva. *Countering the Terrorist Threat: The 3rd Battalion, 87th Infantry*. Washington, DC: Office of the Chief, Army Reserve, 1993.

Brooks, Thomas R. *The War North of Rome, June 1944–May 1945*. Edison, NJ: Castle Books, 2001.

Brower, David R. *Remount Blue: The Combat Story of the 3rd Battalion, 86th Mountain Infantry*. Originally published in 1948; reprinted in 2020 (Chicago: Barajima Books).

Burkhardt, Joseph M. *Annual Historical Summary, 10th Mountain Division Light Infantry, 1 January 2003—31 December 2003*. 10th Mountain Division Light Infantry G3, 2003.

Burton, Hal. *The Ski Troops*. New York: Simon and Schuster, 1971.

Bynum, Bill. "Stories of an Influenza Pandemic." *The Lancet* 373 (March 14, 2009): 886.

Calkins, Derreck T. "A Military Force on a Political Mission: The Brazilian Expeditionary Force in World War II." Georgia Southern University Electronic Theses and Dissertations, 2011. https://digitalcommons.georgiasouthern.edu/etd/600, retrieved April 18, 2020.

"Camp Taji Handover: A Significant Milestone and New Phase in Ensuring the Enduring Defeat of Daesh." Global Coalition, August 26, 2020. https://theglobalcoalition.org/en/camp-taji-handover/, retrieved October 4, 2020.

The Capture of Attu: Tales of World War II in Alaska, as Told by the Men Who Fought There. Edmonds, WA; Alaska Northwest, 1984.

Carter, Kit C., and Robert Mueller. *US Army Air Forces in World War II Combat Chronology, 1941–1945*. Washington, DC: Center for Air Force History, 1991.

Casewit, Curtis W. *Mountain Troopers: The Story of the Tenth Mountain Division*. New York: Thomas Y. Crowell, 1972.

Casper, Lawrence E. *Falcon Brigade: Combat and Command in Somalia and Haiti*. Boulder, CO: Lynne Rienner, 2001.

Castagno, Margaret. *Historical Dictionary of Somalia*. Lanham, MD: Scarecrow, 1975.

Catton, Bruce. "Grant at Shiloh." *American Heritage* 11, no. 2 (February 1960). https://www.americanheritage.com/grant-shiloh#7, retrieved October 24, 2020.

Chabalko, Justin J. *Forging the 10th Mountain Division for War, 1940–1945: How Innovation Created a Highly Adaptive Formation*. Fort Leavenworth, KS: US Army Command and General Staff College, 2017.

Chapman, Dennis P. *Manning Reserve Component Units for Mobilization: Army and Air Force Practice*. Land Warfare Paper 74. Arlington, VA: AUSA Institute of Land Warfare, 2009.

———. "Our Ambivalent Iraqi-Kurdistan Policy." *Small Wars Journal*, June 13, 2010. https://smallwarsjournal.com/jrnl/art/our-ambivalent-iraqi-kurdistan-policy, retrieved September 24, 2020.

———. *Planning for Employment of the Reserve Components: Army Practice, Past and Present*. Arlington, VA: AUSA Institute of Land Warfare, 2008.

———. *Security Forces of the Kurdistan Regional Government*. Costa Mesa, CA: Mazda, 2011.

"Charles Minot 'Minnie' Dole." National Ski Patrol Eastern Division. https://www.nspeast.org/minnie-dole-hof.html, accessed February 8, 2020.

Charles, Roland W. *Troopships of World War II*. Washington, DC: Army Transportation Association, 1947.

Chihaya, Masataka, Katsuya Susaki, and Walter Black (English-language sequences). *Taiheiyô kiseki no sakusen: Kisuka* ("Miraculous military operation in the Pacific Ocean"), also known as *Retreat from Kiska* (story "Taiheyo kaisen saidai no Kiseki"). Directed by Seiji Maruyama. Produced by Toho, 1965.

Clark, Mark W. *Calculated Risk*. New York: Harper & Brothers, 1950.

Clay, Steven E. *US Army Order of Battle, 1919–1941*. Vol. 1, *The Arms: Major Commands and Infantry Organizations*. Fort Leavenworth, KS: Combat Studies Institute Press, 2010.

Coffman, Edward M. *The Regulars: The American Army, 1898–1941*. Cambridge, MA: Belknap Press of Harvard University Press, 2004.

Cole, Ronald H. *Operation Just Cause: The Planning and Execution of Joint Operations in Panama, February 1988–January 1990*. Washington, DC: Joint History Office of the Chairman of the Joint Chiefs of Staff, 1995.

The Combat Arms Regimental System: Questions and Answers. Washington, DC: Center of Military History, 1978.

Combat History of the 10th Mountain Division, 1944–1945. From the files of the US Army Infantry School Library, Fort Benning, GA. Privately published by Earl E. Clark, 1977.

Coquoz, Rene L. *The Invisible Men on Skis*. Boulder, CO: Johnson, 1970.

The Crusader: 86th Inf Regt, 1955–56. N.p., 1956.

Cubbison, Douglas R. *10th Mountain Division (Light Infantry) Annual Historical Summary, 1 January 2005–31 December 2005*. 10th Mountain Division Command Historian, 2006.

———. *10th Mountain Division (Light Infantry), Annual Command History, 1 January 2006–31 December 2006*. 10th Mountain Division, 2007.

Cullen, Pete, and Larry May. *The Trip to Vietnam on the Buckner*. http://alphaassociation.homestead.com/files/index1.htm, retrieved July 10, 2020.

David, Saul. *The Force: The Legendary Special Ops Unit and WWII's Mission Impossible*. New York: Hachette Group, 2019.

Denfeld, Duane Colt. "Clark, General Mark Wayne (1896–1984)." https://www.historylink.org/File/9004, retrieved August 8, 2020.

DeSantis, Judith M. *Fort Drum / 10th Mountain Division Public Affairs Office Annual Historical Review, 1 October 1987–30 September 1988*. Washington, DC: US Army, 1989.

Dixon, James C., Jr. *United Nations Operation in Somalia II: United Nations Unity of Effort and United States Unity of Command*. Carlisle Barracks, PA: US Army War College, 1996.

"Djibouti." In *The World Factbook*. Central Intelligence Agency, 2020. https://www.cia.gov/library/publications/the-world-factbook/geos/dj.html, retrieved August 15, 2020.

Doherty, Richard. *Victory in Italy: 15th Army Group's Final Campaign, 1945*. Havertown, PA: Pen & Sword Military, 2014.

Dole, Charles Minot. *Adventures in Skiing*. New York: Franklin Watts, 1965.

Dole, Charles Minot, chairman, Editorial Board. *The National Ski Patrol System Manual*. New York: National Ski Patrol System, 1941.

Donnelly, Thomas, Margaret Roth, and Caleb Baker. *Operation Just Cause: The Storming of Panama*. New York: Lexington Books, 1991.

Doughty, Robert A. *The Evolution of US Army Tactical Doctrine, 1946–76*. Fort Leavenworth, KS: Combat Studies Institute, 1979.

Doyle, David. *M29 Weasel Track Cargo Carrier & Variants: Rare Photographs from Wartime Archives*. Images of War. Barnsley, UK: Pen and Sword Military, 2019.

Dunnigan, James F., and Albert A. Nofi. *Victory at Sea: World War II in the Pacific*. New York: William Morrow, 1995.

Dusenbery, Harris. *The North Apennines and Beyond with the 10th Mountain Division*. Portland, OR: Binford & Mort, 1998.

———. *10th Mountain Division Italian Diary of Harris Dusenbery Hq. Co. 1st Bn. 86th Mountain Infantry and Riva Ridge Operation 1st Battalion Journal*. Typescript, n.d.

———. *Ski the High Trail: World War II Ski Troopers in the High Colorado Rockies*. Illustrated by Wilson P. Ware. Portland, OR: Binford & Mort,1991.

Earle, George F. *Birth of a Division*. Syracuse, NY: Signature, 1993.

———. *History of the 87th Mountain Infantry, Italy 1945*. Denver, CO: Bradford-Robinson, 1945.

Elliott, Stacy. *Operation Just Cause, 3rd Platoon, A Co, "JAGUARS," 5-87 INF*. Fort Benning, GA: US Army Infantry School, 1992.

Elliston, H. B. *Finland Fights*. Boston: Little, Brown, 1940.

English, John A. *On Infantry*. New York: Praeger, 1984.

Field Manual 23-41, Submachineguns, Caliber .45 M3 and M3A1. Washington, DC: Headquarters, Department of the Army, June 1974.

15th Army Group. *A Military Encyclopedia Based on Operations in the Italian Campaigns, 1943–1945*. N.p., 1945.

15th Army Group History, 16 December 1944–2 May 1945. Nashville: Battery, 1989.

Fifth Army History. Headquarters, 5th Army, 1945.

Finito! The Po Valley Campaign, 1945. Headquarters, 15th Army Group, Italy, 1945.

Finlayson, Kenneth. "Operation Cottage: First Special Service Force, Kiska Campaign." *Veritas* 4, no. 2 (2008).

"1st Brigade Combat Team." US Army, Fort Drum. https://home.army.mil/drum/index.php/units-tenants/1st-BCT, retrieved August 15, 2020.

Fisher, Ernest F., Jr. *Cassino to the Alps*. Washington, DC: Center of Military History, 1993.

"548th Combat Sustainment Support Battalion." GlobalSecurity.org. https://www.globalsecurity.org/military/agency/army/548csb.htm, retrieved August 12, 2020.

Fleming, Colin M. *Leonard Wood: Operational Artist or Scheming Careerist?* Fort Leavenworth, KS: School of Advanced Military Studies, 2012.

FM 7-5, Organization and Tactics of Infantry, the Rifle Battalion. Washington, DC: US War Department, 1940.

FM 7-10, Rifle Company, Rifle Regiment. Washington, DC: US War Department, 1942.

FM 25-100, Training the Force. Washington, DC: Department of the Army, 1988.

FM 27-10, The Law of Land Warfare. Washington, DC: US War Department, July 1956.

FM 31-72, Mountain Operations. Washington, DC: Department of the Army, January 1959.

FM 44-2, Light Antiaircraft Artillery (Automatic Weapons). Washington, DC: Department of the Army, July 1956.

FM 70-10, Mountain Operations. Washington, DC: US War Department, September 1947.

FM 100-5, Operations. Washington, DC: Department of the Army, 1982.

FM 100-17, Mobilization, Deployment, Redeployment, Demobilization. Washington, DC: Department of the Army, 1992.

Fontenot, Gregory, E. J. Degen, and David Tohn. *On Point: The United States Army in Operation Iraqi Freedom*. Fort Leavenworth, KS: Combat Studies Institute, 2004.

Forces Command Hurricane Andrew Response After Action Report. Part 1. Forces Command, n.d.

Forces Command Hurricane Andrew Response After Action Report. Part 2. Forces Command, n.d.

Ford, Corey. *Short Cut to Tokyo: The Battle for the Aleutians*. New York: Charles Scribner's Sons, 1943.

Fort Drum Economic Statement Economic Impact Statement Fiscal Year 2000. Washington, DC: US Army, 2000.

"Fort Pike." New York State Military Museum. https://dmna.ny.gov/forts/fortsM_P/pikeFort.htm, retrieved August 9, 2020.

Fort Riley, Kansas. N.p., ca. 1951.

Forty, George. *Fifth Army at War*. New York: Charles Scribner's Sons, 1980.

Foster, Hugh, Lt. Col. (USA, Ret.). "The Infantry Organization for Combat." 70th Infantry Division Association, April 26, 2000. https://www.trailblazersww2.org/history_infantry-structure.htm, retrieved May 8, 2020.

Fuchida, Mitsuo, and Masatake Okumiya. *Midway: The Battle That Doomed Japan, the Japanese Navy's Story*. Annapolis, MD: Naval Institute Press, 1955.

Garrett, William B., III. *Fratricide: Doctrine's Role in Reducing Friendly Fire*. Fort Leavenworth, KS: School of Advanced Military Studies, 1993.

Golding, J. A. *Shifta*. Edinburgh: Pentland, 1993.

Goldstein, Donald M., and Katherine V. Dillon. *The Williwaw War: The Arkansas National Guard in the Aleutians in World War II*. Fayetteville: University of Arkansas Press, 1992.

Goodman, Paul. *A Fragment of Victory: The 92nd Infantry Division in World War II*. Nashville: Battery, 1993.

Govan, Thomas P. *History of the Tenth Light Division*. Alpine Study 26. Washington, DC: Historical Section, Army Ground Forces, 1946a.

———. *Training for Mountain and Winter Warfare*. Army Ground Forces Study 23. Washington, DC: Historical Section, Army Ground Forces, 1946b.

Griess, Thomas E., ed. *Atlas for the Second World War: Europe and the Mediterranean*. Wayne, NJ: Avery, 1985.

———. *The Second World War: Asia and the Pacific*. Wayne, NJ: Avery, 1984.

———. *The Second World War: Europe and the Mediterranean*. Wayne, NJ: Avery, 1984.

Grinspan, Jon. "How a Ragtag Band of Reformers Organized the First Protest March on Washington, DC." *Smithsonian Magazine*, May 1, 2014. https://www.smithsonianmag.com/smithsonian-institution/how-ragtag-band-reformers-organized-first-protest-march-washington-dc-180951270/, retrieved May 25, 2020.

G3 Section, 15th Army Group. *A Military Encyclopedia Based on the Operations in the Italian Campaigns, 1943–1945*. 15th Army Group, 1945.

Hackworth, David H., and Tom Mathews. *Hazardous Duty: One of America's Most Decorated Soldiers Reports from the Front with the Truth about the U.S. Military Today*. New York: Avon Books, 1996.

Hagan, Kenneth J. *This People's Navy: The Making of American Sea Power*. New York: Free Press, 1992.

Hagedorn, Hermann. *Leonard Wood: A Biography*. New York: Harper & Brothers, 1931.

Haggerty, Richard A., ed. *Dominican Republic and Haiti: Country Studies*. Washington, DC: US Army, 1991.

Hampton, Lt. Col. Henry J. "Report on the Mancinello-Campiano Ridge Operation of the 1st Battalion, 86th Mountain Infantry, June 12, 1945." In *The North Apennines and Beyond with the 10th Mountain Division*. By Harris Dusenbery, . Portland, OR: Binford & Mort, 1998.

Handleman, Howard. *Bridge to Victory: The Story of the Reconquest of the Aleutians*. New York: Random House, 1943.

Harper, Frank. *Military Ski Manual: A Handbook for Ski and Mountain Troops*. Harrisburg, PA: Military Service Publishing, 1943.

———. *Night Climb: The Story of the Skiing 10th*. New York and London: Longmans, Green, 1946.

Harris, Russell D. *The Finnish Campaigns: Failure of Soviet Operational Art in World War II*. Quantico, VA: USMC Command and Staff College, 2013.

Headquarters and Headquarters Detachment, 92d Military Police Battalion Lineage. Washington, DC: Center of Military History, 2006. https://

history.army.mil/html/forcestruc/lineages/branches/mp/0092mpbn.htm, retrieved August 7, 2020.

Headquarters, 37th Infantry Brigade Combat Team (Buckeye). Washington, DC: Center of Military History, 2017. https://history.army.mil/html/forcestruc/lineages/branches/div/0037inbdect.htm, retrieved June 7, 2020.

Headquarters, 193d Infantry Brigade Lineage. Washington, DC: Center of Military History, 2007. https://history.army.mil/html/forcestruc/lineages/branches/div/193infbde.htm, retrieved August 7, 2020.

Hemming, Henry. *The Ingenious Mr. Pyke: Inventor, Fugitive, Spy.* New York: Public Affairs, 2015.

Henry, Merton G. *History of Military Mobilization in the United States Army, 1775–1945.* Washington, DC: Department of the Army, 1955.

"Historical Madison Barracks." https://madison-barracks.com/historical-madison-barracks/, retrieved August 9, 2020.

Hewes, James E., Jr. *From Root to McNamara: Army Organization and Administration, 1900–1963.* Washington, DC: Center of Military History, 1975.

Historic Naval Ships Association. "USS *Massachusetts* (BB-59)." https://web.archive.org/web/20071014043205/http:/hnsa.org/ships/bbma.htm, retrieved April 11, 2020.

History of the 86th Mtn Inf Regt 10th Mtn Div. Typescript, n.p., n.d., est. 1945.

History of the 5th Battalion, 87th Infantry (Light). Washington, DC: US Army, n.d. Copy available at the US Army Heritage and Education Center Library, Carlisle Barracks, PA.

"History." US Army, Fort Drum. https://home.army.mil/drum/index.php/about/history, retrieved August 9, 2020.

"History: 6th Army Group." 70th Infantry Division Association. https://www.trailblazersww2.org/history_6thgroup.htm, accessed April 4, 2020.

Höhne, Markus V. "Political Identity, Emerging State Structures and Conflict in Northern Somalia." *Journal of Modern African Studies* 44, no. 3 (2006): 397–414.

Hooker, R. D., Jr. "Hard Day's Night: A Retrospective on the American Intervention in Somalia." *Joint Forces Quarterly* 54, no. 3 (2009): 129–35.

Hopkins, Joseph G. E., ed. *Concise Dictionary of American Biography.* New York: Charles Scribner's Sons, 1964.

House, Jonathan M. *Toward Combined Arms Warfare: A Survey of 20th Century Tactics, Doctrine, and Organization.* Fort Leavenworth, KS: Combat Studies Institute, 1984.

"HQ, 27th Infantry Brigade Combat Team, NYARNG." http://dmna.ny.gov/units/?unit=1227543580, retrieved August 8, 2020.

Huebner, Klaus H. *Long Walk through War: A Combat Doctor's Diary.* College Station: Texas A&M University Press, 1987.

Huff, William Harrison, IV. "The United States 1989 Military Intervention in Panama: A Just Cause?" MA thesis, Louisiana State University, 2002.

Huston, John, dir. *Report from the Aleutians.* Washington, DC: US Army Signal Corps and Office of War Information, 1943.

Iker, Brandon J. *10th Mountain Division Light Infantry Annual Historical Summary, 1 January 2004–31 December 2004.* 10th Mountain Division Light Infantry G3, 2005.

Imbrie, John. *Chronology of the 10th Mountain Division during World War II, 6 January 1940–30 November 1945.* Houghton, NY: National Association of the 10th Mountain Division, 2004.

Imbrie, John, and Hugh W. Evans, eds. *Good Times and Bad Times: A History of C Company 85th Mountain Infantry Regiment, 10th Mountain Division.* Quechee, VT: Vermont Heritage, 1995.

"Infantry—25th Infantry Division Association." https://www.25thida.org/units/infantry, page 25, retrieved June 1, 2020.

Information Handbook for the Soldiers: 10th Infantry Division, Fort Riley, Kansas. Fort Riley, KS, ca. 1952.

"Information Paper, Subject: Major Army National Guard Units." NGB-ARF-I, August 14, 1992.

"Iraqi Elections: January 30, 2005." US Department of State, Bureau of Public Affairs, 2005. https://2001-2009.state.gov/documents/organization/41314.pdf, retrieved September 29, 2020.

Jackman, Albert H. "The Tenth Mountain Division." *American Alpine Journal*, Special War Number, 1946 (reprint edition, 1991), 13–18.

Jackson, W. G. F. *The Battle for Italy*. New York: Harper & Row, 1967.

Jay, John C. *The History of the Mountain Training Center*. Army Ground Forces Study 24. Washington, DC: Historical Section, Army Ground Forces, 1948.

Johnson, David E., Adam Grissom, and Olga Oliker. *In the Middle of the Fight: An Assessment of Medium-Armored Forces in Past Military Operations*. Santa Monica, CA: RAND Arroyo Center, 2008.

Johnson, Robert L., Jr. *Aleutian Campaign, World War II: Historical Study and Current Perspective*. Fort Leavenworth, KS: Command and General Staff College, 1992.

Johnson, Stuart E., John E. Peters, Karin E. Kitchens, Aaron Martin, and Jordan R. Fischbach. *A Review of the Army's Modular Force Structure*. Santa Monica, CA: RAND, 2012.

Johnson, William Page, II. "Where Honor Is Due: Fairfax County Casualties of World War I; A Requiem." *Fare Facs Gazette* 15, no. 1 (Winter 2018).

Joint Task Force Andrew After Action Report (AAR). Vol. 1. Forces Command, n.d.

Jones, Kenneth J. *The Enemy Within: Casting Out Panama's Demon*. El Dorado, Panama: Focus, 1990.

Kasukabe, Karl Kaoru. *The Aleutians Front Graphics*. Nagoya, Japan: Commercial Arts Center, 1986.

Keegan, John. *The Price of Admiralty*. New York: Viking, 1989.

Keravuori, Jouni. *The Russo-Finnish War, 1939–1940: A Study in Leadership, Training, and Esprit-de-Corps*. Carlisle Barracks, PA: US Army War College, 1985.

Kerekes, Carl D. *Recollections: Company B, 85th Regiment, 10th Mountain Division, US Army, WWII; The Italian Campaign, Ski Troups [sic] at War*. N.p., 1998.

Kern, Philip R. "The Studebaker M29 Weasel, Part II." *Military Vehicles* 43 (May 1994): 12–18.

Kion, George Paul. "Army Town Kansas: The History of a World War I Camp Town." Abstract of thesis, Kansas State University of Agriculture and Applied Science, 1960.

Knowles, John. *A Separate Peace*. New York: Macmillan, 1960.

Kostka, Del C. "Operation Cottage: A Cautionary Tale of Assumption and Perceptual Bias." *Joint Forces Quarterly* 76, no. 1 (2015): 93–100.

Kreidberg, Marvin A., and Merton G. Henry. *History of Military Mobilization in the United States Army, 1775–1945*. Washington, DC: Department of the Army, 1955.

Kretchik, Walter E., Robert F. Baumann, and John T. Fishel. *Invasion, Intervention, "Intervasion": A Concise History of the US Army in Operation Uphold Democracy*. Fort Leavenworth, KS: US Army Command and General Staff College Press, 1998.

Landsea, Chris. "Hurricane Andrew's Upgrade." Atlantic Oceanographic and Meteorological Laboratory, Hurricane Research Division, 2002. https://www.aoml.noaa.gov/hrd/hurdat/andrew.html, retrieved August 12, 2020.

Lane, David A., Robert Gumerove, and Elizabeth W. Holtzworth. *Operation Gyroscope in the United States Army, Europe*. Washington, DC: US Army Current History Branch, Historical Division, 1957.

Lanning, Michael Lee. *Vietnam, 1969–1970: A Company Commander's Journal*. New York: Ivy Books, 1988.

Leach, David M. "The Impact of the Tenth Mountain Division on the Development of a Modern Ski Industry in Colorado and Vermont: 1930–1965." Student thesis, Middlebury College, 2005.

Lee, R. Alton. "The Army 'Mutiny' of 1946." *Journal of American History* 53, no. 3 (December 1966).

Leonhard, Robert. *The Art of Maneuver: Maneuver-Warfare and Airland Battle*. Novato, CA: Presidio, 1994.

Lerwill, Leonard L. *The Personnel Replacement System in the United States Army*. Washington, DC: Department of the Army, 1954.

Lewis, John P. *The Army National Guard: Meeting the Needs of the National Military Strategy*. Fort Leavenworth, KS: School of Advanced Military Studies, 1993.

Lilley, Kevin. "CAB for Past Conflicts? 5 Things You Should Know." *Army Times*, April 4, 2015. https://www.armytimes.com/news/your-army/2015/04/04/cab-for-past-conflicts-5-things-you-should-know/, retrieved May 24, 2020.

Lineage and Honors, 1st Battalion, 7th Field Artillery. Washington, DC: Center of Military History, 2012. https://history.army.mil/html/forcestruc/lineages/branches/fa/0007fa01bn.htm, retrieved August 9, 2020.

Lineage and Honors, 2nd Battalion, 7th Field Artillery Regiment. Washington, DC: Center of Military History, 2012. https://history.army.mil/html/forcestruc/lineages/branches/fa/0007fa01bn.htm, retrieved August 10, 2020.

Lineage and Honors Information, 10th Signal Battalion. Washington, DC: Center of Military History, 1995. https://history.army.mil/html/forcestruc/lineages/branches/sc/0010scbn.htm, retrieved August 10, 2020.

Lineage and Honors Information, 3rd Squadron, 17th Cavalry Lineage. Washington, DC: Center of Military History, 1996. https://history.army.mil/html/forcestruc/lineages/branches/armor-cav/017cv003sq.htm, retrieved August 10, 2020.

Lineage and Honors, 1st Battalion, 22nd Infantry Regiment. Washington, DC: Center of Military History, 2009. https://history.army.mil/html/forcestruc/lineages/branches/inf/0022in001bn.htm, retrieved August 9, 2020.

Lineage and Honors, 2nd Battalion, 22nd Infantry Regiment. Washington, DC: Center of Military History, 2016. https://history.army.mil/html/forcestruc/lineages/branches/inf/0022in002bn.htm, retrieved August 9, 2020.

Lineage and Honors, 2nd Battalion, 25th Aviation Regiment. Washington, DC: Center of Military History, 2018. https://history.army.mil/html/forcestruc/lineages/branches/av/025av002bn.htm, retrieved August 10, 2020.

Lineage and Honors, 3rd Battalion, 25th Aviation Regiment. Washington, DC: Center of Military History, 2011. https://history.army.mil/html/forcestruc/lineages/branches/av/025av003bn.htm, retrieved August 10, 2020.

Lineage and Honors, 59th Chemical Company. Washington, DC: Center of Military History, 2011. https://history.army.mil/html/forcestruc/lineages/branches/chem/059cmco.htm, retrieved August 10, 2020.

Lineage and Honors, 1st Battalion, 87th Infantry Regiment. Washington, DC: Center of Military History, 2015. https://history.army.mil/html/forcestruc/lineages/branches/inf/0087in001bn.htm, retrieved August 10, 2020.

Lineage and Honors, 2nd Battalion, 87th Infantry Regiment. Washington, DC: Center of Military History, 2015. https://history.army.mil/html/forcestruc/lineages/branches/inf/0087in002bn.htm, retrieved August 10, 2020.

Lineage and Honors, 1st Battalion, 41st Infantry. Washington, DC: Department of the Army, October 26, 2014.

Lineage and Honors, 3rd Battalion, 41st Infantry. Washington, DC: Department of the Army, March 18, 2011.

Lineage and Honors, 5th Battalion, 20th Infantry (Sykes' Regulars). Washington, DC: Department of the Army, August 19, 2014.

Lineage and Honors, 41st Engineer Battalion. Washington, DC: Center of Military History, 2018. https://history.army.mil/html/forcestruc/lineages/branches/eng/0041enbn.htm, retrieved August 9, 2020.

Lineage and Honors, Headquarters and Headquarters Company, Combat Aviation Brigade, 10th Mountain Division. Washington, DC: Center of Military History, 2018. https://history.army.mil/html/forcestruc/lineages/branches/div/010mdCAB.htm, retrieved August 10, 2020.

Lineage and Honors, Headquarters and Headquarters Company, 1st Brigade Combat Team, 10th Mountain Division. Washington, DC: Center of Military History, 2016. https://history.army.mil/html/forcestruc/lineages/branches/div/010md1bct.htm, retrieved August 9, 2020.

Lineage and Honors, Headquarters, 2nd Brigade Combat Team, 10th Mountain Division (Commandos). Washington, DC: Center of Military History, 2013. https://history.army.mil/html/forcestruc/lineages/branches/div/010md2bct.htm, retrieved August 9, 2020.

Lineage and Honors, Headquarters, 3rd Brigade Combat Team, 10th Mountain Division. Washington, DC: Center of Military History, 2011. https://history.army.mil/html/forcestruc/lineages/branches/div/010md3bct.htm, retrieved August 15, 2020.

Lineage and Honors, 4th Battalion, 31st Infantry Regiment (the Polar Bears). Washington, DC: Department of the Army, 2018. https://history.army.mil/html/forcestruc/lineages/branches/inf/0031in004bn.htm, retrieved September 20, 2020.

Lineage and Honors Information, Headquarters, 4th Brigade Combat Team, 10th Mountain Division (Patriot Brigade). Washington, DC: Center of Military History, 2007. https://history.army.mil/html/forcestruc/lineages/branches/div/010md4bct.htm, retrieved August 15, 2020.

Lineage and Honors, Headquarters and Headquarters Battalion, 10th Mountain Division. Washington, DC: Center of Military History, updated October 26, 2015. https://history.army.mil/html/forcestruc/lineages/branches/div/010mdhqtbn.htm, retrieved July 24, 2021.

Little, Becky. "Duck Boats Offered a Unique Solution to a World War II Problem." History.com, August 30, 2018. https://www.history.com/news/duck-boats-world-war-ii-d-day, retrieved May 30, 2020.

Lively, Steve. *Annual Historical Summary, 10th Mountain Division Light Infantry, 1 January 2001–31 December 2002*. 10th Mountain Division Light Infantry G3, 2002 [Note: The period covered runs through December 31, 2001, and the actual publication is dated May 2001; these are obvious typographical errors].

———. *Annual Historical Summary, 10th Mountain Division Light Infantry, 1 January 2002–31 December 2002*. 10th Mountain Division Light Infantry G3, 2003.

Lockwood, Theodore, ed. *Mountaineers*. Artcraft / 10th Mountain Alumni Association, ca. 1945.

Loveland, Michael C. *10th Mountain Division (Light Infantry) Annual Command History 2014 and 2015*. 10th Mountain Division (Light Infantry), 2016.

Lujan, Thomas R. *Legal Aspects of Domestic Deployment of the Army*. Carlisle Barracks, PA: US Army War College, 1996.

Lyskowski, Roman, and Steve Rice, eds. *The Big One: Hurricane Andrew*. Kansas City, MO: Andrews and McMeel, 1992.

Mac Hugh, Robert E., ed. *38th Regimental Combat Team Mountain and Winter Warfare, Annual 1947–1948 APHOREC (Army PHOtographic RECord)*. Pueblo, CO: O'Brien, 1948.

"Madison Barracks." New York State Military Museum. https://dmna.ny.gov/forts/fortsM_P/madisonBarracks.htm, retrieved August 9, 2020.

Mahon, John K., and Romana Danysh. *Infantry*. Part I, *Regular Army*. Army Lineage series. Washington, DC: Center of Military History, 1972.

Mapcarta. https://mapcarta.com/N3025050852, retrieved April 18, 2020.

Marshall, S. L. A. *Commentary on Infantry Operations and Weapons Usage in Korea: Winter of 1950–51*. Chevy Chase, MD: Operations Research Office, Johns Hopkins University, 1951.

Marzoli, Nathan A. "'The Best Substitute': US Army Low-Mountain Training in the Blue Ridge and Allegheny Mountains, 1943–1944." *Army History* PB 20-19-4, no. 113 (Fall 2019).

Mascarenhas de Moraes, J. B. *The Brazilian Expeditionary Force, by Its Commander*. Washington, DC: US Government Printing Office, 1966.

Masseck, C. J. *Official Brief History, 89th Division USA, 1917–1918–1919*. G-2, 89th Division, 1919.

Matthews, Matt M. *The US Army on the Mexican Border: A Historical Perspective*. Long War series, Occasional Paper 22. Fort Leavenworth, KS: Combat Studies Institute Press, 2007.

McCann, Irving Goff. *With the National Guard on the Border: Our National Military Problem*. St. Louis, MO: C. V. Mosby, 1917.

McGillis, Gay M. *Organizing NORTHCOM for Success: A Theater Special Operations Command*. Fort Leavenworth, KS: School of Advanced Military Studies, 2003.

McGrath, John J. *The Brigade: A History, Its Organization and Equipment in the US Army*. Fort Leavenworth, KS: Combat Studies Institute Press, 2004.

McMichael, Scott R. *A Historical Perspective on Light Infantry*. Research Survey 6. Fort Leavenworth, KS: Combat Studies Institute Press, 1987.

McMurry, Donald L. *Coxey's Army: A Study of the Industrial Army Movement of 1894*. Boston: Little, Brown, 1929.

Meinke, Albert H., Jr. *Mountain Troops and Medics: Wartime Stories of a Frontline Surgeon in the U.S. Ski Troops*. Kewadin, MI: Rucksack, 1993.

Metz, Helen Chapin, ed. *Somalia: A Country Study*. Washington, DC: Headquarters, Department of the Army, 1993.

Middleton, Jacob. *Calling the Cavalry: Disaster Relief and the American Military*. Maxwell Air Force Base, AL: School of Advanced Air and Space Studies, 2011.

Miles, Nelson. *Serving the Republic*. New York: Harper & Brothers, 1911.

"Minnie Dole Biography." New England Ski History. https://newenglandskihistory.com/biographies/doleminnie.php, retrieved February 8, 2020.

Morton, Desmond. *A Military History of Canada*. Edmonton AB: Hurtig, 1985.

Mountain Search and Rescue Operations. Grand Teton Natural History Association, 7th printing, 1972.

"Mount Belvedere." Musea Diffuso dela Linea Gotica Montese. http://www.lineagoticamontese.eu/en/the-trails/monte-belvedere/72-mount-belvedere.html, retrieved April 18, 2020.

Ngadiman, Naomi. "A Historical Review of the Influenza Outbreaks within Military Settings and Understanding the Viral Spread of the 1918 Influenza Pandemic." Atlanta: Georgia State University School of Public Health Capstone Project, 2018.

19 Days: From the Apennines to the Alps. Fifth Army, 1945.

Oland, Dwight D. *North Apennines*. CMH Pub. 72–34. Washington, DC: Center of Military History, n.d.

Ollila, Mylon. "Finland in Crisis: Finnish Relations with the Western Democracies, 1939–1941." MA thesis, University of Waterloo, 2012.

Operation Just Cause: XVIII Airborne Corps and Joint Task Force South. History Office, XVIII Airborne Corps and Joint Task Force South, n.d. https://history.army.mil/documents/panama/taskorg.htm, retrieved July 25, 2020.

Operational Report: Lessons Learned, Headquarters, 1st Logistical Command, Period Ending 31 October 1969. Washington, DC: Department of the Army, December 18, 1969.

Order of Battle of the United States Land Forces in the World War, Zone of the Interior: Territorial Departments, Tactical Divisions Organized in 1918, Posts, Camps, and Stations. Vol. 3, Part 2. Washington, DC: Center of Military History, 1988.

Owskey, Thomas C. *Fratricide: The Result of Undisciplined Aggressiveness*. Carlisle Barracks, PA: US Army War College, 1996.

Palmer, Robert R., Bell I. Wiley, and William R. Keast. *The Army Ground Forces: The Procurement and Training of Ground Combat Troops*. Washington, DC: Historical Division, Department of the Army, 1948.

Panamanian Defense Force Order of Battle: Operation Just Cause. Fort Bragg, NC: History Office, XVIII Airborne Corps and Joint Task Force South, n.d. https://history.army.mil/documents/panama/pdfob.htm, retrieved July 26, 2020.

Paton, Bruce C. "Cold, Casualties, and Conquests: The Effects of Cold on Warfare." In *Medical Aspects of Harsh Environments*. Vol. 1. Edited by Kent B. Pandolf and Robert E. Burr, 313–49. Falls Church, VA: Office of the Surgeon General, United States Army, 2001.

"Pete Seibert of 10th Mountain Division." World War II in Color, February 28, 2016. http://ww2colorfarbe.blogspot.com/2016/02/pete-seibert-of-10th-mountain-division.html, retrieved May 11, 2020.

Phillips, R. Cody. *Operation Just Cause: The Incursion into Panama*. CMH Pub. 70-85-1. Washington, DC: Center of Military History, 2004.

Pollack, Kenneth M. *Arabs at War: Military Effectiveness, 1948–1991*. Lincoln: University of Nebraska Press, 2002.

Poole, Walter S. *The Effort to Save Somalia, August 1992–March 1994*. Washington, DC: Joint History Office, 2005.

Poore, Brad. "Somaliland: Shackled to a Failed State." *Stanford Journal of International Law* 45 (2009): 117.

Potter, E. B., ed. *Sea Power: A Naval History*. Annapolis, MD: Naval Institute Press, 1981.

Pride, W. F. *The History of Fort Riley*. N.p., 1926.

Queen, Stuart, narr. "Operation Gyroscope." In *The Big Picture*. Army Signal Corps Pictorial Center, ca. 1955.

———. "Strategic Army Corps (STRAC) Fourth." In *The Big Picture*. Army Pictorial Service, ca. 1960.

Ralston, Robert M., and Douglas L. Horn. "Engineers Respond to Operations Other Than War." *Engineer* 23 PB 5-93-2 (April 1993).

"Rebuilding Iraq: US Assistance for the January 2005 Elections." US Government Accountability Office, 2005. https://www.gao.gov/new.items/d05932r.pdf, retrieved September 29, 2005.

"Re-creation through Recreation: Chapter III, World War II and the 10th Mountain Division." www.heritageaspen.org/recre3.html, retrieved July 2, 2008.

Regan, Geoffrey. *Blue on Blue: A History of Friendly Fire*. New York: Avon Books, 1995.

Rel, Stephen A., and Randy Stoehr. *Front End Analysis of Armored Vehicles for the Chemically and Biologically Protected Shelter*. Natick, MA: US Army Natick Research, Development, and Engineering Center, June 1994.

Richmond, Melvin E. *Combat Operations in Mountainous Terrain: Are the US Army Light Infantry Divisions Preparing Properly?* Fort Leavenworth, KS: US Army Command and General Staff College, 1987.

Riehm, Peter J. A. "The USS *Harlan County* Affair." *Military Review* 77 (July–August 1997). file:///C:/Users/Dennis/Downloads/427.pdf, retrieved September 13, 2020.

Riehm, Richard R. *Pictorial History: Thirty-Seventh Infantry Division, Camp Polk, Louisiana, 1952*. Columbus, OH: F. J. Heer, 1952.

Rivera, José G. Vega. *The Mexican Expeditionary Air Force in World War II: The Organization, Training and Operations of the 201st Squadron*. Montgomery, AL: Air Command and Staff College, 1997.

Road to Rome. Fifth Army, 1945.

Romjue, John L. *A History of Army 86, Volume II: The Development of the Light Division, the Corps, and Echelons above Corps, November 1979–December 1980*. Fort Monroe, VA: US Army Training and Doctrine Command, 1982.

———. *The Army of Excellence: The Development of the 1980s Army*. Fort Monroe, VA: US Army Training and Doctrine Command, 1993.

Rommetveit, Karl. *Narvik 1940: Five-Nation War in the High North*. Forsvarsstudier 8/1991. Oslo, Norway: Institutt für Forsvarsstudier, 1991.

"Sackets Harbor Forts." American Forts. https://www.northamericanforts.com/East/New_York/Sackets_Harbor/Sackets_Harbor.html, retrieved August 9, 2020.

Sanders, Charles J. *The Boys of Winter: Life and Death in the Ski Troops during the Second World War*. Boulder: University of Colorado Press, 2005.

"Santa Maria Infante, 351st Infantry, 11–14 May 1944." In *Small Unit Actions*. Washington, DC: War Department Historical Division,

Center of Military History; reprint as CMH Pub. 100-14, 1986.

Sarkis, Sierra. "The 25th Anniversary of Hurricane Andrew." Atlantic Oceanographic and Meteorological Laboratory. https://www.aoml.noaa.gov/keynotes/keynotes_0817_andrew25.html, retrieved August 12, 2020.

Sawicki, James A. *Infantry Regiments of the US Army*. Dumfries, VA: Wyvern, 1982.

"2d Infantry Division." *Army Information Digest*, August 1962.

2nd Battalion, 9th Infantry. Army & Navy Publishing, n.d.

"2nd Brigade Combat Team." US Army, Fort Drum. https://home.army.mil/drum/index.php/units-tenants/2nd-BCT, retrieved August 15, 2020.

2nd Infantry Division, Company A, First Battle Group, Eighty-Seventh Infantry. Albert Love, n.d.

Semiannual Report to Congress, April 1, 2011– September 30, 2011. Washington, DC: DoD Inspector General, 2011.

Setzekorn, Eric B. *Joining the Great War, April 1917–April 1918*. CMH Pub. 77-3. Washington, DC: Center of Military History, 2017.

A Short History of the 85th Mountain Infantry Regiment. N.p., November 1945.

Shrader, Charles R. *Amicicide: The Problem of Friendly Fire in Modern War*. Fort Leavenworth, KS: Combat Studies Institute, 1982.

"69 anos da tomada de Monte Castelo." http://www.defesanet.com.br/ecos/noticia/14284/69-anos-da-tomada-de-Monte-Castelo/, retrieved April 18, 2020.

Smallman, Shawn C. "The Official Story: The Violent Censorship of Brazilian Veterans, 1945–1954." *Hispanic American Historical Review* 78, no. 2 (1998): 229–59.

Smart, A. G. *Military Support to Domestic Disaster Relief: Doctrine for Operating in the Wake of the Enemy?* Fort Leavenworth, KS: School of Advanced Military Studies, 1993.

Smith, Jean Edward. *Grant*. New York: Simon and Schuster, 2001.

Smith, Scott. *Operation in Panama*. Fort Benning, GA: US Army Infantry School, n.d.

Smyth, Donald. *Pershing: General of the Armies*. Bloomington: Indiana University Press, 1986.

The Soviet-Finnish War, 1939–1940 / The Campaign in Norway, 1940. West Point, NY: US Military Academy, Department of Military Art and Engineering, 1948.

Sparrow, John C. *History of Personnel Demobilization in the United States Army*. Department of the Army Pamphlet 20-210. Washington, DC: Department of the Army, July 1952.

Sperberg, Robert J. *Major General Leonard Wood: A Study of Leadership in an Army of Transition*. Carlisle Barracks, PA: US Army War College, 1992.

"SS Argentina." http://www.moore-mccormack.com/SS-Argentina-1938/SS-Argentina-1938-Timeline.htm, retrieved April 4, 2020.

Stanley, Bruce E. *Military Operations Other Than War: One Soldier's Story*. Fort Leavenworth, KS: US Army Command and General Staff College, 1999.

Stanton, Martin. *Somalia on $5.00 a Day: A Soldier's Story*. Novato, CA: Presidio, 2001.

Stanton, Shelby L. *Vietnam Order of Battle*. New York: Galahad Books, 1986.

Starr, Chester G. *From Salerno to the Alps: A History of the Fifth Army, 1943–1945*. Washington, DC: Infantry Journal Press, 1948.

St. Clair, Matthew G. *The Twelfth US Air Force: Tactical and Operational Innovations in the Mediterranean Theater of Operations, 1943–1944*. Maxwell Air Force Base, AL: School of Advanced Air and Space Studies, 2007.

Steinweg, Kenneth K. *Piercing the Fog of War Surrounding Fratricide: The Synergy of History, Technology, and Behavioral Research*. Carlisle Barracks, PA: Army War College, 1994.

Stewart, Richard W. *The United States Army in Somalia, 1992–1994*. Washington, DC: Center of Military History, 2002.

Stouffer, Edwin P. *Fort Drum / 10th Mountain Division Bi-annual Historical Review for October 1, 1984–September 30, 1986*. Washington, DC: US Army, 1987.

"Strategic Army Corps (STRAC) and Strategic Army Forces (STRAF)." *Army Information* 355-201-1 (August 1961).

Strawson, John. *The Italian Campaign*. New York: Carroll & Graf, 1988.

Studebaker. *The Weasel: Snow, Mud and Deep Water Operations, US M-29*. Studebaker, January 1944. Reprint, Andover, NJ: Portrayal, n.d.

Sullivan, Charles J. *Army Posts & Towns: The Baedeker of the Army*. New York: Free Press, 1926.

Sutcliff, Rosemary. *The Eagle of the Ninth*. Oxford: Oxford University Press, 1954.

Talley, Thomas F. *Is Reorganization of the Army under the Unit-of-Action and Unit-of-Employment Concept Consistent with the Army's Identity?* Fort Leavenworth, KS: US Army Command and General Staff College, 2004.

10th Infantry Division, Fort Riley, Kansas, 1950, Company K 87th Infantry. Marceline, MO: Walsworth Brothers, 1950.

10th Infantry Division, Fort Riley, Kansas, 1952, Company I 86th Infantry. Marceline, MO: Walsworth Brothers, 1952.

10th Infantry Division, Fort Riley, Kansas, 1953, Company M 85th Infantry. Marceline, MO: Walsworth Brothers, 1953.

10th Infantry Division: 1957. Dallas: Taylor, 1957.

10th Mountain Division (Light Infantry) Division Capabilities Book, Pamphlet 10-1. 10th Mountain Division (LI) and Fort Drum, May 1, 1997.

"10th Mountain Division's 4th Brigade Transforms to 3rd Brigade." *Beauregard Daily News*, February 28, 2015. https://www.beauregard-dailynews.net/article/20150228/NEWS/150229708, retrieved August 9, 2020.

"10th Sustainment Brigade." https://home.army.mil/drum/index.php/units-tenants/10th-Sustainment, retrieved August 12, 2020.

"3rd Brigade Combat Team." US Army, Fort Drum. https://home.army.mil/drum/index.php/units-tenants/3rd-BCT, retrieved August 15, 2020.

"36th Infantry Division, the 'Texas' Division." Texas Military Forces Museum. http://www.texasmilitaryforcesmuseum.org/texas.htm, retrieved August 15, 2020.

TM 9-772, Carrier, Cargo M29; Carrier Cargo M29C. Washington, DC: US War Department, July 5, 1944. Reprint, Andover, NJ: Portrayal.

Touri, Antti. *The Winter War*. Beaverton, ON: Aspasia Books, 2003.

Tubbs, James O. *Beyond Gunboat Diplomacy: Forceful Applications of Airpower in Peace Enforcement Operations*. Maxwell Air Force Base, AL: Air University Press, 1997.

"27th Infantry Brigade Combat Team." GlobalSecurity.org. https://www.globalsecurity.org/military/agency/army/27in-bde.htm, retrieved August 8, 2020.

"27th Brigade Combat Team History." https://web.archive.org/web/20181210213302/http://ny.ng.mil/27bct/Pages/History.aspx, retrieved August 8, 2020.

US Army, Europe & Seventh Army Fact File, History: 18th Military Police Brigade. USAREUR and Seventh Army Public Affairs, 2007. https://web.archive.org/web/20081230113537/http://www.hqusareur.army.mil/factfiles/factfile_history-018MP_2007-12.pdf, retrieved July 20, 2020.

US Army in Germany. "8th Infantry Division (Mech)." https://usarmygermany.com/Sont.htm?https&&&usarmygermany.com/Units/8th%20Inf%20Div/USAREUR_8th%20Inf%20Div.htm, retrieved July 8, 2020.

———. "Locations of 8 Infantry Division (M), Based on Station List for 1974." https://usarmygermany.com/Sont.htm?https&&&usarmygermany.com/Units/8th%20Inf%20Div/USAREUR_8th%20Inf%20Div.htm, retrieved July 8, 2020.

US Army North. "History." https://www.arnorth.army.mil/about/pages/history.aspx, retrieved April 7, 2020.

"US Troops Complete Their Withdrawal from Iraq." *Herald Sun News*, December 18, 2011. https://web.archive.org/web/20140304204059/http://www.heraldsun.com.au/news/breaking-news/us-troops-complete-their-withdrawal-from-iraq/story-e6frf7jx-1226225154019, retrieved October 4, 2020.

Valle, Ramon. *Is a Deployable Joint Task Force Augmentation Cell (DJTFAC) a Viable Tool*

for US Northern Command during Consequence Management Operations? Fort Leavenworth, KS: School of Advanced Military
Studies, 2003.

Vaughan, Curry N., Robert E. Neiman Jr., Vasco
J. Fenili, et al. *Mud, Mountains and Armor:
The 1st Armored Division from Rome to the
Alps*. Fort Knox, KY: Armored School Officers
Advanced Course, 1949.

Vega Rivera, José G. *The Mexican Expeditionary
Air Force in World War II: The Organization,
Training and Operations of the 201st Squadron*.
Maxwell Air Force Base, AL: Air Command
and Staff College, 1997.

"War Brides." https://jhgraham.com/2017/10/08/
war-brides/, retrieved April 4, 2020.

Watson, Thomas Terry. *History of the 720th
Military Police Battalion*. Book II, Vol. 1,
Vietnam Journal. Edited by Robert P. Schmitz.
Alpharetta, GA: Booklogix, 2013.

"'The Weasel': The Studebaker M29 Cargo Carrier."
Center of Military History. https://history.
army.mil/museums/artifacts/0010_theWea-
selM29.html, retrieved March 3, 2020.

Wellborn, Charles. *History of the 86th Mountain
Infantry in Italy*. Originally published in 1945.
Digitized and edited by Barbara Imbrie, 2004.
www.skitrooper.org/86.htm, retrieved April
19, 2020.

Wellons, Dave. *Doctrine for Domestic Disaster
Response Activities*. Fort Leavenworth, KS:
School of Advanced Military Studies, 2000.

Whayne, Tom F., and Michael E. DeBakey. *Cold
Injury, Ground Type*. Washington, DC: US
Army Medical Department, Office of the
Surgeon General, 1958.

White, D. Fedotoff. *The Growth of the Red Army*.
Princeton, NJ: Princeton University Press,
1944.

Wiese, Carl, field ed. *8th Infantry Division,
Gyroscope 1956*. Dallas: Miller, 1956.

Wiley, Bell I. *Training in the Ground Army,
1942–1945*. Study XI. Washington, DC:
Historical Section, Army Ground Forces,
1948.

Wilson, John B. *Armies, Corps, Divisions, and
Separate Brigades*. Army Lineage Series.

Washington, DC: Center of Military History,
1993.

———. *Maneuver and Firepower: The Evolution
of Divisions and Separate Brigades*. Army
Lineage Series. Washington, DC: Center of
Military History, 1998.

Wilson, Ross J. *History of the First Battalion, 87th
Mountain Infantry*. N.p., 1991.

The Winter Line. Washington, DC: Historical
Division, US War Department, 1945.

Wondolowski, Peter S. *History of the IV Corps,
1941–1945*. IV Corps Headquarters, 1945.

Woo, Elaine. "John Jay: Descendant of Chief
Justice Pioneered Ski Films." *Los Angeles
Times*, December 15, 2000. https://www.la-
times.com/archives/la-xpm-2000-dec-15-
me-328-story.html, retrieved July 24, 2021.

Woods, Jeff. *Studebaker M29 Weasel*. London:
ISO, 1985.

Woodward, Bob. *The Commanders*. New York:
Simon and Schuster, 1991.

Woolridge, Eugene R., III. *Challenges and
Considerations for Employing Military
Chaplains in the Homeland in Support of US
Northern Command*. Carlisle Barracks, PA:
US Army War College, 2005.

"World War I: Birth of the Modern Army Division."
Washington, DC: Center of Military History.
https://history.army.mil/html/bookshelves/
resmat/wwi/wwi_bomad/index.html, retrieved
April 12, 2020.

*World War II in Alaska: A Historic and Resources
Management Plan*. 2 vols. Anchorage, AK:
Army Corps of Engineers, Alaska District,
1987.

Wright, Donald P., James R. Bird, Steven E. Clay,
et al. *A Different Kind of War: The United
States Army in Operation Enduring Freedom,
2001–2005*. Fort Leavenworth, KS: Combat
Studies Institute Press, 2010.

Wright, Donald P., and Timothy R. Reese. *On
Point II: Transition to the New Campaign;
The United States Army in Operation Iraqi
Freedom, May 2003–January 2005*. Fort
Leavenworth, KS: Combat Studies Institute,
2008.

Zirkle, Robert Allen. *Communities Rule: Intra-service Politics in the United States Army.* Cambridge: Massachusetts Institute of Technology, 2008.

Official Documents

Headquarters Tenth Division, Discharge Orders, Charles Miller, Headquarters Company, 41st Infantry, Camp Funston, Kansas, February 20, 1919.

Other Sources

Comacho, Harry Blanco, Dennis Chan, and Tito Sablan, interviewers. Library of Congress American Folklife Center, Veteran's History Project. http://memory.loc.gov/diglib/vhp/story/loc.natlib.afc2001001.111011/, http://stream.media.loc.gov/vhp/video/afc2001001_111011_mv0001001_640x480_800.mp4, retrieved July 23, 2020.

Hubert, Robert E. Co. E, 85th Infantry Regiment, 10th Infantry Division. Personal letter dated February 1, 1953.

INDEX

Regiments

Named Operations